# A Voyage Through the
# NEW TESTAMENT

## Catherine Cory
*University of St. Thomas, Minnesota*

PEARSON

Prentice
Hall

Upper Saddle River, New Jersey 07458

**Library of Congress Cataloging-in-Publication Data**

Cory, Catherine A.
  A voyage through the New Testament / Catherine Cory.—1st ed.
    p. cm.
  Includes index.
  ISBN-13: 978-0-13-049495-5
  ISBN-10: 0-13-049495-X
  1. Bible. N.T.—Criticism, interpretation, etc. I. Title.
  BS2361.3.C67 2008
  225.6'1—dc22

                                                    2007019941

**Editor in Chief:** Sarah Touborg
**Editorial Assistant:** Carla Worner
**Assit. Marketing Manager:** Sasha Anderson-Smith
**Senior Managing Editor:** Joanne Riker
**Production Liaison:** Fran Russello
**Manufacturing Buyer:** Christina Amato
**Cover Design:** Bruce Kenselaar
**Cover Illustration/Photo:** The Art Archive/Bodleian Library Oxford
  (Bodley 352 folio 4v)
**Cartographer:** Justin M. Trupe
**Director, Image Resource Center:** Melinda Patelli
**Manager, Rights and Permissions:** Zina Arabia
**Manager, Visual Research:** Beth Brenzel
**Manager, Cover Visual Research & Permissions:** Karen Sanatar
**Image Permission Coordinator:** Richard Rodrigues
**Photo Researcher:** Teri Stratford
**Composition/Full-Service Project Management:** Suganya Karuppasamy,
  GGS Book Services
**Printer/Binder:** RRDonnelley & Sons Company

Credits and acknowledgments borrowed from other sources and reproduced, with
permission, in this textbook appear on appropriate page within text or on page 525.

Pearson Education LTD. London
Pearson Education Singapore, Pte. Ltd
Pearson Education, Canada, Ltd
Pearson Education–Japan
Pearson Education Australia PTY, Limited

Pearson Education North Asia Ltd
Pearson Educación de Mexico, S.A. de C.V.
Pearson Education Malaysia, Pte. Ltd
Pearson Education, Upper Saddle River,
  New Jersey

10  9  8  7  6  5  4  3  2  1
ISBN-13: 978-0-13-049495-5
ISBN-10:    0-13-049495-X

*To my students who, over several years, have helped to shape this book through discussions and projects which gave us opportunities to break open the scriptures together. I am grateful for their stimulating questions and rich insights that continually challenge me to see the biblical text with new eyes.*

*And to my colleagues in the Theology Department at the University of St. Thomas, whom I deeply respect and admire for their dedication to our double mission of teaching and scholarship. They have inspired me to do my best to teach with wisdom and humility and to engage in scholarly activity that serves the common good and provides an avenue for the flourishing of human culture.*

# Brief Contents

# CONTENTS

# PREFACE

We are about to embark on a most amazing voyage, a voyage through the New Testament of the Christian Bible. Upon first hearing the term *voyage* applied to the New Testament, you might think that this is a bit strange. Many people think of a voyage in terms of a sea cruise or a long trip by boat. In fact, most of the activities and events of the New Testament took place in and around the Mediterranean Sea, but that observation does not warrant calling our study of the New Testament a sea cruise! Consider some other meanings of the word *voyage*. As a noun, *voyage* can describe a journey to some distant place. In a literary sense, it can also refer to a story of an exploratory trip. Recall, for example, the 1961 Irwin Allen film *Voyage to the Bottom of the Sea*. As a verb, *voyage* means to make a long journey to (and often back from) a faraway place, even into a different dimension.

Now that we have expanded our definition of *voyage* a bit, we can talk about how the voyage metaphor can be a helpful way of understanding our study of the New Testament. First, our study of the New Testament will take us to a faraway place, almost halfway around the world to the Middle East and eastern Mediterranean lands, and into cultural environments that are quite unfamiliar to most Westerners. It will also take us into a time very different from our own, some two thousand years ago. Finally, there is the dimension of story. This voyage through the New Testament involves the unfolding of a human story about suffering and hope, expectation and promise, death and new life. Whether you are a religious person or not, perhaps you will find your own life story somewhere in these pages. For some, the New Testament is the unfolding of a story about God's encounter with humanity and an invitation to enter more deeply into the realization of God's kingdom in our midst. Others are simply curious about these ancient writings that continue to have influence on contemporary cultures across the world. Here, too, the voyage metaphor is apt. Hopefully, our journeying will bring us back to this time and place with new insights and deeper understandings of a text that is ancient and ever new.

As with any voyage of this sort—not just a vacation—we need to do our homework in order to make the experience as memorable as possible. Some introductory textbooks on the New Testament spend a lot of time telling you about the New Testament, even summarizing the contents of each book, but at the end of your studies, you may discover that you have not been challenged to read the New Testament for yourself. To use our voyage/journey motif, we can compare that approach to New Testament studies to the experience of reading a tour book on Uganda but not actually going there! In the end, it's not very satisfying. The goal of this textbook is to give you the tools and resources to study the New Testament and then accompany you on the journey so that you can experience the New Testament for yourself.

Therefore, we will not be treating any one book of the New Testament in its entirety. Instead, we will look at two or three key themes or topics in detail and then invite you to investigate others on your own, using the commentary in the textbook as background or sometimes even a template for your own inquiry. You will not feel very adept at first, but this is the kind of journey that you can take again and again. As your knowledge increases and your skills improve, you will be able to explore more deeply the story that awaits you.

One of the most important skills you will need as you embark on this journey through the New Testament is the ability to do a close reading of a text. Biblical scholars and teachers of the Bible, who are adept at reading ancient texts, often take this skill for granted, but for many people, this is strange territory. Whether in your professional career or as a leisure activity, you learned reading techniques that served as a means to an end—skimming, synthesizing, looking for the most important points, and so on—but you probably did not learn to focus on the act of reading itself and how texts makes meaning. Thus, close reading of texts requires a whole new set of skills, and there is no simple formula for learning how to do it. Rather, it takes practice and more practice. The "Questions for Reading" at the end of each chapter are designed to guide you in developing these skills of close reading of individual New Testament books.

Perhaps the greatest challenge to learning the techniques of close reading is our natural tendency toward a naïve reading of ancient texts. Most people have very limited experience with literature from times and cultures that are different from their own. As a result, they are often unaware of how important it is to know and understand the historical, cultural, and literary contexts of the documents they are reading. By default, they want to read every historical text as if it was documentary history. This is where critical thinking skills come into play. This textbook provides materials on the historical, religious, cultural, and literary backgrounds needed to understand each New Testament book and an overview of its major themes. As you work to assimilate this material and bring it to your reading of the New Testament, you will be sharpening your critical thinking skills, which, in turn, will give you the tools to dig more deeply into the biblical text. This process will not be easy, but if you persist, most certainly it will be rewarding.

To support our goal of developing critical thinking skills and learning to do close readings of texts, this textbook includes regular discussion of the background of particular New Testament books (authorship, date of composition, and initial audience) and investigation of controversial interpretations of individual texts. This textbook summarizes not only the majority view of biblical scholars but also some of the minority views. It also explains, as briefly and simply as possible, why and how biblical scholars have come to these conclusions. In addition, each chapter of the textbook contains at least a few step-by-step examples of how to read and interpret excerpts from a New Testament book with attention to its historical, cultural, religious, political, and literary contexts.

Occasionally, the textbook includes brief excerpts from other scholars' commentaries and critical studies to illustrate how the insights of particular historical and literary critical methodologies and various advocacy approaches to scripture can help in the analysis of the biblical text. Finally, to further broaden our awareness of the range of contemporary interpretations of the New Testament that are available in our global context today, this textbook provides examples of interpretations that arise out of cultural perspectives or worldviews that are different from our own. Hopefully, by modeling the use of critical thinking skills and techniques of close reading in the analysis of biblical material, you will gradually come to understand and appreciate the significance of the questions that biblical scholars ask and the methods they bring to bear on the study of scripture and even begin to develop your own skills of analytical reasoning.

My second goal in writing this textbook also relates to our voyage motif. In fact, it may be the distinguishing factor in characterizing this textbook as a journey through the New Testament and not simply an exercise in learning about the New Testament. In today's sometimes fractious and contentious cultural environment, people tend to talk in terms of "either/or" and erect barriers instead of bridges. We see this in politics and religion, and it is made manifest as culture wars or class warfare, so we should not be surprised that it extends even to the study of the New Testament. Some people think that being a believer (whatever one's religious affiliation) means that you cannot ask questions of the sacred text or challenge its meaning, since it is divinely inspired. Others are inclined to say that sound study and analysis of the biblical text require a totally objective approach that is untainted by faith biases.

The authors of most textbooks intended for the academic study of the New Testament are very deliberate about excluding any mention of churches' faith claims relative to their reading of the Bible. Certainly, there are sound reasons for this approach. However, the implicit—and sometimes explicit—message that these authors send is that faith and reason are incompatible and that faith claims have no place in an academic setting. Thus, we have created a situation in which faithful Christians are resistant to learning about historical, cultural, and literary approaches to the study of scripture because they see these approaches as a threat to faith. As a consequence, they retreat to a naïve and often misdirected interpretation of scripture, and we are all the poorer for it. In essence, we have created an either/or situation: either faith or reason, but not both.

Instead of building barriers between faith and reason, I would like to propose an approach that appreciates the compatibility of faith and reason. Thus, this textbook seriously engages Christian churches' faith claims regarding the New Testament, but it does so in a way that is compatible with contemporary historical- and literary-critical readings of the biblical text. Whether you are enrolled at a public institution or a church-based school, many of you were probably initially attracted to the study of the New Testament because it inspires faith and calls people to a more meaningful or ethical life. However, even if your motivation is simple curiosity, hopefully this approach gives us common ground for the study of the New Testament and for the exploration of the ways in which religion shapes culture and is shaped by it. Therefore, where appropriate, this textbook includes commentary on the ways that particular New Testament texts relate to the doctrinal teachings or religious practices of various Christian communities. Likewise, in the "Activities for Learning" in each chapter, you will have opportunities to explore the ways that different Christian churches have incorporated particular biblical texts into the life of their communities of faith and how their interpretations of these texts impact their interactions with the larger human community.

Finally, in designing this textbook, I have tried to provide an abundance of learning aids and resources so that everyone will be able to find something that furthers their particular academic goals and supports their distinctive learning styles. Perhaps one activity or another will also inspire you to launch into your own self-directed study. Here is a list of the learning aids that you will find in this textbook:

- "Overview" at the opening of each chapter, highlights the major topics of that chapter and, where appropriate, summarizes the basic background information about a particular New Testament book (authorship, date of composition, and initial audience).

- A brief "Time Line" at the opening of many chapters will help you place a particular biblical book in its historical context.

- Chapter insets explain, in simple terms, how to use the insights of various historical and literary critical methodologies for the analysis of a particular biblical text. Occasionally, they will include brief excerpts from New Testament commentaries and critical studies to illustrate a particular methodological approach to the study of scripture and to broaden our exposure to diverse interpretations of biblical texts.

- Excerpts from nonbiblical materials that are roughly contemporaneous with the New Testament can be used for purposes of comparison with the New Testament.

- A variety of charts, maps (ancient and contemporary), and photographs illuminate the content of each chapter.

- "Key Terms" at the end of most chapters highlight important concepts discussed in the chapter. Many of these terms are also defined (briefly) in the Glossary at the end of the textbook.

- "Questions for Reading" at the end of most chapters guide you in a close reading of the biblical text.

- "Questions for Reflection" at the end of each chapter identify topics or issues that might make the New Testament more relevant for contemporary readers. These can be used in a variety of ways: as a topic for classroom discussion, as a starting point for web-based bulletin board discussions, or as subject matter for journal-writing exercises.

- "Activities for Learning" at the end of each chapter offer ideas for active learning projects related to the biblical texts and the methodologies being studied or to the ways in which various Christian churches have incorporated particular biblical texts into their religious practices.

- "Sources and Resources" at the end of each chapter provide the bibliography for the chapter but also direct you toward resources that might be helpful for your own study.

I recognize that I have laid out a rather challenging agenda for this textbook, but hopefully it is one that will serve us well on our voyage through the New Testament and produce good fruit in terms of the dialogue among teachers and learners, for whether we are instructors or students, we are all learners. Welcome to the journey!

## ACKNOWLEDGMENTS

My special thanks to Justin Trupe, geography major and graduate of the University of St. Thomas, who under the guidance of his mentor, Dr. Catherine Hanson, prepared all of the maps for this book. I would also like to thank the following reviewers who so generously gave of their time and expertise to provide feedback on the manuscript: Mark G. Boyer (Southwest Missouri State University), Mikeal C. Parsons (Baylor University), Nancy Hardesty (Clemson University), Paul Qualis (Gardner-Webb University), Paul L. Redditt (Georgetown College), D. Gregory Sapp (Mercer College), and Mark D. Given (Southwest Missouri State University).

Catherine Cory
*Director, University of St. Thomas*

# Introduction

Welcome to a most exciting adventure! We are about to launch into the study of the New Testament, a body of literature that is already almost two thousand years old. It comes from a part of the world that is little known to Western cultures like our own, but amazingly it continues to have wide-ranging appeal to people all over the world, scholars and nonscholars alike. Some are drawn to the New Testament as a historical document that provides a window into the sociopolitical world of the ancient Middle East. Others use the New Testament as source material for understanding the role of religion in cultural anthropology. Still others investigate the New Testament to see how literature makes meaning for its readers and how various literary genres and rhetorical techniques affect the meaning of a text. Of course, many Christians look to the New Testament to inspire faith and to provide guidance for the way they live their lives.

At first glance, these might sound like contradictory or competing interests and concerns, but they are not. People of faith can come to better understand the message of the New Testament by drawing on the insights of historical analysis, cultural anthropology, and literary theory. In fact, teachers and scholars of the New Testament would argue that we cannot fully comprehend this literature without investigating its historical setting, the sociopolitical environment in which it was composed, the cultural conventions that were in place at the time of its writing, and the literary forms and techniques that first-century writers had at their disposal.

Perhaps we can use the analogy of travel to a distant location, like India or China, to make our point. Using modern means of transportation, you can get to India without too much trouble. If you are visiting some of its major cities, you may encounter many things that look and sound familiar to you. You may even find a number of people who speak English and dress in clothing similar to yours. But can you say that you know India? Not at all! To really know India, you need to live there awhile. You need to learn about its history and religious and cultural practices. You need to understand the worldviews of various groups within Indian culture and how they relate to each other. You also need to know the languages its people speak.

So it is with the New Testament. We can read the text without much knowledge of how it was composed, and we might think we understand it. However, it is quite possible that we are seeing only a reflection of our own religious and cultural worldviews. To really understand the New Testament, we need to study the historical, religious, cultural, and literary contexts out of which it came and within which we interpret it today. That is what we will be trying to do with this introduction to the New Testament. In addition, we will explore today's new literary theories to see how they help us unlock deep and rich interpretations of the New Testament for contemporary readers. Likewise, liberationist and feminist interpretations, as well as various cultural readings of scripture, can reveal truths about the biblical text that people of earlier generations might never have considered.

We begin our study of the New Testament by describing the "big picture." What is contained in the New Testament? How were these books composed? How were they collected into this larger document we call the New Testament? What kind of authority does the New Testament have for Christians? Before tackling these questions, however, we have to establish the context for our investigation. The New Testament belongs to a larger unit of Christian scriptures known as the Bible. Thus, our first step will be to briefly describe the nature of the Bible so that we can situate the New Testament within that larger document.

## THE BIBLE, THE SCRIPTURES OF CHRISTIANITY

The title of a book often can be helpful in determining its contents or at least in raising our curiosity about what we will find between its covers. The Greek term *ta biblia*, from which the English word **Bible** is derived, means "the books." Thus, the literature that Christians call the Bible is actually a collection of books. Composed over the course of more than one thousand years, some of these books were written a very long time ago and some relatively recently—the latest ones being almost two thousand years old now. Some are rather long, while others are very short. One is only a single page in English translation! Some books contain legends and stories about important historical figures in ancient Judaism and early Christianity. Others consist of prayers and sayings about how to live a good life. Still others provide laws and prescriptions about how to honor and worship God. In sum, the Bible is a very compact library of a wide variety of literature.

The first thing a new reader of the Bible will notice is that it is divided into two parts. Traditionally, these two major units of the Bible have been called the Old Testament and the New Testament. The word **testament** means "covenant" or "agreement." You've probably heard the phrase "last will and testament," referring both to the legal agreement that a person makes to ensure that his property is properly disposed of after death and to the parting words of the deceased. However, when used in a religious sense, as in the Bible, the term *testament* refers to God's covenant relationship with humanity. Thus, to describe the second part of the Bible as the New Testament is to suggest that it proclaims the new covenant established in Jesus the Christ.

However, this terminology poses a problem because some people might be tempted to think that the books identified as the Old Testament proclaim an old covenant, basically one that is no longer valid or effective. In fact, such a view would be entirely wrongheaded for at least two reasons. First, these books include the sacred scriptures of Judaism, which proclaim a living and enduring covenant between God and God's chosen people, the Jews. Second, although individual Christian churches might interpret these books differently, the books of the Old Testament enjoy the same status and authority within the Bible as do the New Testament books.

What, then, shall we call these two parts of the Bible? Some have suggested that the Bible be called Christian Scriptures. If we accept this term for the Bible, then the books we have traditionally called the New Testament could be identified as the Christian Testament, and the books that Christians call the Old Testament could be named the Hebrew Scriptures. This solution resolves the difficulties that arise by labeling the covenant of Judaism "old." However, the term *Hebrew Scriptures* misrepresents this collection of books because not all of these books were written in Hebrew and they do not exactly correspond with the scriptures of Judaism.

Although other potential solutions have run into similar difficulties, the motive for seeking alternative descriptions of the Old and New Testaments is a positive one: respect for Judaism as the elder brother or sister of Christianity. This textbook will use the "*Old Testament*" and "*New Testament*," because these terms have a history within Christianity and because we do not, as yet, have a more satisfactory solution. However, we need to recognize that these are explicitly Christian designations, which reflect Christianity's theological interpretation of the document. Christians do understand Jesus Christ to be the embodiment of a new covenant with God and the New Testament to be the proclamation of that covenant. At the same time, the use of these terms is not intended to deny the unique and privileged status of God's covenant with Israel, manifested as it is in Judaism today.

Christian teaching dictates that both testaments be regarded equally as the sacred word of God. Although different Christian traditions might interpret these two testaments differently, one is not more important or of higher status than the other. Christianity has its origins in Judaism. Its central figure, Jesus of Nazareth, was a Jew. So were the early Jesus followers. Christianity's earliest and most important prayers have their roots in Jewish worship, and its values of justice and charity have ties to Jewish religious practice. Simply stated, Christianity owes its origins and much of its identity to its elder sibling, Judaism.

We now survey these two parts of the Bible.

## DIVISIONS OF THE OLD TESTAMENT

The books of the Old Testament are not arranged chronologically but are grouped (more or less) according to types of literature. Judaism calls its scriptures, which are roughly equivalent to the Christian Old Testament, the **TaNaK**. The name is an acronym based on the scriptures' three parts: Law (the Hebrew word is *Torah*), Prophets (the Hebrew word is *Nevi'im*), and Writings (the Hebrew word is *Ketuvim*). If you look at the table of contents of an English translation of the TaNaK, you will see that the books are arranged in order according to these three categories.

Whether for study or personal and spiritual enrichment, the Bible is perhaps the most frequently read of all Christian books.

Already by the third century B.C.E., Jews were reading their scriptures in a Greek translation that came to be known as the **Septuagint**, often represented by LXX, the Roman numeral 70. The name is derived from a legend recorded in the second-century B.C.E. document, called the *Letter of Aristeas to Philocrates*, in which the Egyptian king Philadelphus (285-246 B.C.E.) requested a Greek translation of the Law (Torah) for his library at Alexandria. In response, the Jerusalem high priest Eleazar sent 72 Jewish elders (six from each of the twelve tribes) to complete the job to the satisfaction of all involved. Later, the Septuagint came to include Greek translations of the prophets and writings, as well as the books of Torah. It also contained a selection of books and parts of books, which Protestant traditions call the **Apocrypha** (Greek, meaning "hidden" or "concealed") and that the Roman Catholic Church and some Eastern Christian churches call **Deuterocanonical** books (meaning "second canon," i.e., literature that was given biblical status at a second or later stage of development). The Septuagint is arranged in order according to the following four categories:

Pentateuch (Greek, meaning "five roll;" the first five books of the Bible)

Historical books

Prophets

Wisdom books

## CALENDAR DESIGNATIONS

As you probably know, people of different cultures in today's world use different ways of marking time. The Chinese calendar, for example, is a lunar calendar (based on the phases of the moon) of twelve months in a year, named after the Chinese signs of the zodiac. Five cycles of twelve years complete a unit in the calendar. According to one legend, the twelve years of the cycle got their names when Buddha invited all of the animals of the earth to say goodbye to him as he was about to leave the earth. Only twelve came, and he honored them by naming the years after them, each in the order of their arrival: the rat, the ox, the tiger, the rabbit, the dragon, the snake, the horse, the sheep, the monkey, the rooster, the dog, and the boar. The Jewish calendar is a modified version of a lunar calendar, but with a standard length to each month and the periodic inclusion of additional months to bring the lunar calendar back into conformity with the solar calendar. The Chinese calendar dates back more than 4,600 years, while the Jewish calendar year is nearing the year 5770.

Of course, the most familiar calendar for people of Western cultures is the Christian calendar, also called the Gregorian calendar. Based on the sixth-century Julian calendar, which was constructed around what they thought, at the time, was the year of the birth of Jesus, the Gregorian calendar uses the designations B.C., meaning "Before Christ," and A.D., meaning "anno Domini" or "Year of the Lord." However, you will notice that biblical scholars tend to use C.E., meaning "Common Era", instead of the more familiar A.D., and B.C.E., meaning "Before the Common Era," instead of the more familiar B.C. The Common Era refers to the shared history of Judaism and Christianity. Biblical scholars are not using a different calendar than the one to which you are accustomed. They simply describe it differently in an effort to respect Judaism's relationship to Christianity and its place in history.

If you have a study Bible (a Bible with study aids), you will likely find a listing of the books that belong in each of these categories in its introductory sections.

## DIVISIONS OF THE NEW TESTAMENT

Like the Old Testament, the books of the New Testament are grouped according to types of literature and are not arranged chronologically. The New Testament is usually divided into four sections: gospels, Acts of the Apostles, letters, and Revelation. Let us look more carefully at the content of each of these sections.

1. **Gospels.** These are the books that tell the story of the life of Jesus. Our English term **gospel** comes from the Anglo-Saxon *god-spell*, which means "good tidings." The Greek word for gospel, *euangelion*, means "good message" (of Jesus Christ). Thus, the term itself suggests that these gospels should not be treated as objective

historical or documentary accounts of the events of Jesus' life, but rather as proclamations of believing communities' faith in Jesus and celebrations of their experience of Christ in their midst.

The New Testament contains four gospels. Although Matthew's gospel appears first, most biblical scholars agree that the Gospel of Mark was written first and that the Gospels of Matthew and Luke are dependent on it. These three similar gospels—Matthew, Mark, and Luke—are called **synoptic** gospels, from the Greek *synoptikos*, because they can be "seen together" or they read the same. In other words, these gospels tell the same general story of Jesus in the same kind of way and with more or less the same chronology.

Biblical scholars think that the Gospel of John was written somewhat later and by an author who did not have access to the synoptic gospels in their written form. When you read the Gospel of John, you will see that it is quite different from the other three canonical gospels in terms of style, content, chronology, and theological perspective, and, therefore, it must be read with different expectations.

2. **Acts of the Apostles.** This book is the second part of a two-part salvation history and a continuation of Luke's gospel. Acts of the Apostles tells the story of the origins of Christianity from the time immediately after the death and resurrection of Jesus through the time of Paul's preaching in Rome—the period covering approximately 35–64 C.E. Its date of composition is usually given as the last quarter of the first century, after the destruction of Jerusalem (70 C.E.).

At first glance, Acts of the Apostles looks like a relatively uncomplicated history (as modern people understand history) or an eyewitness documentary of the early church. However, a closer examination reveals that something quite different is going on in this book. For example, the reader will notice that the author of Acts is being very selective in his telling of the story because he focuses on only two principal characters, namely, Peter and Paul. Moreover, although Acts appears to give us a good deal of information about Paul's missionary activity, the historical details are not always consistent with what Paul tells us in own letters, raising additional questions about the historicity of Acts of the Apostles. However, these are not significant problems because, as we shall see, Acts of the Apostles was not intended to be a documentary account of the early years of Christianity. Rather, it gives us a religious interpretation of or theological perspective on the events associated with the beginnings of Christianity.

3. **Letters.** After the gospels and Acts of the Apostles, the New Testament contains twenty-one letters (also called epistles). Seven are undisputedly **Pauline**: the Letter to the Romans, the two Letters to the Corinthians, the Letters to the Philippians and the Galatians, the First Letter to the Thessalonians, and the Letter to Philemon. They are called Pauline because New Testament scholars are convinced that they were written by Paul himself. Another three letters attributed to Paul are called **Deutero-Pauline** letters, meaning that they probably were written not by Paul himself but by one of his disciples. These are the Letters to the Ephesians and the Colossians and the Second Letter to the Thessalonians. Three others—the two Letters to Timothy and the Letter to Titus—are known as the **pastoral** letters because they are addressed to pastors of churches. Although they bear Paul's name, they appear to be much later compositions, written after his death.

We have now accounted for thirteen letters. What about the other eight letters of the New Testament? The Letter to the Hebrews has no named author, though it was sometimes (wrongly) associated with Paul. We probably should not even call it a letter since it does not follow the typical pattern of a letter. However, since it has traditionally been included among the letters, we will treat it there. Seven other letters are called **catholic**, meaning "general or universal," because they were intended not for a single faith community but generally for all churches. These are also sometimes called **apostolic** letters because they are attributed to some of Jesus' disciples and apostles. This group consists of one letter attributed to James, two letters attributed to Peter, three letters attributed to John, and one bearing the name of Jude.

It is difficult, if not impossible, to make many generalizations about this section of the New Testament. Some of these letters are addressed to communities, while others are addressed to individuals. Most follow the conventional style of a letter, but some do not. Some are formal in style and content, but others are very informal and personal. Thus, as we shall discover, each must be addressed individually and in its own context in order to be properly understood.

4. **Revelation.** This book consists of a series of visions given to John—not the gospel writer but an otherwise unknown Christian prophet with the same name. The Greek word for "revelation" is *apocalypsis*, and, therefore, this book is sometimes called the Apocalypse. It belongs to a special type of literature known as **apocalyptic**, which employs language and imagery associated with the events of the end time. However, if we were to think of the Book of Revelation simply as a "road map" of the end time, we would miss its primary message. The Book of Revelation, and apocalyptic literature in general, addresses some important questions about the problem of evil in the world, and it asserts the sovereignty of God in all things. Thus, it conveys a message of hope and a promise of a return to the paradise of the Genesis creation stories—a fitting way to end the New Testament and the Bible.

## THE QUESTION OF CANON

Another introductory question to be considered is how the collection of documents now called the New Testament was compiled. Why did some religious writings get into the New Testament, while others did not? Implied in this question is the assumption that the books of the Bible did not suddenly appear bound together as we see them today. We can safely say that none of the biblical authors expected that his book would become part of the New Testament when he wrote it. Rather, early Christian communities had access to a variety of religious literature from which they chose the books that would later become the New Testament. Likewise, biblical scholars agree that early Christian communities did not sit down with a predetermined set of rules to decide "This one stays," but "This one goes." However, we may be able to reconstruct, to some extent, the criteria of canonicity, that is, the principles that guided the selection of books to be included in the New Testament. Before we get into the question of the criteria of canonicity, let's take a moment to define terms.

The term **canon** means "rule" or "standard," like a measuring stick. It was first used in early Christian literature to refer to the "rule of faith," that is, the norm or measure of religious truth in the Christian tradition. The first Christian canons were **creeds**, that is, statements of belief. However, today the word *canon* is most often used to describe the collection of authoritative writings of a particular religious group. For example, the canon for Islam includes the Koran, while the canon for Judaism is the TaNaK, roughly what we call the Old Testament; the Mishnah, a collection of Jewish oral law attributed to Jewish teachers dating from 50 B.C.E. to 200 C.E.; and the Palestinian and Babylonian Talmuds, which are commentaries on the Mishnah. To say that the Bible, including the New Testament, is the canon of Christianity is to declare that Christianity's self-understanding is somehow dependent on it. It also means that the Bible carries a level of authority that directs the Christian community's way of being in the world. But how did Christians get the canon they have?

**A THEORY ABOUT THE FORMATION OF THE NEW TESTAMENT CANON** When we consider the development of the New Testament, we need to remember that the first Christians—before they were even called Christian—had no distinctively Christian scriptures. Instead, because the first Christians were Jews and people who were interested in Judaism, they were studying and praying over the Jewish scriptures in order to make sense of their experience of Jesus and this new Jesus movement. For Paul, the apostles of Jesus, and their immediate circle of believers, "scriptures" meant Jewish scriptures. Gradually, as Christians began to put together their own distinctive scriptures, they did so not all at once but in stages.

**First Stage.** The earliest Jesus followers shared stories about Jesus—what he did to care for people, who he taught, how he came to be crucified, and how they knew he was raised from the dead—and they reminisced about his teachings. What they knew about Jesus lived on in the memories of his disciples and the apostles and was passed on by word of mouth, perhaps for thirty years or more. However, we might imagine that they eventually began to write down collections of Jesus sayings that were used in teaching new members about Jesus, hymns and creeds (short statements of belief), and even some individual stories about Jesus.

**Second Stage.** Many Christians are surprised to discover that the first collections of Christian texts did not include the gospels. Rather, they probably consisted of some of the letters of Paul. In the Second Letter of Peter (c. 100–125 C.E.), the author says

> So also our beloved brother wrote you according to the wisdom given him, speaking of this as he does in all his letters. There are some things in them hard to understand, which the ignorant and unstable twist to their own destruction, as they do the other scriptures. (2 Pet. 3:16)

Although the Greek word that is translated here as *scriptures* can simply mean "writings," many biblical scholars take this verse as our earliest clue that Christians were beginning to collect Christian literature in order to create their own canon. It is also our first evidence that the letters of Paul had earned the status of sacred Christian scripture, much like the TaNaK was sacred scripture for Judaism.

**Third Stage.** Eventually, the early Jesus traditions were organized into written gospels (stories about the life of Jesus or collections of his teachings). There were many so-called gospels in the early years of the church. From writers like Clement of Alexandria (c. 150–215 C.E.), Origen (185–254 C.E.), and Epiphanius of Salamis (c. 315–403 C.E.), we know of the Gospel to the Hebrews, the Gospel of the Egyptians, the Gospel of the Ebionites, the Gospel of Peter, and the Gospel of Thomas, but only four obtained the status of sacred scripture: the gospels of Matthew, Mark, Luke and John. Our earliest evidence for this canonization process comes from Justin Martyr, writing in the middle of the second century C.E. In his comments on how Eucharist was celebrated in the early Christian churches, Justin mentions that either the "memoirs of the apostles" or the writings of the prophets were being read at liturgy (*First Apology* 67). The phrase "memoirs of the apostles" most likely refers to the gospels, and Justin appears to be giving them the same status as the books of the prophets, which were already part of the Jewish scriptures.

A few decades later, Irenaeus (c. 180 C.E.) was the first early Christian writer to single out as authoritative the four gospels that would later become part of the New Testament (*Against Heresies* 3.11.8). He also provides evidence that, already in the late second century C.E., people were beginning to distinguish between orthodox and heretical gospels. For example, he dismisses the Gospel of Truth because it "agrees in nothing with the gospels of the apostles" (*Against Heresies* 3.11.9) and he condemns the Gospel of Judas as a "fictitious history" (*Against Heresies* 1.31.1).

**Fourth Stage.** Paradoxically, Marcion (c. 140 C.E.), a Christian preacher in Rome, was responsible for the first canon of the New Testament. Failing to appreciate the richness and complexity of the scriptures that the earliest Christians had inherited from their Jewish brothers and sisters, he created a very restrictive canon of Christian scriptures that excluded all of the Old Testament scriptures. Apparently, he viewed the Old Testament as filled with internal contradictions that could not be resolved. Likewise, he could not reconcile the Old Testament's portrayal of God as a violent and vengeful God with the New Testament's portrayal of God as the God of goodness. He understood Jesus Christ to be the son of the God of goodness and not the messiah of the Jewish God of justice. As a consequence, he also rejected much of Christian literature that had Jewish overtones, accepting only the edited gospel of Luke and ten of the letters attributed to Paul as his canon.

Marcion's teaching quickly prompted a hearing before other clergy in Rome that resulted in his condemnation in 144 C.E. Soon afterward, other church leaders began to form their own canons or lists of approved books. The most famous of these was the Muratorian canon, an official list of books probably developed in Rome in the latter part of the second century C.E. It included the four gospels, the Acts of the Apostles, thirteen letters attributed to Paul (excluding Hebrews), Jude, 1 John, 2 John, the Wisdom of Solomon (today included in the Old Testament apocrypha or deuterocanonical books), Revelation, and the Apocalypse of Peter (today included among New Testament apocrypha). Other lists or partial lists can be found in the writings of Origen (c. 185–254 C.E.) Tertullian (c. 155–230 C.E.), and Eusebius of Caesarea (c. 260–340 C.E.).

Although these early canons sometimes vary a great deal, you will notice that they consistently include the four gospels, Acts of the Apostles, and Paul's letters. Athanasius, in his Festal Letter of 367 C.E., was the first to name the current twenty-seven books of the New Testament as canonical. Thus, the canon of the New Testament as we know it today may have been in flux until the middle of the fourth century. Even so, it was not until the Council of Trent in 1546 that the Catholic Church made an official statement concerning the canon of the Bible, listing—as a response to the Protestant reformers—the books that it considered to be sacred and canonical.

Most religions go through a similar process in the formation of canon, though they may not actually use the term *canon* to describe their authoritative literature. Judaism's formation of the Hebrew canon is a good example. The oldest Jewish canon probably consisted of the Torah, the first five books of the Bible, which are also called the Pentateuch. These books took their final form and were considered authoritative within Judaism not earlier than the end of the sixth century B.C.E. and not later than the fourth century B.C.E. Most Jews at the time of Jesus appear to have accepted a second canon called the Prophets, which may be almost as old as that of the Torah. It included the historical books (Joshua, Judges, 1–2 Samuel, 1–2 Kings), Isaiah, Jeremiah, Ezekiel, and the twelve Minor Prophets. It was of somewhat lesser authority than the Torah, however—what Christians might call a "canon within a canon." In the gospels, we will see several references to "the Law" or "the Law and the Prophets," the latter referring to the Jewish canon of the first century C.E.

However, the Jewish scriptures, as they are known today, also include a collection of books called Writings. Even though many of these books, like the Psalms, had already been in existence for a long time, the Writings apparently were not accepted into the Jewish canon until after the destruction of Jerusalem (70 C.E.). In other words, the Jewish canon was in a state of flux for approximately five hundred years before it reached its final form and was still in flux during the time of Jesus. In the end, Jews did not all agree on the content of their canon, so Samaritans, for example, have a different canon from other Jews. We should not be surprised to learn that the canon of the New Testament also evolved over a long period of time, since the processes of canon formation were likely quite similar for both testaments.

**FACTORS THAT AFFECTED THE DEVELOPMENT OF CANON** How did Christians ultimately decide which religious writings would be included in the New Testament and which ones would not? When we look back on historical evidence of the process of canon formation, we can see a few factors at work. In some cases, we might call these factors criteria because they resulted in the acceptance of some religious writings as authoritative for communities of faith and the rejection of others. However, we should note that early Christian communities did not start out with a set of guidelines for selecting New Testament books. In retrospect, we can identify priorities that seemed to govern the process and, as a result, think the process was fairly straightforward; in reality, the process was probably quite messy.

> Factors that affected the development of the New Testament canon:
>
> (a)  Apostolic origin
> (b)  Theological correctness
> (c)  Authority of church leaders to determine what was appropriate
> (d)  Widespread appropriation by the churches

The first criterion, apostolic origin, suggests that only books written by an apostle or a disciple of an apostle should be included in the Christian canon. However, the application of this criterion is not as straightforward as it might appear on the surface because many of the early Christian texts that later came to be viewed as sacred scripture were not autographed. For example, none of the four gospels of the New Testament was signed by its author. Instead, the names of apostles or disciples of apostles were attached to these anonymous works sometime in the second century C.E. in order to help establish their authority among the churches. Other writings, like the letters of Paul, are problematic because Paul was not an apostle, at least not in the usual sense of the word.

Sometimes it appears that this criterion was used in reverse fashion. For example, some early church historians and theologians questioned whether the Letter to the Hebrews and the Book of Revelation ought to be included in the Christian canon because they could not verify that Paul and John, the son of Zebedee, were their respective authors. However, apostolic origin was probably not their primary concern. Instead, it may have been that how and where the books were used made them suspect. Today we understand the notion of apostolic origin in the broadest sense, meaning that the book has some connection to the traditions associated with a particular apostle or with the period of the apostles in general.

The second criterion, theological correctness, suggests that some religious documents were not included in the Christian canon because they were judged to contain statements that were not consistent with the "rule of faith," that is, the creeds and the teachings that support them. Teachings that are consistent with the "rule of faith" are called **orthodox**, while those that deviate from it are called **heretical**. Of course, we can safely say that people did not set out to be heretics. Instead, it is far more likely that they were wrestling with a particular theological problem or trying to emphasize an aspect of a difficult teaching and they simply were not able to recognize the negative implications of the alternative they put forward. Unfortunately, these judgments about the orthodoxy of a particular writing were not clearly articulated at the time such decisions were made, so sometimes we are left to guess at the issues that pastors and teachers were struggling to resolve.

The Gospel of Peter provides a good example of the complexities of this criterion. First, we should say that we no longer possess this entire gospel. All that remains of the book today is the story of the trial, death, and resurrection of Jesus. Today's reader might be tempted to reject it because it sounds like an ancient version of our science-fiction comic books and could not possibly be historically accurate. It is a strange gospel, complete with enormous angels and a cross that talks! However, this is not the reason why early Christian churches rejected it. The fourth-century historian Eusebius recounts that Bishop Serapion of Antioch (c. 190 C.E.) told Christians not to read it because some of those who held it as sacred were led into heresy (wrong teaching) by its words. As a consequence, he also challenged the apostolic origin of the Gospel of Peter. An excerpt from Eusebius's *Ecclesiastical History* follows:

> "We brethren," says Serapion, "receive Peter and the other apostles as Christ himself. But those writings which falsely go under their name, as we are well acquainted with them, we reject, and know also, that we have not received such handed down to us. But when I came to you, I had supposed that all held to the true faith; and as I had not perused the gospel presented by them under the name of Peter, I said, 'If this be the only thing that creates difference among you, let it be read;' but now having understood, from what was said to me, that their minds were enveloped in some heresy, I will make haste to come to you again; therefore, brethren, expect me soon. But as we perceived what was the heresy of Marcianus, we plainly saw that he ignorantly contradicted himself, which things you may learn from what has been written to you. For we have borrowed this gospel from others, who have studied it, that is, from the successors of those who led the way before him, whom we call Docetae, (for most opinions have sprung from this sect.) And in this we have discovered many things, superadded to the sound faith of our Savior; some also, attached that are foreign to it, and which we have also subjoined for your sake." Thus far of the works of Serapion. (*Ecclesiastical History,* VI 12.3–6)

The wrong teaching to which Serapion referred is called **docetism**, a tendency among some early Christians to consider the suffering and death of Jesus as "mere seeming." One can imagine them characterizing Jesus in this way to emphasize his superior heroism, but others saw this as a refusal to acknowledge the humanity of Christ. Thus, the decision to exclude the Gospel of Peter from the canon of the New Testament appears to have been a judgment of orthodoxy or right doctrine.

Likewise, the Gospel of Thomas, although apparently popular within some Christian circles in the mid–second century C.E., probably did not achieve canonical status because of questions of orthodoxy. The Gospel of Thomas is very difficult to understand unless you know something about Gnosticism (see Chapter 11). This gospel does not contain many of the details we typically associate with gospels. For example, it has no miracle stories and no story of the death and resurrection of Jesus. Rather, it consists of 114 sayings (i.e., short teachings that sound like proverbs) attributed to the "living Jesus," many of which are also found in the canonical gospels (the Gospels of Matthew, Mark, Luke, and John). It describes the true disciples of Jesus as "enlightened ones" who seek to rid themselves of the things of the world in order to become "single ones," that is, pure spirits. They apparently thought of the physical world as evil; they recognized that they came from the divine realm and wanted to return there as quickly as possible.

Even with limited exposure to the Gnostic worldview, you are probably thinking, "But I thought Christians believed that God created the world as good?" You are right! This is just one of the theological problems raised by the Gospel of Thomas. But is this the only reason why early Christians rejected this gospel? We don't know for certain. Early church writers who comment on this gospel say that, because certain heretical groups read it, Christians of the true faith should avoid it. You can imagine them saying, "If those guys are reading that gospel, there must be something wrong with it!"

Our reflections on the Gospel of Thomas and Eusebius's quotation of Serapion's assessment of the Gospel of Peter suggest yet another factor that contributed to the formation of the New Testament canon, namely, the authority of church leaders to determine what was appropriate reading for their Christian communities. As pastors and overseers, they were responsible for the well-being of their churches. The pastoral letters of the New Testament (1–2 Timothy and Titus) make it clear that a chief obligation of the pastor is to restrain false teaching. Therefore, Eusebius's account of Serapion making judgment on the Gospel of Peter was probably not exceptional.

A fourth factor, closely related to the third, is widespread appropriation by the churches. By this, we mean that either the majority of Christian churches in several geographic locations or the most important churches with the greatest amount of influence saw these books as valuable for the development of the faith, preserved them, and passed them on. Thus, Christian literature like the Testament of Mary, which was popular only in Syria, did not become part of the canon of the New Testament, in part because it was not widely known. In some cases, churches like those of Greece and Turkey (then called Asia Minor) collected sacred documents and distributed them to other churches. Paul's letters are a good example. Almost right away, it appears, people started to collect his letters and pass them on to other churches. If those earliest church communities had not chosen to share Paul's writings, they might not have been available to us today.

These four factors appear to have been the most important for canon formation. However, other factors may have affected this process and simply may not have left enough evidence for historians to recognize their significance. For example, some early Christian literature that might otherwise have been included in the canon of the New Testament simply disappeared for reasons that are unknown to us. Today we have only brief quotations from them or commentary on them in other early Christian writings, making us aware that documents like the Gospel to the Hebrews and the Gospel of the Ebionites existed, but we do not know their content or why they were not included in the New Testament canon. But for those writings that were included in the New Testament, we can safely conclude that early Christian communities and their leaders judged them to be more or less universally accepted as authoritative for guiding faith and useful for inspiring and building up communities of believers.

## Key Terms

| | | |
|---|---|---|
| Bible | Synoptic | Canon |
| Testament | Pauline | Creed |
| TaNaK | Deutero-Pauline | Orthodoxy/orthodox |
| Septuagint | Pastoral | Heresy/heretical |
| Apocrypha | Catholic | Docetism |
| Deuterocanonical | Apostolic | |
| Gospel | Apocalyptic | |

## QUESTIONS FOR REFLECTION

1. What difference, if any, does it make that Christians do not all share the same canon of the Bible? For example, what implications might the lack of a common canon have for dialogue among Christian churches? What other consequences might you imagine?

2. As described above, the books of the New Testament are arranged according to the different categories of literature and, within those categories, sometimes according to the length of the books. What if the New Testament was organized differently, perhaps according to the order in which the books were written? How might people's perception of the significance of the various parts of the New Testament and/or their relevance for Christian believers be altered?

## ACTIVITIES FOR LEARNING

1. Select a Christian church tradition with which you are familiar, whether your own or the tradition of a friend or family member. Find out whether the Christian church you selected accepts the Apocrypha (also called Deuterocanonical books) as part of its canon of the Bible. You might also try to locate official documents that describe that church tradition's understanding of the value of the canon of the Bible, with or without the Apocrypha, for its teachings and religious practice. You might start your investigation by going to www.wabashcenter .wabash.edu/Internet/front.htm, where you will find links to the official websites of a large number of American Christian churches.

2. Do some research on the notion of canon in a faith tradition other than Christianity (e.g., Judaism, Islam, or Buddhism). What materials are included in its canon? How did these works come to have the status of canon? If possible, interview someone who belongs to that faith tradition, and ask that person to talk about his/her understanding of the place that scripture has in his/her belief system or religious practice. *Note:* Other faith traditions most likely will not use the word *canon* because of its Christian connotations. What you are asking about is the faith tradition's religious writing, which are considered authoritative with regard to who they are, what they believe, and how they behave.

## SOURCES AND RESOURCES

Barton, John. *Holy Writings, Sacred Text. The Canon in Early Christianity.* Louisville, Ky: Westminster John Knox Press, 1997.

Brueggemann, Walter. *The Book That Breathes New Life: Scriptural Authority and Biblical Theology.* Minneapolis, Minn: Fortress, 2005.

Cruse, C. F., trans. *Ecclesiastical History.* Eusebius Pamphilus. Grand Rapids, Mch.: Baker Book House, 1955 (repr.).

Gamble, H. Y. *The New Testament Canon: Its Making and Meaning.* Philadelphia, Pa: Fortress, 1985.

Lienhard, J. T. *The Bible, the Church, and Authority.* Collegeville, Minn.: Liturgical Press, 1995.

McDonald, L. M. *The Formation of the Christian Biblical Canon.* Peabody, Mass.: Hendrickson, 1995.

———— and Sanders, James A. eds. *The Canon Debate.* Peabody, Mass.: Hendrickson Publishers, 2002.

# BEFORE WE BEGIN

For Christians, the Bible is perhaps the most important document for articulating their identity, providing a foundation for their doctrines (i.e., religious teachings), and establishing guiding principles for the way they live their lives. This has been true from the beginnings of Christianity in the first century C.E. and continues to be true for contemporary Christians. However, the Bible, and even the New Testament, is a deceptively difficult document to read and interpret because it is an ancient piece of literature from a culture and historical time period vastly different from our own. Thus, the first major part of this book is devoted to giving the beginning reader of the New Testament some of the skills and tools, as well as the background knowledge, necessary to more fully appreciate the beauty and richness of the biblical text.

Chapter 1 addresses some of the issues that affect the quality of our interpretation of the New Testament, including the assumptions we bring to the process of interpretation. We begin by looking at how our knowledge of genres and literary forms affects interpretation. We also investigate theological concerns like inspiration, inerrancy, and the authority of the Bible and consider the implications of these ideas for literalist and contextualist interpretations of scripture. Finally, we examine post–Age of Enlightenment perspectives on biblical interpretation by comparing them to medieval approaches to scripture, and we conclude with some principles of a contextualist interpretation of the New Testament. Chapter 2 introduces some of the methods of biblical study that have been developed in this post–Age of Enlightenment period as well as basic resources for the study of scripture.

Chapter 3 surveys the historical, political, economic, and cultural factors that impacted first-century authors of the New Testament. When we look at the writings of contemporary authors, we often do not think about how much their works are shaped by the culture in which they live, in large part because we tend to take for granted our own cultural reality. Only when we are confronted by people whose cultural experiences are very different from our own do we stop to think about how our own cultural "lens" colors our view of the world. Likewise, when we read the New Testament, we must recognize that we are entering a world vastly different from our own—a world that is almost two thousand years in the past and located in the

Mediterranean and Middle East, almost half a world away. The best way to appreciate that cultural "lens" and its impact on the meaning of New Testament texts is to learn what we can about the first-century Greco-Roman world.

Chapters 4 and 5 address two other very important aspects of the background of the New Testament, namely, Israel's story of salvation and the religious and cultural world of first-century Judaism. Novice readers of the New Testament often do not stop to consider that Jesus was a devout Jew and that his first followers were Jews like himself. He and his disciples went to synagogue, studied Torah, and participated in the pilgrimage feasts just like other Jews of his day. Jesus also had to contend with Judaism's elite power structure just like the vast majority of his contemporaries who were not among the wealthy and powerful of Palestinian Judaism. Likewise, novice readers of the New Testament do not think about how its original audiences would have viewed Jesus' teachings and activities in the context of Israel's long and rich story of its relationship with a personal God committed to its well-being. For Christians, this story is told in the Old Testament. Unless you have at least a basic familiarity with the major themes of this story, you will not be able to appreciate the message of the New Testament.

As you can see, we have a great deal of groundwork ahead of us, even before we begin to engage the New Testament text. However, as with any successful and rewarding journey, preparation is key. At the same time, we need to be clear that these chapters provide only the briefest introduction to topics like Greco-Roman culture, the literature of the Old Testament, and first-century Judaism. In fact, entire books and full courses have been devoted to any one of these topics. Therefore, it is our hope that these very small surveys will entice you to explore further the topics that are of particular interest to you. Why? The more we can understand about the social, cultural, and political world of the New Testament authors and their original audiences, the richer will be our own experience of reading the New Testament.

# ISSUES OF INTERPRETATION

People who have limited experience with reading ancient texts sometimes wonder, "How do I know when I have discovered the right meaning?" Others struggle with how to resolve several apparently divergent interpretations of the same text, thinking, "Only one of these can be right!" Still others are content to say, "Meaning is whatever you want to make of it"; that is, interpretation is a matter of personal opinion. Underlying these statements is something that scholars call **hermeneutics**, the study of the principles and techniques of interpretation. The first step to a rich and reliable interpretation of a biblical text is recognition of the presuppositions that we bring to the process of interpretation. Thus, in this chapter, we will begin to identify some of the presuppositions that impact the outcome of the process of interpretation.

## WHY GENRE MATTERS

Suppose you are about to sit down to read a book. Whether you are aware of it or not, you make certain judgments about that book even before you start reading. These presuppositions, in turn, affect how you understand the meaning of the book and the significance you attach to it. For example, if you pick up a grocery-store romance novel, you expect to read about broken hearts, extramarital affairs, and numerous other sexual exploits, but you certainly do not expect to read an enduring literary work of art that later generations will read in their English literature courses. If you go to your local library and find a book on the Vietnam war or the Iraq war, you expect to read about the historical events that led up to the conflict or the political maneuverings that eventually brought it to conclusion.

However, you do not expect to find a travelogue of "must see" places to visit in Saigon or Baghdad. That kind of thing would be totally inappropriate!

When you make interpretational judgments about different types of literature, you are making decisions about the genre of the work. The word **genre** is used in a wide range of studies of literature and fine arts to refer to categories of artistic endeavors that share the same form, content, or artistic technique. For example, in music, most people can distinguish jazz from folk music. Composers and performers of these musical genres know that there are certain rules that govern their work. Sometimes they deviate from these rules in order to create interest or excitement, but when they go too far, they find themselves working in a different genre or possibly even creating a new genre. The same is true for literature. When you decide, "Oh, this is a romance novel," or "That's science fiction," or "These are biographies," you are determining the genre of a work. Sometimes you encounter a piece of literature that isn't quite like a history or a romance novel or some other genre with which you are familiar. The author may have been experimenting with variations of a genre or trying to create a new genre. Either way, you might find yourself struggling with its meaning. That's because knowing the genre of the work is an important first step in understanding how to interpret it.

Genres often contain smaller units of artistic activity that share similarities in form, content, or technique. In literature, these are called **literary forms**. An example of a genre with various literary forms is your local or regional newspaper. Most people can recognize the newspaper genre because, despite differences in political and cultural biases, the rules for newspaper writing and layout are more or less the same throughout the world. However, most people also know that you cannot read every part of the newspaper with the same presuppositions in mind. Instead, without even thinking about it, you shift your reading expectations as you page through the paper or scroll down the on-line edition. You read the front-page stories with one set of expectations, the editorial columns with another set of expectations, and the comic strips with yet another set of expectations. Most of us engage in this process of identifying genres and literary forms quite automatically, but that doesn't mean it is not important. Imagine how absurd it would be to read a comic strip as if it was a front-page story!

Given that most people know how to read newspapers, political satires, graphic novels, and other contemporary genres, how shall we handle ancient writings or literature that comes from a cultural setting that is very different from our own? Suddenly, we discover that we do not know the rules for interpretation. Worse yet, we might think we know how to read a particular text, and instead we find ourselves making serious errors in interpretation because we have not fully appreciated the genre of the literature we are reading or the social, political, and cultural circumstances of the author who created the work. This problem is especially compelling when reading the New Testament because the literature is at once ancient and from a faraway part of the world and, at the same time, considered vital to the faith of contemporary Christian readers throughout the world.

Let's look at a couple of instances where proper understanding of the genre of New Testament books can dramatically impact interpretation. Some people look at the gospels, for example, and are tempted to think of them as histories (in the modern sense of the word) or eyewitness accounts of the life of Jesus. However, research into the gospel writers and their original intended audiences shows that the original authors and hearers of the gospels understood the gospels to be faith proclamations for communities committed to belief in Jesus as the Christ. Thus depending on your expectations for the gospel genre, you might be reading the gospels to learn the "facts" about Jesus' crucifixion, or you might be trying to uncover the early church's understanding of the meaning and significance of Jesus' crucifixion, as explained through story. As you can imagine, these differences in expectations about literary genre will produce dramatically different results in terms of interpretation. If you are reading the gospels primarily to collect historical facts about the life of Jesus, you might be missing what some consider the more substantial and edifying message of the gospel—what it means for your life today. You might also be looking in the text for answers to questions that the author never intended to answer.

Similarly, some people read the Book of Revelation and think it will give them a "road map" of the events that must take place before the end of the world. Armed with this road map, they listen to the news and observe world events, carefully looking for confirmation of the world's end. However, without a proper understanding of the apocalyptic genre, they will miss the intended message of Revelation. Apocalypses employ language and imagery associated with the events of the end time, but the writers of apocalypses saw them as calls to conversion for a particular people in a particular place and time—much like the prophetic literature of the Old Testament. Apocalyptic literature also addresses the problem of evil by asserting that God will vindicate the righteous and punish the wicked and by declaring faith in God who is sovereign and just. Therefore, although the Book of Revelation appears to be about the end time, its real concerns are quite contemporary: Why does God allow good people to suffer? What is the proper human response in the face of evil? How will God assert sovereignty over evil in the world?

Because understanding the genre of a document is essential for knowing how to interpret it, we will ask about the genre of each New Testament book as we study it.

## THEORIES OF INSPIRATION

In addition to questions of genre, Christians who look to the Bible and the New Testament as a source of religious teaching or for insight concerning the way they live their lives bring to their reading a system of theological presuppositions that affect interpretation. These presuppositions revolve around the Christian community's understanding of **inspiration** and the related notions of inerrancy and the authority of the Bible. Perhaps every Christian tradition would agree that God is the author of the Bible. This is what people mean when they say that the Bible is inspired. Of course, the next question is, In what sense is it inspired? Some church traditions would say that God is the author of the Bible in the sense that God actually dictated the words of the Bible to human writers who recorded the words verbatim. Other church traditions hold the view that the human authors of the Bible are real authors in every sense but that the words of scripture are still somehow what God wanted communicated to humanity.

In fact, Christian churches hold a wide range of views on inspiration and, more specifically, on the relationship between the divine author, God, and the human authors of the Bible. Even within a particular church tradition, you will encounter people with differing views on inspiration, not all of which correspond with the church's official teaching on inspiration. The situation is similar for other "religions of the Book," that is, religions that share the stories and traditions of the Torah (also called the Pentateuch), in particular, the stories of Abraham and Moses and teachings about creation and belief in one God. For example, there is no single Jewish position on the inspiration of the TaNaK. Likewise, not all Muslims share the same view about the inspired character of the Koran. For the purpose of showing how views on inspiration affect the related notions of inerrancy and the authority of the Bible, we will select two positions on the spectrum of Christian views on inspiration. For ease of reference, we will call these two positions literalist and contextualist. However, to be clear, individual churches' understandings of inspiration are much more complex than our descriptions of these two approaches might suggest.

A **contextualist** approach to inspiration allows that God is the author of the Bible without describing exactly how the Bible is inspired except to assert that the freedom, individuality, and creativity of the human author are preserved. Thus, a contextualist might say that the Bible is the Word of God communicated through the words of its human authors. This is not to say that the human author worked by himself to create the written document. However, neither was he a puppet, simply recording the dictated words of God without reference to the world in which he lived. Rather, a contextualist who believes in the inspired character of the Bible would say that the human author used his own words and his own knowledge of science, history, and culture to express what God wants us to know about God's self and about God's relationship with creation.

The United Methodist Church's Book of Discipline provides an example of a contextualist understanding of inspiration, as follows:

> United Methodists share with other Christians the conviction that Scripture is the primary source and criterion for Christian doctrine. Through Scripture the living Christ meets us in the experience of redeeming grace. We are convinced that Jesus Christ is the living Word of God in our midst whom we trust in life and death.
>
> The biblical authors, illumined by the Holy Spirit, bear witness that in Christ the world is reconciled to God. The Bible bears authentic testimony to God's self-disclosure in the life, death, and resurrection of Jesus Christ as well as in God's work of creation, in the pilgrimage of Israel, and in the Holy Spirit's ongoing activity in human history.
>
> As we open our minds and hearts to the Word of God through the words of human beings inspired by the Holy Spirit, faith is born and nourished, our understanding is deepened, and the possibilities for transforming the world become apparent to us. . . .
>
> We are aided by scholarly inquiry and personal insight, under the guidance of the Holy Spirit. As we work with each text, we take into account what we have been able to learn about the original context and intention of that text. In this understanding we draw upon the careful historical, literary, and textual studies of recent years, which have enriched our understanding of the Bible.
>
> (*Book of Discipline*, §63, p. 75)

According to this view of inspiration, the Bible is God's revelation to the world. But this view also allows for the possibility that God continues to reveal God's self in a similar way through the works of creation, through the church's tradition, through the sacraments, and through other human beings. By extension, the interpretation of scripture—that is, how we make sense of the scriptures in our own time—also belongs to God's revelation in history. Moreover, because the Bible is the Word of God through the words of human beings, it is rightfully and appropriately interpreted in light of historical, literary, and textual studies of the scriptures.

Another example of a contextual understanding of inspiration can be found in the *Decree on Divine Revelation*, also known as *Dei Verbum*, which was promulgated in 1965 at the Roman Catholic Church's Second Vatican Council. An excerpt from this document follows:

> Those divinely revealed realities which are contained and presented in sacred Scripture have been committed to writing under the inspiration of the Holy Spirit. Holy Mother Church, relying on the belief of the apostles, holds that the books of both the Old and New Testament in their entirety, with all their parts, are sacred and canonical because, having been written under the inspiration of the Holy Spirit (cf. Jn 20:31; 2 Tim 3:16; 2 Pet 1:19–21; 3:15–16) they have God as their author and have been handed on as such to the Church herself. In composing the sacred books, God chose men and while employed by Him they made use of their powers and abilities, so that with Him acting in them and through them, they, as true authors, consigned to writing everything and only those things which He wanted.

> (*Dei Verbum*, §12)

Again, you will notice that this church document does not attempt to explain the mechanics of divine inspiration. However, it states clearly and unequivocally that the human authors acted within their own powers and abilities *as true authors*—that is, even with their limitations—when they composed the sacred text.

A **literalist** approach to inspiration would assert that God chose human beings and used them as instruments to record the divine words that were dictated to them. Sometimes this is called **verbal inspiration**. In this view, the human instrument can be likened to a scribe or secretary, writing down exactly what God told him to write. The human author is understood to have had little influence on the way in which God's word was communicated. As a consequence, there is little attention given to understanding the historical and cultural context in which the document was composed except insofar as it enriches our understanding of what is already written. The literalist interpreter is unlikely to ask, "What did the historical author intend to say?" simply for the purpose of understanding the human author and his historical context because the human author was only a conduit for the Word of God. Who he was and when and where he lived had little influence on the character of God's word communicated in scripture.

Again, some examples will help to illustrate the difference between a literalist approach to inspiration and a contextualist approach. The following statement from the official website of the Christian Reformed Church represents a literalist view of inspiration:

> The beliefs and doctrine of the Christian Reformed Church are based on the Holy Bible, God's infallible written Word contained in the 66 books of the Old and New Testaments.

> We believe that it was uniquely, verbally and fully inspired by the Holy Spirit and that it is the supreme and final authority in all matters on which it speaks. (http://www.crcna.org/crbe/index.htm)

A similar, though more fully explicated, approach can be found in the official teachings of the Missouri Synod of the Lutheran Church:

> We believe, teach and confess that all Scripture is given by the inspiration of God the Holy Spirit and that God is therefore the true Author of every word of Scripture. We acknowledge that there is a qualitative difference between the inspired witness of Holy Scripture in all its parts and the words and the witness of every other form of human expression, making the Bible a unique book.
>     We therefore reject the following views:
>
> 1. That the Holy Scriptures are inspired only in the sense that all Christians are "inspired" to confess the lordship of Jesus Christ.
>
> 2. That the Holy Spirit did not inspire the actual words of the Biblical authors but merely provided these men with special guidance.
>
> 3. That only those matters in Holy Scripture were inspired by the Holy Spirit which directly pertain to Jesus Christ and man's salvation.
>
> 4. That noncanonical writings in the Christian tradition can be regarded as "inspired" in the same sense as Holy Scripture.
>
> 5. That portions of the New Testament witness to Jesus Christ contain imaginative additions, which had their origin in the early Christian community and do not present actual facts.
>
> (*A Statement of Scriptural and Confessional Principles*, p. 2)

As you can see, a literalist view of inspiration gives absolute priority of place to the Bible as God's direct verbal revelation to the believer.

Critics of a contextualist view of inspiration might argue that, for all intents and purposes, it denies the divine authorship of the Bible because it is impossible to assert the human character of the sacred scripture and still insist that it is the authentic Word of God. Critics of a literalist view of inspiration might argue that it denies the free will of the human author and that it assumes a view of the human person as a creature who is fundamentally flawed and incapable of participating in God's revelatory activity. Some would go so far as to say that it denies the incarnation (i.e., "enfleshment") of the word of God and by extension the incarnation of Jesus, who is the Word of God. They reason as follows: Jesus, the Son and the Word of God, brought about the salvation of the world by becoming fully a part of the created world. Likewise, the Bible, which is necessarily "enfleshed" in the language, culture, and history of the created world, is the source of salvation and means of encounter where God engages humans on their own turf, so to speak. Therefore, to deny the enfleshment of the sacred scripture in human culture is to deny the incarnation of the Son of God.

As students engaged in an academic study of the New Testament, our task is not to determine which understandings of inspiration are correct for particular Christian churches. However, we do need to recognize that people from different faith traditions understand inspiration differently and, as a consequence, produce somewhat different interpretations of biblical texts. As we shall see in the next two sections of this chapter, they will also describe inerrancy differently and attribute a different level of authority to the Bible in determining what they believe and how they live their lives as Christians. Simply stated, how a particular church understands inspiration makes all the difference!

## NOTIONS OF INERRANCY

Although inspiration and inerrancy are related concepts, they are not identical. The term **inerrancy** means literally "without error." However, when applied to the Bible, it can have quite different meanings depending on one's understanding of inspiration. If one holds a literalist view of inspiration, inerrancy means that the Bible is without error in every way—for example, grammatically, historically, scientifically, and, of course, theologically. Because the Bible represents the actual words of God dictated directly to the human author, it can have no errors of any kind. To say otherwise is to admit the possibility that God can make errors. Likewise, someone who holds a literalist understanding of inerrancy must assert that the human author did not influence, in any way, the content or expression of God's word.

An example of a literalist view of inerrancy can be seen in this excerpt from the Southern Baptist Convention's *Chicago Statement on Biblical Inerrancy*:

- Being wholly and verbally God-given, Scripture is without error or fault in all its teaching, no less in what it states about God's acts in creation, about the events of world history, and about its own literary origins under God, than in its witness to God's saving grace in individual lives.

- The authority of Scripture is inescapably impaired if this total divine inerrancy is in any way limited or disregarded, or made relative to a view of truth contrary to the Bible's own; and such lapses bring serious loss to both the individual and the Church. (www.namb.net/site/c.9qKILUOzEpH/b.238325/k.AC1C/Chicago_ Statement.htm)

Likewise, the Lutheran Church—Missouri Synod has a view of inerrancy that is consistent with its understanding of inspiration:

With Luther, we confess that "God's Word cannot err" (LC, IV, 57). We therefore believe, teach, and confess that since the Holy Scriptures are the Word of God, they contain no errors or contradictions but that they are in all their parts and words the infallible truth.

We hold that the opinion that Scripture contains errors is a violation of the *sola scriptura*, for it rests upon the acceptance of some norm or criterion of truth above the Scriptures. We recognize that there are apparent contradictions or discrepancies and problems which arise because of uncertainty over the original text.

(*A Statement of Scriptural and Confessional Principles*, p. 5)

For some Christian churches, this view of inerrancy extends also to the translation of the Bible into other languages.

Churches that hold a contextualist view of inspiration understand inerrancy quite differently. For these traditions, the Bible's inerrancy consists primarily in its being a trustworthy guide to salvation, but it does *not* mean that the Bible is devoid of errors in areas of science, history, or grammar. Again, a couple examples will help to illustrate a contextualist approach to inerrancy. *Dei Verbum*, the *Decree on Divine Revelation*, of the Roman Catholic Church's Second Vatican Council describes inerrancy in this way:

> Since everything asserted by the inspired authors or sacred writers must be held to be asserted by the Holy Spirit, it follows that the books of scripture must be acknowledged as teaching firmly, faithfully, and without error that truth which God wanted put into the sacred writings for the sake of our salvation. Therefore "all scripture is inspired by God and useful for teaching, for reproving, for correcting, for instruction in justice; that the man of God may be perfect, equipped for every good work"
>
> (2 Tim 3:16–17, *Dei Verbum*, §12)

Similarly, the Lutheran Church—ELCA describes the trustworthiness of sacred scripture in this way:

> The New Testament is the first-hand proclamation of those who lived through the events of Jesus' life, death, and resurrection. As such, it is the authority for Christian faith and practice. The Bible is thus not a definitive record of history or science. Rather it is the record of the drama of God's saving care for creation throughout the course of history. (www.elca.org/communication/brief.html#thebible)

As you can see, a contextualist approach to inerrancy not only allows for the study of the historical, cultural, social, and political contexts in which the biblical books were written but also requires this kind of study. How else will the believing community be able to discern the truth of scripture for religious teaching and as a guide to salvation?

## AUTHORITY OF THE BIBLE

Hopefully, you have already begun to see that the authority Christian churches give to the Bible is closely linked to their understanding of what it means to say that the Bible is inspired and inerrant. Another factor to consider is whether and to what extent they accept other forms of revelation apart from the Bible. The Roman Catholic Church, for example, gives considerable weight to the revelatory character of the church's tradition, saying "[s]acred tradition and Sacred Scripture form one sacred deposit of the Word of God, committed to the Church" (*Dei Verbum* §10). By **tradition** is meant the accumulated wisdom of the church that has been developed and passed on through the centuries and is manifested in the teachings of its religious leaders who speak under the guidance of the Holy Spirit. Protestant churches are much more cautious about giving authoritative status to tradition, but many allow for the possibility that God's revelation comes to us in a variety of forms. See, for example, the United Methodist Church's *Book of Discipline.*

While we acknowledge the primacy of Scripture in theological reflection, our attempts to grasp its meaning always involve tradition, experience and reason. Like Scripture, these may become creative vehicles of the Holy Spirit as they function with the Church. They quicken our faith, open our eyes to the wonder of God's love, and clarify our understanding.

(Book of Discipline, § 63, p. 76)

Concerning the authority of the Bible, churches that hold a contextualist approach to inspiration and inerrancy might say that the Bible is best described as compelling and persuasive. In theological terms, contextualists could argue that the Bible has authority insofar as it *compels* a believer to respond with faith, hope, and love. Further, it does not legislate a particular moral action in response to a particular situation, but it provides direction or a series of guidelines whereby Christians ought to reflect on modern issues and concerns. In contrast, Christian traditions that have a literalist view of inspiration and inerrancy take a rather different approach to the authority of the Bible because they see the scripture as directly dictated by God. Thus, they would teach that the Bible provides an absolute guide to the moral life of the Christian and a singular response to a particular issue or concern. In essence, it is the "rule book" for the Christian life.

William Countryman, a theologian and professor of the New Testament, explains the authority of scripture in this way. The Bible by itself is not a complete authority but rather a historical record of the exercise of authority. God is the absolute authority. At the same time, the church community to which the believer belongs is the practical and accessible authority for the Christian life in a particular space and time, since humans do not commonly have direct access to God. The church participated in the Bible's creation and acts as its interpreter, but the Bible acts as the church's judge, constantly calling it to conversion (Countryman, 1994, pp. 52–57). Therefore, the authority of the Bible is closely connected to the fact that it is read and interpreted within Christian communities of faith that believe in its power to transform.

## CONTEXTUALIST AND LITERALIST APPROACHES TO SCRIPTURE: A SUMMARY

The above discussion of inspiration, inerrancy, and the authority of the Bible may seem very complicated to the beginner. Even so, we need to remember that we may have already oversimplified the discussion by adopting these two categories, which we have described as the literalist and the contextualist approaches to scripture, to represent the full spectrum of Christian understandings of inspiration. In practice, a particular church's approach to reading the Bible most likely will not appear so neat and tidy. However, our summary categories can help us recognize the extent to which a particular faith tradition's understandings of inspiration, inerrancy, and the Bible's authority must cohere, that is, fit together in a coherent whole. You cannot expect someone who holds a literalist view of inspiration to be able to embrace a contextualist's view of the authority of the Bible or vice versa. Why not? Because the way that each Christian community understands inspiration has direct impact on its understanding of the inerrancy of the Bible and the authority it ascribes to the Bible. One necessarily flows from the other.

Again, at the risk of oversimplification, we can use the following table to illustrate how the related notions of inspiration, inerrancy, and the authority of the Bible cohere.

| | CONTEXTUALIST READER | LITERALIST READER |
|---|---|---|
| | Approaches the Bible with attention to the context in which it was written (history, culture, social situation) and the kind of literature being read. | Approaches the Bible with attention to what the text says insofar as it was dictated by God. |
| INSPIRATION | God is the author of the Bible. It is the Word of God in the words of human authors. | God is the author of the Bible. It is the Word of God communicated directly to its human recipients. |
| THE HUMAN AUTHOR'S ROLE IN INSPIRATION | Being true authors, the human writers of the Bible retained their ability to write in their own languages, from their own perspectives, and with their own (limited) knowledge of the world. | The human writers of the Bible were instruments through whom God communicated his word, but they did not influence the way in which the word was communicated. |
| INERRANCY | Although the Bible can contain errors of history, science, or grammar, it cannot contain errors of faith. It is a trustworthy guide for salvation. | The Bible is without error of any kind, including historical, scientific, or literary errors. |
| THE BIBLE'S AUTHORITY | The Bible is the authority of the church as it invites and inspires the community to action. It also serves as the conscience of the church, calling it to conversion. The church's teachers/tradition serves as the guide for interpretation. | The Bible is the sole authority for the believer, serving as the "rule book" for Christian living. |

## THE PERSPECTIVE OF THIS TEXTBOOK

This textbook takes as its starting point an understanding of inspiration and inerrancy that accepts the full and free involvement of the Bible's human authors. Thus, the Bible is the inspired Word of God expressed in human words from and for people who lived in particular historical and cultural contexts. This approach to the Bible is called contextualist because the reader needs to take into account the historical, political, cultural, literary, and religious contexts in which the document was written. As we have already indicated, this approach is most compatible with contemporary historical and literary methods of studying the Bible.

## BIBLICAL INTERPRETATION: A VERY SHORT HISTORY

Although Christians have studied and written about the New Testament from its origins, they have done so differently in different historical periods. This is to be expected, since people of every historical period wrestle with their own unique problems and, as a consequence, have different perspectives on the world in which they live. The modern period, which was ushered in by the Age of Enlightenment (roughly speaking, the eighteenth century), represents a worldview that is unique when compared to that of any other period in recorded history. As a consequence, the questions that it raised concerning the study of the New Testament are distinctively different, too. To illustrate the difference, we will look briefly at the way in which scriptural texts were investigated in the medieval period and then compare it to modern approaches to studying scripture.

A word of caution, however. What follows is a greatly abbreviated survey of the history of biblical interpretation with special attention to the medieval and modern periods. In fact, much has been written about the history of biblical interpretation. If you wish to study this topic further, you can begin with the "Sources and Resources" section at the end of this chapter.

PRECURSORS TO MEDIEVAL INTERPRETATIONS OF SCRIPTURE   In the medieval period, scriptural study was characterized by what are sometimes called the "Four Senses" of scripture. The idea that a particular biblical text could have multiple meanings was not new to this period, however. In fact, even in the era of the early church, biblical commentators argued over different meanings of biblical texts. Take, for example, the two early Christian approaches to biblical interpretation known as the Alexandrian school and the Antiochene school. These two approaches were named for the cities in which their most important scholars practiced their craft of biblical interpretation: Alexandria in Egypt and Antioch in Syria.

The Alexandrian school, whose most famous commentators were Clement of Alexandria (c. 150–215 C.E.) and Origen (c. 180–251C.E.), believed that every biblical text had a spiritual or moral sense but that not every text had a historical or literal meaning. Especially problematic for them were certain Old Testament texts that did not lend themselves well to Christian reinterpretation. In order to make these texts relevant, the Alexandrian school relied on allegorical interpretations of scripture. **Allegory** is a kind of literature in which characters and events are presented as symbols with some deeper spiritual or moral meaning. In a sense, it is an extended metaphor (comparison). When scripture was read in this way, the event, as narrated in scripture, was understood to point to the Christ event (i.e., Jesus' incarnation, death, resurrection, or presence in the sacraments). Thus, the goal of an allegorical reading of scripture was to assist the reader in encountering Christ in the scriptures, whether or not the scriptural passage itself made any direct reference to Christ.

However, the Alexandrian school was not responsible for inventing this way of reading scripture. Irenaeus of Lyon (c. 130–202 C.E.), for example, also advocated this approach:

> If any one, therefore, reads the Scriptures with attention, he will find in them an account of Christ, and a foreshadowing of the new calling. For Christ is the treasure which was hid in the field [Matt. 13:44], that is, in the world (for "the field is the world" [Matt. 13:38]); but the treasure hid in the Scriptures is Christ, since He was pointed out by means of types and parables.
>
> (*Against Heresies* 4.26, Cited in Yarchin, 2004, xviii)

We can go back even further in history to find other examples of allegorical interpretation of scripture. Take, for example, the Jewish philosopher and biblical scholar Philo of Alexandria (c. 20 B.C.E.–50 C.E.), who was considered to be a master of allegorical interpretation. In the following excerpt, Philo is commenting on the phrase "eat freely" from the Septuagint translation of the Genesis story of Adam and Eve in the garden of Paradise, which is the command God gives to Adam that allows them to eat from all the trees of the garden except for the tree of the knowledge of good and evil (Gen. 2:15–17):

> And the recommendations that [God] addresses to [Adam] are as follows: "Of every tree that is in the Paradise though mayest freely eat" (Gen 3:23). He exhorts the soul of man to derive advantage not from one tree alone nor from one single virtue, but from all the virtues; for eating is a symbol of the nourishment of the soul, and the soul is nourished by the reception of good things, and by the doing of praiseworthy actions.
>
> (*Allegorical Interpretation* XXXI [97])

Here Philo understands Adam to represent the human soul, while the act of eating represents the means by which the human soul is nourished and the trees of the garden represent the virtues (good actions and dispositions). Thus, the point of Philo's allegorical interpretation is that God intended that the human soul be nourished by practice of the virtues.

In contrast with the Alexandrian school, the Antiochene school was generally opposed to allegorical interpretation because its practitioners tended to deny or ignore the **literal sense** of scripture. The literal sense of scripture is not so much "what the words say" as it is the events as narrated, or what some might have called history. Therefore, it should not be confused with today's literalist readings of scripture. Moreover, the goals of history writing in the ancient world were quite different from what we expect today. In our contemporary context, we are inclined to read history to determine the factual details surrounding an event. Ancient peoples thought of history as uncovering the lesson that the event might teach. In that regard, the Antiochene school was not all that different from the Alexandrian school: Both approaches sought to unlock the meaning of the biblical text so that the people who read it could grow in their faith and put it into practice. However, the Antiochene school focused on the rhetoric of the biblical text and the story as a whole as the vehicle that conveyed the lesson for faith, and it generally rejected allegorical approaches as not being faithful to what the biblical author intended.

This is what Theodore of Mopsuestia (350–428 C.E.), a representative of the Antiochene school, had to say about the failures of the allegorical interpreters:

> Countless students of scripture have played tricks with the plain sense of the Bible and want to rob it of any meaning it contains. In fact, they make up inept fables and call their inanities "allegories." They so abuse the Apostle's paradigm as to make the holy texts incomprehensible and meaningless. They go to much trouble to say just what the Apostle says, "This is by way of an allegory," but they have no idea how far they stray from what Paul is saying here. That is because he neither dismisses the historical narrative nor is he adding new things to an old story. Instead, Paul is talking about events as they happened, then submits the story of those events to his present understanding.
>
> (*Commentary on Galatians* 1.75, Cited in Yarchin, 2004, 80)

The apostle to whom Theodore is referring is the New Testament writer Paul. The phrase "This is by way of an allegory" refers to Paul's allegory concerning Abraham's two sons, Ishmael and Isaac, which he includes in his Letter to the Galatians (Gal. 4:21–31). Theodore's point is this: Paul knew the correct way to allegorize—by remaining true to the historical narrative and not adding new details to the story—while Theodore's contemporaries did not. They would do better to focus on the "plain sense of the Bible" and write about biblical events "as they happened."

Before moving to the medieval period, we need to mention briefly one more interpretative approach that was popular in the early church, namely, typological interpretation. The term **type** describes an Old Testament character or event that serves as a pattern or model for the later, more perfect New Testament character or event. The excerpt that follows is a fragment of a larger work called *Cantena on Genesis*. It is often attributed to Melito of Sardis (late second century C.E.), but Alexander of Alexandria (d. 326 C.E.) has also been suggested as its author. Here the author is commenting on the story of Abraham's near sacrifice of his son Isaac (Gen. 22:1–19). He begins with a brief allegorical interpretation of the Abraham story in the first two paragraphs of this excerpt but then shifts to a typological interpretation. Here Isaac and the ram caught in the thicket are both types of Jesus Christ, while Abraham is a type of God the Father. Of each of these characters of the story, we can say that the former prefigures the latter and the latter perfects the former:

> In place of Isaac the just, a ram appeared for slaughter, in order that Isaac might be liberated from his bonds. The slaughter of this animal redeemed Isaac from death. In like manner, the Lord, being slain, saved us; being bound, He loosed us; being sacrificed, He redeemed us. . . .
>
> For the Lord was a lamb, like the ram which Abraham saw caught in the bush Sabec. But this bush represented the cross, and that place Jerusalem, and the lamb the Lord bound for slaughter.
>
> For as a ram was He bound, says he concerning our Lord Jesus Christ, and as a lamb was He shorn, and as a sheep was He led to the slaughter, and as a lamb was He crucified; and He carried the cross on His shoulders when He was led up to the hill to be slain, as was Isaac by his father. But Christ suffered, and Isaac did not suffer: for he was but a type of Him who should suffer. Yet, even when serving only for a type of Christ, he smote men with astonishment and fear.

For a new mystery was presented to view—a son led by his father to a mountain to be slain, whose feet he bound together, and laid him on the wood of the sacrifice, preparing with care whatever was necessary to his immolation. Isaac on his part is silent, bound like a ram, not opening his mouth, nor uttering a sound with his voice. For, not fearing the knife, nor quailing before the fire, nor troubled by the prospect of suffering, he sustained bravely the character of the type of the Lord. Accordingly there lies Isaac before us, with his feet bound like a ram, his father standing by, with the knife all bare in his hand, not shrinking from shedding the blood of his son.

(*Ante-Nicene Fathers*, vol. 8, pp. 759–760)

Notice how the author compares the preparations for sacrifice that Isaac endured to those that Jesus suffered in preparation for his crucifixion. In this sense, Isaac is a type of Christ, providing a blueprint or model of what was to come. However, he is an imperfect model of the more perfect reality because God made it possible for Abraham to spare Isaac's life by providing a ram as a replacement sacrifice. The ram/lamb, of course, is Jesus, God's own son.

Although both involve comparison, typological interpretation is different from allegorical interpretation insofar as the former accepts the literal sense of scripture (i.e., the events as narrated) and then employs typology to establish its relevance for the contemporary reader. The latter does not concern itself with the literal sense of scripture except insofar as it provides insight into the symbolic meaning of the various components of the biblical story.

**THE MEDIEVAL FOUR SENSES OF SCRIPTURE** The major contribution of the medieval period to the history of biblical interpretation is not so much creating new approaches to the interpretation of the Bible as it is organizing them into a kind of formula called the Four Senses of scripture. This approach to scripture is best illustrated by a Latin verse attributed to Augustine of Denmark (thirteenth century C.E.). Translated, the verse reads:

The literal sense shows what happened,
the allegorical what you are to believe,
the moral what you are to do,
the anagogical where you are headed.

(Cited in Montague, 1997, 53)

Let us "unpack" this Latin verse and explain the Four Senses of scripture in more detail. As in the ancient world, medieval peoples understood the literal sense of scripture to be the events as narrated, or what some might have called history. Medieval biblical scholars who were seeking the literal sense of scripture were asking questions that were more or less comparable to the historical questions that biblical scholars might ask today: What did the author intend? What were the circumstances to which the biblical writer was responding? What did the text mean for its original hearers?

The **allegorical sense** of scripture, to which Augustine of Denmark refers, was concerned with finding a metaphor (comparison) that could help explain the meaning of the biblical text and the place of this event in the story of salvation. Thus, as we have seen in the examples above, the goal of an allegorical reading of scripture was to assist the reader in encountering Christ in the scriptures, whether or not the scriptural passage itself made any direct reference to Christ.

The third of the Four Senses of scripture, the moral or **tropological sense**, was not so much about searching out a list of ethical regulations within scripture as about responding to its call to conversion. Therefore, properly speaking, the moral sense relates to the believer's response to the Christ encounter that was elicited through the allegorical reading of scripture. Having encountered Christ in the scriptures, the reader is now invited to respond by changing his or her way of living in the world in order that his or her actions might correspond to the inner change of heart that has already taken place.

Finally, the **anagogical sense** of scripture was understood to relate to humanity's final goal, heaven, or to one's reflection on these final things. Think of it as reading the biblical text through the lens of the afterlife and as a metaphor of the end time. Thus, the anagogical sense of a biblical text addressed questions like these: What awaits the believer at the end of life? Why should believers anticipate their end with joy and hope? Why must the believer behave righteously in this life?

An example from Thomas Aquinas's commentary on Paul's Letter to the Galatians will help to explain further. Thomas is reflecting on the words that God spoke in the first creation story of the Book of Genesis, "Let there be light" (Gen. 1:3):

> When I say, "let there be light," literally referring to material light [of the first creation], this belongs to the literal sense. If "let there be light" is understood as Christ being born in the church [baptism was known as "illumination"], this is the allegorical sense. If "let there be light" means that through Christ we are led to glory, this is the anagogical sense. If "let there be light" means that by Christ we are illuminated in mind and inflamed in heart, this is the moral sense.

(Cited in Montague, 1997, pp. 58–59)

For Thomas, then, the literal sense or plain meaning of Genesis 1:3 concerns the creation of the light that is generated in the sun and stars and reflected in the moon. The allegorical sense of Genesis 1:3 relates to the believers' encounter with Christ in baptism, the sacrament of illumination. The tropological sense of Genesis 1:3 concerns the way in which the believers' encounter with Christ, the Light of the World, gives them insight into right living and the passion to act on it. Finally, the anagogical sense of Genesis 1:3 relates to the believers' destiny, the eternal light and glory that is God.

Among medieval biblical scholars, almost any biblical text could have an allegorical, a moral, and an anagogical sense. However, not all biblical texts were thought to have a literal sense. For example, these scholars would have said that certain difficult Old Testament texts were never intended to have a historical meaning that would edify the Christian believer but only metaphorical meanings. On the other hand, only the literal (i.e., historical) sense of scripture was thought to be useful in

Thomas Aquinas (1225?–1274) wearing his Dominican habit and holding a crucifix and a book.

arguments with nonbelievers. Therefore, the Four Senses of scripture depended not only on the content of the biblical text but also on the audience for which the interpretation was being done.

## THE AGE OF ENLIGHTENMENT

The **Age of Enlightenment** represents the beginning of the modern period of history and the emergence of entirely new ways of thinking about the world, God, and ourselves. Great thinkers in the area of philosophy—Immanuel Kant and René Descartes, to name only two—began to focus on the value of reason and the necessity of empirical evidence as proof for statements of belief. It was no longer acceptable to say that something was true because God had revealed it. Rather, one had to be able to demonstrate a truth through the collection of observable data. Christianity has a long tradition of recognizing the compatibility of faith and reason. One of the traditional definitions of theology—faith seeking understanding—

René Descartes (1596–1650), French philosopher, mathematician, and scientist, seated at table with a quill pen and a book.

is a good example of Christians' understanding of the relationship between faith and reason. However, in the modern period, reason and empirical evidence began to dominate discussions of truth and even counter long-standing religious assertions. Faith claims that could not be proven using the new Age-of-Enlightenment ways of thinking were to be rejected. Included in these faith claims were theological teachings about the existence of God, resurrection of the dead, and Christ's presence in the sacraments.

The Age of Enlightenment also marked the emergence of modern scientific methods and new understandings about the universe. As late as the seventeenth century, most scientists saw the earth as the center of the universe. Beyond the planets and the stars, people thought that there was a place where God resided with the angels. When Copernicus (1543) and later Galileo (1610) began arguing that the earth was not the center of the universe—rather, the earth revolved around the sun—people were not happy, but Galileo even claimed to have evidence to support this theory. The problem was that this view of the universe did not correspond with biblical references that suggested that the sun rotated around the earth. It also did not allow for a place for God to dwell. Worse yet scientists began to develop mathematical formulations to explain the laws of nature, something that previously had been attributed to the direct and personal interaction of God with the world.

German scientist and philosopher Immanuel Kant (1725–1804), seated at his desk with an astrolabe at his side. *Courtesy of the Library of Congress.*

In the same vein, modern scientific approaches to history became popular during this period. Whereas ancient historians were primarily concerned with honoring their heroes and teaching moral lessons, these new historians were seeking an "objective" view of history, based on verifiable data like archival records, letters, and legal documents. They saw this approach to history as untainted by subjective biases and therefore better or truer. The implications for study of the Bible were enormous. Historians began to scour the gospels, for example, for verifiable historical information about Jesus of Nazareth, only to conclude that there was little to be found. The gospels were fiction, they reasoned and therefore not a valid source of information about Jesus. Inevitably, this new approach to history presented a challenge to the authority of the Bible itself.

# RESPONSES OF CHRISTIAN CHURCHES TO THE DEVELOPMENT OF MODERN BIBLICAL SCHOLARSHIP

Throughout the early stages of this movement toward modernity, Christian churches generally opposed these new approaches to learning because they believed them to be a threat to religion and religious belief. In many ways, they were. As a consequence of the historical, scientific, and philosophical developments of the eighteenth century, people began to raise a variety of religious questions never entertained before. And the conclusions they reached appeared to leave no place for God or belief in God. Moreover, since the Bible is the foundation for Christian belief, it became the focus for these apparent attacks against religion.

Eventually, when Christian churches could no longer avoid the theological problems posed by the Age of Enlightenment, some began to apply these new developments in science and historical investigation to the study of the Bible. German biblical scholars led the way in this effort in the nineteenth and early twentieth centuries, and we owe a debt of gratitude to them for their role in the development of modern methods of studying the Bible. However, not all churches considered this the best approach. Roman Catholic scholars, for example, were not allowed to use the modern scientific methods of biblical scholarship in their teaching and writing until 1943, when Pope Pius XII issued an encyclical (a public letter to the church members) entitled *Divino Afflante Spiritu.* It says, in essence, that the scriptures cannot be viewed as existing in a vacuum, as if God had directly deposited them into the hands of the human reader. They must be read contextually—that is, in the light of the historical and scientific developments of the time in which they were written and with an awareness of the literary techniques used by the human author.

What follows is an excerpt from *Divino Afflante Spiritu:*

What is the literal sense of a passage is not always as obvious in the speeches and writings of the ancient authors of the East as it is in our own times. For what they wished to express is not to be determined by the rules of grammar and philology alone, nor solely by the context. The interpreter must go back wholly in spirit to those remote centuries of the East and with the aid of history, archeology, ethnology and other sciences, accurately determine what modes of writing the authors of that period would be likely to use, and in fact did use.

For the ancient peoples of the East, in order to express their ideas, did not always employ those forms or kinds of speech which we use today; but rather those used by the men of their time and centuries. What those exactly were, the commentator cannot determine, as it were, in advance, but only after a careful examination of the ancient literature of the East. The investigation carried out on this point during the past forty or fifty years with greater diligence and care than ever before, has more clearly shown what forms of expression were used in those far-off times, whether in poetic description or in the formulation of laws and rules of life or in recording the facts and events of history.

(*Divino Afflante Spiritu,* §35–36)

Although Pope Pius XII succeeded in opening the door for Catholic scholars to use these new methods of studying the Bible, these approaches were not always well received at first because they seemed only to raise more questions about the truth of the Bible. It was not until the Second Vatican Council issued *Dei Verbum* (*Dogmatic Constitution on Divine Revelation*) in 1965 that historical and scientific approaches to biblical interpretation were fully accepted.

Some Christian churches dealt with modernity's threat by rejecting rationalism and theological liberalism as contrary to "the fundamentals of the faith." Thus, these churches are sometimes described as **fundamentalist**. The name originated from a series of booklets called "The Fundamentals" that were published between 1910 and 1915. These booklets contained essays from leading conservative Protestant pastors and theologians on a variety of issues related to the problems of modernity, including the use of modern historical and scientific methods for the study of the Bible. Although Christian fundamentalism has changed over the century since its inception, it continues to hold verbal inspiration of the Bible. Christians who hold this view assert that the biblical text is to be understood as literally and entirely factual in its history, in its scientific principles, and even in its literary expression. They reject the idea that biblical books might have had multiple authors who drew on oral and written source material in the composition of their texts. This approach is sometimes called *literalist*. It is not the same thing as what was earlier called the literal sense of scripture. Neither is it what modern biblical scholars call the literal meaning (what the author intended to say).

The Roman Catholic Church and a number of Protestant churches warn against this position for a variety of reasons. First, they charge that literalist approaches to scripture tend to reduce all of the literature of the Bible to one genre—something resembling documentary history—and do not allow for the use of symbolic or metaphorical language or imagery. Second, they do not allow for the possibility that the biblical text could be influenced by the historical or cultural setting in which it was written. A recent Roman Catholic document, "The Interpretation of the Bible in the Church," goes so far as to say that fundamentalism actually invites people to "a kind of intellectual suicide" (Pontifical Biblical Commission, Origins 23 [1994] 510). These are strong words, to be sure. However, the point to be made here is that there ought not be any incompatibility between a faithful reading of the scriptures and the historical or literary methods used to study the scriptures.

## SOME GUIDELINES FOR INTERPRETING THE BIBLE

The question of right interpretation of scripture is a difficult one. One thing should be clear, however. Right interpretation cannot be simply a subjective thing. That is, it is not correct to say that people can interpret scripture any way they want. If you belong to a Christian tradition, there are rules for correct interpretation of scripture, which are dependent on the tradition's beliefs concerning revelation, inspiration, inerrancy, and the authority of the Bible. If you do not belong to a Christian tradition or if you wish to approach the New Testament simply as historical literature, you need to be attentive to the historical and literary contexts of the text. That is, you cannot propose an interpretation of a text that is not grounded in or consistent with the author's intended meaning (historical context) or with the way that the text makes meaning today (literary context).

In the broadest sense of the term, biblical *hermeneutics* describes a field of theological study that deals with the interpretation of scripture. It embraces both the study of the principles of biblical interpretation and the process through which such interpretation is carried out in order to make the biblical text relevant for modern readers. We will address this question in greater detail in the next chapter of this textbook, but for now we will suggest some basic rules for interpretation. These are adapted from Mary Ann Tolbert's Sowing the Gospel: Mark's World in *Literary-Historical Perspective* (1989, 10–13). As you can see, she takes a contextualist approach to scripture.

1. The biblical text is the Word of God but written in the words of human beings. Therefore, in order to understand the Word of God, the reader must ask, What was the intent of the human author?

2. The biblical text has a timeless and universal message. At the same time, it comes out of a particular faith community and represents a particular faith perspective. Therefore, the reader must pay attention to the theology of a particular book of the Bible.

3. When interpreting a biblical text for modern Christianity, the reader should be aware of the general historical, cultural, sociological, and literary setting out of which the text comes.

4. If a reader has done a good interpretation of a biblical text, then he or she should be able to demonstrate its points from the text itself, without drawing on other books of the Bible.

5. An interpretation of a particular biblical passage within a larger document must be consistent with the whole of the document.

6. Ancient texts cannot be expected to reflect modern concerns, but modern interpreters can be expected to address modern concerns when reflecting on the biblical text. However, they must do so self-consciously and responsibly out of their own moment in history.

As we make our way through the New Testament, you may want to refer to this list periodically. In addition, you may want to consider ways to refine and/or expand this list of hermeneutical guidelines. Which of the principles listed above are most beneficial to your understanding of a particular book of the New Testament? Would you rewrite any of these principles to better express your understanding of a contextualist approach to scripture? Are there any principles you would like to add to this list? Are any of these principles applicable to a literalist approach to scripture?

## KEY TERMS

Hermeneutics

Genre

Literary form

Inspiration

Contextualist

Literalist

Verbal inspiration

Inerrancy

Tradition

Allegory

Literal sense (of
    scripture)

Type

Allegorical sense

Tropological sense

Anagogical sense

Age of Enlightenment

Fundamentalist

## QUESTIONS FOR REFLECTION

1. In your own words, how would you explain the concept of inspiration as it pertains to a particular book of the New Testament, for example, a gospel? How would your explanation be different if your audience consisted of believing Christians? Persons of another faith (e.g., Judaism, Islam, Buddhism)? Agnostics?

2. What would you say about the relationship between one's understanding of inspiration and one's understanding of concepts like inerrancy and the authority of the Bible?

## ACTIVITIES FOR LEARNING

1. Investigate how the notions of inspiration and the authority of the Bible are understood within your own church tradition or the church tradition of a friend or family member. If possible, interview the pastor or someone who is active in ministry within that church tradition. You might also try to locate official documents that describe that church tradition's views on inspiration and the authority of the Bible. One place to start your investigation is the Wabash Center website, www.wabashcenter.wabash.edu/Internet/front.htm, where you will find links to the official websites of a large number of American Christian churches.

2. Find some examples of literalist interpretations of scripture, perhaps on the internet, in magazines, or in newspaper articles—for example, creationist views of the origin of the world or the practice of snake handling in certain churches of southern United States. What clues did you find to help you determine that the interpretations are literalist? What are some of the attractive elements of this approach? What do you think are some its hazards? Give examples to explain.

3. Find some examples of contextualist interpretations of scripture, perhaps on the internet, in magazines, or in newspaper articles—for example, arguments against slavery, explanations of the phenomenon of speaking in tongues, also called glossalalia. What clues did you find to help you determine that the interpretations are contextualist? What are the benefits of this approach? What do you think are some of its hazards? Give examples to explain.

4. Research the history of the development of fundamentalism during the Age of Enlightenment and society's movement toward modernity. What were the circumstances that gave rise to this movement? What fundamentals of the faith did fundamentalists seek to preserve? To what extent are the values and priorities of fundamentalist movements similar or different today?

## SOURCES AND RESOURCES

Borsch, Frederick Houk, ed. *The Bible in Today's Church*. Valley Forge, Pa.: Trinity Press International, 1993.

Countryman, L. William. *Biblical Authority or Biblical Tyranny? Scripture and the Christian Pilgrimage*. Valley Forge, Pa.: Trinity Press International, 1994.

C. D. Yonge, trans. *The Works of Philo*. Peabody, MA: Hendrickson, 1993, p. 36.

Fischer, James A. *Interpreting the Bible. A Simple Introduction*. New York: Paulist, 1996.

Fowl, Stephen, ed. *The Theological Interpretation of Scripture: Classic and Contemporary Readings*. Oxford, England: Blackwell, 1997.

Froehlich, Karlfried, ed. and trans. *Biblical Interpretation in the Early Church: Sources of Early Christian Thought*. Philadelphia: Fortress Press, 1984.

Gorman, Michael J. *Scripture: An Ecumenical Introduction to the Bible*. Peabody, Mass.: Hendrickson, 2005.

Grant, Robert M., and David Tracy. *A Short History of the Interpretation of the Bible*. Philadelphia: Fortress, 1984.

Hagan, Kenneth, ed. *The Bible in the Churches: How Different Christians Interpret the Scriptures*. 2nd ed. Milwaukee, Wis.: Marquette University Press, 1994.

Lindsey, Paige, and Shaw Lewis, trans. *Theodore of Mopsuestia's Commentary on the Epistle to the Galatians*. 2 Vols. Cambridge: Cambridge University Press, 1880–1882.

Lutheran Church—Missouri Synod. *A Statement of Scriptural and Confessional Principles*. St. Louis, Mo.: Concordia Publishing House, 1973.

Montague, George T. *Understanding the Bible: A Basic Introduction to Biblical Interpretation*. New York: Paulist, 1997.

Olson, Harriett Jane, et al. eds. *The Book of Discipline of the United Methodist Church*. Nashville, Tenn.: United Methodist Publishing House, 1996.

Ord, David Robert, and Robert B. Coote. *Is the Bible True? Understanding the Bible Today*. Maryknoll, N.Y.: Orbis, 1994.

Pontifical Biblical Commission. The Interpretation of the Bible in the Church. *Origins* 23 ( January 6, 1994) 498–524.

Pius XII, Pope. Encyclical Letter of Pope Pius XII: On Promotion of Biblical Studies (*Divino Afflante Spiritu*). Washington, DC: National Catholic Welfare Conference, 1943.

Roberts, Alexander, and James Donaldson, eds. *Ante-Nicene Fathers*. Vol. 8. Grand Rapids, Mich.: Eerdmans. 1981

Second Vatican Council. *Dei verbum* (*Dogmatic Constitution on Divine Revelation*). In *Documents of Vatican II*. Walter M. Abbott, ed. New York: Guild Press, 1966.

Tolbert, Mary Ann. *Sowing the Gospel: Mark's World in Literary-Historical Perspective*. Minneapolis, Minn.: Fortress, 1989.

Trigg, Joseph. *Biblical Interpretation*. Wilmington, Del.: Glazier, 1988.

Yarchin, William. *History of Biblical Interpretation: A Reader*. Peabody, Mass.: Hendrickson Publishers, 2004.

# CONTEMPORARY METHODS OF STUDYING THE BIBLE

How do we traverse the distance of time, history, culture, and geography so that we can understand the New Testament in the context in which it was written and then give it meaning for our own time? We need to know the kinds of questions to ask in order to better understand the New Testament, and we need to know where to go for answers to our questions. To use our voyager metaphor, the place to start is with the resources that make for successful travel. Suppose you are planning a trip to Beijing, China. To make your journey enjoyable and rewarding, you need to gather some resources and learn some skills that will allow you to make the most of your experience. For example, you will want to study the history of some important places like the Great Wall of China and the Forbidden City. You will also want to learn some basic phrases in Putonghua, the official language of China, or at least know how to deal with translation issues. If you really want to appreciate Beijing on its own terms, you will also need to learn about its cultural expectations and values, art and literature, religious traditions, and music and dance. That's a lot to manage, and most of us will not be able to conduct our travel with great skill. However, even if we can do only a little preparation our trip will be a richer experience than it would be without any planning at all.

The same is true for our voyage through the New Testament. We need to gather certain resources and learn some skills that will make our voyage as rewarding as possible. Some of the skills we need to develop in order to better understand the New Testament can be grouped together into what biblical scholars call **biblical critical methods**. For those of you who are new to biblical studies, the word *critical* might sound strange in this context. Why would anyone want be critical of a document like the New Testament, which is understood by millions of individuals and religious groups to be a sacred text? Isn't that disrespectful? Perhaps, but it depends on one's understanding of the term and the activities associated with it. Biblical scholars use the term *critical* in a technical sense to mean "analytical" or "investigative" and the term *criticism* to mean "method of analysis."

Anyone who has conducted an in-depth study within a particular academic discipline like sociology, biology, chemistry, or English literature knows the importance of having carefully articulated methods of analysis for the discovery of new knowledge. The same is true for biblical studies. Simply stated, we would not be able to advance our knowledge of the New Testament without these biblical critical methods. Another image that might help people understand the role of biblical critical methods in the study of scripture is that of a jeweler polishing the facets of the diamond. As we apply different biblical critical methods to the study of the New Testament, we polish its facets so that we can better see the magnificence of the diamond that we have before us.

Some biblical critical methods are called historical because they are primarily concerned with historical questions of authorship, setting, and audience. The historical methods answer these questions: What was the historical author's intended meaning? How would the original audience have understood the biblical text? What source materials did the historical author incorporate into his writings and why? As scientific approaches to the study of the Bible go, historical critical methods have been around for a century and more. In recent decades, biblical scholars have also begun to draw on the methods of the social sciences to help us better understand the cultural contexts of the Bible. This is called social science criticism.

Other biblical critical methods are called literary because they are concerned primarily about what the text says now in its final form, regardless of our ability (or inability) to find answers to historical questions about the text or its author. Literary critical methods answer questions like these: How does the text make meaning? How does the reader make meaning in the process of reading the text? How does our understanding of the rhetoric used by a biblical author affect the meaning of the text?

Finally, because their starting point is the text itself, we will include in this category postmodernist approaches to the text. Postmodern methodologies are difficult to describe, but simply stated, these approaches challenge the assumptions we make about the meanings of biblical texts. They answer questions like the following: How does language work as a "sign system" to give the biblical text meaning? What is the deep structure of particular types of biblical narrative that drives the plot forward and makes them effective? What are the fault lines in a biblical text that make its meaning unravel or implode?

Still other methods might be called advocacy criticisms, for lack of a better term, or ideological approaches to reading the New Testament. Instead of claiming to provide an "objective" analysis of the biblical text, scholars who employ these methods state their biases clearly and up front. In fact, they become the starting point for their work. For example, an Afrocentric approach to scripture has as its starting point the assertion that African contributions to world civilization have not been recognized and have been downplayed and even been erased from history. For biblical studies, then, the challenge is to highlight or sometimes even reconstruct the contributions of Africans to the developing biblical tradition. Approaches such as this one also help us appreciate the multicultural dimension of the Christian story. After all, the personages of the New Testament were almost entirely from Africa, the Middle East, and areas of the eastern Mediterranean. Few, if any, could claim ties to Europe, and certainly none was American, but this fact is often forgotten.

This category can include a wide variety of criticisms, from Asian and Hispanic biblical interpretation to feminist, postcolonial, and liberation readings of scripture. Depending on how you define advocacy criticisms, you might even include some theological methods like canonical criticism (discussed below). Moreover, any of these larger categories of biblical critical methods can be reconfigured and further subdivided to represent or reflect the inquirer's focus on different aspects of the text, the reader's experience of the text, and/or the text's historical context. In sum, there is a large and ever-growing collection of biblical critical methods. Therefore, as you read various commentaries on books of the New Testament, you also need to read the introduction to find out what kind of methodology the researcher is using. When you know the methodology and recognize what kinds of questions are being asked, then you also know what significance to attach to the resultant interpretation. If the researcher is asking about the sources that the biblical author was using when he put together his text, you will most certainly *not* learn about how Hispanic Christian communities make meaning of the biblical text.

Our goal in this chapter is not to make you an expert at employing the full range of methods for the study of scripture. Even biblical scholars would not presume to be specialists in all of these approaches. Rather, our goal is much more modest. We want to introduce briefly some of the more popular and easily accessible kinds of historical, literary, and advocacy criticisms so that this chapter can serve as a reference for the varieties of methodological questions we will encounter as we make our voyage through the New Testament. Later, if you want to investigate one or more of these approaches further on your own, you will have a place to start your studies.

However, before we can even talk about the methods we might use in interpreting a particular biblical text, we need to know exactly what the biblical text is. Again, this might sound like a strange statement to make. Can't you just open your Bible and see the text? Well, yes, but most likely you are reading the Bible in translation, not in the languages in which it was originally written. For example, the New Testament was written in Greek, but you are probably reading it in English or Spanish or one of a number of Southeast Asian languages. And even if you were able to read the New Testament in Greek, the text you would have in front of you is not the original collection of documents because none of those exists anymore. Instead, you are reaping the benefits of text criticism. Different from any of the biblical critical methods that we have mentioned already, text criticism is sometimes called lower criticism. All other methodologies depend on it, and only a few highly trained specialists are able to do the work. So what is text criticism?

## TEXT CRITICISM

Whether you are aware of it or not—and most beginning Bible students are not—you enjoy the fruits of **text criticism** whenever you read the Bible. Why? Because none of the original manuscripts (literally, "handwritten") of any biblical book has survived into the modern period. Instead, we have only copies (of copies of copies) available to us today. Some inevitably deteriorated over time or were destroyed, others were lost, and some may even have been reused for other purposes. Among those that did survive, all books had to be copied by hand, at least until the invention of the printing press in the fifteenth century. Some copyists were better spellers than others and some had poorer handwriting than others, creating the possibility that a scribe might misread the manuscript he was copying and introduce errors into a later manuscript copy. Sometimes a scribe would lose his place while copying and inadvertently omit or repeat a line of text. Since scribes had access to libraries and were often well educated, some would jot notes and commentary into the margins of a manuscript they were copying or correct parts of the text that they thought were wrong. A later scribe would then copy these notes into the text, not realizing that they were not part of the original document. As a result, although we possess some relatively reliable manuscript copies, none is an exact replica of the now-lost originals.

This reality is not cause for despair, however. The text critic's task is to reconstruct insofar as possible the original document by taking all of the available ancient manuscripts and comparing them word for word. Sometimes there are huge numbers of copies to compare. In the case of the New Testament, sometimes we possess as many as 200 or more manuscripts of a single book. When text critics identify a difference in wording, called a **variant**, they have to determine whether the variant represents the original reading or whether it is the result of a copyist's error or an intentional addition of some sort. When they complete this process for all variants in a particular book—deciding from among all possible readings which one is the most authentic—they will have created the best possible reconstruction of the original text.

But not all manuscripts carry the same weight when it comes to reliability. Some have a tendency for more errors than others. Some have rather early dates—our earliest New Testament manuscripts are thought to come from the second century C.E.—while others are relatively late. Most of our New Testament manuscripts date from the fourth century C.E. and later. However, the oldest manuscripts are not necessarily the most reliable because it is just as likely that an error could have been introduced into an early manuscript and copied again and again over the centuries as it is for an error to be introduced late in the history of a manuscript

---

### TASKS OR TECHNIQUES EMPLOYED BY THE TEXT CRITIC

1. The text critic uses the clues of spelling, manuscript styles, and types of writing materials to date the manuscripts.

2. When discerning errors in copying, the text critic attempts to isolate the reading that most easily explains the existence of other variant readings.

3. Since scribes sometimes expanded the original document by adding explanations, commentary, or even biblical texts of similar content, the shortest version is often the preferred version.

4. Since scribes had a tendency to bring similar texts into conformity with one another or to correct what they thought were grammatical or logical errors in the manuscript that they were copying, the text critic assumes that the more difficult reading is probably the original.

family (i.e., a group of manuscripts that can be traced back to an earlier scribe's work). Therefore, text critics also try to date the manuscripts, decide which manuscripts are the most reliable, and identify the relationship of one manuscript to others of its manuscript family.

Text criticism is a very specialized area of study, not only because it requires a very thorough knowledge of ancient languages but also because text critics need to know other scientific fields such as archeology and paleography. Therefore, as a student, you will not do textual criticism yourself, but you benefit from the text critics' work when read your Bible because without them we would not have a common biblical text to read. Sometimes your Bible translation will give you an indication of

LUKE 12:18–37

Saec. III

Manuscript page that contains Luke 12:18–37. Notice how the papyrus has been torn, cracked, and frayed over time, creating lacunae (gaps) in the text. Papyrus[45] from the Chester Beatty collection, third century C.E. Hatch, *The Principal Uncial Manuscripts of the New Testament*, Plate XIV.

textual questions that may affect the way you interpret a particular passage from scripture. These are usually highlighted in the notes at the bottom of the page with the phrase "Other ancient authorities read. . . ."

Having clarified how it is that we even have a New Testament to read today, we can finally turn to our survey of biblical critical methods. We will begin with the oldest, the historical critical methods. Then we will turn our attention to social science criticism, literary and postmodern criticism, and finally advocacy criticism.

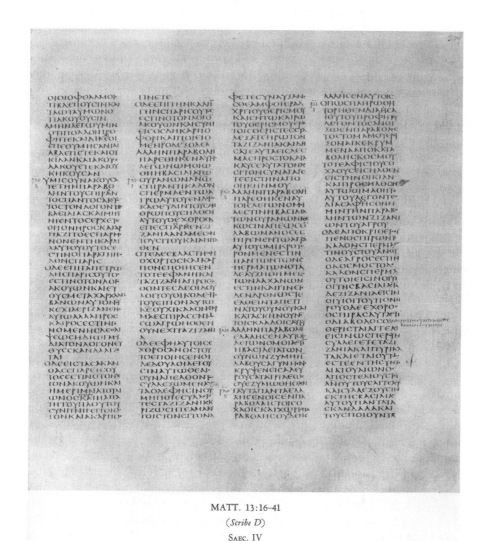

MATT. 13:16–41

(*Scribe D*)

Saec. IV

Manuscript page that contains Matthew 13:16–41. As with most early manuscripts, there are no separations between words, no accent marks, and little punctuation, making translation difficult at times. This manuscript also contains evidence that later scribes made additions or corrections to the text. Codex Sinaiticus, fourth century C.E. Hatch, *The Principal Uncial Manuscripts of the New Testament*, Plate XVI.

## HISTORICAL CRITICAL METHODS

Although there are several methodologies that fall under the category of historical criticism, all are primarily concerned about historical questions such as these: What do we know about the author of a particular book of the Bible? What can we learn about the community to whom the author was writing? Can we uncover the sources that the author used to compose his work? What information can we discover concerning the author's social and cultural situation that will help us understand the meaning of the biblical text in question?

Historical critical methods of studying scripture emerged out of the Age of Enlightenment's interest in scientific method and modern notions of history. When people who were influenced by this Age-of-Enlightenment worldview began to raise questions about certain religious claims, including the reliability of the gospels, biblical scholars responded from within the same worldview, eventually producing a full range of historical criticisms. The goal was to uncover a single objective interpretation of the biblical text that might be best described as the author's "intended meaning."

The following list of historical critical methods is not exhaustive. Rather, we are presenting only those that are relatively accessible to the beginning Bible studies student. If you desire more information about any of these methods or an introduction to other historical criticisms, please consult the "Sources and Resources" section below.

SOURCE CRITICISM The task of **source criticism** is to inquire whether the biblical writer has incorporated excerpts from other written documents into the final text. The source critic must determine precisely what the source was, what that text meant in its original context, and what changes in meaning might have occurred in the transfer of the source material into its new context. Sometimes the source material is no longer **extant** (i.e., preserved or still in existence today). Then the problem becomes one of reconstructing the original source(s). Take, for example, early Christian hymns, creeds, baptismal formulas, and Eucharistic prayers that no longer exist as independent works but that can be detected as having been incorporated into New Testament books. Historically, however, the most important use of source criticism was in determining which of the gospels of the New Testament might have been written first and which ones depended on another gospel as a written source. We will learn more about this later when we investigate the synoptic problem (Chapter 10).

When you begin reading the New Testament, you will observe that the biblical author sometimes indicates directly that he is using source material. The phrase that tells you this is "as it is written." When this phrase is used in the New Testament, it probably means that the quotation comes from the Old Testament. That's helpful to know, but if you had to read the entire Old Testament to find the quotation, you would likely give up before you found it. On the other hand, if you have a study Bible, the work of the source critic is easily available to you through the footnotes or cross-references located at the bottom of the pages or in the margins of your Bible. You will want to familiarize yourself with your Bible's study apparatus in order to have access to this information. By itself, source criticism likely will not add a great

> ### Techniques Employed by the Source Critic
>
> 1. The source critic looks for repetitions and inconsistencies in the final text. He/she also looks for elements in the text that appear to be uncharacteristic of the author or for places where the author seems to correct what he/she just said. These "literary seams" suggest the incorporation of source material.
>
> 2. When possible, the source critic compares the original source material to the final text and describes what changes in meaning might have occurred in its transfer to the new context.
>
> 3. When the source material is not extant, the source critic attempts to reconstruct the original work from which the author borrowed. When he/she is successful, sometimes the reconstruction will reveal an interesting insight about the literary world of the author.

deal to your understanding of a particular biblical text. However, it is an important first step to redaction criticism, which we will discuss below.

**FORM CRITICISM  Form criticism** is the process of discovering the original units of oral tradition that stand behind the written text and establishing the history of these units. When biblical scholars first developed this method, they hoped that it would help them uncover the "setting in life" (*Sitz im Leben*) from which these traditions arose. For New Testament studies, that meant helping biblical scholars understand the earliest church—that is, the church that emerged sometime after the death and resurrection of Jesus and before there were any written accounts of its existence—in terms of both how it operated and what it valued. The use of the German phrase *Sitz im Leben* reflects the fact that biblical scholars in Germany were pioneers of this methodology. The first form critics believed that there was a direct correlation between the way in which a unit of oral tradition was told (its form) and the type of situation in which it was being used. They thought that oral traditions, which were the product of a community and not individual authors, belonged to a concrete setting (baptism preparation, preaching, worship, etc.) that revealed something about the life of the community.

Today biblical scholars are less apt to engage in form criticism in order to learn about the "setting in life" of the early church because they agree that the results were not very reliable or helpful. Instead, form critics focus on the formal (i.e., structural) elements of a particular oral tradition in order to determine how the oral tradition was incorporated into the final text. They also expanded their work to include examination of the literary forms of smaller units of written material located within a larger genre—for example, miracle stories within a gospel. After establishing that the story is indeed a miracle story, for example, then the form critic compares the formal elements of this story to the formal elements typically found in miracle stories. Did the author add any features to the original oral tradition or literary unit? Did he alter or omit any of the elements usually found in that literary form? If so,

> ## TECHNIQUES OF THE FORM CRITIC
>
> 1. In the same way that a source critic isolates written sources from the final text, the form critic isolates an original unit of oral tradition from the final text.
> 2. The form critic identifies the literary form of the text being studied or the category of oral tradition to which the unit belongs (e.g., parable, miracle story, creed, or hymn) and compares its formal (structural) elements to the formal elements usually found in that type of oral tradition.
> 3. If the unit of text does not belong to an already identified literary form, then the form critic tries to determine whether this text represents a new literary form or category of oral tradition or whether it is a variation of an already identified form.

how do these changes or omissions affect the significance of that oral tradition or literary unit for the author's intended message?

Admittedly, in the abstract, all of this sounds very complicated. However, if you think about certain kinds of literature that you regularly encounter today or audio-visual arts like movies or television shows, you often know what to expect before it happens because you know the formal elements of that kind of literature or audio-visual art. For example, everyone knows that "reality TV," perhaps a serial like *Survivor*, is going to have a character that everyone loves to hate and a variety of "challenges" designed to get a reaction from the audience. In addition, you can be sure that there will be scenes of treachery, deceit, and whining. These observations are the starting point for a form critical analysis of the art form to which *Survivor* belongs. Of course, ancient literature is more difficult to analyze because the forms are unfamiliar, but with the help of commentaries (see below), you can do a limited amount of form criticism on parts of the New Testament or at least follow someone else through the process.

**REDACTION CRITICISM** The term *redaction* simply means "editing." When doing **redaction criticism**, the critic starts with the results of source criticism and form criticism and then analyzes the biblical text under investigation in order to understand how and why the author gathered and ordered various oral traditions and written materials as he did. In other words, the redaction critic is trying to map out the author's process of composition, looking for clues of inclusion and redaction of oral and written source materials and trying to figure out why the author adapted those materials as he did. After accumulating a number of examples of the biblical author's editorial work, the redaction critic uses the patterns he/she observes to describe the theological message of the biblical text and the social situation or worldview of the author and his community.

Among the various historical critical methods, redaction criticism is perhaps the most helpful in giving the reader insight into the mind of the author of a particular

**TECHNIQUES OF THE REDACTION CRITIC**

1. The redaction critic uses the clues of source and form criticism to uncover the layers of literary composition, trying to explain how and why this final document was put together the way it was.

2. Having uncovered the layers of redaction in the text, the redaction critic then attempts to articulate the theological perspective or worldview of the author.

3. Depending on the redaction critic's findings, he/she might be able to reconstruct the situation of the author or his original audience, which prompted the writing of the document.

book of the Bible. Biblical scholars use this process to discover "the intent of the author."

For the person who reads the New Testament simply as interesting ancient literature, these historical critical methods are not any different from what you might use in studying Shakespeare or Plato. Those who read the Bible as a religious document and who understand inspiration of the Bible as the Word of God communicated through human words use precisely the same methods. In other words, both groups read scripture as contextualists. The difference? The second group also wants to appreciate how the faith of the human author became a vehicle for God's revelation in a particular place and time so that it can be a vehicle for their own encounter with God. However, for those who are literalist readers of the Bible, understanding inspiration as direct and unmediated dictation from God, all of these historical critical methods will likely be a source of frustration because the emphasis is on the motive and activity of the human author in his historical and cultural setting, not on the divine author per se.

## SOCIAL SCIENCE CRITICISMS

Technically speaking, it is not entirely accurate to call social science criticism a single methodology because it actually describes a variety of approaches to the study of scripture, all of which relate to the social historical background of the biblical text, its author, or its original audience. In some books on biblical interpretation, this approach is called *questions of introduction* and the analyst is called a *social historian*. The methodologies that this approach draws on include the social sciences—especially sociology and anthropology but also archeology and related fields. For example, the social critic might draw on archeology or nonbiblical writings of the New Testament period to inquire about first-century housing, occupations, social classes, clothing, economic systems, and so on. He or she might also ask about the social history of a Christian community as it developed during the period in which the New Testament was written.

In some cases, social critics draw on the information of cultural anthropology, using themes or models that are common to all cultures—for example, honor and shame, sacred and profane, purity and pollution—to better understand the values and images of a biblical book. The social critic might also ask about the worldviews of particular groups for which a biblical book was written and the ways in which their worldviews affected their social ordering in the larger society.

## Literary and Postmodernist Approaches

Whereas historical critical methodologies represent the concerns of the Age of Enlightenment and the movement into modernity, literary criticisms have sometimes been described as the product of postmodernism or late modernity. What is postmodernism? What characteristics are ascribed to this worldview? Both questions are difficult to answer because of the complex issues involved and the variety of academic disciplines through which it is studied, but we will attempt a brief, albeit simplistic, response. Postmodernism is characterized by the recognition that the Age-of-Enlightenment goal of discovering a single objective meaning through the careful application of scientific methods is not possible, nor is it necessarily desirable. Postmodernism not only allows for multiple meanings and approaches but also assumes that to be the case.

Here are a few examples of postmodernism drawn from other academic disciplines. Art that brings together a variety of styles to create a new eclectic form, a collage of sorts, is called postmodern. From a philosophical perspective, a worldview that gives priority to the particular over the universal and the irrational over the rational is called postmodern. In the study of literature, postmodernist interpretations are characterized by a "decenteredness" of meaning (the recognition that the individual human experience of the reader or writer affects meaning) and an appreciation of the variety of cultural perspectives on the writing or reading process. It is less focused on the strictly rational aspects of reality and more attentive to irony and the playfulness of language.

When it comes to biblical studies, there are a number of methods that fit under the category of literary critical and postmodernist approaches to the Bible. However, all are primarily concerned with the text and how the text makes meaning for the reader. The literary critic considers the text as a world in its own right, irrespective of the historical and cultural setting of its author. He or she investigates the overall structure of the text, identifying its artistic and rhetorical elements and exploring how they add to its stylistic beauty or dramatic force. The literary critic asks questions about the *function* of a particular text within its larger context (e.g., transitional, climactic, illustrative), about the *placement* of the text within the larger context, and about the literary *mood* of the text (e.g., ironic, poetic, liturgical, polemical, comic). The literary critic also asks how the reader receives the text: What clues does the reader find within the text to help him or her create meaning? How does the reader's experience act as an interpretive "lens" through which meaning is made?

Literary criticism is a relatively new area of exploration, emerging only in the 1970s and 1980s, and new methodologies are still being developed, some of which are very technical. Therefore, this list will not be exhaustive. Instead, we will focus only on those literary critical methods that are reasonably accessible to beginning students of the Bible.

**NARRATIVE CRITICISM** As the term suggests, **narrative criticism** can be an effective method for understanding and interpreting narratives or stories. The narrative critic is not particularly concerned about historical questions like these: Who wrote the story? In what setting was the story first told? Rather, the narrative critic wants to discover how the story—as it exists now, without reference to its historical author or audience—conveys meaning. Therefore, the narrative critic inquires about the narrator, characters, plot, and setting of the story. Concerning the characters, he or she wants to understand how they are known. For example, does the narrator simply tell us about them, or are we allowed to see them in action or hear them speak? How does this information affect our impression of the characters? What is the point of view of each character? What is the point of view of the narrator? What is the relationship between the narrator and the characters of the story? The narrative critic also analyzes the setting—where and when the story takes place—to determine its contribution to the meaning of the story as well as to the plot of the story. How does the story move forward? What is its climax? How is the story brought to conclusion? Finally, the narrative critic analyzes the rhetoric of the story, that is, how it is told. Again, the goal is to discover how the story conveys meaning.

In New Testament studies, our best examples of narrative criticism relate to the gospels, since they contain many narratives (i.e., stories). As a beginning Bible studies student, you can do a simplified version of narrative criticism like the one described above quite effectively and with very little outside assistance. In fact, you may already be familiar with these techniques from your literature classes. The method is basically the same; only the literature is different.

---

### TASKS AND TECHNIQUES OF THE NARRATIVE CRITIC

1. Identify the place of the narrator in relation to the story being told. What is the narrator's vantage point? What is the narrator's point of view? What do the narrator's vantage point and point of view contribute to the telling of the story?

2. Identify the characters of the story and discover what kinds of characters they are, how they relate to each other, and what function they play in the story.

3. Analyze the temporal and spatial setting of the story. What does the setting contribute to the meaning of the story?

4. Analyze the plot of the story. What makes the story move forward? What is its climax? How is the climax resolved?

5. Analyze the rhetoric of the story. What images and word associations are incorporated into the story? Does it employ certain literary techniques or perhaps a "turn of phrase" designed to elicit meaning?

READER-RESPONSE CRITICISM Like narrative criticism, **reader-response criticism** is not particularly concerned about historical questions like the identity of the author and the community to which the author was writing. However, reader-response criticism differs from narrative criticism because it is not so much concerned with the text being read as it is with the reader's experience of reading the text. This methodology is difficult for the beginning reader of the Bible—or any document, for that matter—to comprehend because we tend not to think about our reading processes. Imagine standing outside of yourself, watching your other self make meaning as you read. This is what the reader-response critic does.

The reader-response critic looks for places in the text where the reader might be prompted to think back to earlier parts of the story or to look forward in anticipation, asking how the reader is acquiring meaning or understanding at this particular moment in the reading process. He or she might focus on gaps in the story, asking how the reader is able to construct meaning to fill those gaps. He or she also asks how the reader deals with irony in the text or with aspects of the text that seem to self-destruct—that is, aspects of the text that build meaning for the reader and then suddenly make that meaning collapse in front of the reader. Finally, the reader-response critic examines how the reader deals with parts of the text that are offensive or troubling to the reader.

Admittedly, there is a certain amount of subjectivity in this methodology because every reader makes meaning differently. However, the cultural context of the reader limits, to a large extent, the range of possible meanings. For example, biblical words like *law* and *righteousness* already have a complex of meanings attached to them, meanings that come from within the reader's cultural context. Unless something in the text forces the reader to reexamine these culturally conditioned meanings, they will be imported intact into the reader's experience of reading. In other words, the reader-response critic is not analyzing an individual reader's experience of reading so much as a community's experience of reading.

---

### TECHNIQUES OF THE READER-RESPONSE CRITIC

1. The reader-response critic attempts to take a position as an outsider watching a reader read a text.

2. When a reader-response critic asks questions about the process of reading, he/she focuses on pivotal moments in reading.

   a. What is the effect of the accumulation of words/images on the meaning of the text for the reader?

   b. When, how, and for what purpose is the reader called to look forward or to look back?

   c. How does the reader handle gaps? With what does the reader fill them?

   d. How does the reader deal with parts of the text that he or she finds troubling or offensive?

Although reader-response criticism can be rather technical, the greatest difficulty that the beginning reader of the New Testament encounters with this method is trying to assume a position as observer of the reading process. For most of us, the process of making meaning from our reading is largely unconscious, and analyzing how a person reads to acquire meaning is quite a different task than simply reading for ourselves. However, when we force ourselves to take this position as outside observer, we can focus on the text in ways that we would not do otherwise, and hopefully we can discover deeper and more nuanced meanings in the text than we ever thought possible.

**Structuralism and Deconstruction**  In addition to narrative and reader-response criticism, there are a couple of other postmodern methods that deserve mention here, even though they are too difficult for beginning readers of the New Testament to do on their own. If you encounter these in your reading, at least you will be able to recognize the methodology and identify its presuppositions. The first, **structuralism**, is actually the oldest of the literary critical methods. It uses the assumptions and techniques of semiotics to analyze the symbol systems of language and to investigate how the meanings we attach to symbols (i.e., combinations of letters that make up words with particular meanings) and the relationships among these symbols make communication possible. For example, how do the meanings we attach to the combination of letters and words in the sentence "My cat is fluffy" come together to convey a meaningful idea? When it comes to gospel stories, the structuralist is trying to uncover the "deep" structure (symbol system) of the narrative to see how it makes meaning.

The second postmodern method we need to mention here is **deconstruction**, which draws heavily on the insights of the French philosopher Jacques Derrida. This methodology (if it can be called a methodology) critiques the commonly held assumption that the world is organized in terms of binary opposites—for example, light/darkness, soul/body, rationality/irrationality, consciousness/unconsciousness, literal/metaphorical, maleness/femaleness—where the first has always been viewed as superior to the second. Imagine how the meaning of a text would change if you gave priority of importance to femaleness, metaphorical meanings, and irrationality, instead of maleness, literal meanings, and rationality, in the reading process! Deconstructionism also has as one of its presuppositions the idea that language is fluid and has within itself the tendency for its meaning to implode or collapse in on itself. Therefore, when applied to scripture, this method does not necessarily result in a new interpretation of a biblical text. Rather, it challenges all prior interpretations of the text and forces the interpreter into creative thought by turning upside down people's assumptions about how the text makes meaning.

## ADVOCACY CRITICISMS AND IDEOLOGICAL READINGS OF THE BIBLE

Finally, there are several other approaches to the study of scripture that might better be described as advocacy criticisms or ideological readings of the Bible. Instead of having their own distinctive methodologies, these approaches use either historical or literary critical methods, or sometimes both, but they take as their starting point an expressed bias or worldview. **Feminist criticism**, which has as one of its starting points the assertion that gender delineation is a social construct, is a good example. You could investigate the social-historical background of a particular gospel story, or you could use narrative criticism to analyze the characters, plot, and setting of the same story. However, when you give special attention to questions of gender, the analysis becomes feminist criticism. What difference does it make that certain characters in the story are male and others are female? Is there a connection between the content of the story and the gender of its major characters? Are male and female characters introduced in the same way or differently? What gender roles or relationships are at work in the gospel story? How do our assumptions about these gender roles affect the meaning of the story? These are just a few of the questions you might ask when doing a feminist reading of a gospel text.

Liberation readings of scripture, also called **liberation hermeneutics** or socioeconomic criticism, take a similar approach. A wide variety of methodologies can be applied to a particular biblical text, but it becomes liberation hermeneutics when special attention is given to the relationships of power and economic inequity described in the text. The expressed bias of this approach is that God is on the side of the poor and oppressed and that anyone who wishes to be in a relationship with God needs to be on the side of the poor, too. Some of the earliest work in liberation hermeneutics was done from a Latin American perspective, but you can now find biblical scholars who do liberation hermeneutics from a wide range of perspectives, including African-American, African, and Asian theologies.

Sometimes people object to these advocacy approaches because, they say, they are blatantly biased. Against this objection, scholars who engage in these approaches respond that all biblical critical methods, historical and literary, are biased. Therefore, it is wrong to say that advocacy approaches are less valid simply because their biases are more transparent. Further, they argue that those who claim that their approach is objective are more dangerous because their biases are operative, whether or not they recognize them. Better the biases we acknowledge, they say, than the ones we refuse to acknowledge because we can mistakenly give those biases a veil of "truth," allowing them to have more authority than they deserve. Finally, they argue that their expressed bias—e.g., God is on the side of the poor—is more consistent with the overall message of the Bible than their critics' hidden but no less operative bias—human structures of oppression are divinely sanctioned. This critique was originally directed against historical critics, who, for the most part, were well-educated, white, male Europeans and Americans. However, in today's pluralistic and globally conscious world, the same critique can be leveled at Western readers in general. Dominant cultures and people of power tend to assume that their view of the world is the only "right" view. Advocacy criticisms challenge us to rethink that assumption.

Related to the two advocacy criticisms described above is a category of biblical interpretations that could be called **cultural hermeneutics**. Here, again, the focus is on the experience of the interpreter. Cultural hermeneutics works from the presupposition that no interpretation is purely objective and that being attentive to the social and cultural context of the interpreter is a good thing. However, cultural hermeneutics can take us a step further into the meaning of a biblical text by drawing on traditional myths, stories, and imagery of cultures that are less like the postindustrial Western world and more like the cultures of the Bible. Most notable, perhaps, are African and Asian interpretations of scripture, in which stories from tribal religions or religious imagery of other-long enduring faiths like Buddhism and Hinduism are used to illuminate the meaning of the biblical story.

These methodologies also remind us that Christianity is never culturally neutral. Ethiopian Christians and Korean Christians, for example, think about biblical stories or theological topics differently than do Euro-American Christians because their cultural experiences shape the way they view the world. Again, the goal of cultural hermeneutics is not to create a single "objective" interpretation of a biblical text but to awaken our minds and hearts to multiple new ways of thinking about the biblical text. Another beneficial outcome of these methodologies is that they foster better understanding among peoples of different faiths and among Christians from cultural backgrounds other than our own.

Some biblical scholars would add another methodology to this category of advocacy criticisms and ideological readings, namely, **canonical criticism**. Others call it theological criticism. Although this methodology is difficult to describe, it shares some of the techniques of historical and literary criticisms, except that it is not concerned with the early stages in the development of a biblical book or with how the literary features of the text help to make meaning for the reader. Instead, it focuses on the final form of the Bible and how it functioned for the communities who first received it. Canonical criticism also focuses on how the developing traditions became authoritative for the community of faith. By analyzing these dynamics, the canonical critic hopes to uncover the locus of authority that resides in the whole canon, which, in turn, provides the lens through which individual texts are read.

Having completed our survey of some of the more popular and easily accessible biblical critical methods, we turn our attention now to some resources that will provide you with the background information we need to begin our voyage through the New Testament.

## Resources for the Study of the Bible

Students have a variety of resources available for the study of New Testament, resources that provide basic information and summaries of research on particular books of the Bible. You may want to visit your library and locate these resources so that you know how to use them when you need them.

**Bible Translations** Beginning Bible studies students sometimes forget that when they are reading their Bible, they are reading a translation of the text. The various books of the Bible were originally composed in Hebrew, Aramaic, or Greek. It would be wonderful if everyone studying the Bible could read the text in its original languages, but few are actually able to do so. Instead, we need to rely on translations. Of course, not all translations are identical because each translation group has a particular audience in mind and particular goals it hopes to accomplish. To further complicate the situation, some of our English translations are already one step removed from the original languages of the Bible. For example, some English translations are based on an earlier Latin translation of the Bible. The introduction to each Bible translation should give you information about how the translation was done and what text the translation is based on.

Most regular readers of the Bible use the same edition all the time, mostly because they have become comfortable with its layout and they know where to find things. However, if you are going to do an intensive study of a particular passage from scripture, it would be especially important to read several translations of the text as a first step in your research. The various translations will give you a better sense of the nuances of the meaning of the text in its original language. For those who are inexperienced at comparing various translations of the biblical text, be aware that you need to focus your attention on subtle differences in wording. For example, the Greek word *krisis* in John 3:19–21 can be translated as "judgment" or "condemnation." The careful reader will notice that these two English words have very different connotations. The first implies a decision between good and bad or right and wrong behavior, while the second always has a negative outcome. Therefore, you will get a somewhat different impression of the meaning of John 3:19–21, depending on the translation that you use. A helpful tool for comparing different translations of a biblical text is a parallel Bible, which contains four or more different translations on the same page of text. If your library uses the Library of Congress system, you will locate various Bible translations in the BS 190 section. You can also locate a number of Bible translations on-line.

**BIBLE ATLASES** As you are reading a particular biblical text, you will find references to cities and geographical regions that are unfamiliar to you. A modern map will not be helpful in locating these places because many no longer exist today. Instead, you need to consult a Bible atlas. Bible atlases contain a collection of maps based on different historical periods (e.g., Egypt and Sinai during the Exodus, Palestine during the time of Jesus). Be careful to select the map that is appropriate for the biblical book you are reading. Some atlases will also provide time lines and brief descriptions of various locations, perhaps even adding a note on their significance for the history of Israel. Depending on the size of your local library, you may find a variety of different Bible atlases available there, including *Hammond's Atlas of the Bible Lands*, *HarperCollins Concise Atlas of the Bible*, *Oxford Bible Atlas*, and *Collegeville Atlas of the Bible*. If your library uses the Library of Congress system, you will locate these atlases in the BS 630 section.

**BIBLE DICTIONARIES** Because the Bible was written in a temporal (i.e., related to time) and cultural location quite different from the world in which we live, it often contains references to historical events, objects, or cultural practices that are unfamiliar to us. For example, few Americans today understand the complexities of ancient techniques of metal smithing, wine production, or pottery making. How are we, then, to appreciate the nuanced interpretations of biblical texts that compare God to a refiner tending his fire, a potter making clay pots, or a wine maker treading grapes? Bible dictionaries can be helpful in providing information about these elements of ancient cultures. Some Bible dictionaries, like the *HarperCollins Bible Dictionary*, *Mercer Dictionary of the Bible*, or *Eerdmans Dictionary of the Bible*, are intended for the beginner and therefore have very brief (paragraph-length) entries arranged alphabetically. Others, like the six-volume *Anchor Bible Dictionary* or the three-volume *Illustrated Bible Dictionary*, contain fairly extensive entries, along with bibliographies for further study. If you do not find what you are looking for in one dictionary, try another. In libraries that use the Library of Congress system, you can locate these Bible dictionaries in the BS 440 section.

CONCORDANCES Sometimes, when reading a biblical text, you might recall another passage pertaining to the same topic, but you cannot locate it. What do you do? Try a **concordance**. This resource book contains a list of every word of the Bible, arranged alphabetically, and a list of citations telling you where you can find this word in every book (chapter and verse) in which it occurs. However, since you probably will be using an English concordance, you need to take notice of the translation on which the concordance is based. For example, if the Bible translation you are reading is the New American Bible, you need to use a concordance that is keyed to the New American Bible. You can usually find this information on the title page of the concordance. If your library uses the Library of Congress system, you can locate these concordances in the BS 425 section. Two of the more commonly used concordances are *The New Strong's Exhaustive Concordance of the Bible*, *The NRSV Concordance*, and *Nelson's Complete Concordance of the New American Bible*. You can also find good online concordances. See, for example, http://bible.crosswalk.com/Concordances. However, remember that whatever concordance you use it must be keyed to your particular Bible translation.

COMMENTARIES There are a large number of different kinds of **commentaries** available for the study of New Testament books. Generally speaking, commentaries provide you with the results of scholars' investigations of biblical books. Some commentaries are what we call single-volume commentaries (e.g., *HarperCollins Bible Commentary*, *Mercer Commentary on the Bible*, and *The New Jerome Biblical Commentary*). These commentaries treat all of the books of the Bible in a single volume. Therefore, as you would expect, they give you only a small amount of information about any one book of the Bible. Multivolume commentaries like *The New Interpreter's Bible* give you a bit more information because they might treat only a few books of the Bible in one volume. You will also find a large number of commentaries that treat a single book of the Bible—for example, the Gospel of Mark. These will provide you with considerably more information on the book that you are studying than a single- or multivolume commentary.

Commentaries usually include an introductory section that answers questions about the author of the book, the audience to which the author was writing, the structure of the book, and the book's major themes. Following the introduction, the commentator provides a section-by-section or verse-by-verse explanation of the biblical book under investigation. Some commentaries are written with the nonspecialist in mind, while others can be very technical and are meant for other biblical scholars to read. Therefore, you will want to skim several commentaries before selecting the ones that might be most helpful to you.

If you intend to do an in-depth analysis of a biblical text, you will need to consult several commentaries for comparison because all commentaries are interpretations of the biblical text and each commentator works with a particular set of presuppositions and methodological approaches. That is not to say that one scholar is right and the others are wrong. Rather, there is a range of possible interpretations available for a particular book. You need to read with a critical eye to determine whether a particular scholar's interpretation is coherent and competent. You also need to be attentive to the methodology being employed in the commentary, since the assumptions and objectives of a particular methodology will greatly affect the outcome of the scholar's interpretation. The more you read, the better equipped you will be to make this assessment.

Single- and multivolume commentaries are usually found in the reference section of your library, beginning with the BS 491 section. Commentaries for individual books are found in your library stacks. Consult the library catalogue under the subject "Bible N.T.—commentaries" to locate commentaries for a particular book of the Bible.

With this brief introduction to the methods and resources of biblical studies, we have made our first big step in preparation for our voyage through the New Testament. The next three chapters will add to our preparations. Chapter 3 will investigate the political world of Palestine, the setting for the New Testament gospels, and the social, political, religious, and cultural world of the Roman Empire. Chapter 4 provides an overview of the major themes of the Hebrew scriptures, otherwise called the Old Testament, without which much of the New Testament would not make sense. Finally, Chapter 5 will help us to understand more about first-century Judaism, which is the religious and cultural world of Jesus and his first followers.

## KEY TERMS

| | | |
|---|---|---|
| Biblical critical methods | Redaction criticism | Feminist criticism |
| Text criticism | Social science criticisms | Liberation hermeneutics |
| Variant | Narrative criticism | Cultural hermeneutics |
| Source criticism | Reader-response criticism | Canonical criticism |
| Extant | Structuralism | Concordance |
| Form criticism | Deconstruction | Commentary |

## QUESTIONS FOR REFLECTION

1. What kind of information might we learn about the biblical text from each of the types of biblical criticism discussed in this chapter? That is, what kinds of questions are appropriate to ask of a biblical text when employing these methods?

2. What are the limitations of the various methods discussed in this chapter? That is, what kinds of things would you expect *not* to discover when employing any one of these methods?

## ACTIVITIES FOR LEARNING

Select a favorite gospel story, preferably something relatively simple like a miracle story or a parable, and follow the directions below to discover information about your gospel story.

1. Use your Bible's footnotes or cross-references to determine whether there are any excerpts in other books of the Bible that relate to the gospel story you are studying. List any biblical texts you find, and write two or three paragraphs explaining what these texts helped you understand about the passage you are studying. If your passage has no cross-references, simply make note of that.

2. Read your gospel story carefully, making note of any references to persons, places, or events contained in it. Use a Bible dictionary to find out whatever you can about these details and write a two- to five-paragraph summary of your findings. Include a bibliography of your source(s).

3. Identify any key terms or potentially important phrases in your gospel story. Use a concordance to find out whether these terms or phrases are used anywhere else in that gospel. Make a list of any references you find and then write two or three paragraphs explaining how the gospel writer uses these terms or phrases elsewhere. How do these other uses help you understand the meaning of these words in the story you are studying?

4. Find at least two other translations of your gospel story that are different from the one you are currently using. For example, if you are using the New Revised Standard Version (abbreviated NRSV), then choose two of the following: the New American Bible translation (NAB), the New International Version (NIV), and the New Jerusalem Bible translation (NJB). Write out (or copy) the three translations of your biblical text in parallel columns. Compare the translations and then write two to five paragraphs explaining how the translators' word choices help you to understand the nuances in meaning of the key terms or potentially important phrases you identified in activity 3 above.

5. Locate at least two commentaries that treat your gospel story. One should be a single-volume commentary, and another should be a commentary that treats only the gospel from which your story is taken (e.g., the Gospel of Mark). Compare your commentaries and comment on the differences in quantity and quality of information you find about your gospel story. Using the summary descriptions of biblical critical methods contained in this chapter, see if you can determine what methodologies your commentators are using. Provide a rationale for your determination.

## SOURCES AND RESOURCES

Anderson, Janice Capel, and Stephen D. Moore. *Mark and Method: New Approaches in Biblical Studies*. Minneapolis, Minn.: Augsburg Fortress, 1992.

Fee, Gordon D. *New Testament Exegesis: A Handbook for Students and Pastors*. Philadelphia: Westminster, 1983.

Harrington, Daniel. *Interpreting the New Testament: A Practical Guide.* Wilmington, Del.: Glazier, 1982.

Hayes, John H., and Carl R. Holladay. *Biblical Exegesis: A Beginner's Handbook.* Atlanta, Ga.: John Knox Press, 1982.

Knight, Douglas A., ed. *Methods of Biblical Interpretation.* Nashville, Tenn.: Abingdon Press, 2004.

McKenzie, Steven L., and Stephen R. Haynes, eds. *To Each Its Own Meaning: An Introduction to Biblical Criticisms and Their Application.* Louisville, Ky.: Westminster John Knox Press, 1999.

Newsom, Carol A. Contemporary methods in biblical study. In *The New Oxford Annotated Bible with the Apocrypha/Deuterocanonical Books,* edited by Michael D. Coogan. 3rd ed. Oxford, England: Oxford University Press, 2001.

Tuckett, Christopher. *Reading the New Testament: Methods of Interpretation.* Philadelphia: Fortress, 1987.

Yarchin, William, ed. *History of Biblical Interpretation: A Reader.* Peabody, Mass.: Hendrickson Publishers, 2004.

# THE FIRST-CENTURY GRECO-ROMAN WORLD

People who are planning to go on a voyage of the sort that we have been talking about—one that takes us far away to a different place and time in order to encounter the unfolding of a story about suffering and hope, expectation and promise, death and new life—will want to learn as much as possible about that place and time before embarking. They will want to know what the political system is like. They will also want to know how the society is organized and what is distinctive about its cultural practices. In addition, they will want to know what role religion plays in this society. Otherwise, they will not have any reference points for understanding what they will see and hear, and they will not be able to interact with the people who live there. They might as well stay home!

The same is true for our journey through the New Testament. In order to understand the appeal of the Jesus movement for Gentiles (non-Jews) in the first century C.E., as well as the challenges the movement faced, we need to know something about the wider world in which it began to flourish. Politically, the years 30 B.C.E.– 235 C.E. were characterized by relative peace and prosperity in the Roman Empire. However, it was a paradoxical time in many respects. For example, the society was marked by considerable conservatism in many aspects of the culture, but it was also a world that was beginning to experience the breakdown of old social structures. People tended to be suspicious of things that were different or innovative, even while things were changing before their eyes. This atmosphere of quiet unrest affected almost every aspect of life, including trade and the development of cities, family life, religion, and philosophy.

## THE POLITICAL WORLD OF PALESTINE

**Palestine** is the name that the Greeks and later the Romans gave to the land of Israel, previously known as Canaan. Ironically, the Greek term has its origin in the name of the land of the Philistines, once Israel's archenemy at its western border along the Mediterranean Sea. The boundaries of Palestine—and, in fact, most ancient nations—fluctuated considerably at different points in their history. However, Palestine was never a large nation by comparison to its neighbors. In the first century C.E., it measured approximately 150 miles from north to south and 60 miles from east to west, making it approximately the size of the state of Vermont. Palestine had few natural resources and still fewer harbors, even though it was located on the Mediterranean. At the same time, it played an important role in the region because it served as a land bridge between what we now call the African and European continents. Thus, it was an important link in the trading industry, but in its long history, it also fell victim to many conquering armies: Egypt, Assyria, Babylonia, Persia, and Greece, to name a few.

Palestine first came under Greek rule as part of a massive campaign by Alexander the Great (336–323 B.C.E.) that began with the conquest of Persia and expanded to Mesopotamia, Phoenicia, and Egypt during the period 334–330 B.C.E. Although Alexander the Great's political prowess was cut short by his untimely death only a few years later, at the age of thirty-three, the influence of Greek culture on conquered peoples took firm hold and flourished for many centuries after his death. This process is called **Hellenization**, and it was characterized by the blending of Greek culture with indigenous cultures and by the adoption of the Greek language throughout its conquered lands. This explains the need for the Septuagint within first-century Judaism, for example (see the Introduction).

Later, in 63 B.C.E., Palestine came under Roman rule when Pompey took over Jerusalem and incorporated Palestine into the Syrian province of the Roman Empire. Yet, even after the Romans conquered these lands, the influence of Greek culture persisted. In fact, the Romans were not especially well known for their original contributions to the arts. Rather, they prided themselves in the massiveness of their building projects and in their ability to manage their conquered peoples. Thus, the period of Roman rule, as it was still heavily influenced by Greek culture, is sometimes called the **Greco-Roman** period.

The New Testament mentions or alludes to only a few of the first-century Roman emperors. The Gospel of Luke identifies Gaius Octavian, also known as **Caesar Augustus** (27 B.C.E.–14 C.E.), as emperor of Rome at the time Jesus was born (Luke 2:1). Luke also mentions his stepson **Tiberius** (14–37 C.E.), who was Caesar during Jesus' adult life (Luke 3:1). Likewise, he is the one referred to in the gospel story about the payment of taxes to Caesar (Matt. 22:15–23; Mark 12:13–17; Luke 20:20–26). Tiberius was succeeded by Gaius (Caligula) (37–41 C.E.) and then Claudius (41–54 C.E.). Acts of the Apostles identifies Claudius as the one who expelled the Jews from Rome on account of riots there (Acts 11:28–30). Claudius was succeeded by **Nero** (54–68 C.E.), Vespasian (69–79 C.E.), Titus (79–81 C.E.), and **Domitian** (81–96 C.E.). Scholars of the Book of Revelation think that the author is alluding to both Nero and Domitian when he writes about the beasts of the land and the sea (Rev. 13:1–18).

According to the New Testament gospels, the ruler of Palestine at the time of Jesus' birth was **Herod the Great.** He was appointed by the Roman Senate in 40 B.C.E. but was not well received by the populace of Palestine. In fact, he had to conquer Jerusalem in order to become its ruler. Although Jewish, he was from Idumea, an ancient enemy of Israel. Gradually, he extended the boundaries of his kingdom to include most of the land that once belonged to King David. He apparently was an

---

### ROMAN EMPERORS OF THE NEW TESTAMENT PERIOD

| | |
|---|---|
| 27 B.C.E.–14 C.E. | Gaius Octavian (Augustus) |
| 14–37 C.E. | Tiberius |
| 37–41 C.E. | Gaius (Caligula) |
| 41–54 C.E. | Claudius |
| 54–68 C.E. | Nero |
| 68–69 C.E. | Galba; Ortho; Vitellius |
| 69–79 C.E. | Vespasian |
| 79–81 C.E. | Titus |
| 81–96 C.E. | Domitian |
| 96–98 C.E. | Nerva |
| 98–117 C.E. | Trajan |
| 117–138 C.E. | Hadrian |

---

excellent administrator, and extremely loyal to Rome, but he was also noted for his cruelty toward any who would oppose him. It is said that he even killed one of his wives and two of his sons in order to suppress threats to his authority. To his favor, he was also noted for his enormous building campaigns, including seven fortresses spread throughout Palestine, the port city of Caesarea, and the remodeling of the Jerusalem Temple. He started the Temple remodeling project in 20 B.C.E., but it was not actually completed until 62 C.E., only eight years before it was finally destroyed. Herod the Great's reign extended from 37 B.C.E. to 4 B.C.E., shortly after the birth of Jesus.

When Herod the Great died, his kingdom was divided among his three surviving sons. Philip (4 B.C.E.–34 C.E.) was given the territory to the north and east of the Sea of Galilee. Herod Antipas (4 B.C.E.–39 C.E.) was given Galilee and the area to the east of the River Jordan. Herod Archelaus (4 B.C.E.–6 C.E.) was given Judea, Samaria, and Idumea. The New Testament gospels identify **Herod Antipas** as the one who beheaded John the Baptist (Matt. 14:1–12; Mark 6:14–29; Luke 9:7–9) and the one who questioned Jesus during his trial before Pontius Pilate (Luke 23:6–12). However, we know nothing of Philip or Archelaus from the gospels. The Romans removed Herod Archelaus from office and banished him to Gaul (modern-day France) because of his cruelty. After that, Judea, Samaria, and Idumea came under the direct authority of the Roman emperor, as part of the province of Syria, and were administrated by a prefect or governor.

The New Testament gospels identify **Pontius Pilate** (26–36 C.E.) as the prefect of Palestine at the time of the death of Jesus (Matt. 27:1–2; Mark 15:1; Luke 23:1; John 18:28–32; see also Tacitus *Annals* 15.44). Two first-century Jewish writers, Philo of Alexandria and Flavius Josephus, write about Pilate's rule in very negative terms. Josephus describes how Pilate, at the beginning of his reign, directed his armies to

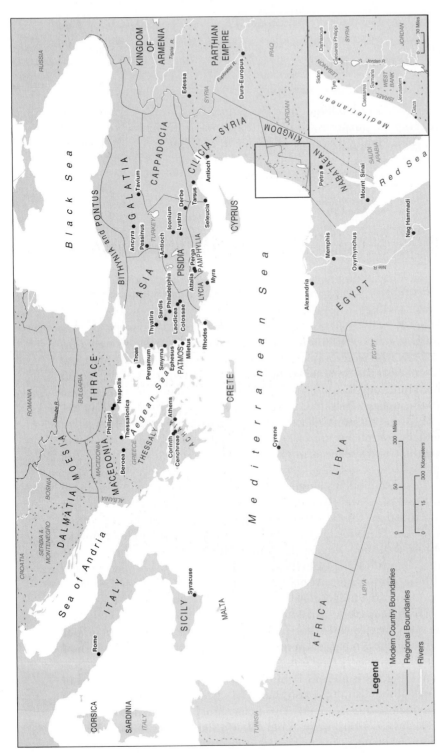

First-century Roman Empire. The inset highlights first-century Palestine.

bring their military standards decorated with the emperor's image into Jerusalem by night (*The Jewish War* 2.9.169–174). Jews considered this to be a shameful act of idolatry, and he relented only after a massive nonviolent protest. Philo writes of a similar event involving the installation of golden shields in Pilate's Jerusalem residence (*Legatio ad Gaium*, 299–305). That situation was resolved only by the intervention of the emperor. Concerning Pilate's brutality toward the population of Palestine, Josephus describes an incident toward the end of his governorship in which he attacked and killed a large group of Samaritans who had gathered at Mt. Gerizim for religious purposes, thinking that it was an insurrection (*Jewish Antiquities* 18.4.85–97). Finally, there is a reference in Luke's gospel to an incident in which Pilate apparently killed some Galileans and mixed their blood with the sacrifices they were about to offer at temple (Luke 13:1). These stories contribute to a portrait of Pontius Pilate as a ruthless and power-hungry ruler.

Stone inscribed with the name of Pontius Pilate (reigned 26–37 C.E.), Caesarea, Israel. The first line reads "TIBERIEUM," referring to Tiberius Caesar. The second line reads "(PON)TIUS PILATUS." The third line reads, "(PRAEF)ECTUS IUDA(EAE)," referring to his position as prefect of Judea. *Ancient Art & Architecture/DanitaDelimont.com.*

Acts of the Apostles makes reference to two later governors of Palestine, namely, **Felix** (52–60 C.E.) and **Festus** (60–62 C.E.). From the writings of Josephus, as well as of the Roman historian Tacitus, it appears that Felix had a reputation for violence similar to that of Pontius Pilate. The author of Acts describes Felix as presiding over Paul's trial after he had been arrested in Jerusalem. When Felix did not receive the bribe for which he hoped, he apparently left Paul to sit in prison for two years, until the new governor, Festus, came on the scene and took charge of his case (Acts 23:11–25:12). On occasion, the gospels also mention the presence of Roman armies in Jerusalem and the surrounding environs. Remember that these were occupied lands.

## The Social and Economic World of the Roman Empire

It is very difficult to speak briefly about the social world of first-century Palestine because the social system was at least as complex as that of our own world. Four languages were spoken in Palestine. Hebrew was used in religious services and in Jewish schools. However, Aramaic was the common language of most Jews and was used in some sacred literature. Jesus probably spoke Aramaic. Since the time of Alexander the Great, Greek was the universal language of the Mediterranean world, and although it existed in several different dialects, Koine Greek was the most prevalent. As the "common" Greek dialect, it tended to assimilate the basic elements of several dialects to produce a form of Greek that was more accessible to non-native Greek speakers. Across the empire, it was the language of business and commerce, diplomacy and administration. The New Testament was written in Koine Greek. Latin was the language of Roman soldiers and some Roman officials in the East. Archeology has uncovered Latin inscriptions on building projects in first-century Palestine. However, it was not widely used by the indigenous population.

Agriculture was the mainstay of the economy throughout the Roman Empire of the first century C.E.. This was also true in Palestine, especially in Galilee in the north, where the soil was fertile and the land received as much as forty-five inches of rain per year. Its climate is Mediterranean, so temperatures are moderate and it has a rainy season from November to February. Farmers raised wheat, barley, grapes, figs, and olives. In the south, where there is little rain and the soil is rocky, people herded sheep and goats. Palestine also had some mining and fishing.

In addition, this period was beginning to see an emerging merchant and artisan class, throughout the Roman Empire and in Palestine, though still as small as 5 percent of the population. As people gravitated toward the cities and as travel for the purpose of trade became more common, there came to be a division between the rural agrarian culture and the urban culture. The rural peoples were generally less well educated and more conservative, since they were also less likely to be exposed to new ideas and new ways of thinking. In contrast, urban cultures tended to be more diverse and more open to new ideas. Social class was determined by one's birth line and legal status in the Roman Empire. Someone born into the aristocracy always belonged to the aristocracy, whether rich or poor. In contrast, the new wealthy— successful merchants from among the lower classes, for example—could never "buy" themselves a place among the aristocracy. A slave who managed to gain manumission and become a freedman would never be considered of the same social status as a freeborn person. Honor and status was a matter of inheritance and social relationships, not economics.

Scholars are extremely cautious about assigning numbers to ancient populations because of the difficulty of assessing the evidence, but some suggest that the aristocracy made up only 1 or 2 percent of the population. The vast majority of the population—perhaps as much as 75 percent—were peasants (small landowners, tenants, day laborers, and slaves). Below the peasants were the "unclean" and the "throwaways" of the society (e.g., beggars, the disabled, and people with certain illnesses). Some scholars speculate that these groups accounted for as much as 10 percent of the population. There was no large middle class, as Americans might expect today.

Not everyone had equal status under Roman law, even among those who were citizens of Rome, and in the provinces Roman citizenship was rather unusual. Some scholars estimate that although the numbers were rising considerably in the mid–first century C.E., only 7 to 9 percent of the population of the empire had the status of citizen. The most common way to become a Roman citizen was to be born of parents who had Roman citizenship. Otherwise, a person might be granted citizenship as a reward for an act of bravery in battle or outstanding service to the emperor, or he might purchase it for a great sum of money. Yet the vast majority of people living in the Roman Empire did not have the status or protection of citizenship. At the same time, we learn from Acts of the Apostles that Paul was a Roman citizen (Acts 22:22–29). Prejudice as we know it today apparently did exist in the ancient world, but it was more likely to be based on social class than on race or religion.

Greco-Roman society operated on what is called a **patron-client system**. The various units of the society were arranged according to relationships in which the patron, usually a man and always of higher social status, provided protection and provisions in return for services—and, in case of war, loyalty and military support—from the client. The behavior of the patron was that of a father toward those in his care. Thus, the different units of society functioned as larger versions of the family unit, which was also often dominated by men: husbands over wives, fathers over children, and masters over slaves. Even the most powerful of society were engaged in patron-client relationships. For example, Herod the Great's relationship with the emperor was that of a client king. There were also intermediaries or "brokers," who made connections between prospective patrons and clients. Virtually everyone was connected to others in the population as patron or client. Without these relationships, survival would have been quite difficult.

Although diminishing somewhat in the first-century Greco-Roman world, slavery was commonplace. However, the situation of these slaves was quite different from America's tragic story of African slavery. The major sources of slaves were conquests in war and piracy, after which these captives would be sold as property in major marketplaces. Others became slaves because of inability to pay debts. Some slaves lived in terrible poverty, doing only the least desirable of work in rock quarries and on galley ships, but others were highly educated, owned property, and operated businesses of their own. The slaves of wealthy persons could be teachers, librarians, craftsmen, managers of the family businesses, and traders of merchandise. They were able to marry and have families of their own, and there were laws that protected them from abuse. Some slaves even owned other slaves. Sometimes masters would reward their most dedicated slaves with manumission. They would then become clients of their former master. Some eventually were able to buy their own freedom. These former slaves were called freedmen.

Women's circumstances also were dependent on social status and economic wealth. Although the vast majority of women did not have positions of authority in the public realm, they were the primary managers of the household (including children, extended family members, and slaves). In that capacity, they were responsible for the household's finances and oversight of the production of all the necessities of the household, including weaving and making clothes; planting, harvesting, and preserving food; and producing oil and soap. Almost everything a family needed was made within the confines of the home, so you might think of these women as managers of multiple home-based businesses. Occasionally, women of high social class received formal education, and wealthy widows, for example, sometimes had their own businesses. Of course, among the poor and those of lower social status, there were many fewer opportunities for women. In fact, life was quite desperate for poor widows who had no male family members to support them.

Given the situation of women in the first-century Greco-Roman world, it is somewhat remarkable that women figure prominently in many of the stories of the gospels and that the New Testament mentions a number of women who held leadership roles within the early Christian communities. For example, Acts of the Apostles names female models and mentors, such as Priscilla (Acts 18:1–11, 24–28), Tabitha (Acts 9:36–43), and Lydia (Acts 16:11–15, 40), among the members of the early Jesus movement. Paul, too, includes a number of women among those whom he called deacons, missionaries, and apostles—Phoebe, Julia, Mary, an unknown woman identified as Rufus's mother, and another described as Nereus's sister, to name a few (Rom. 16:1–16). The New Testament also suggests that the early Christian communities included people who had substantial financial resources as well as those who were peasants, slaves, and freedmen. In sum, in its earliest days, Christianity appears to have been somewhat radical in the fact that it valued, at least in theory, a community in which social class and gender were not barriers to participation.

The economy of the Roman Empire was closely connected with the patron-client system. The emperor, as principal patron of the empire, bestowed privileges on his client kings and, in return, expected financial and military support for his throne. In turn, client kings extracted support for favors granted to their administrative assistants and other elites who were their clients. Ultimately, this chain of compensation was funded by taxes extracted from the peasant class: small farmers, tenants, and day laborers. Since very few farmers owned their own land, they also had to pay rent on their property. Some studies suggest that Herod the Great's taxes on Palestine's farmers and orchard keepers ranged from 33 to 50 percent of the total value of their crops. In addition, there were poll taxes, transit taxes, and market exchange fees. **Tax collectors** made their living by collecting more taxes than they were contracted to deliver and pocketing the surplus. Such a system ensured that the wealthy elite maintained their positions of power in the economy, while the peasant class continued to sink deeper and deeper into debt. Thus, more than 80 percent of the population in Palestine, for example, lived at or below subsistence level in the economy.

There was a banking system of sorts in the Greco-Roman world. However, it was not like the banks we know today. Likewise, money functioned differently than it does today. On the local level and among peasant populations, bartering was the usual mode of operation; people traded goods that were needed for everyday living in the village markets. Occasionally, coinage was used to supplement the bartering process—for example, "I'll give you three loaves of bread and two coins in exchange for a flask of wine"—but not as a substitute for bartering. Among the elite, however, money was an important way to store wealth and to demonstrate their social status. Coinage was minted in gold and silver because of their value as precious metals and stored in banks or treasuries in major cities throughout the empire. Gold and silver were also used to finance the caravans that moved goods and natural resources across the empire and beyond, but profit from this kind of import/export activity was available only to the elite.

Because there was no common monetary system in the Greco-Roman world, **moneychangers** were an important part of the economy. The emperor, as principal patron, minted coinage that was stamped with his image or a symbol of his accomplishments, and client kings did the same. Because much of the Roman Empire consisted of conquered lands, regions within the empire had older monetary systems that were still in use alongside the emperor's or client king's money. However, taxes and certain debts that involved contracts had to be paid with Roman coins. Likewise, Jews had to pay the Jerusalem Temple tax in approved coinage. Thus, the

Marble sarcophagus thought to have come from Viale del Re, Rome, showing a moneychanger at his counter. *Museo della Civilta Romana Rome/Picture Desk, Inc./Kobal Collection.*

moneychangers provided an important service in making these various transactions possible. For that service, of course, they extracted a transaction fee. For peasants who operated on the barter system, paying taxes and meeting other debt obligations required that they surrender large quantities of goods (crops, household products, etc.) that had been determined to be equivalent to the value of the Roman coinage. In this way, the money of the elite never fell into the hands of the peasant class, making it impossible for lower classes to use money to make money.

## Religion in the Greco-Roman World

Whatever their social or economic status, religion affected everyone in the Roman Empire of the first century C.E. Here **religion** is used, in general terms, to describe one's obligation to perform or participate in certain sacred rituals for the welfare of the community. Today, especially in Western cultures, we tend to think of religion as a purely voluntary activity designed to benefit the spiritual or inner life of the individual. However, in the Greco-Roman world, religion was understood to benefit the community—in this case, the Roman Empire—because people could not conceive of separations among the social, cultural, political, and religious aspects of human experience.

**The Roman Cult** The Roman **cult** (i.e., the worship of the Roman deities) did not possess a **creed** (i.e., a set of beliefs or doctrines). Rather, it consisted of a series of **rites** (i.e., rituals or religious acts) performed by professionals in order to ensure the peace and prosperity of the empire and win right relationship between the gods and humanity. Common public worship of the Roman gods was a symbol or proof of a united empire. Failure to participate in the Roman cult was considered a threat to the welfare of the state and a treasonous or subversive act. Jewish subjects had been given certain privileges that exempted them from obligation to the Roman cult, but few others had such an option.

**The Emperor Cult** One aspect of the social or civic religions of the Greco-Roman world was the **emperor cult**. Scholars are not sure exactly how the emperor cult developed or what status it had in the first- and second-century Roman Empire. At a minimum, we can say that it probably was understood differently in Rome itself than in the provinces. In general, Romans were cautious about attributing divinity to their emperors, at least while they were still alive. However, emperors who excelled in their activities as rulers were given divine honors, that is, an official recognition that the deities worked through them. They were also given titles such as Lord, God, Son of God, and Savior. At the same time, in the provinces, some began to think of the living Roman emperor as the earthly manifestation of a deity, perhaps because of Egyptian and other Middle Eastern beliefs about the divinity of the pharaoh or oriental king. Some scholars think that the emperor cult was an extension of the worship of the traditional Roman deities, while others think it was a new kind of religion. Either way, Christians came into conflict with the Roman authorities because they refused to worship the emperor and therefore were considered a threat to the empire.

Participation in Roman rituals did not prevent people from taking part in alien (i.e., non-Roman) cults. In fact, Roman authorities were rather tolerant of most religious activity unless it offended the laws and practices of Roman life or in some way threatened the peace and prosperity of the empire. Therefore, although people might have been suspicious about "new" religious groups, persecutions were not widespread. When they did take place, they usually focused on individuals or groups in particular locations but not on the religion as a whole. The criteria used to judge alien cults were simple: If the foreign deities appeared to threaten the prestige of Roman gods, they were suppressed. If the rites gave rise to scandal, their adherents were punished. Christianity was classified as one of these "foreign" cults, as were the mystery cults, but even these were at least minimally tolerated except when they were the source of scandal.

THE MYSTERY CULTS While the emperor cult and the worship of Roman deities served the needs of the Roman Empire (or, more specifically, its aristocracy) for a stable government, the common people looked to the **mystery cults** for a sense of safety and purpose of life. The Greek term *musterion*, usually translated as *mystery*, means "secret" or "hidden". Paul uses the term several times in his letters to describe the mystery of God's plan of salvation, meaning a plan so vast and rich that humans cannot plumb the depths of it (see, for example, 1 Cor. 2:1–13). However, when used in the plural form (mysteries), it usually refers to the secret rituals that were used for initiation into the mystery religion.

The more popular mystery cults of the first- and second-century Greco-Roman world included the Isis cult, the Eleusian mysteries, the cult of Mithras, and the cult of Dionysus (Bacchus). Although the mystery cults demonstrated considerable diversity in their rituals and deities, many shared a myth with a common theme: A wife or mother loses a son, daughter, or husband, usually through death, but in the end, the lost one is restored to the wife or mother to live a new life. In other words, the myths of the mystery cults are refinements of even more ancient legends of growth-death-rebirth that could be seen in the change of the seasons. Most had an initiation rite that allowed the initiate to enter into a special relationship with the god and receive special knowledge of the heavenly realm or obtain some kind of promise of salvation. They also had a ritual reenactment of the myth, which usually included a sacred meal. The main theme of the mystery religions was that a person could conquer the powers of chaos and fate through knowledge of and identification with the god or goddess.

What follows are very brief descriptions of some of these mystery cults. They are offered here only for the purpose of giving you a sense of the religious landscape of the Greco-Roman world. If you wish to explore any of these cults further, you are encouraged to consult the "Sources and Resources" at the end of this chapter and do some investigations of your own.

**Dionysian (Bacchic) cult.** This cult gets its name from Dionysus (called Bacchus by the Romans), the son of Zeus and the god of wine, who was murdered and devoured by the Titans. The Dionysian cult appealed primarily to women, at least in its early stages, and was noted for ceremonies characterized by ecstatic frenzy. Since, according to the cult's myth, human beings descended from the Titans, the cult members believed that they, too, had within them the divine spark that belonged to Dionysus. Thus, by drinking wine and entering into an ecstatic frenzy, the female initiate could access the divine forces hidden in nature and human beings and even have visions of the god Dionysus. Initiates believed that, through mystical union with Dionysus, they could purge themselves of the earthly element and enter more closely into the divine life. The symbol associated with the Dionysian cult is the ivy wand.

The Dionysiac Mysteries from the Villa of the Mysteries (c. 79 C.E.) in Pompeii, Italy. This fresco shows a female initiate during a ritual flogging alongside of a nude dancer with cymbals. *A.K.G., Berlin/Superstock.*

Although information about the rituals themselves is limited, it appears that the secret celebrations took place in the forests at night and the initiation ritual involved certain aspects of promiscuity—at least that's what their detractors said. Euripides describes one of these Dionysian initiations in his writings. According to this account, a group of women, in a state of frenzy, killed and dismembered what they thought was a wild animal about to attack them. In fact, it was the local king, the son of the leader of the Bacchantes (members of the cult). Thus, his mother stood by, directing the destruction of her own son! The Roman historian Livy recalls that many of its initiates were killed when the Roman government decided that its rituals were a threat to society.

**Isis (Serapis) cult.** Isis was the thousand-named Egyptian goddess who had conquered destiny by bringing back to life her consort and brother, Osiris. He had been murdered and dismembered by his enemies, but she searched the Nile in order to find what she could of his dismembered body. Because the fish of the Nile ate some of his body parts, he became the god of the underworld and judge of the dead, returning to the earth for part of the year, after the flooding of the Nile. The son she conceived with Osiris was named Horus (sun). The Greek form of the rites included sprinkling water on the initiates, fasting, and being clothed in a white linen robe. At sunset, the initiates were taken on a journey into the underworld, later dressed as the sun god, and deified. Isis was also the patron of expectant mothers. Women prayed to her to become good mothers and to have a safe childbirth.

**Eleusian mysteries.** Demeter was the goddess of grain and mother of the earth. According to the myth of the Eleusian mysteries, Pluto (also known as Hades), a god of the underworld, stole Demeter's daughter, Persephone. Demeter grieved so greatly over the loss of her daughter that she neglected the vegetation of the earth and it died. The other gods had to intervene and convince Pluto to release Persephone for part of the year in order that the crops would grow again. This myth explained the change of seasons and productivity of the fields: Each year when Persephone would leave Demeter for the underworld, Demeter would grieve, and all the earth would become dormant. When Persephone was allowed to return, the earth would again begin to flourish. Symbols associated with the Demeter cult include grain, baskets in the form of a womb, a winnowing fan (used for harvesting), and the serpent that was sacred to Demeter. The ritual included the eating of a sacred meal.

**Mithras cult.** Mithras was a god of light who slew a white cosmic bull and released creative energy into the world. In some versions of the myth of Mithras, the creatures of the world are born from the carcass of the slaughtered bull. Imported from Persia (modern Iran) into the Roman Empire in the first century B.C.E., this cult was reserved to men, mostly soldiers. Its rituals included baptisms; purification with honey; meals of bread, water, wine, and meat; crowning with garlands; and tests of valor. The final ritual took place in a cavelike room covered by a grate, over which a bull would be sacrificed. In a liturgical text from the Mithras cult, Mithras is addressed as follows: "You have rescued us, too, by shedding the blood that makes us immortal." The language sounds a lot like Christian statements about baptism and Eucharist.

By the end of the third century C.E., Mithraism had become the official cult of the Roman Empire. Since Mithras was associated with the sun, cult members celebrated his birth on December 25, then thought to be the date of winter solstice, when the divine sun was reborn and the days began to lengthen. In the fourth century C.E., when Christians began to celebrate Christmas, we might imagine that they chose this date for the birth of Jesus as a countercelebration to Mithras's birthday, supported by their belief that God's son was the Light of the World. Before that time in the West, and still today among Eastern Christians, the major feast of the incarnation (referring to the embodiment of God in the person of Jesus) was not Christmas but the Epiphany, the manifestation of the child Jesus to the magi (see Matt. 2:1–23), which is traditionally celebrated on January 6, though many Christian traditions have now shifted the feast day to a Sunday at the beginning of January.

A Roman bas relief sculpture showing the sun god Mithras slaughtering a bull. He is accompanied by torchbearers. Mithras is often depicted wearing a cape lined with star constellations. The bull is thought to represent the constellation of Taurus. *Louvre Museum, Paris/Alinari-Scala/Art Resource.*

**ASTROLOGY AND MAGIC** At this point in history, little progress was being made in science and technology, certainly not of the sort that we are accustomed to seeing today. Believing that impersonal forces ("chance," also known as the god Tyche) ruled the world, people focused their attention on astrological and metaphysical speculations as a way of controlling their fates. Thus, astrology, which had existed since the sixth century B.C.E., enjoyed new popularity. Astrology was based on careful observations of the activity of the planets, stars, sun, and moon, with the understanding that the movements of the heavenly bodies gave information about what would happen in the earthly realm. Even though humans could not control fate, they believed that, by enlisting the services of an astrologer, they could at least anticipate fate's agenda and plan for it. Because calculations had to be done by hand, astrological readings were very expensive and therefore available only to the elite. However, archeological artifacts suggest that most people would have known at least the basic vocabulary of astrology and the signs of the zodiac.

Likewise, magic gained greater popularity in the first century C.E. than it had had in previous centuries. It was attractive to the populace because it claimed to give people some kind of control over the gods. Magic books were published with recipes and formulas, mostly for warding off evil, disease, and demons. The effectiveness of the magic depended on the precise performance of the ritual and recitation of the formula. Folk healers used magical formulas along with their herbal remedies to restore people to health.

A synagogue floor (third–fifth century C.E.) illustrating the signs of the zodiac, Hamat Tiberius, Israel. The stones lined up through the midsection of the mosaic are the remains of a later construction on the same site. *Ancient Art & Architecture/DanitaDelimont.com.*

A closer view of the synagogue floor at Hamat Tiberius. The zodiac sign is Capricorn, depicted as part goat and part fishlike creature. *Ancient Art & Architecture/DanitaDelimont.com.*

## Philosophy in the First Century C.E.

The spread of Greek culture to large parts of the ancient world fostered an interest in the study of Greek philosophy. However, as schools of Greek philosophy were introduced to other cultures, their intellectual systems were sometimes simplified and otherwise adapted to accommodate local traditions. As a result, new levels of complexity and variation were added to these philosophical schools. Additionally, because people who were not philosophers by profession also were attracted to their teachings to gain understanding of life's difficult questions, there occurred a certain level of harmonization and popularization of ideas from different philosophical schools. All of these factors make it difficult to easily summarize the philosophical landscape of the first-century C.E. Mediterranean world. However, because philosophy played a significant role in shaping Greco-Roman culture, we cannot fail to at least mention it here.

**Three Popular Philosophical Systems** What follows are very brief descriptions of three philosophical systems that were popular in the first century C.E. These were chosen because some biblical scholars have suggested that certain New Testament authors were influenced, at least in a superficial way, by their vocabulary or systems of thinking.

A note of caution before we begin: Philosophy, whether ancient or contemporary, is an extremely complex discipline, with its own vocabulary and rules for discourse. Therefore, our brief descriptions will most certainly be lacking. If you wish to explore any of these philosophies further, you are encouraged to consult "Sources and Resources" at the end of this chapter and do some investigations of your own.

**Epicureanism.** Founded by Epicurus of Samos (432–370 B.C.E.), Epicurean philosophy's main theme could be described in this way: Fear is the root of all evil. The Epicureans argued that religion was nothing more than a deceptive attempt on the part of individuals or groups to instill fear in people (cf. Acts 17:21, 25). They believed that the gods, having achieved perfect bliss, have no more need for inter-action with human beings. Thus, the gods are unaffected by human activity like prayer and sacrifice. An Epicurean burial inscription of circa 200 C.E. reads as fol-lows: "There is nothing to fear in God. There is nothing to feel in death. Evil can be endured. Good can be achieved."

Although Epicureanism has been stereotyped as a philosophy that teaches self-indulgence, its ideal is more correctly described as freedom from disturbance, that is, inner harmony. This peace of mind, they said, should come from the knowledge that the universe operates according to a fixed plan that humans cannot control and that the gods have no interest in. They taught that humans must find happiness in this life because there is no life (and no reward) after death. There is no immortal soul to sur-vive death, but death should not be feared, since it is only a long, untroubled sleep. Further, the Epicureans taught that happiness is found in friendship and in just deal-ing with others. This kind of philosophy led its adherents to take up a passive attitude toward life and to withdraw from the activities of citizenship and the like.

**Stoicism.** Founded by Zeno of Cittium (fourth century B.C.E.), the main theme of Stoicism is this: Happiness consists only in the practice of virtue. Virtue, for the Stoics, meant that the inner self lives according to reason. Thus, the goal of Sto-icism is to be indifferent to external attractions and human emotions. They believed that the universe is proceeding on a predetermined course that no human agency can alter and that when unity (i.e., perfect harmony) is achieved, the world will be purged and absorbed by God, so that a new cycle of time and a new universe can begin. Further, they believed that there is no hope of immortality for the indi-vidual beyond the memory of his virtuous deeds.

The Stoics rejected the Platonic notion of reality as ideas that exist outside and independently of the physical world. Instead, they argued that the real world is the world of material bodies in interaction with one another. They believed that just as a human body is energized by a soul (i.e., reason), the universe has a world-soul that enlivens it and makes it operate as a harmonious whole, an ordered universe. This soul, which resides within each human being, is part of the divine reason—the Greek word is *logos*—that underlies all of life (cf. Acts 17:28). However, humans pos-sess only a tiny fragment of the seminal word or universal reason. Therefore, their task is to live in harmony with the universe. Goodness is defined as living in harmony with the universe (cf. Acts 17:26), while sin or evil is the disruption of this harmo-nious relationship.

**Cynicism.** This philosophy, also popular in the first-century C.E., is usually credited to Diogenes of Sinope (c. 400 –325 B.C.E.). He advocated a life of self-sufficiency and simplicity in which needs were kept to a minimum. Cynicism was not a school, as such, with teachers and an established body of doctrine (official teachings), but people sometimes tried to imitate the lifestyle of the cynics. Cynics believed that living simply was living according to nature. Therefore, they often led a wander-ing life, possessing no goods or property and preaching voluntary poverty. They also believed that a life of virtue could be attained through one's moral effort. They would seek dishonor among the people in order to attain hardness, apathy (literally "no passion" or "no emotion"), and freedom—for example, they used abusive language and wore filthy garments in public so that people would shame them. They were known for their boldness of speech in the public assembly. They also had a distinctive dress: a woolen coat, walking stick, beggar's bag, and long beard.

Paul's writings contain a number of allusions to the popular philosophies described above, though it is doubtful that he was actually trained in any of these philosophies. More likely is the possibility that he picked up "bits and pieces" from his cultural environment. The author of Acts of the Apostles describes a scene in which Paul is called a "seed picker" (Acts 17:18). This was not a compliment because a seed picker was someone who collected bits of philosophical vocabulary and used it indiscriminately without regard for its meaning. In fact, the phrase "seed picker" was a derogatory term directed at wandering philosophers like the Cynics. Whether or not Paul actually was a Cynic—some scholars argue that he was—this remark suggests that Paul was a product of his time, shaped and informed by the rich and diverse cultural environment in which he lived.

**EARLY CHRISTIANITY'S ENGAGEMENT WITH PHILOSOPHY** Despite a number of statements to the contrary, especially from second- and third-century C.E. Christian writers, Christian theology depended on philosophy from its beginnings for some of its basic notions about God and humanity's relationship to God. In particular, Christianity drew on the Platonic notion of reality as the idea or universal pattern of an object. This pattern exists outside and separate from the particular object, which is only an imperfect copy of reality. In Christian thinking, this meant that the physical world in which we live is not reality itself but rather an imperfect copy of the (real) spiritual world. Change—in particular, corruptibility (i.e., tendency toward decay)—belonged to the physical world.

Therefore, God, who belonged to the spiritual world, necessarily was incorruptible, immutable (i.e., unchangeable), and immune to injury. Likewise, by using philosophical terms like *substance*, *person*, and *nature*, early Christians were able to explain how God could be "one and three," referring to the Christian doctrine of the Trinity, and how the Son of God could have been fully human and fully divine. This is just one way in which early Christians engaged and interacted with the social and cultural world in which they lived as they learned how to express their faith.

## KEY TERMS

| | | |
|---|---|---|
| Palestine | Herod the Great | Moneychangers |
| Hellenization | Herod Antipas | Religion |
| Greco-Roman | Pontius Pilate | Cult |
| Caesar Augustus | Felix, Antonius | Creed |
| Tiberius | Festus, Porcius | Rites |
| Nero | Patron-client system | Emperor cult |
| Domitian | Tax collectors | Mystery cults |

# QUESTIONS FOR READING

Read Josephus's *Antiquities* 18.3.4 on the Isis cult. Use evidence from this text to answer the following questions. *Note:* In order to locate a citation like *Antiquities* 18.3.4, you need to know that the first number (18) refers to a major section, called a book, within the larger work; the second number (3) refers to the chapter; and the third number (4) refers to the verse. There are a number of hard-copy English translations of Josephus's works, but you can also find the Whiston translation on-line at www.earlyjewishwritings.com, www.ccel.org/j/josephus/JOSEPHUS.HTM or www.perseus.tufts.edu/cache/ perscoll_Greco-Roman .html#text1 (scroll down to Flavius Josephus and select the desired title).

1. Describe in your own words the situation that developed around Decius Mundus's infatuation with the woman named Paulina. How did she happen to come to the temple of Isis?

2. Who was Ide? What was her role in Mundus's deception of Paulina? What role did the priests of the Isis temple play in this deception?

3. Based on Josephus's writing about Paulina's experience in the temple, see if you can reconstruct key elements of this Isis ritual. In what kinds of activities did people engage when they came to the temple? *Note:* Anubis was an Egyptian deity. A son of Osiris, he was the guide of the dead and the patron of embalming and was later adopted by Isis.

4. According to Josephus, what did people expect to happen to them when they participated in the Isis ritual?

5. Clearly, Josephus thought that mystery religions such as the Isis cult were dangerous. Why?

# QUESTIONS FOR REFLECTION

1. How would you describe the possible or potential appeal of mystery religions for ancient peoples? Would they have a similar appeal for modern peoples? What, if anything, does interest in the mystery cults tell us about human nature?

2. How does modern American culture influence the ways in which Christianity is practiced or its values are lived out? Give examples to explain. Are there ways in which Christianity influences the development of modern American culture? Give examples to explain. Are there ways in which Christianity ought to be different from modern American culture? Give examples to explain.

# ACTIVITIES FOR LEARNING

1. Research one or more of the mystery cults described in this chapter, beginning with the relevant works in "Sources and Resources." What is the origin of the mystery cult that you are investigating? What is its central myth? What appeal might it have had for the people of its day?

2. Research one or more of the philosophical systems described in this chapter, beginning with the relevant works in "Sources and Resources." What is the origin of this philosophical movement? What is its worldview and what are its major principles? To what audience would it have appealed the most? Why?

## SOURCES AND RESOURCES

Branham, R. Bracht, and Marie-Odile Goulet-Caze, eds. *The Cynics: The Cynic Movement in Antiquity and Its Legacy.* Berkeley: University of California Press, 1996.

Brunschwig, Jacques, and Geoffrey E. R. Lloyd, eds. *Greet Thought: A Guide to Classical Knowledge.* Cambridge, Mass.: Belknap Press of Harvard University Press, 2000.

Chancey, Mark A. *Greco-Roman Culture and the Galilee of Jesus.* Cambridge, England: Cambridge University Press, 2005.

Dickie, Mathew. *Magic and Magicians in the Greco-Roman World.* New York: Routledge, 2001.

Furley, David, ed. *From Aristotle to Augustine.* London: Routledge, 1999.

Hanson, K. C., and Douglas E. *Palestine in the Time of Jesus: Social Structures and Social Conflicts.* Minneapolis, Minn.: Fortress, 1998.

Harding, Mark. *Early Christian Life and Thought in Social Context: A Reader.* London: T & T Clark International, 2003.

Klauk, Hans-Josef. *The Religious Context of Early Christianity: A Guide to Graeco-Roman Religions.* Edinburgh: T & T Clark International, 2000.

Koester, Helmut. *Introduction to the New Testament.* Vol. 1, *History, Culture, and Religion of the Hellenistic Age.* Philadelphia: Fortress, 1982.

Martin, Luther H. *Hellenistic Religions: An Introduction.* New York: Oxford University Press, 1987.

Meyer, Marvin W., ed. *Ancient Magic and Ritual Power.* Leiden, Netherlands: Brill, 2001.

_____. *The Ancient Mysteries: A Sourcebook.* San Francisco: Harper & Row, 1987.

Stambaugh, John E., and David L. Balch. *The New Testament in Its Social Environment.* Philadelphia: Westminster Press, 1986.

Valantasis, Richard, ed. *Religions of Late Antiquity in Practice.* Princeton, N.J.: Princeton University Press, 2000.

# ISRAEL'S STORY OF SALVATION

## TIMELINE

| | |
|---|---|
| **c. 1850 B.C.E.** | Abraham and Sarah, Isaac and Ishmael |
| **c. 1250 B.C.E.** | Moses and the Exodus |
| **c. 1200 B.C.E.** | Joshua and the Hebrew peoples enter the Promised Land |
| **1050–1000 B.C.E.** | Saul is first king of Israel |
| **1000–961 B.C.E.** | David is king of Israel; takes Jerusalem as his city |
| **961–928 B.C.E.** | Solomon is king of Israel; builds the Temple in Jerusalem |
| **928 B.C.E.** | The united kingdom is divided: Israel (northern kingdom); Judah (southern kingdom) |
| **722 B.C.E.** | Conquest of Israel by the Assyrians |
| **597 B.C.E.** | Conquest of Judah by the Babylonians |
| **587 B.C.E.** | Jerusalem Temple is destroyed; Babylonian Exile |
| **538 B.C.E.** | Return from Exile and rebuilding of the Temple |
| **334–323 B.C.E.** | The Greek Alexander the Great is king; conquered the Persian Empire |
| **175–164 B.C.E.** | Antiochus IV is king of the Seleucid Empire, including Palestine |
| **166 B.C.E.** | Judas Maccabeus and his brothers revolt against Antiochus IV; known as the Maccabean Revolt |
| **63 B.C.E.** | The Roman commander Pompey captures Jerusalem |
| **37–4 B.C.E.** | Herod the Great is king of Palestine; remodels the Temple |

As we have already noted, the key to a successful trip is doing your homework before you leave. We already have done a great deal of preparation for our voyage through the New Testament. We have examined the overarching structure of the New Testament and the Bible (Introduction) and explored some of the issues of interpretation of scripture (Chapter 1). We have surveyed methods of biblical scholarship and resources that will assist us in our studies (Chapter 2), and we have examined the social, political, and religious world out of which the New Testament emerged, namely, the Hellenistic and Greco-Roman cultures (Chapter 3). But our preparations are not yet complete. Before we can launch into our study of the New Testament, we need to understand and appreciate Israel's story of salvation and the Jewish world of Jesus. This is the task of our next two chapters.

Why is it necessary for a reader of the New Testament to be at least minimally familiar with Israel's story of salvation? Scholars of the New Testament and the history of the early church agree that the first Christians—even before they were called Christians—came from within Judaism. These early Christians were Jews who believed that Jesus was the fulfillment of their expectations concerning the messiah. Biblical scholars call them Christian Jews or **Jewish Christians**. Jesus, of course, was a Jew, as were his disciples. Many of the early missionaries of the Jesus movement— Peter, Paul, Barnabas, Apollos, and Priscilla and Aquila, to name a few—were Jews. Likewise, many of the authors of the religious literature that later came to be known as the New Testament were Jewish Christians or Gentiles whose experience of the risen Jesus had been shaped by their encounter with early Judaism. In sum, the earliest Christian communities emerged out of Judaism, they held the scriptures of Judaism as their own sacred scriptures, and they saw themselves as a continuation, or refinement, of all that was Judaism.

Israel's story of salvation is contained in the Jewish scriptures, the TaNaK, which is roughly equivalent to what Christians call the Old Testament (see the Introduction). The TaNaK is a vast and complex collection of documents, deserving a study in their own right. However, since we cannot investigate the whole of this literature in preparation for our study of the New Testament, we will examine only those stories that are absolutely necessary for our understanding of the New Testament. These are the stories of Abraham and Sarah, Moses and the Exodus, and David and the messianic promise. We will also take a brief look at the literature of the prophets and Old Testament wisdom literature, since both are employed in the development of New Testament themes and concepts.

First, we need to say a word about the structure of this chapter. For each section, you will find a very short summary of one part of Israel's story of salvation, followed by a brief introduction to the type of literature under investigation or its central themes. Then you will be asked to read a section from the Bible and answer some questions (located at the end of this chapter) that are designed to assist you in doing a close reading of selected biblical texts. For new readers of the Bible, one of the major obstacles to overcome is the fear that they cannot understand such strange and foreign literature. Learning how to do a close reading of a biblical text will help to alleviate that fear. More experienced readers of the Bible sometimes face a quite different problem. They have heard the stories, so they think they know them, when, in fact, they have not really read them. Their assumptions about the meaning of the story get in the way of a more thorough understanding of the text. Here, too, learning how to do a close reading will greatly benefit the reader.

Let us begin our overview of Israel's story of salvation and our exercises in the close reading of biblical texts with the stories of Abraham and Sarah.

## ABRAHAM AND SARAH

Abram, whose name was changed to **Abraham**, is sometimes called the father of Judaism because his encounter with God marks the beginning of Israel's story of salvation. Abram's story began in Ur of the Chaldees (in the southern part of modern Iraq, near Basra), perhaps around 1850 B.C.E. His family migrated to Haran (near the northern border of modern Syria) and eventually to Canaan (modern Israel). God made a promise to Abram, saying that God would bless him and that he would have his own land and many descendants. But God's promise faced many threats, not the least of which was the fact that Abram's wife Sarai, later renamed Sarah, could not bear children.

Fearing that he would have no heirs, Abraham had a son by Hagar (Sarah's maid servant), and he named him Ishmael. Eventually, however, God gave Abraham a son through Sarah, whom they named Isaac. Finally having a child of her own, Sarah urged Abraham to send Hagar and Ishmael away so that Isaac would be the sole inheritor of the promise. Abraham relented only after God promised that Ishmael, too, would be the father of a great nation. Today Islam traces its heritage as children of Abraham through Ishmael. But then, as a test, God asked Abraham to sacrifice Isaac as a burnt offering on a mountain in the land of Moriah (perhaps a reference to Jerusalem). As Abraham was about to kill his son, an angel appeared and told Abraham to sacrifice a ram that God had provided in his place. Thus, Isaac's life was spared. Later Isaac became the father of Esau and Jacob, the latter of whom received the birthright and his father's blessing by trickery and deceit. Jacob became the father of twelve sons, later to be identified with the twelve tribes of Israel. Among the twelve sons was Joseph, who is an important character in the next scene of Israel's salvation story. In connection with these stories, God is identified as "God of Abraham, Isaac, and Jacob."

The stories of Abraham and Sarah are found in the Book of Genesis, which gets its name from its opening phrase, "In the beginning. . . . " Although Abraham and Sarah probably lived sometime around 1850 B.C.E., their stories derive from oral traditions that began to take written form approximately 1000 B.C.E. The book itself probably was completed in the sixth century B.C.E. The Abraham stories are best described as **legend**. As a literary genre, the term *legend* is used in a technical sense to describe stories that have some basis in history—for example, the people actually existed or the event actually took place—but the story itself is probably not historical, or, at least, it cannot be verified by independent oral traditions or written records. Every culture has its own legends. In the United States, you might think of legends such as the stories of Johnny Appleseed: Paul Bunyan and Babe, the blue ox; and George Washington and the cherry tree. Legends are entertaining, of course, but their primary purpose is to inspire and edify. The same is true for the legends of Abraham and Sarah.

The stories of Abraham and Sarah are theologically significant because they give us the Bible's first major references to the covenant theme, which is important for both Judaism and Christianity. A **covenant** is a formal agreement or contract made between a superior (e.g., king, landlord, master) and an inferior (e.g., vassal, farmer, slave). We have examples of these ancient covenants that have been

A mosaic on the floor of the Bet Alpha Synagogue (sixth century C.E.) illustrating Abraham's near sacrifice of Isaac (Gen. 22:1–19).

preserved and translated into English so that you can actually read them today. Some covenants were in the form of a royal grant (i.e., a gift with no obligation on the part of the subject) to a favorite servant of the king. Others were mutual obligation treaties (i.e., the superior grants his subject some kind of favor in return for the subject's commitment to fight his wars, etc.). The stories of Abraham and Sarah include examples of both kinds of covenant. Christians, of course, understand this covenant as extending to Christian believers as a result of the death and resurrection of Jesus.

The New Testament contains a number of references to the stories of Abraham and Sarah, most notably in the letters of Paul. In his Letters to the Galatians and Romans, for example, he appeals to the example of Abraham as a model of faith for Gentile Christian believers, and he uses Abraham's story as the basis of his teaching on justification by faith. Elsewhere, the early church used the story of Abraham's near sacrifice of Isaac to explain the significance of the death of Jesus by describing Isaac as a type of Christ. The term **type** refers to an Old Testament character or event that serves as a pattern or model for the later, more perfect New Testament character or event. Isaac is a type of Christ in the sense that he carried the wood for his own sacrifice up the mountain, and the ram that was sacrificed in his place is a type of Christ insofar as it rescued Isaac from death and brought him salvation. We should be clear, however, that this typological interpretation of Abraham's sacrifice is not what the author of Genesis intended to communicate. Instead, it is a Christian reinterpretation of the Genesis stories.

With this background in mind, read Genesis 15:1–21 and 22:1–19 from your Bible. Use evidence from the biblical text to answer Question 1 in "Questions for Reading" at the end of this chapter.

---

### AN EXAMPLE OF A CLOSE READING OF GENESIS 15:1–21

Your task is to describe the ritual of covenant performed by Abram and God in Genesis 15:1–21.

1. Read the entire unit of text so that you are familiar with its contents.

2. Read the text again, focusing on details that relate to the question you are trying to answer. Underline or highlight any relevant information that you find. For an example, see below.

3. Explain in your own words your answer to the question, using the material that you highlighted as evidence to support your response. Be careful to stay within the confines of the biblical book that you are reading. Do not incorporate information from other sources unless you can demonstrate that it is relevant.

. . . 7 Then he said to him, "I am the Lord who brought you from Ur of the Chaldeans, to give you this land to possess." 8 But he said, "O Lord God, who am I to know that I shall possess it?" 9 He said to him, **"Bring me a heifer three years old, a female goat three years old, a ram three years old, a turtle dove, and a young pigeon." 10 He brought him all these and cut them in two, laying each half over against the other, but he did not cut the birds in two.** 11 And when birds of prey came down on the carcasses, Abram drove them away. . . . 17 When the sun had gone down and it was dark, **a smoking fire pot and a flaming torch passed between these pieces. 18 On that day the Lord made a covenant with Abram, saying, "To your descendants I give this land, from the river of Egypt to the great river, the river Euphrates."**

(Genesis 15:7–18)

---

## THE EXODUS AND GOD'S COVENANT WITH MOSES AND THE HEBREW PEOPLES

The next scene of Israel's salvation story takes place in Egypt. Joseph's family migrated to Egypt during a famine, not knowing that Joseph, the brother whom they had sold into slavery earlier, now held a position of power in the pharaoh's government. After Joseph revealed his identity, they were invited to stay in Egypt under his protection, but much later, when Joseph's contributions to Egypt were no longer remembered, the Hebrew peoples were enslaved there. As their suffering grew more intense, God chose **Moses** and sent him to the pharaoh to gain their release from slavery. When Moses made his request, of course, the pharaoh refused, so God sent a plague to "persuade" him to let the Hebrew peoples go. Under the burden of the plague, pharaoh gave permission for Moses to lead the slaves out of Egypt, but as soon as the plague was lifted, he changed his mind.

This happened nine times, but then God sent a tenth plague that destroyed all of the firstborn of Egypt. Finally, the pharaoh let the slaves go free. Thus began a forty-year Exodus—forty is a symbolic number indicating transition and change—that took Moses and his followers from Egypt to the land that God had promised them and in the process made of them one people of God. The feast of **Passover** has its origins in this tenth plague: As God prepared to send the Angel of Death to kill the Egyptians' firstborn, Israelite families were told to slaughter a lamb and place its blood on the lintel and doorposts of their homes so that the Lord's angel would pass over their houses and God would spare them from the suffering of the tenth plague. Thus, this day became a festival of celebration for what God had done on their behalf.

Again and again, during the Exodus journey, God showed his benevolence toward the people whom he had chosen. God allowed them to pass through the Red (or Reed) Sea as on dry land but quickly closed the water route on pharaoh's armies, who were in hot pursuit in an attempt to force them back into slavery. God also gave them a cloud by day and a pillar of fire at night to show them the way through the wilderness. In the course of their journey, they arrived at Sinai, where God made a covenant with Moses and the people and gave them the Law as the means by which they were to keep covenant with God. When they were thirsty, God gave water from the rock to drink. When they were hungry, God gave manna, from which they made bread, and quail to eat.

Finally, God led them to the entrance of the Promised Land. As the story is told, Moses was not permitted to enter the land of Canaan (modern Israel and the Palestinian territories). Instead, Joshua took the people across the Jordan River along with the Ark of the Covenant, the symbol of their journey in the desert. Although details about the Ark are now lost in history, apparently it was a wooden box that contained the stone tablets of the Moses covenant, a jar of manna from the wilderness, and the rod (a symbol of authority) of Aaron, Moses' brother and assistant. Moses and the people carried it at the front of the caravan to protect and guide them as they made their way to the Promised Land. The Jordan River crossing parallels the Red Sea crossing, with the water separating so that they could pass through as on dry land. Thus, the Jordan River crossing marks the end of the Exodus and the beginning of a long period of establishing settlement in the land of Canaan.

The Moses stories are told in the Book of Exodus, together with materials from the Books of Numbers and Deuteronomy. The term **Exodus** derives from a Greek word meaning "going forth." The Exodus event is generally dated around 1300–1250 B.C.E. The stories associated with the Exodus began to be collected approximately 1000 B.C.E., but the final form of the Book of Exodus can perhaps be dated to 500 B.C.E. The narrative is legend of the sort we discussed in connection with the Abraham and Sarah stories, but the Book of Exodus contains many other types of literature as well: hymns, ritual traditions, and legal codes, to name just a few. Some of these traditions are very old.

The stories of the Exodus are theologically significant because they continue the covenant theme and the Jewish notion of Law as well as the feast of Passover, all of which are important for understanding the New Testament. Passover was perhaps the most important feast of early Judaism. The first Christians would have celebrated Passover, as did Jesus and his family. The synoptic gospels describe Jesus celebrating his last meal before his death with the disciples on Passover. The Gospel of

A fresco panel from the ancient synagogue at Dura Europos (c. 239 c.e.), depicting the rescue of baby Moses from the Nile River by the pharaoh's daughter. The biblical story can be found in the Book of Genesis (Gen. 1:15–2:10).

John places Jesus' crucifixion on Passover, corresponding with John the Baptist's description of Jesus as the Lamb of God. In connection with these Exodus stories, God is identified as "God who brought us out of Egypt." Recalling the story of Moses' first encounter with God at the burning bush (Exod. 3:1–15), God is also known as YHWH, generally translated "I am (who am)." The author of the Gospel of John appeals to this notion as he writes about Jesus' identity and his activity on behalf of God.

The Passover ritual is still celebrated today and is designed around the understanding that the Jewish people are commanded to remember God's loving care of their people throughout their covenant history. It also celebrates, in anticipation, the ultimate liberation of the Jewish people in the messianic age. In other words, it has elements of looking backward and looking forward. Of course, Christians celebrate this ritual event as the first Eucharist, also called the Lord's Supper by some. Thus, the Christian Eucharist is closely tied to the ritual of Passover and its theological themes. You might consider whether or to what extent the Eucharist ritual also has elements of looking backward and looking forward.

A key event of the Exodus journey was the covenant on Mount Sinai, which marks the giving of the Law to Moses. Known as a **suzerainty treaty**, this kind of covenant ritual was rather common in the ancient world. A king would make an agreement with his subjects in which he would grant them protection from their enemies or other favors. In return, they had to abide by certain rules set by the king. They owed

---

### WHAT IS RITUAL?

Ritual is a powerful, though not fully appreciated experience. People have bedtime rituals and rituals associated with certain holidays. Clubs and organizations have rituals for the incorporation of new members. Fraternities and sororities have rituals of initiation. Important life events like birth, marriage, and death are marked by ritual. Some are private and secret; others are public. Given the fact that rituals are used in so many different settings, it is easy to conclude that the term *ritual* also can have a wide range of meanings for people. Here are two quite different definitions of the term.

1. Ritual consists of "those carefully rehearsed symbolic motions and gestures through which we regularly go, in which we articulate the felt shape and rhythm of our own humanity and of reality as we experience it, and by means of which we negotiate the terms or conditions for our presence among and our participation in the plurality of realities through which our humanity makes its passage" (Roland Delattre, p. 282). One way of restating this definition is to say that ritual is an essential part of the continuum of life and it helps us to know who we are.

2. Ritual is "a means of performing the way things ought to be in such a way that this ritualized perfection is recollected in the ordinary, uncontrolled, course of things" (Jonathan Z. Smith, pp. 124–125). One way of restating this definition is to say that ritual has the capacity to transform our social reality.

These two definitions of ritual hint at the importance of Passover for Israel's story of salvation—it helped Israel understand its identity, and through regular participation in this ritual, it transformed Israel from "no people" to "God's people." Because of the close connection between Eucharist and Passover, you might consider whether or to what extent Eucharist both helps Christians understand who they are and makes them who they ought to be.

---

the king loyalty, which they demonstrated by fighting in his army or working his fields. Ordinarily, the ritual contract associated with a suzerainty treaty consisted of the following elements:

1. Preamble stating the names of the parties
2. Historical listing of the good things that the king has done for the vassal
3. Laws and obligations that the vassal must perform
4. Directive that the document be saved and read publicly
5. List of gods who witness the king's treaty with his vassals
6. Lists of the curses that the gods will bring on those who break the treaty and the blessings promised to those who keep it

The only elements of the suzerainty treaty not found in the Exodus account of the covenant at Sinai are the last two. The reason is simple: the king who made covenant with the Israelite people is the only God, YHWH. There are no higher deities for God to call upon to witness this treaty, nor does God need to call upon other deities, since God is above all other powers and creatures. Further, since YHWH is all-powerful, God does not require the assistance of other gods who are only stone and metal—the gods of Israel's pagan neighbors—to effect curses on those who break covenant with God or to bestow blessings upon those who keep it.

Applying the elements of the suzerainty treaty to the Sinai covenant, what Christians call "the ten commandments" is, in fact, part of the covenant obligations that the vassal, the Israelite people, had to perform in order to keep covenant with God. Unfortunately, many Christians do not appreciate the significance of the Sinai covenant and the giving of the Law. Instead, they think of Judaism as "rule bound" and fixated on the "letter of the law." Actually, this is furthest from the truth. The **Law of Moses** (Torah) is not an arbitrary list of rules to be obeyed but a concrete expression and a living symbol of a special covenant relationship that God had established with the Jewish people. Covenant relationships involve obligations for both parties. In the case of the Sinai covenant, God keeps covenant with the Israelites by being their God and relating to them as God's people. The Israelite people keep covenant with God by obeying the Law of Moses and accepting their role God's chosen ones to whom they promise loyalty. (see element 3 above). For Jews of all time, failure to keep the Law of Moses constitutes a rejection of God's covenant, something like turning your back and walking away from the most important relationship in your life.

We have already mentioned how New Testament gospel writers incorporated the Passover story into the life of Jesus. Other imagery associated with the Exodus also permeates New Testament literature. In the Gospel of Matthew, for example, Jesus is portrayed as the great teacher like Moses (Matt. 5:1–7:29). Other books of the New Testament, like Acts of the Apostles and Revelation, make reference to the Exodus as an example of God's continued care of the covenant people, even in the giving of his Son, Jesus (e.g., Acts 7:17–53; Rev. 16:1–21). Still others, like the Letter to the Hebrews, use the Exodus event to show how Moses is a type of Jesus who is "faithful in all God's house," the former being God's servant while the latter is God's son (Heb. 3:1–19). The author of the Letter to the Hebrews includes Moses and the participants in the Exodus in his litany of the faithful witnesses who preceded Jesus, the ultimate example of faith (Heb. 11:1–12:2). He also describes Jesus as the mediator of a new covenant, alluding to Moses' role as the mediator of the covenant on Sinai (Heb. 12:18–29).

With this background in mind, read Exodus 12:1–13:22 from your Bible. Use evidence from the biblical text to answer Question 2 in "Questions for Reading" at the end of this chapter.

## DAVID AND THE MESSIANIC PROMISE

At the conclusion of the Exodus journey through the wilderness, when the Israelite people finally entered the Promised Land, then called Canaan, they first had to carve out a place for themselves. So begin the stories about Joshua's conquest of the

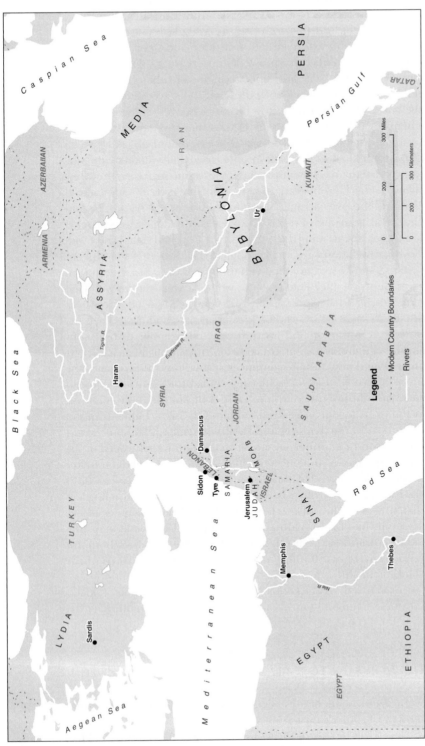

Near East in the time of the Babylonian Empire (seventh–sixth centuries B.C.E.), including modern boundaries. The Babylonian Exile in 586 B.C.E. involved the deportation of the ruling class and craftspeople of Judea to Babylon. Many centuries earlier, the Abraham stories (c. nineteenth century B.C.E.?) trace his migration from Ur through the Fertile Crescent (in the area of the Tigris and Euphrates Rivers) to Haran, and ending in Canaan (later known as Israel). The Moses story (c. thirteenth century B.C.E.) takes place in Egypt and the Sinai region, ending with Joshua's entrance into Canaan. The stories of David (1000–961 B.C.E.) are situated in Canaan, where he established the kingdom of Israel, which was eventually split into the northern and southern kingdoms of Israel and Judea after the death of his son Solomon (961–928 B.C.E.).

land of Canaan, the stories of the judges (in Hebrew, *shofet*, meaning "one who establishes or maintains God's justice") whom God called on periodically to rescue the Israelite people from their enemies, and the story of Israel's choice of its first king, Saul (who reigned circa 1025–1005 B.C.E.). Symbolically, this decision to anoint a king marks a transition from the Israelites' nomadic way of life to a time in which Israel became synonymous with the land and its king. However, Israel's kingship period was fraught with difficulty because of the kings' tendency to abuse their power and enter into alliances that compromised Israel's status as God's holy people. God is Israel's only true king and no one can take his place.

The most famous of Israel's kings was **David**. Reigning from approximately 1005 to 965 B.C.E., he was the second king of the united kingdom of Israel, the one who established its capital in Jerusalem, and perhaps the one who initiated the idea of a dynastic kingship for Israel. He was honored as a great warrior and statesman, but

A stone pediment containing a carved image of David and Bathsheba from the Coptic or pre-Coptic period (third–fourth century C.E.). Coptic Christianity has a very long and rich history, tracing its origins to Mark, the evangelist who is said to have introduced Christianity into Egypt circa 62 C.E. *Coptic Museum Cairo/Picture Desk, Inc./Kobal Collection.*

he also had his dark side, as demonstrated by the story about his affair with Bathsheba and his murder of her husband, Uriah (2 Sam. 11:1–27). Tragically, the child that was born from David and Bathsheba's union died, which David took to be just punishment for his terrible deed. Later they had another son, whom they named **Solomon**. He became the third king of Israel and reigned from approximately 965 to 922 B.C.E.

Although David wanted to build a temple for God in Jerusalem, it was Solomon who accomplished the task. Solomon is remembered for his lavish building projects, which placed heavy burdens on the kingdom's economy and required an extensive international trade system. In addition, the Bible attributes to Solomon the gift of wisdom and even ascribes several books to him—Song of Songs, parts of Proverbs, Wisdom of Solomon, and Ecclesiastes. However, his many marital alliances and his oppressive rule resulted in the breakup of the united kingdom at his death in 922 B.C.E., after which there was Israel in the north and Judah in the south. The Assyrians conquered the former in the eighth century B.C.E., and the Babylonians conquered the latter in the sixth century B.C.E. The Temple in Jerusalem was destroyed during the Babylonian conquest of Judah in 586 B.C.E., rebuilt after the return from the Babylonian Exile in approximately 530 B.C.E., and remodeled by Herod the Great in 36 B.C.E., only to be destroyed by the Romans in 70 C.E. and never again rebuilt.

The Second Book of Samuel reflects some of David's story in the well-known prophecy that Nathan delivers to David after David expresses his desire to build a temple for God. Nathan's first response is to affirm David's decision, but in the night he receives a message from God in a vision, which he, in turn, delivers to David. This vision is recounted in 2 Samuel 7:1–29. Notice how the prophet plays on the word *house*, which can mean "temple," "palace," or "dynasty," depending on the context. The vision recalls the Israelites' experience in the wilderness during the Exodus, when God moved among them in the Ark of the Covenant (see Exod. 37:1–9; Josh. 3:1–17). It also recalls David's humble beginnings as a shepherd boy and youngest of the family of Jesse (1 Sam. 16:1–13). Through the words of the prophet, God promises David that one of his offspring will build God's house and establish an everlasting kingdom. God will be as a father to him and he will be God's son.

On some level, this promise was fulfilled in Solomon. He was the one who built the Temple in Jerusalem, as we have already mentioned, and in every way its magnificence was legendary. Nathan's promise to David that God would one day send a royal messiah from the dynasty of David who would rescue God's people, once and for all times, from their oppressors might also have appeared to be fulfilled in Solomon. As king, he had a celebrated reputation for power, wealth, and wisdom. But all this glory was short-lived. After Solomon's death his kingdom was divided into two much smaller kingdoms: Israel in the north and Judah in the south. Over time, these two tiny kingdoms were battered on all sides by much more powerful forces near and far. Meanwhile, the Israelite people continued to wait in hope for the fulfillment of God's promise to David to build him another kind of house an everlasting dynasty.

Early Christians took Nathan's prophecy to David as the basis for understanding Jesus as the messiah, the everlasting king and heir to the throne of David who would usher in God's eternal kingdom, and the Son of God (see also Psa. 2:7–9). The word **messiah** comes from a Hebrew word meaning "anointed one." The opening verse of Matthew's gospel refers to Jesus as the Son of David (Matt. 1:1). The synoptic gospels describe a scene in which Jesus poses a riddle, asking how the messiah could be David's son and yet David calls him Lord, referring to Psalms 110:1, perhaps reflecting early Christians' belief concerning Jesus' status as the messiah and the Son of God (Matt. 22:41–46; Mark 12:35–37; Luke 20:41–44). They also tell a story about a blind man who addresses Jesus as the son of David (Mark 10:46–52; Luke 18:35–43; cf. Matt. 20:29–34).

With this background in mind, please read 2 Samuel 7:1–29 from your Bible. Use evidence from the biblical text to answer Question 3 in "Questions for Reading" at the end of this chapter.

## THE PROPHETS

Although the Israelite people had prophets before they had kings—Moses and Samuel are examples—the beginnings of the monarchy marked a time of heightened activity for the **prophets**. The prophets served several important functions in ancient Israelite life. Some were court prophets, acting as advisors to the king. Others were cult prophets, associated in one way or another with the worship of the Israelite community. Still others operated outside of these social structures, on the margins of society, challenging the powerful elite of Israel's society to live and act in a way that is true to God's covenant with them. Whatever their specific role, prophets acted as God's voice in the world and as the conscience of the king and his people.

Two key events during the period of Israel's kings brought about an explosion of written prophetic activity. The first was the conquest of the northern kingdom, Israel, by the Assyrians in 722 B.C.E. The second was the conquest of the southern kingdom, Judah, by the Babylonians in 597 B.C.E. and the destruction of the Temple and exile of Jerusalem's elite to Babylon in 587 B.C.E. This second event is often called the **Babylonian Exile**. Prior to these events, in both the north and the south, numerous prophets appeared with warnings about the anticipated downfall of their respective kingdoms. But these prophets also wrote and spoke about the **remnant**, that is, a small group from among God's covenant people who would be saved from destruction because they repented of their wrongdoing or stayed faithful to God against all temptations. In this way, God's covenant would never be broken.

Because the prophets were so much a product of their own history and the particular situation in which they spoke, it is difficult to generalize their message. However, there are at least a few themes that are common to the prophets. First, the prophets held the belief that Israel/Judah is God's chosen people. They acknowledged that this special relationship of **election** carried with it privileges for God's people but also obligations. When Israel and Judah rebelled against God, the prophets warned the people that they would be punished for their failure to fulfill the requirements of the covenant. Hence, the second major theme of the prophets' message is the need to return to the covenant. The third major theme is justice for the disadvantaged. The prophets constantly reminded their hearers that God is a God of the poor and that he does not tolerate those who cause them harm. Thus, the prophets spoke to real, concrete situations of injustice and abuse in their own historical contexts and demanded from the people nothing less than conversion, a complete change of heart.

Despite their numerous warnings, the prophets' message is ultimately one of hope and promise. After the destruction of the two kingdoms of Israel and Judah—and particularly during the Babylonian Exile, when Judeans in exile feared that God had utterly abandoned them—the prophets' message turns to one of consolation. They proclaimed that God will once again fill Jerusalem with people, come to dwell again in the holy Temple, and raise up an everlasting king from David's lineage. The people should not despair in these dark times because God will always be faithful and will return blessings and protection to the chosen people once they have changed their ways.

Finally, in 538 B.C.E., the Judean people were allowed to return from exile to rebuild their homeland and their Temple. It was during this post-Exile period, in approximately 450 B.C.E., that written prophetic activity gradually ended. However, it is reasonable to assume that prophecy continued, in one form or another, into the first century C.E. The Jewish historian Josephus writes about the activities of Jewish prophets or would-be prophets during that period. Likewise, in the New Testament, John the Baptist is identified as a prophet, Jesus of the gospels warns about false prophets, and early Christians are described as engaging in prophetic activity.

The prophets of the Old Testament are important for our understanding of the New Testament for several reasons. First, Jesus is portrayed as the *Prophet par excellence* in some of the gospels, especially in parts of the Gospels of Matthew, Luke, and John. Second, the writers of the New Testament, especially the gospel writers, borrow and reinterpret certain Old Testament prophetic texts and apply them to Jesus or to the events surrounding his life. We should be clear, however, that these are Christian reinterpretations of the prophetic writings. If we accept a contextualist reading of scripture, we must acknowledge that the prophetic authors of the TaNaK were writing within their own historical situations and were not intending to say anything about Jesus as the messiah or about his role in salvation. To argue otherwise is to deny the contextual character of the writing.

Among the more famous prophecies that Christians have reinterpreted to relate to Jesus is Isaiah's suffering servant song (Isa. 52:13–53:12). It is the fourth of Isaiah's servant songs—the others are Isaiah 42:1–4, 49:1–6, and 50:4–11. All of them have as their central character an individual who is described as "the Lord's servant" and "the chosen one." This fourth servant song probably dates back to the Babylonian Exile, a time of great distress for the Judean people, when it appeared that God had broken the covenant with them. Why would they have thought this way? Because everything that represented the covenant—the Temple, the monarchy, and the nation—had been destroyed. The author of the fourth servant song does not tell us the identity of the servant, but today most biblical scholars think that the servant represents the remnant of Israel, those Jews who remained faithful to God's covenant even during the darkest years of the Exile. They humbly and patiently bore God's punishments for Israel's sins in the hope that God would rescue them and restore Israel to right relationship with God.

With this background in mind, please read Isaiah 52:13–53:12 from your Bible. Use evidence from the biblical text to answer Question 4 in "Questions for Reading" at the end of this chapter.

# THE WISDOM OF GOD

In our survey of Israel's story of salvation and the literature of the Old Testament, we have touched on several of the major sections of this testament. However, there is one more collection of books that deserve our attention, namely, the **wisdom literature** (Job, Psalms, Proverbs, Ecclesiastes, Son of Songs, Wisdom of Solomon, and Sirach). Notice that some of these are apocryphal or deuterocanonical books (see the Introduction). This is the part of the Bible that people tend to know least well, even though it is a rich and varied body of literature that has universal applicability for people of many faith traditions. In some of these books, the **sage** (i.e., the wise teacher) communicates wisdom about life experience: what brings happiness, why honesty matters, how to be a good friend, and so on. This wisdom usually takes the form of short sayings or proverbs. The Book of Proverbs provides the best illustration of this type of literature. See, for example, Proverbs 23:19–21:

> Hear, my child, and be wise,
> and direct your mind in the way.
> Do not be among winebibbers,
> or among gluttonous eaters of meat;
> For the drunkard and the glutton will come to poverty,
> and drowsiness will clothe them with rags.

Other wisdom literature addresses the question of **theodicy** (the problem of the suffering of good people and the existence of evil). In most cases, it speaks with a clear conviction that God is just and sovereign, so good people should be comforted in the fact that God will reward their good deeds somehow and somewhere, regardless of how things might otherwise appear. The Book of Job is a good example of a response to the theodicy question. However, sometimes the answer is less satisfying, as in the case of the Book of Ecclesiastes. Qoheleth, its author, speaks about the futility of seeking wisdom:

> I, the Teacher, when king over Israel in Jerusalem, applied my mind to seek and to search out by wisdom all that is done under heaven; it is an unhappy business that God has given to human beings to be busy with. I saw all the deeds that are done under the sun; and see, all is vanity and a chasing after wind.

> (Eccl. 1:12–14)

Qoheleth's gloomy demeanor to the contrary, other wisdom literature praises wisdom and invites the reader to seek after it. Wisdom is one of the attributes of God, but in praising wisdom, the sages gave it personal characteristics. In other words, they personified the wisdom of God as **Sophia** (the Greek noun meaning "wisdom" is feminine in gender). Thus, they presented Sophia as a beautiful and alluring woman who invites the wise to come to her banquet to partake of her bread and drink her wine. She is God's throne partner and God's craftsperson, the one who assisted God in the process of creation. She is pure light, and she reflects the radiance of God. The Old Testament texts that best demonstrate the personification of Wisdom are Proverbs 8, Job 28, and Wisdom of Solomon 6–9. Sirach 24 goes a step further and associates personified Wisdom with the Torah.

> Some of the wisdom books of the Old Testament, like Proverbs and Psalms, are very old. Others, like the apocryphal/deuterocanonical Wisdom of Solomon, may not have been written until the mid–first century C.E. Moreover, the wisdom books apparently did not acquire canonical status until the end of the first century or the beginning of the second century C.E. Therefore, except for the Psalms, the wisdom books are seldom (if ever) quoted in the New Testament. However, the authors of the synoptic gospels appear to portray Jesus as a sage, particularly in their presentation of the teaching materials (parables and sayings of Jesus). Moreover, the author of the Gospel of John uses imagery associated with personified Wisdom to describe Jesus as the one who "enlightens everyone" and comes to "dwell with his own."
>
> (John 1:9–14)

With this background in mind, please read Sirach 24:1–22 and Wisdom 6:12–8:21 from your Bible. Use evidence from the biblical text to answer Question 5 in "Questions for Reading" at the end of this chapter.

## KEY TERMS

| | | |
|---|---|---|
| Jewish Christians | Exodus | Babylonian Exile |
| Abraham | Suzerainty treaty | Remnant |
| Legend | Law of Moses | Election |
| Covenant | David | Wisdom literature |
| Type | Solomon | Sage |
| Moses | Messiah | Theodicy |
| Passover | Prophets | Sophia |

## QUESTIONS FOR READING

1. Read Genesis 15:1–21 and 22:1–19. Use evidence from the biblical text to answer the following questions. *Note:* For those who are unfamiliar with biblical citations, the number immediately after the name of the book and before the colon is the chapter number. The numbers after the colon are the numbers of the smaller units, called verses, within that chapter. For example, in the citation Genesis 15:1–21, the number 15 is the chapter to be read, and 1–21 are the verses. If you do not know the abbreviations for particular biblical books, you should be able to find them in the introductory sections of your Bible.
   a. Describe the ritual of covenant performed by Abram and God in Genesis 15:1–21 and the vision that Abram was permitted to witness.
   b. Identify the prophetic language in the Genesis 15 account of God's covenant with Abram. What hints about the Exodus are you able to find here?

    c. In Genesis 15:1–21, why was Abram accounted or reckoned as righteous before God? What do you think is the significance of the choice of the word *accounted* or *reckoned* (instead of saying that Abram earned righteousness)?

    d. What does Genesis 22:1–19 say about why Abraham took Isaac up the mountain with the wood and fire for the sacrifice? Was anyone else with them? How old was Isaac in this story? What happened to Isaac at the conclusion of the story? *Note:* Abram and Abraham are the same person. Genesis 17 contains a story about how God changed Abram's name to Abraham, meaning "Father of Nations." In the ancient world, a name change meant a change in destiny.

    e. What details in the story of the sacrifice of Isaac (Gen. 22:1–19) might early Christians have wanted to reinterpret to help them explain the significance of the death of Jesus? Explain.

2. Read Exodus 12:1–13:22. Use evidence from the text to answer the following questions. *Note:* In the case of Exodus 12:1–13:22, you begin reading at chapter 12, verse 1, and continue through chapter 13, verse 22.

    a. Describe the original ritual associated with Passover.

    b. What event does Passover commemorate? Why was the blood of the Passover lamb sprinkled on the lintel and doorposts of the Israelites' homes?

    c. According to the author of the Exodus story, why are the people required to celebrate the feast of Passover each year? Why are they commanded to explain to their children the meaning of the feast?

3. Read 2 Samuel 7:1–29. Use evidence from the text to answer the following questions. *Note:* The number in front of the name of the book tells you that there is more than one book (or letter, if you are looking for a New Testament text) by that name. In the case of 2 Samuel 7:1–29, the number 2 means that you want the second book named Samuel.

    a. Who is Nathan? What is his relationship to David?

    b. Describe briefly the prophecy made by Nathan to King David. Explain the author's play on the words *house* and *dynasty*.

    c. What circumstances prompted Nathan to make this prophecy?

    d. What details might early Christians have seen in this story and in Nathan's prophecy that would have helped them explain their understanding of Jesus' identity as the messiah?

4. Read Isaiah 52:13–53:12. Use evidence from the text to answer the following questions.

    a. What promise does God make, through the prophet, regarding the servant's future? Why? What happened to him?

    b. How do kings and nations react to the servant? Why?

    c. How does the servant respond to his suffering? Is his suffering deserved or undeserved? Explain.

    d. According to the prophet, what good result or outcome will come from the servant's suffering?

    e. As you read the suffering servant song of Isaiah, what clues can you find that would confirm biblical scholars' theory that the author of Isaiah was referring to the remnant of God's people in exile when he used the term *servant*?

    f. What details from this prophecy might have appealed to early Christians who were trying to make sense of the death of Jesus?

5. Read Sirach 24:1–22 and Wisdom 6:12–8:21. Use evidence from the text to answer the following questions.
   a. According to Sirach 24, how did Wisdom come into being? Where was her original home?
   b. What does Sirach say about how Wisdom came to dwell on earth? With whom did she come to dwell? Why?
   c. Sirach uses imagery of vegetation (trees and vines) and perfume to describe Wisdom's presence on earth. What do these images say about Wisdom's influence?
   d. In Sirach 24, Wisdom invites humans who desire her to come to her. Why should they? What will they gain?
   e. According to Wisdom 6–8 how did Wisdom come into being? Where is her home?
   f. What does Wisdom of Solomon say about the things (values, traits, or attitudes) that humans who seek Wisdom will gain?
   g. According to Wisdom 6–8 what things (values, traits, or attitudes) have no place alongside of Wisdom, or what things will Wisdom not tolerate?
   h. According to Wisdom 6–8 what attributes are ascribed to Wisdom? What activities does she perform on God's behalf?
   i. What does Wisdom of Solomon say about Wisdom's relationship to God?
   j. What details might early Christians have seen in these descriptions of Wisdom that would have helped them explain Jesus' relationship with God and his role in the world?

## QUESTIONS FOR REFLECTION

1. What is the function of ritual in the lives of modern people? Do you think rituals are as important for people today as they were for ancient peoples? Give examples to explain.

2. Can you think of any modern examples of covenant that carry the same weight as the Old Testament notion of covenant? Where does the notion of covenant come into Christian belief?

3. If the Christian ritual of the Eucharist should be interpreted against the backdrop of Passover, how would you describe some of the important elements of Eucharist and its theological significance?

## ACTIVITIES FOR LEARNING

1. Identify some sort of religious ritual. It may be a ritual of baptism or marriage for a Christian church with which you are familiar or a marriage or life-transition ceremony for another faith tradition. Carefully examine its prayers and sacred actions. Use the two definitions of ritual given above as a starting point for describing the meaning and significance of this ritual. What does the ritual signify? What does it effect—that is, make into a reality?

2. Identify a contemporary of our time who might be considered a prophet in the biblical sense—someone who calls people to conversion of heart and challenges them to live justice. Some famous examples are Martin Luther King, Jr., Bishop Desmond Tutu, Mahatma Gandhi, Thomas Merton, Mother Teresa of Calcutta, and Dorothy Day, but there are others as well. Do some research on that person's life, the social and cultural circumstances in which that person lived, and the prophetic message he or she communicated. In what ways is this person like the biblical prophets?

## SOURCES AND RESOURCES

Bandstra, Barry L. *Reading the Old Testament: An Introduction to the Hebrew Bible.* Belmont, Calif.: Wadsworth, 1995.

Barton, John, and Julia Bowden. *The Original Story: God, Israel and the World.* Grand Rapids, Mich.: Eerdmans, 2005.

Beasley, James R., *An Introduction to the Bible.* Nashville, Tenn.: Abingdon Press, 1991.

Birch, Bruce C., Walter Brueggemann, Terence E. Fretheim, and David L. Petersen. *A Theological Introduction to the Old Testament.* Nashville, Tenn.: Abingdon Press, 2005.

Boadt, Lawrence. *Reading the Old Testament: An Introduction.* New York: Paulist, 1984.

Brueggemann, Walter. *An Introduction to the Old Testament: The Canon and Christian Imagination.* Louisville, Ky.: Westminster John Knox Press, 2003.

Ceresko, Anthony R. *Introduction to the Old Testament: A Liberation Perspective.* Maryknoll, N.Y.: Orbis Books, 2001.

Coggins, Richard J. *Introducing the Old Testament.* New York: Oxford University Press, 2001.

Collins, John J. *Introduction to the Hebrew Bible.* Minneapolis, Minn.: Fortress Press, 2004.

Crenshaw, James L. *Old Testament Story and Faith: A Literary and Theological Introduction.* Peabody, Mass.: Hendrickson Publishers, 1992.

Delattre, Roland. "Ritual Resourcefulness and Cultural Pluralism." In *Soundings* 61 (1978) 281–301.

Drane, John. *Introducing the Old Testament.* Minneapolis, Minn.: Fortress Press, 2001.

Flanders, Henry Jackson, Jr., Robert Wilson Crapps, and David Anthony Smith. *People of the Covenant: An Introduction to the Hebrew Bible.* New York: Oxford University Press, 1996.

Gottwald, Norman K. *The Hebrew Bible: A Socio-Literary Introduction.* Philadelphia: Fortress, 1985.

Nigosian, Solomon Alexander. *From Ancient Writings to Sacred Texts: The Old Testament and Apocrypha.* Baltimore, Md.: Johns Hopkins University Press, 2004.

Smith, Jonathan Z. "The Bare Facts of Ritual." In *History of Religions* 20 (1980) 112–127.

# FIRST-CENTURY JUDAISMS

## TIMELINE

| | |
|---|---|
| **37 B.C.E.** | Herod the Great takes up his kingship in Palestine. |
| **4 B.C.E.** | Herod the Great, king of Palestine, dies; his kingdom is divided among three sons: Archelaus, Herod Antipas, Philip. |
| **4 B.C.E.–39 C.E.** | Herod Antipas, son of Herod the Great, is tetrarch of Galilee and Perea. |
| **6 C.E.** | Judea and Samaria become a Roman prefecture; revolt of Judas the Galilean. |
| **44–46 C.E.** | Revolt of Theudas. |
| **52–60 C.E.** | Revolt of the Egyptian false prophet. |
| **62–64 C.E.** | Jesus, son of Ananus, prophesies in Jerusalem. |
| **66–70 C.E.** | Jewish War. |
| **70 C.E.** | Destruction of Jerusalem and the Temple. |
| **80–90 C.E.** | Flavius Josephus writes *The Jewish War* and *Jewish Antiquities.* |
| **132–135 C.E.** | Revolt of Bar Kochba, whose name means "Son of the Star." |

Finally, our preparations are almost complete. We are about to launch out on our journey into the New Testament, but there is one more topic that we need to address before we can begin. In order to understand the New Testament—and in particular, the gospels—you need to know something of the historical, political, religious, and cultural world in which Jesus and his earliest followers lived, namely, early Judaism. Without this background, it is difficult to appreciate the significance of Jesus' life or why people responded to his message as they did. This chapter will provide only a brief sketch of the Jewish world of Jesus in its Greco-Roman context, with the hope that you will continue to read about the historical and cultural aspects of early Judaism as you study the New Testament itself.

**100**

The period we are surveying here is part of what is called **Second Temple Judaism**. It extends from approximately 520 B.C.E. to 70 C.E.—that is, from the period of the rebuilding of the Jerusalem Temple after the return from the Babylonian Exile (587–539 B.C.E.) up to and including Rome's destruction of the Temple during the Jewish War (66–70 C.E.). The Jewish religion of this period is often called Early Judaism in order to distinguish it from Rabbinic Judaism, which emerges after the Jewish War. Whichever term you choose to use, we must also recognize that Judaism toward the end of this period was rich and varied—hence, the title of this chapter, "First-Century Judaisms."

## GALILEE, SAMARIA, AND JUDEA

Three geographic areas of first-century Palestine are mentioned with regularity in the gospel story: Galilee, Samaria, and Judea. After Herod the Great's death (4 B.C.E.), the northern part of Palestine—**Galilee** and Perea—came under the rule of his son Herod Antipas, who made his capital at Tiberius, on the western shore of the Sea of Galilee. His failed attempt in 39 C.E. to secure the kingdom of his deceased brother, Philip, from Herod Agrippa I ended with his exile to Gaul (modern France). However, until that time, Antipas's long reign was relatively free of political upheavals, suggesting that he was a competent and effective king. If we add to this positive political environment the fact that Galilee was relatively fertile and well-watered, then it is reasonable to assume that the people living in first-century Galilee enjoyed a fairly comfortable existence compared to some of their neighbors. For the most part, they would have been farmers and fishermen. However, they also would have benefited from the trading prowess of their Phoenician neighbors and from the caravans that passed nearby.

Galilee enjoyed a fairly substantial population in the first century C.E. The Jewish historian Josephus mentions that Galilee had 204 villages (*Life of Flavius Josephus* 45.235) during this period, and archeological work in this area gives scholars little reason to doubt his claim. A quick look at a map of Palestine will show that the region of Galilee was less than forty-five miles long, north to south, and less than twenty-five miles wide. If we divide the square miles of the region by the estimated number of villages, we find that Galilee averaged approximately one village for every five square miles, meaning that these villages were only a few hours' walking distance apart.

We should also mention that first-century Galilee apparently was quite thoroughly Jewish in its religious, political, and cultural background. An example of Jewish influence on the region's political climate can be found in the gospel story of the beheading of the Jewish prophet John the Baptist. According to the story, John accused Herod Antipas, the king of Galilee, of breaking Jewish law regarding the marriage of his brother's wife, which made Herod Antipas fearful enough to put him in jail (Matt. 14:12 and parallels; cf. Lev. 18:16; 20:21). Galilee's shift to a predominately Jewish culture began after the Maccabean Revolt in 166 B.C.E. and continued through the second century C.E., at which point Galilee was considered a center of Jewish scholarship. Biblical scholars think that the Mishnah was written there, as was the Palestinian Talmud, both important Jewish religious works. We

First-century Palestine and adjoining areas, including modern boundaries.

also have archeological evidence that Galilee was home to a large number of synagogues during this period.

The southern region of Palestine was **Judea**. After the death of Herod the Great, his son Archelaus inherited this region, along with Idumea (further south in Palestine) and Samaria (central Palestine). Archelaus continued his father's building projects, but his reign was marked by mass murders and considerable brutality toward the people of Judea and Samaria. The people revolted and, finally, in 6 C.E., Archelaus was removed from office and replaced by a prefect (i.e., governor) who had been appointed by the emperor but who reported to the proconsul (i.e., president) of the Syrian province. This prefect ruled from Caesarea, a port city in the northwestern part of Samaria. Pontius Pilate is probably the most well known of these prefects.

In many ways, Judea was quite different from Galilee. For example, the situation of the peasant population was much less secure in Judea than in Galilee, and political unrest was common. Second, Judea did not have direct access to trade routes, and the land was mostly desert. Therefore, agrarian life consisted mostly of herding sheep and producing grapes and olives. Third, the population was not spread across the land, as it was in Galilee; most people lived in and around Jerusalem. Instead of economic diversity, the financial well-being of the region depended principally on the operation of the Jerusalem Temple.

Between Galilee and Judea was **Samaria**. Like Judea, this region was under the rule of the prefect from Caesarea for much of the first century, before the Jewish War in 70 C.E. Its capital, originally also known as Samaria, had been lavishly rebuilt and remodeled by Herod the Great around 30 B.C.E. and renamed Sebaste, in honor of Emperor Augustus, whose Greek name was Sebastos. The city and the region had a long-standing reputation for wealth and prosperity, which has been verified by archeological discoveries in that area. It also appears that Samaria made good use of trade relations with its Phoenician neighbors. In sum, the region and its capital appear to have enjoyed an open exchange of cultures and a stable economy that contributed to the welfare of its people.

The **Samaritans** had a place of worship on Mt. Gerizim, in central Samaria, and they continue to live and worship there today, near the modern city of Nablus. If you have read the New Testament gospels and Acts of the Apostles before, you probably recognize this group. The Gospel of John has a story of Jesus' encounter with a Samaritan woman who eventually brings her whole village to meet Jesus (John 4:4–42). In the Gospel of Luke, Jesus tells a story about a Samaritan who came to the aid of a victim of robbery to teach what it means to love your neighbor (Luke 10:29–37). Acts of the Apostles describes the successful missionary activity of the apostle Philip in Samaria (Acts 8). At the same time, the Gospel of Luke and Acts of the Apostles include some less-than-sympathetic stories about Samaritans: one about the Samaritan magician Simon Magus (Acts 8:9–13) and another about some Samaritans who rejected Jesus (Luke 9:52–59). The Old Testament also contains several negative references to the Samaritans (2 Kings 17; cf. Sir. 50:26; 2 Macc. 6:2), and the first-century Jewish historian Josephus frequently describes the Samaritans in hostile terms.

Who are these Samaritans? What was their relationship to the Judaisms of first-century Palestine? Unfortunately, we do not have a great deal of constructive data with which to answer these questions. As we have already seen in the preceding paragraph,

Samaritan priest holding an ancient Torah scroll. Photo by Rev. David Smith. Used with permission.

much of the textual evidence is highly polemical (i.e., hostile to Samaritans), so it is not very helpful in reconstructing the origins of the Samaritans. Scholars of several decades ago had assumed that the Samaritans were the product of intermarriage between the Israelites of the northern kingdom of Israel and Assyrians who had been resettled in their land after the Assyrian conquest of 722 B.C.E. This would account for the Jewish view that the Samaritans were worse than "foreigners." However, there is little evidence to support this view.

Today scholars gather clues from the Samaritans' own documents and traditions and conclude that first-century Samaritans were a conservative branch of Judaism—taking only the Pentateuch as their scriptures and strictly observing Sabbath regulations, for example—whose worship at Mt. Gerizim developed as an alternative to (and perhaps a protest against) the Jerusalem Temple worship. Some scholars think that the Samaritans began to develop their distinctive identity as early as the sixth century B.C.E., but clearly by the first century C.E. Jews considered them not to be Jews, while Samaritans thought of themselves as the true inheritors of the Mosaic covenant. In other words, the harsh rhetoric against the Samaritans found in the writings of people like Josephus likely is the fallout of an intrafamily fight—Jews fighting their fellow Jews over everything from their place of worship to the content of their scriptures.

## THE PURITY SYSTEM

Before we can investigate Jewish feasts and Temple worship, we need to understand something about the Jewish purity system. When you are reading a New Testament text and come across words like *unclean, defiled,* and *polluted,* you are dealing with the purity system. Likewise, when you see words like *clean, pure, holy, spotless, blameless,* and *undefiled,* you are dealing with issues of purity. This language is very foreign to today's readers, particularly those who belong to Western cultures. However, the purity system is very important to one's understanding of the significance of certain activities within first-century Jewish cultures. Scholars who attempt to reconstruct the purity system of first-century Judaism often rely on the insights of cultural anthropology for models of purity and defilement and for the principles behind purity systems. With this information, they develop "maps" of persons, places, things, and times that are clean and unclean. Such maps help us understand what Judaism valued in terms of social order.

An important tool for building these social maps is the principle of purity, which has to do with things being in the right place. If something is out of place, then it is unclean. For example, a bird that does what birds do (fly in the air) and eats what birds eat (seeds and insects) is considered clean, but an animal that does not behave like it is supposed to behave or that is used in a capacity for which it is not intended is considered unclean. This notion of order extends to the human body and to relationships among persons. Rashes or breaks in the skin (i.e., the surface of the body) make a person unclean because they do not belong there. Likewise, body fluids that are not where they belong make a person unclean. Things that indirectly affect the purity of a person or another object also belong to the system of purity. For example, hands and dishes have to be properly cleaned or else they pollute the food and subsequently the body of the person eating the food. People who regularly come in contact with unclean people (lepers, sinners, women who are menstruating) are also considered unclean, even when they are not touching them. Likewise, people who do not (or cannot) properly participate in Temple worship or abide by other religious obligations are considered unclean.

Needless to say, the rules of first-century Judaism's purity system are much more complicated than what we have summarized here. Hopefully, however, this brief survey will help us appreciate the implications of the purity system for social order. The priests of the Temple and other religious elites played an important role in defining and maintaining the purity system, which, in turn, ensured their position as the elite of the society. Others who, because of poverty, illness, work, or social associations, did not or could not observe the rules of the purity system also knew their place: They were the unclean. Thus, purity was not an individual and private religious matter. Rather, it affected every aspect of first-century Jewish society, from what people ate to the kind of work they performed, where they traveled, and the people with whom they associated.

## JERUSALEM TEMPLE WORSHIP

Jerusalem and its Temple were the political and religious centers of Judea during the first century C.E. Although Jesus and his disciples were from Galilee and were very much a part of Galilean Judaism, they also made pilgrimage to Jerusalem, as many observant Jews did. The gospels suggest that they went at least once and perhaps several times. The **Temple** had religious significance for Judaism because it was the place where God "came down" to be with Israel. It was God's dwelling place, also called the "house" of God. The Temple Mount—that is, the platform on which the Temple was located—was called "the mountain of the Lord's house" (Isa. 2:2).

The first Temple was built during the reign of King David's son, Solomon, in 961–922 B.C.E. This Temple was later destroyed during the Babylonian conquest of Judea in 587 B.C.E., and a second Temple was built on the same site after the Babylonian Exile in the late sixth century B.C.E. Herod the Great launched a major remodeling of the Temple in 20 B.C.E., but the Temple complex was not completed until 62 C.E. Ironically, Herod's Temple was destroyed during the Jewish War of 66–70 C.E. which Emperor Nero initiated when he sent his military commander Vespasian to crush a rebellion there. Jews still come to pray at the Wailing Wall, one of the walls of the Temple Mount, but the Temple itself no longer exists. However, the Dome of the Rock, a Muslim holy site is located in roughly the same place as the Temple once stood.

The major activity that took place in the Temple was **sacrifice**. The word *sacrifice* comes from a Latin word that means "to make holy." Sacrifices were offered to God for a variety of reasons: to give thanks, to petition for favors or protection, and to ask forgiveness for wrongdoing. Since they were intended as gifts for God, only the objects that were considered *acceptable to God* could be offered as sacrifice: the best of the grain harvest, the most perfect lambs from the flock, and the finest of wines from the vineyards. It was the duty of the **priests** (guardians of the Temple, responsible for various duties associated with the operation of the Temple) and the **Levites** (originally descendants of the tribe of Levi; in the New Testament period, temple attendants) to select and prepare the offerings and, in general, to take care of the Temple. In return for their service, the priests and Levites were permitted

Jewish worshipers gathered at the Wailing Wall (Temple Mount) on the eve of Shabbat. Photo by Catherine Cory.

The Dome of the Rock on the Temple Mount. Muslims honor this place as the site from which the prophet Muhammad ascended to God in the heavens, consulted with Moses, and was given the Islamic prayers that are required of all Muslims today. The original structure dates to 688–691 C.E., but the magnificent tile work was completed in the sixteenth century, and the gold covering on the dome was done in 1965.

to use parts of the offerings for their own livelihood. In addition, Jews paid a special tax for the upkeep of the Temple. In first-century Palestine, before the destruction of the Temple, the annual tax was apparently two denarii for every Jewish male. A denarius was the going rate for a full day's work for a day laborer (Matt. 20:1–13).

Based on literary descriptions and archeological evidence, biblical scholars think that the temple complex was rather large. After Herod the Great's expansion, the Temple Mount measured approximately 1,500 feet from north to south. On the southern end, it was approximately 920 feet wide, and on the northern end, it was approximately 1,020 feet wide. These calculations assume an equivalency of 18 inches per "cubit." However, there was an alternative measure whose equivalency is approximately 21 inches per cubit, which would make the measure of the Temple and Temple Mount somewhat larger.

The Temple complex consisted of two major areas: the Temple proper and the outer court of the Temple Mount. Gentiles (i.e., non-Jews) were not permitted any farther than this outer court area. The Temple itself was situated slightly off-center in the northwest quadrant of the Temple Mount. Scholars think it was separated from the rest of the Temple Mount by a wall that was approximately 4$\frac{1}{2}$ feet (i.e., 3 cubits) high. The wall's length from east to west was approximately 480 feet, and its width was approximately 200 feet. Inside of this wall was another wall that surrounded the Temple itself. This area was further divided into areas of increasing holiness: the court of the women, the court of the Israelites, the court

Model of Herod's Temple. It is part of a much larger display of first-century Jerusalem (scale 1:50) at the Holyland Motel in Jerusalem. This reconstruction was first completed in 1964–1967 but is periodically updated when new archeological evidence becomes available. Photo by Catherine Cory.

of the priests, and the Holy of Holies, which was the innermost room within the Temple. The Holy of Holies might have measured 30 feet by 30 feet. The altar of sacrifice, located in the court of the priests, was approximately 48 feet by 48 feet. Compared to the tiny homes and apartments of the peasant classes, this sacred space would have been unbelievably massive and ornate, truly fitting as a "house" of God.

Because the Temple was the major economic institution of Jerusalem and the region, a large number of people were required to maintain it, but, because of purity regulations, not just anyone could perform these tasks. Here are just a few of the services that were needed to operate the Temple. Certain people were charged with making religious objects used for sacrifices like ritually correct breads, oil, wine, linens and religious garments, and incense. Others provided the wood for sacrificial fires. Still others were charged with caring for the ritually pure animals for sacrifices. In addition, there were the carpenters, craftsmen, stonemasons, metalworkers, roofers, and engineers who made repairs and upgrades to Temple property and created the sacred objects for Temple worship. Still other people were charged with gathering the resources for the operation of the Temple and transporting them to Jerusalem from throughout Palestine and beyond. Finally, to accommodate the large number of pilgrims who came to Jerusalem for the major feasts, they needed innkeepers, shops where pilgrims could buy food, people to copy sacred documents, sellers of approved items for sacrifice, and moneychangers. Needless to say, this was big business.

# THE ELITE OF JERUSALEM AND PALESTINE

As discussed in Chapter 3, the elite of the Greco-Roman world probably made up only 1 to 2 percent of the population, and we have no reason to believe that the situation was different in Palestine. The vast majority of the population belonged to the peasant class, sometimes known by the descriptor *am ha aretz*—literally, "the people of the land." In the New Testament gospels, they are often identified simply as "the crowd." In contrast with the elite, who were assumed to be ritually clean, the *am ha aretz* were generally assumed to be unclean. Who were the elite of Palestine? They included the High Priest, chief priests, Sadducees, scribes, and possibly Pharisees. What follows is a brief description of each, along with a few terms we are likely to encounter in our reading of the gospels.

Among the Jewish elite of first-century Palestine, the one with the highest position of power was the **High Priest** of the Jerusalem Temple. Herod the Great, and later the Roman prefects, assumed the authority to appoint the High Priest in an effort to control the activities of the Temple. However, members of the leading priestly families, also called the **chief priests**, managed to keep a tight hold on the powerful office, perhaps by buying the appointment or making certain agreements with the Roman prefect. The High Priest was the spokesperson for the Jewish people in their relations with the Romans. He also had a certain amount of political and governing authority in issues pertaining to his own people. More importantly, in the purity system, the High Priest was considered the holiest among the Jewish population and therefore the only human who could enter the Holy of Holies.

Another group among the Palestinian elite was the **Sanhedrin** (Greek, meaning "council"). The Sanhedrin apparently functioned as the supreme judicial council of the Jews. However, we do not know the exact nature of the Sanhedrin. It may have been an established, and somewhat permanent, assembly of Jewish religious leaders (e.g., Sadducees, priests, and scribes), or it may have been a rather transient group of Jewish aristocrats who were convened to deal with a particular issue— much like today's grand juries. It is also possible that they had some administrative duties, since it was the practice of Roman leadership in the provinces of the empire to assign the local elite to assist them in various activities of governance. The gospels identify the Sanhedrin as standing in opposition to Jesus and participating in his trial before the High Priest.

The **Sadducees** were another of the Jewish aristocratic groups of first-century Palestine. Scholars do not know for certain where their name originated. According to one theory, it derives from the Hebrew word for "righteous ones." Another theory suggests that they got their name by association with the High Priest Zadok, making the Sadducees descendants of the High Priest. The Sadducees were responsible for the operation of the Jerusalem Temple, but they depended on the Romans for their power and status, and even for access to the Temple. Therefore, they were obligated to function as collaborators with the Roman authorities. As a result, they were not well liked or trusted by the majority of the Jewish population. After the destruction of the Jerusalem Temple, it appears that they ceased to exist as a separate group.

Outside of the New Testament, our major source of information about the Sadducees comes from the first-century historian Josephus. He explains that the Sadducees were conservative in their theology, allowing no interpretations of

Jewish law beyond the literal sense. They did not accept such teachings as reincarnation, the immortality of the soul, the resurrection of the dead, or the presence of angels. Concerning fate and free will in the activities of the world, the Sadducees allowed no power to fate, arguing that God was the supreme ruler, untouched by any other power, human or divine. Thus, they held humans responsible in every way for their destiny, whether good or bad.

Also frequently mentioned in the gospels are the **Pharisees**. Their name, we think, means "separated ones." One theory is that this descriptor is indicative of their desire for holiness. Another is that the Pharisees received their name from the Sadducees, who considered them to be their opponents, making it a derogatory term. Our first-century historian Josephus suggests that ordinary Jews looked up to the Pharisees as models of Jewish piety and as teachers and interpreters of the Jewish law. The Pharisees were especially concerned with making the Torah meaningful to their contemporaries by coming up with interpretations of Jewish law that were appropriate for the way people lived in their own time. Again, according to Josephus, they were rather progressive in their theology, believing in such things as reincarnation, the immortality of the soul, the resurrection of the dead, and the presence of angels. Concerning the role of fate and free will in people's lives, the Pharisees allowed that some things were controlled by fate, and yet humans were fully responsible for their actions. God ruled supreme over all of the forces of this world. However, bad things could not be blamed on God.

Because of their negative portrayal in the gospels, many first-time readers think that the Pharisees were wicked people. For example, some think that they were simply "out to get Jesus" at any cost. Others think they were hypocritical, obsessing about the externals of religious practice and disregarding the true intent of the Jewish law. However, again we need to be cautious about our conclusions because Josephus expresses just the opposite bias concerning the Pharisees, saying that they were much loved and respected by the people! Other Jewish writings describe them as having a reform agenda for Judaism that involved finding ways to apply the holiness system to all Jews, not just the elite (see "The Purity System" above). If you look carefully at the gospel stories involving conflicts between Jesus and the Pharisees, you will notice that their debates center on right application of Sabbath and purity regulations. Therefore, perhaps a better way of making sense of the evidence is to say that Jesus had a reform agenda for Judaism and so did the Pharisees, but they disagreed on the kind of reform that was needed. Another possible reason for the gospel writers' apparent fixation on the Pharisees as opponents of Jesus is that Jewish groups associated with the Temple had ceased to exist by the time the canonical gospels were written (70–100 C.E.) so the evangelists no longer considered them a threat.

Another group that deserves mention here is the scribes. The **scribes** were professional copyists who served as secretaries for the priests and other religious leaders. Because they were trained in reading and writing, they were sometimes also the teachers of the Torah, which they memorized and recited for the people. The New Testament suggests that they also functioned as lawyers and judges. Sometimes they are mentioned alongside the Pharisees and other times alongside the Sadducees or the Sanhedrin, which probably reflects their position as "support staff" for these other groups. In other words, the scribes were identifiable as a group because of their occupation and not so much because of their way of being Jewish. Their level of education and society's demand for their reading and writing skills placed them among the elite of Palestine, but most likely they also belonged to wealthy families because only wealthy families had easy access to formal education.

## OTHER FIRST-CENTURY JUDAISMS

Another kind of Judaism found within first-century Palestine is the Essene movement. According to Josephus, there were two kinds of **Essenes**. The monastic community at Qumran near the Dead Sea is the one with which most of us are familiar because of the **Dead Sea Scrolls**, which were discovered there only in the past century (1947–1960). This group is thought to have consisted of Jewish males who shared all property in common, took vows of celibacy, and lived an ascetic lifestyle of fasting and meditation. They developed their own purity regulations and religious rituals, apparently in protest against activities of the Jerusalem Temple. Their origin is unclear, but it is usually traced to the Hasideans, a group of pious Jews who supported the Maccabean Revolt in 166 B.C.E. and opposed Jonathan's ascent to the position of High Priest in Jerusalem (152 B.C.E.). Their leader was called the Teacher of Righteousness. The writings that were preserved at Qumran include some community documents like the *Manual of Discipline* and our earliest available manuscripts of books of the TaNaK, the scriptures of Judaism, together with commentaries on various parts of the TaNaK.

Josephus mentions another group of Essenes who lived outside of the Qumran community in the cities and villages of Palestine. We do not know a lot about

Cave 4 at Qumran, where some of the Dead Sea Scrolls were found. The archeological remains of Qumran are located on the western shore of the Dead Sea. Photo by Catherine Cory.

Several columns of a manuscript of the Book of Isaiah found in Cave 1 at Qumran. The Dead Sea Scrolls include fragments of every book of the Old Testament except the Book of Esther.

them except that they apparently allowed marriage, but only for the purpose of having children, and owned their own property. One of their obligations was to provide hospitality to fellow Essenes traveling through their village. Like the monastic community, this group apparently was concerned about ritual purity and strict observance of community rules. After the Jewish War and the destruction of the Jerusalem Temple, both of these groups disappeared from history without a trace.

Yet another group mentioned by Josephus is the **Zealots**. Josephus describes them as operating throughout much of the first century C.E., but most scholars agree that the Zealots probably did not exist as an identifiable group or in any organized fashion until shortly before the Jewish War in 66 C.E. Their name comes from the fact that they had *zeal* (i.e., enthusiasm) for the reign of God. They declared God their only king and refused to pledge allegiance to any earthly ruler, especially the Romans. They were so dedicated to this principle of liberty that they were willing to die for the cause. From this group came the Sicarii, who were undercover assassins of sorts, killing Jews who collaborated with the Romans. Josephus blames the Zealots for the revolt against the Romans, a revolt that led to the destruction of the Temple in 70 C.E. However, we need to weigh his statements carefully because his harsh rhetoric clearly betrays his biases against the Zealots.

## Jewish Feasts and Religious Observances

First-century Judaism celebrated a number of feasts and festivals of different types throughout the year. Some were celebrated primarily within the home, while others were associated with the Temple. Because we do not have the time or space to treat all of the feasts of the Jewish calendar, we will focus on those that are mentioned in the New Testament. However, it is important for today's reader to remember that Jesus and his disciples were thoroughly Jewish, so the rhythm of Jewish feasts and festivals would have been an important part of their lives.

The Jewish feast that is mentioned most frequently in the New Testament is **Passover**. This seven-day feast commemorates the events associated with the Hebrews departure from Egypt and their sojourn in the wilderness before they entered the Promised Land (see Chapter 4). Passover gets its name from the story about the tenth plague, when God's angel "stood over" or "straddled" (Hebrew, *pasach*) the homes of the Israelites, protecting them from the plague that resulted in the death of the Egyptian firstborn (Exod. 12:13). The ritual foods associated with this feast include bitter herbs, to recall the bitterness of slavery, and unleavened bread (i.e., bread containing no ingredient to make the dough light and fluffy), to recall the haste with which the Hebrew people had to leave Egypt. Originally, this feast was celebrated entirely within the home. However, by the first century C.E., Jews who were able to travel to Jerusalem gathered there for the Feast of Unleavened Bread on the first day of the seven-day feast. This was the same day that the lambs for the Passover feast were sacrificed in the Temple. The gospels describe Jesus' crucifixion as taking place on or near the feast of Passover. Passover begins on the fourteenth of the first month, Nisan, in the Jewish religious calendar (March/April).

Another Jewish pilgrimage festival that is mentioned in the New Testament is the spring harvest festival of grain. It was called the Feast of **Weeks** or the Feast of First Fruits because they allowed seven weeks to pass from the Feast of Unleavened Bread and then presented an offering of **First Fruits** (i.e., the first and best of the harvest given to God in recognition that the whole harvest belonged to God) in the Jerusalem Temple. Greek-speaking Jews called the feast **Pentecost**, meaning "fiftieth," for the seven weeks plus a day between the Feast of Unleavened Bread and this pilgrimage feast. The Feast of Weeks is celebrated on the sixth day of Sivan (usually in May). According to Acts of the Apostles, after the resurrection of Jesus, the Holy Spirit descended on the disciples in flames of fire on Pentecost (Acts 2:1–4); as a result, Christians have adopted Pentecost as one of their feasts as well.

The third of the pilgrimage festivals mentioned in the New Testament is the fall harvest festival of fruits and olives. This feast is called **Tabernacles**, and is also known as Booths or Sukkoth, because the Jewish pilgrims lived in tents during the seven-day feast to remind them of their journey in the desert during the Exodus. In first-century Jewish practice, the feast included a ritual of water pouring to pray for rain for the upcoming planting season. At night, the people lit enormous lamps in the Temple precincts, which flooded the area with light, and they danced and held processions around the Temple area with the lulab, an olive branch decorated with a myrtle branch (an evergreen shrub symbolizing peace, justice, and joy), a willow branch (a tree associated with water), and an etrog (a large lemonlike fruit). The feast is celebrated on the fifteenth day of Tishri (late September/early October). In John's gospel, in a scene that takes place during the feast of Tabernacles, Jesus declares himself to be the source of "living water" (John 7:37–38) and the "light of the world" (John 8:12).

Another Jewish feast that has historical connections to the Temple is **Yom Kippur**, the Day of Atonement, a day of fasting on which God's people ask forgiveness for

A page from a fourteenth-century Hebrew manuscript containing a prayer for the feast of Tabernacles. The man depicted in the upper right-hand margin of the manuscript is holding a lulab and an etrog. *Ancient Art & Architecture/DanitaDelimont.com*.

their past wrongs. Historically, on this day, the High Priest selected two goats: One was offered as a sin offering to God and the other sent out into the wilderness with the sins of the people on its head. This is the same day that the High Priest entered the Holy of Holies with an incense offering, symbolizing God's forgiveness of Israel's sins. This feast continues to be celebrated today on the tenth day of Tishri, according to the Jewish calendar—that is, in late September or early October. Today, of course, Jews do not use animal sacrifice in their worship. Rather, this feast is celebrated with fasting and prayer, both in the synagogue and at home. It comes ten days after Rosh Hashanah, the Jewish New Year. When the New Testament author of Hebrews writes about Jesus as the perfect High Priest who offers once and for all the perfect sacrifice of atonement (Heb. 7:11–28), he is referring to Yom Kippur.

The Jerusalem Temple was not the only place where first-century Jews came together for worship. As is the case today, many sacred moments were celebrated within the home. Perhaps the oldest and the most frequently mentioned in the New

Testament is Sabbath observance. **Sabbath** is celebrated on the last day of the week beginning at sundown—the Jewish day begins at sundown—and therefore extends from sundown on Friday to sundown on Saturday. Although the origins of Sabbath are unclear, most scholars agree that the focus on Sabbath rest is reflected in, or patterned after, the first creation story in Genesis, which describes God as resting on the seventh day (Gen. 2:2–3).

The New Testament and early rabbinic literature do not tell us what rituals were performed within Jewish homes on Sabbath, but they do tell us a lot about prohibitions against work. By the first century C.E., it appears that the only time that Sabbath rest could be broken was when life was endangered. Thus, babies could be delivered on Sabbath and animals that fell into a pit could be rescued on Sabbath, but other types of work were prohibited, especially if they could wait until another day without threatening life. Today observant Jews celebrate Sabbath with a special meal that begins just before sundown on Friday evening with the lighting of the Sabbath candles. A festive celebration, it includes prayers, singing, and blessings over the Sabbath cup of wine and a special kind of bread called challah. The rest of the day is dedicated to restful family activities and to the study of Torah. Some Christian groups, like the Seventh Day Adventists, continue Sabbath observance, but most celebrate on the first day of the week, Sunday, in commemoration of the day that Jesus was raised from the dead.

Although ancient **Diaspora** Jews—that is, Jews living outside of Palestine (the Greek word means "to scatter")—attempted to travel to Jerusalem at least once in their lifetimes, regular participation in the Jewish pilgrimage festivals was extremely difficult for most people. Thus, the study of Torah and preaching and teaching in the synagogue gradually began to take precedence over Temple sacrifice. The word *synagogue* comes from a Greek word meaning "assembly" or "gathering." It is a place where people gathered to read and study the Torah, to pray, and to receive instruction. Archeologists have found a number of structures from the third century C.E. onward that were specifically designated as synagogues. However, in the first century C.E. it appears that Jewish communities met in a room within someone's house or took over an already existing building and converted it into an assembly room.

Scholars do not know much about when or how synagogues first got started. Some say that they were developed as a replacement for the Temple during the Babylonian Exile (586 B.C.E.), after the Temple had been destroyed and Jerusalem's inhabitants exiled. Others argue that the synagogue was developed as a protest against forced Hellenization, after the conquests of Alexander the Great (334–323 B.C.E.). Whatever their origin, by the first century C.E., synagogues were well established and located throughout the Roman Empire.

The synagogue differed from the Temple in several significant ways. First, there was only one temple site and it was located in Jerusalem—though, in fact, not all first-century Jews accepted Jerusalem as the legitimate location for temple worship. Recall, for example, the descriptions of the Samaritans and Essenes above. In contrast, synagogues could be located almost anywhere. However, no sacrifices were performed in the synagogue. Moreover, as their name suggests, the synagogues were important gathering places for Jews. When Paul and the first disciples of Jesus went outside of Palestine to spread the "good news" of Jesus, they went first to the synagogues. We'll learn more about this practice when we read Acts of the Apostles.

## APOCALYPTICISM

Judaism experienced a number of theological or ideological developments in the Hellenistic and Greco-Roman periods that later had significant impact on early Christianity. Perhaps the most important is apocalypticism. Apocalypticism belongs to a larger category of ideas called **eschatology**—that is, teaching about the end time and humanity's destiny. Apocalyptic literature uses symbolic language to express an expectation that this earthly situation will come to an end very soon, usually in some worldwide catastrophe, and that the world will be transformed in such a way that God's rule is made manifest and the wicked are destroyed. On this account, it also addresses an important question for persecuted peoples: How will God reward the righteous and punish the evil ones? For Jews who felt disenfranchised and marginalized and who saw the social, political, and cultural situation around them as opposed to God, the apocalyptic worldview was sure to provide consolation and a reason to stay faithful to God's will.

Christians who are familiar with the Book of Revelation—or the *Left Behind* series, which claims to be derived from it—might recognize its apocalyptic character from the descriptive definition above. However, they probably do not know that Jewish literature already boasted a large number of apocalyptic works before Christians took up this worldview. Daniel 7–12 and Zechariah 9–14 are two examples that can be found in the Bible, but there are several other Jewish apocalyptic writings that were not included in the Bible: 1 Enoch, the Ascension of Moses, the Sibylline Oracles, the Testament of the Twelve Patriarchs, and several community documents from among the Dead Sea Scrolls. If you are interested in reading any of these Jewish religious writings, they are available in English translation in books called the Old Testament Apocrypha (see "Sources and Resources" below).

## MESSIANIC EXPECTATIONS

Today's Christians, who have grown up with the idea of Jesus as the Christ or messiah, assume that first-century Jews were united in their understanding that the messiah would be the divine Son of God and that he would be easily recognizable to anyone who observed his actions or heard him speak. Actually, Judaism had a wide variety of expectations about the person and mission of the messiah. They also witnessed a number of charismatic figures who claimed to be messiah but quickly came to a sad end. The first-century Jewish historian Josephus describes several prophetic and messianic figures of the first and second centuries C.E., among them Judas the Galilean (6 C.E.), Theudas (44–46 C.E.), the Egyptian false prophet (52–60 C.E.), and Jesus, son of Ananus (62–64 C.E.). Later there was Bar Kochba (132–135 C.E.), whose name means "Son of the Star." The dates associated with each of these figures represent the period of his messianic activity.

Thus, as Josephus suggests, first-century Judaisms were characterized by the emergence of a number of prophetic and messianic personalities. The term *messiah* in Hebrew (*christos* in Greek) means "anointed one." In Old Testament history, anointing was reserved for persons singled out by God for some special office—in particular, the office of king. The king was called "God's anointed" and "son of God." As a result, among those who awaited the coming of the messiah, many had an expectation that he would be a powerful political king who would arise from the lineage of David. Nathan's prophecy to David (2 Sam. 7:1–17) reflects this expectation. Others thought he would be a religious figure, perhaps the High Priest *par excellence*. Still others, because of certain Old Testament prophecies, expected the messiah to be a great prophet like Moses (Deut. 18:15–22). With the rise of apocalyptic expectations in the first century B.C.E. and first century C.E., still others expected the messiah to be an eschatological (i.e., end time) warrior or judge who would ride the clouds of heaven and do battle against the forces of evil (Dan 7:13). Some, like the Essenes, expected two messiahs—a High Priest and a king!

One thing is certain. Jesus did not meet any of these expectations of Jewish messiahship, and no one expected the messiah to be charged with terrible crimes and die a shameful death by crucifixion. Among those who were not Jesus followers, Jesus was simply another itinerant Jewish radical reformer who died at the hands of the Romans, and his followers' claim that he had been raised from the dead was foolishness. At the same time, we should note that first-century Jews were not staying up late at night, waiting for the messiah to show up. In other words, messianic expectation was not an all-consuming idea for most first-century Jews, just like the end-time return of Christ is not an all-consuming, immediate expectation for many of today's Christians.

## KEY TERMS

| | | |
|---|---|---|
| Second Temple Judaism | Sanhedrin | Pentecost |
| Galilee | Sadducees | Tabernacles |
| Judea | Pharisees | Yom Kippur |
| Samaria | Scribes | Sabbath |
| Samaritans | Essenes | Diaspora |
| Temple | Dead Sea Scrolls | Synagogue |
| Sacrifice | Zealots | Eschatology |
| Priests | Passover | Messiah |
| Levites | Weeks | |
| High Priest | First Fruits | |
| Chief priests | | |

## QUESTIONS FOR READING

From Josephus's *Jewish War*, read 2.8.2–13, and from *Antiquities of the Jews*, read 18.1. 3–6 on first-century Palestinian religious groups. Likewise, from Josephus's *Jewish War*, read 2.8.5 and 6.5.3, and from *Antiquities of the Jews*, read 10.5.1 on Jewish prophets and messiahs. Use evidence from the texts to answer the following questions. Note: There are a number of hard-copy English translations of Josephus's works, but you can also find the Whiston translation on-line at www.earlyjewishwritings.com, www.ccel.org/j/josephus/JOSEPHUS.HTM or www.perseus.tufts.edu/cache/ perscoll_Greco-Roman.html#text1 (scroll down to Flavius Josephus and select the desired title).

1. For each of the Jewish groups described by Josephus, summarize their teaching or the ideals to which they aspired. What might have been their appeal or general accessibility to ordinary Jews of first-century Palestine? Which group might have been most receptive to Jesus? Why? Note Josephus's biases as he describes these groups. Which groups does he like? Dislike?

2. Examine Josephus's accounts of messianic figures in the first century C.E. See if you can identify his bias against certain of these figures. For what reason does Josephus favor Jesus, son of Ananus?

## QUESTIONS FOR REFLECTION

1. How do you think modern Christians' reading of the New Testament would be different if they could more fully appreciate that Jesus was a Jew and that the earliest Christians were Jewish?

2. One of the issues that early followers of Jesus had to face was explaining why people should accept Jesus as the messiah, especially in light of early Judaism's expectations about the messiah. How would you have addressed this problem?

## ACTIVITIES FOR LEARNING

1. Investigate how Jews today celebrate Yom Kippur, Passover, or Tabernacles. If possible, interview a local rabbi about how the families of his or her synagogue celebrate these feasts.

2. Do some research on activities associated with the synagogue as it serves, its Jewish community today. Contact a local synagogue to see if you might visit a Sabbath service and observe their worship activities. What surprised you? What would you like to learn more about?

3. Find some information about the Dome of the Rock on the Jerusalem Temple Mount. When was it built? By whom and why? What does it commemorate or what is its significance for Islam? What kinds of activities take place there?

## SOURCES AND RESOURCES

Borowski, Obed. *Daily Life in Biblical Times*. Atlanta, Ga.: Society of Biblical Literature, 2003.

Charlesworth, James H., ed. *Jesus' Jewishness: Exploring the Place of Jesus within Early Judaism*. New York: Crossroad, 1991.

Freyne, Seán. *The World of the New Testament*. Wilmington, Del.: Glazier, 1980.

Hanson, K. C., and Douglas E. Oakman. *Palestine in the Time of Jesus: Social Structures and Social Conflicts*. Minneapolis, Minn.: Fortress, 1999.

Harding, Mark. *Early Christian Life and Thought in Social Context: A Reader.* London: T & T Clark International, 2003.

Hjelm, Ingrid. *The Samaritans and Early Judaism: A Literary Analysis.* Sheffield, England: Sheffield Academic Press, 2000.

Horsley, Richard A., and John S. Hanson. *Bandits, Prophets, and Messiahs: Popular Movements at the Time of Jesus.* Minneapolis, Minn.: Winston, 1985.

Jaffee, Martin S. *Early Judaism.* Upper Saddle River, N.J.: Prentice Hall, 1997.

Jeremias, Joachim. *Jerusalem in the Time of Jesus.* Philadelphia: Fortress, 1969.

Levine, Amy-Jill, ed. *"Women like This": New Perspectives on Jewish Women in the Greco-Roman World.* Atlanta, Ga.: Scholars Press, 1991.

Malina, Bruce J. *The Social World of Jesus and the Gospels.* London: Routledge, 1996.

Murphy, Frederick J. *Early Judaism: The Exile to the Time of Jesus.* Peabody, Mass.: Hendrickson, 2000.

Neusner, Jacob. *Judaism When Christianity Began: A Survey of Belief and Practice.* Louisville Ky.: Westminster John Knox Press, 2002.

Rohrbaugh, Richard, ed. *The Social Sciences and New Testament Interpretation.* Peabody, Mass.: Hendrickson, 1996.

Russell, D. S. *From Early Judaism to Early Church.* Philadelphia: Fortress, 1986.

Talmon, Shemaryahu, ed. *Jewish Civilization in the Hellenistic-Roman Period.* Philadelphia: Trinity Press International, 1991.

VanderKam, James C. *An Introduction to Early Judaism.* Grand Rapids, Mich.: Eerdmans, 2001.

# THE GOSPELS

Finally, we are ready to launch our journey through the New Testament! Our first stop will be the gospels, not because they were the first written documents of the collection that came to be known as the New Testament but because they tell the story of Jesus, the one who gives the rest of the New Testament its meaning. But what is a gospel? Our English term comes from the Anglo-Saxon *god-spell*, which means "good news." The Greek word *euangelion* means "good message" (of Jesus Christ). The writer of a gospel is called an evangelist, that is, someone who proclaims the good news. The Gospels of Matthew, Mark, and Luke are called synoptic gospels, from the Greek word *synoptikos,* which means "seeing the whole together." These gospels tell the same general story of the life of Jesus, and they tell it more or less in the same kind of way. As we shall see later, the Gospel of John is quite different in the way that it tells the story of Jesus.

Several pieces of information can help us be clear about the presuppositions we bring to a contextualist reading of the gospels. (See the Introduction for an explanation of the difference between contextualist and literalist readings of scripture.) First, we need to be clear that the way the gospels came to be written differs greatly from the way modern books are written. Second, we need to understand and appreciate the gospel genre; that is, we need to determine what type of literature a gospel is. We will briefly address both of these issues in this introduction to the gospels.

## THE COMPOSITION OF THE GOSPELS

Suppose you wanted to write a book. First, you would have to decide on the kind of book you wanted to write. Next, you would need to draft a book proposal, develop an outline of the book, and write a chapter or two. Then you would have to solicit a publisher to publish your book, negotiate a contract, and finish the manuscript. If everything goes well, you might be able to write the book in a year or less, depending on the topic and type of book. However, it could take you several years to finish your book, especially if the work is very technical and the amount of research required to write the book is extensive. Perhaps you would enlist the assistance of an editor to help with final corrections or copyright permissions. Once the writing and editing are complete, the publishing company might take another six to nine months to get it into the bookstores, or you might significantly shorten the publication timeline by making your manuscript available as an e-book. Although the process might sound complicated, it is relatively self-contained; that is, your book-writing experience has a clear beginning and a clear end. Likewise, the question of authorship is clear. It is your creation and you are responsible for its content—even if you have a "ghost writer" do the writing for you, your name is still attached to the work and people will refer to you as the author.

Although we do not have much direct evidence about gospel writing in the first century C.E., biblical scholars think the process was quite different from the way that people write books today. Of course, the materials used in writing the gospels were different, and so were the rhetorical techniques and styles of expression, but another difference is that we cannot easily determine the starting and ending points for gospel composition like we can with modern works. Scholars who study the origins of the gospels suggest that, rather than being written by a single author who worked over a limited period of time, they went through several stages of development over several decades. Therefore, when we talk about the "author" of a gospel, we are not necessarily referring to a single historical writer. Instead, we may be talking about a name, usually that of a famous figure from the earliest decades of Christianity, who has become associated with a community's sacredly held traditions about Jesus.

How, then, did the written gospels come into being? Most biblical scholars agree that the first stage of the development of the gospels was preliterary—that is, taking place before anything was actually written down. This is the stage of oral tradition, during which people shared stories about Jesus, sang hymns to Jesus and God, and put together collections of the words or sayings of Jesus, which were used in introducing new converts to Christianity. The second stage is when people began to write down the stories and sayings of Jesus. The earliest Christians would not have seen this as necessary activity because they thought the end-time return of Jesus was going to take place very soon, certainly before their deaths. However, when the first disciples and eyewitnesses to Jesus' life began to die, individuals and communities became aware of the need to preserve Jesus' teachings for future generations.

The third stage is called the editing or redactional stage. In this stage, the author or a later redactor attempts to refine the community's oral and written traditions and create a coherent story by filling in the gaps with other oral or written traditions or by adding transitions, explanations, and clarifications to make a written gospel. Sometimes the redactor "corrects" parts of the tradition that he thinks will be problematic or controversial.

**STAGES IN THE DEVELOPMENT OF THE GOSPELS**

Stage One: Oral Traditions

Stage Two: Written Traditions

Stage Three: Redaction

Although New Testament scholars are quite certain that the gospel-writing process began with oral tradition and ended with redaction (editing) of the final document, they also recognize that these stages were not necessarily mutually exclusive or consecutive. In fact, these three stages were most likely overlapping and not sequential, continuing throughout the thirty or more years that it took to write the gospels. Some traditions likely continued to be passed on orally even after communities began to write down the story. Likewise, some written traditions may have been reworked a number of times to suit the needs of particular faith communities before they found their way into a final written gospel.

Chronologically, where should we situate the written gospels in relationship to the life of Jesus? Most biblical scholars agree that Jesus was born approximately 6–4 B.C.E. and was crucified around 30 C.E. The dates assigned to the New Testament gospels are listed below:

Mark (c. 70 C.E.)

Matthew (c. 80–90 C.E.)

Luke (c. 80–90 C.E.)

John (c. 90–100 C.E.)

In other words, after the death and resurrection of Jesus, at least thirty-five years and as many as seventy years had passed before the New Testament gospels took their final form. This means that few, if any, of the eyewitnesses to the life of Jesus were still alive when these gospels began to circulate among the Christian communities.

## THE GENRE OF THE GOSPELS

Having reviewed what most biblical scholars agree are the stages of gospel composition, we turn now to the question of the genre of the gospels. The term *genre* is used to describe a type of literature: history, short story, poetry, legend, fairy tale, and comic book, to name a few. Knowing the genre of a document is important because this information tells us how to read and interpret books of that type. For example, you would not expect to read a book described as a history of the Civil War in the same way as you would the novel *Gone with the Wind*, even though they refer to the same period of history. However, because you've read plenty of histories before, you know that you ought to read a history of World War I and a history of the Civil War with the same interpretative expectations. Sometimes you can find out the genre of a book by reading its title. For example, you would expect a book called *The Poetry of Robert Frost* to contain writings that belong to the genre of poetry. At other times, you might have to examine the form (the structure or organizational elements) of a book to determine its genre. For example, if you are reading a short story that has talking animals as its major characters and that ends with a moral, you can be quite sure that it is a fable, and you will know that you need to interpret it as such.

On the question of genre, the New Testament gospels are somewhat problematic because no written works called gospels existed before Christians began writing gospels about Jesus Christ. As a result, we cannot look to earlier books with the same title to figure out how to interpret the Christian gospels. Likewise, there is little evidence to suggest that the gospel writers themselves intended to call their books gospels. Mark introduces his work using the term *gospel* (Mark 1:1), but New Testament scholars are quite certain that he was not describing the genre or *form* of his work. Instead, he was referring to the *content* of his message—namely, a proclamation of the "good news" of Jesus Christ. Matthew calls his work a "book" (Matt. 1:1), *biblios* in Greek, and nowhere does he mention the word *gospel*. John, too, describes his work as a "book," written so that people might "believe that Jesus is the Messiah, the Son of God" (John 20:30–31). Luke indicates that he is following his predecessors in writing a "narrative of the things accomplished among us" (Luke 1:1). What does Luke intend to do differently? He tells us in his prologue that he will write in an "orderly way" (Luke 1:3); that is, he will arrange the traditions so that those in his audience can understand the truth they should get from the story of Jesus.

Did the Christian gospel writers create a new genre that was unique among religious literature of the first century C.E.? Until quite recently, biblical scholars thought so, but today scholars are answering this question somewhat differently. Studies on the development of new genres indicate that the process takes place gradually. An author begins writing within a particular genre and then, to emphasize a point or to create a certain literary effect, alters the genre somewhat or incorporates aspects of other genres. Over time, other writers, whether intentionally or by happenstance, make the same kinds of adaptations. Eventually, a new genre emerges that is distinct from other genres. The same was likely true of the Christian gospels. As soon as the earliest gospels began to circulate among Christian communities, other gospel writers adopted (and adapted) the form of the gospel and gradually a distinctive gospel genre emerged. Thus, even though we cannot point to a collection of literature called gospels that existed before the Christian gospels were written, we ought to be able to identify a genre on which the gospels were patterned. This is important because knowing the genre of a written work helps us know how to interpret it.

But what ancient genre was the basis for this developing gospel genre? That is, what kind of literature did those earliest gospel writers think they were adopting and adapting? There are at least three possibilities: the history, the biography, and the tragic drama. Given what we know today about these ancient genres, the most likely predecessor of the gospels is the ancient biography, which was designed to tell the story of a famous person in history. In contrast to modern biographers, the ancient biographer cared little about the actual historical events of the person's life or even about the chronological order of things. Instead, the ancient biography was designed to praise the character or virtue of the hero and teach a lesson or provide a model by which to live.

The biography contained *topoi* ("elements") common to other ancient *bioi* ("lives")—an unusual birth; a stellar ancestry, often including the gods; stories about the deeds and character virtues of the person; an account of death accompanied by unusual signs—which the author could use to make a point about the person's character. Sometimes stories were recycled to be included in several biographies; the author would simply change the names of the characters and the details of the setting. The reader would recognize these *topoi* and conclude, "Oh, this person was courageous" or "He was an honest man." Additionally, the events of the person's life were usually arranged thematically, rather than chronologically, in order to emphasize a particular virtue or character trait. When these *topoi* were gathered together into a biography, they tended to amplify the person's positive attributes and minimize his negative qualities. Thus, the ancient biography was *historical* (i.e., based on the life of a real historical person) but was not history or biography, at least not as we understand these genres today. Among the canonical gospels, Matthew's gospel is closest to an ancient biography.

Although a majority of biblical scholars today see the Christian gospels as modified biographies, there are two other ancient genres that may have influenced the development of the gospel genre. The first is the ancient history. An ancient history told a story of a person or event with references to political events and activities of the rulers of that time period. Like the ancient biographies, ancient histories were not designed to be objective reports about historical events or persons. Rather, they were written primarily to cherish the examples of the ancestors. Therefore, one must expect varying degrees of reliability with respect to the historical references provided within these ancient histories. Likewise, ancient histories often contain speeches by their major characters. These are not records of actual historical speeches but literary compositions developed by the authors to express their interpretations of events. Finally, ancient histories have a deliberate political bias that favors those in power.

In some ways, ancient histories are not altogether different from modern histories, since modern histories are also written with a bias. In fact, biases are unavoidable. However, modern historians at least have the intention of being objective. Also, modern historians have the advantage of techniques of record keeping that were not available to ancient historians. Among the canonical gospels, Luke's gospel is closest to an ancient history. It makes several references to political events surrounding the life of Jesus, and it is written with a pro-Roman bias.

A second ancient genre that may have influenced the development of the gospels is the tragic drama. Tragic dramas were religious in origin and dealt with religious questions, and in that sense, they have the greatest similarity to the gospels. However, they were extremely diverse in form and function, therefore giving us few clues concerning techniques for their interpretation. Common to tragic dramas was a structure that included a prologue (introduction), a complication ("tying the knot"), a crisis or confrontation, a resolution of the crisis ("untying the knot"), and an epilogue (conclusion). The main character of the tragic drama is especially striking because of his/her moral purpose, and although presented realistically, he/she remains true to character throughout the play. The play is designed to evoke a response from the listener. Among the canonical gospels, Mark's gospel bears the greatest similarity to tragic drama because the story is dominated by the crisis that reaches its climax in Jesus' death and is resolved in his resurrection. However, there are also significant differences, the most substantial being that the Gospel of Mark is more conversational and less poetic than the typical ancient tragic drama.

The question of the origin of the gospel genre is still an open one, and biblical scholars continue to investigate connections with other ancient genres. The important thing for us to remember here is that the gospel writers were not doing something entirely new when they wrote their stories of Jesus, since it is unlikely that the gospel genre simply appeared out of nowhere. The gospel writers were real people who wrote from within their historical contexts, using the literary genres that were available to them and gradually adapting them to create the gospel genre that we know today.

## Implications for Gospel Interpretation

What do these theories about the composition of the gospels and the emergence of the gospel genre suggest about how we ought to interpret the gospels? First, it should be quite clear that we ought not to read them as eyewitness or documentary accounts of the life of Jesus. There is little evidence to suggest that the Christian gospel writers intended to provide their communities with an unbiased record of the words and deeds of Jesus, as they actually occurred, simply for the sake of recording history. However, this is not to say that they were intentionally falsifying the historical events in the life of Jesus. Rather, as the word *gospel* suggests, the writer shaped the oral and written traditions that were available to him in order to proclaim (in story form) the "good news" of the community's faith in Jesus the Christ.

Are the so-called words of Jesus contained in the gospels *exactly* the words that Jesus spoke some forty or more years earlier? Perhaps, in some cases, they are, but to fixate on that question is to miss the point of the gospels. They are proclamations of faith by and for communities who believed that Jesus of Nazareth was the messiah of God. Thus, we have four (or more, if you include the non-canonical gospels) rather distinctive portraits of Jesus of Nazareth. To put this in the simplest of terms, Mark's gospel presents Jesus as the suffering Son of Man, while Matthew's gospel presents Jesus as the new Moses and Son of God. Luke's Jesus is the prophet *par excellence*, while John's Jesus is the pre-existent (i.e., having no beginning) Son of the Father. Each gospel portrait is unique and yet compatible with the others. We cannot say that one is true and the others are not. Rather, each tells the truth about that community's experience of the Christ in whom they put their trust. This is the richness of the gospel tradition.

## Sources and Resources

Aune, David. *The New Testament in Its Literary Environment.* Philadelphia: Westminster Press, 1987.

Bock, Darrell L. *Studying the Historical Jesus: A Guide to Sources and Methods.* Grand Rapids, Mich.: Baker Academic, 2002.

Burridge, Richard A. *What Are the Gospels? A Comparison with Graeco-Roman Biography.* Grand Rapids, Mich.: Eerdmans, 2004.

Cartlidge, David R., and David L. Dungan, eds. *Documents for the Study of the Gospels.* 2nd ed. Philadelphia: Fortress, 1994.

Collins, Adela Yarbro. *Is Mark's Gospel a Life of Jesus? The Question of Genre.* Milwaukee, Wis.: Marquette University Press, 1990.

———. *The Beginning of the Gospel: Probings of Mark in Context.* Minneapolis, Minn.: Fortress, 1992.

Stuhlmacher, Peter, ed. *The Gospel and the Gospels.* Grand Rapids, Mich.: Eerdmans, 1991.

Talbert, Charles H. *What Is a Gospel? The Genre of the Canonical Gospels.* Philadelphia: Fortress, 1977.

Thomas, Christine M. *The Acts of Peter, Gospel Literature, and the Ancient Novel: Rewriting the Past.* Oxford, England: Oxford University Press, 2003.

Tolbert, Mary Ann. *Sowing the Gospel: Mark's World in Literary-Historical Perspective.* Minneapolis, Minn.: Fortress, 1989.

# CHAPTER 6

# THE GOSPEL ACCORDING TO MARK

## OVERVIEW

- AUTHORSHIP: Anonymous; traditionally associated with Mark, a disciple of Peter in Rome, or John Mark, a one-time disciple of Paul
- DATE OF COMPOSITION: 65–70 C.E.
- INITIAL AUDIENCE: An unknown Gentile Christian community living outside of Palestine; traditionally associated with Rome
- MAJOR TOPICS: Literary Features of the Mark's Gospel; Titles of Jesus in the Gospel of Mark; The Messianic Secret; Mark's Miracle Stories; The Problem of the Disciples in Mark's Gospel; Apocalyptic Christianity; The Passion Narrative of Mark's Gospel; The Postresurrection Narrative

## TIMELINE

| | |
|---|---|
| **37 B.C.E.** | Herod the Great takes up his kingship in Palestine. |
| **6–4 B.C.E.** | Jesus of Nazareth is born. |
| **4 B.C.E.** | Herod the Great, king of Palestine, dies. His kingdom is divided among three sons: Archelaus, Herod Antipas, and Philip. |
| **4 B.C.E.–39 C.E.** | Herod Antipas, son of Herod the Great, is tetrarch of Galilee and Perea. |
| **6 C.E.** | Annas (Ananus I) becomes High Priest of the Jerusalem Temple. |
| **18 C.E.** | Caiaphas, the son-in-law of Annas, becomes High Priest of the Jerusalem Temple. |
| **26–36 C.E.** | Pontius Pilate is prefect of Judea and Samaria. |
| **c. 28 C.E.** | John the Baptist is executed by Herod Antipas. |
| **c. 30 C.E.** | Jesus is crucified, dies, and is resurrected. |
| **c. 41–44 C.E.** | The apostle James, the brother of John, is martyred. |
| **64 C.E.** | Peter and Paul are martyred in Rome. |
| **65–70 C.E.** | **The Gospel of Mark is written.** |
| **66–70 C.E.** | The Jewish War occurs. |
| **70 C.E.** | Jerusalem and the Temple are destroyed. |

We are finally ready to begin our voyage through the New Testament. Our first stop will be the Gospel of Mark. Neither the first book of the New Testament nor the oldest, it is, at least, the oldest of the gospels and certainly the strangest. Like the other gospels, this story takes place in ancient Palestine. Unlike the other gospels, Mark's Jesus is presented as a man racing against time. He is also presented as the unrecognized messiah who must suffer and die. His disciples are portrayed sometimes as clueless and at other times as hard-hearted, but almost never are they examples to be emulated by those who want to be Jesus followers. The story ends strangely as well, with the witnesses of the resurrection running away afraid and failing to proclaim the good news. Welcome to this first leg of our adventure!

However, before we investigate these topics related to Mark's gospel, we need to pause to find out what scholars have determined about its author and his audience.

## AUTHORSHIP

When investigating any piece of literature, it is helpful to know who wrote it, when he or she wrote it, and something about why he or she wrote it. Unfortunately, the study of ancient religious literature is difficult in this regard because the author seldom gives us this information directly. In the case of the New Testament gospels, for example, these authors did not give us their names or date their works; neither did they provide background notes to help us answer our questions about when and where and for whom they wrote the gospels. Yet we can sometimes piece together at least a few clues about the author, the date of composition, and the initial audience of the gospel from the book itself or from other early church authors who mention the book in their writings.

The traditional view is that this gospel was written by Mark, who was identified as a companion of Peter in Rome. The source of this tradition is Papias (c. 120 C.E.), whose words are recorded in Eusebius's *Ecclesiastical History* (3.39.15; see also 1 Pet. 5:13). But who was Mark, if indeed that is the name of the author of this work? Since Mark appears to have been a rather common name in the first-century Roman Empire, the name alone gives us little information about the identity of the author. Some have identified him with John Mark, a cousin of Barnabas and a one-time companion of Paul (Acts 12:12, 25; 15:37–30). Still others connect the gospel writer with the Mark mentioned in some of the letters of the New Testament (Phlm. 24; Col. 4:10; 2 Tim. 4:1). The gospels name twelve apostles, but there is no one named Mark among them. Therefore, this evangelist likely was not an apostle. It is also possible that he had no direct connection with Peter. As you read Mark's gospel, you will observe that the author portrays Peter and the other disciples of Jesus in a very negative light. If the author of this gospel was a disciple of Peter, surely he could have found something good to say about him!

What, then, shall we make of the Papias tradition? Scholars of the New Testament agree that the gospels were not given titles until sometime in the second century C.E. For Mark's gospel, this means that it circulated for thirty or more years without a title. Who would have remembered or even cared about the identity of the author except insofar as his name added credibility to the gospel? Perhaps Papias, knowing a tradition about a certain Mark who was a disciple of Peter, chose to identify this gospel with him in order to verify its authority, or perhaps this tradition was already circulating and Papias simply repeated it. Early Christians acknowledged Peter and the other apostles as the inheritors of Jesus' teaching authority, so written works associated with them also had authority for the communities of faith who read them. However, without any other evidence to support the Papias tradition, most biblical scholars today say that the gospel was written anonymously.

Sometimes a beginning reader of the Bible may find scholars' uncertainty about the identity of the gospel writer or his audience a bit unsettling. They may even see these questions as a challenge to the authority or authenticity of the gospel. However, this need not be the case. Whether or not we can correctly identify the author of a particular gospel or its date of composition, its authenticity remains intact because the authority of the gospel lies in the fact that it can be traced back to the traditions of the apostolic period and, as such, has been read and interpreted as the transformative Word of God by communities of faith through the centuries. Information about the author or the community for which he was writing would be helpful in better understanding the message of the text, but it does not change its authoritative status for communities of believers.

Even though we do not know his name, we will call the author of this gospel Mark, simply for the sake of convenience.

## DATE OF COMPOSITION

Assigning a date of composition to ancient literature, when no date is given, is usually accomplished by looking for historical references in the document and by consulting other documents that mention the writing in question. In the case of the gospels, the authors are recounting the story of Jesus, but they are writing it at some point later in time. This makes the task of dating even more difficult. However, some biblical scholars detect a somewhat obscure reference in Mark 13:2 and 14 that suggests Jerusalem either is about to be destroyed or has just recently been destroyed. The date of the destruction of Jerusalem and its Temple is 70 C.E. In addition, when we compare Mark's gospel to the other synoptic gospels, Mark's appears to be the most primitive and the one that was used as source material for Matthew's and Luke's gospels (see "The Two-Source Hypothesis" in Chapter 10). Therefore, scholars have assigned a date of 65–70 C.E. to the composition of Mark's gospel. This means that the Gospel of Mark was written some thirty-five to forty years after the death and resurrection of Jesus.

## INITIAL AUDIENCE

When asking about the initial audience of an ancient writing, we are usually asking for whom it was written and where that individual or group was located. Assuming that a gospel is the product of the community for which it was written, the location of the initial audience might also be the place where the gospel was written. Unfortunately, the gospels provide us with very little information to either confirm or negate this assumption. Therefore, any conclusions we might draw about the location of the community for which a gospel was originally written or about its author are speculative at best.

With this caveat in mind, what can we say about the initial audience of Mark's gospel? The tone of the gospel suggests that it was written for a community that was undergoing persecution of some sort. Again based on comments by early church writers, the traditional view is that the Gospel of Mark was written in Rome sometime after the martyrdom of Peter and during the persecutions conducted by Emperor Nero (64 C.E.) (see, e.g., Irenaeus, *Against Heresies* 3.1.1). Alternatively, some scholars of Mark's gospel have pointed to its references to Tyre and Sidon (Mark 3:8; 7:24, 31) in southern Syria and to the author's focus on Galilee as the center of Jesus' ministry for the first half of the gospel to argue that its initial audience was located closer to Palestine, perhaps in southern Syria, during a time when the Christian community was in exile from Jerusalem after the Jewish War.

When we examine the text of the gospel itself, there is no evidence to indicate that it was written in Rome or for a Roman Christian community and not a great deal of evidence to prove that it was written in Syria either. Historians of the early church tell us that persecutions of early Christian communities were often sporadic and localized rather than widespread and sustained. Thus, Mark's gospel could have been written in any number of Christian communities, and we have to conclude that the location of its intended audience is unknown.

What else can we say about the initial audience of Mark's gospel? It appears that the gospel was written for Gentile (non-Jewish) Christians. Scholars have noted, for example, that the writer of Mark's gospel assumes that his readers are familiar with the Greek translation of the Jewish scriptures, known as the Septuagint (LXX). At the same time, the gospel contains indicators that the author does not expect his original audience to know the details of Jewish laws and institutions or to attach much value to these things (see Mark 7:1–23; 11:15–19). Mark also translates Aramaic terminology (Mark 5:41) and explains Jewish customs (Mark 7:3–4)—something that would have been unnecessary for a Jewish Christian audience but probably would have been helpful for a Gentile Christian audience.

Remember that Christianity originated not as a separate religion alongside of Judaism but as a reform group within Judaism. However, it appears to have spread very quickly into Gentile territories, beginning with Gentiles who were proselytes (i.e., persons learning about a religion with the goal of converting) to Judaism or who had otherwise associated themselves with a Jewish synagogue. The audience of Mark's gospel may have come from among these Gentiles. From Paul's letters, we know that some Gentile Christian communities were already in existence by 50 C.E.

To sum up, then, we have to say that we do not know the location where this gospel was written, but the community was probably made up of Gentile Christians. More important is the observation that the community was undergoing persecution because that reality likely shaped the content of the gospel in general and its portrayal of Jesus in particular. People who were themselves suffering persecution would have been able to relate to the notion of a suffering messiah. Likewise, they might have been comforted by the possibility that the disciples whom they admired were bumbling and clueless, as Mark portrays them, and sometimes even hard-hearted.

## OUTLINE OF THE GOSPEL OF MARK

Each of the gospel writers tells the story of Jesus somewhat differently, but these differences are not immediately evident until one analyzes the text carefully. An outline of the gospel is a good place to start:

1. Mark 1:1–6:6a—The nearness of the kingdom proclaimed in powerful words and deeds throughout Galilee
2. Mark 6:6b–8:21—Jesus' ministry extended to Jews and Gentiles beyond Galilee
3. Mark 8:22–10:52—Jesus begins his journey to Jerusalem; instruction of the disciples in the meaning of Jesus' life and death (10:45) and the cost of discipleship (8:34–38; 10:42–45)
4. Mark 11:1–13:37—Messianic actions and teachings of Jesus in Jerusalem
5. Mark 14:1–16:8—Suffering, death, and resurrection of Jesus
6. Mark 16:9–20—Longer ending (a later addition to the gospel?)

Although there is usually more than one way to outline a text, this outline gives attention to the geographical markers in the story. In so doing, we discover that the gospel has several corresponding themes: miracle working (in Galilee), discipleship (on the way to Jerusalem), and the suffering Son of Man (in Jerusalem). Refer to the map of first-century Palestine in Chapter 5 to follow the geographic markers of the gospel story.

After studying this outline, perhaps you noticed that Mark's gospel has this longer ending (Mark 16:9-20), which serves as an **epilogue** for the gospel. An epilogue is a speech or a dramatic scene added to the conclusion of a story to explain what happened after the original story ended. In this case, after the gospel's abrupt ending—when the women at the empty tomb ran away afraid and told no one what they saw (Mark 16:8)—there is a second (and perhaps a third) ending, explaining how the message of the resurrection got out to the believers. Most scholars of Mark's gospel think that these endings were added to the finished gospel at some later time to give it a conclusion that was more like the endings of the other three gospels. Hopefully, you also noticed that Jesus' journey to Jerusalem begins at the midpoint of the Gospel of Mark. This has led some New Testament scholars to describe his gospel as a **passion narrative** (i.e., the story of Jesus' trial, suffering, and death) with a long introduction! Again, Mark's gospel is focused on Jesus as the suffering messiah.

### GUIDE FOR INTERPRETING THE GOSPEL OF MARK

The goal of each of the textbook chapters is to give you the tools to read the New Testament yourself. Therefore, we will not be summarizing the contents of the Gospel of Mark in this chapter. Instead, we will offer a kind of tour book for your journey through the gospel—highlights and "things to see" on your tour. We will start off by describing some of the literary features of the Gospel of Mark. We will also look at some of the titles given to Jesus in this gospel as well as the gospel writer's use of miracle stories and what some biblical scholars have called the Messianic Secret. Finally we will look at some of the gospel's major themes like discipleship, and we will examine its strange ending. First, let's look at Mark's literary features. At the conclusion of this chapter, you will be invited to read Mark's gospel for yourself. The "Questions for Reading" section will guide you.

## Literary Features of the Mark's Gospel

While beginning readers of the gospel tend to focus on the content of the story, we also need to pay attention to how the story is written. After all, if the manner in which the story is communicated doesn't matter, we need only one gospel. As it is, we have four canonical gospels. Each gives a particular perspective on an early Christian community's understanding of the significance of Jesus for faith. In writing this gospel, Mark used traditional material from his community of believers, but he also used a variety of literary techniques to shape these traditions. These two things—the traditional material and the techniques of storytelling—make Mark's gospel different from other stories of Jesus.

Several of the more obvious literary techniques of Mark's gospel are summarized below. Watch for these literary features as you read the gospel because the way in which Mark employs them will give us clues to his theology and his worldview.

1. Mark's gospel contains *transitional summaries* (e.g., Mark 1:14–15, 32–39; 3:7–12), which link together two or more scenes that are otherwise independent of each other. Sometimes these transitional summaries also anticipate an account of a later event. This puts the reader in the privileged position of having a hint of what is to come or of having insights about some aspect of the story that are otherwise not available to the characters of the story.

2. Mark's gospel contains several **frame stories**. You know that you have found a set of frame stories when you encounter a second story that is almost identical to a story you read a few pages earlier. This is not an editorial slipup by the author. Rather, these two stories provide a "frame" around a collection of stories and teachings that highlight a certain theme. The gospel writer does not simply announce the theme, however. You have to figure it out by examining the common elements in the stories and teachings that come between the two frame stories. But don't despair! Mark gives some helpful clues about how to interpret the intervening stories and teachings in the two frame stories. Identify their similarities and, more importantly, their differences, and you should be able to discover the central theme of this literary unit.

3. This gospel also contains several **intercalations**, also called Markan sandwiches. Here the writer begins to tell a story and, just when things start to get exciting, interrupts it with another story. Thus, the reader is made to wait while the narrator finishes the second story, and only then does the reader find out what happened in the first story. The two stories usually share some common vocabulary or imagery, suggesting that the gospel writer deliberately

put them together. Typically, the "inner" story explains the "outer" one or focuses it in a special way, so if you look carefully at the second (inner) story, you can usually figure out why the gospel writer told the first (outer) story. However, the central message of the intercalation is usually found in the inner story. Think of it as the "meat" or "filling" of the sandwich.

4. Although this next literary feature is not as easy to spot in the English translation as it is in Greek, much of the narrative of the Gospel of Mark is written in what is called the *historical present*. Contrast this with the past tense, which is usually used in storytelling. Instead of saying, "Jesus *did* this and then he *said* that," Mark's narrator says, "Jesus *does* this and then he *says* that." In this way, the gospel writer describes a rapid succession of events (with few details) as if they are all happening right before your eyes. In addition, Mark connects most of these stories with the word *and*. He also includes words like *now* and *immediately* at every opportunity. The overall effect is a gospel story that carries a heightened sense of immediacy or urgency. Simply stated, Mark portrays Jesus as a man running a race against time!

## TITLES OF JESUS IN THE GOSPEL OF MARK

In all of the gospels, Jesus is given a variety of titles, each of which tells us something about who the gospel writers and their respective communities believed him to be. Three titles are important to the Gospel of Mark and its theology: the Christ or Messiah, the Son of God, and the Son of Man. In fact, these titles figure prominently in all of the canonical gospels. We will treat them at some length here so that you can refer to them again later as you need them. Be aware, however, that each gospel writer uses titles and attributions of Jesus in a slightly different way and toward a different end. Mark uses them to highlight the fact that Jesus, as the Christ, must suffer and die.

**THE CHRIST/MESSIAH** Read Mark 1:1; 8:29; 14:61; and 15:32. Some people mistakenly think of the word **Christ** as the second part of Jesus' name, somewhat like a surname. However, it is actually a title, derived from a Greek word meaning, "anointed." The word **messiah** is its Hebrew equivalent. These titles were originally used to describe an anointed royal figure (i.e., a king) who would restore David's rule. Later they came to be used for other priestly or prophetic figures who were sent to rescue God's people from harm. Mark uses them in the broadest sense—one who comes to establish God's reign—though not in the expected sense of a king or other public political figure.

After the opening line of the gospel, in which the narrator of the story introduces Jesus as the messiah (Mark 1:1), the reader sees Jesus doing work that demonstrates the establishment of God's reign on earth—the miracles (see below). However, in the stories about Jesus' conflict with the religious authorities, the reader also sees evidence that God's kingdom will be opposed. At the midpoint of the gospel, Peter identifies Jesus as messiah, but Jesus' cautionary response to Peter should warn the reader that Peter just doesn't get it (Mark 8:27–33). The only time that Mark's Jesus affirms anyone's claims about his messiahship is toward the end of the gospel, when he is on trial before the High Priest. Of course, this affirmation leads to charges of **blasphemy** (i.e., disrespect for God and holy things) and calls for his death (Mark 14:53–65). Thus, Mark uses the gospel story to explain the true meaning of Jesus' messiahship: He must suffer and die.

**THE SON OF GOD** Read Mark 1:1, 11; 3:11; 5:7; 9:7; 14:61; and 15:39. When Christians today hear the title **Son of God**, they immediately think of the unique Son, begotten of God, and therefore divine. However, as this phrase is used in the Bible, it does not necessarily imply divine nature. Rather, it describes a special relationship to God. Old Testament kings, angelic beings, and righteous people were called sons of God.

Mark uses the title Son of God in a way that coincides with his use of the titles messiah and Christ. For example, the readers of this gospel see God declaring Jesus to be his Son, first at Jesus' baptism by John (Mark 1:11) and again at his transfiguration (Mark 9:7). We even see the demons calling him Son of God (Mark 5:7), but no human being correctly identifies Jesus as the Son of God until the Roman centurion's **confession** (i.e., declaration of faith), when he witnesses Jesus' death (Mark 15:39). A **centurion** was a Roman military person in charge of a century of soldiers. Remarkably, the centurion's statement, "Truly, this is God's son," corresponds with the opening of the gospel, "The beginning of the gospel of Jesus Christ, the Son of God" (Mark 1:1).

Thus, the "good news" concerning the Son of God, which Mark announces at the start of his gospel, comes to climax only when Jesus dies. Likewise, humanity's proclamation of Jesus as Son of God means acknowledging his obedient death on a cross. Such irony! Imagine the impact of this message on Mark's original audience—a crucified Son of God! Nothing in Israel's tradition would have prepared Jews to accept the notion of a suffering messiah. Likewise, Gentiles would have viewed such an idea as pure foolishness. After all, the messiah was supposed to rescue them from their enemies. How could they acknowledge a so-called messiah who was beaten and put to death as a criminal?

**THE SON OF MAN** In each of the gospels, the term **Son of Man** is used on several levels. In Mark's gospel, it can have at least one of three meanings: (1) a human being—the son of a man is a man—who has some kind of power or authority (Mark 2:10, 28); (2) the heavenly warrior/judge who battles the evil one at the end of time and subsequently is given power, honor, and glory (Mark 8:38; 13:24–26; 14:62; cf. Dan. 7:13–27); and (3) the one who must suffer, die, and be raised up (Mark 8:31; 9:9, 12, 31; 10:33, 45; 14:21, 41). In Greek, the word translated as "must" is, literally, "it is necessary that," meaning "God determined that" or "God intended that." In other words, it was God's plan that Jesus must suffer, die, and be raised up. In Mark's gospel, this third meaning is the one that causes the greatest consternation for the disciples. They do not want to accept the reality of suffering, especially Jesus' suffering. However, it is precisely this notion that the gospel writer wants to highlight when he uses the title Son of Man.

As you read the first chapters of Mark's gospel, pay careful attention to when, how, and by whom these terms are used to describe Jesus. What words, events, or images does the gospel writer associate with descriptions of Jesus as Son of Man? When and by whom is Jesus called Son of God? When is the title messiah rightly or wrongly used? Attention to these details will help you better understand and appreciate Mark's theology concerning Jesus.

## THE MESSIANIC SECRET

Biblical scholars use the term **Messianic Secret** to describe those strange scenes in Mark's gospel where someone (correctly) identifies Jesus as the messiah or Son of God, or otherwise calls attention to his activities on behalf of God's reign, and Jesus tells them not to tell anyone. Perhaps the most striking example is the scene in which Peter confesses Jesus as the messiah (Mark 8:27–33). Jesus asks Peter who he is. Peter responds first by saying what others have said about Jesus, but then, when pressed further, he identifies him as the messiah (Mark 8:29). Jesus responds by ordering him not to tell anyone and by saying that the Son of Man must suffer, die, and be raised up (Mark 8:30–31). The narrator adds, "This he said quite openly!" (Mark 8:32), referring to Jesus' announcement that he must suffer.

It is at this point in the story that we know for certain that Peter did not understand what he was saying when he confessed Jesus as the messiah because he scolds Jesus (Mark 8:32), telling him that he's got it all wrong! Jesus responds by scolding Peter, telling him that he's the one who's got it all wrong (Mark 8:33). Following this confrontation with Peter, Jesus goes on to teach his followers about the demands of discipleship: They will have to take up their cross and go the same way that he must go—to death (Mark 8:34–9:1). Later, when Jesus is revealed in the transfiguration event, he again tells his disciples that the Son of Man must suffer (Mark 9:9).

In other scenes in Mark's gospel, Jesus drives out demons and orders them to be silent about his identity (Mark 1:21–28) and Jesus heals a leper and orders him to tell no one (Mark 1:40–45). These are also part of the Messianic Secret. Biblical scholars suggest that Mark expected to communicate at least two things by introducing this notion of the Messianic Secret. First, he wanted to say that Jesus' messiahship is directly connected with the triumph of God's reign, and because the message of the coming kingdom of God is so powerful, it cannot be kept hidden, no matter how hard people try (see also Mark 4:21–24). Therefore, Mark portrayed the demons as shouting out Jesus' identity (Mark 1:21–28) and the leper as going away to tell everyone what Jesus did for him (Mark 1:40–45), even when they were told to keep silent.

Second, Mark wanted to say that the traditional understandings of messiahship did not apply to Jesus. He was not the king or political leader for whom people had hoped or the great prophet of whom Moses spoke. Instead, Jesus' true identity was revealed *in his death*. But this is the same message that the gospel writer was communicating with his use of the title Son of Man. Jesus is the messiah—yes! But he is the messiah in the same way that he is the Son of Man: He must suffer and be put to death.

## MARK'S MIRACLE STORIES

All of the canonical gospels contain miracle stories, but Mark's gospel, and especially its first half, contains a rather large number of miracle stories when compared to the other gospels. In the synoptic gospels, the Greek word is *dynameis*, meaning "mighty works." It is this same Greek word that is the root of our English words *dynamic* and *dynamite*. In most of the miracle stories in Mark's gospel, the person requesting healing must have faith, however imperfect, before the miracle can take place. If he or she does not have faith, Jesus cannot perform the miracle (cf. Mark 9:23–24). However, faith should not be understood as some kind of mental assent to religious teachings (i.e., agreeing to something in your mind). Rather, it means trust.

The writer of Mark's gospel makes several other important theological points using miracle stories. For example, he presents miracles as a demonstration of the power of God, which is manifest in Jesus as Jesus does battle against the powers of Satan (Mark 1:23–28; cf. Mark 3:22). He also uses miracle stories to show that Jesus is a prophet who is mighty in word and deed (Mark 1:27; 2:12; 6:1–6) and exalted above others who would make claims to divine power (Mark 13:21–22). Finally, Mark shows Jesus' healing action as a foretaste of eschatological (i.e., end-time) salvation. Thus, the reader should see in the miracle stories of Mark's gospel a preview of what God will do for the believer in the end time, when God will triumph over all of the forces of evil and reign supreme over all creation.

Miracles pose a difficulty for modern peoples because we tend to think of them as suspensions of the laws of nature. As a result, when people talk about miracles today, most listeners respond with suspicion. They assume that an event that cannot be explained by the principles of science must be a hoax or the product of someone's overactive imagination. However, the ancients understood miracles in a very different light than we do. They believed that God or gods inhabited the upper world above the firmament; that good spirits dwelt in the heavens, the space between the firmament and earth; and that evil powers inhabited the underworld or netherworld (see diagram below). Thus, living on the earth, human beings understood themselves to be in close proximity to both good and evil spirits. They were not surprised by miracles. Rather, they expected their lives would intersect with the spirit world in one way or another.

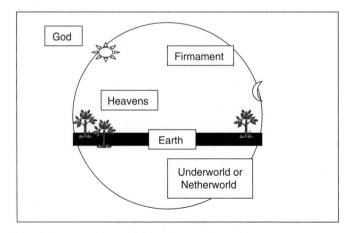

A representation of first-century peoples' understanding of the cosmos.

Certainly, not all Christians today deny that Jesus was able to work miracles. However, among those who accept his miracle-working abilities, some assume that Jesus was the only miracle worker in history, going so far as to say that Jesus' miracles prove his divinity. This view can be problematic as well because miracle stories were common to a variety of religious traditions in the ancient world. Here are two examples of ancient miracle stories, neither of which belongs to a Christian context.

### AN INSCRIPTION FOUND AT THE TEMPLE OF ASKLEPIOS IN EPIDAUROS

Cleo was pregnant five years. She, already five years pregnant, was brought prostrate in bed to the God as a supplicant. Immediately as she came from him and from the temple, she bore a boy; as soon as he was born, he washed himself in the spring and walked around with the mother. After she had accomplished this, she wrote about it on the votive offering. One should be amazed not at the greatness of the tablet, but at the God. Five years Cleo bore the burden in her womb until she slept in the temple and she became healthy. (Cartlidge and Dungan, 1994, 151)

### CHANINA BEN DOSA'S SINLESSNESS

Our rabbis say, once upon a time a poisonous snake was injuring people. They went and made it known to Rabbi Chanina ben Dosa. He said to them, "Show me its burrow." They showed him its burrow and he placed his heel upon the mouth of the hole. It came forth and bit him—and it died. He put that snake on his shoulders, went to the House of Study (beth ha-midrash), and said to them, "See, my sons; it is not the snake that kills but sin that kills." Then they said, "Woe to the man a snake attacks and woe to the snake which Rabbi Chanina ben Dosa attacks! (Berakoth 33a; Cartlidge and Dungan, 1994, 158)

These are only two of a relatively large number of stories about Roman and Greek heroes and even Jewish rabbis who performed miracles similar to the ones found in the Gospel of Mark. If you wanted to argue that miracle stories prove Jesus' divinity, you would have to argue that all of these other stories are fiction and only the miracle stories of Jesus are factual, but this claim would be difficult to defend. You would also have to account for the fact that the New Testament contains stories of Paul and of Jesus' apostles also performing miracles. Does the presence of these stories mean that Paul, Peter, and the other disciples of Jesus were also divine?

Again, the first-century audiences of these ancient stories would not necessarily have assumed the divinity of the miracle worker, nor would they have been terribly amazed by the details of the miraculous event because they expected miracles. Biblical scholars think that these ancient peoples were primarily concerned about the *revelatory character* of miracle stories. In other words, they looked to the miracle story to reveal something about the gods who were the source or cause of the miracle worker's miraculous deed. In Mark's gospel, the stories of Jesus working miracles do not prove his divinity. Rather, they reveal a message about God and the establishment of God's kingdom on earth. To search for something else in the stories is to miss the point.

Miracle stories typically make mention of the disposition of the one being healed. In many of the nonbiblical miracle stories, faith is the consequence of the miracle.

People come to the god as unbelievers, but because they have been healed, they become believers. Some of the New Testament miracle stories have a similar view about the disposition of faith. That is, sometimes when Jesus performs a miracle, the person wishing to be healed goes away strengthened in faith. However, much of the time, the stories describe people coming to Jesus *with faith*. In these stories, especially in Mark's gospel, faith is a prerequisite of the miracle, and there is no miracle if there is no faith. For example, in describing Jesus' visit to his hometown, the author of Mark's gospel says that Jesus could do no miracles there because of the people's lack of faith (Mark 6:1–6).

In some miracle stories—there are several in the Gospel of Mark—it is not Jesus' words but the faith of the petitioner that makes him or her well. For example, in Mark's story about a woman who suffered from hemorrhages, Jesus appeared not to know that the woman was healed until the deed was already done (Mark 5:25–34). But, again, faith is not about accumulating religious knowledge or willing the mind to think certain things. It is about trusting in God's ability to establish God's kingdom on earth. Another feature of Mark's miracle stories is the juxtaposition of faith and fear. See, for example, the story of the man from the Gerasene area who was possessed by thousands of demons (Mark 5:1–20). When Jesus drove out the demons, the townspeople were so frightened that they asked Jesus to leave their town. Likewise, the disciples responded with great fear when Jesus calmed a storm on the sea. The narrator of the gospel, commenting on the miracle, adds that "their hearts were hardened" (Mark 6:47–52).

---

### FORM AND REDACTION CRITICISM AS TOOLS TO BETTER UNDERSTAND MIRACLE STORIES

We can use the techniques of form criticism to analyze a New Testament miracle story. After categorizing the story as a miracle story, we identify its structural elements so that we can reconstruct the oral tradition in the form in which it might have existed before its inclusion in the gospel. Miracle stories are generally grouped into four categories: healings, exorcisms, nature miracles (e.g., calming the sea), and resuscitations. The structural elements, or formal characteristics, of a miracle story are as follows: (1) a description of the sick person's condition, (2) the healing action, and (3) a testimony by someone or another kind of evidence that the miracle actually took place.

After we complete the work of form criticism, we can use the techniques of redaction criticism to determine how the author edited the original version of the story in order to incorporate it into his gospel. In particular, we will want to see whether the gospel writer omitted or altered one of the structural elements of the miracle story or added other details to the story. These redactional (i.e., editing) changes will give us clues about the message that the author wanted to convey through the story. Finally, after investigating the author's pattern of redaction in several miracle stories, we might be ready to draw some conclusions about the author's worldview or theological perspective concerning miracles.

Take, for example, the story about Jesus healing the Syro-Phoenician woman's daughter (Mark 7:24–30). The story involves an **exorcism** or casting out of an unclean spirit. However, when you look at the structural elements of the story, you will notice that Jesus does not actually do or say anything to heal the girl (element 2 above). Rather, he simply announces that the healing has taken place. This fact is then confirmed when the woman returns and sees her healed daughter lying on the bed (element 3 above). Therefore, according to the story, the impetus for the healing did not come from Jesus but rather from the woman's words to Jesus, her act of faith.

If you look carefully at the story of the healing of the Syro-Phoenician woman's daughter, you will also notice a rather cryptic dialogue between Jesus and the woman that comes at the center of the story. Using the findings of form criticism, we can deduce that the original story known to Mark was rather brief: a Gentile (non-Jewish) woman has a daughter who is possessed by a demon. Jesus heals her and the mother goes home to find that the child is well. Using the techniques of redaction criticism, we can speculate that Mark may have created a new setting for the story—a home in the region of Tyre—and inserted the dialogue. In addition, he may have redacted (edited) the structural elements of the story to make the woman responsible for her daughter's healing. "For saying that, you may go—the demon has left your daughter" (Mark 7:29).

However, form criticism and redaction criticism still do not provide a definitive answer to the question of how this story should be interpreted. Does Jesus speak to the woman the way he does to insult her or to elicit from her a profession of faith? When the woman responds to Jesus, is she simply consenting to Jesus' authority, or is she teaching (perhaps even scolding?) him that he needs to expand his mission beyond Judaism to the Gentile world? The gospel text does not favor one interpretation over the other, but hopefully this investigation into Mark's miracle stories can help us appreciate the richness of the Gospel of Mark.

A careful reader of nonbiblical miracle stories will discover that the miracle stories in Mark's gospel have for the most part the same form (i.e., structural elements) as miracle stories in nonbiblical literature. Likewise, Hellenistic and Jewish rabbinic miracle stories tend to exhibit the same categories of miracles as biblical miracle stories. At the same time, there are differences that should not be overlooked. The miracle stories of Mark's gospel differ from nonbiblical miracle stories primarily in their content and in the actions and dispositions of their major characters. For example, the stories of some ancient miracle workers show that the miracle workers' motivation was money and power—quite different from Jesus' motivation, which was to usher in God's kingdom. We also find that Jewish rabbinic miracle workers are presented as more skeptical of the "marvelous" than other ancient miracle workers. Their storytellers are quite explicit about not giving any special attention to the human miracle worker but instead referring all power to God, who is the source of the miracle.

## THE PROBLEM OF THE DISCIPLES IN MARK'S GOSPEL

One of the most problematic features of the Gospel of Mark is its portrayal of the disciples. In the opening scenes of the gospel, Jesus calls the disciples and they follow immediately (Mark 1:16–20). Later they are described as being "with him" and doing the things he does; they proclaim the message about the coming kingdom of God and exorcise demons (Mark 3:13–19). But soon the reader discovers that, although the disciples are privileged to witness Jesus' power as he performs miracles (Mark 4:35–41; 5:37–40), they misunderstand his mighty deeds and his teachings (Mark 4:40; 7:18; 8:16–21). Before long, their misunderstanding turns to astonishment and disapproval and even hardness of heart (Mark 6:47–52; 8:14–21). In the end, when Jesus is arrested, they all run away, abandoning him (Mark 14:50).

Mark's very negative portrayal of Jesus' disciples prompts the question, What is the meaning of discipleship? If you go back to the beginning of the gospel and pay attention to the characters who do believe in Jesus and who want to be with him, you will see that they are the "little people." Thus, the real models of discipleship in this gospel are the marginalized of society—the ones who believe in the midst of their suffering: the woman with the hemorrhage (Mark 5:21–43), the Syro-Phoenician woman (Mark 7:24–30), the blind Bartimaeus (Mark 10:46–52), the widow at the Temple treasury (Mark 12:41–44), and the woman who anoints Jesus before his arrest (Mark 14:3–9). Then, if you go back and look for all of Jesus' teachings on discipleship, you will notice that Jesus repeatedly teaches that the true disciple must be willing to walk in his footsteps and carry his cross. He or she must be willing to suffer as Jesus suffered. No wonder Jesus' disciples had a hard time accepting his teaching! Further, by looking at the disciples' behavior throughout the gospel, you get a glimpse of some of the stumbling blocks to being a good disciple: desire for power, status, and money; fear; hard-heartedness.

In his story of the arrest of Jesus (Mark 14:43–50), Mark softens his picture of the disciples a bit by suggesting that the scriptures predicted that they would abandon him. This is the first indication that all is not lost for the disciples, even though they come off very badly throughout most of the gospel. Pay close attention to how the disciples are portrayed throughout Mark's story of the death and resurrection of Jesus. Do they abandon their hard-heartedness in the end? Does the risen Jesus still consider them to be his chosen disciples? What message do you think Mark was trying to convey by portraying Jesus' disciples in this way?

## APOCALYPTIC CHRISTIANITY

Mark's gospel contains a section that biblical scholars call the Little Apocalypse (Mark 13). Similarly, Matthew's and Luke's gospels have apocalyptic discourses. What is an **apocalypse**? The word translated means "revelation." It is used to describe a genre or type of literature that includes revelations about heavenly realities, the end of the world, and God's ultimate triumph over the forces of evil. Apocalyptic writings were fairly common among religious literature of the first century C.E., both Jewish and Christian. In fact, some scholars believe that the early Christian church originated in a highly apocalyptic milieu—that is, in a setting in which people were keenly aware of the stranglehold that evil had on their world, so much so that they thought the world would be destroyed. Communities with an apocalyptic worldview usually feel marginalized from the rest of society. They also tend to have a strong group identity, seeing those outside of their community as part of the realm of evil.

On the surface, apocalyptic literature appears to be a prediction about the future end of the world. However, scholars have noticed that apocalyptic literature has some affinities with prophetic literature—not prophecy in the sense of predicting the future but, like the prophecies of the Old Testament, a critique of the situation in which the author and his community were living. Apocalyptic writers formulated their responses to the problems of the day in mythic terms, using cosmic imagery to describe the battle between good and evil and to assert their belief in God's ultimate sovereignty over evil. In sum, apocalyptic literature gives the appearance of being about some future time, but it is really about the author's own time.

When you read the apocalypses of the synoptic gospels (i.e., Matthew, Mark, and Luke), you will notice that they contain descriptions of the signs of the end time, including the appearance of false messiahs or false prophets who claim to be the Christ, wars and rumors of wars, famines and earthquakes (marking the beginning of the sufferings), and persecutions instigated by the synagogue, the government, and even family members (Matt. 24–25; Mark 13; Luke 21). They also include signs in the sun, moon, and stars and a vision of the Son of Man coming on the clouds of heaven with power and glory to gather his elect from the ends of the earth. Many of these same signs of the end time are found in Jewish and Christian biblical and nonbiblical apocalyptic literature. Modern readers sometimes want to use these signs to calculate the actual date or time of the end of the world, but the signs were never intended to be used in that way. Rather, the authors of these works used them to demonstrate the extent to which the entire world would be affected by the struggle of good and evil, a struggle that they believed God would surely win.

Synoptic gospel apocalypses also include a section of *paraenesis* (moral exhortation or teaching). Thus, for the persecuted, this literature not only was a source of hope that God would vindicate them by punishing their enemies but it also taught them how the authentic Christian ought to live in troubled times. What is the appropriate stance of authentic Christians with regard to the coming of the end time? They should be confident about God's sovereignty over the forces of evil, but they should also be prepared to endure patiently. They should be vigilant, always ready for the messiah's return, and never lose hope. Endurance is the virtue to be cultivated (see, e.g., Mark 13:13).

It appears that early Christians expected the return of the messiah (and, with it, the end time) within a relatively short period of time. However, as years passed without the messiah's return, early Christians had to deal with the problem of the delayed end time. In response to that problem, they taught this lesson: Be ready because you do not know the time when the messiah will return. While most modern readers do not expect the immediate end of the world, the message of these apoca-lyptic discourses is still relevant—believing Christians ought to be ready and stay alert for the coming of God's reign.

## THE PASSION NARRATIVE OF MARK'S GOSPEL

The story of Jesus' arrest by Roman authorities, trial and condemnation, and his death on the cross is called a **passion narrative**. It gets its name from the Latin word that means "suffering." Even though the chronology of events is more or less the same in all of the gospels, each evangelist tells the story of the death of Jesus a bit differently, perhaps reflecting the fact that each gospel writer and his community had their own theology of the cross—that is, their own way of making sense of the crucifixion of Jesus and its implications for discipleship. What follows is a brief reflection on Mark's theology of the cross as expressed in his passion narrative.

Almost every scene in Mark's passion narrative is characterized by **irony**. Irony is a literary device designed to catch the readers' attention and make them feel like insid-ers to the story, even though they were not present for the event itself. There are at least two kinds of irony. One is *verbal irony*, which occurs when a character in the story makes a comment that he or she intends to be sarcastic, derogatory, or unflattering. Sometimes the character's statement is simply inadequate. However, because of the way the narrator tells the story, the reader recognizes that the character has unwit-tingly made a more profoundly truthful statement than he or she intended to make.

Take, for example, Jesus' words in defense of the woman who anointed him at the start of the passion narrative (Mark 14:3–9). Scolding her accusers, Jesus tells them to leave her alone because, he says, "She has done what she could; she has anointed my body beforehand for its burial" (Mark 14:8). Jesus' statement is at least partially true insofar as his disciples will not be able to give him a proper burial because he will be executed as a criminal. However, for the reader, his statement contains a pro-found truth that even Jesus does not appear to recognize. First, he will not need an anointing for burial after death because God will raise him from the dead before anyone has a chance to anoint his body. Second, whether or not the woman under-stood what she was doing when she anointed Jesus, Jesus' statement about the pur-pose of the anointing does not reveal the whole truth. Why? Because the reader knows that the woman's act of anointing publicly designates Jesus as the messiah (messiah means "anointed"). His messiahship can now be revealed because his death is imminent and there can be no mistake: He is the *suffering* messiah.

Another type of irony is *situational irony*. Mark's passion narrative contains many instances of situational irony. For example, in Mark's telling of the story of Jesus' trial, Pilate makes an offer to release to the crowd one of two men: Jesus or Barabbas, who is described as a murderer and insurrectionist (Mark 15:6–15). The crowd chooses Barabbas, whose name (ironically) means "Son of [my] Father," for release. However, the reader knows that the crowd's choice will result in the condemnation of an innocent man, who is the Son of the Father. Later the soldiers dress Jesus in a purple robe and mock him as "King of the Jews" (Mark 15:16–20). While the soldiers in the story think that they are making fun of Jesus, the reader knows that Jesus really is a king—not just any king but God's chosen one who is about to usher in God's kingdom.

Another way that Mark uses the passion narrative to illuminate his theology of the cross is by juxtaposing two or more stories. In this way, he draws attention to a character or event and lets that character or event "speak" on Mark's behalf. Here are two examples:

1. The author inserts the story of the anointing of Jesus by an unnamed woman (Mark 14:3–11) into the story about Judas's role in the plot to kill Jesus (Mark 14:1–2; 10–11)—an intercalation. Contrast the extravagant generosity of the woman and her public display of faith in Jesus with Judas's offer to betray Jesus and turn him over to the religious authorities for the promise of money. It goes without saying that the intercalation makes a profound statement about the nature of true discipleship in the shadow of the cross.

2. Mark frames the story of the Last Supper (Mark 14:22–25) with two prophecies that threaten the intimacy of the disciples' Passover meal with Jesus—Judas' betrayal (Mark 14:17–21) and Peter's denial along with the disciples' abandonment (Mark 14:26–31). Perhaps he includes these details simply to show that Jesus fully recognized what was in store for him in the hours and days that would follow this meal. The Last Supper story is the foundation for the Christian sacrament of the Eucharist or the Lord's Supper, although Jesus followers had been celebrating the Eucharist for twenty years or more before this gospel was written. By juxtaposing the prophecies of betrayal and of denial and abandonment with the story of Jesus' last meal with his disciples—the Passover meal, in fact—Mark shines a bright light on Jesus' role at the meal. Who among us would knowingly sit at table with our soon-to-be betrayers and still treat them as friends? What does Mark want us to understand about the meaning and significance of the Eucharist, given that he places its founding story in this setting of betrayal and denial?

Perhaps the most important scene of Mark's passion narrative is the one in which the centurion declares Jesus to be the Son of God. In order to grasp the significance of this scene, it is important to recognize what event prompts the centurion's confession of faith—quite simply, he watches Jesus die (Mark 15:39). Matthew's and Luke's passion narratives also include the story of the centurion. However, in one case, the centurion says something quite different—he declares Jesus to be an innocent man (Luke 23:47)—and in the other, it is a different event that prompts his confession of faith—the earthquake and other signs of the end time (Matt. 27:54). For the early preachers of the gospel, Jesus' crucifixion was a major obstacle. Why should people believe that this man who was condemned to death as an insurrectionist and a blasphemer is the messiah and Son of God? After all, crucifixion was reserved for the worst of criminals. Mark doesn't try to explain away the crucifixion. Rather, he says that Jesus is the messiah and Son of God by virtue of the fact that *he had to suffer and die.* Mark's message must have made his original hearers really sit up and take notice. At the same time, if biblical scholars are correct in thinking that Mark's community was suffering persecution, the notion of a suffering messiah could have been a source of hope and consolation: Jesus, the one we call messiah and Son of God, suffers with us.

## THE POSTRESURRECTION NARRATIVE

Although all four canonical gospels narrate the story of the trial and death of Jesus, none describes the actual resurrection of Jesus. Instead, as proof of the resurrection, they include stories about people who witness the empty tomb or see the risen Christ. These are called **postresurrection narratives**. Mark's postresurrection story is particularly troubling because the narrator tells the readers of this gospel that the only witnesses to the resurrection—a group of women—ran away afraid and told no one what had happened there (Mark 16:1–8). You have to ask yourself, then, Where is the good news? The other gospels have stories about the women spreading the message about Jesus' resurrection, as well as stories about his appearances, suggesting

---

### TEXT CRITICISM: WHAT IT TELLS US ABOUT THE ENDING(S) OF MARK'S GOSPEL

When you read the Gospel of Mark, you will notice that it has several endings. Scholars of Mark's gospel agree that the gospel originally ended at Mark 16:8 and that Mark 16:9–20 are later additions to the gospel. However, if the scholars are right and Mark's gospel originally ended at 16:8, we are left with some troubling questions. The women who had been following Jesus in life come to his tomb only to discover a messenger who tells them to go and announce to the disciples that Jesus has been raised. But what do they do? They run away and say "nothing to anyone for they were afraid" (Mark 16:8).

If the women told no one, how is the reader supposed to know about the resurrection? After Jesus has endured so much conflict, opposition, betrayal, denial, and even death, we have finally arrived at the "good news" of the story. Should it not be proclaimed? Are we to conclude that fear ultimately extinguishes the message? Apparently, some of the earliest readers of this gospel— Christian scribes, perhaps—were also troubled by the "unanswered" questions of Mark's ending and therefore crafted new conclusions to his gospel. Do we have evidence to support this theory? Yes, actually we do. We have manuscripts (i.e., hand-written copies) of the Gospel of Mark—some from as early as the second century C.E. and others from as late as the ninth century C.E.—that contain different endings. But which manuscripts represent the original ending of the gospel and which ones are later additions? Here's where the work of the text critic comes into play.

The task of the text critic is to examine all available textual evidence— Greek manuscripts of the gospel as well as manuscripts in translation and quotations from other literature—in order to reconstruct, insofar as possible, the original wording of the gospel. The first thing that text critics noticed is that none of these additional endings is found in any of the earliest manuscripts of Mark's gospel. However, they were able to determine that Mark 16:9–20, often called the Longer Ending, is quite old. Most think it was composed sometime in the second century C.E., in order to give this gospel an ending that looks more like those in Luke's and John's gospels, with stories about the appearances of the risen Jesus and even a story about Jesus' ascension into heaven (see Luke 24; John 20). At the Council of Trent, in the sixteenth century C.E., this Longer Ending was officially accepted as part of the canonical gospel.

The ending marked Shorter Ending is believed to be a much later addition. It is usually placed between verse 8 and verse 9, and it reads as follows:

> And all that had been commanded them they told briefly to those around Peter. And afterward Jesus himself sent out through them, from east to west, the sacred and imperishable proclamation of eternal salvation.

The manuscripts that contain this ending belong to the seventh to the ninth centuries C.E. The Shorter Ending attempts to downplay the problems of the original ending by simply stating that the women actually did tell Peter's companions what happened that Easter Sunday at the empty tomb.

Finally, there is the ending marked Freer Logion, which was inserted between verse 14 and verse 15 of the Longer Ending in a manuscript from the fourth or fifth century C.E. You will probably find it in your Bible's footnotes. It gets its name from the location in which the manuscript is preserved: the Freer Gallery of Art in Washington, D.C. Some scholars have suggested that the Freer Logion is an attempt by a scribal editor to put the disciples in a better light. Even a cursory reading of Mark's gospel will reveal why a scribe might have thought that was necessary. Dumb, fearful, and stubborn, the disciples certainly do not make a very good showing of themselves. This scribal addition attributes the disciples' lack of faith to the forces of Satan. It also describes the risen Christ as saying that he died for them so that they could "return to the truth."

Most of us, even many New Testament scholars, are not going to do text criticism because the work requires highly technical skills, but what should the everyday reader of the Gospel of Mark glean from the work of the text critic? This particular example helps us appreciate how strange and challenging the original ending of Mark's gospel is. We are able to see how the scribes who copied the gospel struggled to resolve its strangeness. Perhaps it also prompts us to reflect on our own reaction to the incongruities of this gospel. What will you do when you hear the "good news"? Will you run away afraid or will you proclaim it?

that traditions about the resurrection developed gradually over time. One can almost imagine the other evangelists trying to answer the questions that Mark left unanswered: Was Jesus the Christ actually raised from the dead? Is he still with us? What are we to do now? Mark, however, leaves us holding our breath.

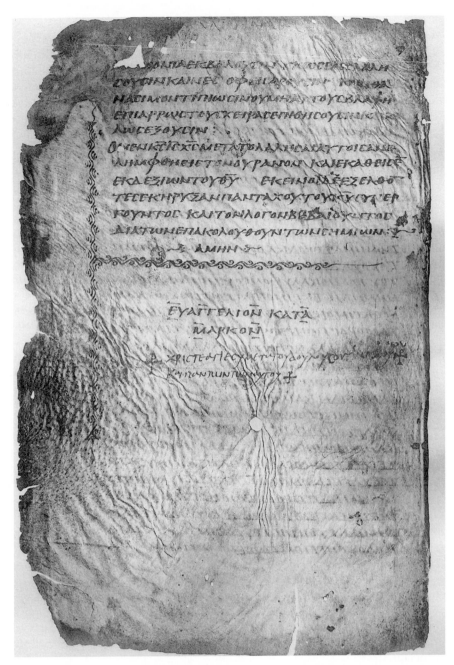

The New Testament manuscript page from Codex Washingtonianus containing Mark 16:17–20. Other images of manuscript pages from Codex Washingtonianus can be found at http://www.beloit.edu/~classics/GospelOfMark. Links for images of other biblical manuscripts can be found at http://www.ntgateway.com/resource/image.htm.

Modern Christians who have grown up hearing about the resurrection of Jesus probably cannot appreciate the significance of this event for early Christians. Among first-century Judaisms, scholars were already debating about resurrection from the dead in the end time. From the information available to us, it appears that Pharisees believed in the possibility of resurrection from the dead for God's righteous ones, but Sadducees did not. For those who did believe, resurrection from the dead was understood to be God's way of rewarding the righteous ones who had suffered unjustly at the hands of their enemies.

Therefore, when Jesus was raised from the dead, the earliest Christians saw this as God's act of vindicating Jesus (i.e., declaring him as righteous and clearing him of any suspicion of guilt in his death). They also thought of it as one of the first signs of the end time, since, according to their belief, resurrection of the dead would happen only in the end time. Jesus was resurrected as God's Righteous One, and thus, they believed, all the rest of God's righteous ones would soon follow. In this way, belief in the resurrection was laden with eschatological (i.e., end-time) expectation, and many New Testament scholars think that early Christian communities were born out of this highly apocalyptic milieu.

## KEY TERMS

| | | |
|---|---|---|
| Epilogue | Son of God | Paraenesis |
| Passion narrative | Confession | Irony |
| Frame stories | Centurion | Postresurrection |
| Intercalations | Son of Man | narratives |
| Christ | Messianic Secret | |
| Messiah | Exorcism | |
| Blasphemy | Apocalypse | |

## QUESTIONS FOR READING

Read the Gospel of Mark, and use evidence from the gospel to answer the following questions. Refer to the directions in Chapter 5 of this textbook to learn how to do a close reading of a biblical text.

1. Make a list of the titles given to Jesus in the first two chapters of the gospel and note the context in which each title is mentioned. Based on your reading of the biblical text, what conclusions can you draw about whom people in the story thought Jesus was? About whom Mark thought Jesus was?

2. Using Mark 1:1–11 as your resource, explain what the reader is told about John the Baptist's identity. What can you say about his message, his relationship to Jesus, and his role in this gospel?

3. Comment on the meaning of the first preaching message of Jesus: "This is the time of fulfillment. The kingdom of God is at hand. Repent, and believe in the gospel" (Mark 1:15). Having heard this statement, what expectations would Jesus' listeners have had about Jesus?

4. Repeatedly in the first five chapters of the gospel, Mark comments that "the people were astonished." About what things are they astonished or amazed? How is the author using the word *astonished*? Were they pleasantly surprised? Offended? Find one or two examples to explain.

5. In Mark 2:1–3:6, the author provides several scenes in which Jesus comes into conflict with the religious authorities. Comment on the reason for the conflict and the manner in which the conflict gets resolved (if it does).

6. In Mark 6:14–29, what was Herod's opinion about who Jesus was? What similarities exist, if any, between the story of the death of John the Baptist and that of the death of Jesus? *Hint:* You will have to read the story of Jesus' death in Mark 14:32–15:47 in order to compare the two death stories.

7. After a brief dialogue between the Syro-Phoenician woman and Jesus, Mark has Jesus say, "For saying this, you may go" (Mark 7:29). What did she say to Jesus and what did her words mean in this context?

8. In the story of Peter's confession (Mark 8:27–33), Peter identifies Jesus as the messiah, but Jesus' reactions to Peter's words suggest that Peter does not understand the meaning or significance of what he said. What is it about the messiahship of Jesus that Peter does not understand? *Hint:* Pay careful attention to the narrator's words in verses 30 and 32.

9. In Mark 9:2–13, the story of the transfiguration, there are several details that hint at Jesus' anticipated resurrection, but there are also several clues indicating that Jesus will have to suffer. Comment on both aspects of the story.

10. In Mark 10:35–45, what do James and John seek from Jesus? What does Jesus promise them in return?

11. Mark 11:1–12:44 includes several stories involving conflicts between Jesus and the religious authorities in Jerusalem. Comment on the source of the conflicts and their place in developing the plot of the gospel.

12. In Mark 13, identify what the author considers to be the signs of the end time. What does this section tell us about the author's understanding of its significance or relevance for his community of believers (i.e., what they thought the end time represented)?

13. From Mark 13, summarize the author's paraenesis (moral exhortation) for his community as it anticipated the coming of the end time.

14. Outline the events of the passion (i.e., trial and death) and resurrection of Jesus as told in Mark's gospel. Make note of the details that surprised you. What were the charges for which Jesus was put to death in Mark's gospel?

15. What characteristics does Mark ascribe to Jesus as he faces death? To his disciples? Be prepared to give concrete evidence from the gospel to support your position.

## QUESTIONS FOR REFLECTION

1. What overall impressions do you get from Mark's portrayal of Jesus? Is this the type of Jesus to which you would be attracted? Why or why not? Be prepared to give concrete evidence from the gospel to support your position.

2. What overall impressions do you get from Mark's portrayal of Jesus' disciples? Are these the kind of disciples you would have expected Jesus to have? Why or why not? Based on Mark's gospel, what would it mean to be a true disciple today? Be prepared to give concrete evidence from the gospel to support your position.

3. How would you characterize modern attitudes toward miracles? Would some of Mark's miracle stories be more readily acceptable than others today? What aspects of ancient understandings of miracles would be useful in helping us appreciate the significance of biblical miracles today?

4. In Mark's Little Apocalypse, Jesus warns, "False messiahs and false prophets will arise and will perform signs and wonders in order to mislead" (Mark 13:22). What might end-time false messiahs and false prophets look like in our modern world? In what ways might they be attractive (and misleading) to today's audience?

5. If, as many scholars believe, Mark's gospel originally ended with Mark 16:8, what difficulties might this conclusion have posed for early Christians? What difficulties does it pose for modern Christians?

## ACTIVITIES FOR LEARNING

1. Locate two or three examples of ancient miracle stories not contained in the Bible and compare them to examples of miracle stories in the Gospel of Mark. One place to begin your search is Cartlidge and Dungan (1994). In what ways is the style/form of Jesus' miracle stories similar to, or different from, that of these nonbiblical miracle stories? In what ways is the content of Jesus' miracle stories similar to, or different from, that of these nonbiblical miracle stories? What, if anything, can you conclude about the distinctiveness of Jesus' miracle working, as told by Mark?

2. Search newspapers, magazines, or websites to find two or three stories about modern miracle workers or about modern claims that a miracle was performed on someone's behalf. In what ways are these accounts similar to or different from ancient miracle stories? What can you detect about the reporter's attitude toward miracles or the reporter's expectations about the readers' attitudes toward miracles? How might you determine whether or not claims of modern miracle working are authentic? In your opinion, what motivates modern peoples to seek out miracles and/or to report on claims of miracle working? How are these motives similar to or different from the purposes of gospel miracle stories?

3. Write your own miracle story using the formal categories and structural elements of traditional miracle stories. Add details to the story to make your own theological statement about Jesus, the miracle worker, but write it in such a way that it is consistent with the rest of the Gospel of Mark.

4. Investigate what archeologists and historians have been able to discover about the Romans' use of crucifixion as a form of capital punishment. Who could be crucified and under what conditions? How was a crucifixion conducted? What purposes did crucifixion serve? What happened to the bodies of the crucified?

## SOURCES AND RESOURCES

Achtemeier, Paul J. *Mark.* Philadelphia: Fortress, 1986.

Beavis, Mary Ann. "Women as Models of Faith in Mark." *Biblical Theology Bulletin* 18:3–9, 1988.

Beck, Robert R. *Nonviolent Story: Narrative Resolution in the Gospel of Mark.* Maryknoll, N.Y.: Orbis Books, 1996.

Blount, Brian K. *Go Preach: Mark's Kingdom Message and the Black Church Today.* Maryknoll, N.Y.: Orbis Books, 1998.

Cartlidge, David R., and David L. Dungan, eds. *Documents for the Study of the Gospels.* 2nd ed. Minneapolis, Minn.: Fortress, 1994.

Donahue, John R., and Daniel J. Harrington. *The Gospel of Mark.* Collegeville, Minn.: Liturgical Press, 2002.

Fowler, Robert M. *Let the Reader Understand: Reader-Response Criticism and the Gospel of Mark.* Minneapolis, Minn.: Fortress, 1991.

Harrington, Daniel J. *What Are They Saying About Mark?* New York: Paulist, 2004.

Horsley, Richard A. *Hearing the Whole Story: The Politics of Plot in Mark's Gospel.* Louisville, Ky.: Westminster John Knox Press, 2001.

Juel, Donald. H. *A Master of Surprise: Mark Interpreted.* Minneapolis, Minn.: Fortress, 1994.

————. *Gospel of Mark.* Nashville, Tenn.: Abingdon Press, 1999.

Kingsbury, Jack Dean. *Conflict in Mark: Jesus, Authorities, Disciples.* Minneapolis, Minn.: Fortress, 1989.

LaVerdier, Eugene. *The Beginning of the Gospel: Introducing the Gospel According to Mark.* Collegeville, Minn. Liturgical Press, 1999.

Levine, Amy-Jill, and Marianne Blickenstaff, eds. *Feminist Companion to Mark.* Sheffield, England: Sheffield Academic Press, 2001.

Malbon, Elizabeth Struthers. *In the Company of Jesus: Characters in Mark's Gospel.* Louisville, Ky.: Westminster John Knox Press, 2000.

Malina, Bruce J., and Richard L. Rohrbaugh. *Social-Science Commentary on the Synoptic Gospels.* Minneapolis, Minn.: Fortress, 2003.

Maloney, Elliott C. *Jesus' Urgent Message for Today: The Kingdom of God in Mark's Gospel.* New York: Continuum, 2004.

McKenna, Megan. *On Your Mark: Reading Mark in the Shadow of the Cross.* Maryknoll, N.Y.: Orbis Books, 2006.

Miller, Susan. *Women in Mark's Gospel.* London: T & T Clark International, 2004.

Minor, Mitzi. *The Power of Mark's Story.* St. Louis, Mo.: Chalice Press, 2001.

Mitchell, Joan. *Beyond Fear and Silence: A Feminist-Literary Approach to the Gospel of Mark.* New York: Continuum, 2001.

Moloney, Francis J. *The Gospel of Mark: A Commentary.* Peabody, Mass.: Hendrickson, 2002.

Rhoads, David. *Reading Mark: Engaging the Gospel.* Minneapolis, Minn.: Fortress, 2004.

————, Joanna Dewey, and Donald Michie. *Mark as Story: An Introduction to the Narrative of a Gospel.* Philadelphia: Fortress, 1999.

Sabin, Marie Noonan. *The Gospel According to Mark.* Collegeville, Minn.: Liturgical Press, 2006.

Senior, Donald. *The Passion of Jesus in the Gospel of Mark.* Wilmington, Del.: Glazier, 1984.

Tolbert, Mary Ann. *Sowing the Gospel: Mark's World in Literary-Historical Perspective.* Minneapolis, Minn.: Fortress, 1989.

Trainor, Michael F. *The Quest for Home: The Household in Mark's Community.* Collegeville, Minn.: Liturgical Press, 2001.

Witherington, Ben. *The Gospel of Mark: A Socio-Rhetorical Commentary.* Grand Rapids, Mich.: Eerdmans, 2001.

Wright, N. T. *Mark for Everyone.* London: SPCK; Louisville, Ky.: Westminster John Knox Press, 2004.

# CHAPTER 7

# THE GOSPEL ACCORDING TO MATTHEW

## OVERVIEW

- AUTHORSHIP: Anonymous but most likely not an eyewitness to the life of Jesus; traditionally associated with Matthew, the "tax collector," who was perhaps identical to Levi, the tax collector who is named among the apostles in Mark's gospel
- DATE OF COMPOSITION: 80–90 C.E.
- INITIAL AUDIENCE: Probably Jewish Christians—that is, Jews who accepted Jesus as the messiah—with openness to including Gentiles in the community; most likely in Antioch, Syria
- MAJOR TOPICS: The Nature of Infancy Narratives; Matthew's Story of the Birth of Jesus; Jesus, the Teacher Like Moses; Matthew's Sermon on the Mount; Matthew's Teaching on the Kingdom of Heaven; Parables and Their Interpretations; The Establishment of the Church; Reconciliation in the Community; Discipleship; Woe to You Hypocrites; The Coming of the End; Testimony to Jesus' Resurrection

## TIMELINE

| | |
|---|---|
| 37 B.C.E. | Herod the Great takes up his kingship in Palestine. |
| 6–4 B.C.E. | Jesus of Nazareth is born. |
| 4 B.C.E. | Herod the Great, king of Palestine, dies. His kingdom is divided among three sons: Archelaus, Herod Antipas, and Philip. |
| 4 B.C.E.–39 C.E. | Herod Antipas, son of Herod the Great, is tetrarch of Galilee and Perea. |
| 6 C.E. | Annas (Ananus I) becomes High Priest of the Jerusalem Temple. |
| 18 C.E. | Caiaphas, the son-in-law of Annas, becomes High Priest of the Jerusalem Temple. |
| 26–36 C.E. | Pontius Pilate is prefect of Judea and Samaria. |
| c. 28 C.E. | John the Baptist is executed by Herod Antipas. |
| c. 30 C.E. | Jesus is crucified, dies, and is resurrected. |
| c. 41–44 C.E. | The apostle James, the brother of John, is martyred. |
| 64 C.E. | Peter and Paul are martyred in Rome. |
| 65–70 C.E. | The Gospel of Mark is written. |
| 66–70 C.E. | The Jewish War occurs. |

| **70** C.E. | Jerusalem and the Temple are destroyed. |
|---|---|
| **80–90** C.E. | **The Gospel of Matthew is written;** the Gospel of Luke is written. |
| **90–100** C.E. | The Gospel of John is written. |
| **c. 180** C.E. | Irenaeus of Lyons writes *Against Heresies.* |
| **c. 310** C.E. | Eusebius of Caesarea completes *Ecclesiastical History.* |

The second stop on our journey through the New Testament is the Gospel of Matthew. Some of what we shall see looks a lot like the Gospel of Mark. For example, like Mark's gospel, the story takes place in ancient Palestine and Jesus is its central character. However, lest you think that this stop in our travels will be "more of the same," the Gospel of Matthew differs from Mark's gospel in important ways. For example, Matthew's Jesus is presented as another Moses, the fulfillment of Israel's hopes, and not as a man racing toward his death. His disciples are still sometimes clueless, but Matthew is more sympathetic toward them, treating them with greater kindness than Mark does.

There are other differences, as well. Some are substantial and noticeable even to the novice reader. For example, whereas Mark's gospel introduces Jesus by describing the situation of his first preaching (Mark 1:15) and by recalling stories about his activities as an adult, the Gospel of Matthew begins with infancy narratives of Jesus, that is, the stories of Jesus' birth and early childhood. Additionally, Matthew's gospel has a large section, traditionally known as the Sermon on the Mount, that is nowhere to be found in Mark's gospel. Other differences are subtler—consisting of a few sentences added here or there, a variation in setting, or a rearrangement of stories—but to the careful reader, they can be equally dramatic.

Our approach to Matthew's gospel, in this chapter, and Luke's gospel, in the next, will be to focus on aspects of the gospel under consideration that are different from those of Mark's gospel. While there are other possible approaches we could take, by focusing on these differences we can find important clues to the theology or worldview of these gospel writers. This approach can also help us understand why the early church might have seen fit to preserve several versions of the gospel story. The canon contains four gospels, which, in turn, give us four distinct portraits of Jesus. If the gospels were simply history, then multiple gospels would become somewhat problematic because it is impossible to reconcile all of the apparent contradictions in the gospels' stories. However, when we view the gospels as faith proclamations—remember that *gospel* means "good news"—we can begin to see that these four distinctive portraits of Jesus provide at least as many opportunities for believers to encounter the risen Jesus in the gospels' proclamation of faith.

However, as a first step in our study of Matthew's gospel, we need to pause to find out what scholars have been able to determine about its author and his audience. This information will, in turn, provide a context for our investigation of the unique features of Matthew's gospel.

## AUTHORSHIP

When we search through the New Testament, we find four lists of the followers of Jesus, all of which include someone named Matthew (Mark 3:18; Matt. 10:3; Luke 6:15; Acts 1:13). Only in this gospel is he identified as a "tax collector" (Matt. 10:3; cf. Matt. 9:9). Elsewhere, Mark and Luke name Levi as the tax collector (Mark 2:14; Luke 5:27). As a result, people have often concluded that Matthew and Levi are the same person and that he became an apostle of Jesus, one of the twelve, after he gave up his career as a tax collector. This is the traditional view (i.e., the view that became popular in the time of the early church) concerning the author of Matthew's gospel.

Another theory about the authorship of Matthew's gospel also has roots in early Christian tradition. The fourth-century historian Eusebius supposedly preserved a quotation from a second-century bishop named Papias, who wrote, "Then Matthew put together the sayings [of Jesus] in the Hebrew [Aramaic?] dialect and each one translated them as he was able" (Eusebius, *Ecclesiastical History* 3.39.16). This led biblical scholars to speculate that perhaps the name of the apostle Matthew got attached to this gospel because its author used as his source another, earlier gospel attributed to Matthew—specifically, a "sayings" gospel. A sayings gospel is simply a collection of the words (i.e., sayings) of Jesus, one following the other like a list of quotations, without any story line or narrative to connect them (see the noncanonical Gospel of Thomas for an example). Unfortunately, this gospel, if it ever existed, is no longer **extant;** that is, it is no longer in existence, or at least no one has yet recovered a copy of it.

The majority of biblical scholars today conclude that the author of the Gospel of Matthew is anonymous, most likely someone who was not an eyewitness to the life of Jesus, but who depended on written and oral traditions about Jesus to construct his gospel. Most biblical scholars also agree that he probably was a Christian Jew or a Jewish Christian—that is, a Jewish person who accepted Jesus as the messiah—because of his liberal use of Jewish scriptures as well as his knowledge of Jewish traditions and his interest in Jewish religious themes. At the same time, this author appears to have been open to the possibility that the good news about Jesus could be preached to Gentiles (non-Jews). Therefore, at the very least, we can say that this gospel writer viewed the Jewish Christian community not as exclusive but as one that should be open to non-Jewish believers as well. For the sake of convenience, we will call him Matthew, even though we do not know his name.

## DATE OF COMPOSITION

Most biblical scholars assign a date of 80–90 C.E. to this gospel. This date of composition is based on the theory that Mark's gospel was the earliest among the synoptic gospels and that Matthew depended on Mark's gospel as one of his written sources. If you carefully compare the content of Mark's and Matthew's gospels, you will discover that Matthew incorporates approximately 90 percent of the Gospel of Mark—something that would be incomprehensible if we were to assume that Matthew was an eyewitness to the life of Jesus. However, this proposed date of composition also means that fifty years or more have passed since the death and resurrection of Jesus. It means that Matthew is writing his gospel at least a generation after the death of Jesus and that he is writing it through the lens of the resurrection. Obviously, his worldview would have greatly affected the way he told the traditional stories of Jesus and even his selection of stories. Thus, we will assume that Matthew (like Mark) was intending not to preserve documentary history of the life of Jesus—a phenomenon unknown to ancient writers—but to give a theological interpretation of their experience of the one whom they called the Christ and of the reason for their faith.

## INITIAL AUDIENCE

Because this gospel contains a large number of references to important Jewish figures and symbols of the Jewish faith—all presented with little explanation—the community for which Matthew was writing appears to have consisted of Jewish Christians, for the most part. However, the gospel also provides a number of clues to suggest that the community's situation was much more complicated. In the story of the sending out of the twelve (Matt. 10:5–6), the gospel writer describes Jesus as telling them not to go to the Gentiles or to the Samaritans and instead to proclaim the "good news" to their Jewish brothers and sisters (see also Matt. 15:24). Yet, at the end of the gospel, Jesus tells the disciples, "Go therefore and make disciples of all nations" (Matt. 28:19). Likewise, early in the gospel, Matthew describes Jesus as affirming Jewish law and insisting that his disciples strive to fulfill to the fullest extent possible the spirit of the law (Matt. 5:18–48). However, he also rails against the Pharisees, whom he sees as obsessed about details of the law and bent on manipulating it to their own good (Matt. 23:1–36). Returning to the story of the sending of the twelve, Matthew's Jesus predicts that the disciples will be handed over for judgment and beaten in the synagogues (Matt. 10:17), probably reflecting the fact that such things were happening to Jewish Christians in Matthew's day (see also Matt. 23:34). Likewise, in other parts of the gospel, Jesus is presented as teaching in *their* synagogues (Matt. 4:23; 9:35; 10:17; 12:9; 13:54), as if Jesus was not himself a Jew! Since these statements do not describe Jesus' historical relationship with the synagogue, they must reflect the experience of Matthew's community.

And so it appears that the community for which Matthew's gospel was written was beginning to separate from Judaism at the time that its author was writing the gospel. Community members may have chosen this separation; that is, they may have decided to leave the synagogue of their own accord. However, it is also possible, perhaps probable, that they left under duress or were even expelled from the synagogue. At the same time, it appears that the community behind Matthew's gospel was trying to decide whether to include Gentiles. Perhaps that outward mission—beyond Judaism and into the Gentile world—was already under way.

What location in the late-first-century-C.E. Mediterranean world would best accommodate this scenario? The city of Antioch in Syria is most often suggested as the location of the community for which the Gospel of Matthew was written. Archeological evidence suggests that Antioch had a large Jewish population in the first century C.E., and Acts of the Apostles also indicates that it was the place where Jewish Christian missionary activity first took root among Gentiles (see Acts 11:19–20). In early Christian tradition, Peter is associated with missionary activity in Antioch, and Matthew's gospel portrays him positively as the leader and representative of Jesus' disciples, adding to the possibility that this gospel was written for the Christian community in Antioch.

## OUTLINE OF THE GOSPEL OF MATTHEW

As we noted in our study of the Gospel of Mark, there are a number of ways to outline any biblical text, depending on the features that the analyst wishes to highlight. The following outline focuses on the Gospel of Matthew's long discourses (i.e., teaching units).

1. Matthew 1:1–2:23—Introduction: stories surrounding the birth of Jesus
2. Matthew 3:1–7:29—The beginning of Jesus' ministry
   Discourse: Sermon on the Mount (Matt. 5:1–7:29)
3. Matthew 8:1–11:1—The authority of Jesus
   Discourse: Teaching on the mission of the disciples (Matt. 10:1–42)
4. Matthew 11:2–13:53—The coming of the kingdom of heaven
   Discourse: Parables of the kingdom (Matt. 13:1–52)
5. Matthew 13:54–19:2—Life in the community of believers
   Discourse: Forgiveness and the community (Matt. 18:1–35)
6. Matthew 19:3–26:2—Conflict between Jesus and the Jewish leaders
   Discourse: Teaching about the end time (Matt. 24:1–25:46)
7. Matthew 26:3–28:20—Passion and resurrection stories

This outline highlights five long discourses, which are interspersed with sections of narrative. Some Matthean scholars have suggested that these discourses are supposed to recall the five books of the Torah, a reminder of the Jewishness of this gospel.

Outlines like this one can be very helpful in providing some kind of map of the literature. However, they should always be used with care because outlines reflect particular interpretations of a literary work. For example, this outline presents Matthew as writing with a clear and deliberate literary plan in mind, and you can see this pattern of stories and speech quite clearly in the earlier chapters. However, when you get to chapters 10 through 24, you will observe that the pattern appears to break down a bit. The narrative sections are no longer so clearly distinguished from the teaching material. If the early chapters of Matthew's gospel had not disposed biblical scholars to look for these long discourses, they might not have come up with this theory that Matthew was writing in imitation of the five books of the Torah.

Despite such potential difficulties, outlines are important tools. In this case, it gives us a sense of the terrain of the gospel, providing some markers to get us started on our journey through Matthew. This particular outline helps to highlight the emphasis that Matthew places on portraying Jesus as paradigmatic teacher like Moses.

## GUIDE FOR INTERPRETING THE GOSPEL OF MATTHEW

Again, the goal of each of our textbook chapters is to give you the tools to read the New Testament on your own. Think of this chapter as the tour book that will assist you in making your way through Matthew's gospel. We will not be summarizing the contents of the Gospel of Matthew. Instead, we will offer some insights into interpreting infancy narratives, some clues to help you understand the Sermon on the Mount, and an overview of the major themes of the gospel. At the conclusion of this chapter, you will be invited to read Matthew's gospel for yourself. The "Questions for Reading" section will guide you.

## THE NATURE OF INFANCY NARRATIVES

**Infancy narratives** (stories about the births of important historical persons) are not unique to the gospels. For example, there is the story of the birth and infancy of Moses in the book of Exodus. It describes how the infant was saved from death at the hands of the Egyptian pharaoh when his mother hid him in the Nile River and how he was later rescued and raised by the pharaoh's daughter (Exod. 2:1–10). There is also a story about the miraculous birth of the philosopher Plato, whose parents tried and tried to conceive a child but could not. Finally, when they had given up all hope of becoming pregnant, she conceived by the god Apollo, and thus Plato was born (Diogenes Laertius, *Lives of the Eminent Philosophers* 3.1–2, 45). Setting aside the question of the historical accuracy of these stories, the one thing they have in common is that they explain how or why these people were destined for great things.

The same is true for the gospel stories of the birth and infancy of Jesus. While it might be interesting to know the historical details of Jesus' birth, we simply do not have evidence to make those determinations. However, we can uncover in the stories what the gospel writers intended to convey—namely, why Jesus was born and what he was destined to be and do for humanity. In other words, we can use the infancy narratives of the gospels to inquire about the *theological significance* of Jesus' birth. For Christians who read the gospels to inspire faith, this is the central question.

## MATTHEW'S STORY OF THE BIRTH OF JESUS

Matthew's gospel opens with a genealogy of Jesus' family, beginning with Abraham and ending with Jesus (Matt. 1:1–17). Today people research their genealogies, or family trees, because they want to learn more about their history but mostly because they enjoy the search. For example, someone might travel to a county courthouse, looking for birth, marriage, or death records of a family member, and suddenly discover that he or she had a great uncle that no one knew about. Now the hunt is on to find more information about this long-lost family member! For some, it can be a hobby that lasts a lifetime. However, in ancient cultures, and even today in cultures that have a strong sense of identity with their ancestors, people grew up knowing their genealogies. It was a way of saying, "This is who I am: the son of ——, who was the son of ——, who was the son of ——." As we might expect of patriarchal cultures, these family trees were almost always traced through fathers and sons. When women were included, it was because something very unusual or very significant happened on their account.

Matthew's report of Jesus' genealogy is arranged in a pattern of three groups of fourteen generations. Right away, this numerical pattern suggests that Matthew's first objective is not to give us a history lesson but to provide an explanation of Jesus' significance as the messiah of God. Although modern readers could not possibly guess on their own why fourteen generations were used, Matthew's original audience probably grasped the symbolism right away. The number 14 represents David's name in Hebrew numerology, a "science" that was popular among Jewish rabbis, in which numbers were associated with a person's name or an event to provide commentary on that person or event. Here is how it worked. Neither Hebrew nor Greek has a separate set of symbols for numerical values. Instead, their alphabets serve both functions. Take the name *David* in Hebrew. Transliterated it reads dvd. However, the letter d in dvd also represents the number 4, while the v is 6. Add up the numbers associated with each letter, and dvd becomes $4 + 6 + 4$, for a total of 14. In Hebrew numerology, this indicates that Jesus' destiny or purpose in life is somehow associated with David. By the way, people still use numerology today—based on their own alphabet, of course—to predict their futures or learn about their destinies.

As mentioned above, Matthew's account of the genealogy of Jesus begins with Abraham (Matt. 1:2). Later he uses the name of David and a reference to the Babylonian Exile to punctuate the three groups of fourteen generations (Matt. 1:6, 11–12). Abraham is significant because he was the one to whom God first made the promise that he would become a great nation (see Gen. 12:1–9). David is significant because he was considered to be the greatest king of Israel and the one to whom God promised an heir who would reign over an everlasting kingdom (see 2 Sam. 7:1–17). The Babylonian Exile is significant because it marked one of the lowest points of Jewish history, when God appeared to abandon his covenant with Israel. Thus, Matthew's genealogy presents Jesus as the promised messiah who is destined to be many times more than what David was for Israel and who will rescue them from disaster and restore the covenant first promised to Abraham.

The reader of Matthew's genealogy should notice that he includes five women in this long list of fathers and sons: Tamar; Ruth; Rahab; Bathsheba, the wife of Uriah; and Mary, the mother of Jesus. This is unusual for Matthew's gospel, which does not otherwise give much attention to women (in contrast to Luke's gospel, as we shall see). Who are these women? Why did Matthew include them here? Tamar was Judah's daughter-in-law and was sent back to her father's house when her husband died. Judah later raped her, thinking that she was a local temple prostitute. Ironically, it is one of her twin sons who continues the lineage to David (see Gen.

38:1–30). Tamar was not an Israelite, but neither was Rahab, the next woman in Matthew's genealogy of Jesus. She was a prostitute from Jericho who befriended and provided a hiding place for spies from Joshua's armies, allowing him to capture Jericho in his establishment of the Promised Land. Joshua's armies rescued her and her family when the city fell and brought them to live among the Israelites (see Josh. 2:1–21; 6:17–25). Rahab became the mother of Boaz, who is an important figure in the story of Ruth, the third woman in Matthew's genealogy.

Like Tamar and Rahab, Ruth was not an Israelite, but she married an Israelite. When her husband died, her widowed mother-in-law, Naomi, encouraged Ruth to go back to her family because she had no remaining male family members to care for her, but Ruth insisted on staying with Naomi. Eventually, they went to Bethlehem, where they met Boaz, a distant relative of Naomi, who married Ruth and provided her with a son named Obed, who became the father of Jesse and the grandfather of David (Ruth 1:1–18; 4:13–18). Perhaps you know this story. It is often used in Christian marriage ceremonies because of its famous statement of faithfulness until death: "Where you go, I will go; where you lodge, I will lodge. . . . Where you die, I will die" (Ruth 1:16–17).

Next comes Bathsheba, who is known in Matthew's genealogy only as the wife of Uriah. Perhaps this is a reminder of David's sin in arranging for her husband's death after David learned that she was carrying his child. David was having an affair with her while Uriah was away fighting in the war (2 Sam. 11:1–26). Finally, when Joseph is named as "the husband of Mary, of whom Jesus is born" (Matt. 1:16)—not the father of Jesus—it becomes quite clear that Matthew is trying to say that Mary shares something in common with these other four women. All of these women had extraordinary marital unions, but all played key roles in the plan of salvation. Without them, the messiah would not have been born!

After the genealogy, Matthew describes the story of Mary's extraordinary impregnation and Jesus' subsequent birth (Matt. 1:18–25). Mary and Joseph were already engaged; that is, their families had already contracted with one another to join their children in marriage. Thanks to social science criticism, we know something about first-century cultural expectations concerning marriage, which can help us appreciate the significance of this story. For example, Matthew does not tell us how old Mary and Joseph were at the time of their engagement, but we know that these arrangements were usually made by the time the children reached the age of ten or twelve. The marriage itself usually took place when the girl was twelve to fifteen years old and the boy was fifteen to twenty years old. The children probably had little to say about their families' marriage arrangements, and the engagement contract was considered just as binding as the marriage contract, so a family that wanted to break an engagement was obligated to go through the procedures of divorce. Also, there were very severe sanctions against women who were involved in sexual activity outside of marriage, whether voluntary or forced, because it was considered a violation of a father's or a husband's property.

Matthew's gospel provides an interesting portrait of Joseph as well. He is described as "righteous" because he wanted to divorce Mary *quietly* when he found out that she was pregnant (Matt. 1:19). What is the significance of this detail? He and his family could have demanded very serious consequences for this violation of their honor: public humiliation of Mary's family, at least, and perhaps even Mary's death.

Thus, Joseph is willing to risk his own honor to spare Mary such harm. But then an angel appears to Joseph to explain the plan of salvation that will unfold on account of Mary. "The child conceived in her is from the Holy Spirit," he tells Joseph. "She will bear a son, and you are to name him Jeshua" (literally, "God saves") (Matt. 1:20–21). In this way, Matthew describes Jesus' origins—conceived as Son of God and born of a virgin mother.

Finally, Matthew reinforces and enhances the message of this infancy narrative by incorporating a quotation from the Old Testament prophet Isaiah to indicate that, far from a source of embarrassment, Mary's conception of Jesus should be seen as part of God's plan of salvation.

> All this took place to fulfill what had been spoken by the Lord through the prophet: "Look, the virgin shall conceive and bear a son and they shall name him Emmanuel." (Matt. 1:22–23; cf. Isa. 7:14)

The name **Emmanuel,** also spelled Immanuel, means "God-with-us." Throughout Matthew's gospel, you will find a number of Old Testament quotations like this one. Matthew introduces each one with a phrase like the one you see above: "All this took place to fulfill what had been spoken . . . through the prophet" (Matt. 1:23). For this reason, biblical scholars often call them **fulfillment citations**.

Roman Catholics have used Matthew's story of the conception and birth of Jesus as a basis for the doctrine (i.e., teaching) about the perpetual virginity of Mary. The phrase "perpetual virginity" implies that Mary was a virgin before the birth of Jesus and remained a virgin after his birth. Against popular misconceptions, the writer of this gospel did not intend the statement "he had no marital relations with her until she had borne a son" (Matt. 1:25) to be a description of Mary and Joseph's sex life but rather a *theological statement* about Jesus' divine origin and his unique status as the only Son of God. Later, as Christians began to develop the notion of original sin to explain the human condition, especially its tendency toward sinfulness and the inevitability of suffering, as something humanity inherited on account of the sin of Adam and Eve (Gen. 3:1–24), Matthew's story of the conception of Jesus explains (theologically) how the Son of God can be fully human and yet untouched by original sin.

Like Matthew's story of Jesus' conception, his stories of the magi (Matt. 2:1–12) and the massacre of the babies of Bethlehem (Matt. 2:13–18) provide a theological interpretation of Jesus' identity and the role he was destined to fulfill. The **magi**, sometimes translated "astrologers," were scholars of the esoteric sciences (e.g., magic, astrology, dream interpretation) from the East, perhaps Persia or some other place in the Orient. We can assume that they were Gentiles, not Jews, so it is significant that Matthew describes them as the first to encounter Jesus. And already they know something of his destiny. The magi describe Jesus as "king of the Jews," which is consistent with Matthew's emphasis on Jesus as royal messiah (see the discussion of genealogy above), but this title also anticipates the mockery by the soldiers at his crucifixion, when they dress Jesus in a scarlet robe and put a crown of thorns on his head (Matt. 27:29). It also anticipates the scene in which Pontius Pilate commands that the inscription "the King of the Jews" be placed on the cross (Matt. 27:37). Finally, these the words that the mocking crowds use when they call for Jesus to come down from the

## SOURCE CRITICISM AND REDACTION CRITICISM AS TOOLS TO BETTER UNDERSTAND MATTHEW 1:23

The author of Matthew's gospel alerts his readers to the use of a written source when he writes, "All this took place to fulfill what was spoken by the Lord through the prophet" (Matt. 1:23). Since the use of chapter and verse numbers in biblical books is a much later development, the gospel writer could not use these to tell his readers the exact location of his quotation. Instead, he would have had to depend on his readers' knowledge of the writings of the prophet Isaiah. However, when source critics seek to locate Matthew's quotations from the Old Testament, they cannot always be sure even what version of the Old Testament he was using. Sometimes he appears to be using a Hebrew text; at other times, he may have been using a Greek translation or even an Aramaic version of the Old Testament.

The Hebrew version of this quotation from Isaiah reads as follows: "The young (or newly married) woman (*alma*) will conceive and bear a son, and she will call his name Emmanuel (God-with-us)" (Isa. 7:14). However, in this case, biblical scholars have argued that Matthew probably took this quotation from a Greek translation of Isaiah, since, instead of "young (or newly married) woman," he uses the technical term for virgin—*parthenos*—which is also found in the Septuagint version of Isaiah that is available to us today. This wording may have appealed to Matthew because it asserts, in very concrete language, his conviction about God's intervention in history through the conception and birth of Jesus.

But was this the original intended meaning of Isaiah 7:14? When we read this section of Isaiah, we soon discover that Isaiah gave this prophecy as a sign to King Ahaz (735–715 B.C.E.), when he was facing attack from neighboring kings after he had refused to join them in alliance against the Assyrian powers that were threatening their lands. Should he follow Isaiah's advice and stand firm, refusing all alliances and trusting God's power to protect them? As "proof" that his advice was trustworthy, Isaiah gave Ahaz this sign concerning a woman in his harem: "[T]he young woman is with child and shall bear a son, and shall name him Immanuel" (Isa. 7:14). Immanuel means "God-with-us." This much is clear: The Isaiah prophecy in its original context says nothing about Jesus. However, both the announcement of the child's birth and the assignment of the name Immanuel recall God's covenant with Israel. Perhaps this is why Matthew was attracted to the quotation. He saw the birth of Jesus as the fulfillment of God's covenant with David, and the name Immanuel richly expressed his conviction that Jesus is "God with us."

In sum, Matthew's story of the conception of Jesus is a great example of theology in story form, and who doesn't love a great story!

cross (Matt. 27:42). Surely Matthew's audience understood the irony of the magi's words, since they knew the whole story of Jesus' life!

The magi's gifts are rather puzzling, and Matthew gives us no clues about their intended meaning, but later Christian tradition associated the three gifts with kingship (gold), divinity (frankincense), and suffering (myrrh)—three important aspects of the identity of Jesus as the Christ. Moreover, frankincense was used for burial, and myrrh was a powerful painkiller. Both of these details hang like a "dark cloud" over this otherwise sweet Christmas scene because the reader knows that this gospel will eventually include the story of Jesus' suffering and death.

Matthew's infancy narratives also contain a story about Jesus and his family fleeing to Egypt to avoid Herod the Great, who wanted to kill Jesus. To explain how this story fits into God's plan of salvation, Matthew adds that it was "to fulfill what had been spoken by the Lord through the prophet: 'Out of Egypt I have called my son'" (Matt. 2:15; cf. Hos. 11:1). This is a reference to the story of Moses and the Exodus. Likewise, the massacre of the infants of Bethlehem is a reminder of the massacre of the Hebrew children at the time Moses was born, but Matthew associates it with a quotation from the prophet Jeremiah to add another layer of meaning: Rachel's sadness over the exile (Jer. 31:15). Rachel was Jacob's favorite wife, the mother of Joseph and Benjamin, and it was on account of Joseph that the Hebrew peoples came to Egypt in the first place. However, Jacob's other name was Israel—the same as the nation of Israel—so Rachel's weeping over her children becomes, for Jeremiah (and now Matthew), a symbol of Israel's grief over the Babylonian Exile (and ultimately the exile of the Holy Family). Thus, by incorporating these two Old

*Adoration of the Magi* by Sandro Botticelli (Florentine, 15th century). The story of the magi who come to greet the newborn Jesus is told only in the Gospel of Matthew.

Testament quotations, Matthew makes the point that Jesus, likewise, went through an exodus *and* he came back from an exile. He is the new Moses and the one who will be God's instrument in saving the people from their sin.

## JESUS, THE TEACHER LIKE MOSES

Because Matthew's infancy narratives introduce Jesus as another Moses, we should not be surprised that Matthew also focuses on Jesus as the teacher and lawgiver, attributes that were traditionally associated with Moses. Moses is the one who encountered God on Mount Sinai and received the Law (the obligations of the covenant), which it became his responsibility to communicate to the people. Meanwhile the people, whom Moses left at the foot of the mountain, began to say among themselves that Moses was not returning and that they should make gods for themselves, which they did (Exod. 32:1–34). Unfortunately, they failed in their devotion to the God of their ancestors, not just this one time but also many other times during their desert wanderings, and they complained against God, who gave them manna from heaven and water from the rock (Exod. 16–17). Contrast this story with Matthew's story of the beginning of Jesus' ministry. The Spirit leads Jesus into the wilderness, where he fasts for forty days and is tested by Satan. Notice that Satan even debates scripture with him! (Matt. 4:1–11). At the end of the forty days—a number symbolizing transition and transformation—Jesus emerges triumphant from his desert testing, having reversed the pattern established by the Israelites' sinfulness.

## MATTHEW'S SERMON ON THE MOUNT

The story of Jesus' temptation in the wilderness is Matthew's introduction to the Sermon on the Mount (Matt. 5:1–7:28), the first and best known of the five long discourses in this gospel. The setting for Jesus' sermon is an unnamed mountain. The disciples form an "inner circle" around Jesus; the crowds are the "outer circle." Jesus takes the "sitting" position, the position of teacher. From here, he gives a new or fuller interpretation of God's covenant Law. Thus, the unnamed mountain recalls Sinai, the mountain of revelation, and Jesus is presented as the new Moses.

In terms of content, Matthew's Sermon on the Mount constitutes a new covenant ethic for his mostly Jewish Christian audience, who understood themselves in some way as reformers within Judaism, not as founders of a new religion. The sermon affirms the basic validity of Torah (Law), though it makes no mention of the necessity of circumcision (i.e., ritual cutting of the foreskin of a Jewish male as symbol of God's covenant with Abraham's people; see Gen. 17:9–14), and it calls its hearers to greater righteousness within the Law. Again, Law does not describe a set of regulations in this context but rather a covenant relationship with God. In sum, the principles for this new ethic are firmly rooted in the covenant relationship that God established with the Israelites through Moses.

The Sermon on the Mount is long, spanning three chapters of the Gospel of Matthew, and somewhat cumbersome, because it does not have a thesis and supporting arguments like some of us might expect in a speech. Rather, it consists almost entirely of a collection of sayings held together by common themes or similar forms. A brief outline of the sermon is given below so that you can pick out its major parts.

A. Matthew 5:3–16—Introduction: beatitudes and sayings on salt and light
B. Matthew 5:17–7:12—Covenant ethic
  1. Basic legal principles (5:17–20)
  2. Six antitheses (5:21–48)
  3. Works of piety (6:1–18)
  4. Further instructions ending with the Golden Rule (6:19–7:12)
C. Matthew 7:13–27—Conclusion

Anyone who has ever heard of the Sermon on the Mount is probably familiar with its opening statements, usually called the **beatitudes**. These are the statements that begin "Blessed are you . . . " or "Happy is the one. . . . " They can be found throughout the New Testament, but only here and in Luke's Sermon on the Plain (Luke 6:17–49) do we find a series of beatitudes used to introduce ethical teaching. In general, beatitudes express divine approval of certain attitudes or behaviors on the part of God's holy ones. They also have an "already, though not yet" quality to them. That is, they carry a hope and an expectation that blessings are already becoming reality or will become reality in the very near future, even though the current situation of those to whom the beatitude is addressed might not be particularly joyous.

Sometimes biblical scholars describe Matthew's beatitudes as a spiritual ethic. However, we must be careful not to conclude that Matthew's Jesus is calling people to a privatized "me and Jesus" way of life. Rather, as the rest of the sermon confirms, Matthew's beatitudes are focused on doing good deeds with the right attitude. For example, "Blessed are the poor in spirit" (Matt. 5:3) means that we ought to be poor *in the right way*—that is, with an attitude of complete detachment. The beatitude "Blessed are those who mourn" (Matt. 5:4) means that we must take seriously the Law's obligation to bury the dead. We can't say, "It's not my problem." Likewise, although Judaism has a long and rich tradition of working for justice, Matthew's beatitude says, "Blessed are those who *hunger and thirst* for justice" (Matt. 5:6). In other words, working for justice cannot be something we do when it is convenient or it makes us feel good. Rather, we have to have a "matter of life and death" passion for justice. This is the greater righteousness.

Likewise, the six antitheses (the statements that are built around the phrases "You have heard that it was said . . . " and "But I say to you . . . "; see Matt. 5:21–48) should be understood in the sense of fulfilling the full meaning of the Law, not contradicting or negating it. Thus, the first half of the antithesis, the "You have heard that it was said" statement, is a reiteration of Torah and the second half of the antithesis, the "But I say to you" statement, is Jesus' reinterpretation of Torah, which includes even those kinds of behaviors or dispositions that could lead to an infraction of Torah. For example, Torah says that people should not kill. Matthew's Jesus articulates the full meaning of the Law by saying, "Do not even harbor anger against your neighbor." The Jewish rabbis called this "making a fence around

Torah." Note the use of hyperbole—that is, exaggeration designed to make the reader take notice and consider the matter seriously. The six antitheses, which represent the Matthean Jesus' interpretation of Torah Law, are summarized below:

- The Law not only forbids murder. It even forbids expressions of anger toward another (Matt. 5:21–26)
- The Law prohibits adultery in deed, but it also prohibits adultery in thought (Matt. 5:27–30)
- The Law says that the divorced wife has a right to a document of dismissal (for her protection and so that she can marry again). But the Law intends that the marriage bond is indissoluble. Therefore, the husband who is responsible for the divorce is guilty of adultery (Matt. 5:31–32)
- The Law forbids the taking of oaths, because it involves pronouncing the divine name aloud, but if one speaks the truth simply there is no need even to take an oath (Matt. 5:33–37)
- The Law places limits on retaliation—the injured party can demand no more than payment in kind for what was done to him—but the better righteousness is to respond with nonviolence (Matt. 5:38–42)
- The Law requires love of neighbor but, just as God allows his benevolence to extend to everyone, the Law ought also to include love of enemies (Matt. 5: 43–48)

Similar to the way that Matthew's Jesus reinterprets the Law, the sermon's message concerning the three major aspects of Jewish piety (i.e., religious activity)—almsgiving, prayer, and fasting—constitutes a Jewish rabbi's interpretation of what righteousness means. The Gospel of Matthew's teachings on piety are summarized below:

- Almsgiving. Almsgiving means giving charity for the needy. Ordinarily, this was something very public and highly valued and praised, but now they are told to do it in secret. The gospel writer's concern is purity of intention.
- Prayer. Matthew's Jesus is not against synagogue worship, but now people are told to worship in private. The gospel writer's concern is sincere and personal communion with God.
- Fasting. Fasting is the discipline of restricting your food intake or denying yourself other pleasures as a way of humbling yourself before God and preparing yourself for prayer. The gospel writer's concern is again purity of intention. Fasting should be directed toward God, not used to draw attention to yourself.

Just to clarify, Matthew is not saying that people should discard these religious practices. Rather, he is using hyperbole to challenge those who know well they are required to give alms, pray, and fast and to do so with purity of intention.

Finally, the conclusion of the sermon confirms what we have already heard many times—Matthew's Jesus does not intend to throw out the ideals of Judaism but rather to get to the heart of their meaning and make them applicable to people's everyday lives. Thus, the conclusion also reaffirms another theme of the sermon: greater righteousness. Three points are worthy of note:

- The "two ways" teaching concerning the wide gate and the narrow gate (Matt. 7:13–14) is very Jewish. The theme is used frequently in Jewish literature for the purpose of moral teaching. Only the fool would take the wide gate or the way of destruction.

- Prophecy is also a typically Jewish phenomenon (Matt. 7:15–20). Notice that Matthew is concerned about *regulating* prophecy, not abolishing it.

- The references to the last judgment reaffirm that only genuine love of God and justice toward all, and not just nice words or lofty deeds, will be rewarded (Matt. 7:21–27). In other words, it is not sufficient to say the right words or do the things that get you noticed. In fact, these things may actually backfire and become your condemnation! Instead, the Christian believer must live out the full meaning of the Law without concern for honor or personal gain.

Thus, Matthew's Sermon on the Mount is an interpretation of the covenant ethic of Moses that calls for greater righteousness. It also reflects the belief of some early Christians that Christianity was not intended to be a new independent religion but rather was a reform movement from within Judaism itself.

## MATTHEW'S TEACHING ON THE KINGDOM OF HEAVEN

Each of the gospels of the New Testament mentions the **kingdom of God** or, in Matthew's case, the **kingdom of heaven**. In Mark's gospel, Jesus' first words of preaching are about the kingdom: "The time is fulfilled, and the kingdom of God has come near" (Mark 1:15; cf. Matt. 3:2). Where or what is this kingdom? Certainly, it is not located in an earthly place, as one might speak of the British Empire or the kingdom of Morocco. However, it should not to be equated with Christian notions of heaven either. Perhaps we get a clearer understanding of the concept of the kingdom of God or kingdom of heaven if we think in terms of the reign of God. The gospels proclaim the reign of God on earth, which is manifested in the coming of the Son, in the Spirit's presence among us, and in the conviction that God's grace is greater than all the powers of evil in the world. In other words, the kingdom of God is about a time when God's sovereignty (i.e., power and authority) is fully manifest in the world.

Matthew 11:1–13:53 describes what the author and his community expect to see in the coming of the kingdom of heaven. When John the Baptist's disciples come asking whether Jesus is the messiah, Matthew's Jesus responds: "Go and tell John what you hear and see: the blind receive their sight, the lame walk, . . . the dead are raised and the poor have the good news brought to them" (Matt. 11:4–5). This is the in-breaking of the kingdom of heaven, the manifestation of the reign of God over the forces of evil in the world. Matthew's Jesus goes on to warn about the kinds of problems that the kingdom will encounter in its coming—it will suffer violence—and to condemn those people who refuse to repent after seeing the signs of the kingdom

(Matt. 11:11–24). Those who take these words to heart know that this coming of the kingdom will not be easy! However, they should also be encouraged because, in the end, God will triumph over all the forces of evil.

## Parables and Their Interpretations

Matthew's Jesus uses parables to further describe the nature of the kingdom of heaven. In fact, the third major discourse in this gospel is made up mostly of parables. The classical definition of a **parable** comes from the biblical scholar C. H. Dodd. He describes a parable as "a metaphor or simile drawn from nature or common life, arresting the hearer by its vividness or strangeness, and leaving the mind in sufficient doubt about its precise application to tease it into active thought" (1961, 5).

In order to better understand this definition, let us investigate it in its parts. First of all, a parable is a metaphor or simile, that is, a comparison. Thus, parables can often be identified by their characteristic introductory formula—"The kingdom of heaven is like . . . " or "The kingdom of God can be compared to. . . . " Second, parables employ imagery from nature or common life—that is, things that people know and understand. In first-century agrarian cultures, these things involved farming, sheepherding, bread baking, and fishing. Of course, this aspect of parables is problematic for some of us today because the imagery can be strange and unfamiliar. Today's readers might do better if the parables were about computers, cell phones, supermarkets, office jobs, and airplane travel!

Third, the effectiveness of a parable depends on the hearer being able to appreciate the "twist" or "surprise" of the story. Parables are riddles—a very ordinary situation ends in a very extraordinary way. Their "twist" is designed to make the listener sit up and take notice. Again, the modern reader can sometimes be at a disadvantage. When Matthew's Jesus compares the one who hears the word of the kingdom to good soil, yielding a thirty, sixty, or hundredfold harvest (Matt. 13:1–23), the contemporary reader who has little experience of farming might simply conclude, "Hearing God's word and acting upon it is a good thing." What the reader will fail to appreciate is the unimaginable level of productivity that is promised here. A harvest of thirtyfold means that, on average, every seed that is planted germinates and every plant produces thirty grains of fruit (barley or wheat, perhaps). Even in high-technology farming regions today, this would be considered an excellent crop. Consider, then, what first-century subsistence farmers would have thought when they heard this parable. They would have been shaking their heads, muttering "Impossible!"

Whether we are reading Matthew's gospel or another of the synoptic gospels, there are a few things we should keep in mind when we read and try to interpret parables. First, parables are concise *fictional* narratives. Insofar as they are stories, they have a plot and characters, but they are not accounts of actual historical events, and they seldom have a single meaning. Another thing to know about parables is that they are not context specific. That is, if you lift the story from its literary context and place it in a new context, its meaning will change somewhat to accommodate the new context. Therefore, in order to properly understand the message of a parable, you need to study carefully the introduction and conclusion that the gospel writer has provided for it. Additionally, because the gospel writer is responsible for the parable's introduction and conclusion, you should not assume that it has exactly the same meaning in the gospel as it had when the parable was first taught.

Third, parables intentionally have multiple interpretations, but like any simile or metaphor, the imagery cannot be pushed to the extreme. In other words, you cannot expect to assign meaning to every element of the story or to push the comparisons of the parable further than their immediate meanings. If you do, the metaphor may yield some rather strange results. Finally, the reader of the gospels should remember that each gospel writer incorporated the parables of Jesus into his gospel for different reasons. Mark portrays Jesus as teaching in parables in order to "harden the hearts" of outsiders (Mark 4:10–11). This is probably the *last* thing we think of when we ask the question, Why did Jesus teach in parables? However, in Mark's gospel, it makes sense. In contrast, Luke's parables are better described as example stories because they are used to illustrate Jesus' teaching, not to hide their message from others. Compare these two perspectives on the purpose of parables to that in Matthew's gospel, which presents Jesus as teaching in parables as a fulfillment of Isaiah's prophecy about people who listen but do not understand (Matt. 13:10–17; see Isa. 6:9–10). For Matthew's Jesus, some will hear and understand the parables and others will not—that's just the way it is—but in the end, whatever happens is all part of God's plan.

What then does Matthew's parables chapter (Matt. 13:1–53) teach about the kingdom of heaven? Basically, it is a message of encouragement and a call to action. Matthew teaches that the kingdom of heaven will triumph over every obstacle, despite poor soil, evil weeds, and even the tiniest of beginnings. Matthew's gospel also teaches that the kingdom is worth the struggle; like a great treasure or a fine pearl, it should be sought at all costs.

## THE ESTABLISHMENT OF THE CHURCH

While Jesus himself did not seek to establish a Christian church separate from Judaism, Matthew's gospel does describe how the church (i.e., the community of believers) should live in anticipation of the coming kingdom of heaven. Among the gospels, the word *church* appears only in the Gospel of Matthew. However, we need to be careful not to apply current imagery and ideas about church to Matthew's world. When we talk about church, we usually think of institutions and buildings, but in Matthew's gospel, the Greek word is **ecclesia**, meaning "assembly." This is where we get our English adjective *ecclesiastical*, which means "church-related"—as in *ecclesiastical office*. In contrast with our contemporary models of church—clergy, buildings, and organizational structures—Matthew understood the church as the assembly or community of believers. The term is thought to have connections with the notion of the Jewish synagogue, which also means "assembly."

Matthew 16:13–19 is an important text for understanding Matthew's concept of church. It begins with Simon Peter's confession (i.e., profession of faith) that Jesus is the messiah and Son of God. Matthew's Jesus describes Peter's words as a revelation from God, not something that Peter was able to discern on his own. He then renames Simon, calling him Cephas (Aramaic; the Greek term is *Petros*) or Peter

Statue depicting the confession of Peter near the Franciscan chapel of the Primacy of Peter, located near Tabgha on the northwestern shore of the Sea of Galilee. Photo by Catherine Cory.

(cf. Mark 3:16; Luke 6:14; John 1:42). Traditionally, a name change meant a change in destiny and that appears to be the case here as well. Using a play on words, Matthew's Jesus continues, "You are *Petros* (translated, "Peter") and on this *petra* (translated, "rock") I will build my *ecclesia* (translated, "church") (Matt. 16:18). The church, he says, will stand strong against the forces of evil and never be overcome. Peter, he says, will be given the keys (i.e., controlling access) to the kingdom and his "binding and loosing" will be effective in heaven as it is on earth.

Scholars are sharply divided on the meaning of these statements. Who or what is the "rock" on which the church is built? Is it Peter? Is it Jesus? Or is it an attitude of perseverance and faith that makes the church strong? Roman Catholics interpret the text in such a way that Peter is the rock and the one on whom the church was established. Thus, it is the text that Catholics use to support the notion of papal primacy—that is, the view that the pope, the bishop of Rome, is the first among all the bishops and the successor of Peter. For Christian churches that do not accept the authority of the pope, this interchange between Jesus and Peter is interpreted in a variety of other ways, all of which are possible because of slight ambiguities in the Greek text. For example, one could take Jesus' words about building the church on rocky ground simply to mean that the community of believers should be confident that it will endure because it can depend on God's protection, regardless of who its leader might be.

Likewise, scholars are unclear about the meaning of Matthew's statement about "binding and loosing." A similar saying in John's gospel makes it clear that the binding and loosing is about forgiveness of sin (John 20:23). But what did Matthew intend? In the section immediately preceding this story, Matthew's Jesus warns about the teaching of the Pharisees and Sadducees (Matt. 16:1–12), and later he criticizes the scribes and Pharisees for "locking" people out of the kingdom (Matt. 23:13). In light of these two statements, the New Testament scholar Raymond Brown suggested that the "binding and loosing" should be understood in terms of the activities of the rabbis, who taught and guided their communities in observance of Jewish law (1973, 95–101). In other words, we should see Peter as the chief rabbi of the Christian community, who guides his community in the observance of Jesus' law of greater righteousness. Of course, this perspective on Peter belongs to the time of the Matthew's community rather than to the time of Jesus.

## RECONCILIATION IN THE COMMUNITY

Matthew 18 is the fourth major discourse of this gospel. It is an important chapter for Christian theology because of its teaching on the attributes of church. It describes how the early Christian assembly and its leaders should function as a community of faith and what its priorities should be, namely, forgiveness and reconciliation. The discourse begins with a teaching about who is greatest in the kingdom of heaven, and Matthew's Jesus tells his audience that only those who become humble like a child can enter the kingdom (Matt. 18:1–5). Notice that the discourse is addressed to the disciples, the eventual leaders of Christian communities, and not simply the crowds. He warns them about being a stumbling block or causing scandal for God's little ones (Matt. 18:6–7). Using a bit of hyperbole, he also impresses on them the seriousness of this offense by saying that it is better for them to cut off a hand or foot than let themselves be a cause of scandal (Matt. 18:8–9).

Likewise, the parable of the lost sheep (Matt. 18:10–14) is addressed to the community leaders. Matthew's Jesus tells them that they are responsible for seeking out those who have strayed from the community. However, he also indicates that these shepherds (the community leaders) may not be successful and that some of those who have gone astray will not return. As a consequence, what follows is a teaching on how to handle a situation when someone refuses to heed the correction of the community. The answer? You need to work until you exhaust *every* possibility (Matt. 18:15–20). Finally, Matthew concludes the chapter with a lengthy parable that acts as a warning to those who refuse to forgive other members of the community (Matt.

18:21–34). One can only imagine the power of such communities of reconciliation. They are, as the opening of this discourse suggests, a "first taste" of the kingdom of heaven!

## DISCIPLESHIP

When we compare Matthew's portrayal of the disciples to Mark's, we notice right away that Matthew describes them in a much more positive light. They are no longer the ignorant, bumbling, and hard-hearted people whom Jesus had to bring along "kicking and screaming." Rather, they are open and willing, if not always understanding. For example, in the story of Jesus stilling a storm (Mark 4:35–41; Matt. 8:23–27), Mark portrays the disciples as complaining that Jesus doesn't care about their safety and Jesus as scolding them for their lack of faith. When Jesus successfully calms the sea, Mark describes them as responding with "a great fear." Matthew changes the disciples' complaint to a plea for Jesus to save them. He also presents the disciples as marveling at what they have experienced.

Another difference between Matthew's and Mark's portrayal of the disciples is that Matthew highlights Peter, sometimes as the model disciple and as the first among equals. Peter is the spokesman for the disciples, answering Jesus' questions and making requests on their behalf (e.g., Matt. 15:15; 18:21). He is also the one to whom people go when they wish to question Jesus or make a request of him (e.g., Matt. 17:24–25). Mark does not show such favoritism to Peter. However, as we shall see in its concluding chapters, Matthew's gospel does not rehabilitate the disciples entirely. Although Peter is positively portrayed in much of the gospel, he still denies Jesus, even with an oath (Matt. 26:69–75; cf. Mark 14:53–72). Likewise, Matthew still describes the other disciples as fleeing when Jesus is arrested (Matt. 26:56; cf. Mark 14:50).

Through its portrayal of Peter and the other disciples, Matthew's gospel says that Jesus continues to stand with his fallible disciples. The term *disciple* means "follower" or "one who learns from a master teacher." At the conclusion of this gospel, the risen Christ meets his disciples again on the mountain and sends them out to "make disciples of all nations" (Matt. 28:19). Thus, they become Jesus' apostles in the world. The term *apostle* means "one who is sent." But they need not fear. Matthew's Jesus, the one called Emmanuel (God-with-us) before he was born, promises them, "I am with you always, to the end of the age" (Matt. 28:20; cf. Matt. 1:23).

## WOE TO YOU HYPOCRITES!

Beginning readers of Matthew's gospel might be taken by surprise by the abrasive language that Jesus uses against the Sadducees, Pharisees, and scribes in the fifth major section of this gospel (Matt. 23:1–36). Matthew's Jesus strongly warns his disciples and followers, saying, "Do whatever they teach and follow it, but do not do as they do" (Matt. 23:3). Calling them hypocrites and blind guides, he charges them with practicing their religion for show so that others will think they are righteous but failing at the more important matters of Jewish Law—"justice and mercy and faith" (Matt. 23:23). Perhaps you have already noticed that these are the same themes that we saw in the Sermon on the Mount (Matt. 5–7), namely, greater righteousness and purity of intention. Thus, it is possible to think of this harsh rhetoric as part of the gospel's larger agenda of reform within Judaism because the elite of Jerusalem would have had both access and power to make change, but they also had the potential to be the greatest obstacle to change.

However, there may be something more going on here in Matthew's gospel. Even though biblical scholars are quite certain that Matthew's gospel was written by a Jewish Christian for a Jewish Christian audience, other parts of the gospel have what appears to be a very strong anti-Jewish message. Take, for example, the scene in which Jesus is brought to trial before Pontius Pilate (Matt. 27:11–23). Pilate wants to release Jesus but doesn't know how to handle the crowds, so he announces publicly that he is not responsible for Jesus' death. The crowd answers, "His blood be on us and on our children" (Matt. 27:25). Later, after Jesus' burial, the Jewish leaders demand that Pilate place a guard at the tomb, and when Pilate refuses, they place their own Temple guard there (Matt. 27:62–66). Matthew also recounts a rumor that had been circulating among the Jews suggesting that the guards had been bribed to lie about what had happened at the tomb early that Sunday morning (Matt. 28:11–15). And even earlier in the story, Matthew's Jesus makes several references to the synagogue as "their" synagogue, as if consciously excluding himself from association with these other Jews (Matt. 4:23; 9:35; 10:17; 12:9; 13:54; cf. Matt. 23:34).

Scholars are still divided over how to make sense of this apparently anti-Jewish bias in Matthew's gospel. However, what we are probably seeing is a story alongside or on top of another story. You might call it a "two-story" story. Matthew tells the story of Jesus, which took place some fifty years earlier, but on top of that story, he provides little glimpses of the story of the Christian community for which he was writing in his own time. For whatever reasons, the relationship between Jewish Christians, or Christian Jews, and their Jewish brothers and sisters had become extremely tense, even to the point of persecution by the dominant group. The majority Jews would have viewed these Christian Jews as threatening their Jewish way of life and therefore might have tried to force them back into conformity. Matthew gives voice to his own and his community's frustrations by incorporating responses to their persecution into his story of the life of Jesus. In other words, what we see here are the remnants of a big family fight—among Jews and Christian Jews—and not a message of hatred against all Jews. Anything else would be inconsistent with the rest of the gospel, which clearly locates Jesus and his disciples within Jewish tradition and practice.

## THE COMING OF THE END

As Matthew understands it, the fulfillment of the kingdom of heaven is something still in the future. This is the subject of the fifth discourse (Matt. 24–25). This discourse has some similarities with the Little Apocalypse of Mark's gospel (Mark 13:5–37). The earliest Christians believed that the *parousia* (the "coming") of the Son of Man, an event that they understood to mark the arrival of the end time, would occur very soon after Jesus' resurrection. However, when some twenty years or more had passed, people began to wonder. Matthew's gospel addresses this question by suggesting that Christians who just sit and wait for the coming of the end time, when God will come and rescue them, are in for a big surprise!

In order to make this point about the delay of the end time, Matthew adds three parables and a "last judgment" scene to the latter half of his "apocalypse" (Matt. 24:36–25:46). He talks about the rewards that will come to a faithful servant and the punishments that will be inflicted on a wicked servant (Matt. 24:45–51). He also talks about five foolish virgins who are excluded from the wedding banquet because they didn't have enough oil to keep their lamps burning through the night (Matt. 25:1–13) and about a frightened servant who was severely punished for hiding and not taking a risk with the money his master had given him to invest (Matt. 25:14–30). Finally, Matthew's Jesus describes a "sheep and goats" judgment scene in which the criteria for reward and punishment must have sounded quite surprising! Those who are given the right to enter into the heavenly kingdom are those who have cared for the littlest ones of society—the poor, the hungry, the homeless, and those in prison (Matt. 25:31–46). In other words, if you sit around doing nothing as you wait for the coming of the end, you may well find yourself among the goats.

## TESTIMONY TO JESUS' RESURRECTION

Matthew's gospel tells the story of Jesus' resurrection using some of the same details found in Mark's version. However, Matthew also addresses one important question that must have been nagging at people, both believers and nonbelievers: Maybe someone simply stole Jesus' body? The story about the guards posted at Jesus' tomb functions as "proof" that his disciples could not have entered the tomb unnoticed and dragged out his corpse (Matt. 27:62–66). Of course, the larger underlying question is, How do we know for certain that Jesus was raised from the dead? The resurrection of Jesus is one of the basic tenets of the Christian faith, yet none of the gospels claims to be able to give eyewitness testimony to the actual event of the resurrection. Matthew addresses this question by adding two stories about the appearance of the risen Jesus—first to the women at the tomb (Matt. 28:1–10) and later to the disciples (Matt. 28:16–20). In Luke's gospel, we shall see that he also includes stories about the risen Jesus, even about witnesses who saw him eat and were invited to touch him (Luke 24:36–43). In other words, it was not a ghost that they saw, but Jesus truly is raised from the dead.

## KEY TERMS

| | | |
|---|---|---|
| Extant | Magi | Parable |
| Infancy narratives | Beatitudes | Ecclesia |
| Emmanuel | Kingdom of | Disciple |
| Fulfillment citations | God/heaven | Apostle |

## QUESTIONS FOR READING

Read the Gospel of Matthew. Use evidence from the text to answer the following questions.

1. Read carefully Matthew's story of the events surrounding Jesus' birth (Matt. 1:1–2:23). Make a list of details that surprised you. Make another list of Christmas stories that you expected to find here—but did not. Make a third list of events surrounding the birth of Jesus that Matthew understood to be fulfillment of Old Testament prophecies. What overall impressions do you get from Matthew's stories of the birth of Jesus?

2. What is the point of Matthew's description of the escape of Mary, Joseph, and Jesus to Egypt and their later return to Nazareth (Matt. 2:13–23)? How does Matthew make his point?

3. In the story about Jesus' temptation in the wilderness (Matt. 4:1–11), what are the three temptations or challenges that Jesus successfully overcomes? How does he overcome them?

4. From Matthew's Sermon on the Mount (Matt. 5:1–7:29), find at least two teachings in which Jesus calls his listeners to a "greater righteousness"—that is, not simply to observe the basic requirements of Jewish Law but also to fulfill its fuller intended meaning. Provide a brief explanation of each.

5. Examine the miracle stories that are recounted in Matthew 8:1–9:38. In what ways are these miracle stories similar to or different from the miracle stories recorded in Mark's gospel? Look, for example, at the kinds of miracles contained here, the order of their appearance in the gospel, and the role of faith in these miracle stories. *Hint:* Using your Bible's cross-references or a gospel synopsis can save you a lot of work.

6. Matthew 10:1–12:50 describes the mission of the apostles and the opposition that Jesus and his followers faced in their ministry. Who is opposed to Jesus? Why? What does Matthew say about what the disciples of Jesus ought to expect as they begin their mission?

7. What is the common thread that holds together the parables chapter of Matthew's gospel (Matt. 13:1–53)? Compare this to the common thread that holds together the parables chapter of Mark's gospel (Mark 4:1–41). How are they similar? Different?

8. Mark 4:10–11 gives a difficult and harsh explanation for the reason why Jesus taught in parables. In what ways does Matthew retain the same explanation? In what ways does he alter it? (Matt. 13:13–16.) Explain.

9. Compare Matthew's story of Jesus walking on the water (Matt. 14:45–52) with Mark's version of the story (Mark 6:15–21). What did Matthew do to change Mark's story? Also, speculate on why he might have changed it as he did.

10. Compare Matthew's story of the Canaanite woman (Matt. 15:21–28) with Mark's version of the story (Mark 7:24–30). What did Matthew do to change Mark's story? Also, speculate on why he might have changed it as he did.

11. Compare Matthew's story of Peter's confession of faith (Matt. 16:13–23) with Mark's version of the story (Mark 8:27–33). What did Matthew do to change Mark's story? Also, speculate on why he might have changed it as he did.

12. Locate and explain at least two elements of the "church" discourse (Matt. 18) that demonstrate its overall theme. How does Matthew's parable about the wicked servant who was forgiven his debt by the king fit into this overall theme?

13. Compare Matthew's version of Jesus' teaching on divorce (Matt. 19:1–12) to Mark's version (Mark 10:1–12). What did Matthew do to change Mark's teaching? Also, speculate on why he might have changed it as he did.

14. Make a list of all the stories in the latter half of the Gospel of Matthew that feature Peter as a central character. What kind of person is he? What role does he play in relation to the other disciples? To Jesus? *Hint:* You can use a concordance to quickly find these stories.

15. Locate the three units (two parables and a teaching) at the end of Matthew's "apocalypse" (Matt. 24:1–25:46) that are not included in Mark's Little Apocalypse (Mark 13). What lesson does each one have for the community of Matthew's gospel?

16. Use your outline of the passion and resurrection narratives in Mark's gospel to identify the special features of Matthew's passion and resurrection narratives. Make a list of any scenes in Matthew's gospel that are absent from Mark's gospel or that have been changed in some significant way. *Hint:* Using your Bible's cross-references or a gospel synopsis also can help you with this question.

## Questions for Reflection

1. Find three sayings in the Sermon on the Mount that you think would apply well to modern culture in the United States. Find three sayings that are less easily applicable to modern Christianity in the United States. Explain why you selected these particular sayings.

2. What overall impressions do you get from Matthew's portrayal of Jesus? Is this the type of Jesus to whom you would be attracted? Why or why not? Be prepared to give concrete evidence from the gospel to support your position.

3. We have already noted several times the significance of the death and resurrection of Jesus for the faith of early Christianity. What about the modern believer? What significance, if any, do the death and resurrection of Jesus have? What would Christianity look like today without the faith claim that Jesus died on a cross and was raised from the dead?

## Activities for Learning

1. Use C. H. Dodd's definition of a parable (see above) to construct a modern parable. Identify a message you wish to convey through the medium of the parable. Construct the comparison using imagery common in modern life. When you

have completed the parable, create a literary context (i.e., setting) for the parable that will indicate to your reader how the parable should be interpreted. See if you can create an alternative literary context that would give your parable a slightly different interpretation. Comment on your observations.

2. Write a series of beatitudes (six or more) that follow the basic form of Matthew's beatitudes and that makes a point about how modern believers who anticipate the manifestation of the reign of God ought to behave. Provide a rationale for your beatitudes: What do they say about your understanding of the reign of God? Notice that beatitudes are not explicitly Christological (i.e., pertaining to Jesus as the Christ). What do you conclude about that observation?

3. Matthew's gospel provides one way of understanding the notion of church: *Ecclesia* is the assembly (community) of believers characterized by reconciliation. Conduct an assessment of a church community in your area. It can be a church community with which you are currently involved or one that you know little about. Attend their church service. Examine the literature they make available to new members. What opportunities for participation does the church provide to its members? What kind of outreach activities does it support? If possible, arrange to interview the pastor, an elder, or someone who works in ministry at that church. Find out how they understand themselves as church. To what extent do the theology and ethical values of the church's tradition (Catholic, Lutheran, Methodist, Baptist, etc.) affect their understanding of church? To what extent does the cultural background (African-American, Hispanic, Hmong, Korean, etc.) of the church community affect how they understand themselves as church? How does what you have learned about this church community compare to Matthew's vision of church?

## SOURCES AND RESOURCES

Anderson, Janice Capel. *Matthew's Narrative Web: Over, and Over, and Over Again.* Sheffield, England: JSOT Press, 1994.

Bauer, D. R. *The Structure of Matthew's Gospel: A Study in Literary Design.* Sheffield, England: Almond Press, 1988.

Brown, Jeannine K. *The Disciples in Narrative Perspective: The Portrayal and Function of the Matthean Disciples.* Atlanta, Ga.: Society of Biblical Literature, 2002.

Brown, Raymond E. *The Birth of the Messiah: A Commentary on the Infancy Narratives in Matthew and Luke.* Garden City, N.Y.: Doubleday, 1977.

_____. *The Death of the Messiah.* 2 vols. New York: Doubleday, 1994.

_____, Karl P. Donfried, and John Reumann, eds. *Peter in the New Testament.* Minneapolis, Minn.: Augsburg, 1973.

Byrne, Brendan. *Lifting the Burden: Reading Matthew's Gospel in the Church Today.* Collegeville, Minn.: Liturgical Press, 2004.

Carter, Warren. *What Are They Saying about Matthew's Sermon on the Mount?* New York: Paulist. 1994.

_____. *Matthew's Parables: Audience-Oriented Perspectives.* Washington, D.C.: Catholic Biblical Association of America, 1998.

_____. *Matthew and the Margins. A Sociopolitical and Religious Reading.* Maryknoll, N.Y.: Orbis Books, 2000.

_____. *Matthew and Empire: Initial Explorations.* Harrisburg, Pa.: Trinity Press International, 2001.

_____. *Matthew: Storyteller, Interpreter, Evangelist.* Peabody Mass.: Hendrickson, 2004.

Cartlidge, David R., and David L. Dungan, eds. *Documents for the Study of the Gospels.* 2nd ed. Minneapolis, Minn.: Fortress, 1994.

Charette, Blaine. *Restoring Presence: The Spirit in Matthew's Gospel.* Sheffield, England: Sheffield Academic Press, 2000.

Deutsch, Celia M. *Lady Wisdom, Jesus, and the Sages: Metaphor and Social Context in Matthew's Gospel.* Valley Forge, Pa.: Trinity Press International, 1996.

Dodd, C. H. *The Parables of the Kingdom.* New York: Charles Scribner's Sons, 1961.

Edwards, Richard A. *Matthew's Narrative Portrait of Disciples: How the Text-Connoted Reader Is Informed.* Harrisburg, Pa.: Trinity Press International, 1997.

Garland, David E. *Reading Matthew: A Literary and Theological Commentary on the First Gospel.* New York: Crossroad, 1993.

Harrington, Daniel. *The Gospel of Matthew.* Collegeville, Minn.: Liturgical Press, 1991.

Horsley, Richard. *The Liberation of Christmas: The Infancy Narratives in Social Context.* New York: Crossroad, 1989.

Kealy, Sean P. *Matthew's Gospel and the History of Biblical Interpretation.* Lewiston, N.Y.: Mellen Biblical Press, 1997.

Keener, Craig S. *A Commentary on the Gospel of Matthew.* Grand Rapids, Mich.: Eerdmans, 1999.

Kingsbury, Jack Dean. *Matthew as Story.* Philadelphia: Fortress, 1979.

————. *Matthew:* Proclamation commentaries. 2nd ed. Philadelphia: Fortress, 1986.

Lambrecht, Jan. *The Sermon on the Mount: Proclamation and Exhortation.* Wilmington, Del.: Glazier, 1985.

Levine, Amy-Jill, and Marianne Blickenstaff, eds. *A Feminist Companion to Matthew.* Sheffield, England: Sheffield Academic Press, 2001.

Long, Thomas G. *Matthew.* Louisville, Ky.: Westminster John Knox Press, 1997.

Malina, Bruce J., and Richard L. Rohrbaugh. *Social-Science Commentary on the Synoptic Gospels.* Minneapolis, Minn.: Fortress, 2003.

Meier, John. *The Vision of Matthew: Christ, Church, and Morality in the First Gospel.* Mahwah, N.J.: Paulist, 1979.

————. *Matthew.* New Testament Message series, vol. 3, Wilmington, Del.: Glazier, 1980.

Montague, George T. *Companion God: A Cross-Cultural Commentary on the Gospel of Matthew.* New York: Paulist, 1998.

Powell, Mark Alan. *Chasing the Eastern Star: Adventures in Biblical Reader-Response Criticism.* Louisville, Ky.: Westminster John Knox Press, 2001.

Reid, Barbara E. *The Gospel According to Matthew.* Collegeville, Minn.: Liturgical Press, 2005.

Senior, Donald. *What Are They Saying About Matthew?* Ramsey, N.J.: Paulist, 1983.

————. *The Passion of Jesus in the Gospel of Matthew.* Wilmington, Del.: Glazier, 1985.

————. *Matthew.* Nashville, Tenn.: Abingdon Press, 1998.

Sim, David C. *The Gospel of Matthew and Christian Judaism: The History and Social Setting of the Matthean Community.* Edinburgh, Scotland: T & T Clark International, 1998.

Stanton, Graham. *A Gospel for a New People: Studies in Matthew.* Louisville, Ky.: Westminster John Knox Press, 1993.

Stock, Augustine. *The Method and Message of Matthew.* Collegeville, Minn.: Liturgical Press, 1994.

Westerholm, Stephen. *Understanding Matthew: The Early Christian Worldview of the First Gospel.* Grand Rapids, Mich.: Baker Academic, 2006.

Wright, N. T. *Matthew for Everyone.* London: SPCK; Louisville, Ky.: Westminster John Knox Press, 2004.

# CHAPTER 8

# THE GOSPEL ACCORDING TO LUKE

## OVERVIEW

- AUTHORSHIP: Traditionally associated with Luke, a physician and a companion of Paul; probably a Gentile Christian who knew the Septuagint (i.e., Greek translation of the Jewish scriptures)
- DATE OF COMPOSITION: 80–90 C.E.
- INITIAL AUDIENCE: Probably a Greek-speaking, Gentile Christian community; location unknown
- MAJOR TOPICS: Themes of the Gospel; Luke's Jesus, the Prophet Who Speaks on Behalf of the Poor; Luke's Infancy Narratives; The Sermon on the Plain; Luke's Travel Narrative; Luke's Story of the Death and Resurrection of Jesus; Luke's Gospel and Liberation Theology

## TIMELINE

| | |
|---|---|
| **37 B.C.E.** | Herod the Great takes up his kingship in Palestine. |
| **30 B.C.E.–14 C.E.** | Augustus is Roman emperor. |
| **6–4 B.C.E.** | Jesus of Nazareth is born. |
| **4 B.C.E.** | Herod the Great, king of Palestine, dies. His kingdom is divided among three sons: Archelaus, Herod Antipas, and Philip. |
| **4 B.C.E.–39 C.E.** | Herod Antipas, son of Herod the Great, is tetrarch of Galilee and Perea. |
| **6 C.E.** | Annas (Ananus I) becomes High Priest of the Jerusalem Temple. |
| **18 C.E.** | Caiaphas, the son-in-law of Annas, becomes High Priest of the Jerusalem Temple. |
| **26–36 C.E.** | Pontius Pilate is prefect of Judea and Samaria. |
| **c. 28 C.E.** | John the Baptist is executed by Herod Antipas. |
| **c. 30 C.E.** | Jesus is crucified, dies, and is resurrected. |
| **c. 41–44 C.E.** | The apostle James, the brother of John, is martyred. |
| **64 C.E.** | Peter and Paul are martyred in Rome. |
| **65–70 C.E.** | The Gospel of Mark is written. |
| **66–70 C.E.** | The Jewish War occurs. |
| **70 C.E.** | Jerusalem and the Temple are destroyed. |
| **80–90 C.E.** | The Gospel of Matthew is written; **the Gospel of Luke is written.** |
| **90–100 C.E.** | The Gospel of John is written. |

| | |
|---|---|
| **c. 180 C.E.** | Irenaeus of Lyons writes *Against Heresies.* |
| **c. 310 C.E.** | Eusebius of Caesarea completes *Ecclesiastical History.* |

We have arrived at the third of the synoptic gospels, the Gospel of Luke. On the surface at least, this stop on our journey will look a lot like what we saw in the Gospels of Matthew and Mark. Again, the gospel takes place in ancient Palestine, Jesus is its central character, and approximately two-thirds of the stories that we find in the Gospel of Luke are also found in Mark's or Matthew's gospel. So why even bother with Luke's gospel? On a tour, sometimes you get to the point that you simply cannot look at another historic site or museum because they all start to look the same! However, our familiarity with Matthew and Mark can provide the opportunity to go deeper into parts of the Gospel of Luke that we would only be able to survey if we had not already studied Matthew's and Mark's gospels. Welcome to the adventure. Hopefully, Luke's gospel will provide some very special surprises!

Our approach to Luke's gospel will be the same as our approach to the Gospel of Matthew in the previous chapter. We will focus on the distinctive features of this gospel so that we can appreciate Luke's unique portrait of Jesus and his interpretation of discipleship, what it means to be church, and how the believer ought to live in the world. However, once again, before we investigate some of these aspects of Luke's gospel, we need to pause to find out what biblical scholars have concluded about the author and his audience.

## AUTHORSHIP

One source of information about the author of this gospel is its opening section (Luke 1:1–4). This section is called a **prologue** because, as an introduction, it appears at the start of the gospel and it provides some background and a context for the book. In the prologue, the gospel writer indicates that he knows that others before him have written orderly accounts (i.e., gospels) of the "events that have been fulfilled among us" (Luke 1:1), meaning the salvation story fulfilled in Jesus. The gospel writer's comments suggest that he is not an eyewitness to Jesus' life; that is, he is not one of the apostles or a disciple of Jesus (Luke 1:2). However, apparently he has studied other gospels and traditions, oral or written, that had their origins in the eyewitnesses of Jesus' life (Luke 1:3). Thus, although the author does not say it in so many words, he seems to be implying that his gospel should be regarded as trustworthy and authoritative because he has based it on the traditions that trace back to the eyewitnesses of Jesus' life.

Like the authors of the Gospels of Mark and Matthew, the writer of this gospel does not give his name. Irenaeus, a theologian of the early church (c. 180 C.E.), is among the first to associate this gospel with Luke. The fourth-century church historian Eusebius records his words as follows: "Luke also, the follower of Paul, put down in a book a gospel (*euangelion*) preached by that one" (*Ecclesiastical History*

5.8.2). The New Testament's three references to a man named Luke who was a companion of Paul have led some scholars to conclude that Luke was a physician and a Gentile Christian (Phlm. 24; Col. 4:11–14; 2 Tim. 4:11).

However, some biblical scholars argue that Luke's gospel is not unlike Matthew's and Mark's gospels on the question of authorship. These gospels were not named until the latter half of the second century, and the circumstances of their naming had more to do with establishing the authority of the gospel by tying them to the eyewitnesses and disciples of Jesus than with identifying their actual historical authors. Other scholars, even those who accept this argument for the anonymous authorship of Matthew's and Mark's gospels, say that Luke's gospel is different. It makes sense that the early church might have made up a tradition that connected Matthew's gospel with the apostle Matthew or another tradition that associated Mark's gospel with a disciple of Peter, who was also an apostle and eyewitness to the life of Jesus. But why would anyone make up a tradition that associated the Gospel of Luke with Luke, a companion of Paul? Paul was not a disciple of the historical Jesus or an eyewitness to his words and deeds. Therefore, some scholars think that the tradition is historically accurate and that Luke was the actual author of this gospel. Leaving open the question of the anonymity of this gospel, we will call the author Luke, as has been the convention.

Another New Testament book, the Acts of the Apostles, provides further insight into the identity of the author of the Gospel of Luke. Both have the same addressee, namely, Theophilus (Acts 1:1–14). The author of Acts of the Apostles, referring to his first book, says that he has written about "all that Jesus did and taught from the beginning until the day when he was taken up to heaven" (Acts 1:1–2). In other words, whoever wrote Luke's gospel also wrote Acts of the Apostles. These two documents together reveal an author who had an extensive vocabulary and considerable skill in Greek composition. They also contain evidence that he knew Greco-Roman literature and philosophy. In other words, this author had a formal education of the sort that was typically available to the elite of Greco-Roman societies.

Biblical scholars have wondered whether Luke was Gentile, as the tradition has suggested, or Jewish. Those who argue that he was Jewish do so because his writings contain numerous references to the Old Testament Septuagint. However, he would necessarily have been a Hellenistic Jew who received training in one of the urban centers of learning around the Mediterranean. If he was Gentile, perhaps he was one of the **God-fearers** (e.g., Acts 10:2): Gentiles who were attracted to Judaism, studied Torah, and participated in Jewish religious practices to the extent that they were allowed to do so but who never actually converted to Judaism. The word *fear* in this context does not mean "to be afraid" but rather "to worship and honor." This would explain the author's knowledge of the Septuagint and his interest in Jerusalem and the Temple.

In sum, Luke's gospel might have been written anonymously or by someone named Luke. Whether Jewish or Gentile, he was Greek-speaking and had received a classical education, most likely in one of the urban centers of learning around the Mediterranean. He was also the author of Acts of the Apostles.

## DATE AND INITIAL AUDIENCE

Most biblical scholars agree that Luke depended on Mark's gospel for source material. Luke incorporates approximately 65 percent of Mark's gospel and to a large extent follows Mark's chronology in the ordering of its stories. If the Gospel of Mark was written about 65–70 C.E., then Luke's gospel likely was written approximately 80–90 C.E., about the same time as Matthew's gospel.

Concerning the gospel's initial audience, Luke's prologue tells us that it was written for someone whom the author describes as **Theophilus**, which means "lover of God." Perhaps Theophilus is this man's proper name. If so, because Luke addresses him as "your Excellency," Theophilus may have been a wealthy patron or a member of the Roman ruling class. However, by addressing this book as he did, Luke might simply be acknowledging the status of its readers as people of faith: They are "lovers of God." In that case, the gospel writer has a more universal audience in mind. The gospel is intended for all who call themselves "lovers of God." Either way, it is clear that this gospel is directed toward people who are already believers in Christ.

Concerning the place of composition or the location of the community for which this gospel was intended—when it comes to the gospels, it is difficult to distinguish one from the other—some scholars have suggested Rome, the place where Acts of the Apostles, Luke's second book, ends (see Acts 28). Others have suggested Antioch because the introduction to a late-second-century-C.E. manuscript of Luke's gospel says that Luke was a Syrian from Antioch. Antioch was a major center of learning at that time, it had a sizable Jewish community, and the Jesus movement expanded to include Gentiles in that place. However, some biblical scholars question whether Luke could have written his gospel from Antioch because Luke's gospel contains some stories and teachings that are very different from Matthew's gospel, which is also associated with Antioch. See, for example, the birth stories of Jesus. Both gospels tell the story of the birth of Jesus, but they have very few details in common. If both gospels were written from the same community, one would expect much more commonality. Other scholars have suggested the region of Boeotia, in Greece, as the place from which this gospel was written because it is the traditional location of Luke's death. However, in the end, we probably have to say that the location of the community or the place from which the gospel was written is unknown.

## OUTLINE OF THE GOSPEL OF LUKE

The writer of Luke's gospel understood his work to be a history, as his own introduction testifies. However, we must be careful not to impose modern understandings of history on this work. The gospel does make references to political events surrounding the life of Jesus, but there is no attempt to provide objective reports about historical events or persons, like we might expect in a documentary history today. Rather, this book has a clear theological agenda, and the story is told in service of that agenda. In the opening section of the gospel, Luke says that he is writing "an orderly account" of all that Jesus said and did so that Theophilus might know "the truth" concerning the things about which he has been instructed—that is, how the salvation story is fulfilled in Jesus (Luke 1:4; cf. Luke 1:1). Thus, the gospel unfolds in a clear and orderly way, as this outline suggests:

1. Luke 1:1–4—Prologue
2. Luke 1:5–4:13—Infancy narratives and the beginning of Jesus' ministry
3. Luke 4:14–9:50—Jesus' ministry in Galilee
4. Luke 9:51–19:27—The journey to Jerusalem, also called the Travel Narrative
5. Luke 19:28–21:38—Jesus' activity in Jerusalem
6. Luke 22:1–23:49—The passion narrative
7. Luke 23:50–24:53—The resurrection and ascension of Jesus

This outline suggests one of the major themes of Luke's gospel—namely, the attention given to Jerusalem and the Temple. We see this already in the infancy narratives, which include two stories of Jesus' early journeys to Jerusalem: the first made when he was a tiny baby so that his parents could fulfill the prescribed purification rituals after his birth (Luke 2:21–38) and the second made when he was twelve years old and his family was on pilgrimage to Jerusalem for Passover, as was their custom (Luke 2:41–51). Both stories are significant for what they say about Jesus' destiny.

This outline also shows how important the Jerusalem theme is for whole of the gospel story. It begins in Jerusalem with the story of Zechariah and Elizabeth, the parents of John the Baptist, and before the readers have traversed 40 percent of the gospel, their eyes will be focused on Jerusalem again, as Jesus and the disciples make their way from Galilee to Jerusalem in a lengthy section of the gospel that has come to be known as the Travel Narrative. Of course, the narratives associated with the death and resurrection of Jesus take place in Jerusalem, but Luke also places the postresurrection appearances of Jesus in and around Jerusalem. All totaled, then, as much as 60 percent of this gospel is focused on Jerusalem.

## GUIDE FOR INTERPRETING THE GOSPEL OF LUKE

Here is your tour book for the Gospel of Luke. Again, we will not be summarizing the entire content of the gospel. Instead, we will offer some insights that will help you with your own reading of Luke's gospel. We will begin by highlighting some of the distinctive themes of the Gospel of Luke and Luke's unique portrait of Jesus as the prophet who speaks on behalf of the poor. We will examine how Luke's infancy narratives differ from those in Matthew's gospel and also how elements of Luke's story have been incorporated into Christian worship and practice over the centuries. We will also compare Luke's Sermon on the Plain with Matthew's Sermon on the Mount to better understand the themes of the Gospel of Luke. Next, we will gather some clues for interpreting his Travel Narrative and some special features of his story of Jesus' death and resurrection. We will conclude by looking at the appeal of Luke's gospel for liberation theology. At the end of this chapter, you will be invited to read the gospel for yourself. The "Questions for Reading" section will guide you.

## THEMES OF THE GOSPEL

Luke works into his gospel a number of themes and literary features that make it unique among the synoptic gospels. Two of these themes—promise and fulfillment and the reversal of fortunes for the oppressed and the powerful—will be addressed later when we investigate the infancy narratives. Another theme that Luke incorporates into his gospel is *universality* or inclusion of all peoples. We see this, for example, in his genealogy of Jesus. Compared to Matthew's genealogy, which begins with Abraham, who is sometimes called the father of Judaism, Luke's genealogy extends back beyond Abraham to Adam and the beginning of the human race (Luke 3:23–28). Similarly, Luke's understanding of God's plan of salvation includes Jews and Gentiles, rich and poor, men and women, and even Samaritans.

In addition to these themes, biblical scholars have frequently observed that *women* play a prominent role in Luke's gospel as compared to the other gospels. This is already evident in the infancy narratives, which devote a considerably large space to Mary and her cousin Elizabeth (Luke 1:5–6, 24–56; 2:1–7, 19, 22–24, 33–35, 41–52). You see this attention to female characters also in Luke's mention of the women who minister to Jesus (Luke 8:1–3) and in the story of Jesus healing a crippled woman (Luke 13:10–17), to name only two. Luke's gospel also has more banquets and scenes of *table fellowship* than any other gospel (e.g., Luke 14:7–14). Likewise, Luke's Jesus has a special *concern for sinners.* You will note several stories about sinners, most of which are found only in Luke's gospel: Zacchaeus in the Sycamore tree (Luke 19:1–10), the rich man and Lazarus (Luke 16:19–31), the cluster of three parables about "the lost" (Luke 15:1–32), and the penitent sinner who was crucified alongside of Jesus (Luke 23:39–43). This gospel also has frequent warnings about the *dangers of wealth* (e.g., Luke 12:13–15).

The special themes of Luke's gospel also include *righteousness* and the *role of the Holy Spirit.* Already in the infancy narratives, we see that Zechariah and Elizabeth, the parents of John the Baptist, are described as "righteous" and "priestly" (Luke 1:5–6). They represent the best of the religion of Israel. This theme continues throughout the gospel and culminates in the centurion's declaration of Jesus as "righteous" in the crucifixion scene (Luke 23:47). Further, Luke situates every important action, including Jesus' activity, in the context of the promptings of the Spirit. For example, at the beginning of his ministry, Jesus was led into the wilderness "full of the Holy Spirit" (Luke 4:1). When he returns from the wilderness and enters the synagogue at Nazareth, Luke's Jesus reads from the Book of Isaiah, "The Spirit of the Lord is upon me" (Luke 4:18; cf. Isa. 61:1–2; 58:6). Later, in Acts of the Apostles, we shall see that Luke associates the receiving of the Spirit with the sacrament of baptism.

Another important theme in Luke's gospel is *prayer.* Luke's Jesus is constantly in prayer, especially before any important event: his baptism (Luke 3:21–22), the selection of the twelve apostles (Luke 6:12–16), Peter's confession about Jesus as messiah (Luke 9:18–20), the transfiguration (Luke 9:28–36), the teaching of the Lord's prayer (Luke 11:1–13), and the garden scene before Jesus' arrest (Luke 22:39–46). Luke also includes stories about right attitudes in prayer, like the story of Mary and Martha (Luke 10:38–42) and the story of the Pharisee and tax collector (Luke 18:9–14).

## LUKE'S JESUS, THE PROPHET WHO SPEAKS ON BEHALF OF THE POOR

Luke uses a number of themes and images to paint his distinctive portrait of Jesus. For example, Jesus is presented as the messiah of God (Luke 9:20), the Son of Man who will come with power in the end time (Luke 22:69; cf. Acts 7:56), and the Suffering Servant of whom Isaiah spoke (Luke 22:37; cf. Acts 8:30–35; Isa. 52:13–53:12). He is also the new Elijah who, when he ascended into heaven, passed on his spirit to the disciples along with the mantle of responsibility to preach the good news of God to the world (Luke 24:44–53; cf. 2 Kings 2:9–12).

However, the description that Luke provides at the beginning of Jesus' ministry is perhaps the clearest and most comprehensive for understanding Jesus' mission and identity. The context for this description is the story of Jesus' unhappy visit to his hometown of Nazareth, which ends with Jesus saying that a prophet is not accepted in his own country (Mark 6:1–6; Matt. 13:54–58; Luke 4:16–30). It is found in all three of the synoptic gospels. Mark places the story partway into Jesus' ministry, as does Matthew, but Luke places it at the start of his ministry, so that the story acts as a lens through which all of Jesus' words and deeds should be viewed.

If you examine the three versions of the account of Jesus' visit to Nazareth in a gospel synopsis, you will discover that Luke retains the general structure of this story with two important exceptions. First, whereas Mark and Matthew comment generally about Jesus entering the synagogue to teach, Luke says that Jesus stood up to do the Sabbath reading and was given the Book of Isaiah to read. This is what follows:

He unrolled the scroll and found the place where it was written:

> The Spirit of the Lord is upon me,
> because he has anointed me to bring good news to the poor.
> He has sent me to proclaim release to the captives
> and recovery of sight to the blind, to let the oppressed go free,
> to proclaim the year of the Lord's favor.

And he rolled up the scroll, gave it back to the attendant, and sat down. The eyes of all in the synagogue were fixed on him. Then he began to say to them, "Today this scripture has been fulfilled in your hearing." (Luke 4:17–21; see also Isa. 61:1; 58:6; 61:2)

Thus, Luke presents Jesus as the prophet *par excellence*, filled with the Holy Spirit and anointed by God to proclaim the good news to the poor and disadvantaged.

Continuing the prophet theme, Luke adds a second unit to the story of Jesus' visit to Nazareth, which is not found in either Mark's or Matthew's version. In Luke 4:25–30, Luke's Jesus recalls two prophets of old, Elijah and Elisha. Both were miracle workers, and both used their miracle-working powers outside of Israel to extend God's care to those who were not among God's covenant people (see 1 Kings 17:8–16; 2 Kings 5:1–14). The people of the synagogue react with fury, forcing Jesus out of his hometown and even attempting to throw him over a cliff to kill him. Thus, Luke's version of this story signals to the reader that, as the prophet *par excellence*, Jesus' ministry will be extended to the Gentiles, even as he is rejected and eventually killed by his own people.

## Luke's Infancy Narratives

When you compare the opening pages of the Gospel of Luke to the Gospel of Matthew, you will notice that Luke's story of the birth of Jesus is completely different from Matthew's version, with the exception of the naming of the major characters: Mary, Joseph, and Jesus. What is said about each character and even the manner in which each is introduced into the story are different from Matthew's gospel. However, the question we should be asking ourselves is not, Which story is historically accurate? Rather, the question should be, What theological statement does each make about Jesus and his place in God's plan of salvation?

Already in the first scene of the gospel (Luke 1:5–80), we see Luke's interest in Jerusalem. Here we encounter Zechariah, a priest in the Jerusalem Temple, who is about to perform his service of the offering of incense. Suddenly an angel appears! Thus begins an extended comparison between Zechariah (together with his wife Elizabeth) and Mary concerning the births of their sons, John the Baptist and Jesus. The stories follow the pattern outlined below:

1. The expectation that neither woman would be pregnant
2. Annunciation of birth by the angel Gabriel

   "Do not be afraid. . . . "

3. Naming of the child

   "You shall name him. . . . "

4. Explaining the destiny of the child
5. Protest (the point at which the two stories begin to diverge)

   "How shall I know this?"

6. Sign/confirmation given by the angel
7. Birth narrative
8. Pronouncement of the significance of John/Jesus for God's plan of salvation

The clear structural parallels between these two stories suggest that we are looking not at historical eyewitness accounts of the births of John and Jesus but rather at a literary creation designed to make a point. What point is the evangelist trying to make? The naming of each child and the explanation of their destinies reveal that John the Baptist and Jesus are joined together as "promise" and "fulfillment." In each case, the angel Gabriel delivers the message concerning the child's destiny. John stands for all the promises that God made for the salvation of Israel up to this time; he will be the one to prepare the way of the Lord (Luke 1:13–17). However, Jesus will be the fulfillment of God's plan of salvation. He will be given the throne of David and will reign forever, for his kingdom will have no end (Luke 1:30–33; see also 2 Sam. 7:13–16).

The story of Mary's visit to her cousin Elizabeth, who is also the wife of Zechariah, (Luke 1:39–56) provides the context for another of Luke's major themes as well as a prayer that eventually becomes part of the Christian spiritual tradition. Mary's response to Elizabeth (Luke 1:46–55) is the prayer that has come to be known as the **Magnificat**, after the Latin translation of the opening phrase, "My soul magnifies. . . ." Most biblical scholars agree that it is not Luke's original composition but perhaps a traditional (Christian?) prayer derived from Hannah's prayer in praise of God upon the birth of her son Samuel, a famous prophet and judge of the Old Testament (see 1 Sam. 2:1–10). This prayer of praise to God is developed around a theme that modern theologians sometimes call **reversal theology**. Mary praises God because she believes that the coming of Jesus is the first step in God's fulfillment of the promise to bring down the mighty and exalt the lowly. It anticipates a reversal of the social system of power and oppression, in which those with little power will be exalted or raised up, while those with great power will be brought down. Obviously, this is a theological worldview that would likely make most rich and powerful people more than a little nervous!

By comparison, Matthew's infancy narratives do not include the stories of the **Annunciation** and the **Visitation.** However, Luke's infancy narratives contain no mention of the magi (Matt. 2:1–12). Instead, Luke includes a scene in which shepherds from the nearby fields receive a heavenly invitation to visit the child Jesus (Luke 2:8–14). This scene is consistent with Luke's interest in the poor and his conviction that God would raise up those who are marginalized in society. Shepherds were not well respected in first-century Palestine. They were nomadic peoples, for the most part, and they were economically poor, ritually unclean, and poorly educated. The religious elite of Judaism considered them part of the *am ha aretz,* "**people of the land**," whose very existence was thought to keep the messianic age from

The Virgin Mary, detail from the *Annunciation* (oil on panel) by Leonardo da Vinci (1472–1475). *Galleria degli Uffizi, Florence, Italy/The Bridgeman Art Library.*

The *Visitation* fresco in the Lower Church of the Basilica of San Francesco in Assisi (Italian, 13th century). *Picture Desk, Inc./Kobal Collection*.

becoming a reality because they would not (or could not) keep all the laws of the Torah. In some sense, then, they were the scapegoats of the society. According to Luke's story, it was to them that the angels first announced the birth of the messiah with the words "Glory to God in the highest . . ." (Luke 2:14). These are also the opening words of a prayer, sometimes called the Gloria, that is spoken or sung in the worship services of several Christian traditions on Sundays and at special feasts.

Even from this brief overview, we can see that Luke's infancy narratives, like those of Matthew's gospel, are vehicles for a well-developed theological message. Therefore, the Christian believer need not be overly concerned about the question of historicity—whether Matthew's or Luke's version of the story is historically more accurate—because that was not the intent of the authors of these gospels. Moreover, the theological messages of these two infancy narratives are entirely compatible. Therefore, the Christian believer need not choose one over the other. Both infancy narratives are true insofar as they tell the truth about God's intentions for humanity and who it is that Jesus was destined to be as the Christ.

## THE SERMON ON THE PLAIN

Luke's gospel contains a sermon, traditionally known as the Sermon on the Plain (Luke 6:20–49), that has some substantial similarities to Matthew's Sermon on the Mount. However, by looking at the differences between these two discourses, we can

## THE INFLUENCE OF LUKE'S GOSPEL ON CHRISTIAN WORSHIP AND DEVOTIONAL PRACTICE

Luke's infancy narratives contain a number of scenes that are celebrated as feast days in the liturgical (worship) calendar of several Christian churches (e.g., Roman Catholic, Lutheran, Episcopalian, Eastern Catholic, and Orthodox churches) and that have been an important source for religious art through the centuries. The scene in which the angel messenger comes to Mary and announces the birth of Jesus (Luke 1:26–38) is called the Annunciation. This subject was especially popular with artists of the Middle Ages and the Renaissance, and anyone who has taken an art history course or visited a museum of art has seen at least a few paintings with this title. Luke's gospel also includes the story of Mary's visit to Elizabeth after the Annunciation (Luke 1:39–56). This event is known simply as the Visitation. Although somewhat less popular than the Annunciation, this scene—usually depicting Mary and Elizabeth in tender embrace—can also be found in religious art from the medieval and renaissance periods.

Luke's accounts of these two events also provide a good opportunity to say a word about the source of some of Christianity's devotional (prayer) practices. Take, for example, the Roman Catholic prayer called the Hail Mary. The opening words are as follows:

> Hail, Mary, full of grace,
> The Lord is with you.
> Blessed are you among women
> And blessed is the fruit of your womb, Jesus.

After reading the Gospel of Luke, you will probably recognize the first two lines of this prayer as the angel's greeting to Mary when it was announced that she would be the mother of Jesus (Luke 1:28). The second two lines are Elizabeth's words to Mary when the child in Elizabeth's womb, later to be named John, leapt at their meeting (Luke 1:42). The remainder of the Hail Mary prayer is this: "Holy Mary mother of God, pray for us sinners now and at the hour of our death. Amen."

The Gospel of Luke contains other prayers that have become part of Christian devotional practice, including the Canticle of Zechariah (Luke 1:68–79), the Canticle of Simeon (Luke 2:29–32), and the Canticle of Mary (Luke 1:46–55), also known as the Magnificat. In addition, its stories have provided inspiration for much of the religious art of the medieval period. If you are interested in exploring this topic further, you might begin with an internet image search using key words like *Annunciation, Visitation*, and *Magnificat* or *Nativity* and *shepherds*. Carefully read the gospel story that was the inspiration for the painting that you selected and then examine it to see how the artist has interpreted (or in some cases reinterpreted) the gospel story. See ACTIVITIES FOR LEARNING below for more information about how to analyze your painting.

A shepherd boy with his sheep, near the Church of the Nativity in Bethlehem. Photo by Catherine Cory.

get some important clues to Matthew's and Luke's theology at work. An outline of Luke's Sermon on the Plain is given below.

1. Luke 6:20–26—Introduction: beatitudes and woes
2. Luke 6:27–36—Love of enemies
3. Luke 6:37–42—Do not judge others
4. Luke 6:42–49—Conclusion

When you read Luke's Sermon on the Plain, the first thing you will notice is that he begins with four beatitudes ("Blessed are you . . . " sayings) and four woes (Luke 6:20–26), instead of the eight or nine beatitudes of Matthew's gospel (Matt. 5:3–12). When we investigated Matthew's beatitudes, we saw that his focus is on attitudinal and behavioral concerns related to "greater righteousness." In contrast, Luke's beatitudes are primarily concerned with social and economic issues. When Luke's Jesus says, "Blessed are the poor," he means the economically poor. Matthew's version contains the additional phrase, "in spirit," meaning those who have no concern for their financial gain or are not burdened down by their wealth. In the Old Testament, and for Jews in general, poverty was no virtue because it kept people from giving right worship to God (sacrifices, etc.) and from supporting the poor, widows, and orphans (one of the basic acts of piety in Judaism). In Old Testament prophetic literature, *woes* are warnings against wrong behavior. Luke's woes are directed against the rich and powerful of society.

Thus, with their emphasis on social and economic concerns, Luke's beatitudes and woes are an example of his reversal theology. They describe how the poor will be given many good things and how the rich will be brought down. This is not a case of good moral behavior being rewarded. The rich are not necessarily wicked in

## "BLESSED ARE YOU NOW": A LIBERATIONIST READING OF LUKE'S BEATITUDES

As mentioned in Chapter 1, liberation hermeneutics is not so much a distinct method of biblical analysis as it is a "lens" through which the biblical text is interpreted—in this case, the lens is the *preferential option for the poor*. Here is an excerpt from John Gillman's study of the theme of wealth and possessions in Luke's gospel. He uses literary critical methodologies and insights from cultural anthropology and then analyzes the text from the perspective of liberation hermeneutics. The subject of this excerpt is Luke's beatitudes (Luke 6:20–23).

> In contrast to the painful reality of their present condition, the poor are called "blessed" (*makarioi*). The good fortune, the happiness, even the "good luck" of the poor is acclaimed. Why? The reasons not given for their blessedness are as enlightening as those that are. The poor are called blessed (1) not because of the miserable condition in which they find themselves—poverty in itself is not acclaimed as a state of happiness, (2) not because of any repentance, virtue, or internal disposition they might have—no prior repentance or virtue is required, and (3) not because they are doers of the Law or faithful to the covenant—their status as keepers of the Law is not addressed. Without any prior qualifications the poor are called happy for one reason: They are the recipients of the reign of God. To them God's message of salvation, realized in the kingdom preaching of Jesus, is made available. Already now the poor, particularly the disciples whose way of life is decidedly marked by following Jesus, experience salvation. There is also a future dimension to their blessed condition. In the eschatological future, the poor will enjoy the fullness of God's reign. This promise of salvation is made to them unconditionally. . . .
>
> God's attitude toward the poor is clear. They do have a privileged place. Singled out from among all others, they are the ones called blessed. Fully aware of their present condition of distress, Jesus offers them the fullness of God's kingdom, where they will be satisfied, where they will laugh, and where they will leap for joy. (1991, 52, 54)

Gillman's book is written with the beginning New Testament reader in mind, so if you find this topic of interest, you might consider reading the entire book. You should be able to find it in a college or university library that has a theology or religious studies department, but you could also obtain it through interlibrary loan at any library.

Luke's gospel. They are simply rich. And the poor are not necessarily righteous in Luke's gospel. They are simply poor. At the same time, Luke is not saying that the rich cannot be saved. Rather, they are called to share their riches with the poor and to be on the side of the poor, just as God is on the side of the poor.

Luke's Sermon on the Plain also differs from Matthew's Sermon on the Mount in that certain characteristically Jewish elements (e.g., the six antitheses and the three acts of Jewish piety) are absent. Likewise, the pattern of conduct to which the Christian believer is called in the Sermon on the Plain is not necessarily the greater righteousness of obeying Jewish law. Rather, it is one that puts no value on self-protection. Thus, the Christian believer is exhorted to bless those who curse him and pray for those who abuse him (Luke 6:28). Luke ends this section of the Sermon on the Plain with a radical reinterpretation of the Golden Rule ("Do unto others as you would have them do unto you"; see Matt. 7:12) by having Jesus say, "Be merciful as your Father is merciful" (Luke 6:38). In other words, "Be to those around you who are in need the same way that God acts in relation to humanity in need." Matthew's parallel statement is "Be perfect as your Father is perfect" (Matt. 5:48). In other words, "Complete in the fullest way possible the obligations of the covenant." The difference is quite significant.

The conclusion of Luke's Sermon on the Plain includes some of the same parables we find in Matthew's Sermon on the Mount (Luke 6:39–49; cf. Matt. 7:1–27). You will notice, however, that Luke interprets differently than Matthew the sayings about good trees and bad fruit (Luke 6:43–45; cf. Matt. 7:15–20). Finally, note the close relationship between Matthew's and Luke's versions of the parable about the man who built his house on sand (Luke 6:46–49; Matt. 7:21–27). The wording is so similar that it appears that one copied from the other or perhaps that they both copied from another source. We will address this question of the sources for the synoptic gospels in Chapter 10.

## LUKE'S TRAVEL NARRATIVE

For the most part, Luke follows the chronology of Mark's gospel except for a very long section called the **Travel Narrative** (Luke 9:51–19:27). This section consists of a series of parables, stories, and other teachings that Jesus delivers to his disciples as they journey to Jerusalem before his death. All three of the synoptic gospels mention this journey, but only Luke includes this extended section of teachings during the journey. Many of the stories and parables are very familiar, even to those who have limited knowledge of the New Testament, and most are unique to Luke's gospel. Here we find the parable of the prodigal son (Luke 15:11–32), the parable of the good Samaritan (Luke 10:25–37), the parable about the rich man and Lazarus (Luke 16:19–31), the story of Zacchaeus in the sycamore tree (Luke 19:1–10), the parable about seating people at a dinner party (Luke 14:12–35), the parable of the persistent widow (Luke 18:1–8), and the parable about the tax collector at prayer (Luke 18:9–14). All of these parables and stories relate to themes that are important to Luke's gospel—especially forgiveness, concern for sinners, the importance of prayer, reversal of fortunes for rich and poor, and universality.

As the narrative is presented, the disciples are the immediate recipients of these stories and teachings. Therefore, we can assume that Jesus' teaching on discipleship is also embedded in the Travel Narrative. For example, Jesus teaches that disciples must pray, and he even gives them a formula for prayer (Luke 11:1–4). Christians today call this prayer The Lord's Prayer or the Our Father, though most tend to use the longer version found in Matthew's gospel (Matt. 6:9–13). Luke's Jesus also teaches his disciples about the necessity of perseverance in prayer and consoles them with the assurance that God, who is insurmountably better than any human father, will answer their prayers of need if they ask (Luke 11:5–13). In addition, Luke's Jesus advises them of the risks of discipleship. They will be dragged before powerful people, he says—people who will try to get them to speak against him and who will even kill them for speaking his name. But they should not worry because the Holy Spirit will teach them what to say (Luke 12:1–48). Finally, Luke's Jesus uses this journey to prepare his disciples for what will happen to him in Jerusalem, warning them that "it is impossible for a prophet to be killed outside of Jerusalem" (Luke 13:33). What more can we say? This is a journey with life-and-death consequences!

---

## A CULTURAL READING OF THE PARABLE OF THE LOST COIN

When people from different cultural backgrounds offer their interpretations of scripture, we have an opportunity to see and understand aspects of the biblical text that might otherwise have been hidden to us. The parable of the lost coin (Luke 15:8–11) is a good example. If you have heard people from a white, middle-class, American background, for example, speak about this parable, they often point to things like the value of the lost coin or the comparison of God with a housewife. A New Testament scholar, Dr. Carol Schursten LaHurd, took a different approach. Working with a theory advanced by Kenneth E. Bailey—that cultural experiences of contemporary Middle Easterners can help us understand the cultural context of ancient Middle Easterners who gave us the New Testament—she asked Christian women who had come to the United States from Lebanon and Egypt to interpret the parable of the lost coin. Here is the summary of her findings:

> They assumed that this woman was married with a family and that her role was to guard the money "earned by men" and to "keep everything in order." They attributed her aggressive searching not to any intrinsic monetary value of the coin itself, but rather to the woman's desire to restore the set of coins to completeness and to fulfill cultural expectations of her as a good wife and housekeeper.
>
> One Egyptian woman marveled at the realism of the oil lamp and of the need for sweeping, as she too had experienced life in a pre-electric arid climate. Even in daytime, she explained, the darkness of a house with few small windows would necessitate a lamp for such a search. She speculated that the broom might have been made of a date palm branch, as its very strong twigs are effective for dealing with the dust that blows into village homes. . . .
>
> All the women interviewed agreed that the housekeeper's celebration with female friends and neighbors was completely normal, as women act as a support network and their homes serve as the same type of gathering place as coffee shops do for men. Indeed, one said it was quite possible that the neighbor women had been asked to join in the search. Another added that the woman's rejoicing was very believable and commented, "Whenever we lose something we pray both before and after finding it." (LaHurd, 2002, 250–251)

## LUKE'S STORY OF THE DEATH AND RESURRECTION OF JESUS

Luke's story of the death and resurrection of Jesus differs from Matthew's and Mark's stories in some of its details, even though the basic story line is the same. As one might expect, the unique theological focus of Luke's story accounts for these differences. For example, only Luke's gospel contains the story about the women who follow Jesus as he is making his way to the place of crucifixion (Luke 23:26–31). As they weep, Jesus stops to address them, asking them to weep not for him but for their children. What Luke has in mind is the apocalyptic expectation of turmoil in the end time. Luke also adds the scene in which one of the two thieves crucified with Jesus defends Jesus' innocence against those who would mock him (Luke 23:39–43). Jesus affirms his good deed and promises him a place in paradise (Luke 23:43).

Luke includes several important stories about appearances of the risen Jesus that are found nowhere else in the synoptic gospels: one involving two disciples walking on the road to Emmaus after the crucifixion (Luke 24:13–35) and another involving the disciples hidden away in the upper room (Luke 24:36–49). Finally, this is the only gospel to describe the **Ascension** of Jesus (Luke 24:50–52). The Ascension is the term given to Christ's return to heaven after a brief period of postresurrection appearances. The Christian feast day by the same name is celebrated forty days after Easter—forty being a number symbolic of transition or change.

Especially in his postresurrection appearance narratives, the writer of Luke's gospel answers this important question: How can we make sense of the fact that the messiah was crucified? This was a very troubling question for the earliest Christians because the messiah was supposed to be their deliverer, but crucifixion was a horrible and shameful form of execution reserved for the most terrible of criminals. How can Christians preach a crucified messiah? Luke's answer, in the words of the messengers at the tomb, is this: "Remember how he told you, while he was still in Galilee, that the Son of Man *must* be handed over to sinners, and be crucified, and on the third day rise again" (Luke 24:7). Later when the disciples encounter the risen Jesus on the road to Emmaus, he tells them, "Was it not *necessary* that the Messiah should suffer these things and then enter into his glory?" (Luke 24:26). The words *must* and *necessary* should be understood to mean "God ordained it that . . . " or "God willed that . . ." In other words, the messiah's death is not a problem to be argued away; simply stated, it was God's plan from the beginning.

## LUKE'S GOSPEL AND LIBERATION THEOLOGY

Luke's stories about the birth of Jesus, his Sermon on the Plain, and many of his parables relate to the concerns of liberation theology and therefore are often cited in its literature. Liberation theology begins with the presupposition that God is on the side of the poor and oppressed—articulated by the phrase "**preferential option for the poor**"—and demonstrates a commitment to the poor and

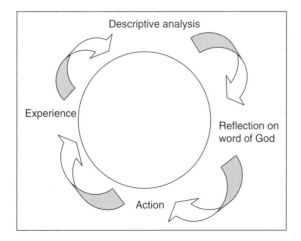

underprivileged that is modeled on God's commitment to the poor and under-privileged. Its ethical position is that those who wish to follow Jesus must stand in solidarity with the poor.

Liberation theology follows the social praxis model: (1) People insert them-selves into the experience of those whom they wish to serve, (2) reflect on their experience (descriptive analysis), (3) ask what the word of God has to say to their experience, and (4) determine what action they must take to make God's word a reality in the world. Thus, liberation theology is a theology of action in the sense that it advocates *application* of the Bible in the form of action on behalf of the poor. It values the Bible as a *transformative* document that actualizes or makes con-crete the ideals of the liberated Christian community and that calls people to conversion. In other words, the source of its theology is the experience of the people and the scripture that articulates this experience. Liberation theologians read the Bible from the hermeneutic perspective of the poor—that is, with the "eyes" of the poor.

This model for doing theology is sometimes called "the circle of praxis," based upon a diagram and description published in Joe Holland's and Peter Henriot's book, *Social Analysis: Linking Faith and Justice* (1980). If you are interested in issues related to justice and peace studies, you may want to read this book for yourself.

## Key Terms

| | | |
|---|---|---|
| Prologue | Reversal theology | Travel narrative |
| God-fearer | Annunciation | Ascension |
| Theophilus | Visitation | Preferential option for |
| Magnificat | People of the land | the poor |

## QUESTIONS FOR READING

Read the Gospel of Luke. Use evidence from the text to answer the following questions.

1. Make a list of the events that are recorded in Luke's infancy narratives (Luke 1:1–2:52), and compare it to the list of the events in Matthew's infancy narratives (Matt. 1:1–2:23) that you made in the preceding chapter (see Chapter 7, Questions for Reading #1). What observations can you make after comparing the two lists?

2. Explain the major themes of the Magnificat (Luke 1:46–55) and the Canticle of Zechariah (Luke 1:68–79) in Luke's gospel. How do these themes relate to the notion of reversal theology?

3. Compare Luke's genealogy (Luke 3:23–38) to the genealogy in the opening of the Gospel of Matthew (Matt. 1:1–17). What do you conclude about the theological meaning of Luke's genealogy?

4. Compare the Sermon on the Plain from Luke's gospel (Luke 6:1–49) to the Sermon on the Mount from Matthew's gospel (Matt. 5:1–7:29). What similarities can you identify in the two versions? Where are the significant differences?

5. The section known as Luke's Travel Narrative (Luke 9:51–18:14) contains a number of teachings that Jesus directed toward his disciples. Based on these teachings, what would you say about the gospel writer's understanding of the ideals of discipleship? Give evidence from the text to support your position.

6. Luke's Travel Narrative contains a number of parables and stories that are contained in no other gospel. Use the cross-references in your Bible (or the lack thereof) to locate at least three and describe their themes. How do these relate to the themes of Luke's gospel overall?

7. Locate at least three stories in Luke's gospel that have a woman or women among their central characters. What common elements can you find in your selected stories? What do you think Luke is saying, through these stories, about Jesus' attitude toward women?

8. Locate at least two stories or sayings that illustrate Luke's message about the dangers of riches. What clues can you find in your two selections that explain why Luke thought riches were dangerous? Explain.

9. Use your outline of the passion and resurrection narratives in Mark's gospel to identify the special features of Luke's passion and resurrection narratives. Make a list of any scenes in Luke's gospel that are absent from Mark's gospel or that have been changed in some significant way. *Hint:* Your Bible's cross-references or a gospel synopsis can help you with this question.

10. Luke's stories about the appearances of the risen Jesus have a common theme: Either a messenger tells people to remember what Jesus told them when he was with them or the risen Jesus himself interprets the scriptures for the disciples. What is Luke's point? Give examples to explain.

## Questions for Reflection

1. What overall impressions do you get from Luke's portrayal of Jesus? Is this the type of Jesus to whom you would be attracted? Why or why not? Be prepared to give concrete evidence from the gospel to support your position.

2. Why might a culture preserve stories associated with the birth of its famous people? What is the function of these stories? Why might the early church have preserved the birth stories of Jesus? How might the stories have been adapted from their original form? Can you identify anything comparable in the cultures of modern peoples?

3. Imagine that you are to do a modern rewriting of Matthew's Sermon on the Mount or Luke's Sermon on the Plain. Identify the modern audience to which it would be addressed. What aspects of Matthew's or Luke's sermon are relevant today, regardless of the differences in cultural or historical context?

## Activities for Learning

1. Locate several artistic representations of the Annunciation or the Nativity of Jesus. You might select from different historical periods or different parts of the world. As you analyze each of the paintings, pay attention to how closely the artist followed the infancy narratives in the Gospel of Luke. Look for other details (colors, objects, etc.) that might have symbolic meaning for the artist. What can you conclude about the artist's theological interpretation of the event? The following questions may help you with your analysis:
   a. Study the artistic representation carefully. What is your first response to the work?
   b. When and where was the work created? Are these circumstances reflected in any way in the presentation of the work? Does it have attributes of a particular culture or time period?
   c. What do we know about the artist? What purpose did the work serve? For example, was it created to stimulate devotion? To teach? To delight? To express a feeling? To illustrate a mystery of faith?
   d. What is the title of the work? Does the title help us understand anything about the intent of the artist?
   e. Observe the medium in which the artist worked (e.g., oil on canvas, carving in wood or stone, pastels or charcoal on paper). What does the artist's medium contribute to your overall impression of the work?
   f. What colors and tones or hues did the artist use? Are the contours (outlines of shapes) of the work strong and hard, or are they irregular and indistinct? What is the level of detail contained in the work? How is perspective used? How do these aspects of the artist's technique affect your overall sense of the work?
   g. What is the central subject of the work? What objects are placed around the periphery? Are any of these objects significant/symbolic in any way?

    h. Identify the major characters depicted in the work. How do these characters relate to one another? How are they situated in relationship to the background of the work? What do these relationships convey about the meaning of the work?

    i. What biblical text appears to have provided the inspiration for the work? To what extent is it simply a retelling of the biblical text and in what ways is it a reinterpretation of the text?

    j. What theological question does the artist's work address or in what sense is it a proclamation of faith? Explain. How does cultural perspective enter into the interpretation of the work or the biblical text on which it is based?

2. Investigate the origins and the history of development of some of the feasts and religious devotions associated with Mary, the mother of Jesus, within one of the Christian traditions that celebrate these feasts or encourage these religious practices. You might select one or more of the following: the Hail Mary prayer, the liturgical feasts of the Annunciation and Visitation, and the rosary. To what extent are these feasts and religious practices biblically based? What other influences have contributed to their development?

3. Investigate some of the faith-based social justice organizations in your city or region. After reviewing their literature or websites, select one that you think might have liberation theology as its theoretical basis for operation. Interview someone from the organization about his or her understanding of the preferential option for the poor and how the organization's work is a necessary expression of its faith commitment. Use Leonardo Boff and Clodovis Boff's book, *Introducing Liberation Theology (1987)*, or a comparable text, to provide yourself with some background with which to formulate your interview questions.

## Sources and Resources

Arlandson, James Malcolm. *Women, Class, and Society in Early Christianity: Models from Luke-Acts.* Peabody, Mass.: Hendrickson Publishers, 1997.

Boff, Leonardo, and Clodovis Boff. *Introducing Liberation Theology.* Maryknoll, N.Y.: Orbis Books, 1987.

Brawley, Robert L. *Centering on God: Method and Message in Luke-Acts.* Louisville, Ky.: Westminster John Knox Press, 1990.

Brown, Raymond E. *The Birth of the Messiah: A Commentary on the Infancy Narratives in Matthew and Luke.* Garden City, N.Y.: Doubleday, 1977.

_____. *The Death of the Messiah.* 2 vols. New York: Doubleday, 1994.

Cassidy, Richard. *Political Issues in Luke-Acts.* Maryknoll, N.Y.: Orbis Books, 1983.

Darr, John A. *On Character Building: The Reader and the Rhetoric of Characterization in Luke-Acts.* Louisville, Ky.: Westminster John Knox Press, 1992.

Dornisch, Loretta. *A Woman Reads the Gospel of Luke.* Collegeville, Minn.: Liturgical Press, 1996.

Esler, Philip Francis. *Community and Gospel in Luke-Acts: The Social and Political Motivations of Lucan Theology.* Cambridge, England: Cambridge University Press, 1987.

Gillman, John. *Possessions and the Life of Faith: A Reading of Luke-Acts.* Collegeville, Minn.: Liturgical Press, 1991.

Gowler, David B. *Host, Guest, Enemy, and Friend: Portraits of the Pharisees in Luke and Acts.* New York: Lang, 1991.

Grassi, Joseph A. *Peace on Earth: Roots and Practices from Luke's Gospel.* Collegeville, Minn.: Liturgical Press, 2004.

Green, Joel B. *The Theology of the Gospel of Luke.* Cambridge, England: Cambridge University Press, 1995.

Heil, John Paul. *The Meal Scenes in Luke-Acts: An Audience-Oriented Approach*. Atlanta, Ga.: Society of Biblical Literature, 1999.

Holland, J., and P. Henriot. *Social Analysis: Linking Faith and Justice*. New York: Orbis Books, 1980.

Horsley, Richard. *The Liberation of Christmas: The Infancy Narratives in Social Context*. New York: Crossroad, 1989.

Karris, Robert J. *Eating Your Way Through Luke's Gospel*. Collegeville, Minn.: Liturgical Press, 2006.

Kim, Kyoung-Jin. *Stewardship and Almsgiving in Luke's Theology*. Sheffield, England: Sheffield Academic Press, 1998.

Kingsbury, Jack Dean. *Conflict in Luke: Jesus, Authorities, Disciples*. Minneapolis, Minn.: Fortress Press, 1991.

LaHurd, Carol Schursten. "Re-viewing Luke 15 with Arab Christian Women". In *A Feminist Companion to Luke*, edited by Amy-Jill Levine with Marianne Blickenstaff. London: Sheffield Academic Press, 2002.

Levine, Amy-Jill, with Marianne Blickenstaff, eds. *A Feminist Companion to Luke*. London: Sheffield Academic Press, 2002.

Malina, Bruce J., and Richard L. Rohrbaugh. *Social-Science Commentary on the Synoptic Gospels*. Minneapolis, Minn.: Fortress, 1992.

Moore, Stephen D. *Mark and Luke in Poststructuralist Perspectives: Jesus Begins to Write*. New Haven, Conn.: Yale University Press, 1992.

Neale, David A. *None But The Sinners: Religious Categories in the Gospel of Luke*. Sheffield, England: JSOT Press, 1991.

Neogoe, Alexandru. *The Trial of the Gospel: An Apologetic Reading of Luke's Trial Narratives*. Cambridge, England: Cambridge University Press, 2002.

Neyrey, Jerome H., ed. *The Social World of Luke-Acts*. Peabody, Mass.: Hendrickson, 1991.

Patella, Michael. *The Gospel According to Luke*. Collegeville, Minn.: Liturgical Press, 2005.

Phillips, Thomas E. *Reading Issues of Wealth and Poverty in Luke-Acts*. Lewiston, N.Y.: Mellen Biblical Press, 2001.

Reid, Barbara E. *Choosing the Better Part? Women in the Gospel of Luke*. Collegeville, Minn.: Liturgical Press, 1996.

Roth, Samuel John. *The Blind, The Lame, and The Poor: Character Types in Luke-Acts*. Sheffield, England: Sheffield Academic Press, 1997.

Senior, Donald. *The Passion of Jesus in the Gospel of Luke*. Wilmington, Del.: Glazier, 1989.

Shellard, Barbara. *New Light on Luke: Its Purpose, Sources and Literary Context*. London: Sheffield Academic Press, 2002.

Swanson, Richard W. *Provoking the Gospel of Luke: A Storyteller's Commentary, Year C*. Cleveland, Ohio: Pilgrim Press, 2006.

Sweetland, Dennis M. *Our Journey with Jesus: Discipleship in Luke and Acts*. Collegeville, Minn.: Liturgical Press, 1990.

Talbert, Charles H. *Reading Luke: A Literary and Theological Commentary*. Macon, Ga.: Smyth and Helwys Publishers, 2002.

_____. *Reading Luke-Acts in Its Mediterranean Milieu*. Leiden, Netherlands: Brill, 2003.

Tannehill, Robert C. *The Narrative Unity of Luke-Acts: A Literary Interpretation*. Philadelphia: Fortress, 1986.

_____. *Luke*. Nashville, Tenn.: Abingdon Press, 1996.

Tiede, David L. *Prophecy and History in Luke-Acts*. Philadelphia: Fortress, 1980.

Tuckett, Christopher M. *Luke*. Sheffield, England: Sheffield Academic Press, 1996.

Tyson, Joseph B. *Images of Judaism in Luke-Acts*. Columbia: University of South Carolina Press, 1992.

Wenk, Matthias. *Community-Forming Power: The Socio-Ethical Role of the Spirit in Luke-Acts*. Sheffield, England: Sheffield Academic Press, 2000.

Wright, N. T. *Luke for Everyone*. London: SPCK; Louisville, Ky.: Westminster John Knox Press, 2004.

# CHAPTER 9

# THE GOSPEL ACCORDING TO JOHN

## OVERVIEW

- AUTHORSHIP: Anonymous; perhaps a Jewish Christian who was somehow identified with the Beloved Disciple; traditionally associated with John, the son of Zebedee, or John of Ephesus
- DATE OF COMPOSITION: 90–100 C.E.
- INITIAL AUDIENCE: Probably Ephesus, but other locations have been suggested
- MAJOR TOPICS: Sources for the Gospel of John; Literary Features of the Gospel of John; The Eschatology of John's Gospel; Jesus, the Logos and Wisdom of God; Jesus as God's "I Am"; Johannine Discipleship; Signs, Glory, and Glorification in John's Gospel; The "Lifted Up" Sayings; The Bread of Life Discourse; The Foot-Washing Scene; John's Passion and Resurrection Narratives; The Story alongside of the Story

## TIMELINE

| | |
|---|---|
| 37 B.C.E. | Herod the Great takes up his kingship in Palestine. |
| 6–4 B.C.E. | Jesus of Nazareth is born. |
| 4 B.C.E. | Herod the Great, king of Palestine, dies. His kingdom is divided among three sons: Archelaus, Herod Antipas, and Philip. |
| 4 B.C.E.–39 C.E. | Herod Antipas, son of Herod the Great, is tetrarch of Galilee and Perea. |
| 6 C.E. | Annas (Ananus I) becomes High Priest of the Jerusalem Temple. |
| 18 C.E. | Caiaphas, the son-in-law of Annas, becomes High Priest of the Jerusalem Temple. |
| 26–36 C.E. | Pontius Pilate is prefect of Judea and Samaria. |
| c. 28 C.E. | John the Baptist is executed by Herod Antipas. |
| c. 30 C.E. | Jesus is crucified, dies, and is resurrected. |
| c. 41–44 C.E. | The apostle James, the brother of John, is martyred. |
| 64 C.E. | Peter and Paul are martyred in Rome. |
| 65–70 C.E. | The Gospel of Mark is written. |
| 66–70 C.E. | The Jewish War occurs. |
| 70 C.E. | Jerusalem and the Temple are destroyed. |
| 80–90 C.E. | The Gospels of Matthew and Luke are written. |

| 90–100 C.E. | **The Gospel of John is written.** |
| c. 180 C.E. | Irenaeus of Lyons writes *Against Heresies.* |
| c. 310 C.E. | Eusebius of Caesarea completes *Ecclesiastical History.* |

In our journey through the synoptic gospels, we observed that the Gospels of Matthew, Mark, and Luke have certain common elements that lend a sense of coherence to the story of Jesus. At the same time, they differ from one another in ways that are substantial enough to prompt the careful reader to conclude that the synoptic gospels provide us with several distinctive portraits of Jesus. These differences are even more pronounced when we compare them to the Gospel of John. John's gospel is different from the synoptic gospels in chronology, literary style, and even content. Some of the events that the synoptic gospels place at the end of Jesus' life—for example, the scene in which Jesus throws the moneychangers out of the Temple—appear close to the beginning of the Gospel of John. Likewise, some of the kinds of literature that we commonly find in the synoptic gospels (e.g., parables) are nowhere present in the Gospel of John. Add to these differences in content, form, and chronology a distinctive literary style and a unique use of symbolism and we have, in the Gospel of John, another exceptional portrait of Jesus. Thus, the next stop on our voyage through the New Testament will provide us with some interesting opportunities for exploration.

Again, as we have done several times before, let us pause to summarize what biblical scholars have concluded about the authorship and date and location of composition of this gospel before setting out on our journey through its pages.

## AUTHORSHIP

One strand of early church tradition from the second century C.E. connected the author of the Gospel of John with John, the son of Zebedee, one of the twelve named in Mark's gospel. Also circulating in the second century C.E. was a tradition about another John, not an apostle of Jesus, who lived to an old age and who wrote a gospel from his home in Ephesus. Irenaeus apparently conflated these two stories, since he says that the gospel writer was John, the son of Zebedee, who lived a long life in Ephesus and wrote the gospel there (*Against Heresies* 3.1.1). Perhaps in an attempt to clear up the confusion, Eusebius indicates that there were two people named John who were honored and remembered at Ephesus: one who was an apostle and another who was a presbyter (i.e., elder) (*Ecclesiastical History* 7.25.1–16; 3.39.1–7).

Although the author of the Gospel of John does not name himself in the text, the gospel does provide us with a few clues about his identity. Apparently, he was familiar with the geography of Palestine, since he accurately describes the location of certain sites like Solomon's Porch in the Temple (John 10:23) and Bethany (John 11:18). John 21:20–23 suggests that he did not die a martyr's death but lived to an old age. Because the author makes numerous references to Jewish feasts and religious observances, we can be fairly certain that he was Jewish Christian. Further, the gospel indicates that its author, or at least the one who is responsible for the tradition on which it is based, is the "disciple whom Jesus loved" or the **Beloved Disciple** (John 19:35; 21:20–24). He is elsewhere identified in this gospel as the "other" disciple.

Who is this Beloved Disciple? Scholars of John's gospel have explored a number of options over the years. We have already commented on the traditional option, John the son of Zebedee, but here are some others:

- Lazarus, the one whom Jesus loved (John 11:3)
- Thomas, the disciple who was willing to die with Jesus but who later refused to believe until he was directed to touch the risen Jesus (John 11:16; 20:24–29)
- A symbolic figure created by the author of the gospel as a model of true discipleship
- A now unknown historical figure who was part of the ministry of Jesus and who later became the founder or spiritual leader of the community for which the Gospel of John was written.

Most scholars of John's gospel favor the last of these options. According to this view, the gospel traces itself to the apostolic tradition, but its author is unknown.

Such confusion in the early church traditions about the authorship of John's gospel should be a reminder that the early church was not particularly concerned with providing documentary history for future generations but rather with establishing the authority of the biblical text. Apparently, the Gospel of John was extremely popular among second- and third-century Gnostic Christians. In fact, the Gnostic Heracleon was the first to write a commentary on this gospel (see Chapter 11 for more on the Gnostics and Gnosticism. See http://www.webcom.com/gnosis/library/fragh.htm for an English translation of fragments from Heracleon's commentary). At the same time, the orthodox or mainstream churches of the third through fifth centuries depended heavily on the Gospel of John for the development of their teaching on the Trinitarian nature of God (i.e., how God could be "three in one," referring to the relationship of the Father, Son, and Holy Spirit). Perhaps second-century Christian writers also recognized its authority for the churches and articulated their conviction about its reliability as a document of faith by connecting it to the disciple John. Again, for the sake of convenience, we will call this author John, even though we do not know his name.

## INITIAL AUDIENCE AND DATE OF COMPOSITION

Early Christian writings associate the author of the Gospel of John, as well as the community for which it was written, with Ephesus. Since there is little evidence to oppose the traditional view, we should allow the possibility that it was written in Ephesus. However, because the gospel writer shows considerable familiarity with Judea and locations in and around the Jerusalem Temple, some scholars have suggested a Palestinian location for the gospel. Others have suggested Syria, north of Palestine. Further, it appears that the **Johannine** (adj.: belonging to the Gospel of John) **community**—that is, the community for which John's gospel was written—was Jewish Christian, at least when it was first established. This view is supported by the author's liberal use of references to Jewish feasts and religious practices with little or no explanation of their meaning or significance. At the same time, the gospel contains clues that the community for which it was written was already expanding to include Samaritans and Gentiles. The stories of the Samaritan woman who encounters Jesus at a well (John 4:3–42) and the Greeks who ask to meet Jesus (John 12:20–26) are two examples.

However, the Johannine community was not entirely expansive and outward in its movement. The gospel contains evidence that the community for which it was written was engaged in some kind of struggle with fellow Jews, but the evidence is not entirely unambiguous. Occasionally, "the Jews" is used in a value-neutral way to refer to Jewish people who are undecided about Jesus (e.g., John 2:18–20; 3:1; 6:41–42, 52), or to Jewish friends of characters who are devoted to Jesus (e.g., John 11:45). More often than not, however, "the Jews" is used in a negative sense to refer to people who were opposed to Jesus. They are portrayed as harassing Jesus at every turn and even seeking to kill him (John 5:18; 7:1, 13; 8:59). Likewise, John presents Jesus as harshly criticizing "the Jews," charging them with doing the work of their father, the devil (John 8:39–44). He also tells a story about a blind man who, after being healed by Jesus and professing faith in him, is thrown out of the synagogue (John 9:1–41).

Most biblical scholars see these comments about "the Jews" as expressions of concern from the gospel writer and his community in the latter part of the first century C.E. and not as belonging to the time of Jesus and the first disciples. This observation has led some to describe the Gospel of John as a two-level drama, a "two-story" story, or a story alongside of a story. As such, the gospel is an account of the life of Jesus, but embedded in it is a reflection on the later Christian community's history. The story of the healing of the blind man (John 9:1–41) is a good example of this two-level drama. Notice, in particular, the parents of the blind man who refuse to stand up for their son because they are afraid of getting kicked out of the synagogue (John 9:22). It is highly unlikely that Jews in Jesus' time were being excluded from the synagogue for listening to Jesus' teaching, but it is entirely possible that Jewish Christians, a generation or two after the death and resurrection of Jesus, were suffering such a fate. Thus, the dialogue that follows the story of the healing of the blind man (John 9:8–41) may well reflect the situation of the Johannine community: They have been thrown out of the synagogue!

Whatever the problems of the community and the identity of "the Jews"—most Johannine scholars think that they were the Jewish religious authorities in Jerusalem or a literary symbol of all who are opposed to Jesus—the author of the Gospel of John apparently perceives the situation to be beyond repair. Thus, the gospel has the tone of *fait accompli*. Anyone who is "sitting on the fence" cannot sit there for long because people involved in this story fall into one of two camps. Some belong to Jesus and are "from above." These are already saved. Others who refuse to believe have no hope because they are already condemned.

Concerning the date of composition for the Gospel of John, the author writes into the story of Jesus a statement about the Pharisees' fear that the Romans will come and destroy their Temple and their nation (John 11:48)—almost as a retrospective look at an event that had already taken place. Therefore, we can safely conclude that the Gospel of John was composed sometime after the destruction of Jerusalem in 70 C.E. On the other end of the time line, scholars think that the gospel was already in circulation before the mid-second century because we possess a manuscript fragment that dates to approximately 125 C.E.. To date, it is the earliest manuscript evidence that we possess of any part of the New Testament. Most Johannine scholars assign to the Gospel of John a date of composition that is in the middle of

Fragment of St. John's Gospel – second century
*John Rylands Library, Manchester*
(Actual size)

Rylands Papyrus 457, an early-second-century manuscript fragment that contains parts of John 18:31–33, 37–38. Plate XIV in *Our Bible and the Ancient Manuscripts* by Sir Frederick Kenyon (1895 – 4th ed. 1939).

this range, approximately 90–100 C.E. because it appears that the split between Jewish and Jewish Christian communities was beginning to take place at that time.

## SOURCES FOR THE GOSPEL OF JOHN

Even a casual reading of the Gospel of John will show that it does not have a great deal in common with the synoptic gospels. At the same time, a careful reader of John's gospel might notice that some of its stories appear to be very old and some of its speeches seem to be "variations on a theme," incorporated into the gospel without appropriate transitions or conclusions. These observations prompted some biblical scholars of the past century to ask whether John was using written source materials to construct his gospel. Rudolf Bultmann, writing in the 1950s, suggested that John used three such sources: a discourse source (from which the author drew the gospel's speeches or sermons), a signs source (from which he selected its miracles), and a passion story (1976, 6–7). Ultimately, Bultmann's theory concerning the discourse source and the passion source did not gain much acceptance among scholars, but the **signs source** is considered a good possibility.

Other scholarly investigations into the sources of John's gospel have focused on similarities with the synoptic gospels. Though limited, these similarities, where they exist, are significant. For example, both Mark and John have similar stories of Jesus feeding 5,000 in the wilderness and Jesus walking on water, and they appear in the same order in both gospels (Mark 6:30–52; John 6:1–21). Further, in both feeding stories, the disciples comment that it would take 200 denarii (each denarius equaling about a day's wages) to feed the crowd (Mark 6:37; John 6:7). Mark's and John's gospels also share some details concerning the story of the woman who anoints Jesus. Both authors describe the ointment as "costly perfume of pure nard" (Mark 14:3; John 12:3), and someone among the crowd complains that the ointment could have been sold for 300 denarii (Mark 14:5; John 12:5).

Likewise, Luke's and John's gospels have some important similarities. For example, they include several characters—Mary, Martha, and Lazarus— that are not found anywhere else among the canonical gospels. In both gospels, Mary and Martha are sisters (Luke 10:38–42; John 11:1–44). Both gospels give an account of Lazarus's death (Luke 16:19–31; John 11:1–44). However, in Luke's gospel, Lazarus is portrayed as a poor beggar who used to lie starving at the gate of a rich man's house (Luke 16:19–31), whereas John's gospel depicts Lazarus as the brother of Mary and Martha and, as a family, certainly not in danger of starvation (John 11:1–44). Additionally, both Luke's and John's gospels include the story of the risen Jesus appearing to the disciples in Jerusalem and inviting them to touch him (Luke 24:36–43; John 20:26–29), and both have a story about a miraculous catch of fish (Luke 5:1–11; John 21:4–8).

Do these shared stories mean that John had Luke's and Mark's gospels in front of him when he wrote his gospel? Not necessarily, but they do suggest that the author of John's gospel knew some of the same oral traditions—that is, the stories that were being passed on by word of mouth among communities of faith. Most historical critics (see Chapter 2) believe that the Gospel of John underwent several stages of development within the community before it was edited into its final form, much like the synoptic gospels did. Its double ending (John 20–21) suggests that the completed gospel also went through a final redaction before it was allowed to circulate among communities of faith.

## An Outline of the Book

Apart from its introduction and conclusion, the Gospel of John can be divided into two large sections: the **Book of Signs** (John 1:19–12:50), which recounts Jesus' miracles and is interspersed with several large sections of dialogue and discourse, and the **Book of Glory** (John 13:1–20:31), which recounts the story of the passion, death, and resurrection of Jesus and is punctuated by an extended farewell discourse, or perhaps more than one farewell discourse.

1. John 1:1–18—Prologue: the divine Logos
2. John 1:19–12:50—Book of Signs
3. John 13:1–20:31—Book of Glory
   a. Last Supper (John 13:1–38)
   b. Farewell discourses and prayer for the church (John 14:1–17:26)
   c. Passion and resurrection narratives (John 18:1–20:31)
4. John 21:1–25—Epilogue: appearances in Galilee

Notice that John's gospel has a prologue. As you may recall, we saw an example of a prologue in Luke's gospel. However, John's prologue is different from Luke's because it provides us with a poetic synopsis (summary) of the entire gospel story, whereas Luke's prologue is more like a preface, explaining how and why he came to write his gospel. John's gospel also has an epilogue. An epilogue, as you know, is a follow-up to a story. We saw one (or several) of these at the conclusion of Mark's gospel. An epilogue might address questions that were left unanswered by the original story or tell the reader what happened to its major characters after the conclusion of the original story. The epilogue of John's gospel does both.

### GUIDE FOR INTERPRETING THE GOSPEL OF JOHN

What follows is your tour book for the Gospel of John. Again, we will not be summarizing the entire content of the gospel. Instead, we hope to offer some insights on certain parts of the gospel that will allow you to interpret John's gospel for yourself. We will begin with an explanation of some of the literary techniques that John used in writing his gospel story. We will also provide some background into the eschatology of John's gospel and some insights into his understanding of discipleship. After addressing these introductory topics, we will provide brief analyses of some of the gospel's more important (and in some cases, more difficult) segments. We will give particular attention to John's prologue and its presentation of Jesus as the Logos and Wisdom of God as well as the gospel's "I am" sayings. At the conclusion of this chapter, you will be invited to read the gospel for yourself. The "Questions for Reading" section will guide you.

## LITERARY FEATURES OF THE GOSPEL OF JOHN

We have already indicated that John's gospel differs from the synoptic gospels in its chronology and in some of its characters. However, perhaps its symbolic language and its use of literary techniques that are not found in the synoptic gospels are the most striking ways in which the Gospel of John distinguishes itself from the synoptic gospels. What follows is a brief survey of Johannine symbolic language and literary techniques. You may want to keep this list near you while you read the gospel because, once you are able to recognize John's literary techniques, you will be able to more fully appreciate the rich, multilayered meanings of this gospel.

First, the author of the Gospel of John uses the literary technique of **double meanings** and **misunderstanding**. John has Jesus say something that is deliberately ambiguous, usually having both a plain meaning and a symbolic meaning. The characters in the story understand only the plain meaning of Jesus' words, while Jesus *intends* the deeper meaning. When the characters say something that indicates their misunderstanding, then, much of the time, though not always, John has Jesus clarify the meaning of his words by giving a short speech, which biblical scholars call a discourse. The character in the story still may not understand the intended meaning of Jesus' words, but hopefully the reader or hearer of the gospel does.

As you will see, this gospel contains many examples of double meanings and misunderstanding. Here are a few examples. Jesus receives a message that his friend Lazarus is ill (John 11:3). After waiting around for a couple days, Jesus tells his disciples that Lazarus is asleep, but he's going to go wake him up (John 11:11). They say, "But you should let him sleep. If he's sleeping, he'll be fine!" (John 11:12). However, Jesus meant that Lazarus was dead and he is planning to go to Bethany to resuscitate him. But the story contains not a single clue that the disciples understood what Jesus was about to do. Likewise, in his dialogue with Nicodemus, Jesus tells him that the believer must be born *anothen* (John 3:3). The Greek word *anothen* can mean "from above" or "again." Nicodemus thinks that Jesus is saying that he must literally be born again—a ridiculous statement, to be sure—but Jesus is saying that he must be born from above and goes on to clarify what that means in a short discourse (John 3:5–8). Later, in Jesus' dialogue with the Samaritan woman, Jesus offers to give her "living" water (John 4:10). She thinks he is referring to "flowing" water—that is, fresh spring water—but he really means "eternal life" (John 4:14).

Somewhat related to the technique we just surveyed is John's use of **irony**. Although it is often hard to define, most people know irony when they see or hear it. In fact, that is what makes irony work! If the hearer or observer does not recognize something as ironic, then it fails to be effective. In the Gospel of John, certain characters do or say something that they intend to be derogatory, sarcastic, incredulous, or otherwise inadequate in the sense they intend. However, the reader knows that the statements or actions of these characters are more profoundly true or more meaningful than the story characters realize (John 4:12; 7:35, 42; 8:22; 11:50). For example, the Samaritan woman says to Jesus in what appears to be a scorning voice, "Surely, you're not greater than our father Jacob, are you?" (John 4:12). But that is precisely the point. He *is* greater than Jacob. In fact, he is greatest among all of the symbols of the Jewish faith. Likewise, after Jesus' arrest, when the soldiers dress him in a purple robe, place a crown of thorns on his head, and shout, "Hail, king of the Jews" (John 19:2–3), clearly they intend to mock him, but the reader knows that Jesus really *is* the king of the Jews! In fact, many biblical scholars think this is the central theme of John's passion narrative.

Another important feature of John's gospel is its long **symbolic discourses**. Compare these discourses to the teaching material of the synoptic gospels. In Matthew's gospel, for example, Jesus' discourses usually consist of short sayings, called *aphorisms*, linked together by a common theme or by catchwords. Other teaching material consists of brief stories that end in a saying of Jesus. These are called *apothegms* or *pronouncement stories*. In contrast, John's gospel contains long symbolic discourses, which are usually initiated by a misunderstanding on the part of some character in the story. Individual sayings cannot be excerpted to stand alone, as they do in the synoptic gospels, because the discourse is designed as a coherent whole. It is in these discourses that you will find characteristically Johannine themes and vocabulary like "my hour," "the Father's glory," and "abide in me." Finally, in the transition from dialogue to discourse, the careful reader will notice that Jesus' audience often appears to expand, or even change, from the narrow circle of the characters of the story to the larger circle of the readers of the gospel.

John also employs a literary technique called the **explanatory note**, which keeps the reader informed about what is going on in the story through the words of the narrator. More than simply telling the story, the narrator appears to step aside to speak directly to the reader, adding brief commentary where needed. In some cases, these notes provide explanations of names (John 1:38, 42) or symbols (John

2:21; 12:33; 18:9). Sometimes they correct misunderstandings (John 4:2, 6:6) and remind the reader of related events (John 3:24; 11:2) or clarify the identity of certain characters (John 7:50; 21:20). Thus, the reader always knows more than any of the gospel's characters, so much so that the reader becomes a privileged participant in the story, even equal to the narrator.

In addition, the author of the Gospel of John uses **chiasms**, or inverted parallelisms, to highlight its important themes. These are often difficult to identify in our English translations, but ancient audiences were well attuned to their artistry and likely would have recognized them right away. Chiasms are constructed in such a way that the first unit of a gospel passage corresponds to the last unit of the same passage, the second unit corresponds to the second to the last unit of the passage, and so on (e.g., John 6:36–40, 18:28–19:16). If the chiasm has an even number of units, the outermost elements are the ones that the gospel writer wants to highlight. If the chiasm has an odd number of units, then the focal point is the central element. An example is given below:

    A.  John 7:1–2: Before the feast, the "Jews" seek to kill Jesus.

        B.  John 7:3–5: The brothers demand that Jesus manifest himself to the world.

            C.  John 7:6: Jesus' response: "his time" has not yet come.

                D.  John 7:7: The world hates Jesus because of his testimony against it.

            C'.  John 7:8–9: Jesus' repeated response: "his time" is not yet fulfilled.

        B'.  John 7:10: Jesus goes up to the feast—not openly but in secret.

    A'.  John 7:11–13: At the feast, the "Jews" seek Jesus.

Notice that the first and last units (A and A') of this chiasm refer to the feast of Tabernacles and describe how "the Jews" (not the Jewish people but perhaps a symbol of those who are dualistically opposed to Jesus and refuse to believe in him; see "Anti-Judaism in the Early Church" in Chapter 11) are seeking Jesus in order to kill him. The second and second to the last units (B and B') are about whether Jesus should manifest himself to the world or keep secret his identity and mission. The third and third to the last units (C and C') describe Jesus' time as "not yet." Since this chiasm has an odd number of units, its focal point is the central unit (D), which describes the world's hatred of Jesus because of his testimony against it. In fact, this is one of the central themes of the entire gospel.

Another important feature of the Gospel of John is its dualism. In the simplest of terms, **dualism** has to do with polar opposites, but there are many kinds of dualism. For example, we could talk about ethical dualism, which places persons and activities that represent goodness in stark contrast with persons and activities that represent evil. One might also talk about the dualism of body and soul or spirit. As we shall see, the dualism of the Gospel of John is neither ethical nor anthropological (having to do with the human person). Here is a list of some of the dualistic pairs found in John's gospel:

| | |
|---|---|
| Light | Darkness |
| Truth | Falsehood |
| Life | Death |
| Of God | Of Satan |

| From above | From below |
|------------|------------|
| Spirit     | Flesh      |

By carefully analyzing the literary context in which these dualistic pairs appear throughout the Gospel of John, we soon discover that their common denominator is belief and unbelief. Of course, John's understanding of belief is quite different from that of many modern believers, who think it involves some sort of mental assent to the official teachings of a particular religious group. For John, and for most of the New Testament writers, belief is best described as trust, specifically trust in Jesus. In John's gospel, those who believe or trust in Jesus are said to walk in the light and belong to God. They are from above and have eternal life. Those who refuse to believe in Jesus walk in the darkness and belong to Satan. Because they are from below, they are already perishing.

## THE ESCHATOLOGY OF JOHN'S GOSPEL

The dualism that we find in the Gospel of John prompts a discussion of another feature that makes this gospel unique—its eschatology. The word comes from the Greek *eschaton*, which means "last," as in the last or end of a thing. Thus, **eschatology** refers to teachings about the end time: For what are we destined? When and how will the end time come? What awaits us after death? How will the righteous be rewarded and the wicked punished? Generally speaking, the synoptic gospels have what is called future eschatology, though their views on the end time are not identical. Mark's gospel, for example, focuses on the nearness of the *parousia* (second coming of the messiah), while Matthew acknowledges its delay but still expects the end will come relatively soon, and Luke pushes it into the distant future. Whether near or far, all three synoptic gospels expect that the end time will come sometime in the future and that it will be ushered in by the return of the risen Jesus.

Like the synoptic gospels, John's gospel contains some statements that reflect future eschatology. See, for example, John 5:28, in which Jesus says, "Do not be astonished at this; for the hour is coming when all who are in their graves will hear his voice and will come out—those who have done good, to the resurrection of life, and those who have done evil, to the resurrection of condemnation." However, the vast majority of eschatological statements in this gospel can be described as **realized eschatology**. This observation has led biblical scholars to conclude that the community for which John's gospel was written believed that the end-time reign of God had already come, at least in a partial way, and that its realities were already present in Christ and in the Christian community. Thus, you will hear the Jesus of John's gospel saying, "Anyone who hears my word and believes him who sent me *has* eternal life, and does not come under judgment, but has passed from death to life" (John 5:24). Elsewhere he says that "those who do not believe are condemned *already*" (John 3:18) and "whoever believes *has* eternal life" (John 6:47). That is, regardless of what happens in life or death, the believer is already enjoying eternal life and those who oppose Jesus are already perishing. The time for decision has passed and each person's destiny is set. You either belong to the light or walk in the darkness; you are already part of the believing community or you are lost. Thus, you can see how such a view of the end time is consistent with John's dualism.

## JESUS, THE LOGOS AND WISDOM OF GOD

Let us turn now to John's portrait of Jesus. The author of the gospel employs the literary techniques that we have described above, the dualism of belief and unbelief, and realized eschatology to tell his story of Jesus and explain how and why he believes that "Jesus is the Messiah, the Son of God" (John 20:31). Key to understanding John's portrait of Jesus is the prologue of his gospel (John 1:1–18). As with most prologues, it was probably written after the main part of the gospel was completed and with the goal of providing a lens for the interpretation of the gospel. In this case, John's prologue focuses the gospel on the Son, whom John calls the Word, and on his relationship with God the Father, with creation, and with the believer. However, before we can elaborate on John's portrait of Jesus as introduced in the prologue, we need to say something about his use of the word *Word* to describe the Son of God (John 1:1, 14).

John begins his gospel, "In the beginning was the Word and the Word was with God and the Word was God" (or godlike) (John 1:1–2). The Greek word is **logos**, which can be translated as "word" or "reason." The philosopher Heraclitus, in the sixth century B.C.E., was apparently the first to introduce the term into philosophical circles, where it was used to describe the unifying principle of the created world and the power that underlies all of creation. For the Stoics, the logos represented the mind of God, which was responsible for the order and harmony of the universe. In the first century C.E., the Jewish philosopher Philo adopted some of this philosophical logos language to speak about Israel's God and God's relationship to creation. He wrote about the Logos as God's intermediary with the created world—a second god, in a sense—and about how the Logos gave meaning and order to creation (*On the Confusion of Tongues* 62–63; *On the Cherubim* 125–127). He also wrote about how the Logos is a pattern for the human soul. Thus, like divine Logos, which mediated between God and the created world, the logos within the human person is capable of uniting humanity with God. Philo even used the phrase "Son of God" to describe the Logos (*On the Confusion of Tongues* 146–147).

We cannot say with any certainty that John borrowed directly from the Greek philosophers when he wrote about the Logos in his prologue. However, the connections are illuminating. Concerning creation, John writes that "all things came into being" through the Logos (John 1:3). John also attributes to the Word the special status of being God's only Son (John 1:14, 18). Further, John describes the mediating role of the Logos in humanity's encounter with God, saying, "No one has ever seen God. It is God the only Son . . . who has made him known" (John 1:18). Likewise, he describes the Logos as the means by which humanity is united to God, saying, "To all who received him . . . he gave power to become children of God" (John 1:12).

In addition to or aside from Greek philosophy, John very likely drew on Jewish wisdom literature and its depiction of Wisdom (see Chapter 4) to flesh out his portrayal of Jesus as the Logos of God. In Jewish wisdom literature, Wisdom—also known as *Sophia* (Greek for "wisdom")—is a personified power of God, possessing certain divine attributes. The sages (i.e., wise teachers) describe her as dwelling with God from the beginning (Sir. 24:4, 9; Wis. 9:9) and as coming forth from the mouth of God (Sir. 24:3; Wis. 9:1–2). Further, they write that Wisdom participated with God in the act of creation as God's craftsperson (Prov. 8:22–23, 27–30; Sir. 24:9; Wis. 7:22; 9:9). She is also described as the glory of God and the brilliance of eternal light (Wis. 7:25–26). She is light and life for humanity, a light that darkness cannot overcome (Prov. 8:35; Wis. 7:29–30). Finally, the sages describe Wisdom as coming into the world and making her dwelling among the people of Israel through the covenant that God gave to Moses (Sir. 24:8, 10–12), but she was also rejected by Israel when it refused to keep the covenant (Wis. 9:10; Sir. 24:8ff).

John's prologue contains much of this same Wisdom imagery in its references to the Word. For example, John describes the Word as being "in the beginning with God" (John 1:2; cf. John 1:15). In theological terms, scholars refer to this notion as the **preexistence** (i.e., existence at an earlier time and in a different state) of the Word, who is the Son of God. He also describes the Word as a participant in creation, saying, "All things came into being through him, and without him not one thing came into being" (John 1:3). Further, the Word is "the true light, which enlightens everyone" (John 1:9); the light that "shines in the darkness," which the darkness cannot overcome (John 1:5); and the glory of God (John 1:14)—all descriptors of personified Wisdom. Later in the gospel, we discover that the gospel writer understands Jesus to be the light insofar as he sheds light on or exposes those who walk in the darkness (e.g., John 3:19–21; 9:3–5, 39–41). In other words, in John's gospel, light is an image that evokes judgment. John also writes in his prologue about how the Word became flesh and "made his dwelling" among God's people (John 1:14)—in theological terms, the **incarnation** (literally taking on flesh) of the Son—and about how some rejected him (John 1:10–11) as they had rejected Wisdom.

We have already mentioned how Jewish wisdom literature associates the sending of personified Wisdom with the Mosaic covenant and the giving of the Law (see Sir. 24:8, 10–12). Likewise, John's prologue describes the Word-made-flesh in terms of covenant imagery. For example, John's description of the believing community as children of God (John 1:14) has covenant overtones. In addition, the phrase "grace and truth" (John 1:14, 17) has parallels with the Old Testament covenant phrases "loving kindness" and "faithfulness," which are associated with the expression of God's love for Israel in the covenant (e.g., Dan. 9:4; Isa. 54:10; Psa. 89:34–35). Finally, John's reference to Moses and the Law (John 1:17) reflects the theme of covenant—in this case, the famous covenant at Sinai. However, John goes a step further, suggesting that Jesus is the *fullness* of the covenant and the one from whom we receive "grace upon grace" or inexhaustible grace (John 1:16–17).

After the prologue, John no longer refers to Jesus as the Word, and nowhere in the gospel does he actually call Jesus the Wisdom of God. However, the themes associated with these two attributions continue to appear throughout the gospel. For example, in keeping with the idea that the Logos mediates between God and humanity, John presents Jesus as the revealer of God and the only way to the Father (e.g., John 14:6). Likewise, the theme of seeking and finding and the phrase "Come and see," which appear again and again in John's gospel, recall personified Wisdom's invitation to the wise to "come and see" and her declaration that many may seek but only the wise will find wisdom (Prov. 1:28; 3:13; 8:1–5, 17, 35; 9:3–6). As you carefully read the Gospel of John, you will find evidence of these two themes throughout the gospel.

## JESUS AS GOD'S "I AM"

John's portrait of Jesus is further enhanced and more finely nuanced by the inclusion of his characteristic **"I am" sayings**. Sometimes the "I am" sayings stand alone, without an object, as in John 6:20, when Jesus speaks to his frightened disciples, saying, "It is I," when they see him near the boat in the midst of a terrible storm. His statement, "It is I," or *eigo emi,* is the Greek equivalent of the Hebrew "YHWH," translated "I am (who am)." This is the divine name, which was revealed to Moses at the burning bush (Exod. 3:13–15).

However, many times John's "I am" sayings include an object, as in the following examples:

- I am the Bread of Life (John 6:35)
- I am the Living water (John 7:37)
- I am the Light of the world (John 8:12)
- I am the Door of the sheep (John 10:7)
- I am the Good shepherd (John 10:11)
- I am the Resurrection and Life (John 11:25)
- I am the Way, truth, and life (John 14:6)
- I am the True vine (John 15:1)

Most draw on Old Testament imagery or imagery associated with Jewish feasts. For example, the "bread of life" imagery is an allusion to the manna that God provided to the Israelites to save them from starvation as they wandered in the wilderness during the Exodus (Exod. 16:1–8; cf. Num. 11:1–9). Similarly, the "living water" imagery likely alludes to the water-drawing ritual that was part of the feast of Tabernacles, in which the Jewish priests carried water from the Pool of Siloam to the Temple as a reminder of the water from the rock that God provided to the Israelites during the Exodus (Num. 10:2–13).

When you first see these "I am" sayings, you might be tempted to think that they are simply poetic metaphors: "What is Jesus like? He is like the light!" However, on a deeper level of meaning, they relate to the manner in which Jesus is the **agent of God**. First-century peoples were familiar with this notion of agency because they saw how the emperor's or king's messengers acted on behalf of their superiors. When the messenger came with a ruling or a demand from the emperor, they listened and obeyed as if the emperor was actually standing there in front of them. To honor the messenger was to honor the emperor; to disrespect the messenger was to disrespect the king. In other words, the messenger, as agent of the king, manifested the king's presence in that place and time. In the same way, John presents Jesus as the agent of God. These "I am" sayings describe how God, revealed through Jesus, acts in the world. God sent Jesus and therefore Jesus speaks and acts on God's behalf, doing only what God has commanded him to do and speaking only the things God has instructed him to speak. In this way, he is the "I am" of God. He is God manifest in the world.

## JOHANNINE DISCIPLESHIP

When you compare the Gospel of John to the synoptic gospels, you will notice that John's gospel differs somewhat from the other gospels in its understanding of discipleship. Take, for example, John's version of the call of the disciples (John 1:35–51). Whereas the synoptic gospels describe Jesus as going out to look for his disciples and commanding them, saying "Follow me" (Matt. 4:18–22; Mark 1:16–20; Luke 5:1–11), John portrays them as seeking Jesus. Jesus' question, "What are you looking for?" (John 1:38), introduces the theme of seeking and finding that will appear again at several important moments in John's gospel (cf. John 7:32–36; 8:21–30; 18:1–11). Jesus' new disciples call other disciples, using Jesus' own words, "Come and see" (John 1:39; cf. John 1:46), and gradually Jesus' identity is revealed to the reader:

- Jesus is the Lamb of God (John 1:29, 36)
- Jesus is the Messiah (John 1:41)
- Jesus is the One about whom Moses and the prophets wrote (John 1:45)
- Jesus is the Son of God (John 1:49; cf. John 1:34)
- Jesus is the king of Israel (John 1:49)
- Jesus is the Son of Man on whom the angels of God ascend and descend (John 1:51)

Even the word for discipleship is different from that used in the synoptic gospels. John calls it *abiding*, sometimes translated as "staying" or "remaining" or "dwelling." However, **abiding** is not concerned with physical presence as much as with a relationship so intense that one appears to dwell in the other. In sum, the Johannine notion of abiding is an *in-dwelling*.

Shortly after the story of the call of the disciples (John 1:19–51), John introduces two characters who are found only in this gospel: Nicodemus (John 3:1–10) and the Samaritan woman (John 4:3–42). Through the use of Johannine dualism, irony, and the literary techniques of double meanings, misunderstanding, and clarification, the gospel writer portrays one of these characters as a positive model of discipleship and the other as a negative model of discipleship. Study the two narratives carefully and see if you can discover which one is the positive model of discipleship and which one is the negative model of discipleship. What makes each one what he or she is?

### THE SAMARITAN WOMAN AND THE "I AM" OF GOD

The first "I am" saying of John's gospel is found in the story of the Samaritan woman (John 4:3–42). This story is rich in symbolism, and biblical scholars through the centuries have written a great deal about the meaning of this story. In particular, they have commented on the way that she gradually comes to an awareness of Jesus' identity until he reveals himself as the "I am" of God (John 4:26). They have also wondered about her marriage situation. Why has she had five husbands? What is this "affair" that she is now engaged in? Is this story another case of Jesus talking to immoral women in need of repentance? Reminding us that the story itself does not describe the Samaritan woman as immoral, the biblical scholar Sandra Schneiders says that people have often missed the more important message—that she is the first person in John's gospel to act as Jesus' apostle! Here is an excerpt from Professor Schneiders' work:

> The story of the Samaritan woman is remarkable for the clarity and completeness of its presentation of this revelation process in the Fourth Gospel. Jesus' self-revelation to the woman as the Messiah whom the Samaritans expect (4:25) is given in the "I am" formula that has such Christological importance in the Fourth Gospel. It is the first use of this absolute formula in the Gospel, and its impact on the woman is that she immediately leaves her water jar where it is and hastens into the town to bear witness to Jesus as the expected Messiah, that is, as the one who would tell them all things (see 4:25 and 29). We should not fail to note the feminine version of the standard Gospel formula for responding to the call to apostleship, namely, to "leave all things," especially one's present occupation, whether symbolized by boats and nets.(e.g., Matt. 4:19–22), or tax stall (cf. Matt. 9:9), or water pot. . . . That her apostleship is fully effective is indicated by 4:41–42, according to which the Samaritans come to full faith in Jesus as Savior of the World. (*2003*, 102–103)

Perhaps the most sustained teaching on discipleship in John's gospel comes in the farewell discourse (John 13:31–16:33). As a literary form, the **farewell discourse** is employed to communicate the sum of a great and holy person's teaching to his disciples. Often called a **testament**, as in "last will and testament" (e.g., Testament of the Twelve Patriarchs or Testament of Moses), it is a discourse delivered by a teacher in anticipation of his death. The topics and themes of Jesus' farewell discourse can be summarized as follows:

- An announcement by Jesus about his departure (John 13:33; 16:5)
- The disciples' question concerning where Jesus is going (John 13:36; 16:5b)
- Jesus' recognition of the sorrow of the disciples (John 14:1; 16:6)
- Several sayings about the Holy Spirit, also known as the **Paraclete** (i.e., the "advocate," as in a court of law), who will be the disciples' teacher and guide after Jesus' departure (John 14:16–17, 26; 16:7–11, 13–15)

- A prediction of the infidelity of the disciples (John 13:38; 16:32)
- References to Jesus' return to the disciples (John 14:18–20; 16:16)
- Comments about the Father's love for the disciples (John 14:21; 16:27)
- A promise that whatever the disciple asks for will be given by the Father (John 14:13; 16:23)

This discourse—or discourses, as there may be as many as three discourse units knit together here—also stresses the importance of staying in union with Jesus and loving one another. In fact, this is the single most important ethical command of John's gospel: "Love one another as I have loved you" (John 13:34). Moreover, it is the true test of discipleship. Thus, Jesus says, "By this everyone will know that you are my disciples, if you have love for one another" (John 13:35).

## SIGNS, GLORY, AND GLORIFICATION IN JOHN'S GOSPEL

John's gospel contains a number of elements that make it different from the synoptic gospels. The author's treatment of miracle stories is one such distinctive element. Whereas the synoptic gospels describe miracle stories as *dynameis* (Greek, meaning "mighty deeds"), John calls them **signs**; signs *point to* something. In the synoptic gospels, sometimes faith is a prerequisite for a miracle, and at other times a miracle results in increased faith. However, in the Gospel of John, "signs faith"—that is, faith that comes *as a result of* signs—is not considered to be real or full faith. If someone believes in Jesus only because he or she has witnessed Jesus' miracles, that person's faith is suspect, and the narrator of John's gospel says that Jesus will not entrust himself to them because he knows what is in their hearts (see John 2:24).

To what do John's signs point? The miracle of changing water to wine at Cana (John 2:1–11) is the first of seven signs in this gospel. The seventh is the raising of Lazarus (John 11:1–44). Concerning the first, the narrator of the gospel says, "Jesus did this, the first of his signs, in Cana of Galilee, and revealed his glory" (John 2:11). It is not altogether clear how John intends this first occurrence of the word **glory** in the Book of Signs (John 1:19–12:50) to be understood, except that it is manifest in or through the miracle. However, gradually as the gospel unfolds, one begins to discover that Jesus is the agent of God, doing only what the Father tells him (e.g., John 5:1–19). Thus, the glory that shines through Jesus in the performance of these mighty deeds is, in fact, God's glory; Jesus manifests the glory of God present in the midst of God's people (e.g., John 2:11; 9:40; 17:4).

However, there is another sense in which the word *glory* is used in relation to the Johannine signs and in the gospel as a whole. Perhaps this second usage is most evident in the seventh sign story, the raising of Lazarus (John 11:1–54), in which the Johannine Jesus says that Lazarus's illness is "for God's glory, so that the Son of God may be glorified through it" (John 11:4). It is the greatest of the signs in John's gospel because it involves the resuscitation of a dead person, something that ancient peoples thought was impossible for folk healers or miracle workers to accomplish—only God could bring the dead back to life! At the same time, this sign is overcast with a sense of foreboding because, as a result of this sign, the religious authorities are compelled to enact their plan to kill Jesus. The narrator describes the situation this way:

> So the chief priests and the Pharisees called a meeting of the council, and said, "What are we to do? This man is performing many signs. If we let him go on like this, everyone will believe in him, and the Romans will come and destroy both our holy place and our nation. . . . So from that day on they planned to put him to death. (John 11:45–48, 53)

In this same scene, the narrator adds a detail about Caiaphas's prophecy that Jesus would die for the nation "and not for the nation only, but to gather into one the dispersed children of God" (John 11:53). Only a few scenes later, when some Greeks approach the disciple Philip to request a meeting with Jesus, Jesus responds, "The hour has come for the Son of Man to be glorified" (John 12:23), followed by some cryptic sayings about dying and eternal life (John 12:24–26). Thus, for John, the **glorification** of Jesus describes his death and exaltation.

In sum, the signs in John's gospel are a manifestation of the divine glory, but they also point to the glorification (death and exaltation) of Jesus. This was hinted at already in the first sign, when Jesus' mother told him that the wedding couple and their families had run out of wine for the celebration. He responded, saying, "My hour has not yet come" (John 2:4). Elsewhere in John's gospel, **"the hour"** refers to the death of Jesus. For example, on two occasions—one when some of the Jerusalemites wanted to arrest Jesus (John 7:30) and another when the Pharisees wanted to arrest him (John 8:20)—the narrator notes that they were not successful because Jesus' hour (the appointed time for his death) had not yet come. Thus, at the conclusion of the first sign story, when the narrator notes that Jesus did this sign "and revealed his glory" (John 2:11), he may be doing more than simply commenting on the miracle. He may be foreshadowing Jesus' glorification as well.

## THE "LIFTED UP" SAYINGS

Another unique, though not immediately obvious, detail of John's gospel is its **"lifted up" sayings**. Like John's miracle stories, these "lifted up" sayings point to the death and exaltation of Jesus. The gospel contains three of these sayings, each appearing in a major discourse (i.e., speech): the Nicodemus discourse (John 3), the Tabernacles discourse (John 7–8), and the discourse delivered upon the arrival of the Greeks (John 12).

> "And just as Moses lifted up the serpent in the wilderness, so *must the Son of Man be lifted up*, that whoever believes in him may have eternal life." (John 3:14–15)
>
> "*When you have lifted up the Son of Man*, then you will realize that I am he, and that I do nothing on my own, but I speak these things as the Father instructed me." (John 8:28)

"Now is the judgment of this world; now the ruler of this world will be driven out. And I, *when I am lifted up from the earth*, will draw all people to myself." He said this to indicate the kind of death he was to die. (John 12: 31–33)

The careful reader will recall that the synoptic gospels also contain prophetic sayings about the death and resurrection of Jesus, often called passion predictions (Mark 8:31, 9:31, 10:33–34, and parallels). However, the Johannine "lifted up" sayings suggest that John has a different understanding of the significance of the death and resurrection of Jesus than do the synoptic gospel writers. What follows is a brief explanation of each of these three "lifted up" sayings as they appear in their respective discourses.

FIRST "LIFTED UP" SAYING In the discourse that follows Jesus' encounter with Nicodemus (John 3:11–21), Jesus declares that the Son of Man (referring to himself) must be "lifted up," just as the serpent was "lifted up" in the desert (John 3:14–15). The literary and historical background for this saying is the Old Testament story of the Exodus wanderings in the wilderness. In Numbers 21:4–9, we hear how the Israelite people complained against God and Moses during their time in the wilderness. In punishment, God sent seraph serpents among the people to bite them. When the people repented of their sin, Moses prayed on their behalf, and God told him to make a bronze serpent and mount it on a pole so that anyone who looked at it would be healed of their snakebites. In John's gospel, Jesus is presented as taking the place of this bronze serpent that saved the people from their afflictions. Thus, John presents the serpent on the pole as a *type* of Jesus on the cross (see Chapter 4). However, John's Jesus promises more than physical healing to those who turn toward him (i.e., believe): He will give eternal life. Further, John declares that God gave his only Son as an act of love for the salvation of the world (John 3:16–17).

SECOND "LIFTED UP" SAYING In the Tabernacles discourse (John 7–8), a long unit of text that gets its name from the fact that its setting is the feast of Tabernacles, Jesus says, "When you have lifted up the Son of Man, then you will realize that I am (John 8:28). In order to make sense of this saying, you first need to know who it is that Jesus is addressing. By looking at the immediate context (John 8:21–30), you soon discover that he is speaking to "the Jews" (again, not the Jewish people but perhaps a symbol of those who are dualistically opposed to Jesus and who refuse to believe in him). The phrase "I am," as we have already mentioned, refers to the divine name, YHWH, which God gave to Moses when he encountered God at the burning bush (Exod. 3:13–15). In other words, in John 8:28, Jesus is confronting his opponents who will soon lift him up (i.e., crucify him) and warning them that, when they do, they will realize that he is the "I am" of God. Their lifting up of Jesus will be his vindication (i.e., proof that he was right) because they will have to acknowledge that Jesus does what he does and says what he says *by the authority of God* (John 8:28; see John 5:18–30). Moreover, Jesus' vindication will be *their condemnation* because, having realized who Jesus is, there will be no more opportunity for them to come to belief (John 8:21–26). Quite simply, it will be too late for them! This is what John's Jesus means when he says, "You will die in your sin" (John 8:21).

The feast of Tabernacles is a remembrance of the time that the Israelites dwelled in tents as they wandered through the wilderness during the Exodus (see Chapter 5).

More importantly, it celebrates the conviction that God will supply all of the people's needs just as God had done in the Exodus (e.g., manna, water from the rock, the pillar of cloud and fire that protected them on their journey). Given this setting for the second "lifted up" saying, we should not be surprised about the confidence with which John's Jesus addresses his opponents who threaten his life: "And the one who sent me is with me; he has not left me alone, for I always do what is pleasing to him" (John 8:29).

**THIRD "LIFTED UP" SAYING** In the discourse that follows a scene in which some Greeks (non-Jews) come to Andrew and Philip asking to meet Jesus, Jesus says that his "lifting up" will bring about the "gathering in" of all peoples, just as John had explained earlier in his expansion of Caiaphas's prophecy of Jesus' death (John 12:32–33; cf. John 11:53). Here the narrator adds an explanatory note— "He said this to indicate the kind of death he was to die" (John 12:33)—showing that "lifted up" does indeed refer to Jesus' crucifixion. This view is consistent with the opening sentence of this discourse, when Jesus says that "the hour has come . . . " (John 12:23; cf. John 12:27). Again, "the hour" refers to the death of Jesus (see John 2:4). However, the Johannine Jesus goes on to identify this as the hour in which "the Son of Man will be glorified" (John 12:23), referring to his exaltation.

In sum, whereas the synoptic gospels explain the problem of the death of Jesus by having Jesus prophesy that he must be humiliated in a shameful death by crucifixion but that later God will vindicate and exalt him in his resurrection, John has joined crucifixion language with exaltation language, making Jesus' crucifixion and exaltation into the single event of his "lifting up." Further, John understands Jesus' lifting up as the venue through which Jesus is glorified and the Father is glorified in him. He also presents the "lifting up" as the moment in which, simultaneously, Jesus is vindicated, his enemies are condemned, and all are gathered to him. For John, Jesus' "lifting up" is God's gift of love to the world so that all who believe might be saved.

## THE BREAD OF LIFE DISCOURSE

As we have already observed, the Gospel of John contains several discourses. The "bread of life" discourse (John 6:35–58) is especially noteworthy because it illustrates a number of themes and literary features of John's gospel, but it also gives us an opportunity to talk about Christian understandings of Eucharist. John begins this section of his gospel with several scenes that sound very much like scenes found in the synoptic gospels: the story of the multiplication of the loaves (John 6:1–15; cf. Matt. 14:13–21; Mark 6:30–44; Luke 9:10–17), the story of Jesus walking on the water (John 6:16–24; cf. Mark 6:45–52), and the demand for a sign (John 6:25–30; cf. Mark 8:11–13). However, at this point in the narrative, John diverges from the traditions underlying the synoptic gospels and inserts a long discourse punctuated by short units of dialogue. This discourse is commonly known as the bread of life discourse.

In the introduction to the bread of life discourse, the narrator of the gospel tells us that a crowd has been looking for Jesus (John 6:24). When they find him, Jesus talks to them about not looking for signs (miracles) but working for food that endures (John 6:26–27). This, of course, prompts the crowd to ask what work they must do, to which Jesus replies that they must "believe in the one whom God has sent" (John 6:29)—that is, "believe in me as God's agent." They, in turn, demand a sign of Jesus. In other words, they want Jesus to "prove" that he is God's agent, and it is in this context that they refer to the scriptures of old: "He gave them bread from the heavens to eat" (John 6:31; see Psa. 78:24; 105:40; Exod. 16:4). Quite simply, they want a sign that is greater than the one that God effected through Moses when he gave the Israelites manna in the wilderness during the Exodus.

The response that John attributes to Jesus is sometimes called **midrash**, a Jewish technique of interpreting scripture in which the interpreter takes each individual word or phrase of the text and gives it a new contemporary meaning. This midrash on the scriptures associated with the manna miracle can be outlined as follows:

## THE BREAD OF LIFE DISCOURSE AS MIDRASH

| PHRASE OF SCRIPTURE TO BE INTERPRETED | INTERPRETATION |
| --- | --- |
| "He gave them" (John 6:31) | Jesus tells the crowd that "it was not Moses who gave you the bread from heaven." Instead, he says, God gives them (now in the present time) bread for the life of the world (John 6:32–33). |
| "bread" (John 6:31) | In response to the crowd's request that Jesus give them this bread always, Jesus says, "I am the bread of life." Unlike the manna in the desert, he says that anyone who believes in him will never hunger or thirst; he will have eternal life (John 6:34–40). |
| "from the heavens" (John 6:31) | In response to "the Jews" who complain that Jesus cannot be from the heavens because they know his family, Jesus says, "No one can come to me unless drawn by the Father who sent me." Jesus is bread "from the heavens" insofar as he was sent by the Father to provide eternal life, unlike the manna, which people ate and still died (John 6:41–51a). |
| "to eat" (John 6:31) | In response to "the Jews" who were disputing how Jesus could give his flesh to eat, Jesus says, "Those who eat my flesh and drink my blood have eternal life" (John 6:54; see John 6:51b–58). |

By reinterpreting the scriptures in this way, the Johannine Jesus provides commentary on the sign that the crowd wants but does not comprehend. It is a sign not unlike the miracle story of Moses and the manna, when God provided "bread from heaven" to save them from starvation, but it is far better insofar as Jesus, the agent of God, will be for them the "bread" that is eternal life. Unlike the manna that came down from heaven in the Exodus, God sends his Son down from heaven to be the bread that gives life to the world. To receive this new bread, the believer need only respond to Jesus' invitation, "Come!" Thus, as Wisdom personified, Jesus is the teacher of God's Word and in this way nourishes and gives life to the world (John 6:34–51a).

Up to this point in the bread of life discourse, one would assume that John intends "bread" to be understood metaphorically: Like bread that nourishes in a physical sense, Jesus nourishes in a spiritual sense. Or does he? In the final section of this discourse (John 6:51b–58), the Johannine Jesus says, "Unless you eat the flesh of the Son of Man and drink his blood, you have no life in you" (John 6:53). This may sound like cannibalism, and the narrator of the story portrays some of the characters as interpreting it that way. Note, for example, the reaction of "the Jews" who say, "How can this man give us his flesh to eat?" (John 6:52) and the disciples' response to Jesus' teaching: "This teaching is difficult; who can accept it?" (John 6:60). John's emphasis on Jesus' flesh as real food and his blood as real drink (John 6:55) further confirms that he is not speaking simply about a spiritual encounter with the Wisdom teacher here.

Many Johannine scholars think that this final section of the bread of life discourse (John 6:51b–58) contains allusions to the Eucharist. If so, we might conclude that the Johannine community believed Jesus was really present in the bread and the wine of the Eucharist and in the ritual associated with it. Teachings of this sort later come to be known as **Real Presence**. But how does this view of Eucharist—eating and drinking the body and blood of the Lord—correspond with the more spiritual view of Jesus as the Wisdom teacher who "nourishes" those who believe? Does this earlier part of the bread of life discourse (John 6:35–51a) also relate to the Eucharist? If so, John may be offering his readers more than one interpretation of the Eucharist.

John's bread of life discourse is significant in light of the fact that this gospel does not contain a "first Eucharist" story like that of the synoptic gospels in which Jesus shares a Passover meal with his disciples and, breaking the bread, says, "This is my body," and, sharing the cup, says, "This is my blood" (Matt. 26:17–30; Mark 14:12–26; Luke 22:7–39). Did the community of John's gospel celebrate a different kind of Eucharist than other Christian communities who reenacted Jesus' Last Supper with his disciples. Certainly, this is possible. The *Didache*, also known as *The Teachings of the Twelve Apostles* (early second century C.E.), contains a Eucharistic prayer that illustrates one of these alternative understandings of Eucharist among Christians of the early church:

Concerning the thanksgiving (*eucharistia*), give thanks thus: First concerning the cup, "We give thanks to you, our Father, for the holy vine of David, your servant, which you have disclosed to us through Jesus your son. To you be the glory unto the ages!" Concerning the broken bread, "We give thanks to you, our Father, for the life and knowledge that you have disclosed to us through Jesus your son. To you be the glory unto the ages! As this broken bread, scattered upon the mountains, has been gathered together to be one, so may your church be gathered together in the same manner from the ends of the earth into your kingdom. For to you is the glory and the power through Jesus Christ unto the ages!" (*Didache* 9.1–4, translated by Rev. J. Michael Joncas. Used with permission.)

The "broken bread," of course, is an allusion to the manna of the Exodus. The holy vine of David is a reference to the prosperity and blessings that will accompany the reestablishment of David's kingship when the messiah comes. Thus, early Christians who accepted the teachings of the *Didache* understood the Eucharist in terms that are reminiscent of Jewish scriptures, calling on the memory of David and Moses, the manna in the wilderness, and the abundant vineyard of the messianic age.

If you belong to a Christian community that celebrates the Eucharist (also called the Lord's Supper) on a regular basis, consider whether John's bread of life discourse corresponds in any way to your church's understanding of Eucharist. Does it prompt you to rethink your understandings of Eucharist in some way? What challenges or opportunities does it present for dialogue among churches that hold differing views of the meaning and significance of the Eucharist?

## THE FOOT-WASHING SCENE

Only John's gospel contains the story of Jesus washing his disciples' feet on the night before he was crucified (John 13:1–20). Some biblical scholars have suggested that it replaces the story of Jesus' Last Supper institution of the Eucharist in the synoptic gospels. Although we have no evidence to argue this point with any certainty, we might at least speculate that the Johannine community shared a ritual of foot-washing in remembrance of Jesus' self-giving act of love. However, there might be an easier explanation for the absence of a Last Supper institution of the Eucharist in John's gospel. Quite simply, John places Jesus' crucifixion on the day of preparation (John 19:28–37), when the lambs for the feast of Passover were being sacrificed in the Temple, not after the first day of Passover (when the Passover meal was celebrated) as the synoptic gospels do. By doing so, he proclaims Jesus to be *the* Passover lamb. John's crucifixion story also recalls one of the opening scenes of the gospel in which John the Baptist testifies on Jesus' behalf, saying, "Look, here is the Lamb of God" (John 1:36; cf. John 1:29).

Thus, John's foot-washing scene is a prelude to the events associated with Jesus' death. It can be divided into three parts: Jesus' action (John 13:1–5), a first interpretation (John 13:6–11), and a second interpretation (John 13:12–20). Jesus' action highlights the service that Jesus is about to perform through his death: "He loved them to the end" (John 13:1). The second interpretation highlights the service to which the disciples are called: "You ought to wash one another's feet" (John 13:14). The phrases "his hour had come" (John 13:1) and "aware that he had come from God and was returning to God" (John 13:3) remind the reader that we are moving from the Book of Signs to the Book of Glory. The phrase "the hour" in John's gospel refers to the death of Jesus, the subject of this second part of the gospel.

But what is the point of the first interpretation (John 13:6–11)? In first-century cultures, foot-washing was a sign of hospitality, much like putting on the pot of coffee or setting the table with the good china is in today's culture. However, when the host welcomed a dignitary to his home, the host's *slaves*, not the host, performed this work. Thus, Peter's question, "Are you going to wash my feet?" (John 13:6), is his way of acknowledging Jesus' superior position but also expressing his shock that Jesus would do something that was so far beneath his dignity. In an honor/shame culture such as this one, a host or guest of honor who does the work of a slave brings considerable loss of honor upon himself. Better for Peter to wash Jesus' feet, but the reader will notice that he does not offer to change places with Jesus. He doesn't want to lose honor either!

After Jesus explains the necessity of this foot-washing, Peter responds in a way that is typical of Johannine misunderstanding. Peter says, "[A]lso my head and hands" (John 13:9), thinking that a full bath is better than simply having washed feet. What he fails to understand is that this foot-washing is the beginning of Jesus' perfect act of love, his death, through which Jesus will return to the Father and the believers will share in Jesus' life with the Father. Even though Peter seems not to understand what's going on, hopefully the reader grasps the significance of this first interpretation (John 13:6–11): those who wish to abide with Jesus must allow themselves to be served by him, trusting in his love even to the point of death. "Whoever has bathed" (John 13:10) may be a symbolic reference to baptism.

Finally, the second interpretation offers a lesson to all disciples who will follow Jesus: "As I have done for you, you should also do" (John 13:15). This is Jesus' teaching on service. Hopefully, the reader of the gospel will remember that Mary, the sister of Lazarus, has already done this act of service for Jesus, even without the benefit of Jesus' teaching or his example (see John 12:1–8).

## JOHN'S PASSION AND RESURRECTION NARRATIVES

Beginning with the earliest chapters of his gospel, John has been writing in symbolic and sometimes veiled language about Jesus' death and exaltation. For example, there are the numerous references to Jesus' hour and his glorification, which we have discussed above. In addition, there are the "lifted up" sayings, which describe Jesus' lifting up in crucifixion and exaltation as the source of salvation to those who walk in the light and as condemnation for those who walk in the darkness. In each case, John has interpreted Jesus' death and exaltation as a single event. Thus, John's passion and resurrection narratives might appear to be an afterthought, or at least disjointed in some way from the rest of the gospel, since they treat the death and exaltation or resurrection of Jesus as chronologically distinct events, similar to the approach used in the synoptic gospels.

And yet the passion and resurrection narratives of John's gospel are quite different from those of the synoptic gospels in their content, presenting Jesus as sovereign and triumphant even as he submits to his arrest, crucifixion, and death. Absent are the scenes of Jesus' agony in the garden (cf. Matt. 26:36–46; Mark 14:32–42; Luke 22:39–46) and his crying out on the cross (cf. Matt. 27:45–53; Mark 15:33–38). Thus, the Johannine Jesus shows no fear or doubt concerning the events that lie before him. Likewise, in the scene of the arrest in the garden (John 18:1–11; cf. Matt. 26:47–56; Mark 14:43–50; Luke 22:47–53), the Johannine Jesus confounds the people who come to arrest him by asking them, "Whom are you looking for?" (John 18:4, 7) and revealing himself as the "I am" of God (John 18:5, 8). Whether or not the characters in the story know it, this is why the author describes them as falling down at Jesus' feet (John 18:6). Prostration is a sign of respect and a ritual of worship.

Other scenes in the Johannine passion narrative present a portrait of Jesus as already vindicated and exalted by God. For example, when Pontius Pilate attempts to interrogate Jesus, it is Pilate who is actually put on trial (John 18:28–19:16) as he moves back and forth from the darkness outside to where Jesus is located inside of Pilate's headquarters. In the central unit of this chiasm (see below), Jesus is mocked by the soldiers who dress him in "royal robes," hail him as "King of the Jews," and beat him (John 19:2–3). Of course, the reader knows the truth: As Son of God, Jesus truly *is* Lord and King. This proclamation is further confirmed in the scene where Pilate orders that an inscription be written and placed on Jesus' cross (John 19:19–22). The narrator notes that some among the crowd wanted the inscription changed, but Pilate refused. The inscription read "Jesus of Nazareth, King of the Jews" (John 19:19).

---

### CHIASTIC STRUCTURE OF JESUS' TRIAL BEFORE PILATE

**Outside** (John 18: 28–32): Pilate with the Jewish religious authorities. When Pilate asks for the charges against Jesus, they give a vague response about him being a criminal. When told to deal with him under their own law, they say, "We are not permitted to put anyone to death" (John 18:31). The narrator notes that their response is fulfillment of Jesus' prophecy about how he would die.

  **Inside** (John 18:33–38a): Pilate with Jesus. Pilate asks, "Are you the king of the Jews?" Jesus answers, "My kingdom is not from this world" (John 18:36) and concludes by saying, "For this I came into the world, to testify to the truth. Everyone who belongs to the truth listens to my voice" (John 18:37).

    **Outside** (John 18:38b–40): Pilate and "the Jews." Pilate addresses those gathered, saying, "I find no case against him" (John 18:38). He offers to release Jesus as an acknowledgment of their Passover feast, saying, "Do you want me to release for you the king of the Jews?" (John 18:39). They answer, "Not this man, but Barabbas" (John 18:40). Ironically, his name means "Son of a father."

      **Inside** (John 19:1–3): Jesus and the soldiers. The soldiers engage in crude and cruel horseplay, dressing Jesus in a crown and purple robe and hailing him as "King of the Jews."

    **Outside** (John 19:4–7): Pilate and the people gathered outside. Pilate announces that he finds no case against Jesus and presents him to the crowd, saying, "Here is the man" (John 19:5). When the Jewish religious leaders call for his crucifixion, Pilate again tries to release Jesus, but they persist: "He ought to die because he claimed to be the Son of God" (John 19:7).

  **Inside** (John 19:8–12): Pilate with Jesus. Pilate asks, "Where are you from?" Jesus refuses to respond. When Pilate attempts to assert his authority over Jesus, he says, "You would have no power over me unless it had been given you from above" (John 19:11). Pilate continues to find a way to release Jesus, but the Jewish religious leaders threaten him with charges of opposing the emperor.

**Outside** (John 19:13–16a): Pilate with "the Jews." Pilate takes his place on the judge's bench and announces to the people gathered, "Here is your king!" The crowd shouts back, "Crucify him!" To Pilate's retort, they respond, "We have no king but the emperor" (John 19:15). With that, Pilate hands Jesus over to be crucified.

The differences between John's gospel and the synoptic gospels extend to the resurrection and appearance narratives as well. In John's gospel, early on the first day of the week after Jesus' burial, we see Mary Magdalene at the tomb in the garden where Jesus had been laid (John 20:1). When she notices that the tomb is empty, she interrupts her grieving to find Peter and the other disciple, most likely a reference to the Beloved Disciple. What follows is a strange scene in which both men come to the tomb, look in, and return home (John 20:23–10), but concerning the Beloved Disciple, the narrator says, "He saw and believed" (John 20:8).

The Risen Christ Appearing to Mary Magdalen. Rembrandt Harmenszoon van Rijn, 1638. Oil on wood. Royal Collection, Buckingham Palace, London. *The Royal Collection (c) 2006, Her Majesty Queen Elizabeth II.*

Meanwhile, Mary Magdalene is standing near the tomb weeping when she encounters two angels and then someone she presumes to be the gardener (John 20:11–18). Each in turn asks her, "Why are you weeping?" (John 20:13, 15). But the supposed gardener—in reality, the risen Jesus—adds, "Whom do you seek?" (John 20:15), recalling the manner in which the first disciples of Jesus were called (cf. John 1:38). After their encounter, the risen Jesus sends her to the "brothers" to deliver the good news, and she declares, "I have seen the Lord" (John 20:1–18). Thus Mary Magdalene takes up the role of apostle.

The Gospel of John contains several other postresurrection narratives, one of which is similar to those in the synoptic gospels in that Jesus appears to the disciples while they are gathered in the upper room of a house (John 20:26–29; cf. Luke 24:36–43). Others are unique to John's gospel, like the tremendous catch of fish (John 21:1–14) and the dialogue between Peter and the risen Jesus (John 21:15–23). By weaving together synopticlike materials and other stories that are important to his own community, John paints a portrait of Jesus as the sovereign king who cannot be overcome by death. What a powerful message of hope for believers, both then and now!

## THE STORY ALONGSIDE OF THE STORY

As we have already observed, each gospel gives us at least a few clues about the community for which it was written. This phenomenon is even more evident in the Gospel of John, prompting some scholars to describe it as a two-level drama, or a "two-story" story. John's gospel is a two-story story in the sense that it provides an account of the life of Jesus but also a reflection on the later Christian community's history. The story of the healing of the blind man (John 9:1–7), and the extended dialogue that follows (John 9:8–41), is a good example of this two-level drama. Notice, in particular, the parents of the blind man who refuse to stand up for their son because they are afraid of getting kicked out of the synagogue (John 9:22). Although it is highly unlikely that Jews in Jesus' time were being excluded from the synagogue for listening to Jesus' teaching, it is quite possible that a generation or two after the death and resurrection of Jesus Jewish Christians were suffering such a fate.

Several scholars of John's gospel have taken clues such as this one from the gospel and attempted to reconstruct the history of the Johannine community. Perhaps the most widely known study of this sort is Raymond Brown's *Community of the Beloved Disciple (1979)*. However, there are also several more recent studies. We cannot spare the time to summarize this research here, but if you find this question of interest, you may want to explore it further on your own. At the very least, research of this sort reminds us that the gospels were not intended to be eyewitness accounts or documentary histories of the life of Jesus. Rather, they are the faith proclamations of communities that had experienced the risen Christ and are "written so that you may come to believe that Jesus is the Messiah, the Son of God, and that through believing you may have life in his name" (John 20:31).

The Pool of Siloam, where, according to John's gospel, Jesus told a blind man to wash his face and thus restored his sight. *Alistair Duncan (c) Dorling Kindersley.*

## KEY TERMS

Beloved Disciple

Johannine
   community

Signs source

Book of Signs

Book of Glory

Double meanings

Misunderstanding

Irony

Symbolic discourses

Explanatory
   note

Chiasms

Dualism

Eschatology

Realized
   eschatology

Logos

Preexistence

Incarnation

"I am" sayings

Agent of God

Abiding

Farewell discourse

Testament

Paraclete

Signs

Glory/glorification

"The hour"

"Lifted up"
   sayings

Midrash

Real Presence

## QUESTIONS FOR READING

Read the Gospel of John. Use evidence from the gospel to answer the following questions.

1. In the prologue (John 1:1–18), what clues can you find concerning the identity of the Word? What does the prologue say about the origin and role or function of the Word?

2. After reading John 1:19–37, what do you conclude about John the Baptist's relationship to Jesus? What is his role or function in this unit of the gospel?

3. According to John 1:35–51, who are the first disciples of Jesus? What are the circumstances under which they begin to follow Jesus?

4. John's gospel describes Jesus' miracles as "signs." What clues, if any, can you find in the story of the miracle at Cana (John 2:1–11) that would warrant its designation as a sign? To what does it point?

5. Locate the story of the cleansing in the Temple in Mark's gospel and compare it to John's version (John 2:13–22). *Hint:* Use your Bible's footnotes or cross-references. What similarities and differences do you observe when you compare these two versions?

6. In the story of Nicodemus (John 3:1–10), locate as many of the following as you can: misunderstanding, double meanings, explanatory notes, dualism, chiasm, and irony. Is Nicodemus a true disciple of Jesus? Why or why not?

7. In the story of the Samaritan woman (John 4:3–42), locate as many of the following as you can: misunderstanding, double meanings, explanatory notes, dualism, chiasm, and irony. Is the Samaritan woman a true disciple of Jesus? Why or why not?

8. Analyze the story of the crippled man (John 5:1–9) using the formal elements that are typically found in miracle stories (see Chapter 6). What, if anything, is unusual or surprising about this story? What is it that Jesus did to make "the Jews" unhappy with him (John 5:10–18)? Why did they wish to put Jesus to death?

9. In John 5:19–30, Jesus responds to the charge brought against him in John 5:18. What are the two things that he says the Son can do because the Father shows him? Is Jesus' response an affirmation or a denial of the charge? Explain.

10. In the Tabernacles discourse, what does Jesus mean when he says that "you will search for me but you will not find me" (John 7:34; 8:21)? To whom is he speaking?

11. In the story of the healing of the blind man (John 9:1–41), describe the steps that the blind man goes through as he comes to believe in Jesus. At what point does the blind man move from being the accused to being the accuser?

12. Concerning Jesus' teachings about the shepherd and the sheep (John 10:1–30), what is the sheepfold? Who is the gate? Who is the shepherd? Who are the sheep? What does John say about the relationship between the shepherd and the sheep?

13. In the story of the resuscitation of Lazarus, who is Lazarus (John 11:1–44)? What were the circumstances that prompted Jesus to bring him back to life? What can you conclude about the message that John wanted to convey through this story?

14. In the farewell discourse, what words of consolation does Jesus give his grieving disciples (John 14–17)? What does he say about the role of the Paraclete after his departure?

15. Explain the imagery of the vine and branches in John 15:1–17. Who is the vine? Who are the branches? What is their fruit? What can you conclude about the message that John wanted to convey through this teaching?

16. Identify at least one scene from John's passion narrative that is absent from Mark's passion narrative. Identify at least one scene that is contained in Mark's passion narrative but is absent from the Gospel of John. How does the inclusion (or absence) of these scenes affect how the reader views John's story of the suffering and death of Jesus?

17. What is the significance of the risen Jesus' threefold question to Peter, "Do you love me?" (John 21:15–23). What does the reader learn from this scene about the relationship between Peter and the Beloved Disciple?

## QUESTIONS FOR REFLECTION

1. Create a modern counterpart for the figure of Nicodemus (John 3:1–12). What attributes would you ascribe to him? Who or what does he represent in the schema of the opening chapters of John's gospel? Make an assessment of him as a model of faith.

2. Create a modern counterpart for the figure of the Samaritan woman (John 4:4–42). What attributes would you ascribe to her? Who or what does she represent in the schema of the opening chapters of John's gospel? Make an assessment of her as a model of faith.

3. Some people clearly prefer one gospel more than another. To what kind of audience would the Gospel of John have the greatest appeal? Explain. What do you think they are hoping or expecting to find in this gospel?

## ACTIVITIES FOR LEARNING

1. Using the language and style of John's gospel, compose your own dialogue between Jesus and his disciples as they might have conversed in the garden prior to Judas' arrival (see John 18:1–2). Incorporate themes from the gospel and references to experiences that Jesus had shared with his disciples during his time of ministry.

2. Interview a pastor or religious educator from a Christian denomination with which you are familiar (e.g., Roman Catholic, United Methodist, ELCA Lutheran, Episcopalian) and ask that person to describe his or her understanding of Eucharist. Compare what you learned from your interview with the various images and interpretations of Eucharist contained in the bread of life discourse (John 6:31–58). What parts of the bread of life discourse best resonate with this denomination's understanding of Eucharist? What parts of the discourse appear to be less important for this denomination's understanding of Eucharist? Explain.

3. Take the story of Jesus' trial before Pilate (John 18:28–19:16a) and rewrite it as a screenplay. Divide the text into its seven scenes, write out the dialogue as you would expect to see it if this was an actual play, and provide stage directions and director's notes. What did you discover about the text that you did not know before you began the screenwriting process? *Note:* The designation 16a refers to the first half of the verse.

## Sources and Resources

Beasley-Murray, George. *John.* Nashville, Tenn.: Thomas Nelson Publishers, 1999.

Bieringer, R., D. Pollefeyt, and F. Vanneuville Vandecasteele. *Anti-Judaism and the Fourth Gospel.* Louisville, Ky.: Westminster John Knox Press, 2001.

Brown, Raymond. *The Gospel According to John.* 2 vols. Garden City, N.Y.: Doubleday, 1966–1970.

————. *The Community of the Beloved Disciple.* New York: Paulist, 1979.

————. *An Introduction to the Gospel of John,* Edited by Francis J. Moloney. New York: Doubleday, 2003.

Bultmann, Rudolf. *The Gospel of John: A Commentary.* Translated by G. R. Beasley-Murray. Philadelphia, Pa.: Westminster Press, 1971.

Coloe, Mary L. *God Dwells with Us: Temple Symbolism in the Fourth Gospel.* Collegeville, Minn.: Liturgical Press, 2001.

Culpepper, Alan. *The Anatomy of the Fourth Gospel: A Study in Literary Design.* Philadelphia: Fortress, 1983.

Dumm, Demetrius. *A Mystical Portrait of Jesus: New Perspectives on John's Gospel.* Collegeville, Minn.: Liturgical Press, 2001.

Fehribach, Adeline. *The Women in the Life of the Bridegroom: A Feminist Historical-Literary Analysis of the Female Characters in the Fourth Gospel.* Collegeville, Minn.: Liturgical Press, 1998.

Fortna, Robert T., and Tom Thatcher, eds. *Jesus in Johannine Tradition.* Louisville, Ky.: Westminster John Knox Press, 2001.

Keener, Craig S. *The Gospel of John: A Commentary.* 2 vols. Peabody, Mass.: Hendrickson Publishers, 2003.

Koester, Craig. *Symbolism in the Fourth Gospel: Meaning, Mystery, Community.* Minneapolis, Minn.: Fortress Press, 2003.

Lee, Dorothy A. *Flesh and Glory: Symbol, Gender, and Theology in the Gospel of John.* New York: Crossroad, 2002.

Levine, Amy-Jill, and Marianne Blickenstaff, eds. *Feminist Companion to John.* London: Sheffield Academic Press, 2003.

Lewis, Scott M. *The Gospel According to John and the Johannine Letters.* Collegeville, Minn.: Liturgical Press, 2005.

Lincoln, Andrew T. *Truth on Trial: The Lawsuit Motif in the Fourth Gospel.* Peabody, Mass.: Hendrickson Publishers, 2000.

Newheart, Michael Willett. *Word and Soul: A Psychological, Literary, and Cultural Reading of the Fourth Gospel.* Collegeville, Minn.: Liturgical Press, 2001.

O'Day, Gail R. *John.* Louisville, Ky.: Westminster John Knox Press, 2006.

Reinhartz, Adele. *Befriending the Beloved Disciple: A Jewish Reading of the Gospel of John.* New York: Continuum, 2001.

Schneiders, Sandra Marie. *Written That You May Believe: Encountering Jesus in the Fourth Gospel.* New York: Crossroad Publishers, 2003.

Sloyan, Gerard S. *What Are They Saying about John?* New York: Paulist, 2006.

Smith, D. Moody. *John.* Nashville, Tenn.: Abingdon Press, 1999.

Talbert, Charles H. *Reading John: A Literary and Theological Commentary of the Fourth Gospel and the Johannine Epistles.* New York: Crossroad, 1994.

Thompson, Marianne Meye. *The God of the Gospel of John.* Grand Rapids, Mich.: Eerdmans, 2001.

Vanier, Jean. *Drawn into the Mystery of Jesus through the Gospel of John.* New York: Paulist Press, 2004.

Wright, N. T. *John for Everyone.* London: SPCK; Louisville, Ky.: Westminster John Knox Press, 2004.

# CHAPTER 10

# THE SYNOPTIC PROBLEM AND HISTORICAL JESUS RESEARCH

It is time to take a little respite from our travels and reflect for a bit on what we have seen and heard in our exploration of the Gospels of Mark, Matthew, Luke, and John. Specifically, we need to address a problem that people who are not otherwise familiar with the synoptic gospels might not have thought much about. When first-time readers take on the project of reading the Gospels of Matthew, Mark, and Luke, one after the other, they soon find themselves saying, "Wait a minute! Didn't I read this part already?" Perhaps your reading of John's gospel sharpened the question for you, because now you can see how different it is from the synoptic gospels. If we accept biblical scholars' theory about the stages of gospel composition (see the introduction to Part II, above), we could argue that the authors of these three gospels individually were familiar with a large body of oral traditions about Jesus and just happened to select the same stories and sayings to incorporate into their written gospels, resulting in the similarities that we find among them.

However, when we examine more closely the similarities and differences among the synoptic gospels, we sometimes—and perhaps more often than we might expect—find word-for-word agreement among comparable texts. That is, where we find a story or saying of Jesus that is present in more than one of these three gospels, we often find exactly the same wording and even the same word order (see the example on next page). Thus, it becomes apparent not only that the synoptic gospel writers knew the same stories that had been passed on through oral tradition but also that one or more of these writers actually copied from a shared written text. In other words, there is a literary relationship among the Gospels of Matthew, Mark and Luke. But who copied whom? This inquiry is called the **synoptic problem**.

## WHAT IS THE SYNOPTIC PROBLEM?

In order to illustrate the synoptic problem, let us look at the three versions of the parable of the mustard seed as it is found in the synoptic gospels. Observe carefully the similarities in vocabulary and sentence structure evident even in this English translation.

| Matthew 13:31–32 | Mark 4:30–32 | Luke 13:18–19 |
|---|---|---|
| 31 He put before them another parable: | 30 He also said, | 18  He said therefore, |
| "The kingdom of heaven | "With what can we compare the kingdom of God, or what parable will we use for it? | "What is          the kingdom of God like?  And to what should I compare it? |
| is like a mustard seed that someone took and sowed in his field; 32 it is smallest of all the seeds, but when it has grown it is the greatest of shrubs and becomes a tree, | 31 It is like a mustard seed, which, when sown upon the ground, is the smallest of all the seeds on earth; 32 yet when it is sown it grows up and becomes the greatest of all shrubs, and puts forth large | 19 It is like a mustard seed that someone took and sowed in the garden;           it grew and      became a tree, |
|                so that the birds of the air come and make nests in its branches." | branches,       so that the birds of the air can make nests in its shade." | and the birds of the air made nests in its branches." |

The similarities among the three versions of the parable of the mustard seed are obvious. All three compare the kingdom to a mustard seed, which, when it grows, becomes something very large so that the birds of the air can find shelter because of it. These similarities are substantial enough to suggest that two or perhaps all three authors copied the parable from another written source. To put it another way, you cannot account for this degree of similarity in wording by saying that the gospel writers simply knew the same oral stories. This is what biblical scholars mean when they talk about literary dependence among the synoptic gospels.

When biblical scholars first began working with the synoptic problem, they would identify corresponding sections of the synoptic gospels that show this literary dependence. That is, they started by looking for similarities in wording. But they did not stop there. They were also interested in the literary differences among comparable texts. Biblical scholars speculated that these differences provided clues about the way in which individual authors, having a written source in front of them, deliberately altered their source for some reason. Again, let's look at our example of the parable of the mustard seed. Matthew's gospel uses the parable to describe the kingdom of heaven, whereas the other two gospels talk about the kingdom of God. Luke's gospel describes the product of the growth of the mustard seed as a tree, while Mark's gospel calls it a shrub. Matthew's gospel calls it both a shrub and a tree. Mark writes that the birds find shelter in the shade of the mustard plant, while Matthew and Luke write that the birds make nests in its branches.

By analyzing a large number of these synoptic gospel texts and looking for patterns in their similarities and differences, biblical scholars were able to speculate about an answer to the question, Who copied whom? That is, which is the earliest of the synoptic

Mustard plants growing through the cracks in some ruins in Jerusalem. Photo by Catherine Cory.

gospels? Again, if we take our example of the parable of the mustard seed, one can imagine Matthew changing Mark's phrase "make nests in its shade" to "make nests in its branches," thinking that he was correcting an error made by the earlier writer, since everyone knows that birds nest in trees, not on the ground! One can further imagine Luke highlighting and expanding Mark's contrast of smallest and largest by changing "shrub" to "tree," even though mustard plants do not make very big trees. We can also imagine Matthew streamlining the somewhat awkward opening sentence of Mark's parable, "With what can we compare the kingdom of God, or what parable shall we use for it?" to conform to the pattern of the previous parable: "Another parable he put before them, saying . . . " (Matt. 13:24; cf. Matt. 13:31). Likewise, it is easier to argue that Matthew received the shared tradition about the "kingdom of God" and changed the wording to "kingdom of heaven" than to argue the other way around—that "kingdom of heaven" represents the shared tradition and that Mark, Luke, and John changed it to "kingdom of God." Thus, this particular example seems to point to Mark as the earliest gospel and the one that Matthew and Luke used as the basis for their gospels.

Again, on the other side of the argument, if we were to suppose that Mark was written later and therefore that its author had Matthew's or Luke's gospel in front of him when he wrote his version of the parable, how would we explain some of his changes? Why would he alter the original story to say that birds nest "in the shade" when it is more common to see birds nesting in branches? Further, if the source material that Mark was using described the seed as being planted in a "field" or a "garden"—places one would expect to plant seeds—why would he change the story to say the seed was planted "on the ground"? And why would he take a story about a seed growing into a "tree" and reduce the metaphor by saying that the seed grows into a "shrub"? Mark's alterations just wouldn't make sense!

## THE TWO-SOURCE HYPOTHESIS

Using techniques like those described above, biblical scholars have investigated a number of solutions to the synoptic problem. Our analysis of the parable of the mustard seed is consistent with the most commonly accepted solution, which is called the **two-source hypothesis**. Extrapolating from this one example and drawing on numerous other sections of text in the synoptic gospels, those who accept the two-source hypothesis say that Mark's gospel is the earliest gospel among the three, written perhaps as early as 65–70 C.E., and that Matthew and Luke had Mark's gospel (or an earlier version of it) in front of them as they wrote, selecting from it a variety of stories and teachings and using them in the creation of their gospels. This explains why some parts of Matthew's gospel are almost identical in wording to Mark's gospel and, likewise, why some parts of Luke's gospel are almost identical to Mark's gospel. Studies have shown that Matthew's gospel incorporates approximately 90 percent of the verses in Mark's gospel, while Luke's gospel incorporates about 65 percent of Mark's gospel, and in both cases, they retain for the most part the chronology of Mark's gospel. We can even find segments that are almost identical in wording *across all three gospels*. These segments are called the **triple tradition**.

Apart from the triple tradition, there are sections of Matthew's and Luke's gospels that show evidence of literary dependence—they share similar wording and even the same word order—while Mark's gospel lacks any such comparable section of text. These segments are called the **double tradition**. An obvious example is the Sermon on the Mount (Matt. 5–7) and the Sermon on the Plain (Luke 6), which are entirely absent from Mark's gospel. Another example of the double tradition is the Lord's Prayer (Matt. 6:9–11; Luke 11:2–4). Because we again find word-for-word similarities in some of this material in Matthew's and Luke's gospels, scholars have suggested that they copied from another common source, which they called **Q** (for the German word *Quelle*, which means "source"). Thus, according to the two-source hypothesis, Mark's gospel and this hypothetical Q make up the written source material for Matthew's and Luke's gospels, thereby explaining the literary relationship among the synoptic gospels. This relationship can be diagrammed as follows:

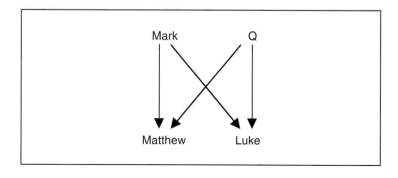

Before proceeding further, we need to say that the Q document (or documents) is not **extant**—that is, it has not been preserved and is no longer available to us today—if, in fact, it even existed as a written document. However, a few biblical scholars have attempted to reconstruct the Q material (see "Sources and Resources" below). The starting point for these reconstructions is the assumption that neither Matthew nor Luke knew or had read the other writer's gospel. With that assumption in place, these scholars examined the double tradition, uncovering what they thought was most likely the earliest version of that tradition, and compiled a collection of sayings and parables that they attributed to Q. Here is a sampling of the kinds of materials that might have been part of Q:

- I tell you, ask and it will be given you; seek, and you will find; knock, and it will be opened to you. For everyone who asks receives, and whoever seeks finds and to the one who knocks it will be opened. (Matt. 7:7–8; Luke 11:9–10)

- Whoever is not with me is against me, and whoever does not gather with me scatters. (Matt. 12:30; Luke 11:23)

- The queen of the south will arise at the judgment with this generation and condemn it; for she came from the ends of the earth to hear the wisdom of Solomon and behold, something greater than Solomon is here. The people of Nineveh will arise at the judgment with this generation and condemn it; for they repented at the preaching of Jonah, and behold, something greater than Jonah is here. (Matt. 12:42, 41; Luke 11:31–32)

As you can see from this small sample, reconstructions of Q consist largely of sayings of Jesus. Thus, biblical scholars often describe Q as a "sayings" source. Later we will read a "sayings" gospel called the Gospel of Thomas (see Chapter 11). The Gospel of Thomas is not Q, but it gives us an idea of what Q might have looked like if, in fact, it ever existed as a single written document.

Of course, any attempt at reconstructing Q is highly speculative, and any reconstruction based on the double tradition gives us, at best, the minimum of what was contained in Q. How do we know that? By comparing Matthew's and Luke's use of Mark. When we examine a large number of synoptic parallels, we find instances where Matthew retained Mark's wording but Luke did not. We also find cases where Luke followed Mark's wording but Matthew omitted the section altogether. Finally, there are sections of Mark's gospel that were not included in either Matthew's or Luke's gospel. There is no reason to think that Matthew and Luke treated Q any differently than they treated Mark. Thus, we should expect that neither Matthew nor Luke felt compelled to include all of Q in their respective gospels. We should also expect that both felt comfortable in adapting the Q material (changing wording, etc.) for their own purposes. Likewise, since Matthew and Luke took liberty in rearranging the material they borrowed from Mark's gospel, we have to assume that they did the same when it came to the order of sayings and parables in the Q material. In other words, despite biblical scholars' best efforts at reconstructing Q, we will likely never know completely what was contained in it, nor will we know the order of its contents.

Apart from these difficulties with the Q sayings source, the two-source hypothesis sounds quite simple and straightforward, and it does make sense of much of the data from the synoptic gospels. However, the gospels also present important exceptions that have prompted scholars to make emendations to the two-source hypothesis. Let's take as an example Matthew's gospel, which contains stories about the birth of Jesus and certain parables that cannot be found anywhere else in the synoptic gospels. Much of this material does not appear to be Matthew's own creation, but rather traditional material known only to his community. The same can be said for Luke's gospel. He includes a collection of stories related to the birth of Jesus that are found nowhere else in the gospels, along with large sections of stories and teachings of Jesus that make up the Travel Narrative (Luke 9:51–18:14). These materials likely belong to the tradition known only to Luke's community. For lack of a better term, we will call them Special Matthew and Special Luke, respectively. With these emendations, the two-source hypothesis can be diagrammed as follows and, in effect, it becomes a four-source hypothesis:

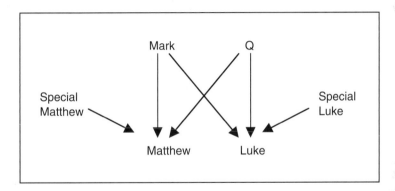

Occasionally, one encounters instances in the triple tradition (stories or sayings of Jesus that appear in all three synoptic gospels) where Matthew's and Luke's gospels agree on the wording, but they differ slightly from the wording of Mark's gospel. In most cases, these very small differences can be explained in terms of grammatical corrections or clarifications that Matthew and Luke just happened to make in the same way. However, sometimes we find variations in the wording of Matthew's and Luke's gospels that cannot be explained as coincidental corrections. In light of these exceptions, scholars have proposed certain adaptations of the two-source hypothesis. One of the most frequently suggested adaptations is that Matthew and Luke used an earlier version of Mark's gospel than the one we currently possess. Scholars call this gospel Proto-Mark. Thus, although the two-source hypothesis sounds quite simple and straightforward, in fact some of its aspects can be quite problematic. Attempts to address these problems have sometimes resulted in extremely complex variations of the two-source hypothesis. If you are interested in studying the two-source hypothesis and its variations further, please consult the "Sources and Resources" section at the end of the chapter.

## OTHER THEORIES OF LITERARY DEPENDENCE

In part because of these exceptions to the two-source hypothesis but also because of the history of the tradition surrounding the development of canon, other theories of literary dependence among the synoptic gospels have been proposed from time to time. The oldest has been attributed to Augustine in the fourth century C.E., who, following the order of the canon, suggested that Matthew's gospel was the first one written and that Mark's gospel is a much-abbreviated version of Matthew's gospel. Today the most notable theory that gives first place to Matthew's gospel is the **Griesbach hypothesis**, which argues that Luke had Matthew's gospel available to him when he wrote his gospel and that Mark used both Matthew's and Luke's gospels in the composition of his gospel. The Griesbach hypothesis can be diagrammed as follows:

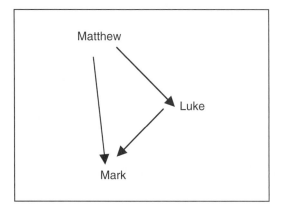

Like the two-source hypothesis, the Griesbach hypothesis helps to explain why the synoptic gospels arrange the stories in the same order and even have similar wording in some sections of the gospels. Those who prefer the Griesbach hypothesis instead of the two-source hypothesis say that it better explains instances in the triple tradition where Matthew's and Luke's gospels agree on the wording, but they differ slightly from the wording of Mark's gospel. More importantly, it does not require speculation about Q source material, for which there is no real evidence beyond the so-called double tradition.

Basically, the Griesbach hypothesis presents the Gospel of Mark as an abbreviation or synthesis of Matthew's and Luke's gospels. However, this theory does not satisfactorily explain why Mark would have knowingly omitted certain parts of the synoptic gospel story, like the infancy narratives and the postresurrection appearance stories, and such important teaching material as the Sermon on the Mount in Matthew's gospel or its parallel Sermon on the Plain in Luke's gospel. In sum, if it is a synthesis or condensation of the synoptic gospels, it is not a very good one!

## WHY CARE ABOUT THE SYNOPTIC PROBLEM?

You might be wondering why anyone would even care about the synoptic problem. Here are a few reasons. First, its solution is an excellent example of source criticism at work (see Chapter 2). However, more than an exercise in source criticism, the search for a solution to the synoptic problem was, at least in the beginning, part of the search for the **historical Jesus**. By this term, biblical scholars mean evidence about the actual historical person named Jesus of Nazareth, whose story has been stripped of myth and exaggeration in order to get at the objective facts concerning his life and death. Scholars thought that, by finding (or reconstructing) the earliest gospel, they would also have uncovered the most historical (and least theologically interpreted) gospel. That gospel, some concluded, was the Gospel of Mark. However, most biblical scholars today would readily acknowledge that Mark's gospel is no less theological than any of the other three canonical gospels. In other words, we cannot look to any of the gospels to provide us with an absolutely unbiased eyewitness account of the life of Jesus of Nazareth. Instead, the gospels are, first and foremost, faith proclamations—, that is, theological works that serve as interpretations of the life of Jesus—and are designed to inspire faith.

However, once we understand the synoptic gospels as theological documents, then the solution to the synoptic problem becomes important for redaction criticism (see Chapter 2). When investigating a passage in Matthew's gospel, for example, biblical scholars often compare it to a parallel text (when available) in Mark's gospel. Using the techniques of redaction criticism, they highlight ways in which Matthew apparently altered Mark's story to make a certain point. In doing so, they are working with the presupposition that the two-source hypothesis best explains the literary relationship among the synoptic gospels. Over time, as this methodological approach is applied to a number of texts from the Gospel of Matthew, biblical scholars arrive at certain conclusions about its author's theology or worldview. However, if we were to work with a different theory regarding the synoptic problem— for example, the Griesbach hypothesis—then a redaction critical analysis of a particular gospel passage would inevitably yield quite different results.

Take, for example, the story of Peter's confession of Jesus' messiahship in Matthew 16:13–20 and its parallel, Mark 8:27–33. If we start with the assumption that Mark's gospel was written last among the synoptic gospels and that Mark had Matthew's gospel in front of him when he composed his gospel, then we have to account for the fact that Mark deliberately omitted Jesus' praise of Peter for his profession of faith. We also have to explain why Mark omitted the reference to the establishment of the church on its rocky foundation. Did Mark have an anti-Peter bias? Was he opposed to the idea of church? Of course, to confirm our conclusions about this particular passage, we need to examine the whole of the Gospel of Mark from this methodological starting point. However, if we start with the presupposition that Mark's gospel was the first one written, we probably will not even be asking these questions about Mark's worldview. Instead, we will focus on Matthew's theological perspectives, as compared to those of Mark.

In sum, our answer to the synoptic problem plays a significant role in our understanding of the theologies of the synoptic gospels. As you might expect from the arrangement of its chapters, this textbook favors the two-source hypothesis. However, because we lack important evidence concerning the development of the synoptic tradition—specifically the Q sayings material—we have to be somewhat tentative about the conclusions we draw based on the two-source hypothesis. Likewise, when you are reading scholarly commentaries on one or more of the synoptic gospels, you need to be aware of how those scholars have resolved the synoptic problem because the analysis they provide will depend on it. Ordinarily, you can find this information by reading the introductory section of the commentary.

## THE HISTORICAL JESUS

Even at this early point in our voyage through the New Testament, you are probably beginning to ask whether any of its literature tells us simply and directly what Jesus actually said and did or thought and felt. You may even be thinking that perhaps these first Jesus followers simply made up the details of their stories about Jesus. First, we have to acknowledge that we possess very little unbiased documentary or eyewitness testimony to Jesus' words and deeds—perhaps none, some would say. The New Testament gospels and letters of Paul, for example, tell us a great deal about the **Christ of Faith** but very little about the historical Jesus. The term *Christ of Faith* describes the resurrected Jesus as he was revealed through the faith experiences of people who had come to believe in him. In contrast, the term *historical Jesus* refers to the historical person, Jesus, son of Joseph of Nazareth, as he can be known through such disciplines as history and archeology.

This lacuna is not as problematic as it sounds. Although evidence from non-Christian writers is extremely limited, it does support some of what the gospels say about Jesus, giving historical validity to the gospel story. At the same time, we should not lose sight of the reason that the gospel writers wrote their gospels and the reasons that early Christians read them: to appreciate, from a theological perspective, the meaning of Jesus' mission in the world and its implications for their lives, not simply to read a biography of Jesus' life. But what can we learn about the historical Jesus? Outlined below are five non-Christian, nonbiblical references to the life of Jesus of Nazareth from the first and second centuries of the Common Era. Although the texts are, for the most part, biased against Christians and their beliefs, it is possible to sift the data and discover some historical information concerning Jesus.

1. The Roman historian Tacitus in his *Annals* of the history of Rome (112–113 C.E.) writes about the Christians who were persecuted by Nero (64 C.E.), saying, "The founder of this sect, Christus, was given the death penalty in the reign of Tiberius [14–37 C.E.] by the procurator Pontius Pilate; suppressed for the moment, the detestable superstition broke out again, not only in Judea where the evil originated, but also in the city [Rome] to which everything horrible and shameful flows and where it grows" (*Annals* XV.44).

2. The Roman historian Suetonius in his *Lives of the Caesars* (121 C.E.) says that Emperor Claudius (41–54 C.E.) "expelled from Rome the Jews who were constantly rioting at the instigation of a certain Chrestus" (*Lives of the Caesars,* Claudius, 25). This is a probable reference to Jews and Jewish Christians who were engaged in a messy debate concerning claims that Jesus was the Christ.

Note that the death and resurrection of Jesus had already taken place before Claudius came to power. Therefore, if "Chrestus" is a reference to Jesus Christ, then Suetonius is mistaken in suggesting that Jesus instigated the riots himself.

3. The Babylonian Talmud Sanhedrin contains a tradition that is thought to go back to the first and second centuries C.E.: "On the eve of Passover they hanged Yeshu [of Nazareth] and the herald went before him forty days saying, '[Yeshu of Nazareth] is going forth to be stoned in that he has practiced sorcery and beguiled and led astray Israel. Let everyone knowing anything in his defense come and plead for him.' But they found no one in his defense and hanged him on the eve of Passover. . . . Yeshu had five disciples, Mattai, Maqai, Metser, Buni, and Todah" (b. Sanhedrin 43a).

4. Pliny (the Younger), writing to Emperor Trajan in approximately 112 C.E., asks for confirmation of his approach to people who had been reported to him as belonging to the Christian sect. Here he reports a summary of his interrogation of Christian prisoners: "But they declared that the sum of their guilt or error had amounted only to this, that on an appointed day they had been accustomed to meet before daybreak, and to recite a hymn antiphonally to Christ, as to a god, and to bind themselves by an oath, not for the commission of any crime but to abstain from theft, robbery, adultery, and breach of faith, and not to deny a deposit when it was claimed. After the conclusion of this ceremony it was their custom to depart and meet again to take food; but it was ordinary and harmless food, and they had ceased this practice after my edict in which, in accordance with your orders, I had forbidden secret societies. I thought it the more necessary, therefore, to find out what truth there was in this by applying torture to two maidservants, who were called deaconesses. But I found nothing but a depraved and extravagant superstition, and I therefore postponed my examination and had recourse to you for consultation" (*Epistulae X* [*ad Traj.*], xcvi.7–8, cited in Bettenson and Maunder, 1999, 4).

5. A reliable but secondary reference to Jesus is found in Josephus's *Antiquities*. He tells the story of the martyrdom of James, the one called the brother of Jesus: "Ananus, therefore, being of this character, and supposing that he had a favorable opportunity on account of the fact that Festus (60–62 C.E.) was dead, and Albinus (62–64 C.E.) was still on the way, called together the Sanhedrin, and brought before them the brother of Jesus, the one they called Christ, James by name, together with some others, and accused them of violating the law, and condemned them to be stoned" (*Antiquities* 20.200).

Although these nonbiblical references might appear, on the surface, to reveal little about the historical Jesus, they actually tell us quite a bit, since they help to confirm some of the things that are said about Jesus in the gospels. With this information from nonbiblical sources and with the use of certain criteria that allow us to separate out the tradition of Jesus from the early church's interpretations of the tradition, we can say these things about the historical Jesus:

1. Jesus was born shortly before Herod the Great's death (4 B.C.E.), perhaps between 6 and 4 B.C.E.. If we assume the gospel accounts that place Jesus'

death on or immediately after Passover and on a Friday are correct, then most likely he was crucified in approximately 30 C.E.

2. He lived in Galilee and probably was from a family of moderate income, but he identified himself with the poor.

3. Concerning other events in the life of Jesus, we can be relatively certain that

    a. Jesus was a healer and miracle worker.
    b. He was a critic of Jewish law.
    c. He told parables as a means of teaching.
    d. He was baptized by John.
    e. Although he called himself the Son of Man, Jesus probably never identified himself as the Christ or the Son of God.
    f. He had disciples and he gathered a community characterized by the notion of discipleship, but he never intended to establish a church as we know it today.
    g. He was crucified by Roman authorities.
    h. The disciples of Jesus had some kind of experience of the risen Christ that changed their lives.

CRITERIA FOR HISTORICAL JESUS RESEARCH  What are some of the criteria that biblical scholars use to sift out the historical data about Jesus of Nazareth from the faith proclamations of the early church? So much has been written on this topic that it can be overwhelming for the beginning reader of the New Testament. Therefore, we will limit ourselves to the "basics" and refer interested readers to the "Sources and Resources" below if they wish to do further reading. In general, scholars of historical Jesus research begin with this question: What guidelines or criteria can we use to strip away theological interpretations of the story of the Christ in order to uncover objective historical data about the historical Jesus?

Scholars of historical Jesus research have proposed a number of criteria for sifting out historical materials from the gospels and other religious literature of the New Testament period. We should be clear from the start that, even though a saying attributed to Jesus or a story from one of the gospels may satisfy one of these criteria, we cannot say with absolute surety that it goes back to the historical Jesus, nor can we say that it does not. If it satisfies several of these criteria, then we can infer with greater certainty that Jesus actually spoke those words or that the story actually took place as described. Yet, when our analysis is done, we have to acknowledge that, although the gospels contain historical information, their authors' objective was not to provide documentary evidence concerning Jesus but to inspire faith in Jesus, whom they believed to be the messiah of God. Therefore, we must always proceed with caution when conducting historical Jesus research.

The most frequently cited criteria for historical Jesus research are summarized below:

1. **Multiple Attestation.** If a saying of Jesus or a detail about the life of Jesus is found in two or more independent sources, then it might be a historical remembrance. For example, the story of Jesus multiplying loaves and fishes to feed the crowds in the wilderness is found in the synoptic tradition (Mark

8:1–10; Matt. 14:13–21; Luke 9:10–17) and in the Gospel of John (6:1–13). These are considered to be independent sources—that is, John had not read and did not copy the synoptic gospels—and therefore the story is considered to be historically reliable.

2. **Dissimilarity (or Distinctiveness).** If a saying of Jesus or a detail about his life is unlike what one might expect from Jesus' Jewish contemporaries or from the early church, then it is likely a historical remembrance. For example, all four of the canonical gospels refer to Jesus' baptism by John the Baptist. However, they also indicate that this is a strange event because John is clearly inferior to Jesus and the superior person should have been baptizing the inferior one, according to their religious hierarchy. Early Christians, too, would have viewed the story of Jesus' baptism by John as an embarrassment, since John's baptism was a baptism of repentance from sin. If Jesus presented himself to be baptized, then his action would be viewed as an admission of sin, but Jesus, as the Son of God, must be sinless. Therefore, because this story would be problematic both to Jesus' Jewish contemporaries and to the early church, they could not have made it up, and it must be historically reliable.

3. **Cultural Inconsistency.** If a saying of Jesus or a story about Jesus contains language or cultural details that are not consistent with early-first-century-C.E. Palestinian life, the saying or story is more likely not historically reliable. For example, in John's gospel, there is a story about a man whose blindness was healed by Jesus (John 9:1–41). Afterward, he becomes the center of controversy with the Pharisees, and the reader is told that his parents refuse to get involved because they are afraid of getting thrown out of the synagogue for believing that Jesus is the messiah (John 9:23). Although it is possible that Jews who believed in Jesus were being excluded from the synagogue toward the end of the first century C.E., there is no reason to think that this was happening in Jesus' time. Therefore, the story of the formerly blind man's controversy with the Pharisees is more likely not a historical remembrance from the life of Jesus but instead a creation of the gospel writer to explain a situation that was of concern to his community.

   Notice that this criterion is expressed in negative terms and its logic cannot be reversed. That is, you cannot say that every saying or story of Jesus that does conform to the language and culture of early-first-century Palestine is historically reliable because the early followers of Jesus were Palestinian Jews and they would have preached and written about Jesus from within that cultural milieu. Some of this material might be historical remembrances, but some might be theological interpretations of the sayings and stories of Jesus, while others might be creations of the gospel writer.

4. **Coherence.** This criterion presumes that you already have developed, through the application of other criteria, a collection of sayings and stories associated with the historical Jesus. If you have another saying of Jesus or story about Jesus that coheres with or is similar to these already accepted sayings and stories, then it, too, is likely to be historically reliable.

These are the most commonly used criteria in historical Jesus research, though occasionally scholars will refine these criteria somewhat, add other criteria, and/or employ combinations of some of these criteria. However, no matter what criteria one employs in trying to "reconstruct" the historical Jesus, the results will never give a full historical presentation of the life and deeds of Jesus of Nazareth. Instead, like the reconstructions of Q that we talked about earlier, these criteria give us only a minimum portrait of the historical Jesus. Let's use criterion two to illustrate. When we sift through the Jesus traditions and pull out only those stories and sayings that are (1) dissimilar from Jesus' Jewish contemporaries and (2) not attributable to his early followers, we can be fairly confident that they go back to the historical Jesus. However, once we eliminate these two groups of stories and sayings, we end up with a rather distorted portrait of the historical Jesus, which is neither particularly Jewish nor recognizable to his followers. What kind of Jesus is this?

Another difficulty with historical Jesus research is that scholars, employing similar criteria, often come to quite different conclusions about what the historical Jesus was like. For example, Markus Borg's (1994) work resulted in a portrait of a charismatic, compassionate sage (i.e., a wise teacher) who had mystical experiences (visions of God and the divine realm). By comparison, E. P. Sanders (1993) describes the historical Jesus as a Jewish prophet of the end of the world. Richard Horsley (1987) portrays the historical Jesus as a social revolutionary who stood against the abusive powers of the elite. Elizabeth Schüssler Fiorenza (1994) examines the wisdom traditions and proposes that the historical Jesus was a wisdom teacher who considered himself a prophet and child of Sophia (personified wisdom). John P. Meier (1991–2000) describes the historical Jesus as a "marginal Jew" who was influenced by John the Baptist and whose ministry was characterized by miracle working and prophecy concerning the end time. All of these are interesting and informative portraits of the historical Jesus, but from a social-scientific point of view, shouldn't the same criteria yield the same result?

Given the substantial difficulties inherent in historical Jesus research, it is probably safe to say that we will never really know exactly what Jesus said or did, much less his inner thoughts and motivations. However, to make this the primary focus of our gospel study would be to miss the point of the gospels entirely. Whether or not we can verify the historical details of Jesus' life, the gospels that convey his story are faith proclamations of communities that had come to believe that Jesus is the messiah and Son of God. We are not saying that history doesn't matter, but whether or not biblical scholars can agree on the historical details of Jesus' life, the purpose of the gospels remains intact—to proclaim and inspire faith in Jesus who is the Christ.

## Key Terms

| | | |
|---|---|---|
| Synoptic problem | Double tradition | Griesbach hypothesis |
| Two-source hypothesis | Q | Historical Jesus |
| Triple tradition | Extant | Christ of Faith |

## QUESTIONS FOR REFLECTION

1. Suppose you are a contextualist reader of scripture who also accepts the divine inspiration of the Bible. How would you reconcile the two-source hypothesis with the view that the synoptic gospels are inspired?

2. Suppose you are a literalist reader of scripture. In what ways or to what extent might you be able to accept the two-source hypothesis as an explanation of the literary relationship among Matthew's, Mark's, and Luke's gospels? Explain. What problems does the theory pose?

3. What do you think might be some of the potential benefits of historical Jesus research for the ordinary (nonscholarly) reader of the gospels? What are some of the possible difficulties it presents? Explain.

## ACTIVITIES FOR LEARNING

1. Locate the three versions of the synoptic gospel story of Jesus healing a leper. The first one is Mark 1:40–45. You will need to use the footnotes or cross-references in your Bible to find the other two versions. Copy them on paper in three columns like the example given above, or locate a gospel synopsis, which has the parallel texts already mapped out in side-by-side columns. Two of the more widely used gospel synopses are Burton Throckmorton's *Gospel Parallels*, Kurt Aland's *Synopsis of the Four Gospels*. Using four colors, underline or highlight the three versions of the "healing of a leper" story as follows:

   | | |
   |---|---|
   | Words or phrases found in all three versions | color #1 |
   | Words or phrases found in Matthew and Mark only | color #2 |
   | Words or phrases found in Mark and Luke only | color #3 |
   | Words or phrases found in Matthew and Luke only | color #4 |

   Examine your results. What observations can you make concerning the synoptic problem? Are there any variations in the three versions of this story that cannot be explained using the two-source hypothesis? Are there other ways to account for these differences?

2. Find the two versions of Jesus' teaching about God answering prayer. The first one is Matthew 7:7–11. Use your Bible's footnotes or cross-references to find the other version or work with a gospel synopsis. Copy them on paper in two columns like the example given above, or make a copy of the appropriate page from your gospel synopsis. Underline or highlight the words or phrases that are found in both Matthew and Luke. Examine your results. What observations can you make concerning the synoptic problem?

3. Locate the three versions of the synoptic gospel story of the empty tomb (Matt. 28:1–10; Mark 16:1–8; Luke 24:1–11). Using the two-source hypothesis as your starting point, determine how Matthew and Luke altered Mark's story. If we assume that they intentionally revised Mark's story, what issues—theological or otherwise—do you think they were trying to address? Are there any new questions

or problems that their revisions create? Using the Griesbach hypothesis as your starting point, determine how Luke altered Matthew's story and how Mark altered Matthew's and Luke's stories. If we assume that these revisions were intentional, what issues—theological or otherwise—do you think the gospel writers were trying to address? Are there any new questions or problems that their revisions create? Based on your analysis of the three versions of the empty tomb story, which of these two theories provides the best solution to the synoptic problem? Provide an argument to support your position.

4. Established in 1985 by Professor Robert Funk, the Jesus Seminar, which is associated with the Westar Institute, is an example of a conference of scholars who are investigating the historical Jesus question. It periodically publishes its findings in the media, so perhaps you have heard about it at some point. Do some research to learn how the group is organized and what criteria its members use in identifying data concerning the historical Jesus. You might begin by looking at the Jesus Seminar's official website, http://www.virtualreligion.net/forum. In addition, see if you can locate statements by some of its critics. What are their objections to the goals and the methods of operation of the Jesus Seminar?

## SOURCES AND RESOURCES

Bettenson, Henry, and Chris Maunder. *Documents of the Christian Church.* 3rd ed. New York: Oxford University Press, 1999.

Aland, Kurt, ed. *Synopsis of the Four Gospels: Greek-English Edition of the Synopsis Quattuor Evangliorum.* Stuttgart, Germany: German Bible Society, 1993.

Borg, Markus J. *Meeting Jesus Again for the First Time.* San Francisco: Harper/Collins, 1994.

Goodacre, Mark S. *The Synoptic Problem: A Way through the Maze.* London: Sheffield Academic Press, 2001.

Havener, Ivan. *Q: The Sayings of Jesus.* Wilmington, Del.: Glazier, 1987.

Herzog, William R. *Prophet and Teacher: An Introduction to the Historical Jesus.* Louisville, Ky.: Westminster John Knox Press, 2005.

Horsley, Richard A. *Jesus and the Spiral of Violence.* San Francisco: Harper, 1987.

Meier, John P. *A Marginal Jew: Rethinking the Historical Jesus.* New York: Doubleday, 1991–2001.

Nickle, Keith F. *The Synoptic Gospels: Conflict and Consensus.* Atlanta, Ga.: John Knox, 1980.

Robinson, James M., Paul Hoffmann, and John S. Kloppenborg. *The Sayings Gospel Q in Greek and English: With Parallels from the Gospels of Mark and Thomas.* Minneapolis, Minn.: Fortress, 2002.

Sanders, E. P. *The Historical Figure of Jesus.* London: Penguin, 1993.

Sanders, E. P., and Margaret Davies. *Studying the Synoptic Gospels.* Philadelphia: Trinity Press International, 1989.

Schüssler Fiorenza, Elizabeth. *Jesus: Miriam's Child and Sophia's Prophet.* New York: Continuum, 1994.

Stein, Robert H. *Studying the Synoptic Gospels: Origin and Interpretation.* Grand Rapids, Mich.: Baker Academic, 2001.

Throckmorton, Burton H., ed. *Gospel Parallels: A Synopsis of the First Three Gospels.* Nashville, Tenn.: T. Nelson Inc., 1992.

Van Voorst, Robert E. *Jesus outside the New Testament: An Introduction to the Ancient Evidence.* Grand Rapids, Mich.: Eerdmans, 2000.

Valantasis, Richard. *The New Q: A Fresh Translation with Commentary.* New York: T & T Clark International, 2005.

Wright, N. T. *The Contemporary Quest for Jesus.* Minneapolis, Minn.: Fortress Press, 2002.

# CHAPTER 11

# NONCANONICAL GOSPELS

## OVERVIEW

The Gospel of Thomas
- AUTHORSHIP: Anonymous; written under the pseudonym of Didymus Judas Thomas
- DATE OF COMPOSITION: Approximately 140 C.E.
- INITIAL AUDIENCE: Perhaps Christians in Syria
- MAJOR TOPICS: Genre of the Gospel; Gnostic Tendencies of the Gospel of Thomas; The Theology of the Gospel of Thomas; Is the Gospel of Thomas a Misogynist Document?

The Gospel of James
- AUTHORSHIP: Anonymous; written under the pseudonym of James, the brother of Jesus
- DATE OF COMPOSITION: Approximately 150–180 C.E.
- INITIAL AUDIENCE: Unknown; perhaps in Egypt
- MAJOR TOPICS: Birth and Childhood of Mary; Mary, the Mother of the Messiah; Answers to Other Questions; Birth Stories of Other Famous People; The Significance of the Birth Stories of Jesus for Christology

The Gospel of Peter
- AUTHORSHIP: Unknown; written under the pseudonym of Peter
- DATE OF COMPOSITION: Approximately 150 C.E.
- INITIAL AUDIENCE: Unknown, though Syria, Asia Minor, and Egypt have been suggested
- MAJOR TOPICS: The Worldview and Theological Perspectives of the Gospel of Peter; Christology of the Gospel of Peter; Anti-Judaism in the Early Church; Contemporary Christian Responses to Anti-Judaism

## TIMELINE

| | |
|---|---|
| **37 B.C.E.** | Herod the Great takes up his kingship in Palestine. |
| **6–4 B.C.E.** | Jesus of Nazareth is born. |
| **4 B.C.E.** | Herod the Great, king of Palestine, dies. His kingdom is divided among three sons: Archelaus, Herod Antipas, and Philip. |
| **c. 30 C.E.** | Jesus is crucified, dies, and is resurrected. |
| **65–70 C.E.** | The Gospel of Mark is written. |
| **66–70 C.E.** | The Jewish War occurs. |
| **70 C.E.** | Jerusalem and the Temple are destroyed. |
| **80–90 C.E.** | The Gospels of Matthew and Luke are written. |
| **90–100 C.E.** | The Gospel of John is written. |

| c. 140 C.E. | **The Gospel of Thomas is written.** |
| 150 C.E. | **The Gospel of Peter is written.** |
| c. 150–180 C.E. | **The Gospel of James is written.** |
| c. 180 C.E. | Irenaeus of Lyons writes *Against Heresies.* |
| c. 310 C.E. | Eusebius of Caesarea completes *Ecclesiastical History.* |

Thus far, our voyage through the New Testament has taken us along some relatively familiar terrain. Most Christians, and even those who are not, know at least the basic elements of the Jesus story. Moreover, once we had thoroughly explored the Gospel of Mark, the other synoptic gospels—namely, those of Matthew and Luke—were not an entirely different experience because they share many stories and teachings and even the same plot line. Now, however, we are going to take a little side trip into the realm of early Christian gospels that are not in the New Testament. We will sample three: the Gospels of Thomas, James, and Peter. These will provide us with some interesting adventures, since each is different from the others and all three are different from the synoptic gospels of the New Testament. Nevertheless, each has some bearing on the New Testament gospels. Hopefully you will enjoy our little side trip.

As already noted, the gospels of the New Testament were not the only gospels that were written and circulated among Christian churches in the first and second centuries C.E. These other gospels are called **extracanonical**, or noncanonical, meaning that they are not part of the canon of Christianity and not authoritative for Christian faith. We do not know exactly how many of these gospels were in existence in the early church or how widely they were read. Some, like the Gospels of James and Thomas, have been preserved more or less intact and are available today in collections of New Testament apocrypha. Others, like the Gospels of the Ebionites and the Hebrews, are known to us only because of brief quotations that survive in other early Christian works. Occasionally, we have the great fortune to discover a manuscript copy of an ancient document that was previously unknown or believed to be lost forever—as, for example, when a collection of works was discovered at Nag Hammadi, Egypt, in 1945. These works include the Gospel of Philip, the Gospel of Truth, the Sophia of Jesus Christ, the Apocryphon of John, the Apocryphon of James, the Gospel of Mary, and the Gospel of Judas, all of which are now available in English translation. Studying these noncanonical gospels can help us understand the theological questions that their authors attempted to address the variety among early Christian churches, and the values and ideals they embraced.

Why choose these three noncanonical gospels for our side trip? The Gospel of Thomas is of special interest for the study of the synoptic gospels because it provides us with an example of a "sayings" gospel, a form that may be similar to the Q material that we discussed in relation to the synoptic problem. The Gospel of James is important because it contains stories related to the birth of Jesus, which is also addressed in the Gospels of Matthew and Luke, and it tells the story of Mary of Nazareth, perhaps in an attempt to explain (theologically) how and why she was chosen to be the mother of Jesus. The Gospel of Peter deserves our attention because the extant excerpt—we do not have the entire gospel—tells the story of the death and resurrection of Jesus not only with some remarkable similarities to the synoptic gospels but also with some important differences. These two events in the life of Jesus were especially important to the early church in its struggle to understand and articulate what it meant to say that Jesus is the Christ or messiah of God. Notice that all three of these gospels are named after apostles of Jesus, one of the techniques used by early Christian writers to establish the authority of religious writings.

## THE GOSPEL OF THOMAS

As one might expect, early Christian communities were quite diverse. There was no single way of believing about Jesus, just as there was no single way of worshiping God. The Gospel of Thomas provides us with a view of early Christianity that is distinctly different from those found in the New Testament even though it contains many synoptic-like sayings. It appears to represent what we might call, in general terms at least, a Gnostic Christianity. For today's readers, this gospel provides an opportunity to raise some important questions about the relationship between a community's theology and its ethics. Believers read the gospels of the New Testament to answer the question, What does it mean to be a Christian living in the world? The Gospel of Thomas answers this question quite differently than the synoptic gospels do.

However, before we launch into commentary about the content of this gospel, let us again take some time to summarize what scholars have determined about authorship, date of composition, and audience.

## AUTHORSHIP

The Gospel of Thomas is attributed to **Didymus Judas Thomas**. The Greek word *Didymus* and the Aramaic word *Thomas* both mean "twin." Although this gospel does not tell us in what sense and with whom he was a twin, other literature associated with Thomas indicates that he was Jesus' twin brother—not in a biological sense but in a spiritual sense: He was Jesus' true friend and recipient of his secret sayings. See, for example, the Book of Thomas, in which Jesus addresses Thomas as follows: "Now since it has been said that you are my twin and my true friend, examine yourself and learn who you are, in what way you exist, and how you will come to be" (*Nag Hammadi Library* II 138, 7–9). Consider also the Acts of Thomas, in which a donkey addresses Thomas as "Twin of Christ, apostle of the Most High and fellow initiate into the hidden word of Christ, who receives his hidden sayings" (Acts Thom. 39; Schneemelcher, 1992, 2.335).

In the canonical gospels and Acts of the Apostles, someone named Thomas is listed among the apostles of Jesus (Matt. 10:3; Mark 3:18; Luke 6:15; John 11:16; Acts 1:13). However, the fourth-century Bishop Cyril of Jerusalem asserted that the author of this gospel was not the apostle Thomas but a follower of the heretic Mani, with whom the Manichaeans were associated (*Catechesis* 6.31). In case you are thinking that Cyril actually had historical information about the author of the Gospel of Thomas, we should clarify that his statement most likely was designed to discredit the gospel by arguing that its author was a heretic (i.e., a teacher of false doctrine).

The Manichaeans originated in the third century C.E. in Persia (modern Iran) and quickly spread to Syria and other regions around the Mediterranean Sea. Their worldview was based on a dualism of light and darkness, in which created beings (humans, animals, and plants) were thought to be prisons of the heavenly light. The goal of their religious practices, which included fasting and a celibate lifestyle, was to free these particles of light and send them back to the heavenly realm. Concerning the Gospel of Thomas, most scholars today agree that the name Thomas is a pseudonym and that its author is anonymous.

## DATE OF COMPOSITION AND INITIAL AUDIENCE

The Coptic Gospel of Thomas was found in December 1945 among the library of manuscripts discovered at Nag Hammadi in Egypt. Before this time, scholars knew about this gospel only because of some quotations that were preserved in other writings. This particular manuscript copy (not the original) has been given a date of approximately 400 C.E., though the gospel itself is thought to be much older. The third-century writer Hippolytus quotes it once and perhaps twice (*Refutation of All Heresies* 5.7.20–21; 5.8.32), which tells us that it had been circulating in its Greek translation already by that time. The Nag Hammadi manuscript is preserved in the Coptic language, an ancient Egyptian dialect, but most scholars think the work was originally written in a Semitic language like Aramaic or Syriac.

At first, Nag Hammadi scholars had few clues concerning the date of composition of the Gospel of Thomas. But then they discovered that three Greek papyri, found at Oxyrhynchus in Egypt and published much earlier (at the end of the nineteenth century and the beginning of the twentieth century), contained sayings that show literary dependence on the Gospel of Thomas. These manuscripts had been assigned a date of approximately 200 C.E., suggesting that the Gospel of Thomas was already in existence by the middle part of the second century and perhaps as early as the latter part of the first century C.E. Thus, this gospel is usually dated to 140 C.E., although a few scholars have given it a date as early as 50 C.E. The argument for this very early date—before Mark's gospel was written—is based on the observation that at least some of its synoptic-like sayings appear in a more primitive form than in the canonical gospels. However, we will follow the majority view and say that the gospel was composed about 140 C.E.

As already mentioned above, the full text of the Gospel of Thomas survives only in Coptic, an Egyptian language. However, the gospel is thought to have originated in Syria because of the strong traditions about Thomas's missionary activity in Syria. The Book of Thomas and the Acts of Thomas are also thought to come from this area, and according to early church tradition Thomas died and was buried in the ancient city of Edessa (modern Urfa) in Syria. Another reason for associating the Gospel of Thomas with Syria is its ascetic spirituality, which was popular there in the early centuries of Christianity. **Asceticism** consists of depriving the body of pleasures by fasting or engaging in other spiritual practices in order to focus one's attention on spiritual matters. Several of the sayings of the Gospel of Thomas suggest that the initial audience for this writing valued asceticism as a way of life.

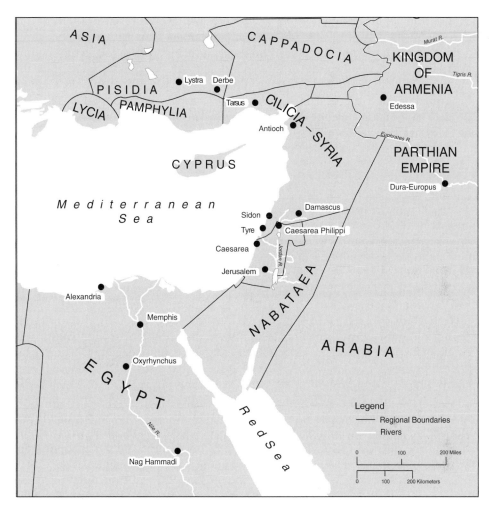

Nag Hammadi, Oxyrhynchus, and Edessa.

## GENRE OF THE GOSPEL

In terms of genre (i.e., type of literature), the Gospel of Thomas is quite different from the canonical gospels. There is no unifying narrative, no stories about the birth or the death and resurrection of Jesus, and no miracle stories. Instead, the Gospel of Thomas consists of a collection of 114 sayings supposedly dictated by the "living Jesus" to Didymus Judas Thomas. Therefore, instead of chapters and verses in your English translation of this gospel, you will find brief numbered units called **logia** (pl.; **logion**, sing.). The Greek term *logion* means "a saying." The Gospel of Thomas appears to have no unifying structure, though occasionally you will find within the larger collections of logia some smaller units that are joined together by a common theme. Other units are joined together by catchwords. For example, the description of disciples as "babies" joins logia 21 and 22, and the mention of "two" joins logia 47 and 48. Beyond these catchwords and small groups of sayings with a common theme, there is little evidence of an organizational plan for this gospel.

Because this gospel has no overarching narrative and, except for parables, none of the story forms that we saw in the synoptic gospels, we quickly notice that the reading strategies we used for studying the synoptic gospels do not easily apply to this gospel. What is the best advice for the new reader of the Gospel of Thomas? Think of each logion (saying) as a tiny riddle, and don't try to connect one riddle to the next. Just enjoy each "wise" saying for what it is.

## Gnostic Tendencies of the Gospel of Thomas

One of the ways of unlocking the meaning of this gospel is to examine its Gnostic tendencies. The Greek term *gnosis* means "knowledge." The Gnostics, then, were "knowing ones." What they claimed to know was the truth about the human self, their status as the saved, and the way of their salvation—, namely, how they could return to their place of origin. Knowledge, of course, does not refer to a biochemical process of the brain but to something more like "experience"—they know in their essence where they came from and where they are destined to return.

We have discovered from the Nag Hammadi Library, as well as from other second- and third-century documents, that there were Jewish texts with Gnostic tendencies, Christian Gnostic texts, and non-Judeo-Christian (pagan) Gnostic texts. What these Gnostic texts share is a presentation of "believers" as enlightened ones, people who are somehow destined to transcend the physical world, which is the domain of evil forces. Some go so far as to say that the origin of this world is an aberration, the result of something that went horribly wrong. Thus, the enlightened ones are described as aliens in the world, always in danger of falling victim to the allure of the physical realm. They seek a life of inwardness and detachment from the world until they can return to their true home, the divine realm.

Technically speaking, the Gospel of Thomas is not a Gnostic document because it does not explicitly refer to the Gnostic myth or otherwise presuppose it. However, understanding the Gnostic myth will provide us a window into the meaning of this gospel. In some versions of the **Gnostic myth**, God sends a savior, one of the divine powers, down to earth to help the soul return to the heavenly realm. Below you will find a synopsis of the Gnostic myth as described by Bentley Layton, a scholar of Gnostic scriptures.

### Myth from the "Hymn of the Pearl"

The First principle of the spiritual realm providentially causes the individual soul to descend past the heavenly bodies into incarnate life in a material body, in order to be educated (get salvation). The soul becomes unconscious and inert because of matter [female principle]. But it disengages itself in response to the savior or the message of philosophy (wisdom). It becomes acquainted with itself and is metaphysically reunited with itself [i.e., becomes solitary] and with the first principle, gains true repose. (Layton, 1987, 367)

The Gnostic myth was told in many forms, but the common elements of all versions of the myth are the heavenly origin, fall, incarnation, awakening, and return of the

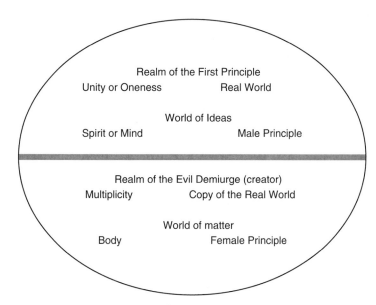

Gnostics' view of the divine and physical realms with their related descriptors.

human spirit (sometimes called the mind) to God (see G. Thom, logia 18, 28, 29, 50). The spirit or mind (which, according to philosophical principles, is the place where the essence of the person resides) is understood to have its origins in the heavenly reality where the fullness of God dwells. When the human spirit begins to lose its focus on the divine reality, it experiences a "fall," and eventually it becomes incarnate (i.e., enfleshed) in a body. The body is the physical matter that the spirit takes on during its human existence. As matter, it is a copy of, and therefore inferior to, the heavenly reality. Although the human spirit must carry around this body while it is on earth, the goal is to quickly shed the body and return to the heavenly reality from which it came.

The Gnostic myth presupposes a **cosmology** (i.e., understanding of the universe) that is based on a philosophical system called Middle Platonism. At the risk of being too simplistic, we might describe the Gnostics' real world as the realm of the divine, while the physical world is merely a copy of the divine realm, and therefore inherently inferior. The divine realm is ruled by the First Principle, also called God, and is characterized by unity or "oneness." This upper world is the realm of ideas, whereas the lower world is the realm of matter and is characterized by multiplicity or "twoness." Finally, the divine realm is associated with the mind and the male principle of the human person, while the physical realm is associated with the body and the female principle of the human person.

Again, at the risk of being overly simplistic, we could say that the Gnostics' **anthropology** (i.e., understanding of the human person) is closely connected with their cosmology. Within different Gnostic writings, the human person is sometimes described as bipartite (body/soul) and other times as tripartite (body/soul/mind). The tripartite division of the human person is probably more useful for understanding the Gospel of Thomas.

### TRIPARTITE DIVISION OF THE HUMAN PERSON

- Mind or spirit (the place where the essence of the person resides)
- Soul (the element that animates the body; also the seat of the emotions)
- Body (the matter or stuff of physical existence)

Again, according to the Gnostic myth, the enlightened ones "know" in their essence that they possess a spark of the divine and that they are destined to return to the divine. However, those who have allowed themselves to become "drunk" with the enticements of the world are like animals—bodies with souls but no minds. Salvation is available only to those who detach themselves from the things of the world to become pure mind. These are the **solitary ones**.

## THE THEOLOGY OF THE GOSPEL OF THOMAS

As we have already noted, Gnostic Christianity had a concept of salvation. However, its answers to questions about what leads to salvation and to whom it is available are quite different from those of orthodox (literally "right thinking," or mainstream) Christianity. The author of the Gospel of Thomas states, at the beginning of the gospel, that the correct interpretation of the sayings of Jesus will result in eternal life: "Whoever finds the meaning of these sayings will not taste death" (G. Thom. logia 18–19). In other words, knowledge (i.e., experience) of Jesus's words is the secret of salvation. Notice that his role in salvation is one of revealer, through whom the "enlightened" ones can understand or learn the meaning of the secret.

The language that the Gospel of Thomas uses to describe salvation is "repose," becoming acquainted with oneself and becoming "solitary" or "a single one." According to this gospel, to know oneself is to know where you come from, namely, from God (G. Thom. logia 50–51). Only the "enlightened ones," who know who they are and where they came from, are capable of becoming solitary. While they are part of the physical world, they are multiple or divided. When they become solitary or single ones, they become one with their divine origin—that is, with the One, the First Principle, or God (G. Thom. logia 16, 23). The ideal disciples—those who have left behind everything that binds them to this world—make themselves free to return to their origins. What does this mean in concrete terms? Salvation is obtained by stripping off everything that is of this world (G. Thom. logia 21a, 37, 56) and liberating the spirit from the body (G. Thom. logia 29, 87, 112).

As already suggested by our discussion of the Gospel of Thomas's understanding of salvation, its understanding of Christology (i.e., the nature and function of Jesus as the Christ) is different from that of the synoptic gospels as well. There are, for example, no sayings about the future coming of the Son of Man or about an eschatological (i.e., end-time) expectation of the coming of the kingdom—sayings that are characteristic of the Q material and the synoptic gospels. There is no assertion that Jesus is the messiah and no mention of his suffering, death, and resurrection. The only title given to Jesus in this gospel is "the living Jesus." Most scholars of the Gospel of Thomas say this is the risen Jesus. However, the gospel itself gives no evidence of this interpretation. Marvin Meyer, a scholar who specializes in the study of the Gospel of Thomas, suggests that the "living Jesus" is the one who "lives" through the sayings (1992, 67). This view is consistent with the gospel's idea of salvation, especially if we think of knowledge as experience. By "knowing" the sayings, the enlightened one gets to experience the living Jesus!

Another way to understand Thomas's notion of the "living Jesus" is to think of him as the one who is fully united with the divine, the one who knows fully where he came from, and therefore the one who is pure spirit. The living Jesus is the one who "comes from what is whole" (G. Thom. logion 61)—that is, God—and in whom the rest or repose (freedom from the things of the world) and the new world are already present (G. Thom. logion 51). In sum, he is the wisdom teacher and the prototype of the real disciple. He will show his disciples how to become "children of the living Father" (G. Thom. logion 3).

What can we say about the Gospel of Thomas's understanding of church? Granted, this gospel contains numerous references to discipleship and the requirements for becoming a disciple of Jesus. There are also a few references to leadership among the disciples. For example, the Gospel of Thomas identifies James the Just, who is elsewhere described as "the brother of the Lord" and the head of the church in Jerusalem, as the one to whom they should go for leadership (G. Thom. logion 12). However, nowhere does the Gospel of Thomas say that the disciples have a mission in the world or as a community. Rather, their journey of becoming solitary is a *solitary* journey. In the synoptic gospels, the mission of the church is closely associated with the realization of God's kingdom in the world. However, when we examine the Gospel of Thomas's frequent references to the "kingdom of the Father," we discover that it is clearly not concerned with the establishment of God's reign in the world. Instead, this kingdom becomes a reality only with the solitary one's return to the divine realm (e.g., G. Thom. logia 76, 96–98).

Thus, the theology and worldview of the Gospel of Thomas have some important implications for the way believers live their lives in the world (i.e., ethics). For example, if one understands that the physical world is ruled by the forces of evil and that God's kingdom rightly resides in the heavenly realm, then there is no reason to be concerned about justice for the poor and oppressed in this world. There is also no need for the church to be a witness to the establishment of God's kingdom in the world or to work for the transformation of human culture. Indeed, there is no need for church in any form, because the quest to become solitary is something that the enlightened soul does alone and apart from the world.

Among modern Christians, we sometimes see some of these same tendencies. We encounter Christians who believe that they can best attain salvation by withdrawing from the mainstream of society in order to protect themselves from the contamination of the world. (This tendency is not to be confused with the vocation of monks who withdraw from public activity so that they can more intensely meditate and pray for the world.) We also find Christians who think their religion should be a private thing between themselves and God and not something that has anything to do with their everyday lives, their work, or their associations in secular society. While the first tendency seems quite laudable and the second sounds at least practical and respectful of others, both tendencies run into difficulties when critiqued by a creation theology that is grounded in the Book of Genesis and confirmed and reinforced in the tradition of the Christian church: God is the creator of all things and God created everything as good; all human beings are created in the image and likeness of God; humans are entrusted with stewardship over creation. Gnostic tendencies are also critiqued by a covenant theology that is founded in Exodus, reinforced in the prophets, and confirmed by the writings of the New Testament and the Christian tradition: God is a personal God; God's relationship to humanity is essentially communal in nature; God's justice and mercy are manifest in humanity's care and concern for the least among human society.

Hopefully, our discussion of the Gospel of Thomas illuminates something of the relationship between theology and ethics. First, consider that the believer's ethics necessarily flow from his or her theology. That is, how one understands the nature of God and God's relationship with creation, including human creatures, should directly impact the way one lives in the world. Likewise, how one lives in the world reflects one's operative theology, regardless of whether or not that theology is clearly acknowledged and articulated. For example, one cannot support the death penalty and also argue that God is the God of mercy. Second, consider that the believer's ethics are (or ought to be) grounded in the faith community to which he or she belongs and that they ought to cohere with the whole of the community's theological tradition. That is, one cannot espouse ethics that advocate separation from the world and, at the same time, hold a theology that says God is the sovereign creator of the world, is incarnate (i.e., enfleshed) in the world, and continues to be actively engaged with the world.

## IS THE GOSPEL OF THOMAS A MISOGYNIST DOCUMENT?

Given our current sensitivities about language and gender, we cannot leave our discussion of the Gospel of Thomas without mentioning the extremely troublesome and apparently misogynist tone of sayings like logion 114:

> Simon Peter said to them, "Make Mary leave us, for females don't deserve life." Jesus said, "Look, I will guide her to make her male, so that she too may become a living spirit resembling you males. For every female who makes herself male will enter the kingdom of Heaven." (Stephen Patterson and Marvin Meyer, trans., "The 'Scholars' Translation' of the Gospel of Thomas," http://www.misericordia.edu/users/davies/thomas/Trans.htm)

How can we make sense of logion 114 and others like it? First, we need to recognize that the document was composed in a highly patriarchal culture and therefore thoroughly influenced by that cultural context. However, a careful examination of the document also suggests that the author is not talking about biology when he refers to males and females. Rather, he intends a metaphorical use of the language, which is directly related to the gospel's understanding of salvation.

For example, logion 22 clarifies that the "solitary one" is the one who has transcended sexuality: He is like a little child (without gender) or like Adam before the fall (G. Thom. logion 37)—a pure spirit that still remembers his existence in the heavenly realm and that has not yet suffered the contamination of this world. Further, these statements presuppose an anthropology in which the masculine element is associated with the mind, which was considered to be the higher, spiritual principle of the human person, while the feminine element is associated with the body, which was considered to be the lower, animal principle of the human person. Thus, logion 114 teaches that the living Jesus will transform the female principle (the body) of the human person who wishes to become "solitary" in such a way that only the male principle (the mind) remains and he or she can be fully reunited with the divine. The readers of the Gospel of Thomas believed this to be the ideal for Christianity.

## THE GOSPEL OF JAMES

The Gospel of James, also known as the Protoevangelium of James or the Proto-Gospel of James, is not necessarily the original title of this document. In a fourth-century-C.E. manuscript, it was known as *Birth of Mary: Revelation of James,* and later it was known by a variety of names, including *Story of the Birth of Saint Mary, Mother of God* and *Birth of Our Lord and Our Lady Mary.* The document tells the story of the miraculous birth of Mary, her early childhood, her engagement and marriage to Joseph, and finally the birth of Jesus. It also includes a story about the martyrdom of Zechariah, the father of John the Baptist, and the death of Herod. The early Christian theologian Origen (c. 185–202 C.E.) appears to be referring to this work when he explains that the brothers of the Lord were sons of Joseph by a previous marriage (*Commentary on Matthew* 10.17).

Once again, before we investigate the content of this gospel, let us take some time to summarize what scholars have determined about authorship, date of composition, and audience.

## AUTHORSHIP

The Gospel of James was written under the pseudonym of James, the brother of Jesus and head of the church in Jerusalem, who was martyred in 62 C.E. (Josephus, *Antiquities* 20.200). In a brief postscript (G. Jas. 25:1–3), the assumed author of the Gospel of James says he was writing from the wilderness where he had escaped to wait out the uproar that took place in Jerusalem after the death of Herod the Great (4 B.C.E.). However, because this gospel contains material that was borrowed from Matthew's and Luke's gospels (80–90 C.E.), clearly it was written much later. Moreover, James could not have been its author, since he was already deceased by the time those gospels were written. Scholars have noted that the author was probably a Gentile Christian because, although he regularly refers to the Greek Septuagint, he seems not to know the geography of Palestine or certain Jewish customs and religious practices. For example, it is almost impossible to imagine a Jewish Christian author thinking that a Jewish girl could be raised in the Jerusalem Temple (G. Jas. 8:1–2). Additionally, the Gospel of James shows that its author had some rhetorical training and therefore was a person of at least modest means and not a simple peasant.

## DATE OF COMPOSITION AND INITIAL AUDIENCE

As noted above, an early reference to this gospel comes from Origen in the later part of the second century or the beginning of the third century C.E. Likewise, Clement of Alexandria (d. c. 212 C.E.) mentions some details about Mary that likely came from this gospel: Mary's baby was delivered by a midwife who declared her to have remained a virgin (*Stromata* 7.16.93). Some scholars think that Celsus (writing approximately 175–180 C.E.) also knew the Gospel of James because he mentions that Mary made her living by spinning thread for weaving and that she had been accused of adultery (Origen, *Contra Celsum* I.28). Justin Martyr (c. 100–165 C.E.) also appears to mention a detail of the Gospel of James: Jesus was born in a cave (*Dialogue with Trypho* 78.5). Therefore, scholars of the Gospel of James usually give it a date of composition in the second half of the second century, perhaps 150–180 C.E.

Because the Gospel of James contains some obvious literary seams and certain parts of the gospel are not included in the earliest manuscripts, scholars think that it underwent significant redaction (i.e., editing) after its original composition. The later additions include Joseph's words when time stands still at the birth of Jesus (G. Jas. 18:2), Salome's prayer when she witnesses Mary's virginity (G. Jas. 20:2), and the story of the murder of Zechariah, the father of John the Baptist (G. Jas. 22–24). Later, when you read the Gospel of James, you might want to note these sections in the text.

The location from which this gospel originated is extremely difficult to determine. Scholars have ruled out Palestine because the author seems not to know its geography (e.g., G. Jas. 21:1) as well as the western portions of Asia Minor (modern Greece) because the literary style lacks the sophistication we might expect from those locations. Some scholars have suggested Syria or Egypt, but there is not a great deal of evidence to support either location. In sum, we have to say that we do not know where the author was located when he wrote this gospel or for whom it was intended.

## BIRTH AND CHILDHOOD OF MARY

Although this gospel includes the story of Jesus' birth, its first concern is the story of the miraculous birth and childhood of Mary. As the story opens, we are introduced to **Joachim**, who was a wealthy and generous man, giving freely to those in need and making lavish offerings with great devotion to God at his place of worship (G. Jas. 1:1). However, when he was about to take his usual first place in the procession of offerings at the great feast, he was told that he could not because he had no children (G. Jas. 1:2). Deeply troubled by this challenge, he went out into the wilderness to grieve (G. Jas. 1:4). In the meantime, his wife, **Anna,** was grieving doubly because she had no children—if a wife was not able to provide children for her husband, it was considered a curse—and her husband had abandoned her (G. Jas. 2:1). But an angel appeared to each to tell them that Anna was pregnant and that they would give birth to a child (G. Jas. 4:1–2). Overjoyed, Joachim came back from the desert and made his offering to God (G. Jas. 4:4). Anna was waiting for him at the city gate, and together they rejoiced over their good fortune (G. Jas. 5:1). When Anna's pregnancy was finished, she gave birth to a girl whom she named Mary (G. Jas. 5:2). Thus, Anna and Joachim became the parents of Mary, who would be the mother of Jesus.

By telling this story as he does, the gospel writer appears to be answering an important theological question: How was it that Mary was chosen to be the mother of Jesus, the Son of God? We are told the story of her miraculous birth from parents who were righteous but unable to conceive a child (G. Jas. 1:2; 2:1)—recalling the situations of other famous persons from the story of salvation like Abraham and Sarah (Genesis 18, 21), Isaac and Rebecca (Genesis 25), and Jacob and Rachel (Genesis 29–30). The angel who announces Anna's conception of Mary prophesies that Mary will be known throughout the world (G. Jas. 4:1)—accounting for the place of importance she has in the Christian salvation story. We also learn that the Jewish priests recognized, in her infancy, the special role she would have in the redemption of God's people (G. Jas. 7:2). Of course, these details are not necessarily historical, but they express the conviction of the author of this gospel and the community for which it was written that it was part of God's plan that Mary be the mother of the messiah.

Birth of Mary, a panel of the altarpiece made for the Church of Ursule in Cologne, Germany. Anonymous (Master of the Life of Mary), 1490. *Bayerische Staatsgemaldesammlungen, Neue Pinakothek, Munich.*

## Mary, the Mother of the Messiah

But why this particular Jewish girl? Were there not other girls who were better suited to be the mother of the savior? The Gospel of James tells us that Mary was dedicated to God from before her birth (G. Jas. 4:1) and that her mother, Anna, did everything she could to protect her holiness, even to the extent of turning her childhood bedroom into a sanctuary and providing special nannies to care for her so that nothing ritually unclean could come into contact with her (G. Jas. 6:1). It also describes Mary as being raised in the Jerusalem Temple—a detail that is historically highly unlikely but theologically very significant—and being fed by angels (G. Jas. 8:2).

When it came time for her to leave the Temple, it was not Joseph's and Mary's families who arranged the marriage, as would have been the custom in first-century Palestine; rather, God selected Joseph from among the widowers of Israel by making a dove fly out of his walking stick and land on his head (G. Jas. 9:1–4). Thus, the priests of the Temple knew that Joseph was the one whom God had chosen. Mary's unique status is further affirmed in the way that she was chosen by lot, as the eighth—one more than the perfect number—virgin of the tribe of David, and given the assignment of weaving the purple and scarlet fabrics for the Temple (G. Jas. 10:1–2). Purple is the color of royalty and scarlet is the color of suffering, perhaps anticipating what would happen to her son, Jesus: He would be called "King of the Jews" and put to death.

## Answers to Other Questions

The Gospel of James addresses a number of questions that the synoptic gospels leave unanswered concerning Joseph's relationship with Mary and Jesus. For example, how do we explain the detail about Jesus' siblings? Answer: Joseph had children from a previous marriage. What was his occupation, and why is he not mentioned again after the story of the birth of Jesus? Answer: He was a carpenter. Already an old man when he took Mary into his house, he most likely was deceased by the time Jesus was an adult (G. Jas. 9:5, 9). How do we know for certain that Joseph was not the father of Jesus? Answer: He was away on a building project from the moment she came to live in his house and he returned home to find her six months' pregnant! (G. Jas. 9:9; 13:1–5). The Gospel of James goes on to assert the virginal conception (i.e., conception without the assistance of a male partner) of Jesus in several ways: the angel's announcement to Mary (G. Jas. 11:4–8); the angel's appearance to Joseph (G. Jas. 14:5–7); the story of Mary's and Joseph's survival of the "water of the Lord's testing," a technique for judging a person's guilt or innocence (G. Jas. 16:1–5); and the story about the midwife Salome, who checks Mary's virginal status after Jesus' birth (G. Jas. 20:1–4).

Finally, of all the noncanonical gospels, this gospel—or in the case of western Christianity, its successor, the Gospel of Pseudo-Matthew—has had the most lasting effect on the imagery that Christians associate with the Christmas event. For example, the Gospel of James gives us the story of Mary's journey to Bethlehem, in which Joseph placed Mary on the back of a donkey and led them down the road, and the story of Jesus' birth in a cave. These are scenes frequently depicted on religious

Christmas cards, for example. It has also inspired much of the devotional art associated with Mary, especially paintings and other types of art that illustrate the Annunciation and the Nativity of Jesus. You may wish to explore some of these aspects of the history of the interpretation of the Gospel of James on your own. You can locate the Gospel of Pseudo-Matthew at http://www.gnosis.org/library/psudomat.htm or at http://www.meta-religion.com/World_Religions/Christianity/Other_Books/New_Testament_Apocrypha/gospel_of_pseudo-matthew.htm.

## BIRTH STORIES OF OTHER FAMOUS PEOPLE

There are certain similarities between the birth stories of Jesus (from the Gospels of Matthew, Luke, and James) and the legendary accounts of other famous persons of the ancient world. For example, Diogenes Laertius tells the story of Plato's birth, most notably the unusual circumstances associated with his conception and his lineage back to the gods, as he received it from the writings of Speusippos (*Lives of the Eminent Philosophers* 3.1–2, 45). According to the story, Plato's father was Apollo, who conceived the child with Plato's mother when her husband had been unable to impregnate her. Similarly, Suetonius repeats a story about the conception of Caesar Augustus that reads as follows:

> In the book, *Theologumenon* by Asclepias of Mendes, I read that when Atia had come in the middle of the night to the solemn rite of Apollo, when her litter had been set in the temple, and while the other women slept, she slept. A snake slipped up to her and, after a little while, went out. When she awoke, she purified herself as if coming from her husband's bed. And immediately on her body there appeared a mark colored like a snake, and she could never get rid of it. Therefore, she always avoided the public baths. Augustus was born in the tenth month after this and because of this was considered the son of Apollo. (*Lives of the Caesars* II.94.4, translated in Cartlidge and Dungan, 1994, 133)

The early church writer Origen comments on these stories, saying that people fabricated them to show that these famous people had more wisdom and power than most (*Contra Celsum* I.37). Origen's pro-Christian biases are quite clear, however. He goes on to say that the stories about the unusual births of people like Plato and Caesar Augustus are merely fables or myths, whereas the stories of the birth of Jesus are reliable and true. We can safely say that Origen's antagonists would have said the same thing about the stories of Jesus' birth—that they are merely fantastic fables! How, then, shall we read these stories?

## THE SIGNIFICANCE OF THE BIRTH STORIES OF JESUS FOR CHRISTOLOGY

**Christology** is a term that refers to the study of the person and nature or function of Jesus as the messiah or the Christ. The earliest years of Christianity saw a variety of Christologies, some giving special attention to the death and resurrection of Jesus, some to his birth (incarnation) or baptism, others to his portrayal as a wisdom teacher or another Moses, and still others to his preexistence with the Father. The following theory has been proposed as an explanation for the expansion of traditions concerning the life of Jesus and their relation to the development of Christology. As we shall see, the infancy narratives play an important role in this chronology.

1. Paul's letters (50–62 C.E.) are the earliest among the writings of the New Testament. Christians before and during the time of Paul had no written gospel as we know it. Instead, they articulated their faith in the form of kerygmatic statements—brief statements of belief used in preaching the faith. These statements identified the death and resurrection as the decisive moment in which Jesus was proclaimed as the divine Son of God and messiah (e.g., Rom. 1:3–5). Their Christology focused primarily on Jesus' role as savior.

2. Later, when Christians began to preserve stories about Jesus' words and deeds, perhaps when the eyewitnesses to the life of Jesus were no longer among them, we can imagine that they began to ask, At what point did God first name Jesus as God's son? The earliest gospel, Mark (65–70 C.E.), identifies the baptism of Jesus as the decisive moment in which Jesus is designated as Son of God by God's own word, "You are my Son, my beloved" (Mark 1:9–11).

3. However, if the baptism of Jesus is the moment in which God designated Jesus as his divine Son, someone might then assume that this was the moment in which God "adopted" Jesus. But this would mean that Jesus was not of the same substance as God, a teaching that eventually was identified as a heresy. So who or what was Jesus before the baptism? Perhaps in response to a question like this, the tradition began to develop stories associated with the birth of Jesus that reveal Jesus' unique relationship with God from the moment of his conception and birth (the Gospels of Matthew and Luke).

4. John's gospel, the most theologically sophisticated of the gospels, pushed the answer even further and said that Jesus always was the divine Son of God, that he preexisted with the Father from the beginning (John 1:1–18). He is thus described as the Logos or Word of God. This Christology focused primarily on Jesus' incarnation (enfleshment).

With this gradual movement backward into the events of Jesus' life, the early church articulated a variety of Christologies, each designed to answer certain questions about Jesus' identity and his place in God's plan for salvation, and each illustrated through stories. In fact, the stories became the medium or vehicle through which the faith was proclaimed. Thus, whether or not we can substantiate the historical details of these gospel stories, the truth of the gospels resides in the theological claims being made by the communities of faith that stand behind the gospels. Are they **myths**? Yes, but not as Origen understood myth or even as many of our contemporaries understand myth—merely fanciful fiction. Rather, they are religious stories that employ symbols and metaphoric language in order to articulate religious truths that otherwise cannot be easily understood through logical reasoning. They tell the truth about fundamental human experiences and answer questions that transcend reason, like these: Why are we here? What is our destiny? Why did God become a person like us? In that sense, myth expresses truth that is weightier than anything that could be documented as historical fact.

## THE GOSPEL OF PETER

The third noncanonical gospel that we explore in this chapter is the Gospel of Peter. Whereas the Gospel of James treats the beginning of Jesus' life and the story of his mother's life up to and including his birth, the excerpt that we possess from this gospel pertains to the end of Jesus' life. Like the Gospel of James, the Gospel of Peter apparently was fairly well known and widely read among early Christian churches. Unlike the Gospel of James, it apparently fell out of favor when people began to raise questions about its orthodoxy. Again, before we look at the content of this gospel, let us summarize what we know about its author, date, and audience.

## AUTHORSHIP

This gospel is attributed to Peter, one of the apostles of Jesus. It was known by this title at least by the end of the second century C.E. However, biblical scholars today are quite certain that Peter did not write it. Some have argued that the author was Jewish Christian, partly because of the gospel's apologetic overtones and partly because of the inclusion of the detail about giant angels who aid the resurrected Jesus in his departure from the tomb. These giant angels are part of the system of angels in Jewish angelology (i.e., teaching about angels). Others have argued that the gospel's harsh polemic against the Jews is evidence that the author was a Gentile Christian. We know from other literature of the time that Christian anti-Jewish rhetoric was already very fierce by the end of the second century C.E. (see below). However, the Gospel of Matthew, which most scholars agree originated in a Jewish Christian context, also has some harsh anti-Jewish rhetoric. In the end, we have to conclude that we do not have enough information about this gospel to determine the background of its author.

## DATE AND INITIAL AUDIENCE

Although several early church writers mention a gospel attributed to Peter, none provides us with a quotation that confirms they are talking about this particular gospel, nor do they give us any descriptions of its content except for a quotation from Bishop Serapion (190 C.E.) that is preserved in the writings of the fourth-century church historian Eusebius (*Ecclesiastical History* VI.12.3–5). If Eusebius can be trusted to accurately convey this quotation from Serapion and if Serapion is referring to this gospel, then we have an outside limit for the date of the Gospel of Peter, namely, 190 C.E. But the gospel was already being read in Christian communities in Serapion's time. In order for it to have been circulated this widely, it had to have been written at least a decade or so earlier, perhaps in the middle part of the second century, perhaps 150 C.E.

Another argument for a mid-second-century date for the Gospel of Peter concerns the observation that the gospel appears to incorporate, perhaps even harmonize, traditions from the canonical gospels. If the last of the canonical gospels was written by 100 C.E. and if we allow a couple decades for those gospels to circulate widely enough that this gospel writer would have known all four canonical gospels, then a mid-second-century date of composition is reasonable. Based on the strength of these arguments, we will follow the majority view and assign it a date in the mid–second century, perhaps 150 C.E. However, others who have studied this gospel see evidence of independent and more primitive traditions that suggests a much earlier date of composition, perhaps even as early as 50 C.E., which would make it earlier than the synoptic gospels. Notice, in particular, some of the details of the resurrection story that are found nowhere else in the synoptic gospels.

Determining the location from which this gospel was written is equally problematic. Most scholars associate it with Syria because Serapion was bishop of Antioch in Syria and the communities with which he was associated appear to have known the gospel fairly well. Others have suggested Asia Minor (modern Turkey) because of the anti-Jewish worldview that this gospel shares with Melito of Sardis's *On Pascha* (see below), which originated in Asia Minor. However, it is also possible that the gospel originated in Egypt, since the only existing manuscript fragment of this gospel was discovered in Akhmim in Upper Egypt in 1886 or 1887. If we had the entire gospel, perhaps we could make a better determination, but without additional evidence, little more can be said about the date or location of composition of the Gospel of Peter.

## THE WORLDVIEW AND THEOLOGICAL PERSPECTIVES OF THE GOSPEL OF PETER

Although the Gospel of Peter is similar to the synoptic gospels in many ways, the differences are also very important. For example, the Gospel of Peter contains a story of the resurrection event itself, not simply the "empty tomb" scene that we find in the canonical gospels. It also incorporates the "testimony" of supposedly unbiased witnesses—that is, the Roman soldiers—of the resurrection event. By examining differences such as these, we can uncover clues that will help us better understand the theology of the Gospel of Peter and the worldview of its author. Here is a list of some of the scenes in which you will find significant differences between the Gospel of Peter and the canonical gospels:

- Herod Antipas (who was Jewish) in place of Pontius Pilate as Jesus' judge (G. Pet. 1–2)
- Jesus' mockery by the crowd and the reference to Jesus as the "Son of God" (G. Pet. 6–9)
- Jesus' silence (G. Pet. 10)
- The narrator's reference to the fulfillment of scripture (G. Pet. 17)
- The Jews' lament after the crucifixion and references to the destruction of the Temple (G. Pet. 25–26)

- The proclamation "Behold how righteous he is!" (G. Pet. 28)
- The Jewish elders' interest in placing guards at the tomb (G. Pet. 29–30, 48)
- Witnesses to the resurrection (G. Pet. 31–43)
- Context for the statement "Truly he was a Son of God" (G. Pet. 45–46)
- The cover-up and Pilate's declaration of innocence in the situation (G. Pet. 45–49)

## CHRISTOLOGY OF THE GOSPEL OF PETER

One of the theological concerns raised by the Gospel of Peter relates to Jesus' silence "as if he had no pain" (G. Pet. 10). At the risk of being overly repetitious, we include Serapion's comments on the Gospel of Peter here. The full quotation can be found in our discussion of canon in the Introduction to this book.

> "We brethren," says Serapion, "receive Peter and the other apostles as Christ himself. But those writings which falsely go under their name, as we are well acquainted with them, we reject, and know also, that we have not received such handed down to us. But when I came to you, I had supposed that all held to the true faith; and as I had not perused the gospel presented by them under the name of Peter, I said, 'If this be the only thing that creates difference among you, let it be read;' but now having understood, from what was said to me, that their minds were enveloped in some heresy, I will make haste to come to you again; therefore, brethren, expect me soon. . . . For we have borrowed this gospel from others, who have studied it, that is, from the successors of those who led the way before him, whom we call Docetae, (for most opinions have sprung from this sect.)" Thus far of the works of Serapion. (Eusebius, *Ecclesiastical History* VI 12.3–6)

The heresy to which Serapion refers is called **docetism**, from the Greek word *dokei*, which means "seemed" or "seeming." Though not a fully formed teaching advocated by any particular group of early Christians, there was a tendency among some to consider the suffering and death of Jesus as "seeming." Thus, certain early Christians were saying that it may have looked like Jesus suffered terribly on the cross, but truly he did not. To be fair, it is unlikely that any of these Christians set out to develop a heresy. Instead, they were trying to resolve the problem of Jesus' crucifixion, which was, in every way, an embarrassment to early Christians. After all, how could anyone in his or her right mind accept the possibility of a suffering savior/king? And as they came to appreciate more fully what it meant to say that Jesus was the Son of God, how could they explain the notion of a suffering deity?

One way that early Christians made sense of a crucified messiah was to acknowledge that indeed Jesus was condemned to crucifixion, but he was unjustly condemned. Thus, God vindicated him by restoring him to life in the resurrection. This approach—sometimes called humiliation-exaltation Christology—is what we have seen in the synoptic gospels. Another way to resolve the problem was to say that Jesus somehow transcended the pain of crucifixion. In other words, he was the ancient equivalent of our contemporary Hollywood superheroes who endure repeated beatings by the bad guys, as well as gunshots, bombings, car explosions, and every other kind of violence, and still manage to stay on their feet, fighting the good fight! This apparently was the approach of the Gospel of Peter.

Of course, a Christology that downplays the suffering of Jesus has implications for other aspects of theology. In his second-century C.E. Letters to the Trallians and the Smyrnaeans, Bishop Ignatius of Antioch rails against certain Christians who say that the suffering of Jesus was "seeming." Calling them the "seeming ones," he argues that their belief about the suffering of Christ negates their claims to believe in his resurrection. In other words, these two elements of theology have to cohere. If Jesus wasn't really crucified, how can you say that he was really resurrected from the dead? Ignatius also charges them with denying the Eucharist, which he associates with the blood of Christ, and with disobeying the bishop, who is the representative of Christ, thereby destroying the unity of the church. However, what appears to pain Ignatius the most is the way that their views call into question the credibility of **martyrdom** (i.e., witnessing to the faith even to the point of being willing to die). If these "seeming ones" do not allow for the suffering of Jesus, then they also invalidate the suffering of the martyr, who lives his or her life in imitation of Christ.

Gradually, early church writers exposed other problems with this docetic tendency that was designed to downplay the suffering of Jesus. Perhaps the most significant problem had to do with how people understand salvation. For those whose Christology—understanding of Jesus as the Christ—focused primarily on Christ's divinity, it would not have been difficult for them to start with a denial of his suffering and end up downplaying his humanity. "So what?" you might say. Irenaeus, a second-century C.E. bishop, answered this question with little explanation, assuming that his colleagues knew the answer well:

> But as our Lord is the only true teacher, he is also the true Son of God, who is good and who suffers in patience—the Logos of God the Father become Son of man. . . . For if a human person had not conquered humanity's foe, that foe would not have been conquered justly. Conversely, unless it was God who conferred salvation, we should not possess it securely, and unless humanity had been closely united to God, it could not have become a sharer in incorruptibility. It was necessary that "the mediator between God and human beings" [1 Tim. 2:5], through his sharing in the life of both, bring the two together in friendship and harmony and bring it about both that humanity is made over to God and that God is made known to human beings. (*Against Heresies* 3.18.6–7)

Clement of Alexandria, one of Irenaeus's contemporaries, said it this way: "The Logos of God had become man so that you might learn from a human how a human may become God" (*Protrepticus* 1.8.4 [GCS 12:9]). Origin, a third-century theologian, wrote, "From Him [Christ] there began the union of the divine with the human nature, in order that the human, by communion with the divine, might rise to be divine" (*Contra Celsum* 3.28; ANF 4.475). Athanasius, a fourth-century bishop, wrote that the Word of God "was made man so that we might be made God" (*De Incarnatione* 54.3). In sum, unless God becomes one of us, there is no salvation.

# ANTI-JUDAISM IN THE EARLY CHURCH

Finally, we cannot leave our discussion of the Gospel of Peter without addressing its strongly anti-Jewish character. Already we have seen the kernel of anti-Jewish sentiments in the synoptic gospels, where the Pharisees are often portrayed as hostile opponents of Jesus over interpretation of the Torah, where the Pharisees and Sadducees plot to have Jesus arrested, and where the High Priest presides over Jesus' trial in front of the Sanhedrin. Of course, the first followers of Jesus were Jews, as was Jesus. The earliest Christian communities were made up of both Jews and Gentiles, and sometimes they found themselves in fierce fights with their Jewish brothers and sisters. Therefore, some of what appears to be anti-Judaism in the New Testament may be the fallout of disputes between Jews who did not believe that Jesus was the messiah and Jews who did. However, as Christianity gained in power and status, eventually becoming the protected religion of the Roman Empire, the rhetoric against Judaism grew in intensity. Jews were branded as "Christ-killers" and charged with deicide (literally, "God-killing"). Regrettably, terrible acts of violence accompanied the harsh rhetoric against the Jews throughout the centuries, even to the present day—all of this fueled by Christians' interpretation of the gospels.

The Gospel of Peter probably reflects the early stages of this growing tendency to blame the Jews for the death of the messiah. Another example can be found in Melito of Sardis's *Homily on the Passover*, written in the late second century C.E.:

> He is the Pascha of our salvation. . . .
> It is he that was enfleshed in a virgin,
> That was hanged on a tree, . . .
> He is the lamb being slain;
> He is the lamb that is speechless; he is the one born from Mary the lovely ewe-lamb;
> He is the one taken from the flock,
> And dragged to slaughter,
> And sacrificed at evening,
> And buried at night;. . .
> It is he that has been murdered.
> And where has he been murdered? In the middle of Jerusalem.
> By whom? By Israel.
> Why? Because he healed their lame
> And cleansed their lepers
> And brought light to their blind
> And raised their dead,
> That is why he died. (*On Pascha*, 69–72; Hall, 1979, 37, 39)

Notice how Melito describes Jesus as the Passover lamb. Notice, also, how he blames Israel for what he calls the murder of Jesus and even assigns a motive to their action: They repaid good with evil. Unfortunately, this is part of the legacy of the early church concerning relations with the Jews.

# CONTEMPORARY CHRISTIAN RESPONSES TO ANTI-JUDAISM

What shall we say about anti-Judaism today? Despite anti-Jewish interpretations of the New Testament, all four of the canonical gospels say quite clearly that the death of Jesus was not the responsibility of the Jewish people, then or now; rather, Jesus' death was part of God's design. The religious leaders of first-century Judaism may have been instruments in that plan because they delivered Jesus to the Roman authorities, but they were no more responsible for the death of the Son of God than the Roman authorities or even the disciples of Jesus, who ran away when he was arrested. Unfortunately, however, Christianity bears at least some responsibility, throughout the centuries, for creating an environment that made possible terrible atrocities against the Jews, thus violating the core message of the gospel—love.

The Second Vatican Council of the Roman Catholic Church attempted to address the problem of anti-Judaism in a document entitled *Nostra Aetate*, also called *The Declaration on the Relationship of the Church to Non-Christian Religions*, which was promulgated in 1965. Today the language of this document may seem somewhat awkward to our ears, but at the time that it was written, it marked a monumental step in opening dialogue between Catholics and Jews. An excerpt from *Nostra Aetate* follows:

> Since the spiritual patrimony common to Christians and Jews is thus so great, this sacred Synod wishes to foster and recommend the mutual understanding and respect which is the fruit above all of biblical and theological studies, and of brotherly dialogues. . . .
>
> The Church repudiates all persecutions against any man. Moreover, mindful of her common patrimony with the Jews, and motivated by the gospel's spiritual love and by no political considerations, she deplores the hatred, persecutions, and displays of anti-Semitism directed against the Jews at any time and from any source.
>
> Besides, as the Church has always held and continues to hold, Christ in His boundless love freely underwent His passion and death because of the sins of all men, so that all might attain salvation. It is therefore the duty of the Church's preaching to proclaim the cross of Christ as the sign of God's all-embracing love and as the fountain from which every grace flows. (*Declaration on the Relationship of the Church to Non-Christian Religions*, § 4)

Of course, the Roman Catholic Church is not the only church to make statements against anti-Judaism (also called anti-Semitism, though perhaps incorrectly). In fact, it was not the first to do so in the period after the Holocaust. The World Council of Churches, in its first assembly in 1948, made the following statement, which it renewed again in its third assembly in 1961:

> We call upon all the churches we represent to denounce anti-semitism, no matter what its origin, as absolutely irreconcilable with the profession and practice of the Christian faith. Anti-semitism is sin against God and man. Only as we give convincing evidence to our Jewish neighbours that we seek for them the common rights and dignities which God wills for his children, can we come to such a meeting with them as would make it possible to share with them the best which God has given us in Christ. (http://www.jcrelations.net/en/displayItem.php?id=1492)

A search of the internet using the key words *Jewish-Christian Relations* will yield many more such statements from individual Christian churches and from committees engaged in ecumenical and interreligious dialogues as well as responses from various Jewish communities. The large number of these statements testifies to the progress that has been made in Jewish-Christian relations in recent decades. However, the persistence of hate crimes against our Jewish brothers and sisters reminds us that much more progress is needed. Hopefully, our study of the Gospel of Peter and the canonical gospels demonstrates that an important starting place is careful and well-informed interpretation of the gospels' passion narratives.

## KEY TERMS

| | | |
|---|---|---|
| Extracanonical | Gnostic myth | Anna |
| Didymus Judas Thomas | Cosmology | Christology |
| Asceticism | Anthropology | Myths |
| Logion/logia | Solitary one | Docetism |
| Gnosis | Joachim | Martyrdom |

## QUESTIONS FOR READING

Read the Gospel of Thomas. Use evidence from the text to answer the following questions. Links to English translations of this gospel can be found at http://www.ntgateway.com and http://www.sacred-texts.com/chr/thomas/htm, or you can do an online search to locate a site of your choice.

1. After reading the Gospel of Thomas, explain how it compares to the synoptic gospels in terms of literary form and overall structure and arrangement. Does it bear any similarities to the synoptic gospels in these areas? How is it different?

2. Locate two or three logia that describe the Gospel of Thomas's understanding of who Jesus is or what he does for the believer. Use these sayings to make your own observations about the Christology of the Gospel of Thomas.

3. Locate two or three logia that describe the Gospel of Thomas's understanding of discipleship. Use these sayings to make your own observations about what it means to be a disciple of Jesus. What might this kind of discipleship look like in our modern context?

4. Use the above descriptions of Gnostic cosmology and anthropology to explain logia 7 and 56.

5. Locate one or two logia from the Gospel of Thomas that espouse asceticism. Explain the meaning of these sayings.

6. Locate two or three logia from the Gospel of Thomas that have parallels in the synoptic gospels. In what ways are the sayings alike? In what ways are they different? Use the results of your analysis to comment on scholars' observation that both the synoptic gospels and the Gospel of Thomas borrowed material from a

"sayings of Jesus" tradition and that the Gospel of Thomas, in some cases, preserves a more primitive version of these sayings.

Read the Gospel of James. Use evidence from the text to answer the following questions. Links to English translations of this gospel can be found at http://www .earlychristianwritings.com/infancyjames.html and http://wesley.nnu.edu/biblical _studies/noncanon/gospels/gosjames.htm, or you can do an online search to locate a site of your choice.

7. After reading the Gospel of James, comment on the author's portrayal of Anna and Joachim, the parents of Mary. What does the gospel suggest about the kind of people they were? Why do you think the gospel writer portrayed them in this way?

8. What details does the author incorporate into the Gospel of James to show that Mary is God's chosen one? Find at least three examples.

9. According to the Gospel of James, how was Joseph chosen to be Mary's husband? What was his reaction to the proposal? Why do you think the gospel writer portrayed him in this way? What was his profession?

10. Examine the story of the birth of Jesus in the Gospel of James. What details of the story have close parallels with the stories of the birth of Jesus in the canonical gospels (specifically, the Gospels of Matthew and Luke)? Use the results of your analysis to comment on scholars' observation that the author of the Gospel of James used Matthew's and Luke's gospels to write his gospel.

11. According to the Gospel of James, how did Mary and Elizabeth escape Herod the Great's attempts to kill them and their children? Can you speculate about the message that the author of the Gospel of James was trying to convey by including these details?

12. According to the Gospel of James, why was Zechariah murdered? Who took his place as priest in the Temple?

Read the extant excerpt from the Gospel of Peter. Use evidence from the text to answer the following questions. Links to English translations of this gospel can be found at http://www.earlychristianwritings.com/gospelpeter.html and http://wesley.nnu.edu/biblical_studies/noncanon/gospels/gospete.htm, or you can do an online search to locate a site of your choice.

13. How are Pontius Pilate and Herod Antipas portrayed in this gospel? Compare their roles in the Gospel of Peter to their roles in the passion narratives of the canonical gospels.

14. How are Jesus and his disciples portrayed in this gospel? Compare their depiction in the Gospel of Peter to their depiction in the passion narratives of the canonical gospels.

15. Compare the resurrection story in the Gospel of Peter to the resurrection stories of the canonical gospels. In what ways are they similar? In what ways are they different?

16. Are there ways in which the Gospel of Peter provides more satisfying answers to questions about what happened to Jesus after his burial? Explain.

## Questions for Reflection

1. What were the most appealing aspects of the Gospel of Thomas for you? What were most problematic for you? Explain.

2. How would you explain the relationship between theology and ethics? Locate an example of a person or group that has a clear understanding of the relationship of theology and ethics. How do you see this relationship manifested in what they say and do?

3. How would you respond to someone who said that, since gospels like the Gospels of Thomas, Peter, and James are not canonical, there is no benefit to be gained by reading them? Explain.

4. What aspects of the Gospel of James were especially interesting or surprising to you? Why?

5. What aspects of the Gospel of Peter's story of the passion and resurrection of Jesus were especially interesting or surprising to you? Why?

## Activities for Learning

1. Using the synoptic gospels and the Gospel of Thomas as your source material, design a short sayings gospel of no less than ten logia. Select your sayings around a theme (or themes) and with a view to making proclamation—gospel means "good news"—on a theological topic like Christology, discipleship, or salvation. You may organize your mini "sayings" gospel in any way you wish, and you may redact the sayings to suit your purposes, but keep track of your source materials. When you have completed your gospel, take some time to reflect on the process. What, if anything, does this process help you understand about the ancient processes of gospel formation? What new questions does your reflection on this process raise for you?

2. The Koran, the sacred scriptures of Islam, contains stories and sayings about Mary, the mother of Jesus, some of which have parallels with the synoptic gospels and the Gospel of James. From the Koran, read surahs 3.37, 3.44, and 19:23–26. What do these verses tell you about how Muslims regard Mary? If possible, interview a scholar of the Koran about how and why Muslims honor Mary, the mother of Jesus.

3. Locate a contemporary culture that preserves stories about the birth and childhood of its leaders. For example, you might investigate the birth stories of North Korean leader Kim Jong-il or stories about the childhood experiences of American politicians. You might also explore the birth totems of Native American cultures. To what extent are these stories intended to be read as documentary history? What role do these stories play in foreshadowing the kind of leader this person will be? Compare these stories to stories about the birth of Mary or Jesus. How do you account for similarities or differences?

4. Select one of the many movies that depict the life of Jesus: for example, *Godspell*, *Jesus Christ Superstar*, *Jesus of Nazareth*, *Jesus of Montreal*, *The Passion of the Christ*, or

*The Gospel of John.* How does your movie selection address the problem of the crucifixion and resurrection of Jesus? Compare its portrayal of the death and resurrection of Jesus to those of the canonical gospels or the Gospel of Peter. To what extent does the movie provide more satisfying answers about the death of Jesus? Give examples to explain. In what ways might the movie portrayal be problematic? Give examples to explain.

5. Investigate the circumstances around the discovery and recent publication of the Gospel of Judas. When and where was the manuscript discovered? How is it being preserved? What challenges did the scholars who transcribed the Coptic text and translated it into English have to face in order to bring their project to completion? What do they hope will be its contribution to our knowledge of the life of the early church?

## Sources and Resources

Cameron, Ron, ed. *The Other Gospels: Non-Canonical Gospel Texts.* Philadelphia: Westminster Press, 1982.

Cartlidge, David R., and David L. Dungan, eds. *Documents for the Study of the Gospels.* 2nd ed. Minneapolis, Minn.: Fortress, 1994.

Cartlidge, David R., and J. Keith Elliott. *Art and the Christian Apocrypha.* London: Routledge, 2001.

Crossan, John Dominic. *The Cross That Spoke: The Origins of the Passion Narrative.* San Francisco: Harper & Row, 1988.

———. *Who Killed Jesus? Exposing the Roots of Anti-Semitism in the Gospel Story of the Death of Jesus.* San Francisco: HarperSanFrancisco, 1995.

Ehrman, Bart D. *Lost Christianities: The Battle for Scripture and the Faiths We Never Knew.* New York: Oxford University Press, 2003.

———, ed. *Lost Scriptures: Books That Did Not Make It into the New Testament.* New York: Oxford University Press, 2003.

Elliott, J. K. *The Apocryphal New Testament: A Collection of Apocryphal Christian Literature in English Translation.* Oxford, England: Oxford University Press, 2005.

Fredriksen, Paula, and Adele Reinhartz, eds. *Jesus, Judaism and Christian Anti-Judaism: Reading the New Testament after the Holocaust.* Nashville, Tenn.: Westminster John Knox, Press 2002.

Hall, Stuart George. *Melito of Sardis: On Pascha and Fragments.* Oxford, England: Oxford University Press, 1979.

Hock, Ronald F. *The Infancy Gospels of James and Thomas: With Introduction, Notes and Original Text Featuring the New Scholars Version Translation.* Santa Rosa, Calif.: Polebridge Press, 1995.

Jenkins, Philip. *Hidden Gospels: How the Search for Jesus Lost Its Way.* New York: Oxford University Press, 2001.

Koester, Helmut. *Ancient Christian Gospels: Their History and Development.* Philadelphia: Trinity Press International, 1990.

Layton, Bentley. *The Gnostic Scriptures.* Garden City, N.Y.: Doubleday, 1987.

Meyer, Marvin. *The Gospel of Thomas: The Hidden Sayings of Jesus.* New York: HarperCollins, 1992.

———. *Secret Gospels: Essays on Thomas and the Secret Gospel of Mark.* Harrisburg, Pa.: Trinity Press International, 2003.

Miller, Robert J. *Born Divine: The Births of Jesus and Other Sons of God.* Santa Rosa, Calif.: Polebridge Press, 2003.

Pagels, Elaine H. *The Gnostic Gospels.* New York: Vintage Books, 1989.

———. *Beyond Belief: The Secret Gospel of Thomas.* New York: Random House, 2003.

Robinson, James M., ed. *Nag Hammadi Library in English.* Leiden, Netherlands: E. J. Brill, 1996.

Schneemelcher, Wilhelm, ed. *New Testament Apocrypha.* 2 vols. Philadelphia: Westminster Press, 1992.

# ORIGINS OF THE EARLY
# CHURCH

The second major section of the New Testament consists of a single book, Acts of the Apostles. It is the story of the origins of the early church from the Ascension of Jesus and the descent of the Holy Spirit on his disciples at Pentecost through Paul's arrest and transport to Rome, covering roughly thirty-five years. Acts of the Apostles has been called a history. Its introduction (Acts 1:1–5) links this book to the Gospel of Luke, in which the author indicates that he is writing an "orderly account" of the events associated with the story of Jesus "after investigating everything carefully from the first" (Luke 1:3). But is this a history as we understand the genre today?

The ancient history narrates the story of a famous person or an important event. Although written with reference to political events and activities of the rulers of that time, the ancient history was not designed to be an objective report about the historical event or person. Instead, it was written primarily to honor an important person or make an example of a particular event. Certainly, its stories have a historical basis, but they are not historically accurate in all their details because the author of the ancient history was given literary license to fine-tune his stories in order to highlight his own agenda. Perhaps the closest contemporary parallel is the historical novel. People who like to read historical novels recognize the historical elements of the story, but precisely because they know the history, they also can recognize where the author has embellished the story with fictional details. Sometimes the embellishments are designed to entertain, other times to edify, and still other times to explain the motivations or inner thoughts of the major characters.

Many of the same things could be said of the ancient history. How do we know? For one thing, we possess several histories from the first century B.C.E. through the second century C.E., from which scholars can reconstruct the formal (i.e., structural) elements of histories. Another way to learn what to expect from ancient histories is to read any existing instructions for writing histories. In this case, we are lucky enough to have a work by Lucian of Samosata entitled "How to Write a History."

Here is what he has to say about how to write an effective history that is both useful and entertaining:

> The task of the historian is similar [to that of a great sculptor]: to give a fine arrange-
> ment to events and illuminate them as vividly as possible. And when a man who has
> heard him thinks thereafter that he is actually seeing what is being described and then
> praises him—then it is that the work of our Phidias of history is perfect and has
> received its proper praise. . . .
>
> After the preface, long or short in proportion to its subject matter, let the transition
> to the narrative be gentle and easy. For all the body of the history is simply a long nar-
> rative. So let it be adorned with the virtues proper to narrative, progressing smoothly,
> evenly and consistently, free from humps and hollows. Then let its clarity be limpid,
> achieved, as I have said, both by diction and the interweaving of the matter. For he will
> make everything distinct and complete, and when he has finished the first topic he will
> introduce the second, fastened to it and linked with it like a chain, to avoid breaks and
> a multiplicity of disjointed narratives; no, always the first and second topics must not
> merely be neighbours but have common matter and overlap. . . .
>
> If a person has to be introduced to make a speech, above all let his language suit his
> person and his subject, and next let these also be as clear as possible. It is then, how-
> ever, that you can play the orator and show your eloquence. (*Lucian*, §§ 51, 55, 58)

Observe how Lucian compares a good history to a great sculpture—Phidias was a
very popular sculptor of Lucian's day. Like great art, Lucian says, you know a history
is well done when you read it and feel like you are actually seeing the story unfold.
He goes on to say how the narrative needs to be neatly constructed so that it flows
easily from one scene to another and illuminates a common theme. Likewise, the
speeches should be carefully crafted so that they are appropriate for each character
and, at the same time, clear and eloquent. Notice that Lucian says nothing about
including only historically accurate materials or having all of your documentation
in place. These modern concerns of history writing simply would have been incomprehensible to someone like Lucian.

Most biblical scholars agree that Acts of the Apostles is a history in the tradition
of ancient histories. As such, it contains several literary forms typically found in histories. Two are important for our reading of Acts of the Apostles: dramatic episodes
and speeches.

*Dramatic episodes* were created not so much to communicate facts and chronology
as to edify the listener. The episodes are usually freestanding—that is, easily
excerpted from the larger text, as if they could have been written for another setting or about another character and have served their purpose just as well. But they
are neatly woven into the larger story so that the reader is able to move quickly and
seamlessly from one scene to the next. The individual scenes also tend to have a
fairly predictable plot. It would seem that part of the enjoyment of the story came
from knowing how it would end!

The primary function of these dramatic episodes was to advance the agenda of
the author who was trying to deliver some sort of message. For example, the story of
Stephen's martyrdom in Acts 6–7 introduces Paul, who is the central figure of much
of the rest of Acts of the Apostles. Here he is called Saul (Acts 7:58). It also provides
an example of how Luke wants to show that the Jews continued to reject the

message of Jesus. They put Stephen to death, says Luke, because he preached to them about Jesus (Acts 7:54, 58). Another dramatic episode, the story of Cornelius's conversion in Acts 10, also demonstrates the author's agenda: The message of Jesus Christ is destined to extend beyond Judaism to the Gentile world. Finally, the story about the Jerusalem Council in Acts 15 describes how even the apostles in Jerusalem agreed to accept Gentile converts without significant restrictions. If these dramatic episodes were intended to be strictly historical accounts, many other things would have been said about each event. Instead, a single message is conveyed: The Jews were the first recipients of God's promise, and some accepted it, but because others did not, God expanded the promise to the Gentiles.

*Speeches* make up the centerpiece of most of the significant scenes in Acts of the Apostles. A quick survey shows that approximately one-third of the book is devoted to speeches, many by Paul but others by Stephen, Peter, and James. Consistent with other histories of its time, the speeches of Acts were created by the author and placed in the mouths of the main characters of the story so that the author could dialogue with his listeners. Thus, the bystanders described in scenes that contain speeches are not the intended audience for the speech. Rather, they are simply characters in the story who provide Luke with the opportunity to expound on his message. Thus, the author is using the medium of a speech to speak directly to his own audience, making the speeches an important tool in developing the themes of Acts of the Apostles.

Of course, we could say much more about ancient historiography (i.e., rules for writing history). Hopefully, this brief overview is sufficient to provide a context for interpreting Acts of the Apostles, a very interesting but sometimes misunderstood book of the New Testament. In sum, we must be careful not to impose on Acts of the Apostles our modern expectations of history. Instead, we should read it as it was intended—as a great story with an enduring message, designed to make you feel like you are right there with the early Christians, sharing in their adventures.

# CHAPTER 12

# ACTS OF THE APOSTLES

## OVERVIEW

- AUTHORSHIP: Traditionally identified as Luke; the same person who wrote the Gospel of Luke
- DATE OF COMPOSITION: Probably 80–90 C.E.
- AUDIENCE: Unknown, though Theophilus is named as its recipient in the prologue
- MAJOR TOPICS: Literary Features of Acts of the Apostles; Peter and Paul; A Spirit-Filled Church; The Early Church's Way of Life; Comments on Acts 28:16–30

## TIMELINE

| | |
|---|---|
| **37 B.C.E.** | Herod the Great takes up his kingship in Palestine. |
| **6–4 B.C.E.** | Jesus of Nazareth is born. |
| **4 B.C.E.** | Herod the Great, king of Palestine, dies. His kingdom is divided among three sons: Archelaus, Herod Antipas, and Philip. |
| **4 B.C.E.–39 C.E.** | Herod Antipas, son of Herod the Great, is tetrarch of Galilee and Perea. |
| **c. 5–10 C.E.** | Saul/Paul of Tarsus is born. |
| **26–36 C.E.** | Pontius Pilate is prefect of Judea and Samaria. |
| **c. 30 C.E.** | Jesus is crucified, dies, and is resurrected. |
| **c. 36 C.E.** | Stephen is martyred; Paul is converted on the road to Damascus. |
| **c. 41–44 C.E.** | The apostle James, the brother of John, is martyred. |
| **49–51 C.E.** | An apostolic conference is held in Jerusalem to decide about inclusion of Gentile believers. |
| **52–60 C.E.** | Felix is procurator of Palestine. |
| **54–68 C.E.** | Nero is Roman emperor. |
| **60–62 C.E.** | Festus is procurator of Palestine. |
| **62 C.E.** | James, the brother of Jesus, is stoned to death. |
| **64 C.E.** | Peter and Paul are martyred in Rome. |
| **65–70 C.E.** | The Gospel of Mark is written. |
| **66–70 C.E.** | The Jewish War occurs. |
| **70 C.E.** | Jerusalem and the Temple are destroyed. |

| 80–90 C.E. | The Gospels of Matthew and Luke are written; **Acts of the Apostles is written**. |
| 90–100 C.E. | The Gospel of John is written. |

Like other books we have encountered thus far in our voyage through the New Testament, this book originally did not have a title. The name that the early church eventually assigned to it—Acts of the Apostles—refers to the deeds (i.e., acts) of the preachers and ministers of the early Christian communities in the period immediately following the death and resurrection of Jesus. Some of these ministers, like Peter and Philip, were apostles in the traditional sense of the word—that is, people who had been disciples of Jesus and were "sent" by him to continue his work. Others, like Stephen and the wife-and-husband team of Priscilla and Aquila, probably did not know the historical Jesus and were not apostles in the traditional sense of the term; however, they were major players in the story of the early church. And, of course, we cannot forget Paul. The author of Acts of the Apostles devotes a great deal of space to Paul, who, though he called himself an apostle, did not know the historical Jesus.

Acts of the Apostles includes stories about these characters in the history of the early church that are inspiring and sometimes even amusing. They also give us some great insights into the life of the earliest Christian communities as we learn about the people who were attracted to Christianity, how they lived, and how they worshiped. However, before we venture into these topics, we need to say something about authorship, date, and initial audience for Acts of the Apostles. Since most scholars agree that Acts of the Apostles was written by the same person who wrote the Gospel of Luke, we will provide only a brief summary here and then refer you back to Chapter 8, on the Gospel of Luke, for more details.

## AUTHORSHIP

Acts of the Apostles is the second of two volumes attributed to Luke—traditionally thought to be Luke, the physician, who is mentioned in Colossians 4:14, Philemon 24, and 2 Timothy 4:11. The claim that he was also a companion of Paul comes from the "**we passages**" in Acts of the Apostles: Acts 16:10–17; 20:5–15; 21:1–18; and 27:1–28:16—all of which are concerned with the missionary activity of Paul. In these segments of the story, the author changes from third-person narration ("he" and "they") to first-person narration ("we" and "us"), suggesting that the author was present with Paul during these travels. Except for this shift from third-person to first-person narration, the literary style of these sections is very similar to that in the rest of the book, prompting scholars to argue that the person who wrote the "we passages" also wrote the other parts of Acts of the Apostles.

Was Luke an eyewitness to the events behind the "we passages"? That's a more complicated question. As we shall soon discover when we read Paul's letters, Luke presents Paul's story in a way that does not always correspond with Paul's own writings, nor does Luke appear to know any of the characteristic aspects of Paul's theology. Thus, some scholars have suggested that Luke did not know Paul or his teachings but somehow had access to the travel diary of one of his now-unknown companions. Wishing to honor Paul's memory, Luke incorporated the travel diary without alteration with the consequence that the "we passages" appear to be Luke's work when, in fact, they are not. At least one scholar has argued that Luke did know Paul's history and his theology but rejected them and instead wrote Acts to "correct" Paul's story and his teachings. In the end, we have to admit that there is not enough evidence to put forward an absolutely convincing argument one way or another about the author of the "we passages" and his relationship to the author of the larger work.

## DATE AND INITIAL AUDIENCE

A late-second-century-C.E. prologue (i.e., introduction) to Acts of the Apostles suggests that this book was written at Boeothia in Greece, where the author, Luke, died at the age of eighty-four. Given the author's interest in Gentile believers, his use of certain techniques of Hellenistic (i.e., Greek-inspired) rhetoric, and the lack of evidence to the contrary, the area of Greece is a reasonable option, though Acts of the Apostles provides few, if any, clues concerning its intended audience, except for his reference to Theophilus (Acts 1:1; see Chapter 8 on the identity of Theophilus). If the Gospel of Luke was written approximately 80–90 C.E.—the date of 85 C.E. is most commonly cited—then it is reasonable to assume that Acts of the Apostles was written around the same time or at least not before 80 C.E. On the other end of the spectrum, Luke did not appear to know about the letters of Paul, which were already being collected and recognized as "scriptures" by the early part of the second century C.E. He also did not seem to know about bishops or other elements of church organization that were in place by the early part of the second century. Thus, Acts of the Apostles had to have been written by 100 C.E. Most scholars give it a date more or less the same as that of the Gospel of Luke, that is, 80–90 C.E.

## OUTLINE OF ACTS OF THE APOSTLES

As we have seen many times before, the outline of a New Testament book can be very helpful in providing a "road map" for our reading and interpretation of the book. However, often there are as many outlines of a particular book as there are biblical scholars studying it because the scholar has to decipher the book's outline based on his or her understanding of the author's intent (using historical critical methods; see Chapter 2) or based on literary clues in the text (using literary critical methods; see Chapter 2). The outline that follows highlights the activities of key figures and geographical references in Acts of the Apostles, including their various travels.

1. Acts 1:1–5—Introduction
2. Acts 1:6–8:1a—Activities in Jerusalem
   a. Ascension of Jesus (Acts 1:6–11)
   b. Selection of replacement apostle (Acts 1:12–26)
   c. Pentecost descent of the Spirit (Acts 2:1–47)
   d. Activities of Peter and John (Acts 3:1–5:11)
   e. Arrest of the apostles (Acts 5:12–42)
   f. Story of Stephen (Acts 6:1–8:1a)
3. Acts 8:1b–13:23—Mission in Judea, Samaria, and Syria
   a. Activities of Philip (Acts 8:1b–40)

Acts of the Apostles begins with the disciples gathered in an upper room in Jerusalem after the resurrection of Jesus. It ends with Paul's arrival as a prisoner in Rome, where he meets with members of the synagogue to talk to them about Jesus. Note the significance of these two cities. The former represented the center of Jewish life and practice. The latter represented the center of the Gentile world. Thus, even the spatial (having to do with place) and temporal (having to do with time) settings of its stories remind the reader that Acts of the Apostles is a *theological interpretation* of the history of the early church, explaining how Christianity began as a sect within Judaism and eventually found its home in the Gentile world.

### GUIDE FOR INTERPRETING ACTS OF THE APOSTLES

Here is your tour book for the next stop on our journey through the New Testament. Again, we will not be summarizing the content of this book. Instead, we will offer some insights into interpreting Acts of the Apostles. We will begin by reviewing the genre and literary forms that Luke used in writing this book. Next, we will examine Luke's presentation of two of its major characters, Peter and Paul. We will also reflect on Luke's appreciation of the presence of the Holy Spirit in the life of the early church. Finally, we will investigate what Luke tells us about the way early Christians tried to live their faith. At the conclusion of this chapter, you will be invited to read Acts of the Apostles for yourself. The "Questions for Reading" section will guide you.

## LITERARY FEATURES OF ACTS OF THE APOSTLES

As already described in the introduction to Part III, Acts of the Apostles is categorized as a history. However, since the ancient genre of history differs considerably from what we call history today, we must be careful not to make incorrect assumptions about the content and purpose of Acts of the Apostles. Unlike history writers today, ancient history writers had no intention of providing an objective, documentary-style account of the people and events of their time. Rather, the goal of ancient histories was to honor a particular individual or individuals or to celebrate a special occasion. To accomplish that goal, ancient history writers used several literary forms, including the following:

> *Dramatic episodes*: short story units that have a basis in historical fact but that have been embellished to illuminate the virtues of a particular person or explain the significance of an event

> *Speeches*: literary creations of the author that are placed in the mouths of major characters of the story, allowing the author to communicate directly with his audience concerning the book's central themes

The author of Acts of the Apostles also used summary statements to move the plot along and provide a transition to the next scene of the story. Here is an example:

> God did extraordinary miracles through Paul, so that when the handkerchiefs or aprons that had touched his skin were brought to the sick, their diseases left them, and the evil spirits came out of them. (Acts 19:11–12)

As you read Acts of the Apostles, be attentive to patterns in the way that the stories are told and to recurring themes in the speeches. It is in these patterns and themes that the central message of Acts of the Apostles is located.

## PETER AND PAUL

Luke gives considerable attention to two important figures of the early church, namely, Peter and Paul. Peter dominates many of the early sections of Acts of the Apostles, where he takes on the role of spokesperson for the apostles. For example, he is the one to convene the believers so they can select a replacement for Judas (Acts 1:15–26). On the Jewish feast of Pentecost (see Chapter 5), after the Holy Spirit descends on those gathered in the upper room, he is the one who stands up to preach to the crowds about Jesus (Acts 2:14–42).

In addition, Acts contains stories about Peter working miracles in the name of Jesus, for example, his healing of a crippled man at one of the gates of the Jerusalem Temple (Acts 3:1–10). We also see Luke using Peter's missionary activity to advance his message about the inclusion of Gentile believers. This is most evident in the story of the conversion of the Roman official Cornelius, in which Peter is told three times that foods previously considered ritually unclean (i.e., not kosher) are now ritually clean (i.e., permissible for Jews to eat) (Acts 10:1–11:18). Peter uses this heaven-sent message to defend his missionary work among Gentile believers against other Jewish Christian leaders who think that Gentiles must become Jews before they can be baptized.

Finally, we read about several incidents in which Peter is arrested for preaching about Jesus. In one story in particular—Acts 12:6–19—we see Luke's flair for the dramatic. Peter had been arrested by Herod Agrippa I and held under heavy guard,

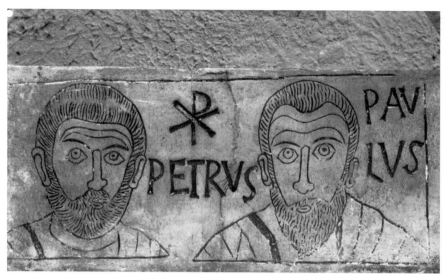

Depictions of Peter and Paul engraved on the sepulcher of Asellus, a Roman child (after 313 C.E.). *Erich Lessing/Art Resource, NY.*

awaiting the end of Passover, and suddenly an angel entered his prison cell and led him out of the jail without anyone seeing them. Even Peter did not know what was happening until he found himself on the street. When Peter realized that he was no longer imprisoned, he went to the home of John Mark's mother and knocked on the door. The female servant who opened the door recognized Peter but was so excited that she slammed the door in his face and ran to tell the others, leaving him standing outside still knocking! Wonderfully entertaining stories like this one make Peter a "larger than life" figure in the early church.

Luke takes a similar approach in his presentation of Paul, making of him a giant among the leaders of the early church. The story of Paul's conversion to faith in Jesus is most notable because Luke includes three versions of the story: one from the mouth of the narrator (Acts 9:1–19) and two from the mouth of Paul himself (Acts 22:3–16; 26:2–18). In Acts 9:1–19, we see Paul—identified by his Hebrew name, Saul—on his way to Damascus to arrest fellow Jews who believe Jesus is the messiah. After his encounter with the heavenly voice, who asks, "Why do you persecute me?" (Acts 9:4), Saul is blinded and can do nothing except await God's next move. God calls Ananias and tells him to go and heal Saul. Ananias's response goes something like this: "I've heard of this guy. Better to leave him blind!" (Acts 9:10–14). Luke uses God's counterresponse to deliver a message about Paul's role in the development of Christianity: He has been chosen to bring Jesus' name "before Gentiles and kings and before the people of Israel" (Acts 9:15). The imagery Luke uses to tell this story recalls the Old Testament stories about the call of a prophet to the ministry of prophecy. Later, as Paul tells his own conversion story, the message is the same: God has sent Paul to be a light to the Gentiles to preach the good news of Jesus Christ to the world.

Using the form of the dramatic episode, Luke tells numerous other stories about Paul and his missionary activity. Several times he describes Paul coming to a city and

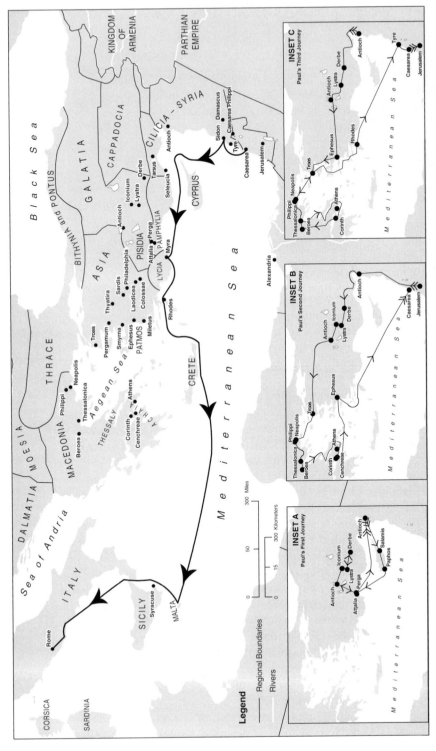

The Roman Empire in the first century C.E., highlighting Luke's account of Paul's missionary travels in Acts of the Apostles. The larger map illustrates Paul's final journey to Rome before his death. The three insets illustrate each of his three missionary journeys across the Mediterranean world.

going first to the synagogue, where he preaches the message of Jesus Christ. Some respond positively to the message, but others reject Paul's words, and before long, as Luke tells it, Paul is driven from the synagogue. But he refuses to be stopped! Immediately, he goes to others in the city who are willing to hear him—the Gentiles—and he preaches the message to them (e.g., Acts 13:13–52; 14:1–7; 21:17–22:21). Luke also tells stories about Paul's gifts as a miracle worker. Once he drives a demon out of a slave who has powers of divination (i.e., fortune-telling), making her useless to her owners, because they have been selling her psychic skills (Acts 16:16–24). Needless to say, they are not happy! Another time Paul heals a boy named Eutychus, who has fallen out a window after slipping into a deep sleep while listening to Paul's all-night preaching marathon (Acts 20:7–12).

Luke also tells stories about the times that Paul is arrested and imprisoned for preaching the message of Jesus Christ. At Philippi, for example, after Paul drives the demon out of the fortune-teller, he and Silas are arrested under the false charge of trying to convert people to Judaism. Suddenly, as they are praying in their prison cell, there comes a tremendous earthquake. It is so strong that the impact unfastens their chains and breaks open the doors. The jailer races in, ready to commit suicide because he thinks that his prisoners had escaped. When he finds them quietly waiting for him, he asks that he and his family be baptized (Acts 16:19–39). Luke also tells of Paul's final arrest, which takes place in Jerusalem and eventually results in his being transported to Rome (Acts 21:27–23:10). Luke provides commentary on the significance of this arrest by including a scene in which the risen Christ stands near Paul that same night and speaks to him, saying, "Keep up your courage! For just as you have testified for me in Jerusalem, so you must bear witness also in Rome" (Acts 23:11). What is the message that Luke wants to convey? The trial in Rome is only the means by which Paul will preach the "good news" to the Gentile world.

These are the stories of Peter and Paul. Luke has made them exciting and entertaining so that his readers get to experience Peter and Paul as he saw them, the superheroes of the early church. Who would not have been edified by their courage and perseverance in times of trouble and their determination to spread the gospel!

## A SPIRIT-FILLED CHURCH

The Holy Spirit is an active presence throughout Acts of the Apostles but especially in its opening chapters. The beginning of the book finds the apostles waiting for the coming of the Holy Spirit, just as they had been instructed to do by the risen Jesus before his ascension into heaven and just as they were promised by God the Father (Acts 1:1–5). A bit later the Holy Spirit gives them discernment in selecting Matthias to replace Judas as one of the twelve apostles, and Peter speaks words of prophecy inspired by the Holy Spirit (Acts 1:15–26). Notice that Luke understands the group called "apostles" to be larger than "the Twelve."

Later, when the Holy Spirit descends on the apostles, it gives them the power to speak and be understood in different languages in order that they might proclaim God's mighty deeds to all peoples and preach about Jesus, crucified and raised from the dead (Acts 2:1–13). When Peter preaches to the crowds, he uses the words of the prophet Joel to suggest that, in these "last days," God is ready to pour out the

Spirit on all humankind (Acts 2:17–36; cf. Joel 2:28–32). And when he calls the people to baptism, he tells them that they will receive the Holy Spirit (Acts 2:38). In sum, this new community of believers is Spirit-filled.

The setting for Luke's story of the descent of the Holy Spirit is **Pentecost**, a Jewish pilgrimage feast, also known as the Feast of Weeks or *Shavuot*. Pentecost originated as a harvest festival of thanksgiving and is celebrated in May or June, depending on the calendar year. However, it eventually became associated with the covenant that God made with Moses and the desert wanderers at Sinai because Exodus 19:1 says that the Sinai event took place on the third new moon (i.e., about a month and a half) after the Exodus out of Egypt. Today Shavuot is celebrated seven weeks after Passover. The imagery Luke uses to describe the descent of the Holy Spirit—fire and rushing wind—ought to remind the reader of Exodus 19, in which smoke and thunder accompanied God's appearance to Moses on Sinai.

Thus, it appears that Luke is quite intentional about placing the story of the descent of the Holy Spirit in a Jewish context. When he describes the crowds who witness this event, he calls them "Jews and proselytes" (Acts 2:11). A **proselyte** is someone who is preparing for formal membership in a group—in this case, someone who was not born Jewish but wishes to convert to Judaism. However, Luke adds the detail about the Jewish crowds coming from all over the Mediterranean and beyond—from Africa, Asia Minor (Greece and Turkey), Arabian countries, and even Rome. This extensive list of witnesses suggests that the new covenant, which God is enacting by the sending of the Spirit, is not limited to a single people in the wilderness but is expanded to include peoples from all over the world. As Luke's story of the early church unfolds, we will see that this community of the covenant expands even further to include Gentiles. Luke attributes this outward expansion to the activity of the Holy Spirit and the fulfillment of prophecy, which is itself a manifestation of the power of the Spirit.

### READING ACTS OF THE APOSTLES FROM THE PERSPECTIVE OF LIBERATION THEOLOGY

The feast of Pentecost is an important one for most Christian communities today. However, many do not fully understand its significance, whether we talk about the Jewish roots of the feast or the Spirit-filled mission to which it calls Christians today and tomorrow. Using the hermeneutical principles of liberation theology, Justo González provides a thoughtful reflection on the significance of the Pentecost miracle—everyone being able to understand the disciples in their own language—for the mission of the church today:

> In order to have the multitude understand what the disciples of Jesus were saying, the Holy Spirit had two options: one was to make all understand the Aramaic the disciples spoke; the other was to make each understand in their own tongue. Significantly, the Spirit chooses the latter route. This has important consequences for the way we understand the place of culture and language in the Church. Had the Spirit made all the listeners understand the language of the apostles, we would be justified in a centripetal understanding of mission, one in

which all who come in are expected to be like those who invite them. However, because what the Spirit did was exactly the opposite, this leads us to a centrifugal understanding of mission, one in which as the gospel moves toward new languages and new cultures, it is ready to take forms that are understandable within those languages and cultures. In other words, had there been an "Aramaic only" movement in first-century Palestine, Pentecost was a resounding no! to that movement. And it is still a resounding no! to any movement within the Church that seeks to make all Christians think alike, speak alike, and behave alike. The first translator of the gospel is the Holy Spirit, and a church that claims to have the Holy Spirit must be willing to follow that lead. (2001, 39)

## THE EARLY CHURCH'S WAY OF LIFE

If Christians have heard anything about Acts of the Apostles, most know Luke's description of the early Christian communities' way of life—how they sold their property and shared all things in common so that no one among them would be needy and how they devoted themselves to prayer and the "breaking of bread" (i.e., Eucharist) (Acts 2: 43–47; 4:32–37). In fact, this continues to be the model for small intentional Christian communities or neighborhood churches today. However, as we shall see, Acts of the Apostles gives us many more clues about the practices of late-first-century Christian communities. Here are just a few examples:

- These early believers were identified as followers of "the Way" (Acts 9:2; 18:25; 22:4) and were first called "Christians" at Antioch in Syria (Acts 11:26).

- At least some of the first converts to Christianity came from among the **God-fearers**—that is, Gentiles who were interested in Judaism and who participated in aspects of Jewish practice that were open to outsiders, like studying Torah and going to synagogue, but never actually converted to Judaism (Acts 10:2).

- Christians practiced baptism as a rite of initiation into the Christian community. Luke describes the rite as being done in the name of Jesus Christ for the forgiveness of sin (Acts 2:38). He also says that the baptized receive the gift of the Holy Spirit or, in some cases, they are baptized because they have received the gift of the Holy Spirit (e.g., Acts 10:44–48).

- Christians celebrated the "breaking of the bread," also known as Eucharist, on the first day of the week, which began on Saturday night, at the conclusion of the Jewish Sabbath (Acts 2:46; 20:7–12; 27:35). Luke assumes that Jewish Christians, and perhaps the God-fearers, also went to temple or synagogue as they had done before (Acts 2:46; 3:1–10; 16:11–15).

- Christian communities commissioned teachers, preachers, and ministers by "laying on hands," which signified sending by the Holy Spirit (Acts 6:6; 13:1–4). Laying on hands was also associated with the reception of the Holy Spirit at baptism (Acts 8:14–17; 19:1–7)

> ### CHRISTIAN COMMUNITIES PATTERNED ON ACTS OF THE APOSTLES
>
> At certain periods of reform in the history of Christianity, communities of faith have attempted to pattern their common life on Luke's description of the early church (Acts 2:41–47). From the period of the Radical Reformation, for example, we have an account of the beginning of the Hutterites, named after one of their early leaders, Jakob Hutter. This is their story:
>
> > Thus some 200 persons, not counting children, gathered outside Nikolsburg. Several people mercifully came from town and wept with them. Others quarrelled with them. Then they proceeded to the vicinity of Tannewitz and Muschau. Here they found a deserted village, stayed for a day and a night, and counseled with one another on account of their present need. They appointed servants of temporal goods, namely Frantz Lutzinger of Leiben in Styria and Jacob Mändel, who had been an official for the Lord of Liechtenstein. Thomas Arbeiter and Urban Bader were appointed assistants. At this time these men spread a coat before the people and everybody laid down his possessions, voluntarily and uncoerced, so that the needy might be supported according to the teaching of the prophets and the apostles. (*Die Älteste Chronik der Hutterischen Brüder*, 87, cited in Hillerbrand, 1979, 270–271)

- The Christian communities recognized prophets and teachers in positions of leadership (Acts 11:27; 13:1), but Luke appears not to know about bishops as overseers of churches, which we find mentioned later in the pastoral letters (cf. 1 Tim. 3:1–7; Tit. 1:7–9).

- Luke's story about the Twelve who appointed seven people—Stephen, the first martyr, among them—to serve (*diakonein*) tables for the widows of the Christian community may reflect the origin of ordained deacons in the churches (Acts 6:1–7). Here table service most likely refers to food distribution to the needy, which was one of the major responsibilities assigned to the deacon. Another was assisting the bishop in the celebration of the Eucharist. See Chapter 19 for more on ministries in the early church.

- Early Christian communities did not have dedicated church buildings in which to meet. Instead, they gathered as "house churches" in the homes of prominent members of the community, who also served as their patrons. Luke seems to suggest that at least one of these house churches was led by a woman, namely, the church that met at Lydia's house (Acts 16:40).

Acts of the Apostles also offers a glimpse of the socioeconomic character of early Christian communities. It is interesting to note that these church communities appear to cross the commonly accepted boundaries of social class and gender. Tabitha was a widow known for her good deeds and someone to whom other Christian widows in Joppa looked for support (Acts 9:36–43). **Timothy**, a fellow missionary with Paul, was the son of a Jewish Christian mother and a Gentile father (Acts

16:1–5). Lydia was a dealer in purple cloth who hosted a house-church at her home after she and her household were baptized (Acts 16:11–15, 40). **Priscilla** and **Aquila** were tentmakers like Paul, and in their preaching ministry, they worked alongside of Paul as a husband-and-wife missionary team (Acts 18:1–28). Though the two are always mentioned together, Priscilla's name is usually listed first, suggesting that she was known to be of higher social status than her husband. **Apollos**, a missionary from Alexandria in Egypt, was trained in Greek rhetoric (Acts 18:24–28) but gave up his lucrative career to preach the Christian message.

## COMMENTS ON ACTS 28:16–30

In the latter sections of Acts of the Apostles, Luke describes how Paul eventually returns to Jerusalem in order to deliver a financial contribution to the Jewish Christian community there (for more on the contribution, see Acts 11:29–30; 24:17). It had been suffering greatly because of the persecutions going on in Jerusalem, and Paul apparently saw this as an opportunity for the Gentile Christian communities to show their support. Having arrived in Jerusalem, he found himself in the middle of a riot when some people began complaining that he was stirring up trouble in Jewish communities of the Diaspora (Acts 21:27–40). The Roman authorities intervened to stop the riot that broke out around Paul. After they arrested him, they allowed Paul to address the crowd, at which point a riot broke out again (Acts 21:37–22:29). When the Roman authorities prepared to "examine" him by flogging, he told them that he was a Roman citizen and that he had a right to a trial before Caesar. Thus begins a very long imprisonment in which Paul is eventually taken to Rome.

Tradition tells us that Paul was martyred (i.e., put to death for the faith) in Rome approximately 62–64 C.E. If Luke simply wanted to honor Paul's memory, we would expect him to use the story of Paul's martyrdom as the climactic conclusion of the book, but he does not even mention Paul's death. Is it possible that Luke did not know about his martyrdom? What is going on here? According to Acts of the Apostles, when Paul finally gets to Rome, he speaks to the Jews who have assembled to meet him (Acts 28:11–22). We know from other ancient literature and from archeological evidence that there existed an important Jewish community at Rome long before Paul's visit. However, Luke presents them as having no information about what is happening among other Jewish communities or about these followers of the Way (i.e., Christianity) except that the sect had been denounced by the Jewish religious authorities.

From a historical point of view, this scenario is quite unlikely, raising the possibility that Luke "constructed" the conclusion of Acts of the Apostles in order to make his point one last time. As a literary construction, the book's concluding scene consists of two parts:

1. Acts 28:17–22. This section describes Paul's first encounter with the Jewish authorities in Rome. He convenes the assembly and speaks his message about Jesus Christ. The Jews find his message worthy of further investigation.

2. Acts 28:23–28. This is Paul's second encounter with the Jewish community in Rome. Paul gives a lengthy exposition of his teaching, but discussions break

down in disagreement. At this point, Paul recites a prophecy from Isaiah in testimony against the Jews' inability to hear and understand. Then he makes his own prophecy about the Gentiles accepting God's salvation, which was rejected by the Jews.

Thus, we can see how the concluding scene of Acts of the Apostles focuses on Luke's assessment of the problem that motivated the writing of this book in the first place: Should Christianity remain a sect within Judaism, or should it spread beyond Judaism to the Gentile world? Luke's answer is clear. The Jews were the first recipients of God's promise, and for this reason, they had a right to be the first to hear the message about Jesus. Some accepted this message; when others did not, God expanded the promise to the Gentiles. But we should not conclude that God changed His mind concerning the Jews or that God was somehow punishing them for their refusal to accept Jesus. Rather, Luke argues, this was God's plan from the beginning: that the gospel (i.e., "good news") would extend from Jerusalem to the entire world.

## Key Terms

| | | |
|---|---|---|
| "We passages" | God-fearers | Priscilla and Aquila |
| Pentecost | Timothy | Apollos |
| Proselyte | | |

## Questions for Reading

Read Acts of the Apostles. Use evidence from the text to answer the following questions.

1. Analyze Peter's speech on the day of Pentecost, after the descent of the Holy Spirit (Acts 2:14–36). What is the main point of the speech? How is the speech organized to convey this message?

2. After healing a lame man and preaching to the people who had gathered around Solomon's Portico, Peter and his colleague were arrested (Acts 3:1–4:31). Why were they arrested? By whom? What point was Luke trying to make by telling this story?

3. What does Luke say about the kind of life the early Christian communities lived together (Acts 2:43–47; 4:32–5:11)? Why were Ananias and Sapphira punished by God?

4. Who was Stephen and what role did he have in the Christian community (Acts 6:1–7)? Why was he arrested? By whom? What charges were brought against him at his trial (Acts 6:8–15)? What is the content of the speech that he made in his defense (Acts 7:1–53)?

5. What incident ultimately led to Stephen's stoning, or what was the precipitating factor in his execution (Acts 7:54–8:1a)? Who was present as witness to the stoning?

6. Based on Luke's telling of the story, what do we know about the Ethiopian eunuch (Acts 8:26–40)? Who was he? What is the significance of the text that he was reading? What prompted him to be baptized? By whom was he baptized?

*Note:* A eunuch is someone who has been castrated. In this case, it may be an indication of this man's high position in the administrative offices of the queen of Candice. His castration would ensure that nothing inappropriate happened between himself and the queen.

7. Describe the circumstances around Saul's conversion (Acts 9:1–19). From the story about God sending Ananias to Paul, what does Luke want us to understand about Paul's mission? *Note:* From this point onward in Acts of the Apostles, Luke refers to Saul by his Greek name, Paul. Saul was his Hebrew name.

8. Based on Luke's telling of the story, what do we know about Cornelius (Acts 10:1–48)? Who was he? What prompted him to be baptized? By whom was he baptized? What point was Luke trying to make by telling this story?

9. Describe Paul's activity in Antioch (Acts 13:13–52). Whom did he visit there? How was he received? What is the point of his speech in the synagogue? How is the speech organized to convey this message? What is the point of the concluding scene where Paul and Barnabas speak out at the assembly?

10. What was the problem that prompted Paul and Barnabas to go to Jerusalem for the council of church leaders (Acts 15:1–35)? According to Luke's telling of the story, how was the problem resolved? Who was present at the meeting?

11. What happened when Paul came to Thessalonica (Acts 17:1–15)? With whom did he meet? How was he received? How does this story fit into Luke's larger agenda in Acts of the Apostles?

12. What happened when Paul came to Corinth (Acts 18:1–17)? With whom did he meet? How was he received? What did he do in response? Who are Priscilla and Aquila? Crispus? Gallio? Sosthenes? How do they fit into the story?

13. According to Luke's telling of the story, what did Paul hope to accomplish in his return to Jerusalem (Acts 21:1–23:10)? What were the circumstances that led to his arrest? By whom was he arrested? Why did the Jewish council of elders (i.e., Sanhedrin) seek to kill Paul? How did he defend himself?

14. What happened when Paul was brought before the procurator Felix for judgment (Acts 24:1–27)? What is the central message of the speech Paul delivered in his defense? How does this relate to Luke's larger agenda in Acts of the Apostles?

15. What were the conditions that led to Paul being brought to trial before Festus, the procurator of Judea (Acts 25:1–26:32)? What is the central message of the speech Paul delivers in his defense? What decision is made at the conclusion of the trial?

16. Outline the events that take place when Paul gets to Jerusalem (Acts 28:14b–31). What is the point of Paul's concluding speech before the Jewish assembly of Rome? How does this speech relate to Luke's larger agenda in Acts of the Apostles?

## QUESTIONS FOR REFLECTION

1. Compared to the early churches portrayed in Acts of the Apostles, in what ways are modern Christian churches different in their governing organization and their patterns of worship? Select one or two contemporary churches that you

want to compare to the early Christian churches of Acts, and be prepared to give concrete examples. Do you see any advantages to the way of life of the early churches as compared to churches of the modern world?

2. What values/ideals or practices do you think modern Christians should attempt to reclaim from the early church as portrayed in Acts of the Apostles? Are there certain problems we should be glad we do not have to deal with today? Explain.

## ACTIVITIES FOR LEARNING

1. Locate the video *Peter and Paul*, distributed by Gateway Films (©1981). If it is not available at your local library, you should be able to find it in a video rental store that specializes in older films. The script for the video comes directly from Acts of the Apostles, with actors acting out selections from the book. After reading Acts of the Apostles yourself and learning about its major themes, do an analysis of the video. What aspects of the film helped you better understand the major theological themes of the book? Were there scenes in the film that could have been presented differently in order to better convey the theological themes of Acts of the Apostles? Explain. Were there sections of Acts of the Apostles that were not included in the film but should have been in order to better convey theological themes of the book? Explain. What overall impressions did you get of Peter from viewing the film? What overall impressions did you get of Paul from viewing the film?

2. Imagine that you are going to start a new Christian church based on the vision and values of Acts of the Apostles. Write a founding document that outlines the following:
   a. How will your church be organized? Who will be its leaders? By what criteria will they be chosen? What are their job descriptions?
   b. Where will the church community meet? How often? What will the members do when they come together? What religious rituals will you share in common?
   c. What are the basic (or defining) theological teachings of your church? That is, what does a member need to accept as truth in order to be part of this church community?
   d. What obligations will community members have toward one another? What can individual members expect from others in the community?
   e. What are the guiding ethical principles of your church community? That is, how do you intend to live out your faith in the world? What behaviors are appropriate? Inappropriate?
   For each of the above points, provide a citation (or citations) from Acts of the Apostles that lends authority to your founding document. Having drafted your church's founding document, would you be willing to join? Why or why not? What might be your church's greatest challenges?

3. Research a contemporary church community that takes seriously the values and vision of Acts of the Apostles, especially in the way they live out the model of church that is described in Acts 2:41–47. The most obvious are the Radical Reformation churches that have been labeled by others as Anabaptist (re-baptizers)—the Amish

and Mennonite churches, for example—but there are others as well. Find out how the church is organized, what kind of leadership structure is has, where and how often its members meet, what their religious rituals are like, what they hold as basic (i.e., defining) theological teachings, and what they value as ethical living. What aspects of this community's life would you find most attractive? What aspects of this community's life would be really challenging for you? Explain.

## SOURCES AND RESOURCES

Borgman, Paul. *The Way according to Luke: Hearing the Whole Story of Luke-Acts.* Grand Rapids, Mich.: Eerdmans, 2006.

Dillon, Richard. "Acts of the Apostles." In *The New Jerome Biblical Commentary,* edited by R. E. Brown, J. A. Fitzmyer, and R. E. Murphy. Englewood Cliffs, N.J.: Prentice Hall, 1990.

Gaventa, Beverly R. *The Acts of the Apostles.* Nashville, Tenn.: Abingdon Press, 2003.

González, Justo L. *Acts: The Gospel of the Spirit.* Maryknoll, N.Y.: Orbis Books, 2001.

Hamm, M. Dennis. *The Acts of the Apostles.* Collegeville, Minn.: Liturgical Press, 2005.

Hillerbrand, Hans, ed. *The Reformation: A Narrative History Related by Contemporary Observers and Participants.* Grand Rapids, Mich.: Baker, 1979.

Johnson, Luke Timothy. *The Acts of the Apostles.* Collegeville, Minn.: Liturgical Press, 1992.

Juel, Donald. *Luke-Acts: The Promise of History.* Atlanta, Ga.: John Knox Press, 1984.

Kee, Howard Clark. *To Every Nation under Heaven: The Acts of the Apostles.* Harrisburg, Pa.: Trinity Press International, 1997.

Pilch, John J. *Visions and Healing in the Acts of the Apostles: How the Early Believers Experienced God.* Collegeville, Minn.: Liturgical Press, 2004.

Robinson, Anthony B., and Robert W. *Called to be Church: The Book of Acts for a New Day.* Grand Rapids, Mich.: Eerdmans, 2006.

Smith, Dennis E., and Michael E. Williams, eds. *Acts of the Apostles.* Nashville, Tenn.: Abingdon Press, 1999.

Soards, M. *The Speeches in Acts.* Louisville, Ky.: Westminster John Knox Press, 1994.

Spencer, F. Scott. *Journeying through Acts: A Literary-Cultural Reading.* Peabody, Mass.: Hendrickson Publishers, 2004.

Talbert, Charles. *Reading Acts: A Literary and Theological Commentary on the Acts of the Apostles.* New York: Crossroad, 1997.

Walaskay, Paul W. *Acts.* Louisville, Ky.: Westminster John Knox Press, 1998.

# THE LETTERS ASSOCIATED
# WITH PAUL

aving completed the first two segments of our voyage through the New Testament—namely, the gospels and an early church history, Acts of the Apostles—we are about to embark on a new kind of adventure. This third segment will take us into a number of cities around the Mediterranean Sea, mostly in the areas that are now known as Turkey and Greece. The journey is not entirely new because Acts of the Apostles traverses the same geography, but we will have a different experience of the terrain in the fact that all of these books are written in the letter genre. Unlike narratives, these letters give us an opportunity to experience directly through the eyes of Paul, the letter writer, his special relationship with the communities to whom the letters are addressed. These letters also provide us with greater insight into some theological issues that have shaped Christianity from its earliest decades all the way to the present.

Our first step, of course, is to investigate the letter genre. The New Testament contains twenty-one books that bear the name "Letter." In addition to these books, we find letters inserted into other documents of the New Testament, for example, Acts of the Apostles and the Book of Revelation. In other words, letters make up a substantial part of the New Testament. Knowing what to expect from first-century letters will help us to ask the right questions about their form and content and to interpret them in a way that can have meaning for Christians today. We will begin our investigation by looking at the form (structure) of Greco-Roman letters and the circumstances in which letters were typically used.

## GRECO-ROMAN LETTER GENRE

Surprisingly, letters of the Greco-Roman period (roughly from the second century B.C.E. to the first century C.E.) were not all that different in form (structure) from modern letters. One of the biggest factors that makes ancient letters different from modern letters is the absence of easy forms of delivery—such as e-mail, fax, Federal Express, or the post office—for the ancient letters. Another difference is that not a lot of people could read or write in the first-century C.E. Mediterranean world, so most people had to depend on scribes (secretaries) whom they paid to write (and read) their correspondence for them. Once a letter was written, it had to be sent to its destination by messenger. The delivery was slow by modern standards and sometimes dangerous because of robbers on the roads and pirates on the seas. Given all of these factors, people made the most of their correspondence, addressing the letter to more than one person or adding a postscript containing messages for other people in the town.

What did the Greco-Roman letter look like? First, it had an opening that identified the sender and the addressee (in that order), together with a greeting. Immediately following the opening, the letter usually included a thanksgiving and a wish for the good health of the addressee. Third, in the body or main part of the letter was the business or content of letter. The final part of the letter, the closing, usually contained greetings and good wishes for other people known to the addressee and a final greeting, wish, or prayer for the addressee.

As for the types of letters that were written and sent in the first-century world, we do not find a lot of surprises either. Archeologists and scholars of ancient manuscripts have found a variety of personal letters, including love letters, letters between friends, private business transactions, and letters of introduction between family or friends. Archeologists have also found business letters dealing with trade, taxes, wills, and land agreements. In addition, historians have preserved official letters from political or military leaders to their constituents, subjects, or superiors. We also know of public letters (e.g., public pleas written in the form of a letter) and philosophical treatises (e.g., letters from Isocrates and Plato).

Finally, scholars have found fictitious letters purporting to come from heaven or from famous figures in history and epistolary novels or pseudonymous letters (e.g., letters of Hippocrates, Letter of Aristeas, and 2 Clement). These literary creations employ the form of the letter for rhetorical effect (to persuade, etc.), but they were never intended to be sent as letters. We can find a similar range of different kinds of letters today, and whether or not we are aware of our process of reading, it is easy to see that we have to treat each of these letter types differently if we are to understand them correctly. The same is true of ancient letters.

---

### A SAMPLING OF ANCIENT LETTERS

A number of different kinds of letters have survived from the Greco-Roman period to the present. Here are two that might sound familiar to you. The first is a letter of introduction and recommendation. The term *dioiketes*, at the conclusion of this letter, is the title of an administrator. The second letter was written by a husband, who was away on an out-of-town job, to his wife back home. He might have used "sister" simply as a term of endearment, but a brother/sister marriage is also a possibility.

Most likely, Berous is the mother of one or, in the case of a brother/sister marriage, the mother of both members of the couple.

### THEON TO TYRANNOS, C. 25 C.E.

Theon to his esteemed Tyrannos many greetings. Herakleides, who carries this letter to you, is my brother. Wherefore, I entreat you with all my power to regard him recommended. I have also asked your brother Hermias through correspondence to talk with you about him. You will grant the greatest favor to me if he receives your attention. Above all I pray that you may have health and fare most excellently, unharmed by enchantment (the evil eye). Good-bye.

Outside address: To Tyrannos, dioiketes. (White, 1986, 118)

### HILARION TO ALIS, 1 B.C.E.

Hilarion to his sister Alis many greetings, likewise to my lady Berous and to Apollonarion. Know that we are even yet in Alexandria. Do not worry if they all come back (except me) and I remain in Alexandria. I urge and entreat you, be concerned about the child and if I should receive my wages soon, I will send them up to you. If by chance you bear a child, if it is a boy, let it be, if it is a girl, cast it out. You have said to Aphrodisias, "Do not forget me." How can I forget you? Therefore I urge you not to worry. (Year) 29 of Caesar, Payni 23.

Outside address: Deliver from Hilarion to Alis. (White, 1986, 111–112)

## PAUL'S LETTERS

Given this general background on Greco-Roman letters, how shall we characterize Paul's letters? Are there things that make his letters distinctive? Many of the concerns that Paul writes about are typical of private letters of the time. Moreover, as one might expect with any private letter, it can be difficult for outsiders to know the letters' context in order to properly interpret them. They were originally intended for single churches or individuals living in Central and Eastern Europe during the middle of the first century C.E. Therefore, when we read Paul's letters today, we have to remember not only that we are reading someone else's mail but also that we are reading mail that belonged to people who lived almost 2,000 years ago and in a part of the world that is quite different from our own. Most of his letters were addressed to churches, so they were probably read aloud at a time when the community was already gathered for worship, which may explain why Paul uses so much liturgical (i.e., worship-related) language in his letters.

Because Paul established most of the churches to which he wrote and felt responsible for them, even to the point of acting like a father to them (e.g., 1 Cor. 4:14–16, 21), his letters also contain *paraenesis* (moral teaching), like you might expect to see in the philosophical letters of his time (see, for example, 1 Thess. 4:1–5:22). Paul also made other modifications in the form and content of the private letter. For example, Paul expanded the thanksgiving section to include a summary of the themes of his letter (e.g., 1 Thess. 1:2–2:16). He often concluded certain sections of his letters (e.g., 1 Thess. 3:11–13) with eschatological comments (i.e., comments concerning the end time). Finally, Paul added a *doxology* (a prayer that begins "Glory to God . . . ") or a *benediction* (blessing) to the standard closing of the letter (see, for example, 1 Thess. 5:28). Thus, the form of Paul's letters can be described as follows:

FORM OF PAUL'S LETTERS

Opening (sender, addressee, greeting)

Thanksgiving (including prayer of intercession and eschatological ending)

Body of the letter

Paraenesis (ethical exhortation)

Closing (greeting, doxology, blessing)

Now that we have identified a general form (structure) for Paul's letters, we have to recognize that, just like his contemporaries, he did not always follow the established form. For example, we will discover that one of his letters—the Letter to the Galatians—has no thanksgiving section. Other letters—for example, the First Letter to the Thessalonians—have more than one conclusion or more than one unit of paraenesis. This should not surprise us because the same thing happens today. Students in school learn the proper way to write a letter but eventually develop their own unique style of letter writing, and sometimes circumstances prompt people to deviate from the established form or even to "create" a new form. A good example might be the business memo or even text messaging, which some would say is a radical revision of the letter form.

Here is another important introductory note about Paul's letters. Although the New Testament includes thirteen letters to which Paul's name is attached, most biblical scholars agree that only seven were actually written by Paul. The others were most likely written by later disciples of Paul, who were either appealing to his authority or honoring his memory, or both, by attributing their letters to him. The thirteen letters attributed to Paul can be divided as follows:

1. Authentic letters of Paul (also identified as Pauline): 1 Thessalonians; 1 Corinthians; 2 Corinthians; Philippians; Philemon; Galatians; and Romans

2. Letters attributed to Paul but probably not actually written by him (also identified as Deutero-Pauline): Ephesians; Colossians; 2 Thessalonians, and the pastoral letters (1 Timothy, 2 Timothy, and Titus)

The pastoral letters are so named because they are addressed to pastors (leaders) of churches. They are usually treated together in scholarly studies because they are grouped together in the canon and because 1 Timothy and Titus share many of the same themes.

Finally, as you begin reading the letters attributed to Paul, you may wonder why they are arranged as they are in the New Testament. As we mentioned earlier in our studies, we have no documentary "history" of the development of the canon (i.e., authoritative list of books) of the New Testament. However, one thing we know for sure is that the Pauline and Deutero-Pauline letters are not arranged chronologically.

That is, the first one listed—the Letter to the Romans—is not the first one written. Rather, they appear to be organized from longest to shortest, with the letters addressed to churches first and the letters addressed to individuals second. The only exception is the Letter to the Galatians, which comes before the Letter to the Ephesians, even though the Letter to the Ephesians is slightly longer. Thus, the canonical order of the letters attributed to Paul is as follows:

LETTERS TO CHURCHES (LONGEST TO SHORTEST)

Romans

1 Corinthians

2 Corinthians

Galatians

Ephesians

Colossians

1 Thessalonians

2 Thessalonians

LETTERS TO INDIVIDUALS (LONGEST TO SHORTEST)

1 Timothy

2 Timothy

Titus

Philemon

Having explained the canonical order of the letters associated with Paul, we should note that we will not study them in this order. Instead, we will treat them chronologically, with a few exceptions. We will begin with the letter that most scholars agree is Paul's earliest—1 Thessalonians—and contrast it with a later Deutero-Pauline work of the same name—2 Thessalonians. Next, we will study another early work—the Letter to the Galatians—and use it as a stepping-stone to Paul's longest work, and perhaps one of his latest, the Letter to the Romans. These two letters share the theme of justification through faith.

Between the Letter to the Galatians and the Letter to the Romans, we will investigate the Letter to the Philippians and the Letter to Philemon. These two letters, the first addressed to a church and the second to an individual, are joined together by virtue of the fact that Paul tells his readers that he is in prison at the time he is writing. From there, we will move to Paul's two letters to the Corinthian church, both of which give us wonderful insight into Paul and his relationship to the churches. After the Letter to the Romans, our penultimate stop will be the Letter to the Colossians and the Letter to the Ephesians. Many biblical scholars agree that both are Deutero-Pauline letters. They also share some significant similarities in themes and structure, so it is appropriate to treat them together. We will conclude our study of the letters associated with Paul with an investigation of the pastoral letters.

Before leaving the topic of how we categorize the letters associated with Paul, we need to say a word about *pseudonymity*. The term means "false name." In biblical scholarship, you will often see it used in conjunction with the word *pseudepigraphy*, which means "false writing." To nonscholars, calling a biblical book pseudonymous can be troubling because it seems to suggest that there is something wrong with the work. However, for biblical scholars, pseudonymity and pseudepigraphy are value-neutral; that is, they say nothing about the intrinsic worth of the documents in question. Rather, these terms simply indicate that the name attached to the work does not correspond with what scholars know about the actual author. An example from today's literary world may help to illustrate. Suppose you recently discovered that Mark Twain was actually Sam Clemens. Would that information negatively affect your assessment of *Huckleberry Finn* or *Tom Sawyer*, two of his major literary works? Probably not. Or what if you accidentally happened upon George Eliot's *Middlemarch* and, in researching the work, discovered that the author was not a man but a woman by the name of Mary Ann Evans? Surely, the pseudonymity of the book does not affect its standing as a great literary work. So it is with the letters of the New Testament.

The early church pastors and theologians who compiled the canon of Pauline and Deutero-Pauline letters and the scribes who copied the manuscripts apparently did not make a distinction between the letters actually written by Paul and those simply attributed to him. This should be a good reminder that questions about the authenticity of authorship are more a product of the world in which we live, whereas they were of less concern to second- and third-century C.E. pastors and students of scripture. However, we should not be so naïve as to think that those early compilers of the New Testament were not aware that some of Paul's letters were written under a pseudonym. For them, the authority of these letters lay in the fact that they were part of the Pauline tradition, not that Paul actually wrote them.

## WHO WAS PAUL?

The letters associated with Paul give us an opportunity to learn something about the man because, unlike the gospels written by authors who remain anonymous, Paul's personality shines through in his letters, and occasionally he even tells us about his life. Paul was born in Tarsus of Cilicia in approximately 10 C.E. The quality of his Greek suggests that he was an educated Hellenistic Jew of the Dispersion (i.e., a Greek-speaking Jew living outside of Palestine). He apparently knew at least a limited amount of Greek philosophy because he alluded to the principles of its different schools in parts of his letters.

His letters also tell us that he was raised as a devout Jew, trained in reading and studying the Law (scriptures), and proud of it; he called himself a Pharisee. Acts of the Apostles suggests that Paul had Roman citizenship, which he apparently inherited from his father (who probably received the honor as a result of some extraordinary service to Rome). Since only a small percentage of the population of the Roman Empire were citizens, Paul should be considered as part of the elite of society. We also know that Paul was trained as a craftsperson, a leather worker/tentmaker. All of these factors suggest that he was not a person of low socioeconomic status in the community but someone who enjoyed some of the "perks" of the society.

---

**A Description of Paul from the Apocryphal Acts of Paul and Thecla (late second century c.e.)**

Even with the limitations of the written word, Paul's letters paint a picture of him as a rather unique and fiery personality. You may even begin to wonder what he looked like! Although not necessarily historically reliable, the *Acts of Paul and Thecla* (late second century c.e.) provides the following colorful description:

> And a man named Onesiphorus, who had heard that Paul was come to Iconium, went out with his children Simmias and Zeno and his wife Lectra to meet Paul, that he might receive him to his house. For Titus had told him what Paul looked like. For (hitherto) he had not seen him in the flesh, but only in the spirit. And he went along the royal road which leads to Lystra, and stood there waiting for him, and looked at (all) who came, according to Titus' description. And he saw Paul coming, a man small of stature, with a bald head and crooked legs, in a good state of body, with eyebrows meeting and a nose somewhat hooked, full of friendliness; for now he appeared like a man and now he had the face of an angel. (*Acts of Paul and Thecla*, 2–3; Schneemelcher,1992, 2:237)

If you can picture this image in your mind, surely you would agree that he likely would have stood out in a crowd!

---

Biblical scholars also think that Paul did not know the historical Jesus. That is, Paul was not a disciple of Jesus, and he very likely did not actually meet Jesus before his death. However, apparently he was familiar with Jesus *traditions*, since we can find the following materials in his writings:

1. Kerygmatic statements (e.g., 1 Cor. 15:3–8). The term *kerygma* is used to describe the kind of preaching that is directed toward people who are just being introduced to the faith. Kerygmatic statements are little "creeds" (i.e., statements of belief) used in preaching and liturgy (i.e., worship). They represent the community's understanding of the core of the faith. In Paul's case, his kerygmatic statements tell us something about his Christology. He focuses on the death and resurrection as the significant events of Jesus' life.

2. Liturgical traditions. At least the Eucharistic tradition (e.g., 1 Cor. 11:23ff), which goes back to the beginnings of Christianity, is included. He also apparently knew about John the Baptist and the baptism of John.

The fact that Paul incorporated these traditions into his writings indicates that, by the time Paul became a Jesus follower and began his ministry of persuading others to join them, people already had an established collection of oral traditions, and possibly some written traditions concerning Jesus. It is through these oral and written traditions that Paul came to learn about what later was known as Christianity.

## THE CHRONOLOGY OF PAUL'S LIFE

Unlike other figures in the history of the early church who are known to us only by name, we are privileged to have a few sources that help us reconstruct the chronology of the life of Paul, although some are more reliable than others. These sources include Paul's own words in his letters (e.g., Galatians 1–2; 1 Corinthians 15–16; 2 Corinthians 8–9; Romans 15); references to Paul's life story in Acts of the Apostles; and the Gallio inscription, found at Delphi, Greece (Achaia) (cf. Acts 18:12–22). The most problematic source is Acts of the Apostles because, in the telling of Paul's story, it sometimes contradicts Paul's own writing.

Here is where it is helpful to remember that the author of Acts was not necessarily trying to give us a historical account of the early church but rather a theological interpretation of its origins. However, the same can be said about Paul's letters. When he writes about his life, he is usually defending himself against one charge or another, and therefore he probably has embellished his story a bit. Despite the problem of sources, scholars have constructed some fairly reliable chronologies of Paul's life. The chronology that follows is an example. The biblical texts that relate to a particular event in Paul's life are included in the third column after the date.

Scholars who attempt to recreate Paul's chronology often use the Gallio inscription, mentioned above, as the linchpin for their presentation. It was found at Delphi, Greece (Achaia), and it reads as follows:

> Tiberius [Claudius] Caesar Augustus Germanicus [Pontifex Maximus, in his tribunician] power [year 12, acclaimed Emperor for] the 26th time, father of the country, [consul for the 5th time, censor, sends greetings to the city of Delphi.] I have long been zealous for the city of Delphi [and favorable to it from the] beginning, and I have always observed the cult of the [Pythian] Apollo, [but with regard to] the present stories, and those quarrels of the citizens of which [a report has been made by Lucius] Junios Gallio my friend, and [pro]consul [of Achaea]. . . (Jackson and Lake, 1920, 460–464; cited in Barrett, 1956, 48).

The twelfth year of the rule of Emperor Claudius was 52 C.E., and apparently Gallio left Corinth at the end of that year. If we follow the chronology of Acts, then Paul's eighteen-month stay in Corinth would have been between 50 and 52 C.E. Acts 18:12–16 describes how Paul was arrested and brought before Gallio for judgment:

> But when Gallio was proconsul of Achaia, the Jews rose up together against Paul and brought him to the tribunal, saying, "This man is inducing people to worship God contrary to the law." When Paul was about to reply, Gallio spoke to the Jews, "If it were a matter of some crime or malicious fraud, I should with reason hear the complaint of you Jews; but since it is a question of arguments over doctrine and titles and your own law, see to it yourselves. I do not wish to be a judge of such matters." And he drove them away from the tribunal. (Acts 18:12–16)

Acts describes how Paul departed the city of Corinth shortly after he was released from Gallio's custody. This means that the first part of Paul's post–Jerusalem Conference travels can be dated to 50–52 C.E. (see below). The events before and after these travels (also called Paul's second missionary journey) are then dated accordingly.

## CHRONOLOGY OF THE LIFE OF PAUL

| EVENT | DATE | BIBLICAL TEXTS | COMMENTARY |
| --- | --- | --- | --- |
| Birth of Paul | c. 10 C.E. | Acts 7:58; Phlm. 9 | There is no biblical account of Paul's birth. This date is suggested based on two general references to his age: when he witnessed the stoning of Stephen and when he wrote his Letter to Philemon. Paul was a contemporary of Jesus, whose birth took place approximately 6–4 B.C.E. and whose crucifixion took place approximately 30–33 C.E. |
| Paul's conversion experience | 32–36 C.E. | Gal. 1:15–16; 1 Cor. 15:8; Acts 9:1–9; 22:4–21; 26:12–18 | Acts provides three versions of the dramatic story of Paul's encounter with the risen Christ on the road to Damascus, but Paul mentions it only briefly. |
| Paul's first visit to Jerusalem | 37 C.E. | Gal. 1:18–19; Acts 9:26–28 | Paul describes a period of at least three years between his conversion experience and his first visit to Jerusalem to meet with Peter and James, during which time he traveled in Arabia (today, southern Israel, southwestern Jordan, and northeastern Saudi Arabia) and later returned to Damascus. Acts presents these two events as happening consecutively. |
| Paul's first missionary journey | 37–49 C.E. | Acts 13–14; Gal. 1:21 | Paul writes only in general terms about his missionary activity, saying that fourteen years passed before he went back to Jerusalem (Gal. 1:21). Acts describes three journeys; the first begins at Antioch and extends to Cyprus, through southern Asia Minor (modern Turkey), and back to Antioch. |
| Jerusalem Conference | 49–50 C.E. | Gal. 2:1–20; Acts 15:1–29 | Paul and Barnabas go to Jerusalem to meet with James and Peter concerning the admission of Gentiles to the community of Jesus followers. |

| EVENT | DATE | BIBLICAL TEXTS | COMMENTARY |
|---|---|---|---|
| Paul's post–Jerusalem Conference travels, traditionally called his second missionary journey | 50–52 C.E. | Acts 15:40–18:22; cf. Gallio inscription from Delphi, Greece. | Acts describes Paul as revisiting sites of his first journey and going on to Galatia and Phrygia. In Macedonia, he visits the cities of Philippi, Thessalonica, Beroea, Athens, and Corinth (today all in Greece). After a lengthy stay in Corinth, he visits Ephesus (today in Turkey) and Caesarea (in northern Israel), before going back to Jerusalem. |
| Part II of Paul's post–Jerusalem Conference travels, traditionally called his third missionary journey | 53/54–58 C.E. | Acts 18:23–21:15 | According to Acts, this period begins with a stay at Syrian Antioch. He then travels through Galatia and Phrygia to Ephesus (all in Turkey), where he stays for three years. After Ephesus, he goes to Macedonia and visits Achaia and Corinth (today in Greece), where he collects funds for the church in Jerusalem. Making his way through Macedonia and down to Tyre and Caesarea (in northern Israel), he eventually arrives in Jerusalem. |
| Paul is arrested in Jerusalem and imprisoned at Caesarea | 58–60 C.E. | Acts 21:15–26:32 | According to Acts, Paul's presence in the Jerusalem Temple results in a riot. Eventually, he is arrested and sent to Caesarea for judgment by the Roman governor Felix, who leaves him sitting in prison for two years. The next governor, Festus, judges him innocent of any crime, but Paul appeals to Caesar and is sent to Rome. |
| Paul is sent by sea to Rome | 60–61 C.E. | Acts 27:1–28:14 | Acts describes a sea voyage that is high adventure and great drama, complete with storms, shipwreck, and a winter spent on the island of Malta. |
| Paul's two-year imprisonment in Rome | 61–63 C.E. | Acts 28:15–31 | According to Acts, Paul is placed under some sort of house arrest where he pays his own living expenses and is allowed visitors, including the Jews of Rome. |
| Paul is killed in Rome | 64 C.E. | Eusebius, *Ecclesiastical History* 2.25.4–8; 1 Clement 5:7 | Acts does not tell the story of Paul's death, but according to tradition, he was martyred in Rome at or near the time Peter was martyred. |

As we read the letters attributed to Paul, you may want to keep this chronology nearby in order to situate his writing within the larger framework of his life. Keep in mind, however, that we cannot rely on this chronology to help us date Paul's authentic letters, except to say that they were most likely written between 50–60 C.E. This means that the authentic letters of Paul precede the writing of the gospels and are among the earliest works of the New Testament. The Deutero-Pauline letters, by contrast, are among some of the latest works of the New Testament.

## Sources and Resources

Barrett, C. K. *The New Testament Background: Selected Documents.* New York: Harper & Row, 1956.

Callan, Terrance. *Dying and Rising with Christ: The Theology of Paul the Apostle.* New York: Paulist, 2006.

Chilton, Bruce. *Rabbi Paul: An Intellectual Biography.* New York: Doubleday, 2004.

Crossan, John Dominic, and Jonathan L. Reed. In *Search of Paul: How Jesus' Apostle Opposed Rome's Empire with God's Kingdom.* New York: HarperSanFrancisco, 2004.

Griffith-Jones, Robin. *The Gospel according to Paul: The Creative Genius Who Brought Jesus to the World.* New York: HarperSanFrancisco, 2004.

Foakes-Jackson, Fredrick J. and Kirsopp Lake. *The Beginnings of Christianity. Part I. The Acts of the Apostles.* New York: Macmillan, 1920.

Murphy-O'Connor, Jerome. *Paul the Letter-Writer: His World, His Options, His Skills.* Collegeville, Minn.: Liturgical Press, 1995.

_____. *Paul: His Story.* Oxford, England: Oxford University Press, 2004.

Richards, E. Randolph. *Paul and First-Century Letter Writing: Secretaries, Composition, and Collection.* Downers Grove, Ill.: InterVarsity Press, 2004.

Roetzel, Calvin J. *Paul: The Man and the Myth.* Minneapolis, Minn.: Fortress, 1999.

_____. *Paul, a Jew on the Margins.* Louisville, Ky.: Westminster John Knox Press, 2003.

Sampley, J. Paul, ed. *Paul in the Greco-Roman World: A Handbook.* Harrisburg, Pa.: Trinity Press International, 2003.

Schneemelcher, Wilhelm, ed. *New Testament Apocrypha.* 2 vols. Philadelphia: Westminster Press, 1990–1992.

Stirewalt, M. Luther. *Paul, the Letter Writer.* Grand Rapids, Mich.: Eerdmans, 2003.

Stowers, Stanley Kent. *Letter Writing in Greco-Roman Antiquity.* Philadelphia: Westminster Press, 1989.

Wallace, Richard, and Wynne Williams. *The Three Worlds of Paul of Tarsus.* London: Routledge, 1998.

White, J. L. *Light from Ancient Letters.* Philadelphia: Fortress, 1986.

Witherington, Ben. *The Paul Quest: The Renewed Search for the Jew of Tarsus.* Downers Grove, Ill.: InterVarsity Press, 1998.

# CHAPTER 13

# THE FIRST AND SECOND LETTERS TO THE THESSALONIANS

# ART AS A MEDIUM FOR BIBLICAL INTERPRETATION

Any student of art history knows that religious symbols and themes dominate much of the art that has been preserved to the present day. This phenomenon gives witness to the priority of place that human cultures have given to religious expression over the centuries and even in early recorded history. Indeed, art has been and continues to be an important medium through which peoples of different times and places can articulate responses to fundamental questions about human existence—How did we come into being? Why are we here? How do we account for evil in the world? What values do we hold dear and what are the virtues to which we ought to aspire? For what are we destined?

For Christians, these questions are addressed most fully and richly in the stories of Jesus and his early followers. Here are some examples of artistic interpretations of the story of the birth of Jesus taken from different historical periods and from different parts of the world. Carefully analyze each work. Consider using the guidelines provided in Chapter 8, Activities for Learning, # 2 (pp. 195–96). To what extent is the artist's work simply a retelling of the biblical text and in what ways is it a reinterpretation of the text? What theological question does the artist's work address or how is it an acclamation of a theological truth?

The Birth of Jesus. From the Life of Jesus Mafa project, North Cameroun, Africa. Website at www.jesusmafa.com.

The Nativity (tempera and oil). Master Francke (c. 1385–c. 1436). Panel from the St. Thomas Altar in St. John's Church, Hamburger Kunsthalle, Hamburg, Germany/The Bridgeman Art Library.

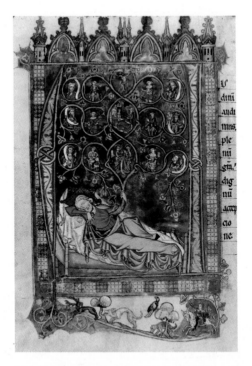

Tree of Jesse with Annunciation, Nativity, Crucifixion and Kings and Prophets. Fourteenth century German/Swiss manuscript; Cistercian Sermologium, Douce 185, fol. IV. Bodleian Library, Oxford.

The Nativity (w/c and gouache on paper). Lisa Graa Jensen (contemporary artist), Private Collection/The Bridgeman Art Library.

Adoration of the Shepherds (oil on canvas). El Greco, 1603–1605.
Museo del Patriarca, Valencia, Spain/The Bridgeman Art Library.

The Nativity. He Qi (contemporary artist). www.heqigallery.com

Mystic Nativity (oil on canvas). Sandro Botticelli, 1500. © The
National Gallery, London.

Nativity of the Virgin and the Massacre of the Innocents
(tempera on panel). Master Bertram of Minden
(c. 1345-c. 1415). Central panel of the Buxtehude Altar.
Kuhnsthalle (museum), Hamburger Kunsthalle, Hamburg,
Germany/The Bridgeman Art Library.

| 80–90 C.E. | The Gospels of Matthew and Luke are written; Acts of the Apostles is written. |
| 81–96 C.E. | Domitian is Roman emperor. |
| 90–100 C.E. | The Gospel of John is written; **the Second Letter to the Thessalonians is written.** |

We are now about to launch out on our voyage into the New Testament letters associated with Paul of Tarsus. One potentially difficult issue that people face when reading Paul's letters is where to begin. Since his letters do not have dates attached to them, we cannot easily say, "Let's start with the first one he wrote." Similarly, we cannot say, "Let's read them according to different themes and different topics" because each of his letters contains numerous themes and topics. Our approach will be to begin with Paul's First Letter to the Thessalonians (abbreviated as 1 Thess.) because it is short and because most scholars agree that it is the first (or among the first) that he wrote. In the second half of this chapter, we will investigate the Second Letter to the Thessalonians (abbreviated as 2 Thess.), which scholars have categorized as a Deutero-Pauline letter. By comparing its style and content to 1 Thessalonians, perhaps you can see why biblical scholars think it was not written by Paul but rather by someone who was writing in Paul's name.

## THE FIRST LETTER TO THE THESSALONIANS

For many of the faith communities to whom Paul wrote, Acts of the Apostles has a corresponding story about his first visit to that city. Luke uses a fairly straightforward pattern to present these stories: Paul enters a city, preaches in the synagogue, gets thrown out of the synagogue, and finally starts a community of believers among the Gentiles. The predictability of the pattern is a good reminder that Luke's purpose in writing was not to provide a documentary account of Paul's life but to offer a theological interpretation of the origins and direction of the earliest Christian communities. However, because Paul's letters support this view, we can safely assume that Paul's communities were as Luke describes them—mostly Gentile believers, together with at least a few Jewish members, from different socioeconomic classes, including some wealthy and influential residents of the city. The Christian community at Thessalonica appears not to be an exception.

## AUTHORSHIP, AUDIENCE, AND DATE OF COMPOSITION

Acts of the Apostles tells a story about a visit by Paul and his companion Silas to Thessalonica (Acts 17:1–9) during his second journey through Europe and Asia Minor, perhaps in 50 C.E. Luke tells us that there was a Jewish synagogue at Thessalonica. Paul and Silas stayed at Jason's house and preached in the synagogue for three weeks until a riot broke out, and they had to escape from the city for fear of being arrested. Luke adds that some Jews from the synagogue became believers on account of Paul's teaching, as did many Greeks (Gentiles) and even a number of the city's leading women (Acts 17:4). If the historical details of Luke's story can be

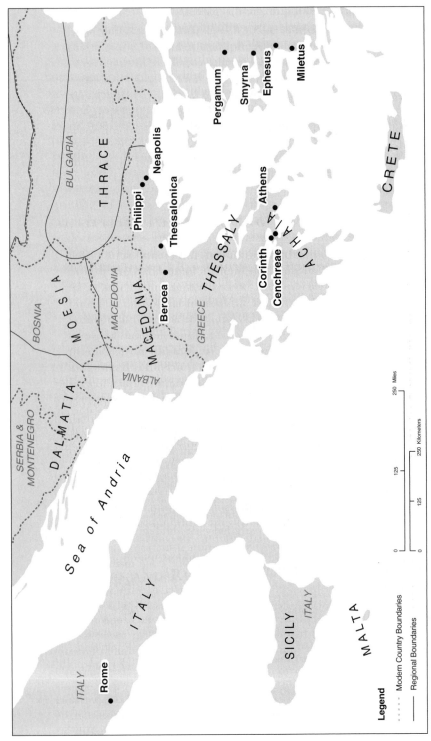

Thessalonica and surroundings in Macedonia, including modern boundaries.

trusted, these people would have comprised the nucleus of the Christian community at Thessalonica. Because Paul was the first to preach the message of Jesus in this community, he is identified as the founder of the church. This First Letter to the Thessalonians appears to have been written shortly after Paul's visit to the city. Most biblical scholars give it a date of 51 C.E.

Named after Alexander the Great's sister, the city of Thessalonica was founded in 315 B.C.E. It was an important trade city, located on the Egnatian Way, the main Roman road across the Balkans. In 146 B.C.E., under the rule of the Romans, it became the capital of the province of Macedonia. Shrines to Roman and Egyptian gods, including Isis, Serapis, Osiris, and Anubis, have been discovered in its archeological remains. The city also has archeological evidence of some aspects of emperor worship. All of these data indicate that Thessalonica was a very cosmopolitan city, open to new ideas and accustomed to receiving travelers from all over the Roman Empire.

## OUTLINE OF THE LETTER

The introduction to Part IV of our textbook provides a "neat and tidy" description of the five parts of Paul's letters. However, as the outline of this letter demonstrates, Paul does not always follow the standard letter form in his writings. When you think about your own letter-writing practices, this is probably not surprising. At some point in elementary or junior high school, you learned the proper way to write a letter, but you probably do not consciously follow those guidelines today except in formal correspondence like job applications, letters of recommendation, or wedding invitations. Instead, your personal and informal correspondence probably is quite fluid. When it comes to letter writing in particular, the medium and the message have considerable impact on the form (structure) of the letter.

We should think of Paul's letters to the churches in a similar vein. When he wrote this First Letter to the Thessalonians, he probably never imagined that he was doing something as formal and definitive as writing a book of the New Testament. Instead, we should envision him writing a personal letter to a community, which he has established and for which he has great affection, giving them guidance as they struggle to live out the gospel (i.e., the good news about Jesus Christ) in their lives. Today we look at this letter and detect two and perhaps three thanksgiving units, along with a section that looks like a conclusion that has been incorporated into the body of the letter. If that's not enough confusion, Paul has interspersed paraenesis (moral exhortation) within the body of the letter. It makes biblical scholars wonder what was going on! The outline below will help you locate these multiple units in the First Letter to the Thessalonians.

1. 1 Thessalonians 1:1—Opening
2. 1 Thessalonians 1:2–10; 2:13; 3:9–10—Thanksgiving
3. 1 Thessalonians 2:1–3:13; 4:13–5:11—Body
4. 1 Thessalonians 4:1–12; 5:12–22—Paraenesis
5. 1 Thessalonians 3:11–13; 5:23–28—Closing

Why did Paul deviate so dramatically from the standard letter form? In this case, the answer might be as simple as this: Proper letter writing wasn't his primary concern; the needs of the community—particularly its members' peace of mind—take priority over rules of style. However, in other letters, the answer might be more complex, as we shall see.

The thanksgiving section(s) will give you clues to the letter's themes, but until you are more familiar with Paul's letters, you may not be able to locate them right away. Therefore, you should plan to go back and reexamine the thanksgiving section(s) after you have completed your study of the letter. However, one theme you will recognize right away in this letter is Paul's interest in the end time. For example, his comment about waiting for God's Son from heaven (1 Thess. 1:10) is a reference to early Christians' expectation about the Risen Christ's return or reappearance on the earth at the end time. They understood this to be the time of their rescue when God would put everything right with the world. Paul will develop this theme more fully in the body of the letter.

## A PERSECUTED CHURCH?

In this First Letter to the Thessalonians, Paul makes several comments about the hardships that community members were facing and how they were enduring persecution on account of their belief in Jesus, even about how they ought to *expect* persecution (e.g., 1 Thess. 1:6; 2:14; 3:2–4). What was going on in Thessalonica? Were members of this Christian community being publicly and actively sought out for arrest, or was their persecution more incidental and sporadic? Maybe they weren't actually being harassed, but perhaps they somehow felt alienated from the mainstream society because of their status as a minority community. And who were their persecutors? We have already mentioned the story from Acts of the Apostles where Luke describes a riot that broke out during Paul's visit to Thessalonica (Acts 17:1–15). Although Paul and Silas were able to hide from the mob and slip out of town, we are told that Jason and some other believers were arrested for providing Paul a place to stay and for "saying that there is another king named Jesus" (Acts 17:7). Is this an example of the kind of thing that was happening to the Christian community in Thessalonica?

Luke blames the riot, and presumably everything that followed, on the Jews of Thessalonica who were jealous of Paul and had refused his teaching. Therefore, some people might conclude that the Jews were somehow responsible for the ongoing persecution of the Christian community in that city. Certainly, tension between Thessalonian Jews and Jewish Christians, or Christian Jews, like Paul, was possible, since Jews would have viewed these Christian Jews as innovators, at best, and as defectors or opponents of the Law, at worst. And, of course, the minority Jewish Christians would have perceived their situation as persecution because, although they were convinced that they were right about Jesus, they must have grieved the break in relations with their Jewish brothers and sisters.

But what does Paul reveal about the Thessalonian community to whom he was writing? Paul's comment about how they "turned to God from idols, to serve a living and true God" (1 Thess. 1:9) suggests that they were Gentile, for the most part. Then who was responsible for persecuting these Gentile Christians? Perhaps Paul gives us a clue when he praises the community for imitating the (Jewish Christian) churches of Judea, adding that they "suffered the same things from [their] compatriots as they did from the Jews" (1 Thess. 2:14). If Paul accurately understood the situation there, then the Thessalonian Christian community's compatriots likely would have been other Gentiles in the town. Even though Thessalonica was a large city and the Christian community was relatively small, we can imagine that the latter's members attracted attention because they behaved differently and held values that were not shared by their neighbors. As a consequence, they may have become a target for persecution when things went wrong. Unfortunately, this same kind of scapegoating continues today as minority communities try to find their place in the majority society.

## CONCERNS ABOUT THE END TIME

The First Letter to the Thessalonians is Paul's response to a report brought by Timothy (a companion of Paul) concerning some among the Christian community in Thessalonica who had mistaken beliefs concerning the fate of those who have died. Their misunderstandings are directly connected to the perceived delay of the **parousia**, the return of the messiah (1 Thess. 4:13). Therefore, this letter is especially important for understanding what early Christians believed about the parousia and the end time. In theological terms, we are investigating the eschatology of Paul's church at Thessalonica. The root of the word **eschatology** is *eschaton*, a Greek word that means "the end." Thus, eschatology means "teaching about the end time."

Following are some of the questions addressed by eschatology: Do created beings continue to exist in some state after death? What is the ultimate destiny of human beings? To what are we referring when we talk about heaven and hell? Some eschatologies are apocalyptic insofar as they are concerned about the immediacy of the end time and the catastrophe that is expected to accompany it. Jewish and Christian apocalyptic eschatologies regularly express the conviction that God's justice will prevail—the wicked will be punished and the righteous will be rescued—and that God is sovereign (i.e., has power over everyone and everything).

The eschatological units of this letter are 1 Thessalonians 4:13–18 and 5:1–11. In the first section, Paul addresses the community members' concern that their dead relatives and friends might be lost because they died before the return of the messiah. Some early Christians (including Paul) believed that Jesus would return to participate in God's triumph over the forces of evil within a relatively short period of time, at least within their lifetimes. Most likely, this expectation was due to the Christian proclamation that Jesus had been raised from the dead. Resurrection from the dead was one of the signs of the end time among some first-century Jewish groups. Awaiting the completion of the end time, these early Christians looked forward to the return of the messiah, when God would rescue the persecuted righteous from the hands of their tormentors and establish a new world order.

However, the lengthy delay of the parousia—by the time of this writing, now twenty years—created problems for these early Christian believers. When members of the Christian community began to die, their relatives questioned how their loved ones could be included in the restored new order. Perhaps they also asked whether these premature deaths meant that their relatives somehow lacked in faith. Paul answers their concerns with consolation: Your deceased relatives are not lost but will be raised up to participate in God's triumphant reign (1 Thess. 4:13–18). Paul goes so far as to "paint a picture" of what this end time event will be like. Reading Paul's explanation of the end time, you can easily imagine that he expected the parousia to be a glorious experience and one to be anticipated with joy, as heavenly trumpets sound, archangels call out to announce the coming of the Risen Christ, and all of God's holy ones—the deceased first—join him in the skies. What a celebration!

In the second eschatological section of this letter (1 Thess. 5:1–11), Paul addresses his own concern about how Christians ought to behave in light of the delay of the end time. Again, his principal message is one of consolation. Here we see some standard eschatological imagery found in many Jewish and early Christian apocalyptic texts: drunkenness, sleep, the labor pains of a pregnant woman, the thief in the night, darkness, and the armor of war. The language is metaphorical and designed to urge Christian believers to stay alert, be vigilant, and persevere in times of trouble. They should not allow the delay of the end time to make them apathetic or complacent. At the same time, they should not worry about being saved because they are all "children of the light" and "children of the day." Salvation is already theirs as long as they persevere. Thus the admonition: "Encourage one another and build up each other, as indeed you are doing" (1 Thess. 5:11). Clearly, Paul's message regarding the end time is one of consolation and joyful anticipation.

## PAUL ON THE DEATH AND RESURRECTION OF JESUS

Because the First Letter to the Thessalonians is most likely the earliest document of the New Testament, it provides important evidence for understanding how the earliest Christian communities, approximately twenty or twenty-five years after the death and resurrection of Jesus, were understanding these defining events. Frequently in this letter, Paul talks about awaiting the return of the Son *whom God raised from the dead* (e.g., 1 Thess. 1:10). He encourages the community to have hope because *God who raised Jesus from the dead* will also rescue them (1 Thess. 4:14). Paul's primary interest is that God had raised Jesus from the dead; he is little concerned about other details of Jesus' life. The wording is very important here. It was *God* who raised Jesus, and in similar fashion, *God* will raise up the community of believers. Paul's focus is on what God has done and what God will do in the future. There is little evidence of the more sophisticated presentations of Jesus as savior, redeemer, or sacrificial offering of atonement, which we see in Paul's later works. Therefore, it is possible that we are seeing a very early stage in the development of Christian doctrine concerning the death and resurrection of Jesus.

## DID SOMEONE TAMPER WITH 1 THESSALONIANS?

One of the questions that biblical scholars ask when studying the letters of the New Testament is whether Paul actually wrote the letters that have been traditionally ascribed to him. In the ancient world, it was fairly common, for writers of religious literature especially, to write pseudonymously, that is, in the name of a famous person.

While we as modern readers might think of this as falsifying documents, ancient readers probably would not have worried about whether Paul actually wrote the letter. Instead, they would have seen this kind of activity as a tribute to a famous person. However, the authenticity of the First Letter to the Thessalonians is seldom questioned. That is, most scholars are certain that Paul actually wrote this letter.

At the same time, some scholars have suggested that certain parts of the First Letter to the Thessalonians might represent later additions by a scribe or a disciple of Paul. The most controversial is 1 Thessalonians 2:13–16, where Paul has been exhorting the community to imitate the Jewish Christian communities in Judea in their response to persecution. The text goes on to describe how the Jews "killed both the Lord Jesus and the prophets" and to announce their condemnation (1 Thess. 2:15–16). Biblical scholars who view these verses as a later addition note that we do not see such hostile rhetoric against fellow Jews anywhere else in the authentic Pauline letters. Those who view these verses as Paul's own words say that they simply reflect the degree of Paul's frustration with the obstacles that have been placed in the way of his preaching.

Although biblical scholars have not yet come to a consensus about whether verses 13 through 16 represent the actual words of Paul, a majority think they are the work of a redactor. In investigating this sort of question, biblical scholars begin by looking for evidence of what they call literary seams, that is, places where an editor appears to have knit the addition into the earlier work. Let's use 1 Thessalonians 2:13–16 as an example. To provide a bit of context, we will begin at verse 11. The first column of the table that appears on the next page contains the biblical text. The second column offers commentary on the parts of the text that are highlighted in italics. Note the literary seams between verses 12 and 13 and again between verses 16 and 17. Observe how you can read verses 11–12 (text in bold face), skip verses 13–16, and begin reading again at verse 17 (text in bold face) without any interruption of the train of thought.

Biblical scholars are interested in redactional questions like this one because the answer could have a substantial impact on how they understand Paul's theology concerning Israel's place in God's plan of salvation. In his Letter to the Romans, Paul treats this topic directly but in a much more positive way. He does not charge the Jews with killing Jesus or with opposing the spread of the gospel (i.e., message of faith in Jesus Christ) to the Gentiles. Instead, he argues that they actually made the Gentile mission possible. See Romans 9–11. If 1 Thessalonians 2:13–16 is a later addition and not Paul's own words, then we can say that Paul has a consistent theology concerning Israel's place in God's plan of salvation, which you can find more fully explicated in his Letter to the Romans. However, if 1 Thessalonians 2:13–16 is Paul's own writing, then the biblical scholar has to find a way to reconcile these two apparently contradictory teachings.

When we talk about redactional activity in biblical texts, some might be asking whether and to what extent this affects the integrity of the text as sacred literature. If we accept the possibility that someone altered or added to Paul's writing, are we suggesting that it is no longer the inspired word of God? Absolutely not, provided that we hold a contextualist understanding of inspiration (see Chapter 1 of this textbook). Just as the gospels were considered the property of communities of faith that shaped the traditions to express their conviction that Jesus was the Christ, so, too, the rest of the New Testament. As Paul's letters gradually acquired the status of scripture, the churches that preserved them and passed them on to other communities of

| 1 THESSALONIANS 2:11–18 | COMMENTARY ON THE TEXT |
|---|---|
| **11 As you know, we dealt with each one of you** *like a father* **with his children, 12 urging and encouraging you and pleading that you lead a life worthy of God, who calls you into his own kingdom and glory.** 13 *We also constantly give thanks to God* for this, that when you received the word of God that you heard from us, you *accepted it not as a human word but as what it really is, God's word, which is also at work in you believers.* 14 For you, brothers and sisters, became *imitators of the churches of God in Christ Jesus* that are in Judea, for you *suffered the same things* from your own compatriots as they did from the Jews, 15 *who killed both the Lord Jesus and the prophets,* and drove us out; they displease God and oppose everyone 16 by hindering us from speaking to the Gentiles so that they may be saved. Thus they have constantly been filling up the measure of their sins; but God's wrath has overtaken them at last. **17 As for us, brothers and sisters, when, for a short time, we were** *made orphans by being separated from you*—**in person, not in heart—we longed with great eagerness to see you face to face. 18 For we wanted to come to you— certainly I, Paul, wanted to again and again—but** *Satan blocked our way.* | A family metaphor used to express concern about the community's well-being.

A "thanksgiving" section that appears to be out of place.

Rapid change of topic, introduction of themes reminiscent of the original letter thanksgiving—on the power of God's word (1 Thess. 1:5); on becoming imitators of Paul and his co-missioners (1 Thess. 1:6–7); on suffering persecution (1 Thess. 1:6).

Anti-Jewish language that is not typical of Paul's authentic writings.

Return to the family metaphor to express deep affection for the community at Thessalonica.

Satan is the chief opponent of God's coming kingdom. See verse 12 above. |

faith also made small emendations to the text, perhaps to clarify something that they thought was unclear or to highlight a point of contact with the community's experience. Whatever the reason, it is the book in its final form that churches consider sacred and canonical.

## THE SECOND LETTER TO THE THESSALONIANS

Paging through your Bible, you probably noticed that there are two letters addressed to the church at Thessalonica. If you knew nothing about these letters, you probably would assume that the first one was written earlier and the second one later, and you would be correct in making that assumption. However, you might be surprised to

Archeological site of the Roman forum of the city of Thessalonica (second century C.E.). The first-century forum is thought to be below or near this site. *www.HolyLandPhotos.org*.

discover that many biblical scholars think that some forty or more years passed between the writing of these two letters. If you read the opening section of each letter, you will notice that they are addressed to the same Christian community of the Thessalonians. They even claim the same author, namely, Paul. However, when you read the two letters, one after the other and very carefully, you may begin to wonder whether they were, in fact, written by the same author because they are very different in tone.

Perhaps the biggest difference you will see between 1 Thessalonians and 2 Thessalonians is the author's attitude toward the end time and his advice to the believing community that is awaiting its arrival. However, before we engage this question any further, let's begin our exploration of 2 Thessalonians by summarizing what biblical scholars have concluded about its author, date of composition, and intended audience.

## AUTHORSHIP, AUDIENCE, AND DATE OF COMPOSITION

The Second Letter to the Thessalonians has some significant similarities to the first letter by the same name, especially in the duplication of certain phrases and sentences. However, most biblical scholars agree that Paul did not write the Second Letter to the Thessalonians. Instead, they categorize this letter as Deutero-Pauline, meaning that it was written under the pseudonym of Paul but was actually written by someone else, perhaps one of his disciples, in order to honor Paul and further his message. Why? A number of arguments have been put forward, and any one by itself is probably not sufficient, but cumulatively they tip the balance toward the probability that 2 Thessalonians was not written by the same author who wrote 1 Thessalonians. We will review a few of the more convincing arguments here, and in the course of our discussion, we will also learn a bit more about 2 Thessalonians.

Our first argument, though not necessarily the strongest, concerns the observation that these two letters share certain phrases and sentences. If you read them very carefully, you will notice that their opening sections contain exactly the same wording, except for a phrase that is added to the greeting in 2 Thessalonians. Compare the following:

> Paul, Silvanus, and Timothy, to the church of the Thessalonians in God the Father and the Lord Jesus Christ: Grace to you and peace. (1 Thess. 1:1)

> Paul, Silvanus, and Timothy, to the church of the Thessalonians in God the Father and the Lord Jesus Christ: Grace to you and peace from God our Father and the Lord Jesus Christ. (2 Thess. 1:1)

Likewise, you will find similar wording in 1 Thessalonians 2:9 and 2 Thessalonians 3:8, where the text describes Paul and his colleagues' labor and toil on behalf of the gospel and how they did not burden the community while they preached among them. Compare the following:

> You remember our labor and toil, brothers and sisters; we worked night and day, so that we might not burden any of you while we proclaimed to you the gospel of God. (1 Thess. 2:9)

> And we did not eat anyone's bread without paying for it; but with toil and labor we worked night and day, so that we might not burden any of you. (2 Thess. 3:8)

Other examples of repetitions or close resemblances between 1 Thessalonians and 2 Thessalonians include the double thanksgivings in both letters (1 Thess. 1:2; 2:13; 2 Thess. 1:3; 2:13), the similar sounding blessings (1 Thess. 3:11–13; 2 Thess. 2:16–17), and the identical closing sentences (1 Thess. 5:28; 2 Thess. 3:18).

At first glance, you might think that these similarities in wording make a good argument in support of the view that Paul wrote both letters. However, none of the authentic Pauline letters shows this degree of repetition of phrases from one letter to the next. Further, if you think about your own letter-writing practices, you might agree that it is hard to imagine Paul repeating himself so precisely, especially with content as inconsequential as this. However, it is fairly easy to imagine a pseudonymous author doing so in an effort to imitate Paul's writing style. Using this argument, we can even account for the additional phrase, "from God our Father and the Lord Jesus Christ," that the author of 2 Thessalonians incorporates into his opening greeting. Stylistically, the phrase is awkward because it appears to duplicate "in God the Father and the Lord Jesus Christ" (2 Thess. 1:1) of the preceding sentence. However, most of Paul's authentic letters have the longer greeting. The author of 2 Thessalonians probably knew that and decided to "correct" the opening greeting of 1 Thessalonians.

Another argument in favor of a pseudonymous author for 2 Thessalonians is the presence of certain themes and vocabulary that resonate better with the later pastoral letters (i.e., 1 Timothy, 2 Timothy, and Titus) than with Paul's authentic letters. Two examples are the multiple warnings to avoid false teachers (2 Thess. 2:2–3, 10–11; cf. 1 Tim. 1:3–7; 4:1–3; 6:3–6) and the call to hold fast to the traditions (2 Thess. 2:15; cf. 2 Tim. 3:14–15; Tit. 1:9). A third argument concerns the highly apocalyptic tone of 2 Thessalonians, with fiery imagery that seems more consistent with the Book of Revelation, which was written toward the end of the first century C.E., than with 1 Thessalonians. Likewise, its symbolic use of temple imagery (2 Thess. 2:4) is consistent with that found in the Book of Revelation (e.g., Rev. 21:22–27), which was written after the Jerusalem Temple had been destroyed.

Recognizing that 1 and 2 Thessalonians have certain similarities but that they also differ from one another in significant ways, what is the best way to answer the authorship question? Those scholars who wish to assert that Paul wrote both letters say that the second letter was written shortly after the first (c. 51 C.E.) and that it was written to tame the community's nervous excitement about the coming end time by saying that "that day will not come unless the rebellion comes first" (2 Thess. 2:3). However, this theory does not explain Paul's rapid change of attitude toward the end time, nor does it account for the high degree of similarity in wording that we find in these two letters. Recall that the message of 1 Thessalonians concerning the end time is consolation and joyful anticipation.

Other scholars have suggested that the author of 2 Thessalonians, writing forty to forty-five years after the first letter had been completed, was using the first letter—particularly its opening and thanksgiving sections, its blessings, and its closing section—as a pattern for his own writing. Clearly, he viewed Paul as a hero of the Christian tradition and considered it an honorable thing to write in his name. However, because the author of 2 Thessalonians was living in a period of time and in a social location that were similar to those of the pastoral letters, he was inclined to use vocabulary and to address issues that were more like those of the pastoral letters (see Chapter 19 of this textbook). In sum, 2 Thessalonians is a pseudonymous work written in approximately 90–100 C.E.

A theory like the one outlined above would account for the similarities *and differences* between the First and Second Letters to the Thessalonians. However, it raises new questions about the intended audience for the letter. The pseudonymous author indicates that the letter is addressed to the Thessalonians (2 Thess. 1:1), but was it necessarily sent to the Thessalonian Christian community, or is this a bit of literary fiction that the author introduced to make the letter seem like a real letter? We cannot know for certain. The Second Letter of Peter, which is dated approximately 100–125 C.E., suggests that by that time letters attributed to Paul were being circulated rather widely (i.e., beyond the boundaries of the individual church or churches to which they were written) (2 Pet. 3:15–16). One can easily imagine a situation in which a disciple or admirer of Paul, wanting to honor him and extend his teaching about the end time to another generation, copies the general form of Paul's First Letter to the Thessalonians—including the addressee of the letter—and writes an "updated" teaching on the end time for the body of the letter. People received the letter as edifying and helpful for living the faith, and gradually the letter joined the collection of letters attributed to Paul and circulated among the churches as such. Thus, it became known as the Second Letter to the Thessalonians.

## OUTLINE OF THE LETTER

This letter follows the pattern of ancient letters with few deviations. Most of the similarities between 1 Thessalonians and 2 Thessalonians are contained in the letter's opening, thanksgiving, and closing.

1. 2 Thessalonians 1:1–2—Opening
2. 2 Thessalonians 1:3–12; 2:13—Thanksgiving
3. 2 Thessalonians 2:1–17—Body
4. 2 Thessalonians 3:1–16—Paraenesis
5. 2 Thessalonians 3:17–18—Closing

Note the inclusion of a second thanksgiving unit in the body of the letter, following the pattern of 1 Thessalonians. Also of interest is the closing of this letter, in which the author writes, "I Paul, write this greeting with my own hand. This is the mark in every letter of mine; it is the way I write" (2 Thess. 3:17). If this letter is pseudonymous, as most biblical scholars agree, how do we make sense of this strange statement by the author? Is he simply lying, or is there another way to account for his writing?

## THE END TIME

The Second Letter to the Thessalonians contains some of the same themes as 1 Thessalonians, particularly with regard to its interest in the end time. However, rather than consoling the believers and assuring them that they are God's children, the Second Letter to the Thessalonians is more interested in identifying the signs of the end time, in warning people about the powers of the Evil One, and in emphasizing the terribleness of the "Day of the Lord" (i.e., judgment day). Moreover, concerning the signs of the end time, it appears that this letter is saying almost the opposite of the first letter. Whereas the first letter assumed that the end would come relatively soon—even though Paul admitted that he did not know the exact time—this letter cautions against being misled by so-called signs, adding that the rebellion must come first.

The author of the Second Letter to the Thessalonians writes at some length about this anticipated rebellion and the Lawless One who is currently being restrained (2 Thess. 2:3–4). He also implies that the end will come when the one who is restraining the Lawless One eventually releases it (2 Thess. 2:7). Who is the Lawless One? And who is the one doing the restraining? What is the rebellion? We have to assume that the original audience for this letter was well aware of who and what the author was talking about. Otherwise, the author would have had to provide more explanation. Unfortunately, however, we have no way of knowing today what the first-century author meant. The only thing we can safely say is that all this is somehow related to Satan and the forces of evil and deceit. None of this language is found in the First Letter to the Thessalonians.

# A Vengeful God and the Lord Jesus

The Second Letter to the Thessalonians differs from the first letter also in its theology of God. In 2 Thessalonians, God is principally a God of retribution and judgment who deludes those who have chosen not to "love the truth" (2 Thess. 2:11) and who afflicts those who have afflicted God's holy ones (2 Thess. 1:5–6). Contrast this view of God with 1 Thessalonians, in which God is portrayed as the one who can be counted on to raise the deceased believers so that they might participate fully in the glorious events of the end time.

Likewise, the author of 2 Thessalonians emphasizes the Lordship of Jesus over the powers of evil, the glory of his might, and his vengeance against those who do not know God (2 Thess. 1:7–8; 2:8–9). Contrast this view of the parousia Christ with 1 Thessalonians, in which the story of the death and resurrection of Jesus is presented primarily as a message of consolation—just as God raised Jesus, you can be certain that he will also raise you in the end time (1 Thess. 4:14).

## Unmasking the Man of Tyranny

In every generation, Christian believers struggle to relate the sacred scriptures to their own life experience so that the Bible can speak in new and meaningful ways to the people of their day. One way this has been done is by paraphrasing the biblical text, using the common language of the day. Sometimes people even substitute contemporary place names or characters into the paraphrase, as a vehicle for making the ancient scriptures speak to a new audience. One such example is *The Cotton Patch Version of Paul's Epistles*, which was composed with special attention to the culture and dialect of the American South and to the issues of race relations and the Civil Rights movement. The author, Clarence Jordan, paraphrases 2 Thessalonians 2:1–12 in this way:

> Brothers, let us speak earnestly to you about the coup of our Lord and our gathering together around him, so that you may not be easily thrown for a loop nor upset by a "spirit" or a message or a letter supposed to be from us stating that the Lord's era has "arrived." Don't let anybody bag you with that kind of foolishness! For unless there first comes the reformation, and the mask is pulled off the Man of Tyranny, the damned bastard, who opposes and lords it over everything called God or sacred; in fact, he sits in God's house and claims that he himself is God. . . . Don't you remember that while I was with you I was telling you these things? Even now you know the Despot, so he may be unmasked in his own time. For already the secret of tyranny is working only until the Despot can be gotten out of the way. And then the Tyrant shall be unmasked and the Lord Jesus will smash him with a sneeze and make him powerless for the ushering in of HIS *coup*. His *coup* is the result of Satan's energy expressed in much activity and charts and phony programs and in much crooked slick talk by those who are going to hell because they spurned the love of the truth whereby they may have been rescued. And that's why God is bringing upon them a "generator of error" that leads them to put stock in the outright lie, so that all who don't trust the truth but delight in wickedness might be brought to judgment. (Jordan, *The Cotton Patch Version of Paul's Epistles*, 136–137)

## RELEVANCE FOR TODAY'S CHRISTIANS

What do these two letters, with their very different perspectives on the end time, have to say to contemporary believers? There are Christians today who view the end time in words and images that are very much like those in the Second Letter to the Thessalonians—worried about the signs of the end time, always on the lookout for the anti-Christ or the Lawless One, and fearful about whether they will survive the trials of the last days. We only need to think about the popularity of the "Left Behind" book series to see this worldview at work in today's culture. But when people immerse themselves so much in a worldview like that of 2 Thessalonians, it is possible that they will miss the more hopeful message of the First Letter to the Thessalonians. Yes, there is evil in the world. No, we have not yet seen the fullness of the kingdom of God. But Christians also believe that God raised up Jesus and just as surely God will restore humanity, which is God's creation. "Therefore encourage one another and build up each other, as indeed you are doing" (1 Thess. 5:11). Thus the words of Paul.

## KEY TERMS

Eschatology                    Parousia

## QUESTIONS FOR READING

Read 1 Thessalonians. Use evidence from the text to answer the following questions.

1. What happened to Paul and his companions at Philippi (1 Thess. 2:2)? *Hint:* Read Acts 16:19–40. What speculation can you make about why Paul alluded to this incident in 1 Thessalonians?

2. In 1 Thessalonians 2:1–7, as Paul writes about his work among the Thessalonians, biblical scholars think he may also be indirectly answering his critics. What are some of the things his critics might be saying about him?

3. How did Paul learn what was going on in Thessalonica (1 Thess. 3:1–10)? Is he encouraged or discouraged by the news he received? Explain.

4. Describe the main points in Paul's teaching about how the Christian community at Thessalonica ought to live (1 Thess. 4:1–12; 5:12–22).

5. Explain the problem about the end time that was troubling the Christian community at Thessalonica (1 Thess. 4:1–13). What does Paul have to say to them in this regard? What evidence does he give them in support of his statement?

6. In 1 Thessalonians 5:1–11, Paul addresses a related question about when the parousia (i.e., the return of Christ at the end time) will take place. When does he think this event will happen? What does he expect the Thessalonian community to do in the meantime?

7. After reading this First Letter to the Thessalonians, what can you deduce about Paul's relationship to the community at Thessalonica? Why does he have this attitude toward the community?

Read 2 Thessalonians. Use evidence from the text to answer the following questions.

8. According to the author of 2 Thessalonians, what is the nature of God's justice (e.g., when, how, why, and against whom) (2 Thess. 1:5–12), and how does this relate to the suffering that Christian believers must face?

9. What attributes or characteristics does the author of 2 Thessalonians associate with the Lawless One (2 Thess. 2:1–12)? What role does Jesus play in relation to the Lawless One?

10. Summarize the main points that the author of 2 Thessalonians makes about how the Christian community ought to live in light of the coming end time (2 Thess. 2:16–3:15). How do these teachings compare to what Paul teaches in 1 Thessalonians on the same topic?

11. Most biblical scholars do not think that Paul wrote 2 Thessalonians. What evidence do you find to be convincing in support of this position? If you do not accept this position, what evidence would you offer in support of the view that Paul *did* write this letter?

12. If Paul did not write this letter, how do you explain the postscript, "I, Paul . . . (2 Thess. 3:17)?

13. After reading both letters to the Thessalonians, how would you compare these two letters on questions about the end time and the events that will signal its arrival? How would you compare them on the attitude or disposition that Christian believers ought to have toward the parousia (e.g., fearful, excited, cautious)?

## QUESTIONS FOR REFLECTION

1. Do the ethical teachings of 1 Thessalonians and 2 Thessalonians have concrete application for the modern Christian? If yes, in what ways? If no, why not? Is one letter more relevant than the other in this regard? Why or why not?

2. For modern Christian communities, what problems are associated with the expectation of the return of Christ? How are they different from those of the early church? If Paul were living today, how would he respond to modern readers on this issue?

## ACTIVITIES FOR LEARNING

1. Study the geographic location of the city to which the letters to the Thessalonians were addressed. What do you notice about its location that would have made it a fitting place for Paul to engage in his preaching mission? Do some research on what archeologists have discovered about the ancient city of Thessalonica. What does this information help us understand about the community (or communities) behind these letters?

2. Suppose Paul were alive today and writing to a faith community with eschatological expectations similar to those of the original audience of 1 Thessalonians or 2 Thessalonians. What would the paraenesis of his letter to that community look like? Sketch out its major components or, better yet, pretend that you are Paul. What would you write to today's Christians?

## SOURCES AND RESOURCES

Beker, J. C. *Paul's Apocalyptic Gospel: The Coming Triumph of God*. Philadelphia: Fortress, 1982.

Gaventa, Beverly Roberts. *First and Second Thessalonians*. Louisville, Ky.: John Knox Press, 1998.

Jordan, Clarence. *The Cotton Patch Version of Paul's Epistles*. New York: Association Press, 1968.

Malherbe, Abraham. *Paul and the Thessalonians: The Philosophic Tradition of Pastoral Care*. Philadelphia: Fortress, 1987.

_____. *The Letters to the Thessalonians: A New Translation with Introduction and Commentary*. Vol. 32B of Anchor Bible. New York: Doubleday, 2000.

Marshall, I. H. *1 and 2 Thessalonians*. Grand Rapids, Mich.: Eerdmans, 1983.

Neyrey, Jerome H. *Paul, in Other Words: A Cultural Reading of His Letters*. Louisville, Ky.: Westminster John Knox Press, 1990.

Reese, J. M. *1 and 2 Thessalonians*. Wilmington, Del.: Glazier, 1979.

Richard, Earl. *First and Second Thessalonians*. Collegeville, Minn.: Liturgical Press, 1995.

Roetzel, Calvin J. *The Letters of Paul: Conversations in Context*. 4th ed. Louisville, Ky.: Westminster John Knox Press, 1998.

Smiles, Vincent M. *First Thessalonians, Philippians, Second Thessalonians, Colossians, Ephesians*. Collegeville, Minn.: Liturgical Press, 2005.

Smith, Abraham. *Comfort One Another: Reconstructing the Rhetoric and Audience of 1 Thessalonians*. Louisville, Ky.: Westminster John Knox Press, 1995.

Wright, N. T. *Paul for Everyone: Galatians and Thessalonians*. London: SPCK; Louisville, Ky.: Westminster John Knox Press, 2004.

# CHAPTER 14

# PAUL'S LETTER TO THE GALATIANS

## OVERVIEW

- AUTHORSHIP: Paul
- DATE OF COMPOSITION: Approximately 54–55 C.E.
- INITIAL AUDIENCE: Most likely Gentile Christian churches of the northern and central plateau region of Asia Minor (modern Turkey)
- MAJOR TOPICS: Paul's Claim to Apostleship; Paul's Opponents; Paul's Teaching on Justification by Faith; Demonstration of Justification by Faith; The Allegory of Hagar and Sarah

## TIMELINE

| | |
|---|---|
| c. 36 C.E. | Paul is converted on the road to Damascus. |
| 49–50C.E. | The Jerusalem Conference is held to decide about the inclusion of Gentile believers. |
| 51 C.E. | Paul writes his First Letter to the Thessalonians. |
| 52–60 C.E. | Felix is procurator of Palestine. |
| 54–55 C.E. | **Paul writes his Letter to the Galatians.** |
| 54–56 C.E. | Paul writes his Letters to the Philippians and Philemon. |
| 54–68 C.E. | Nero is Roman emperor. |
| 55–56 C.E. | Paul writes his First Letter to the Corinthians. |
| 56–57 C.E. | Paul writes his Second Letter to the Corinthians. |
| 57–58 C.E. | Paul writes his Letter to the Romans. |
| 60–62 C.E. | Festus is procurator of Palestine. |
| 64 C.E. | Peter and Paul are martyred in Rome. |

This next stop on our voyage through the New Testament is a group of churches in an area that was called Galatia at the time, now in Turkey. The Letter to the Galatians is perhaps Paul's most fearsome. In it, he rages against those who have deserted the message he taught them when he was with them (Gal. 1:6–10). Interestingly, this letter is also one of only a few instances in which Paul tells his own story. He writes about his life in Judaism before his conversion on the road to Damascus and how he once violently persecuted the "church of God" (Gal. 1:13–24). He also writes about his activities in the years between his conversion and the Jerusalem Conference (c. 49–50 C.E.) (Gal. 2:1–10). Additionally, Paul gives us an inside view of his sometimes tense relationship with Peter (Gal. 2:11–14).

Also noteworthy is the fact that the Letter to the Galatians describes, in abbreviated form, Paul's teaching on justification by faith, which became the foundation for the doctrine that continues to be important for many Christian churches today. Martin Luther, in the sixteenth century, called it his "pet" gospel because, from it, he was able to develop his own understanding about the relationship between faith and works. However, before we investigate these topics, we need to ask what we know about the date of the composition of this letter and the community or communities for which it was written.

## AUTHORSHIP AND AUDIENCE

Biblical scholars agree that the Letter to the Galatians is an authentic Pauline letter—that is, a letter actually written by Paul. As we noted earlier, Paul wrote several letters to individual churches, but this is the only letter addressed to a group of churches, here identified as the "churches of Galatia" (Gal. 1:2). Unfortunately, we do not know the exact location of these churches because the term *Galatia* was used differently by different groups of people in the first century C.E. Long-time inhabitants identified the northern and central plateau region of Asia Minor (now Turkey) as Galatia, but in 25 B.C.E., the conquering Romans linked this area with another region that extended south through the central part of Asia Minor and called the entire region Galatia. The northern part of the region was sparsely populated, but it included the cities of Ancrya, Pessinus, and Tavium. The ethnic Galatians were the descendants of the Celts and Gauls who invaded this land in the third century B.C.E. However, Acts 13–14 describe Paul's travels through the southern part of the expanded region that the Romans called Galatia, including visits to Antioch in Pisidia (Acts 13:14), Iconium (Acts 14:1), Lystra (Acts 14:8), and Derbe (Acts 14:20) to preach his message about Jesus Christ.

To whom was Paul referring when he wrote to the churches of Galatia? Were they churches of the northern region like Ancrya, Pessinus, and Tavium, or were they churches of the southern region? While either region is possible, scholars tend to favor the North Galatia theory because of Paul's use of the word *Galatians* in Galatians 3:1, suggesting not a place but a group of people (i.e., the ethnic Galatians who lived in the northern region). Because of Paul's description of the communities' situation before they became believers—"formerly when you did not know God" (Gal. 4:8)—scholars think they were mostly Gentile. Again, this would be consistent with the North Galatia theory, since Acts describes Paul's mission in the south as targeted to both Gentiles and Jews (Acts 13–14). Little is known about the socioeconomic situation of these communities, but most likely their members came from across the spectrum of social classes (cf. Gal. 3:28).

## DATE OF COMPOSITION

A decision about the date of composition for Paul's Letter to the Galatians depends on whether we follow the North Galatia theory (i.e., Paul is writing his letter to churches in the northern part of the Roman province of Galatia) or the South Galatia theory (i.e., Paul is writing his letter to churches in the southern part of the Roman province

Possible locations of the churches in Galatia, including modern boundaries.

of Galatia). It also depends on how we interpret what Acts of the Apostles has to say about Paul's missionary journeys into these areas. Paul himself says, in the Letter to the Galatians, that he is writing some fourteen years after his conversion (see Gal. 2:1). If we followed the South Galatia theory and use the chronology from Acts 13–14, then the letter could have been written any time after 50 C.E. However, since we have judged the arguments for the North Galatia theory to be stronger, then we can say that the Letter to the Galatians was written in 54–55 C.E., soon after Paul arrived in Ephesus (see Acts 18:23; cf. Acts 16:6). This is the view held by most Pauline scholars.

## OUTLINE OF THE LETTER

As we have noted many times before, an outline can be a helpful tool for beginning our study of a biblical book. This outline highlights the problem that prompted Paul to write the letter—the communities' failure to hold to the gospel he had taught them when he was first with them. Remember, when Paul talks about the gospel, he means "good message"—that is, the proclamation of faith in Jesus Christ—not a written gospel.

1. Galatians 1:1–5—Opening
2. Galatians 1:6–11—Amazement
3. Galatians 1:12–4:31—Body
   a. Paul's call to preach the gospel (Gal. 1:12–2:14)
   b. Paul's teaching on justification (Gal. 2:15–21)
   c. Arguments in support of this gospel (Gal. 3:1–4:31)
      i. The Galatian communities' experience of first receiving the Spirit (Gal. 3:1–5)
      ii. The example of Abraham—a midrash (Gal. 3:6–26)
      iii. Baptism (Gal. 3:27–29)
      iv. The example of Abraham—a midrash (Gal. 4:1–11)
      v. The Galatian communities' experience of first receiving Paul's gospel (Gal. 4:12–20)
      vi. The allegory of Hagar and Sarah (Gal. 4:21–31)
4. Galatians 5:1–6:10—Paraenesis
5. Galatians 6:11–18—Closing

You will notice that Paul deviates from the usual pattern of the letter and replaces the thanksgiving with some very harsh words about the ease with which these communities abandoned Paul's teaching and took up a different gospel than the one he taught when he first founded these churches. There is no mistaking the fact that Paul is angry!

## PAUL'S CLAIM TO APOSTLESHIP

Paul's Letter to the Galatians is important to our study of the New Testament because it contains a small bit of Paul's autobiography, albeit with a particular agenda in mind: to demonstrate his right to be called an apostle of Jesus Christ, even though he did not actually know the historical Jesus. We see this already in the opening section of the letter, in which Paul identifies himself as an apostle (Gal. 1:1)—that is, "one who is sent." He also makes clear the source of his calling— namely, God and the risen Jesus. Thus, Paul says:

> But when God, who had set me apart before I was born and called me through his grace, was pleased to reveal his Son to me, so that I might proclaim him among the Gentiles, I did not confer with any human being, nor did I go up to Jerusalem to those who were already apostles before me. . . . (Gal. 1:15–17)

Of course, he is referring to the story of his conversion on the road to Damascus and the voice that spoke to him from the heavens (cf. Acts 9:1–19). This is why he can claim to be an apostle: He knew the risen Christ, and he was sent by God on this mission to the Gentiles. Can there be a more authoritative sending than that?

## PAUL'S OPPONENTS

Sometimes Christians of the present day, frustrated with divisions and disagreements within and among their faith communities, look back at the time of the early church with the mistaken belief that Christians then all had a clear sense of who they were and that everyone lived and worked together in peace and harmony. However, evidence from the early churches suggests that this view is far from reality. Not unlike our contemporary Christian communities, they fought about what was right teaching and how they ought to behave. Not everyone got along, and certainly not everyone did everything the same way when it came to Christian belief and practice.

Paul is a good example. In this Letter to the Galatians, he refers to a rather fierce disagreement with Cephas over sharing table fellowship with Gentile believers. Paul, of course, thought it should not be an issue, but some Jewish Christians apparently believed that it violated purity regulations. But Cephas "waffled" on the subject and that made Paul really mad (Gal. 2:11–14). And who is Cephas? Most scholars have identified him with Simon Peter (see Matt. 16:13–20; John 1:41–42). Paul situates his complaint against Peter/Cephas in the context of his retelling of the events associated with the Jerusalem Conference. It is interesting to observe that Paul's recollection of the obligations that would be placed on Gentile converts is different from what is recounted in Acts (compare Galatians 2:10 with Acts 15:19–21), as is the delineation of Peter's and Paul's missionary roles.

Acts presents Peter as the one who was chosen, "in the early days," to evangelize among the Gentiles (Acts 15:7), a task that would now be extended to include Paul and Barnabas (Acts 15:22–29). However, Paul apparently interpreted his commission to preach among the Gentiles as the counterpart of Peter's mission to Jewish Christians (Gal. 2:7–8). At any rate, the major participants are the same: Paul and Barnabas (Gal. 2:1; cf. Acts 15:2), who came to meet Peter/Cephas and James (Gal. 2:7–9; cf. Acts 15:7, 13–15) in Jerusalem. In his Letter to the Galatians, Paul vents his anger against Cephas about no longer sharing table fellowship with Gentiles (Gal 2:11–14), but his comments clearly show that the leadership was not of one mind about how they should live their shared life as Jesus followers.

Paul had other opponents as well, or at least people he considered to be opponents. Sometimes these opponents were within the community to whom he was writing, but other times they were competing missionary preachers who had visited his community in his absence. In the case of his Letter to the Galatians, Paul accuses his opponents of perverting the gospel that he taught when he was with the churches (Gal. 1:7–9) by insisting that the Galatians be circumcised (Gal. 5:2; 6:12–13). It appears that they also insisted that these Gentile Christians keep Jewish Law (Gal. 3:2–5; 5:4–6) and observe Jewish religious festivals (Gal. 4:10).

But who were these opponents? Apparently, they were well known to the churches of Galatia because Paul does not feel a need to name them, but his failure to do so makes it extremely difficult for us to identify them today. The most widely accepted view among biblical scholars is that they were Jewish Christians who believed that Gentiles must keep all of Jewish Law—in essence, become Jews—if they wish to be followers of Jesus. In the scholarly literature, they are sometimes called **Judaizers**. However, this term is not Paul's, and it is generally considered to be derogatory. Therefore, it is better to think of these competing preachers simply as Jewish Christians (like Paul)—or perhaps they were Gentile Christians, like the God-fearers of Acts of the Apostles—who advocated the view that Gentiles had to become Jews in order to enter into the community of Jesus believers.

Whoever Paul's opponents were—if, in fact, they were a separate and identifiable group—the Letter to the Galatians makes it clear that Paul did not think that Gentiles had to observe (i.e., obey) Jewish Law in order to become followers of Jesus.

## PAUL'S TEACHING ON JUSTIFICATION BY FAITH

Paul's Letter to the Galatians is important to the study of the New Testament because it provides us with a very succinct account of his teaching concerning justification by faith, which continues to be a central doctrine (i.e., an official teaching) of many Christian churches today. In order to fully appreciate this teaching, we need to recognize that the terminology and imagery Paul uses are thoroughly Jewish and that he develops his ideas about justification by faith as an argument against those who are advocating **righteousness** that comes through obedience to the Law of Moses. Remember that Paul's opponents in these Galatian communities were probably Jewish Christian missionaries or Gentile God-fearers and that Paul himself was Jewish. Righteousness means "right relationship," in the sense of a properly ordered relationship, or "acquittal," as in a court of law. The word is also translated as **justification**.

What did Paul's opponents mean when they talked about righteousness that comes through obedience to the Law? In the covenant that God established with Moses and the Israelite people, the notion of justification or right relationship with God means acknowledging God as God and obeying Torah or Jewish Law. But it is much more than simply "obeying laws." Rather, observance of Jewish Law is the chosen people's *obligation to covenant relationship* with God. By observing Jewish Law, they are doing their part to live out the covenant and maintain right relationship with God. However, apparently some people had the mistaken view that observance of Jewish Law could actually *acquit* a person of all failures against the covenant. The phrase **justification by works** is shorthand for this view.

Paul fiercely scolds the Galatian churches for their placid acceptance of the "different gospel" that his opponents taught in his absence (Gal. 1:6–8). Based on the content of his letter, we know that this "different gospel" has something to do with the idea that these Gentile converts should be required to observe Torah Law. Nowhere does Paul say that Jews, even Jewish Christians like himself, are exempt from observing Torah Law. And we have every reason to believe that Paul continued to practice his Jewish faith after he became a Jesus follower, except perhaps for laws that regulated contact between Jews and Gentiles. Simply stated, this was, and always would be, their obligation to the everlasting covenant that God made with the Jewish people. But why forbid the Gentile Jesus followers from observing Jewish Law? It represented, after all, a highly moral way of life. Because they might conclude that the Law acquits (i.e., dismisses the charges against them). Paul argues that no one is acquitted before God, except by God's free gift, which is Jesus Christ, for those who believe. The phrase **justification by faith** is shorthand for Paul's view.

Both Paul and his opponents are drawing on the language of covenant, but Paul's point is that human beings cannot make themselves righteous (in right relationship with God) by what they do because justification is God's gift to those who believe in Jesus Christ. Again, to be clear, humans cannot earn justification through any means. Because God is the initiator of the covenant, when the covenant is broken, only God can repair it. Paul also argues that observance of the Law does not define the Gentile believers' relationship with God. Rather, faith in Jesus Christ is the defining element of their covenant with God. Today's readers might be tempted to think of **faith** as a set of teachings to which the believer must give mental assent, but what Paul means by faith is "trust." This distinction is important because trust is a disposition

## A TECHNIQUE FOR ANALYZING PAUL'S WRITINGS

In Galatians 2:15–21, Paul makes a succinct (though somewhat difficult to comprehend) statement about the difference between justification by works and justification by faith. One way to "unpack" Paul's theological statements is to diagram them. Perhaps you learned sentence diagramming when you were studying grammar in elementary or junior high school. This process, which is adapted from Gordon Fee's *New Testament Exegesis*, is basically the same. Ideally, we would do this diagramming with the Greek text, but it works well even with the English translation as long as you remember that Paul was writing in Greek and not in English. Let's begin.

1. Work with one sentence at a time. We will start with Galatians 2:15. Find the subject, verb, and object and diagram them as follows.

   | SUBJECT | VERB | OBJECT |
   |---------|------|--------|
   | We      | are  | Jews   |

   Sometimes one or more of these three elements are implied. In that case, you will insert it but place it in square brackets.

   | SUBJECT | VERB      | OBJECT  |
   |---------|-----------|---------|
   | We      | are       | Jews    |
   | [we]    | [are] not | sinners |

2. Next, find the adjectives and adjectival phrases—that is, the words that modify the nouns—and place them under the nouns they modify.

   | SUBJECT | VERB | OBJECT |
   |---------|------|--------|
   | MODIFIER | | MODIFIER |
   | We | are | Jews |
   | ourselves | | by birth |
   | [we] | [are] not | sinners |
   | | | Gentile |

Do the same thing with the adverbs and adverbial phrases—that is, the words that modify the verb in the sentence. Finally, indicate conjunctions (e.g., and, but, or) by incorporating them into the diagram.

| | SUBJECT | VERB | OBJECT | |
|---|---|---|---|---|
| | MODIFIER | | | MODIFIER |
| | We | are | Jews | |
| | ourselves | | | by birth |
| AND | [we] | [are] not | sinners | |
| | | | | Gentile |

3. When you have completed your diagram of the first sentence, repeat the process with the second sentence, and so on, until you have diagrammed the entire unit of text. If you want to make your diagram more elaborate, you may also diagram the adverbial and adjectival phrases after you have subordinated them to the subject, verb, and object of the sentence.

4. When your diagram is complete, you need to look carefully for patterns of sentence construction. For example, you might notice certain nouns or adjectives that are placed in juxtaposition in order to help you better appreciate the author's point of emphasis or his attempt to nuance the meaning of a particular idea. At the very least, the diagramming process will help you do a close reading of the text.

We will not complete the diagram of Galatians 2:15–21 here. Instead, you will be asked to complete it on your own. However, even this first sentence reveals some important insights into Paul's thinking about justification by faith. The first thing we observe is that the meaning of Galatians 2:15–21 depends on knowing who is included in the pronoun "We." They are Cephas and Paul. Paul has already identified Cephas with early Christian missionary activity to the Jews, while Paul claims for himself the mission to Gentile Christians (Gal. 2:7–8), but Paul himself is a Jew. Therefore, "We" refers to Cephas and Paul, who *both* know (or should know) that no one is acquitted by obeying Jewish Law. That is, Jews are not favored over Gentiles when it comes to justification. Our diagram of Galatians 2:15 also reminds us that the context for understanding justification by faith is a problem we have already seen in Acts of the Apostles: What obligations should be imposed on Gentiles who wish to join this Jesus movement? Notice that Paul calls the Gentiles "sinners" and contrasts them with Jews "by birth." This bias probably does not reflect Paul's own thinking, but we can imagine some of his Jewish Christian colleagues, like Peter or James, saying something like this.

or attitude of openness and receptivity, not an activity of the mind and will. Quite simply, it depends on **grace**, that is, God's gift.

Paul will go on to argue how both Jews and Gentiles need justification (i.e., acquittal) because all humanity has broken covenant relationship with God. Moreover, for both groups, justification depends on God's grace and is available to all who trust in Jesus. It has nothing to do with observance of Jewish Law because the Law condemns; it cannot acquit. Simply stated, Paul's teaching on justification by faith is born out of a concern about whether Gentile Jesus followers should be required to observe Jewish Law, as are their Jewish brothers and sisters. This raises an interesting question for today's Christians who struggle with the teaching of "faith versus works," which, although it has its roots in Paul's teaching on justification by faith, has nothing to do with whether Gentile Christians ought to be required to obey Jewish Law. Instead, in the contemporary Christian context, it has become a question of whether good works contribute in any way to one's salvation. Is this a distortion of Paul's teaching on justification by faith? How do we take a teaching like justification by faith, which originated within a specific historical situation, and faithfully reinterpret it for later generations living in a different place and time?

## DEMONSTRATIONS OF JUSTIFICATION BY FAITH

Immediately following his summary teaching on justification by faith (Gal. 2:15–21), Paul provides six demonstrations in support of this teaching. Altogether they make an argument, based on real people's experience, for why justification by faith is the correct way to understand how humanity comes into right relationship with God. These demonstrations can be outlined as follows:

1. The Galatian communities' experience of first receiving the Spirit (Gal. 3:1–5)
2. The example of Abraham—a midrash (Gal. 3:6–26)
3. Baptism (Gal. 3:27–29)
4. The example of Abraham—a midrash (Gal 4:1–11)
5. The Galatian communities' experience of first receiving Paul's gospel (Gal. 4:12–20)
6. The allegory of Hagar and Sarah (Gal. 4:21–31)

If we set aside, for a moment, the allegory of Hagar and Sarah, which serves a dual purpose of demonstrating the difference between justification by faith and justification through works of the Law and advising the Galatian communities on what to do with these preachers of a "different gospel," an interesting pattern emerges. The first and fifth demonstrations are similar insofar as Paul is calling the Galatian communities back to their first encounter when he preached to them the message of Jesus Christ and the moment when they first received the Holy Spirit. Do they really want to give up all that for the sake of this "different gospel" (Gal. 3:6–26; 4:12–20)?

The second and fourth demonstrations go together because they have Abraham as their example. Abraham is an apt choice for these two demonstrations because of the quotation from Genesis: Abraham "believed the Lord and the Lord reckoned it to him as righteousness" (Gen. 15:6). Playing on the meaning of Abraham's name ("Father of Nations"), Paul argues that Christ is the one heir of Abraham through whom the promise is fulfilled for all the Gentiles and that the Law, which came later (through Moses), cannot negate the promise (Gal. 3:6–26). Later, again playing on the theme of inheritance, Paul argues that, as Abraham's children, they are no longer slaves but rather heirs to the promise and children of God. If they accept this "different gospel," they will enslave themselves once again. "Why do you want to do that?" he asks, in apparent dismay (Gal. 4:1–11).

Perhaps you have already noticed. Paul appears to be using a chiasm to structure these five demonstrations into a coherent whole. Again, the chiasm is a literary technique that an ancient writer would use to make a point or highlight a particular theme. It is constructed in such a way that the first unit of text corresponds to the last unit of the same passage, the second unit corresponds to the second to the last unit of the passage, and so on. If the chiasm has an even number of units, the outermost elements are the ones that the writer wants to highlight. If the chiasm has an odd number of units, then the focal point is the central element. In this case, our chiasm has an odd number of elements. Paul has placed in the center of his chiasm a profoundly powerful proclamation of the life they share in baptism:

> As many of you as were baptized into Christ have clothed yourselves with Christ. There is no longer Jew or Greek, there is no longer slave or free, there is no longer male and female; for all of you are one in Christ Jesus. And if you belong to Christ, then you are Abraham's offspring, heirs according to the promise. (Gal. 3:27–29)

What more is there to say about justification or right relationship with God? Because of their baptism into Christ, they ought not to seek justification by works of the Law; they are already justified by God through faith in Christ Jesus.

## THE ALLEGORY OF HAGAR AND SARAH

Let us turn, now, to Paul's sixth demonstration concerning justification by faith. As we have already mentioned, this demonstration is different from the previous five because it not only demonstrates the difference between justification by faith and justification through works of the Law but also advises the Galatian communities about what to do with these preachers of a "different gospel." In essence, it is a call to action. Paul begins with a challenge to the Galatian churches, which, when paraphrased, sounds like this: "So you want to do what Jewish Law requires? You want to embrace this 'different gospel' that those other people taught you? Then listen to what the Law says!" (Gal. 4:21).

Paul develops this sixth demonstration and call to action by means of an allegory about Sarah and Hagar, the wife and the concubine of Abraham, respectively (Gal. 4:22). An **allegory** is a method of interpretation in which characters or events in a story are given a symbolic or spiritual meaning beyond their literal meaning. By mapping out, in table form, what Paul has to say about Abraham's wife and concubine and their two sons in Galatians 4:22–31, we can illustrate his allegorical associations like this:

| Hagar | Sarah |
|---|---|
| A slave woman | A free woman |
| Her son, born according to the flesh (i.e., by Abraham's action) | Her son, born through the promise (i.e., by God's word) |
| Covenant from Mount Sinai, the present Jerusalem | Covenant of Jerusalem above (referring to the restored Jerusalem promised by the prophets but not yet realized; see Isaiah 51:2–6 and Zechariah 2:10–12) |
| A mother bearing children for slavery (i.e., under the Law) | Our mother (referring to Zion, the restored Jerusalem of the prophets' visions; see Psalms 87:5) bearing children for freedom |

After laying out these allegorical parallels, Paul recites a segment from the Law (Jewish scriptures) to demonstrate that God favors Sarah over Hagar (Gal. 4:27). Using the footnotes or cross-references of your Bible, you will see that the quotation comes from Isaiah 54, in which the prophet is speaking God's word of consolation to Jerusalem, whose population had been dispersed through the Babylonian Exile. Paul changes the verb "to be" from future tense to present tense and applies the prophecy to his allegory, suggesting that the prophecy is fulfilled now in the growth of the Christian community. Next, Paul incorporates a detail of the Hagar/Sarah story that comes not from Genesis but from later interpretations of the Hagar story to explain why Sarah demanded that Abraham send Hagar and her son, Ishmael, away from their house: The older Ishmael was picking on the younger boy, Isaac! Thus, Paul says, just as Ishmael persecuted Isaac, so Gentile Christians should not be surprised that they are being persecuted by their Jewish brothers and sisters.

Finally, as Paul brings the allegory to a close, he reminds his readers of his initial challenge. So says Paul (paraphrased), "If you want to be obedient to Torah Law, you must do what the scriptures say: 'Drive out the slave and her child!'" (Gal. 4:30; cf. Gen. 21:9–10). Of course, originally, these were Sarah's words to Abraham, but in Paul's reinterpretation, they have become God's words to the Galatian Christian communities. They are to drive out those people who demand that they observe Jewish Law because that is what the Law (scripture) says! If they do not, they are in danger of submitting again to "a yoke of slavery" (Gal. 5:1); that is, they will lose their status as free children of Abraham.

This is what Paul thinks is at stake in his teaching on justification—the freedom of the children of God. No wonder he addresses the churches in Galatia with such intensity! But, of course, Paul does not employ the word *freedom* in the same way that today's readers, especially those of Western cultures, might understand it—as freedom from encumbrances or freedom to do what we want. Rather, Paul is talking about freedom for commitment to another—that is, the freedom to become children of God through faith in Jesus Christ and freedom to become "slaves to one another" through love (Gal. 5:13). This freedom, he adds, is not contrary to the Law because the Law can be summed up in a single command: "You shall love your neighbor as yourself" (Gal. 5:14).

## Key Terms

Judaizers

Righteousness

Justification

Justification by works

Justification by faith

Faith

Grace

Allegory

## Questions for Reading

Read Paul's Letter to the Galatians. Use evidence from the letter to answer the following questions.

1. To whom is the letter addressed? What, if anything, can we deduce from the letter about the circumstances of the churches who were its initial recipients?

2. From the Letter to the Galatians, what do we learn about Paul, his life before his conversion to the Christian Way, and his understanding of his mission now?

3. Compare Paul's account of the Jerusalem Conference (Gal. 2:1–10) to Luke's account of the same meeting (Acts 15:1–35). Identify any similarities. What inconsistencies do you find?

4. In his Letter to the Galatians, what does Paul have to say about how Jesus followers are justified (Gal. 2:15–21)? What does the term *justification* mean in this context?

5. Describe in your own words the point of each of Paul's demonstrations in support of his teaching on justification by faith.
   a. The Galatian communities' experience of first receiving the Spirit (Gal. 3:1–5)
   b. The example of Abraham (Gal. 3:6–26) *Note:* Pay careful attention to the point Paul makes with his play on the words *cursed* and *covenant*.
   c. Baptism (Gal. 3:27–29)
   d. The example of Abraham (Gal. 4:1–11) *Note:* Observe how Paul compares the believer's life before baptism to that of a minor [nonadult] child.
   e. The Galatian communities' experience of first receiving Paul's gospel (Gal. 4:12–20)
   f. The allegory of Hagar and Sarah (Gal. 4:21–31)

6. In light of the whole of Galatians 5, what does Paul mean by the statement that "the only thing that counts is faith working through love" (Gal. 5:6)? Does this mean that believers do or do not have to do good works? Explain.

## Questions for Reflection

1. Suppose that Paul is writing this letter today to a Christian community that had been prompted to take up a "different gospel." What might that "different gospel" be in our contemporary culture? How do you think Paul would respond today?

2. In response to the question about whether Jesus followers ought to be circumcised or not (i.e., whether converts need to become Jewish first), Paul says that "the only thing that counts is faith working through love" (Gal. 5:6). What do you think this phrase might mean to today's Christian? How might it be a good motto for the moral life?

3. How might Christian churches' activity in the world be different from the way it is now if they were to fully live out Paul's understanding of freedom as being "slaves to one another" through love (Gal. 5:13)?

## ACTIVITIES FOR LEARNING

1. Finish diagramming Galatians 2:15–21 according to the rules given above. What insights did you gain about the meaning of Paul's teaching on justification (Gal. 2:15–21) by using this method of close reading and analysis of a text?

2. Locate the baptism rite/ritual of a couple different Christian traditions. One way to find these rites is to look at the church's official prayer book, if it has one. Here are a few: the *Lutheran Book of Worship*, the Roman Catholic *Sacramentary*, the Episcopalian *Book of Common Prayer*, the Presbyterian *Book of Common Worship*, and the *United Methodist Book of Worship*. If you do an internet search, you might try an advanced search using key words like (1) baptism; (2) prayer, rite, ritual, or prayer book; and (3) the name of the denomination you wish to investigate. As always, when using the internet, be careful to assess the credibility of the source. Official church websites are generally reliable, as are academic websites that publish the work of their faculty.

   Carefully examine the prayers and rituals associated with the baptism rites you have chosen to determine what they tell you about each church's understanding of baptism: What function does baptism serve for the community? What are its effects for the individual, and why should someone want to be baptized? How do these churches' understanding of baptism compare with Paul's understanding of baptism, as described in Galatians 3:27–29?

## SOURCES AND RESOURCES

Beker, J. C. *Paul the Apostle: The Triumph of God in Life and Thought.* Philadelphia: Fortress, 1980.

Braxton, Brad Ronnell. *No Longer Slaves: Galatians and African American Experience.* Collegeville, Minn.: Liturgical Press, 2002.

Ebeling, Gerhard. *The Truth of the Gospel: An Exposition of Galatians.* Philadelphia: Fortress, 1985.

Fee, Gordon D. *New Testament Exegesis: A Handbook for Students and Pastors.* 3rd ed. Louisville, Ky.: Westminster John Knox Press, 2002.

Fitzmyer, Joseph. *Paul and His Theology.* Englewood Cliffs, N.J.: Prentice Hall, 1989.

Gager, John G. *The Origins of Anti-Semitism: Attitudes toward Judaism in Pagan and Christian Antiquity.* New York: Oxford University Press, 1985.

Karris, Robert J. *Galatians and Romans.* Collegeville, Minn.: Liturgical Press, 2005.

Martyn, J. Louis. *Galatians: A New Translation with Introduction and Commentary.* Anchor Bible Series, Vol. 33A. New York: Doubleday, 1997.

Nanos, Mark D. *The Irony of Galatians: Paul's Letter in First-Century Context.* Minneapolis, Minn.: Fortress, 2002.

Neyrey, Jerome H. *Paul, in Other Words: A Cultural Reading of His Letters.* Louisville, Ky.: Westminster John Knox Press, 1990.

Perkins, Pheme. *Abraham's Divided Children: Galatians and the Politics of Faith.* Harrisburg, Pa.: Trinity Press International, 2001.

Roetzel, Calvin J. *The Letters of Paul: Conversations in Context.* 4th ed. Louisville, Ky.: Westminster John Knox Press, 1998.

Smiles, Vincent M. *The Gospel and the Law in Galatia: Paul's Response to Jewish-Christian Separatism and the Threat of Galatian Apostasy.* Collegeville, Minn.: Liturgical Press, 1998.

Soards, Marion L. *The Apostle Paul: An Introduction to His Writings and Teaching.* Mahwah, N.J.: Paulist, 1987.

Wiley, Tatha. *Paul and the Gentile Women: Reframing Galatians.* New York: Continuum, 2005.

Williams, Sam. Galatians. Nashville, Tenn.: Abingdon Press, 1997.

Witherington, Ben. *Grace in Galatia: A Commentary on St. Paul's Letter to the Galatians.* Grand Rapids, Mich.: Eerdmans, 1998.

Wright, N. T. *Paul for Everyone: Galatians and Thessalonians.* London: SPCK; Louisville, Ky.: Westminster John Knox Press, 2004.

# CHAPTER 15

# PAUL'S LETTERS TO THE PHILIPPIANS AND PHILEMON

## OVERVIEW

The Letter to the Philippians
- AUTHORSHIP: Paul, probably while in Ephesus
- DATE OF COMPOSITION: Approximately 54–56 C.E.
- INITIAL AUDIENCE: A mostly Gentile Christian community in Philippi that had been influenced by Jewish Christians (or possibly Gentile God-fearers) who insisted on circumcision and certain other Jewish practices for Gentiles who would join the community
- MAJOR TOPICS: One Letter or Several Letter Fragments; The Transformative Power of Knowing Jesus Christ; The Christ Hhymn

The Letter to Philemon
- AUTHORSHIP: Paul, probably while in Ephesus
- DATE OF COMPOSITION: Approximately 55–56 C.E.
- INITIAL AUDIENCE: Philemon, together with Apphia and Archippus, and the church in his house, probably in Colossae
- MAJOR TOPIC: Paul's Views on Slavery

## TIMELINE

| | |
|---|---|
| **c. 36 C.E.** | Paul is converted on the road to Damascus. |
| **49–50C.E.** | The Jerusalem Conference is held to decide about the inclusion of Gentile believers. |
| **51 C.E.** | Paul writes his First Letter to the Thessalonians. |
| **52–60 C.E.** | Felix is procurator of Palestine. |
| **54–55 C.E.** | Paul writes his Letter to the Galatians. |
| **54–56 C.E.** | **Paul writes his Letters to the Philippians and Philemon.** |
| **54–68 C.E.** | Nero is Roman emperor. |
| **55–56 C.E.** | Paul writes his First Letter to the Corinthians. |
| **56–57 C.E.** | Paul writes his Second Letter to the Corinthians. |
| **57–58 C.E.** | Paul writes his Letter to the Romans. |
| **60–62 C.E.** | Festus is procurator of Palestine. |
| **64 C.E.** | Peter and Paul are martyred in Rome. |

As you already know, this leg of our journey through the New Testament is dedicated to the letters associated with Paul. On this next stop, we encounter two Pauline letters sometimes known as the prison letters. These are the Letters to the Philippians and to Philemon. In Acts of the Apostles, Luke tells of two times when Paul was imprisoned and another time when he was arrested but not put in jail. Paul himself says he was imprisoned many times (2 Cor. 6:5; 11:23). Where was he imprisoned and when was he writing? How does his imprisonment affect his correspondence to the Christian communities to whom these letters are addressed? We will tackle these and other questions as we investigate these two letters.

## THE LETTER TO THE PHILIPPIANS

Paul's Letter to the Philippians is among the most tender of his letters, revealing the genuine affection he has for this Christian community at Philippi. It also contains some of the New Testament's most beautifully poetic and powerful statements about the person and mission of Jesus Christ. Before we explore some of these dimensions of the Letter to the Philippians, however, let's review what biblical scholars are saying about where Paul was located when he wrote this letter and the original audience and date of composition for the letter as well as some questions about the unity of this letter.

## LOCATION AND DATE OF COMPOSITION

In his Letter to the Philippians, Paul indicates that he is in prison even as he is writing to the community (Phil. 1:7, 13, 17; 4:21). Acts of the Apostles mentions two times when Paul was imprisoned. One was in Caesarea in northern Palestine, probably in 58–60 C.E. (Acts 23:33–26:32), and the other was in Rome in 61–63 C.E. (Acts 28:16–30). Acts also describes a time when Paul was arrested at Ephesus (in modern Turkey), though Luke does not say that Paul was actually imprisoned there (Acts 19:23–41). The date would have been around 54–56 C.E. But remember that Luke is not always the most reliable source for historical information about the life of Paul. At any rate, having no better information with which to work, biblical scholars have explored each of these places to determine where Paul was when he wrote the Letter to the Philippians.

The first step in this sleuthing task is to look for clues in the letter itself. We have already observed that Paul was in prison when he wrote the letter. He also indicates that there were members of the "praetorian guard" (Phil. 1:13) in the place where he was imprisoned and that there were Christians among the "emperor's household" in that place (Phil. 4:22). The praetorian guard consisted of servants, guards, and officials of the emperor's administration. Because they belonged to the emperor, they were considered part of his household. There was a large contingent in Rome, of course, but also at major administrative centers throughout the empire, most notably Caesarea and Ephesus.

Wherever Paul is at the time he is writing this letter—Rome, Caesarea, or Ephesus—he has Timothy with him, and he is able to make frequent contacts with the Christian community in Philippi. In fact, there are indications in this letter that this may be Paul's

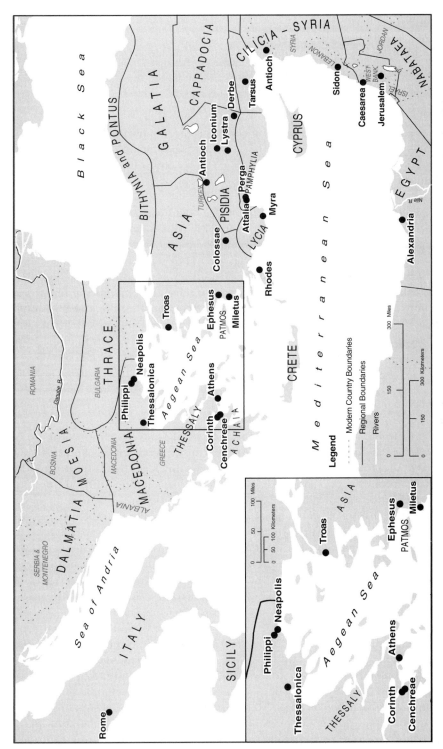

First-century Mediterranean world, showing Rome, Caesarea, Ephesus, and Philippi. The inset in the map is highlighting Ephesus and Philippi.

fifth communication since his imprisonment. The sequence of contacts might have gone like this:

1. The Philippian Christian community learns that Paul is in prison.
2. They send Epaphroditus to Paul with a gift (Phil. 4:15).
3. They find out that Epaphroditus is deathly sick (Phil. 2:26, 30).
4. Epaphroditus learns that they are worrying about him (Phil. 2:26).
5. Paul tells them that he is sending (or has sent) Epaphroditus back to them (Phil. 2:25–30). Paul also writes that he intends to send Timothy to them, presumably with the understanding that he will return to Paul with further news about them (Phil. 2:19–23).

Such frequent and regular contact means that Paul has to be relatively close to Philippi. The distance between Caesarea and Philippi ranges from 900 to 1,100 miles, depending on whether one is traveling by boat or by foot. Likewise, the distance between Rome and Philippi ranges from 700 to more than 900 miles. However, the travel distance between Ephesus and Philippi was more like 400 miles. Given the relative locations of these two cities, the travel time has been estimated at seven to nine days one way, considerably less time than the other two journeys would have entailed. This is the principal reason why biblical scholars think that Paul was imprisoned in Ephesus when he wrote to the Christian community at Philippi. If so, then his Letter to the Philippians most likely was written between 54 and 56 C.E.

## AUDIENCE

Located on the Egnatian Way, part of the Roman highway system used for commerce and for moving troops throughout the empire, Philippi was an important Roman city. Acts 16:12 describes it as a colony, meaning that it was populated by retired Roman military personnel. Alexander the Great's father, Philip II, brought the city under Macedonian rule in 356 B.C.E., and he is the one for whom the city is named. Later, in 168 B.C.E., it was brought under Roman rule. In 42 B.C.E., the city was the site of the battle between Mark Antony and Octavian (also known as **Augustus**) and the assassins of Julius Caesar, Brutus and Cassius. The victorious armies were then settled in the city as reward for their good service. Because the city was a Roman colony, it was governed by Roman law, and Latin was its official language. However, because of its location on a major trade route, people also would have spoken Greek.

According to Acts of the Apostles, Paul may have established the Christian community in Philippi as early as 50 C.E. He had at least some success preaching the gospel among members of the Jewish synagogue there but also among God-fearers— Gentiles who had significant contacts with the Jewish community (Acts 16:11–40). However, like the Galatian Christian communities, this mostly Gentile community appears to have been influenced by certain Jewish Christians (or perhaps other Gentile God-fearers) who insisted on circumcision as a requirement for membership in the community. Apparently, these folks made quite an impression because Paul takes great pains to refute their message. First, he warns the community about accepting their demand for circumcision (Phil. 3:2). Second, he "redefines" circumcision, saying that the truly circumcised are those who worship in the Spirit and boast in Christ (Phil. 3:3). Third, he defends his authority to tell them what to do, saying that he is a member of the tribe of Benjamin, circumcised on the eighth day, trained as a Pharisee, and righteous (blameless) under the Law (Phil. 3:3–6). You can almost hear him saying, "I'm clearly more Jewish than they are, so listen to me on this issue of circumcision!"

We have no reason to think that the Christian community at Philippi was any different from the other communities that Paul founded: mostly Gentile and drawn from a range of socioeconomic classes. However, Acts of the Apostles and the Letter to the Philippians itself suggest that the sociological diversity of the Philippian church extended even to the inclusion of women in important leadership roles in this community. Acts 16:11–16 describes Paul and Silas (and perhaps Luke?) going to a synagogue outside of the city on Sabbath and talking to the women gathered there. One of the women is Lydia, a "worshiper of God" (probably a synonym for God-fearer) and a trader in purple cloth from Thyratira. After listening to Paul's teachings, she asks to be baptized, together with her whole household. Apparently, Paul maintains contact with her, later visiting the Christian community that gathers at her home (Acts 16:40). Further, in his letter to the Philippian community, Paul mentions two women—Euodia and Syntyche—who are having some kind of disagreement. Unfortunately, we don't know the nature of the dispute, but you should notice that Paul calls them "co-workers" and describes them as having struggled beside him "in the work of the gospel" (Phil. 4:3).

## OUTLINE OF THE LETTER

In some respects, this letter is rather straightforward, possessing all of the standard elements of a letter without much deviation:

1. Philippians 1:1–2—Opening
2. Philippians 1:3–11—Thanksgiving
3. Philippians 1:12–3:1a—Body
4. Philippians 3:1b–4:9—Paraenesis
5. Philippians 4:10–23—Concluding comments and letter closing

A couple items are worthy of note, however. First, you will notice that Paul addresses this letter to the church at Philippi together with "the bishops and deacons" (Phil. 1:1). Perhaps you recognize these titles because they describe officeholders in some of today's Christian churches. The Greek word for bishop is *episkopos,* meaning "one who oversees," while the Greek word for deacon is *diakonos,* meaning "one who serves." In Paul's time, these terms likely do not describe ordained members of the community. Rather, they should be viewed simply as Paul's acknowledgment of persons who complete certain tasks for the community. Therefore, we should not assume that the church at Philippi had an organized structure and ordained ministers like those we see by the beginning of the second century C.E. Second, the division between the body of the letter and its paraenesis is somewhat arbitrary, since the body contains moral exhortation, just as the paraenesis contains elements one might otherwise include in the body of the letter.

## ONE LETTER OR SEVERAL LETTER FRAGMENTS?

Biblical scholars have observed that this letter, like the Second Letter to the Corinthians, has several literary seams—that is, breaks or interruptions in the text—suggesting that the letter we possess today is not the same one that Paul first sent to the Philippian community. Instead, it may have been compiled after the fact from letter fragments that had been preserved by Paul's communities. The most obvious of these literary seams is at Philippians 3:1, but scholars have detected other possible literary seams between 4:7 and 4:8 and between 4:9 and 4:10. Some English translations, for example, the New Revised Standard Version, show these breaks in the text by inserting spaces between the verses. Those who think this letter is made up of two letter fragments divide the text as follows:

Letter A—Philippians 3:1b–4:20
Letter B—Philippians 1:1–3:1a and 4:21–23

Archeological remains of a Byzantine church (560 C.E.) built on the ancient palaestra (wrestling school) of Philippi, Greece. *Picture Desk, Inc./Kobal Collection.*

They describe Letter A as the letter Paul sent after having received the gift of the community that was delivered by Epaphroditus, whereas Letter B is the one that Paul sent to the community after Epaphroditus recovered from his illness.

Biblical scholars who think this letter is made up of three letter fragments divide the text as follows:

Letter A—Philippians 4:10–20

Letter B—Philippians 1:1–3:1a, together with 4:4–7 and 4:21–23

Letter C—Philippians 3:1b–4:3 and 4:8–9

According to this theory, Letter A is the letter in which Paul acknowledges the community's gift sent through Epaphroditus, while Letter C is what remains of a "scolding" letter in which Paul warns the community against following a "different gospel" than the one he taught. Letter B appears to be a somewhat generic letter having a theme of rejoicing.

What shall we say? Is the Letter to the Philippians a single letter, or is it a combination of two or even three letter fragments? As we shall see with the Letters to the Corinthians, it is certainly possible that Paul wrote more than one letter to the

Ruins of the gateway into the city of Philippi, which was built for Octavian's sister, Octavia (42 B.C.E.). This was the place where Octavian and Mark Antony defeated Brutus and Cassius, the central figures in an assassination plot that resulted in the death of Julius Caesar (44 B.C.E.).

Philippian community. He indicates as much when he says, "To write the same things to you is not troublesome to me, and for you it is a safeguard" (Phil. 3:1). However, biblical scholars have not been able to agree about whether this letter is a unity (preserved for us as it was originally written) or a redaction of two or more letter fragments. Since the level of disagreement is high and since our understanding of the letter is not substantially enhanced by dividing and rearranging the text, we will read it "as is"—that is, in the form that the early church preserved and passed it on.

## THE TRANSFORMATIVE POWER OF KNOWING JESUS CHRIST

The Letter to the Philippians contains some of the most beautiful and inspiring statements about how Paul's life had been changed by his experience of the risen Christ. You might even think of this letter as a testimonial of someone who "knows" Jesus Christ and has been "born again" through faith in Christ. However, for Paul, faith is not merely an intellectual assent. It is a kind of self-emptying, a total giving over of oneself to Christ. Likewise, knowing Christ is not something that one does with one's mind. Rather, knowing means "experiencing" Christ with one's whole being. For Paul, this means suffering as he suffered. Listen to Paul's own words:

- "Christ will be exalted now as always in my body, whether by life or by death. For to me, living is Christ and dying is gain." (Phil. 1:20–21)
- "And this is God's doing. For he has graciously granted you the privilege not only of believing in Christ, but of suffering for him as well." (Phil. 1:28–29)
- "For his sake I have suffered the loss of all things, and I regard them as rubbish, in order that I may gain Christ. . . . " (Phil. 3:8)
- "I want to know Christ and the power of his resurrection and the sharing of his sufferings by becoming like him in his death, if somehow I may attain the resurrection from the dead." (Phil. 3:10–11)
- "[Jesus] will transform the body of our humiliation that it may be conformed to the body of his glory, by the power that also enables him to make all things subject to himself." (Phil. 3:21)

This is the source and summit of Paul's joy, and in this spirit, Paul urges the Philippian community to "rejoice in the Lord always" (Phil. 4:4; cf. Phil. 1:18; 2:17–18; 3:1; 4:10).

## THE CHRIST HYMN

Known as the Christ hymn, Philippians 2:6–11 contains Paul's most comprehensive statement concerning the transformative power of the death and resurrection of Jesus. A quick review of books and journal articles on the Letter to the Philippians will show that a tremendous amount of time and energy has been devoted to the study of this hymn. Scholars of the Letter to the Philippians have tried to reconstruct the original hymn in order to determine exactly how Paul edited it when he incorporated it into this new literary setting. They have also inquired about Paul's Christology. What did Paul mean when he wrote about Christ being in the "form" of God and taking on the "likeness" of a human (Phil. 2:6–7)? Of what did Christ "empty" himself (Phil. 2:7), and in what sense did he "humble" himself (Phil. 2:8)? What is it that Christ chose not to "seize, cling to, or exploit" (Phil. 2:6)?

You can see that the language of this hymn is rich and multilayered in meaning, giving rise to multiple Christological interpretations. Some scholars read this hymn as a precursor of the later fourth- and fifth-century-C.E. debates about the humanity and divinity of Jesus Christ. They understand Paul to be saying that Jesus Christ is of the same substance or essence as God but that he chose not to exploit his special relationship with God. Instead, he "emptied" himself of his divinity in order to be born in resemblance of human beings. Because Christ went so far as to give over his life in obedience to God's will, God restored him to his rightful place as Lord of creation.

Others say that Paul intended to use an Adam typology when he adapted this traditional hymn. If so, then the hymn would be interpreted as follows: Like Adam, Jesus Christ was created in the image and likeness of God, but unlike Adam, he chose not to seize on that special relationship. That is, he did not try to make himself equal to God, like Adam and Eve did when they sinned against God in the Garden of Eden (cf. Gen. 3:1–7). And unlike Adam, whose pride was his downfall, Christ humbled himself in obedience to God's will, even to the point of death. But humility before God will always be rewarded. Thus, God exalted him in the resurrection, making him Lord of creation.

We may never be able to fully resolve the question of what kind of Christology Paul intended to express in the Christ hymn. However, we can speculate about why Paul incorporated it into his letter. Look carefully at the way he introduces the hymn. He writes, "Let the same mind be in you that was in Christ Jesus" (Phil. 2:5); that is, "Have the same attitude or orientation toward the Christian life, as Jesus Christ" (Phil. 2:5). Paul makes the same point elsewhere in the letter when he exhorts the community to live their lives "in a manner worthy of the gospel of Christ" (Phil. 1:27) and to do nothing out of selfish ambition but to act humbly in putting other people's interests ahead of their own (Phil. 2:3). Thus, Paul exhorts his hearers to imitate the pattern of Jesus' life and death with the understanding that the community will indeed share in Christ's glory if they obediently share in his suffering (cf. Phil. 2:12).

In other words, even though this hymn is important for its Christological message (Who is Jesus as the Christ?), Paul apparently included it for its **soteriological** teaching (How will we be saved?). Thus, he tells the Philippian community that believers must be of the "same mind" as Jesus Christ, imitating him in humility, self-emptying, obedience, and suffering. And just as surely as God exalted Jesus, they can trust that God will reward them on the day of Christ (i.e., the parousia). Is there any better message of joy and consolation? No wonder Paul constantly exhorts the community, "Rejoice in the Lord."

## THE CONTEMPORARY SIGNIFICANCE OF THE CHRIST HYMN

The biblical scholar Robert Karris, OFM, has written an analysis of the major hymns of the New Testament entitled *A Symphony of New Testament Hymns*. Here's what he has to say about the contemporary significance of the Philippians hymn. You will need to have the text of the Christ hymn (Phil. 2:6–11) in front of you as you read Karris's analysis so that you can more easily follow his argument:

> Philippians 2:2–5 and 2:12 are vitally important for interpreting the immediate context of the hymn in Philippians 2:6–11. I treat 2:12 first. From the inferential words "so then," which commences 2:12, it is easy to see that Paul quotes the hymn of 2:6–11 to influence the conduct of the Philippians: "So then, my beloved, obedient as you have always been, not only when I am present but all the more now that I am absent, *work out your salvation with fear and trembling*" [italics mine]. But it is only when we turn to 2:2–5 that we see what conduct Paul is trying to persuade the Philippians to adopt. And we should not be surprised to see that Paul's concern is about unity. . . .
>
> With the evidence in hand of similar terminology in both 2:2–5 and 2:6–8, we can appreciate the argument that some scholars make that the hymn of 2:6–11 is used by Paul to show Christ Jesus is the ethical example to the Philippians. That is, if the Philippians would only follow the example of the self-sacrificing Christ Jesus, there would be greater unity among them. While this argument is helpful and spiritually challenging, it needs to be supplemented by another line of thought to show how Christ Jesus' exaltation (stanzas four through six) is also interpreted by the immediate context of 2:2–5. For surely Christians' imitation of Christ Jesus comes to an insurmountable barrier when we consider that Christ Jesus was exalted by God. That's not in store for us Christians, no matter how perfectly we imitate the humiliation of Christ Jesus, or is it?
>
> Let me highlight this mystery from another angle. Because of the parallel passage of 3:21 we now know more of the import of the drama of 2:6–11 and we realize that this drama is not just Christ Jesus'. It is also ours as we, who are humbling ourselves in imitation of Christ Jesus, await our Savior who will transform us. (Karris, *A Symphony of New Testament Hymns*, 46–47, 49)

As you read Paul's Letter to the Philippians, pay special attention to how he develops this theme of joy and rejoicing. Certainly, he does not mean that they should be giddy with laughter, but what kind of joy does he have in mind? According to Paul, what is the source of this joy? How might it have manifested itself in the Philippian community? The "Questions for Reading" section at the end of this chapter will help you explore some of these questions.

## THE LETTER TO PHILEMON

Like most of the letters we have investigated so far, the Letter to Philemon has Paul as its author. There are a couple things that distinguish it from the others, however. First, it is the shortest of Paul's letters, having only 25 verses and no divisions by chapters. Second, it is the only letter of the New Testament that is addressed to an individual. In addition, its subject is a runaway slave. Why, then, do Christians bother to read it today? Before we attempt to answer this question, let's review what biblical scholars have concluded about the intended audience for this letter and its date of composition.

## LOCATION AND DATE OF COMPOSITION

In the opening section of this letter, Paul describes himself as "a prisoner of Christ Jesus" (Phlm. 1). As already mentioned in our investigation of the Letter to the Philippians, this detail has led biblical scholars to speculate about when and where Paul was in prison. Paul's Letter to the Philippians gave us few clues about where he was located at the time of its writing. Unfortunately, his Letter to Philemon gives us even fewer— only a request that they prepare a room for him for his upcoming visit (Phlm. 22).

Because Paul's letter shows that he expects to get out of his "difficult" situation of imprisonment and because several of the persons named in this letter—most notably, Onesimus, the slave who ran away from Philemon's house, and Archippus— are otherwise associated with Colossae (see Col. 4:9–10, 17), the majority view is that Paul was in Ephesus at the time of this writing. The biblical scholars' reasoning is as follows: An escaped slave might be able to make it to Colossae, approximately 110 miles travel distance from Ephesus, but a trip to Rome or Caesarea would have been impossible without substantial assistance or financial resources. If Paul was in Ephesus at the time this letter was written, then it was probably written between 54 and 56 C.E. and most likely toward the end of this period, since he foresees that he will soon be released.

## AUDIENCE

Paul identifies the recipients of this letter as Philemon, whom he calls a "dear friend" and a "co-worker" in the ministry of the gospel, together with Apphia and Archippus, whom he calls his "fellow soldier" (Phlm. 1), as well as the church in this place. Because this is a personal letter, Paul does not explain who these people are. However, we can safely assume that Philemon was an affluent Christian, since he owned slaves and the local church met at his house (Phlm. 2). Remember that early Christian communities did not have separate church buildings for worship. Instead, a wealthy member of the community hosted the group's gatherings. In many cases, that person also served as the community's leader. Apphia is probably Philemon's wife, but we can only speculate about Archippus's identity. Some have suggested that he is Philemon's son. Others have said that he is the head of this house-church. In fact, we have little evidence to favor one theory over another.

Because Onesimus, Philemon's slave, and Archippus are associated with Colossae elsewhere in the New Testament (see Col. 4:9, 17), most scholars conclude that Philemon and his house-church were located there. The opening and closing sections of the Deutero-Pauline Letter to the Colossians appear to be patterned after the Letter to Philemon, adding further credibility to the theory that this Letter to

Philemon was intended also for the Colossian church (see Phlm. 1, 19; cf. Col. 1:1; 4:18). Colossae was already a very old city at the time of Paul's writing. However, it had declined considerably from its glory days in the fifth century B.C.E., when it was considered a large and wealthy city, known for its wool and cloth-dying industries. A comment by Cicero (*Pro Flacco* 68) suggests that the area in which Colossae was located had a large Jewish population, though Paul's Letter to Philemon does not provide any clues to indicate whether the Christian community there was Jewish Christian, Gentile Christian, or a mix of the two.

## PAUL'S VIEWS ON SLAVERY

The purpose of Paul's Letter to Philemon is to convince Philemon to take back his runaway slave, Onesimus (Phlm. 10–12). Since this is a personal letter between pastor and slave owner, we should not expect to learn how or why Onesimus ran away. However, Paul does make it clear that, once Onesimus found his way to Paul, he has been a devoted servant to Paul in his need (Phlm. 12). Because Paul calls himself Onesimus's father, we can assume that Onesimus was baptized when he was with Paul and now serves under Paul in the ministry of the gospel (Phlm. 10). Concerning Paul's play on the words *useful* and *useless* (Phlm. 11), it might be helpful to know that the name Onesimus means "useful one."

To the observant reader, the Letter to Philemon is extremely problematic because nowhere in this letter does Paul even *hint* at the possibility that slavery is wrong. Certainly, Paul does not condemn the practice. Instead, he blithely engages in an argument designed to get Philemon to take this runaway slave back into his household. Why should a book that allows for such morally reprehensible behavior be considered sacred and canonical? Or does the inclusion of the Letter to Philemon among the books of the New Testament give tacit permission for Christians to own slaves?

Perhaps there is another way to view this letter. Remember that slavery was so much a part of first-century Greco-Roman culture that few people would have been able to gain the perspective of "outsider" in order to challenge the practice. If we looked at certain behaviors and practices among Western cultures of the twenty-first century, we would probably find that we suffer a similar "blindness" because we are simply too close to the situation. For example, depending on your socioeconomic background, you might have never thought about the morality of capitalism. Advocates for the poor argue that capitalism raises some serious moral issues because it works on the presupposition that people become wealthy and powerful at the expense of the poor and weak. However, those of us who benefit from capitalism are usually too close to the situation to see the problems. And what about violence in the media? It has become so thoroughly a part of American music and video experiences that most people no longer register alarm, even when the violence is particularly egregious—that is, not until someone acts out in real life what they have seen in movies or have been playing in video games, and people get killed!

We would have to say, then, that Paul did not recognize the inherent immorality of slavery. At the same time, his letter demonstrates a Christian response to slavery that would have seemed quite radical in his time and place. In this letter, he coaxes and cajoles Philemon to accept Onesimus back and to treat him not as a slave but as a beloved brother in the Lord (Phlm. 16). Imagine how this must have sounded to Philemon's ears, especially in a culture that held such clear divisions of class and economy. We don't know how Philemon responded to Paul's request, but the letter shows that Paul put out his best effort. But does this explain why the early church saw fit to preserve this letter and include it in the New Testament?

Perhaps there is one more thing to consider here. In his Letter to Philemon, we see Paul making concrete what he expressed elsewhere as the essence of baptism and what it means for the way that members of the community of faith ought to behave toward one another. This is what he says about baptism in his Letter to the Galatians:

> As many of you as were baptized into Christ have clothed yourselves with Christ. There is no longer Jew or Greek, there is no longer slave or free, there is no longer male and female; for all of you are one in Christ Jesus. (Gal. 3:27–28)

What Paul is calling for is an egalitarian community of faith—this in a culture that was far from egalitarian. From our social location and temporal perspective, we sometimes look back and notice only that Paul's communities did not realize his vision. But consider Paul's social location. He took a tremendous risk in upsetting the societal order and acted against seemingly impossible odds to advocate for the wellbeing of a single slave. And as we have already seen, this is not the only time that Paul challenged the status quo. If every generation of Christians does what Paul did, heeding his admonition "Imitate me," then perhaps some day Paul's vision will be realized. Thus, the Letter to Philemon stands as a sign of all that is possible for the community of faith and a message of encouragement never to give up the struggle. The community of faith can indeed be a community of equals!

## KEY TERMS

Caesar Augustus                    Soteriological

## QUESTIONS FOR READING

Read Paul's Letter to the Philippians. Use evidence from the text to answer the following questions.

1. Find clues in the Letter to the Philippians that describe Paul's relationship to and his attitude toward this community. How would you describe this relationship? Explain.

2. Are there any clues in this letter concerning Paul's situation, specifically where he's writing and under what conditions? Explain.

3. What arguments does Paul give in support of his right to preach the gospel in the Philippian community? What can you conclude about why he needs to defend himself in the first place?

4. In the Letter to the Philippians, Paul makes several references to the suffering he experiences in his current situation. What does he say about how he makes sense of his suffering or what meaning he attaches to it?

5. In this letter, Paul tells the Philippian community, "Imitate me" (Phil. 3:17). How or in what things does he want them to imitate him?

6. Make a list of all the references to joy and rejoicing in this letter. What does Paul mean when he says "my joy"? Why does he rejoice? Why does he encourage the recipients of this letter to rejoice?

Read Paul's Letter to Philemon. Use evidence from the text to answer the following questions.

7. Who are the recipient(s) of the letter? Find clues in the letter that help us describe Paul's relationship with the recipient(s).

8. Examine the thanksgiving section of this letter (Phlm. 4–7). What does Paul say in order prepare Philemon to hear his request?

9. What does the letter tell us about Paul's relationship to Onesimus? What does it tell us about Onesimus's relationship to Philemon?

10. What problem is Paul attempting to resolve with this letter? How does he propose to resolve it?

11. Describe the kinds of arguments Paul uses to get Philemon to accept his request. To what does he appeal?

## QUESTIONS FOR REFLECTION

1. If we were to take Paul's rejoicing theme from the Letter to the Philippians and translate it into today's context, what would he say about Christians' reason for rejoicing?

2. After reading his Letter to the Philippians, how would you describe Paul's relationship to Jesus Christ? What does he value about this relationship? What aspects, if any, of this kind of relationship might be appealing to Christians today? What aspects might today's Christians find repulsive or difficult to comprehend?

3. While Paul's Letter to Philemon has all the markings of a private letter, it has always been included in the lists of canonical books from the time of Marcion (mid–second century C.E.). See if you can speculate about why early Christian communities might have valued this letter enough to identify it as canonical from the beginning stages of canon formation.

## ACTIVITIES FOR LEARNING

1. Locate two commentaries on the Letter to the Philippians—one that presents the Christ hymn (Phil. 2:6–11) in terms of Adam typology and another that presents it as descriptive of God's "self-emptying" (see above; see also Chapter 1 on

types and typology). Study the biblical scholars' arguments in support of each view. Whose argument is most convincing? Why?

2. Sadly, in the history of the tradition, Christians (even today) have used the Bible to support the right to own slaves as well as the notion that some races of people are inferior to others. In particular, people have cited Genesis 9:18–27 ("the curse of Ham"), Exodus 21 on the buying and selling of slaves, and several New Testament texts including the Letter to Philemon. See if you can locate one of these arguments in favor of slavery so you can see how the argument is constructed and what biblical texts are used to support it. Then locate a contemporary commentary on the same scripture texts to learn how responsible biblical scholars make sense of these texts. Use this information to construct an argument against those who would use the Bible in support of slavery and the inferiority of certain races of people. *Hint:* A good place to begin looking for these arguments is Stephen R. Haynes's book *Noah's Curse: The Biblical Justification of American Slavery.*

## Sources and Resources

Fee, Gordon D. *Philippians.* Downers Grove, Ill.: InterVarsity Press, 1999.

Fitzmyer, Joseph A. *The Letter to Philemon: A New Translation with Introduction and Commentary.* Anchor Bible Series, Vol. 34C. New York: Doubleday, 2000.

Harrington, Daniel J. *Paul's Prison Letters: Spiritual Commentaries on Paul's Letters to Philemon, the Philippians, and the Colossians.* Hyde Park, N.Y.: New City Press, 1997.

Haynes, Stephen R. *Noah's Curse: The Biblical Justification of American Slavery.* Oxford, England: Oxford University Press, 2002.

Karris, Robert J. *A Symphony of New Testament Hymns.* Collegeville, Minn.: Liturgical Press, 1996.

Keegan, Terence J. *First and Second Timothy, Titus, Philemon.* Collegeville, Minn.: Liturgical Press, 2006.

Martin, Ralph P. *The Epistle of Paul to the Philippians: An Introduction and Commentary.* Grand Rapids, Mich.: Eerdmans, 1987.

————. *Ephesians, Colossians, and Philemon.* Atlanta, Ga.: John Knox Press, 1991.

Osiek, Carolyn. *Philippians, Philemon.* Nashville, Tenn.: Abingdon Press, 2000.

Patzia, Arthur G. *Ephesians, Colossians, Philemon.* Peabody, Mass.: Hendrickson, 1990.

Smiles, Vincent M. *First Thessalonians, Philippians, Second Thessalonians, Colossians, Ephesians.* Collegeville, Minn.: Liturgical Press, 2005.

Thompson, Marianne Meye. *Colossians and Philemon.* Grand Rapids, Mich.: Eerdmans, 2005.

Thurston, Bonnie Bowman, and Judith M. Ryan. *Philippians and Philemon.* Collegeville, Minn.: Liturgical Press, 2005.

Wright, N. T. *Paul for Everyone: The Prison Letters: Ephesians, Philippians, Colossians and Philemon.* London: SPCK; Louisville, Ky.: Westminster John Knox Press, 2004.

# CHAPTER 16

# PAUL'S FIRST AND SECOND LETTERS TO THE CORINTHIANS

## OVERVIEW

The First Letter to the Corinthians
- AUTHORSHIP: Paul, perhaps while he was living in Ephesus
- DATE OF COMPOSITION: Probably 55–56 C.E.
- INITIAL AUDIENCE: A Christian community in Corinth; predominantly Gentile but with at least a few members from the Jewish community
- MAJOR TOPICS: Koinonia and the Problem of Factions; Other Problems in the Corinthian Christian community; Paul and Women in Ministry; Paul's Teaching on the Resurrection

The Second Letter to the Corinthians
- AUTHORSHIP: Paul
- DATE OF COMPOSITION: Shortly after the writing of 1 Corinthians, perhaps 56–57 C.E.
- INITIAL AUDIENCE: Same as for 1 Corinthians
- MAJOR TOPICS: The "Tearful" Letter; Paul's Ministry and Ministry in Christ; An Interruption; Paul's Collection for the Jerusalem Church

## TIMELINE

| | |
|---|---|
| c. 36 C.E. | Paul is converted on the road to Damascus. |
| 49–50 C.E. | The Jerusalem Conference is held to decide about the inclusion of Gentile believers. |
| 51 C.E. | Paul writes his First Letter to the Thessalonians. |
| 52–60 C.E. | Felix is procurator of Palestine. |
| 54–55 C.E. | Paul writes his Letter to the Galatians. |
| 54–56 C.E. | Paul writes his Letters to the Philippians and Philemon. |
| 54–68 C.E. | Nero is Roman emperor. |
| 55–56 C.E. | **Paul writes his First Letter to the Corinthians.** |
| 56–57 C.E. | **Paul writes his Second Letter to the Corinthians**. |
| 57–58 C.E. | Paul writes his Letter to the Romans. |
| 60–62 C.E. | Festus is procurator of Palestine. |
| 64 C.E. | Peter and Paul are martyred in Rome. |

Having traveled to Thessalonica and Galatia, in the present-day country of Turkey, for our tour of Paul's Letters to the Thessalonians and Galatians, we are heading for present-day Greece and the city of Corinth. Here we will tour his First and Second Letters to the Corinthians. When compared to the letters we have already investigated, these letters have features that make them at once similar and distinctive. Like 1 Thessalonians, Paul's First Letter to the Corinthians addresses everyday problems specific to that church community. In fact, this letter describes Paul's responses to a long list of practical problems involving members of the Christian church at Corinth, perhaps because he knew this community very well over an extended period of time. Like Paul's letter to the Galatians, 1 Corinthians has some longer teaching units: one on what it means to heed God's wisdom (1 Cor. 1:18–2:16) and another on what one ought to believe about resurrection from the dead (1 Cor. 15:1–58). Further, as he did in his letter to the Philippians, Paul incorporates traditional prayers and poems into the text of his First Letter to the Corinthians.

But how are these two letters different from the others we have investigated so far? More than in his other letters, Paul lets us see who he is in all his passion and frustration, love and devotion, care and concern. Parts of the letters even read like an ancient soap opera! Through a careful reading of 1 Corinthians and 2 Corinthians, it is possible to glimpse the intensity of Paul's personality and to discern his motives and intentions for the community there. Perhaps this metaphor is fitting: Our study of the Corinthian correspondence gives us a chance to pause in our journey through the New Testament, stop being a tourist for awhile, and get to know some of the folks along the way!

## THE FIRST LETTER TO THE CORINTHIANS

The New Testament contains two letters addressed to the Corinthian Christian community. Because the letters of the New Testament are organized, for the most part, according to length and not chronology, we should not automatically assume that a letter labeled "first" was written before a letter labeled "second." However, in this case, scholars agree that 1 Corinthians was written before 2 Corinthians, so, as we have done many times before, let's pause to summarize what biblical scholars have learned about the authorship, date of composition, audience, and the occasion for writing this First Letter to the Corinthians.

## AUTHORSHIP, DATE OF COMPOSITION, AND OCCASION FOR WRITING

Biblical scholars agree that the First Letter to the Corinthians is Pauline, that is, written by Paul. According to Acts of the Apostles, Paul established the community at Corinth during an eighteen-month residence there, perhaps in 50–51 C.E. (Acts 18:11). This letter was written at some point after he had left Corinth, most likely while he lived in Ephesus (1 Cor. 16:8; cf. Acts 19). The date of composition is often disputed among biblical scholars, but 55–56 C.E. is a generally accepted date.

The Corinthian church was a community that Paul knew well, and we can imagine that its members also knew him pretty well. In addition to the time they had together when Paul lived among them, they apparently corresponded regularly. We see evidence of this already in the First Letter to the Corinthians, where Paul says, "I wrote to you in my letter" (1 Cor. 5:9). Unfortunately, that earlier letter was not preserved and is not available to us today. Thus, 1 Corinthians is at least the second letter that Paul wrote to the church at Corinth, and that doesn't count the canonical Second Letter to the Corinthians, which contains fragments of two and perhaps three additional letters to this community.

In the opening chapters of 1 Corinthians, Paul gives at least one reason for writing this letter. He has received a report from Chloe's people about the community at Corinth, a report that makes him very unhappy—there are divisions within the community (1 Cor. 1:11). Although we know little about Chloe's identity, the context suggests that she may have been a merchant. Her "people," then, would have been servants who had traveled to Corinth on business of some sort and then reported to Paul concerning what they had discovered there. Were Chloe and her servants Christians? Perhaps, but because **Chloe** is not mentioned anywhere else in Paul's writings or in Acts of the Apostles, we can only speculate about whether or how she fits into the early Christian story.

Was there yet another reason for Paul's writing? Apparently, he had recently received a letter from them and he is using this opportunity to respond to their questions and concerns (see 1 Cor. 7:1). We do not know the content of this letter from the community, but we can speculate that its members were asking for clarification concerning some of Paul's earlier teachings or were drawing conclusions, based on his earlier teachings, for which they wanted confirmation. The clearest evidence that Paul was responding, in part, to their letter is his statement "Now concerning the matters about which you wrote . . . " (1 Cor. 7:1). Other statements are somewhat more ambiguous, like "All things are lawful for me," to which Paul adds, "but not all things are beneficial" (1 Cor. 6:12). The latter statement is clearly Paul's, but the former almost certainly is not. In many English translations, the statements of the community are placed in quotation marks so that you can distinguish them from Paul's own words.

## AUDIENCE

The Christian community at Corinth appears to have been predominantly Gentile, with at least a small percentage of its members coming from the Jewish community. Although archeologists have found few remains of synagogue life in first-century Corinth, Philo of Alexandria, a Jewish philosopher at the beginning of the era, wrote that the city had a vital Jewish community at that time. Acts 18 suggests that Priscilla and Aquila, both Jewish Christians, were already actively engaged in ministry in Corinth before Paul arrived. Acts also indicates that Paul began his preaching within the Jewish synagogue when he first arrived in Corinth and moved to the house of Titius Justus, a God-fearer, after Timothy and Silas joined him from Macedonia (Acts 18:5). This is the evidence that scholars use to conclude that the Corinthian community consisted of both Jews and Gentiles.

In a world where class and social standing are firmly fixed, Paul's communities are noteworthy because they included people of several social classes. Among the people mentioned in the First Letter to the Corinthians there is **Crispus**, whom Paul baptized and who had been president of a synagogue at Corinth (1 Cor. 1:14; Acts 18:8), and **Gaius**, who apparently was very wealthy, since his house was big enough that it could contain the "whole church"—that is, a collection of house-churches from the area (1 Cor. 1:14; Rom. 16:23; cf. 1 Cor. 14:23). Apollos was a Jewish rhetorician (an occupation as lucrative as the profession of lawyer today) from Alexandria who, when he became a Christian, gave up his practice to become a missionary preacher (1 Cor. 1:12; 4:6; 16:12: cf. Acts 18:24–19:1). Erastus, who is not identified by name in 1 Corinthians, is elsewhere described as an official of the city of Corinth, perhaps the treasurer, and Timothy's companion on a mission trip to Macedonia, which Paul arranged (Acts 19:22; Rom. 16:23; 2 Tim. 4:20).

This community also knew of women who participated in the evangelizing work of the churches and even held leadership roles. For example, there was the husband-and-wife team, Aquila and Prisca (Priscilla in Acts of the Apostles), whom Paul mentions in the conclusion of this letter (1 Cor. 16:19). They were skilled artisans, making them better off than most of the population but not part of the elite (Acts 18:1). When they are referred to as a couple, Priscilla's name is usually given first, leading biblical scholars to speculate that she was of higher social status than Aquila. Paul called them his co-workers (Rom. 16:3), and they were leaders of a house-church of their own (1 Cor. 16:19). They also likely knew of Phoebe, a female deacon (Rom. 16:1), who had a house in Cenchreae very near to Corinth. Because it is identified as *her* house (not her husband's) and because the church apparently met there, most likely she was a wealthy widow and a patron of the church.

Two other persons are mentioned by name in 1 Corinthians. **Stephanas** may have been one of the persons who brought to Paul the letter to which Paul is responding here (1 Cor. 1:14; 16:15; cf. 1 Cor. 7:1). Cephas, who is also mentioned at the beginning of this letter (1 Cor 1:12), most likely is Peter.

## CORINTH, THE CITY

Located on an isthmus (i.e., land bridge) that links the Peloponnesus peninsula to the mainland of Greece and situated between two seaports, Corinth was the central city of the province of Achaia in Greece and an important trade center. Although the site had already been inhabited for many, many centuries, Corinth was relatively new when Paul visited it because the Romans had destroyed the original city in 146 B.C.E. When they reestablished Corinth in 44 C.E., it was as a Roman colony whose first settlers were freedman (i.e., slaves who had been released from their obligations) originally from Greece, Syria, Egypt, and Judea. As a consequence, the city had a tremendously diverse population base. It sported a rising "middle class" (e.g., artisans, traders), whose members once had belonged to the lower classes but who had later become relatively wealthy. Corinth was also home of the Isthmian games, an all-Hellenic festival, second only to the Olympic games in importance (cf. 1 Cor. 9:24–27). Because of the city's status as a trade center, the people of Corinth were exposed to and familiar with a number of religious movements, including the mystery religions. Artifacts from the city suggest that they participated in the emperor cult as well as a variety of Greek and Egyptian religions. In sum, it was a very cosmopolitan city.

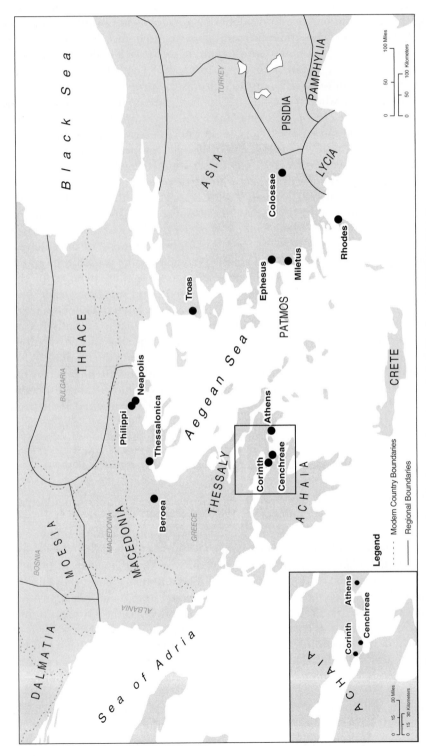

First-century Achaia, Macedonia, and Thrace, including modern boundaries. The inset highlights Corinth.

Whether warranted or not, Corinth also had a somewhat shady or immoral reputation among cities of the area. The Acrocorinth, located on a plateau above the city, was the site of a temple to Aphrodite, the goddess of love, which some say was staffed by as many as a thousand temple prostitutes in its heyday. Archeologists have uncovered the remains of as many as forty-four taverns or liquor stores on the main street of the city, and apparently it was common practice to run a brothel from the same location. Therefore, people used the name of the city to coin words that described the rough and wild lifestyle of Corinth. A "Corinthian girl," for example, was another term for "prostitute." If you wanted to say that you were going out on the town for a night of heavy drinking, you would say that you were going "Corinthying." In other words, Corinth was not altogether different in reputation from the downtown district of a large cosmopolitan city today.

## OUTLINE OF THE LETTER

This outline of Paul's First Letter to the Corinthians is different from some of the ones we have seen earlier insofar as it combines an outline of the formal elements of the letter with summaries of some of its content. Because 1 Corinthians is much longer than the letters we have studied up to this point, an outline of this type can be extremely helpful in keeping track of what is going on in the letter.

1. 1 Corinthians 1:1–3—Opening
2. 1 Corinthians 1:4–9—Thanksgiving
3. 1 Corinthians 1:10–4:21—Body
   a. The problem of factions (1 Cor. 1:10–17)
   b. Teaching on wisdom and the foolishness of the cross (1 Cor. 1:18–2:16)
   c. Application to the Corinthian community (1 Cor. 3:1–23)
   d. Paul's authority (1 Cor. 4:1–21)
4. 1 Corinthians 5:1–14:40—Paraenesis
   a. Sexual sins and immorality in general (1 Cor. 5:1–8)
   b. Avoiding people who are not part of the community (1 Cor. 5:9–13)
   c. Bringing lawsuits before pagan courts (1 Cor. 6:1–11)
   d. Claim of some that "all things are lawful" (1 Cor. 6:12–20)
   e. Marriage and celibacy (1 Cor. 7:1–40)
   f. Christian freedom and the problems of idolatry (1 Cor. 8:1–11:1)
   g. Problems of Christian worship (1 Cor. 11:2–34)
   h. True nature of spiritual gifts (1 Cor. 12:1–14:40)
5. 1 Corinthians 15:1–58—Teaching on resurrection of the dead
6. 1 Corinthians 16:1–24—Additional comments and closing

Notice the amount of space that Paul gives to pastoral problems and ethical teaching in this letter. Spanning nine chapters and parts of other chapters, the paraenesis is massive by comparison to the Pauline letters we investigated earlier. Likewise, this outline highlights some of his longer teaching units, in particular, his teaching on wisdom (1 Cor. 1:18-2:16) and his teaching on resurrection of the dead (1 Cor. 15:1-58), which do not have parallels in the letters we have studied thus far.

## KOINONIA AND THE PROBLEM OF FACTIONS

Already in the thanksgiving section of Paul's First Letter to the Corinthians (1 Cor. 1:4–9), the careful reader can find clues about Paul's major concerns in dealing with this community. The key theme is **koinonia**, a Greek word that means "community" or "partnership." We should not be surprised to hear someone talk about a church community in terms of koinonia, since church always involves groups of people. However, the fellowship to which Paul was calling the community is fellowship with Jesus Christ. For Paul, the community members have fellowship with one another on account of or as a consequence of their shared fellowship with Jesus Christ. Further, Paul grounds this koinonia in the faithfulness of God, who called the community to fellowship by grace. In other words, this is no ordinary partnership. However, the reader of 1 Corinthians soon discovers that partnership is exactly what is lacking in the Christian community in Corinth.

In the first major section of the body of this letter (1 Cor. 1:10–4:21), Paul describes three problems that are creating difficulties in the churches at Corinth, precisely because they disrupt koinonia. The first problem involves a dispute over leadership and people who think they are better than others in the community on account of the person who baptized them (1 Cor. 1:10–2:16). In simple terms, Paul's response would sound something like this: "You may have other guides, but I am your only 'father.' Imitate me." Paul goes on to describe his mission on their behalf: to proclaim the gospel "so that the cross of Christ might not be emptied of its power" (1 Cor. 1:17). Reading between the lines, you have to wonder if members of the Corinthian community were proclaiming a risen Christ and, at the same time, trying to ignore or reason away the difficulty of his crucifixion. This might explain why Paul writes so passionately about God's wisdom and what the world calls foolishness. Human wisdom tells us that a gospel founded on the notion of a crucified messiah is foolishness, but Paul argues that this gospel is the *fullness* of the wisdom of God and something that God had decreed "before the ages" (1 Cor. 2:7), meaning from the beginning of time.

In his argument about God's wisdom, Paul is addressing yet another problem of the Corinthian community: divisions based on some people's claims to possess superior wisdom or knowledge (1 Cor. 3:1–23). Apparently, some people thought that they were spiritually more mature than others in the community of Christians. Paul responds by appealing to commonsense knowledge. He says something like this: "Not many of you are wise—and neither am I!" And against pride, or what he calls being "puffed up," Paul says, "God chooses the weak to shame the wise." Against their claim to have superior knowledge, he tells them that he's only been giving them milk. Why? Because they are spiritual babies! The proof is in their behavior; they hate the brothers and sisters.

The third problem that Paul addresses in the early section of this letter is the community's perceptions of Paul himself—or at least this is Paul's take on the situation. Paul indicates that some are judging him as inadequate, but, in his view, they are the ones who are at fault (1 Cor. 4:1–13). Paul's response goes something like this: "Look at my own life and that of Apollos. We are merely stewards of God's mysteries (i.e., plan). We do not judge ourselves; only God has a right to judge." Paul goes on to charge them with a mistaken sense of self-importance. They should remember that everything they have is a gift and not something that they can claim as their own accomplishment. If they weren't so "puffed up," there wouldn't be factions in the community in the first place.

If you pay careful attention to Paul's rhetoric, you should be able to detect some of his feelings toward this community. The most obvious example is his threat to punish them! Apparently, their behavior has caused him so much pain that he threatens them as a concerned father might threaten his child: "What would you prefer? Am I to come to you with a stick, or with love in a spirit of gentleness?" (1 Cor. 4:21). Of course, Paul's words should not be used to sanction physical punishment of children today—or adults, for that matter. Rather, they simply reflect first-century C.E. child-rearing practices. At the same time, his scolding words reveal just how intensely Paul cares for this community. It's safe to say that he loves them as much as, or more than, any mother could love her biological children, and he aches with pain when they fail him.

Hopefully, these few examples help to show the importance that Paul places on koinonia. But, again, we need to remember that Paul is not concerned simply with "getting along" in this section of his First Letter to the Corinthians. However, we can also see that the biggest threats to koinonia are factions based on people's arrogance or sense of self-importance. In light of this problem, Paul uses another image to describe the Christian community, namely, the temple of God. "Do you not know that you are God's temple and that God's Spirit dwells in you?" (1 Cor. 3:16), asks Paul. Being God's temple requires a holy way of life, and that is the subject of the next section of this letter.

## OTHER PROBLEMS IN THE CORINTHIAN CHRISTIAN COMMUNITY

In the paraenesis of this First Letter to the Corinthians (1 Cor. 5:1–14:40), Paul addresses a number of pastoral questions that were brought to his attention either by Chloe's people or by the Corinthian community itself in their letter to him. In order to understand exactly what is going on, you have to pay careful attention to the way in which Paul introduces the topic he is about to address. For example, in 1 Corinthians 5:1, he says, "It is actually reported." This phrase probably refers to the report Paul received from Chloe's people concerning the things that were going on in Corinth. Likewise, in 1 Corinthians 5:9, Paul says, "I wrote to you in my letter not to associate with sexually immoral persons—not at all meaning the immoral of this world." This comment suggests that part of the problem of the community at Corinth comes from their own *misinterpretation* of Paul's earlier teachings to them.

Another example of the Corinthian community's possible misinterpretation of Paul's teaching concerns the Law. From the Letter to the Galatians, we know that Paul said things like "no one will be justified by the Law" (Gal. 2;16) and "Do not let yourselves become slaves of the Law" (e.g., Gal. 5:1) and "for freedom Christ has set us free" (Gal. 5:1). Hopefully, you have not understood those words to mean that Paul thought he could do anything he wanted without regard for other people's needs. And yet we can imagine some people from the Corinthian community hearing Paul say, "We are no longer slaves of the Law," and *wrongly* concluding, "That's right! No one can tell us what to do!" Thus, Paul's words, "All things are lawful for me" (1 Cor. 6:12a), most likely come from the Corinthian church's letter to him, and he answers, "But not all things are beneficial," in order to correct their thinking (1 Cor. 6:12b).

The pastoral problems that Paul addresses in this section of the letter are enumerated in the outline above. When you examine what Paul has to say about each problem, you first need to accurately identify the problem. For example, when Paul complains about the man who is sleeping with his stepmother (or mother) (1 Cor. 5:1–8), you might jump to the conclusion that he is concerned about immoral sexual behavior—and to some extent he is—but the real problem is the community's apathy about the situation.

Second, you need to pay close attention to the way Paul crafts his response to the community's problems. Let's take the same example. After Paul orders the Corinthians to throw this man out of the community—shunning was supposed to make people examine their ways and change their behavior—suddenly he begins writing about bread, yeast (the ingredient that makes bread soft and light), and Passover. This bread imagery might seem confusing at first, and you might be tempted to think that it's not very important to Paul's point, but quite the opposite is true. In preparation for the celebration of Passover, Jews removed all yeasted bread from their homes, using only unleavened bread in remembrance of the first Passover. In this setting, yeast was thought to be a source of impurity or "uncleanness" (see Chapter 5), and anyone or anything that came in contact with it was also made unclean, or unholy, and therefore unavailable to celebrate Passover. Paul's message: By not dealing with this problem, community members risk the whole community becoming contaminated and being denied participation in the celebration of Christ, the paschal lamb (1 Cor. 5:7–8).

Hopefully, our brief analysis of Paul's advice to the Corinthian community concerning the man who was sleeping with his stepmother also illustrates the importance of knowing the historical and cultural background for Paul's teachings. Of course, you cannot be expected to know this background information without doing some research, but you can get quick access to a summary of this research from biblical commentaries like the ones listed below in the "Sources and Resources" section of this chapter. It won't take a great deal of time, and it's well worth the effort.

Finally, as you analyze Paul's treatment of these various problems in the Corinthian church, you will begin to notice that he has only two basic concerns as he crafts his responses: building up the Christian community and not causing scandal to outsiders. You could say that these two concerns comprise his moral guidelines for decision making. Therefore, if you are unclear about what Paul is saying on a given topic, you might ask yourself, "Is he worried about the community being a source of scandal to outsiders?" or "Does he think that their behavior is a threat to the welfare of the community?" If the answer to either question is "Yes," this is sufficient cause for Paul to say that the behavior is wrong.

# PAUL AND WOMEN IN MINISTRY

Paul's treatment of the problem of Corinthian women who pray and prophesy without covering their heads (1 Cor. 11:2–16) provides a good opportunity to look at Paul's attitudes toward women in ministry. Many people have the perception that Paul was dismissive of women's activities in the churches, at the least, and perhaps was even openly hostile toward women. At the same time, we can find within Paul's writings statements like the following: "There is no longer Jew or Greek, there is no longer slave or free, there is no longer male and female; for all of you are one in Christ Jesus" (Gal. 3:28). Did Paul actually intend to establish an egalitarian community, in which ethnic and religious ties, social class, and gender played no role, or was he the misogynist that many today take him to be? As you might expect, the answer is complex.

Certainly, we can find evidence within the New Testament itself that Paul worked alongside of women in the preaching of the gospel and that he accepted their leadership roles within the churches. Earlier in this chapter, we mentioned Phoebe, whom Paul calls "a deacon of the church at Cenchreae" and one of his benefactors (Rom. 16:2). The term *deacon* means "minister," in this case suggesting that she had a position of leadership in her community. We have also already mentioned Prisca and Aquila, who are identified as Paul's co-workers and leaders of a church in their house (1 Cor. 16:19; Rom. 16:3). Prisca is the same woman who is named Priscilla in Acts 18:1–18. There are others as well. For example, toward the end of his Letter to the Philippians, Paul sends wishes of reconciliation to two women, Euodia and Syntyche (Phil. 4:2–3). The context suggests that they are leaders of the churches in Philippi.

But does Paul regard these women as equal to men in every respect? His teaching about the Corinthian women who pray and prophesy without covering their heads will help to illustrate some of the issues that underlie this question (1 Cor. 11:2–16). Even before Paul names the problem, he lays out a hierarchy that has God as the head of Christ, Christ as the head of a man, and man as the head of a woman. Scholars are divided concerning whether "head" should be understood as "authority" over another—in the sense that a husband has authority over his wife—or as a hierarchy of being—in the sense that God is a greater being than Christ. Some argue that "head" should be understood as "source"—in the sense that God is the source of Christ and man is the source of woman. We cannot say precisely what Paul's intended meaning was, but it is clear that he assumed some kind of difference in the status of males and females. However, the reader of 1 Corinthians 11:2–16 soon discovers that Paul is concerned not about these women's right to take an active role in the worship of the community—something that he takes for granted—but about whether their heads are covered or perhaps how their hair is styled (1 Cor. 11:4–6; cf. 1 Cor. 11:14–15).

Most women in Western cultures today would say that Paul is stressing out about something of little consequence, but he is tenacious in his argumentation. Immediately, he launches another argument—this one based on the creation stories in Genesis. Using Genesis 1:27 as his starting point, Paul argues that man is the "image and reflection" of God but woman is the reflection of man. Referring to Genesis 2:18–23, he further argues that woman was made for man, not man for woman. However, just as quickly, he defeats his own biblical argument concerning the differences between men and women, saying, "In the Lord" women and men are interdependent, all having

God as their origin and source (1 Cor. 11:11–12). "In the Lord" refers to their identity among the baptized. Paul still does not give up. His final argument against women not having the proper hair covering? "We have no such custom, nor do the churches of God" (1 Cor. 11:16)! In other words, in the end this problem comes down to infractions of proper cultural practice. Again, women of Western cultures may not appreciate the weightiness of this situation, but women of Middle Eastern and Eastern cultures, particularly in traditional communities, certainly do!

In sum, when it comes to Paul's attitudes about the social status of women and cultural restrictions on their behavior, he probably is not too much different from others of his background and experience. However, when it comes to ministry in the churches, Paul allows women a substantial role—not as an exception but simply as a matter of everyday life. So why does Paul get such a bad reputation when it comes to his attitudes toward women? Perhaps it's not about Paul at all. The most offensive remarks attributed to Paul regarding women come from the Letter to the Ephesians—"Wives, be subject to your husbands as you are to the Lord" (Eph. 5:22)—and 1 Timothy—"I permit no woman to teach or to have authority over a man; she is to keep silent" (1 Tim. 2:12). However, as we shall later see, these letters were actually written not by Paul but by some anonymous author who was writing under the pseudonym of Paul. One letter belongs to the category of letters called Deutero-Pauline. The other is a pastoral letter. In other words, Paul might not be as misogynistic as some think!

---

### Is 1 Corinthians 14:34–35 an Interpolation?

The careful reader of 1 Corinthians will notice that what Paul says about the proper behavior of women in 1 Corinthians 11:2–16 appears to contradict what he says in 1 Corinthians 14:34–35. In the first statement, he seems to allow women to speak freely and participate openly in worship. In the second, he says that women must keep silent in the churches. How do we reconcile these two apparently contradictory statements? Most biblical scholars agree that 1 Corinthians 14:34–35 is an **interpolation**, that is, a segment of text added by some later editor or copyist.

Why did they come to this conclusion? Because they detect literary seams in the middle of verse 33 (or at the end of verse 33) and again at the end of verse 35 that may have been created when verses 34–35 were inserted into the text. Observe how much more smoothly the text flows when you omit these verses:

> For you can all prophesy one by one, so that all may learn and all be encouraged. And the spirits of prophets are subject to the prophets, for God is a God not of disorder but of peace, [as in all the churches of the saints]. . . . Anyone who claims to be a prophet, or to have spiritual powers, must acknowledge that what I am writing to you is a command of the Lord. Anyone who does not recognize this is not to be recognized. So, my friends, be eager to prophesy, and do not forbid speaking in tongues; but all things should be done decently and in order. (1 Cor. 14:31–33a, 37–40)

Additionally, there are some early manuscripts of 1 Corinthians that place verses 34–35 after verse 40, suggesting that the copyists who were responsible for these manuscripts also recognized that there was something wrong with the text and tried to correct it by moving verses 34–35 to the end of the literary unit.

If we omit verses 34–35, then 1 Corinthians 14:31–37 has a single literary purpose—to provide a fitting conclusion to Paul's teaching on the proper use of the spiritual gifts of prophecy and **glossalalia** ("speaking in tongues"), which began with chapter 12. Then why have these verses been retained in your Bible? Why didn't the scholars who translated your text into English simply leave them out? Because we have other early and reliable manuscripts that include these verses as you see them in your English text and because they are now part of the text that has been passed down through the centuries.

If we have no intention of omitting these problematic verses from the biblical text, should we even worry about whether or not 1 Corinthians 14:34–35 is an interpolation? Actually, yes, we should—at least when it comes to investigating Paul's views on women's role in worship. If we are obligated to treat both 1 Corinthians 11:2–16 (commenting female prophets who prophesy with their heads uncovered) and 1 Corinthians 14:34–35 (saying women must keep silent in the churches) on the same footing, then we have some difficult tensions to resolve. However, if 1 Corinthians 11:2–16 is authentically Pauline and 1 Corinthians 14:34–35 is not, then we can weigh these two texts accordingly and more easily articulate a coherent description of Paul's views on women's role in worship.

## PAUL'S TEACHING ON THE RESURRECTION

If you ask Christians today what they think happens when they die, many might say that their soul goes to heaven, implying that they simply leave their bodies behind. Actually, Christian theology about the resurrection of the dead is much more complicated. Paul argues in 1 Corinthians 15 that Christians must believe in resurrection *of the body*. What is at stake, you ask? According to Paul, salvation itself! Here you will find a detailed outline of Paul's argument concerning the correct understanding of Christian teaching on the resurrection of the body. Keep it close at hand as you read this next section of Paul's letter to the Corinthians.

1. 1 Corinthians 15:3–11: The argument begins with the recollection of a short **creed** (i.e., statement of belief) that was already being circulated in the early churches. Paul adds his own name at the end of the creed, perhaps as an attempt to establish himself as a member of the apostolic circle.

2. 1 Corinthians 15:12–19: Paul argues that denying resurrection of the body results in some logical inconsistencies.

a. Paul identifies the consequences of such an opinion (1 Cor. 15:12-18):

If there is no resurrection of the dead . . .

*then* Christ has not been raised.

*then* our preaching is void and your faith is empty.

*then* we are still in our sin and there is no life for the faithful who have died.

b. He gives his argument a final "punch" by telling the community why this issue should matter to them: "If our hopes in Christ are limited to this life only, we are the most pitiable of humans" (1 Cor. 15:19).

3. 1 Corinthians 15:20–28: Paul returns to his starting point—their shared belief in the resurrection of Jesus—and provides a theological reflection on its significance for those who believe.

a. Christ is the first fruits of those who have fallen asleep (1 Cor. 15:20). The term *first fruit* recalls Temple sacrifice (see Chapter 5). Just as God accepted Jesus as the "first and best" of the harvest offered in sacrifice and raised him to life, so God will accept all who believe. Note also the use of Adam typology (1 Cor. 15:21-22).

b. Paul then explains the sequence of the eschatological events (1 Cor. 15:23-28). Observe that Paul sees both the resurrection of Christ and the resurrection of the dead as essential elements of God's plan of salvation. According to Paul, the events of the end time will take place in this order:

  i. Christ's resurrection,

  ii. His coming/enthronement,

  iii. The resurrection of the dead, and

  iv. Christ's giving over his authority/power to God, who is "all in all."

4. 1 Corinthians 15:29–34: Paul presents another argument about the implications of refusing to believe in resurrection of the dead. He argues that their actions are futile if there is no resurrection for the believer. Compare with 1 Corinthians 15:12–19.

a. Why do we do proxy baptism on behalf of the dead? (1 Cor. 15:29)

b. Why do we allow ourselves to suffer for preaching the gospel? (1 Cor. 15:30-32a)

c. Why do we try to live good moral lives? Why not just "eat, drink, and be merry"? (1 Cor. 15: 32b-34)

5. 1 Corinthians 15:35–49: These next verses are a theological reflection on the properties of the resurrected body. Perhaps someone will say, "How are the dead raised?" (1 Cor 15:35)—This is the crux of the issue!

a. Paul makes a comparison: Just as the "bare kernel" of grain is related to but different from the plant that comes out of the ground, so also their "earthly bodies" are related to but different from their "heavenly bodies" (1 Cor. 15:36–41).

b. Elaboration of the comparison follows (1 Cor. 15:42-44). Paul uses four antithetical parallelisms to explain how the resurrected body is qualitatively different from the physical body.

| Present Body | Future Body |
| --- | --- |
| perishable | imperishable |
| dishonorable | glorious |
| weak | powerful |
| physical | spiritual |

c. A second argument about the distinctive differences between the physical and the resurrected bodies (1 Cor. 15:45-49) depends on Adam typology. Paul argues that the first Adam was physical; the second is heavenly or spiritual. Although the "first Adam" was a "living being," the "second Adam" is endowed with a "life-giving spirit" (Gen. 2:7).

6. 1 Corinthians 15:50–58: Paul concludes his argument concerning resurrection of the dead by addressing the need for transformation of the physical body. The major points in this discussion are as follows:

a. In baptism, believers are freed from the power of sin and the law (1 Cor. 15:56-57).

b. In the resurrection *of the body*, believers are freed from the power of death, which is the consequence of sin (1 Cor. 15:51-55).

When Paul introduces his teaching about resurrection of the body, it is not altogether clear why there is a problem. However, he begins with something that both he and the community agree is truth—a creed concerning the death and bodily resurrection of Jesus (1 Cor. 15:3–7). His next step is to argue that they cannot deny the idea of bodily resurrection if they believe that Christ was raised from the dead. Otherwise, their faith is in vain and they have no reason for hope (1 Cor. 15:12–19).

Returning to his starting point—their shared belief in the resurrected Christ—Paul goes on to explain how Christ's resurrection relates to their own future resurrection from the dead. Using the image of Temple sacrifice, he describes Christ as the "first fruit" that is taken up to God, as a symbol of all who have died—they, too, will be taken up to God (1 Cor. 15:20). He also relates Christ to Adam, who brought sin into the world; Christ has "undone" the sin of Adam, making it possible for humanity to come to new life in him (1 Cor. 15:21).

Midway through Paul's teaching on resurrection of the body, the crux of the problem is revealed. With what kind of body will they be resurrected? If you have been following Paul's argument, you are probably asking the same question! Paul answers with metaphors. The first involves planting grain. To what can we compare the resurrected body? It is like a seed (the physical body) that goes into the ground; what comes up (the resurrected body) is related but different—like a seed is to the plant from which it comes. The second metaphor involves the different bodies that earthly things possess (e.g., humans, animals, plants) and the different bodies that are given to heavenly things (e.g., sun, moon, and stars). Human flesh is one among many kinds of things that dwell on earth; so, too, the resurrected human is one among many kinds of heavenly bodies—related but different. It is in this context that Paul identifies the four qualities that distinguish the resurrected body from the physical: It is imperishable, glorious, powerful, and spiritual.

But how does Paul know that there is such a thing as a spiritual body? Paul's source is sacred scripture and the example of Adam, whom he compares to Christ. He has two texts in mind, both from Genesis and both having to do with God's creation of humans. The highlighted phrases in these quotations are the ones on which Paul will build his argument:

> Then God said, "*Let us make humankind in our image, according to our likeness*; and let them have dominion over the fish of the sea, and over the birds of the air, and over the cattle, and over all wild animals of the earth and over every creeping thing that creeps upon the earth." So God created humankind in his image, in the image of God he created them; male and female he created them. (Gen. 1:26–27)
>
> Then the Lord God formed man *from the dust of the ground,* and breathed into his nostrils the *breath of life,* and the man *became a living being.* (Gen. 2:7)

Alluding to the second text from Genesis, Paul says that the first man, Adam, was *from the earth* and *became a living being* (1 Cor. 15:45a). This is the physical body. But the last (most perfect) Adam, who is Christ, is *of heaven* and became *a life-giving spirit* through his resurrection from the dead (1 Cor. 15:45b). Again, Paul is drawing upon the second creation story, but this time focusing on the second stage of Adam's creation—God's breathing upon him and giving him the *breath of life* (Gen. 2:7). The Hebrew word *ruah* translates as both "breath or wind" and "spirit." Likewise, the Greek word *pneuma* translates as both "breath or wind" and "spirit." Finally, Paul draws upon the phrase "in our image and according to our likeness" in Genesis 1:26-27 to explain how humans bear the image of Adam in their physical bodies, but they bear the image of the risen Christ, the man of heaven, in their spiritual bodies, that is, the bodies that they will receive in the resurrection of the dead (1 Cor. 15:48–49).

In the final section of his argument, Paul's tone shifts to one which is more intimate, more ecstatic, and more triumphant. Now we learn why Paul has been so insistent that the Corinthian community must accept the notion of resurrection of the body and not some other theory about the afterlife. He says that he wants to share with them a "mystery" about a moment when they will all be transformed and their physical bodies will become spiritual bodies. At that moment, death will have no more hold on them! But why insist on resurrection *of the body*? If the body is not raised, Paul says, then sin still has its power because death (which is the consequence of sin) has not been overcome. If the body is not raised, there is no salvation! "But thanks be to God," says Paul, "who gives us the victory through our Lord Jesus Christ" (1 Cor. 15:57).

Columns and other archeological remains of the ancient Temple of Apollo in Corinth.
*Joe Cornish/Dorling Kindersley (c) Archaeological Receipts Fund (TAP).*

## THE SECOND LETTER TO THE CORINTHIANS

Biblical scholars agree that Paul is the author of the Second Letter to the Corinthians. They also agree that he is addressing the same community, though perhaps at a somewhat later time than the first letter, perhaps as late as the fall of 57 C.E. However, biblical scholars are divided about the nature of this letter. Is it a single letter, preserved for us today in the New Testament just as it was originally sent to the Corinthian Christian community? Or is it a collection of fragments that were later arranged to "create" the letter that we read today? One reason that scholars of 2 Corinthians raise this question is that the letter contains several abrupt transitions or literary seams. You will notice these literary seams as you read through the letter and find yourself saying, "Wait a minute! What happened? How did Paul get onto this topic?"

Paul's comments about some kind of rupture in his relationship with the Corinthian community also lead biblical scholars to think that 2 Corinthians might consist of more than one letter fragments. Unfortunately, we never learn exactly what the problem was. However, in some parts of the letter, the relationship appears to be on the mend, but in other parts Paul is writing as if he has not yet confronted the issue that has torn them apart. In other words, there are some serious problems with sequencing in this letter. The letter also contains a couple of sections that do not seem to fit the form and content of the letter for one reason or another. All of these factors contribute to some biblical scholars' speculation that we actually have the remnants of several letters in 2 Corinthians. We'll say more about this later.

## OUTLINE OF THE LETTER

Even though we have already indicated that 2 Corinthians may actually be several letter fragments knit together into a new literary creation, an outline of the entire letter might be a helpful way to begin our investigation. After all, as it exists today, it is a single unified letter, and we have no manuscript evidence to suggest that the fragments ever circulated as independent letters. At the same time, our outline will help us more easily identify some of the literary seams of the letter. It will also reveal some of its major themes.

1. 2 Corinthians 1:1–2—Opening
2. 2 Corinthians 1:3–11—Blessing
3. 2 Corinthians 1:12–13:10—Body
   a. Comments about strained relationships with the community (2 Cor. 1:12–2:13)
   b. Reflections and comments on Paul's ministry (2 Cor. 2:14–6:13, 7:2–16) [Interruption (2 Cor. 6:14–7:1)]
   c. The Jerusalem collection (2 Cor. 8:1–9:15)
   d. Paul answers challenges to his authority; the "tearful" letter? (2 Cor. 10:1–13:10)
4. 2 Corinthians 13:11–13—Closing

The first thing you will notice with this outline is that Paul substitutes a blessing in the place of the usual thanksgiving section. The major themes of the blessing are affliction and consolation. In the immediate context of the blessing, Paul is talking about an "affliction" that he suffered in Asia (modern Turkey) (2 Cor. 1:8), but most likely he is anticipating what he will later say about the mutual suffering that he shares with the community (2 Cor. 2:1–11), a situation for which both sides apparently need consolation.

## THE "TEARFUL" LETTER?

In the first major section of the body of this letter (2 Cor. 2:1–11), Paul writes in vague terms about a difficult and as-yet-unresolved situation that has caused a great deal of pain for both Paul and the community. What happened? Actually, the final section of the body of the letter may provide our best clues. In 2 Corinthians 10–13, Paul scolds the community for being so easily led astray by people who teach a different gospel, and he uses this part of the letter to go after his opponents, whom he calls "super" apostles. Some biblical scholars think this is the "tearful" letter that Paul mentions in 2 Cor. 2:3–5, when he writes:

> And I wrote as I did, so that when I came, I might not suffer pain from those who should have made me rejoice. . . . For I wrote you out of much distress and anguish of heart and with many tears, not to cause you pain, but to let you know the abundant love that I have for you. But if anyone has caused pain, he has caused it not to me, but to some extent—not to exaggerate it—to all of you. (2 Cor. 2:3–5)

However, against the view that 2 Corinthians 10–13 is the "tearful" letter mentioned in 2 Corinthians 2:3–5, some have observed that Paul is apparently referring to a single person here, while 2 Corinthians 10–13 is written with a group of opponents in mind.

Unfortunately, biblical scholars may never be able to determine precisely what happened at Corinth to cause so much hurt, nor will they be able to say with certainty that 2 Corinthians 10–13 is (or is not) the "tearful" letter. However, if you read carefully, you may be able to uncover Paul's perception about the things his opponents were saying about him—of course, this is not necessarily what they actually were saying about him. You may also be able to discern some information about who his opponents were and what they valued. Finally, you can see what Paul valued in people who would call themselves ministers of Christ. In this context, Paul talks about boasting in weakness, the kind of weakness that is really the power of God.

Sometimes it can be difficult to appreciate what Paul is saying unless you recognize the rhetorical techniques he is using. And, again, remember that this letter represents only one side of a written conversation. Take, for example, the opening statement of 2 Corinthians 10–13. Paul writes about being humble when face to face with the Corinthian community and bold when he is away (2 Cor. 10:1). These are not his own words; he is actually repeating his opponents' words against him! Later, when he is writing about how easily they take up a different gospel, he calls them "wise" (2 Cor. 11:19) and says, "To my shame, I must say, we were too weak for that!" (2 Cor. 11:21).

Does Paul really mean what he is saying here? Not at all! In fact, he means quite the opposite. Paul is speaking sarcastically, using harsh and pointed language to say that the Corinthian community is made up of fools and weak-minded people. Later Paul appears to ask forgiveness of the community when he says, "Forgive me this wrong!" (2 Cor. 12:13). Does he mean it? Well, yes and no. He does not regret the way he acted when he taught among them, but he does regret their ingratitude, and he is thinking that things might have turned out differently if he had not made it so easy for them!

Recognizing these rhetorical features in Paul's letters is essential to understanding the message he is trying to convey. If you have difficulty identifying them on your own, you might consider reading the text aloud and stopping periodically to imagine the reaction of Paul's original audience. This practice should help you get a sense of the tone of his letters.

## PAUL'S MINISTRY AND MINISTRY IN CHRIST

The second major section of the body of this letter (2 Cor. 2:14–6:13; 7:2–16) is filled with imagery about the power of ministry in Christ. The first two images are probably the most revealing. First, Paul likens his participation in the ministry of Christ to a procession of victors returning home from war; they cannot claim the victory, but they can participate in its rewards (2 Cor. 2:14). Second is an image of perfume whose fragrance spreads out to fill every space. He tells the Corinthian community that he and his colleagues are the aroma of Christ; they are not the perfume, but they participate in its positive effects (2 Cor. 2:15). In this context, Paul also calls the community his letter of recommendation (2 Cor. 3:2–3), testimony to God's good work among them. In other words, their ministry in Christ is not a reason for them to boast, since everything belongs to God.

Later Paul contrasts this ministry "of the new covenant" with the glory that shone on Moses' face when he came down the mountain of Sinai (2 Cor. 3:7–14; cf. Exod. 34:29–35). This former glory was veiled, Paul says, because Moses did not want people to see that it was fading. But when people turn to Christ, the veil is lifted, and the greater glory of the Lord transforms all who come under its reflection, making them into the image of God (2 Cor. 3:15–18). For Paul, of course, the image of God is Christ (2 Cor. 4:4). In other words, Paul is saying that participation in the ministry of Christ is a transformative experience—they are being transformed into Christ!

Finally, Paul expresses confidence in the power of ministry in Christ by using two more metaphors—clay pots and tents. Beginning with the understanding that everything that he and his fellow ministers do is possible only because of God's mercy, Paul says that they are like clay pots—fragile and of little value—in which God has placed a treasure of enormous proportions (2 Cor. 4:7–14). Similarly, concerning the potential of facing death for the sake of the ministry, he describes his body as an earthly tent groaning and longing to be clothed in its heavenly dwelling place (2 Cor. 5:1–5). These metaphors are especially vivid and obviously intended to inspire! Because their ministry is ministry in Christ, they have every reason to hope and to be joyful. All for the glory of God!

## AN INTERRUPTION?

At the conclusion of this long reflection on the ministry of Christ (2 Cor. 2:14–6:13), Paul appears to return again to the problem of the strained relations between himself and the community. He challenges the community members to make peace, saying that he and his colleagues have opened their hearts to them and charging that they are the ones who are holding back (2 Cor. 6:11–13). Suddenly, without warning, Paul launches into a tirade against associating with unbelievers (2 Cor. 6:14–7:1). Again, without transition, Paul returns to his earlier appeal, pleading with them to open their hearts to him (2 Cor. 7:2).

What is going on here? Where's the logic in Paul's argument? This is another example of the literary seams that biblical scholars look for when they examine questions of redaction (editing). In this case, we can easily see the redactor's work. Look what happens when you read to the end of 2 Corinthians 6:13 and pick up again at the beginning of 2 Corinthians 7:2, skipping the section about staying away from unbelievers (2 Cor. 6:14–7:1):

> We have spoken frankly to you Corinthians; our heart is wide open to you. There is no restriction in our affections, but only in yours. In return—I speak as to children—open wide your hearts also. . . . Make room in your hearts for us; we have wronged no one, we have taken advantage of no one. (2 Cor. 6:11–13; 7:2)

Without 2 Corinthians 6:14–7:1, the text flows smoothly and without interruption. Some scholars suggest that these intervening verses are part of another letter written to the Corinthian community, perhaps even the one mentioned in 1 Corinthians 5:9–11, when Paul says, "I wrote to you in my letter not to associate with sexually immoral persons."

Much more could be said about the letter fragments that may have been incorporated into 2 Corinthians. However, because the task of this textbook is to survey the whole of the New Testament, not to conduct an exhaustive study of 2 Corinthians, we will leave this topic for now. If you wish to further investigate the question of the unity of 2 Corinthians, you may consult the "Sources and Resources" section at the end of this chapter.

## PAUL'S COLLECTION FOR THE JERUSALEM CHURCH

At the conclusion of Paul's First Letter to the Corinthians (1 Cor. 16:1–24), he comments about a collection that is taken up on Sundays and held for Paul's arrival. The plan is for him to take the money with him to the church in Jerusalem (1 Cor. 16:1–4). In 2 Corinthians 8–9, Paul returns to the topic of the Jerusalem collection and treats it in a more sustained way. Because these two chapters do not have strong literary connections to the text that precedes and follows them, several biblical scholars have suggested that they originally circulated as a separate stewardship appeal letter—the kind you or someone in your family might receive during a large capital campaign for your church or some charitable organization to which you belong—and were later incorporated into this new letter created from letter fragments. Some scholars of the Corinthian correspondence even have speculated that we may have two stewardship letter fragments in chapters 8 and 9. Why? Chapter 8 is addressed to the Christian community at Corinth, whereas chapter 9 appears to be addressed to churches in the region of Achaia, the territory in which Corinth was located.

Whether or not these chapters were once one or two letters, chapter 8 indicates that the community had earlier made a commitment to contribute to Paul's collection and then failed to keep that promise. We do not know why the community members never finished the collection, but one thing is clear: It was *not* because they lacked the financial resources, since Paul contrasts their abundance with the neediness of some of Paul's other churches (2 Cor. 8:13–14). He also makes the point that their contribution is warranted because it will bear good fruit for the Jewish Christian church in Jerusalem; in his words, it will "produce thanksgiving to God through us" (2 Cor. 9:11).

When you read this section of Paul's Second Letter to the Corinthians, pay careful attention to the arguments he raises to convince the members of the Corinthian community that they should fulfill their commitment to complete the collection. The argument presented in chapter 8 is somewhat different from the one presented in chapter 9, but both arguments provide some interesting hints concerning the character of the Corinthian community and the nature of Paul's relationship with it. The stewardship letter(s) are also important as a window into the relationships between Jewish Christian churches and their Gentile counterparts in the middle of the first century C.E. One can see, for example, that Paul's concern for the well-being of the Jewish Christian churches was genuine and passionate, even though he saw his mission as belonging primarily to Gentile Christian communities.

Finally, as you reflect on 2 Corinthians 8–9, you might also consider the significance of Paul's message for today's Christian communities. Would he be proud of their practice of charitable giving? In what ways would he challenge them to do better? What would he say about the proper motivation for charitable giving?

## Key Terms

| | | |
|---|---|---|
| Chloe | Stephanas | Glossalalia |
| Crispus | Koinonia | Creed |
| Gaius | Interpolation | |

## Questions for Reading

Read 1 Corinthians. Answer each of the following questions using evidence from Paul's letter.

1. What is the situation in Corinth to which Paul addresses himself in the opening segments of this letter (1 Cor. 1:4–17)? Where did he get his information concerning this problem?

2. What does Paul mean when he speaks about "God's wisdom" (1 Cor. 2:7)? Why does he think that God's wisdom should be preferred over human wisdom?

3. Explain Paul's point when he uses the garden and the building imagery (1 Cor. 3:5–15) to comment on the situation he finds in Corinth.

4. For each of the community problems that Paul addresses in this letter, explain the specifics of the problem, the solution that Paul wants the community to adopt, and his argument in defense of the solution:

   a. Problem: There is a man living with his father's wife (1 Cor. 5:1–8). *Note:* This kind of behavior was forbidden by both Roman and Jewish law, but the community appears to be ignoring the problem.

   b. Problem: Members of the community have mistakenly understood Paul's teaching about not associating with sexually immoral people to mean that they should restrict their contact with people who did not belong to their community (1 Cor. 5:9–12).

   c. Problem: Christians are bringing their legal disputes against fellow Christians into civil courts, where their cases are decided by non-Christians (1 Cor. 6:1–8).

   d. Problem: Some people in the community are saying, "All things are lawful for me," meaning that they do not have to abide by certain moral standards (1 Cor. 6:9–20).

   e. Problem: Some members of the community are advocating asceticism within marriage (i.e., abstaining from sexual activity), saying, "It is a good thing for a man not to touch a woman" (1 Cor. 7:1–7).

   f. Problem: Some people are asking whether virgins (i.e., women who are unmarried), widows, the already married, and even slaves should remain as they are (1 Cor. 7:8–40).

   g. Problem: Arguing that "[a]ll of us know that there is no idol in the world and no god but one," some members of the Christian community are eating meat sacrificed to idols (1 Cor. 8:1–13) and going to the sacrificial banquets at the homes of their friends (1 Cor. 10:1–22).

   h. Problem: Certain women of the Christian community are praying and prophesying in the worship assembly with their heads uncovered (1 Cor. 11:2–16).

*Note:* Just as long hair among men raised suspicions of effeminate behavior and homosexual tendencies, unkempt or close-cropped hair among women suggested prostitution.

    i. Problem: Divisions in the community are evident in the way they celebrate Eucharist (1 Cor. 11:17–34). *Note:* In wealthy homes, the dining room opened into a courtyard. Less important guests were seated there, and even served differently than the more important guests.

    j. Problem: Some members of the Christian community are thinking that they are more important than other members of the community because of the spiritual gifts they possess (1 Cor. 12:131; 14:1–40).

5. Having analyzed Paul's advice on the problems facing the Corinthian community, what common themes, priorities, or concerns were you able to uncover? What do they tell you about Paul's understanding of how Christian communities ought to live?

6. Construct your own detailed outline of Paul's argument concerning resurrection of the body (1 Cor. 15:1–49), or study the one provided above. What does Paul perceive to be the Corinthians' misunderstanding regarding resurrection? Why does he think they must believe as he does? That is, what is at stake in his teaching about Christ's resurrection?

7. Describe the circumstances surrounding the collection that Paul wants the Corinthians to take up (1 Cor. 16:1–4). What is the purpose of the collection?

Read 2 Corinthians. Use evidence from the letter to answer the following questions.

8. Compare the thanksgiving section of 1 Corinthians to the comparable section of 2 Corinthians (1 Cor. 1:4–9; 2 Cor. 1:3–7). In what ways is this section of 2 Corinthians distinctive? Consider not only the content of the unit but also its form (i.e., structure).

9. What does this letter tell us about Paul's past relationship with the Christian community at Corinth? How would you describe his current standing with the community?

10. What appears to be the source of Paul's distress as he writes this letter (2 Cor. 1:12–2:13)? What is the status of his planned trip to visit them?

11. In 2 Corinthians 3:1–18, Paul argues a case for the superiority of his ministry compared to Moses' ministry, using imagery about the old and new covenants. See if you can outline this section of the letter and describe the flow of Paul's argument.

12. In 2 Corinthians 4:7–18, Paul describes his ministry in terms of what some scripture scholars have called "the paradox of God's mysterious ways." Explain this section in your own words.

13. In 2 Corinthians 5:11–21, Paul explains how his is a ministry of reconciliation. What is his point? How does this relate to his talk about "a new creation"?

14. In 2 Corinthians 6:1–7:3, Paul makes two appeals to the Christian community at Corinth. What are these? How are they related? What is Paul's underlying concern?

15. In 2 Corinthians 7:5–16, Paul returns to the situation of the community in Corinth. What has he now discovered? How does he respond?

16. In 2 Corinthians 8:1–15 and 9:1–15, Paul makes two appeals for money. For what purpose? How do these appeals concern Titus? Examine the manner in which Paul makes these appeals. What is the logic of his argumentation? How would you describe the "pathos" of his argumentation—that is, the rhetorical details that are designed to make people feel sad?

17. In 2 Corinthians 10:1–18, Paul indicates that he plans to return to Corinth. What does he hope to find when he returns? How does he expect to behave with the Christian community there?

18. In 2 Corinthians 11:1–21, Paul provides a sarcastic refutation of his opponents' claim to be true apostles. What clues, if any, do we have concerning the basis of the opponents' claim? What, if anything, does Paul's refutation tell us about his understanding of the characteristics of a true apostle?

19. In 2 Corinthians 11:22–12:10, Paul offers a defense of his own right to be called an apostle. What other things can we say about Paul's understanding of the characteristics of a true apostle from this section?

20. Finally, in 2 Corinthians 12:11–13:14, Paul returns to the subject of his plans to return to Corinth. What more does he say about what he hopes to find when he returns? What more does he say about how he expects to behave with the Christian community there?

## QUESTIONS FOR REFLECTION

1. Paul saw the Spirit as the means by which he was persuasive enough to make the Corinthians listen to him (1 Cor. 2:4). He also believed that those who possess the Spirit have the mind of Christ (i.e., know what is truly Christ's). Describe your own understanding of the Spirit and its activity in your personal life or in the lives of people you know. How does this compare with Paul's understanding?

2. Identify at least two moral situations that might occur in your own community (e.g., town, neighborhood, or worship group), and write responses similar to what Paul might have written to the Corinthians. How do the general concerns and priorities underlying modern Christian responses to these problems compare to Paul's concerns and priorities?

## ACTIVITIES FOR LEARNING

1. Do some research on the Pentecostal churches in America or on another charismatic church that celebrates the gifts of the Holy Spirit in the community. What is the worship service like? What priority do church members give to spiritual gifts like glossalalia, prophecy, or spiritual healings? How do they see these activities as manifestations of the Holy Spirit? What biblical texts do they consider helpful or meaningful for understanding these phenomena? If possible, interview the pastor or someone who is active in ministry within that church tradition. You might also try to locate official documents that describe that church tradition's views on the activity of the Holy Spirit. One place to start your investigation is the Wabash

Center website, *www.wabashcenter.wabash.edu/Internet/front.htm,* which has links to the official websites of many American Christian churches.

2. Investigate the megachurch called Toronto Blessing and the phenomenon of "holy laughter." How and when did this church originate? What is its connection to traditional charismatic churches? Does this church have its own set of beliefs? What is its worship service like? How do church members explain the unusual phenomena associated with the blessing? Some have praised the movement and described it as a "renewal" of the church. What do they mean? Others are skeptical about the Toronto Blessing and even say that it is dangerous? Why? What do you think?

3. Paul's concern about individuals who might become the source of scandal for others in the Corinthian community when they take part in activities of the larger culture (e.g., banquets commemorating the Greek and Roman deities; 1 Cor. 10:23–33) may seem antiquated and irrelevant to modern peoples. However, occasionally, we hear of a comparable situation in our contemporary world. One such example came to light in May 2004, when some Israeli Jewish rabbis issued a ruling that Hasidic Jewish women were not allowed to wear wigs made in India (*New York Times,* May 14, 2004). Why was this ruling issued? What kind of response did the ruling receive in the Hasidic and Orthodox Jewish communities? Why? What is the connection with Paul's concern about not causing scandal in 1 Corinthians? *Note:* Hasidic Jewish women have a religious obligation to keep their heads covered. Many wear wigs instead of headscarves to fulfill this obligation.

## SOURCES AND RESOURCES

Beardslee, William A. *First Corinthians: A Commentary for Today.* St. Louis, Mo.: Chalice Press, 1994.

Collins, Raymond F. *First Corinthians.* Collegeville, Minn.: Liturgical Press, 1999.

Hays, Richard B. *First Corinthians.* Louisville, Ky.: John Knox Press, 1997.

Horsley, Richard. *1 Corinthians.* Nashville, Tenn.: Abingdon Press, 1998.

Lambrecht, Jan. *Second Corinthians.* Collegeville, Minn.: Liturgical Press, 1999.

Levine, Amy-Jill, and Marianne Blickenstaff. *A Feminist Companion to Paul.* London: T & T Clark International, 2004.

Matera, Frank J. *II Corinthians: A Commentary.* Louisville, Ky.: Westminster John Knox Press, 2003.

Murphy-O'Connor, Jerome. *1 Corinthians.* Collegeville, Minn.: Liturgical Press, 1991.

Neyrey, Jerome H. *Paul, in Other Words: A Cultural Reading of His Letters.* Louisville, Ky.: Westminster John Knox Press, 1990.

Roetzel, Calvin J. *The Letters of Paul: Conversations in Context.* 4th ed. Louisville, Ky.: Westminster John Knox Press, 1998.

Scott, James M. *2 Corinthians.* Peabody, Mass.: Hendrickson; Carlisle, England: Paternoster Press, 1998.

Soards, Marion. *1 Corinthians.* Peabody, Mass.: Hendrickson; Carlisle, England: Paternoster Press, 1999.

Talbert, Charles H. *Reading Corinthians: A Literary and Theological Commentary.* Macon, Ga.: Smyth & Helwys, 2002.

Wire, Antoinette Clark. *The Corinthian Women Prophets: A Reconstruction through Paul's Rhetoric.* Minneapolis, Minn.: Fortress, 1990.

Witherington, Ben. *Conflict and Community in Corinth: A Socio-Rhetorical Commentary on 1 and 2 Corinthians.* Grand Rapids, Mich.: Wm. B. Eerdmans, 1995.

Wright, N. T. *Paul for Everyone: 1 Corinthians.* London: SPCK; Louisville, Ky.: Westminster John Knox Press, 2004.

_____.*Paul for Everyone: 2 Corinthians.* London: SPCK; Louisville, Ky.: Westminster John Knox Press, 2004.

# CHAPTER 17

# PAUL'S LETTER TO THE ROMANS

- AUTHORSHIP: Paul, perhaps from Corinth
- DATE OF COMPOSITION: 57–58 C.E.
- INITIAL AUDIENCE: A mostly Gentile Christian community in Rome that has at least some Jewish Christians among its members; a community that was not founded by Paul
- MAJOR TOPICS: Paul's Gospel; Paul's Anthropology; Justification Through Faith; Life of the Justified; Roman Catholic/Lutheran Dialogue on Justification; Israel's Place in God's Plan of Salvation; Paul and the Law in a Post-Holocaust World; Church as the Body of the Christ

## TIMELINE

| | |
|---|---|
| **32–36 C.E.** | Paul is converted on the road to Damascus. |
| **49–50 C.E.** | The Jerusalem Conference is held to decide about the inclusion of Gentile believers. |
| **51 C.E.** | Paul writes his First Letter to the Thessalonians. |
| **52–60 C.E.** | Felix is procurator of Palestine. |
| **54–55 C.E.** | Paul writes his Letter to the Galatians. |
| **54–56 C.E.** | Paul writes his Letters to the Philippians and Philemon. |
| **54–68 C.E.** | Nero is Roman emperor. |
| **55–56 C.E.** | Paul writes his First Letter to the Corinthians. |
| **56–57 C.E.** | Paul writes his Second Letter to the Corinthians. |
| **57–58 C.E.** | **Paul writes his Letter to the Romans.** |
| **60–62 C.E.** | Festus is procurator of Palestine. |
| **64 C.E.** | Peter and Paul are martyred in Rome. |

The next segment of our voyage through the New Testament backtracks and picks up where we left off at the end of Acts of the Apostles. Recall that Paul has arrived in Rome under Roman guard and requests a meeting with members of its Jewish community, at which he proclaims to them his message about Jesus Christ. Now, as we investigate Paul's Letter to the Romans, we jump back to the Italian peninsula and to the city of Rome. Paul's Letter to the Romans is among his most difficult for today's readers, perhaps because it is more theoretical than his other letters. This letter is also his longest, and to English-speaking readers at least, its style is very dense. Every word counts!

Another challenge is that Paul's writing appears to be confused and not very logical to Western eyes and ears. Remember that Paul was born and reared in a culture quite different from that of many of us, in a part of the world that is now called the Middle East. Contemporary Western thinkers tend to value linear thinking, calling this approach "logical" and implying that other ways of thinking are illogical. However, not all cultures value the same ways of thinking and the same types of argumentation. This is true today, and we have to assume that the situation in the ancient world was no different.

It has been suggested that the form of Paul's argumentation is more cyclic or spiral than linear. Thus, you will see Paul introduce a topic and then appear to go off on a tangent. When he returns to the topic at some later point, you may wonder where he has been and why he went there. But this does not mean that Paul is being illogical. Each time he revisits the topic, he does so with greater sophistication and more nuances of meaning. Some would say that he is simply arguing like a good Jewish rabbi. With these few words of introduction, let us journey further into Paul's world and explore his Letter to the Romans.

## AUTHORSHIP AND DATE OF COMPOSITION

Biblical scholars agree that the Letter to the Romans is an authentic Pauline letter, that is, a letter authored by Paul himself. A few scholars have wondered whether chapter 16 is a later addition, in part because there is a second-century-C.E. manuscript of the Letter to the Romans that does not include chapter 16 and in part because none of Paul's other letters has such a long list of concluding greetings as we find here. However, the majority of biblical scholars agree that chapter 16 is indeed part of Paul's original Letter to the Romans.

How, then, shall we account for this unusually long list of greetings at the end of the letter? One possible explanation is tied to what Paul says about the reason for writing this Letter to the Romans. In his opening and closing remarks (Rom. 1:10–15; 15:14–33), he tells the Roman Christian community that he is preparing for a long-planned trip to meet them, which he hopes to do soon (Rom. 1:13). He wants to be clear about his motives and assure them that he is not coming to interfere. He wants only to offer them some spiritual benefit, but he also hopes that his visit will be for mutual encouragement for the benefit of their common faith (Rom. 1:11–12). Thus, in light of the fact that Paul did not establish this community and probably was not particularly well known to them, we might conclude that this long list of greetings (Rom. 16:1–16) was meant to serve as a list of references. You can almost imagine Paul saying, "A bunch of recommendations from people they know and respect can't hurt!"

Does Paul provide us with any clues about when this letter was written? In the concluding section of the letter, Paul says that he wants to visit them on his way to Spain, where he plans to begin some new missionary work. He hopes that they will "send him on," perhaps with their prayers and good wishes or even with money for his journey to Spain (Rom. 15:22–24). But first, he says, he has to go to Jerusalem to

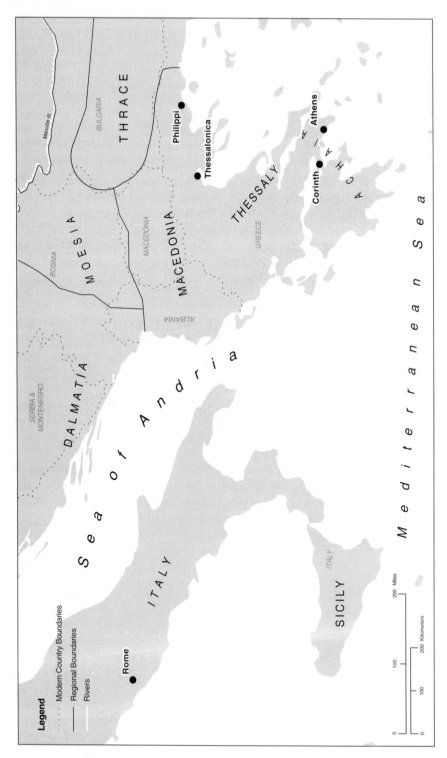

First-century Mediterranean world, showing Rome, Corinth, Jerusalem, and Spain, with modern boundaries.

meet with the Jewish Christian church located there and deliver the money he has been collecting from his Gentile churches in Asia Minor (Rom. 15:25–28). The Jerusalem church, led by James, the brother of Jesus, was suffering persecution from its Jewish neighbors. Apparently, Paul wanted to use the donation not only to express support for this persecuted church but also to show the good will of the Gentile churches toward the Jewish Christian churches. However, we do not have any evidence that Paul ever made it to Spain on his missionary travels. Instead, as Acts of the Apostles tells it, Paul was arrested at the end of the first leg of his journey, when he arrived in Jerusalem (Acts 21:27–40). The date of his arrest is sometime between 58 and 60 C.E.

If the Letter to the Romans was written shortly before Paul's arrest in Jerusalem, at the start of his aborted trip to Spain, then a date of composition of 57–58 C.E. is reasonable. However, we need to restate our earlier cautions about attempting to date Paul's letters with too much precision. The evidence we use to establish these dates comes from two sources: Paul's own letters and Acts of the Apostles. Paul himself gives us too few historical details to be of much use in dating his letters. Acts of the Apostles gives us lots of details about Paul's story, but Luke was not intending to write history as we understand it today, nor does he mention Paul's letter-writing activity. In other words, although Acts is significant for its theological message, it is not necessarily reliable in providing information for reconstructing a chronology of Paul's life. Not to worry, though. While it would be nice to know precisely when Paul wrote each of his letters, the meaning of each letter does not depend on knowing the exact date of composition.

## THE CHRISTIAN COMMUNITY AT ROME

Biblical scholars have theorized that, although the community at Rome was predominantly Gentile at the time of Paul's writing (Rom. 1:13; 11:13), it most likely originated as a Jewish Christian community (Rom. 2:17). Why? The arguments Paul makes in this letter are profoundly Jewish: He uses Jewish vocabulary, he appeals to the authority and tradition of Judaism, he invokes values that are important to Judaism, he frequently cites the TaNaK (the Jewish scriptures), and he uses techniques of interpreting scripture that were well known to Jews. But how did this once Jewish Christian community evolve into a Gentile Christian community?

In answer to this question, scholars have argued for the Roman exile theory. According to this hypothesis, the community at Rome was originally Jewish Christian, but soon it was also receiving Gentile converts. At some point, Jewish Christians were banished from Rome, leaving behind a community of believers that consisted almost entirely of Gentile converts. Then, after a period of years, Jewish Christians began returning to a predominantly Gentile Christian community. This would explain why Paul, toward the end of this letter, takes great pains to remind the Gentile Christians in this community of their debt to Judaism. See Romans 11:13–24.

The external (nonbiblical) evidence used to support this theory comes from the Roman historian Suetonius. He describes an edict of Emperor Claudius dating to about 49 C.E.: "The Jews were expelled from Rome on account of a riot instigated by a certain Chrestus" (*Lives of the Caesars*, Claudius, 25). Who was this

Chrestus? Certainly, it is possible that he was some now-unknown Roman Jewish inhabitant who said or did something so inflammatory that he caused a riot in the Jewish community there. Apparently, Chrestus was a common name in first-century Rome, much like Jesus is in Hispanic communities today. However, a more likely scenario is that Chrestus is a reference to Jesus, the Christ, and that Suetonius had his facts wrong. Jesus' death and resurrection had already taken place almost twenty years earlier, so Jesus certainly did not instigate the riots about which Suetonius is writing.

However, by 49 C.E., one can imagine Jews and Jewish Christians engaged in a heated dispute over Jewish Christian claims that Jesus, whom they called Son of God, was their long-awaited messiah. Emperor Claudius would not have been particularly concerned about the theological nuances of this intracommunity battle. Moreover, to a non-Jew like Claudius, Jews and Jewish Christians all looked alike. This is not surprising, since Christianity began as a reform group within Judaism. Only when the two groups began to separate toward the end of the first century C.E. would any outsider have perceived Christians to be different from Jews. Therefore, in deciding to put a stop to the Jewish riots in Rome, Claudius might have simply chosen to get rid of the whole lot, leaving behind only Gentile God-fearers.

## OUTLINE OF THE LETTER

Paul's Letter to the Romans is an exceptionally long document, and its dense theological content makes it difficult reading. This is a case where we might benefit from two kinds of outlines. The one provided here shows the five formal elements of a letter and gives you an opportunity to grasp the "big picture."

1. Romans 1:1–7—Opening
2. Romans 1:8–15—Thanksgiving
3. Romans 1:16–11:26—Body
4. Romans 12:1–15:13—Paraenesis
5. Romans 15:14–16:27—Closing

Notice how carefully the letter is organized, compared to some others we have seen. Every element of the letter form is appropriately represented. There are no double (or triple) thanksgivings, nor are there large sections of paraenesis mixed into the body of the letter. Pay attention, also, to the length of each letter section. Except for the thanksgiving, every section of Paul's Letter to the Romans is noticeably longer than the comparable section in all of the letters that we have already seen or will see in the entire New Testament.

What this outline does not provide is tools for unlocking the content of the letter. Therefore, as we move into the next sections of this textbook chapter, you will be given some detailed, content-based outlines for certain sections of the Letter to the Romans. These will help you follow the development of Paul's argumentation as he moves from one section to the next. We will begin with the opening section of the letter.

## PAUL'S GOSPEL

As we have already noted, the opening of the Letter to the Romans is longer than any of his other letter openings. This letter opening is remarkable in the fact that it provides us with a succinct description of Paul's gospel. You can uncover it by first isolating the basic elements of the opening: sender, recipient, greeting.

> Paul . . . to all God's beloved in Rome. . . . Grace to you and peace from God our Father and the Lord Jesus Christ. (Rom. 1:1, 7)

Next, isolate the descriptors Paul uses for himself: "a servant [literally, "a slave"] of Jesus Christ, called to be an apostle, set apart for the gospel" (Rom. 1:1). The word *apostle* means "one who is sent." Notice that Paul is using these three descriptors to establish his authority to write to the Roman community. What remains is his gospel—not a written work but his message of proclamation. You will find a flow diagram that illustrates the content of his gospel after the following paragraph.

The Christology (i.e., teaching about Jesus as the Christ) that underlies Paul's gospel as it is described here in Romans 1:1–4 is called a two-stage Christology. It has as its first stage the person of Jesus, the messiah, descended from the line of David. Its second stage concerns the resurrected Jesus declared to be Son of God with power. Contrast this Christology with that of John's gospel, for example, which has a three-stage Christology that can be described as follows: (1) the Son's preexistence with the Father; (2) his incarnation (i.e., enfleshment) as Jesus of Nazareth; (3) the Son's return to the Father at his death and exaltation. The former is sometimes described as a low Christology, because of its starting point. The latter is called a high Christology, because of its emphasis on the Son's divine origins.

```
The gospel
      of God,
         which he promised
                     beforehand
                     through his prophets
                              in the holy scriptures,
   the gospel
         concerning his Son,
                     who    was descended
                              from David
                              according to the flesh

            and [who]  was declared                          to be Son of God
                                                                    with power
                        according to the spirit
                                    of holiness
                                                             by resurrection
                                                                from the dead,
Jesus Christ our Lord. (Rom.1:1b-4)
```

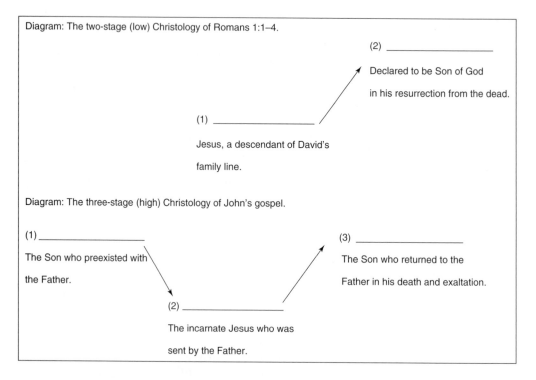

Diagram: The two-stage (low) Christology of Romans 1:1–4.

(2) _____

Declared to be Son of God

in his resurrection from the dead.

(1) _____

Jesus, a descendant of David's

family line.

Diagram: The three-stage (high) Christology of John's gospel.

(1) _____

The Son who preexisted with

the Father.

(3) _____

The Son who returned to the

Father in his death and exaltation.

(2) _____

The incarnate Jesus who was

sent by the Father.

At first glance, you might think that the biblical writer's Christology is not particularly important for our understanding of his New Testament book. In fact, a proper understanding of the book's Christology can provide us with opportunities to flesh out many of its other related topics and themes. For example, John's three-stage Christology can help us more fully appreciate his description of Jesus as the agent of the Father. Jesus is not simply a messenger boy, but he can effect what he is sent to do, because he comes from the Father.

Similarly, the two-stage Christology that is articulated in the opening of the Letter to the Romans helps us appreciate the significance that Paul attaches to the death and resurrection of Jesus. Throughout his letters, Paul appears to be little concerned about the sayings of Jesus, nor does he seem to know the stories of Jesus' healings or conflicts with the Jewish religious authorities—all that matters is Jesus Christ crucified and raised from the dead (see Rom. 1:16–17). For Paul, this is the good news of "Jesus Christ our Lord" (Rom. 1:4). As you read his Letter to the Romans, be attentive to the ways in which his gospel (Rom. 1:1–4) shapes the whole of his letter and, as a consequence, our understanding of its theology.

## PAUL'S ANTHROPOLOGY

After the opening and thanksgiving of this letter, Paul describes what he considers to be the status of humanity's relationship with God "apart from the Law" and without the saving activity of Jesus Christ. In other words, he is describing his **theological anthropology**. Anthropology is concerned with the study of various aspects of human existence, especially culture and the social development of humanity. Theological anthropology is concerned with the origin, development, and destiny of humanity vis-à-vis God. In Romans 1:18–3:20, Paul articulates his own theological anthropology—that is, his understanding of human nature, the origin of evil, and humanity's capacity to know God and of the relative advantage (or disadvantage) of being a Jew. He begins by explaining who is to blame for the broken relationship between God and humanity and why.

As you read this section of Paul's Letter to the Romans, you are invited to use this "read-along" outline so that you can more easily follow the development of his argument. What does he say about the kind of relationship that God intended humanity to have with God? What does he say about the nature of sin? Who does it affect? How and why?

---

### The Nature of Human Sin and Its Consequences

1. Paul describes the human condition and the origin of sin in the world from the perspective of the creation story (Rom. 1:18–32).

   a. No one has an excuse, since knowledge of God has been available to humanity through the elements of creation (Rom. 1:18–21).

   b. People have chosen not to acknowledge God as God, overturning the right relationship between God and created beings (Rom. 1:22–23).

   c. Therefore, God has handed humanity over to self-indulgence (Rom. 1:24–32).

2. As a consequence of humanity's sin, God is right to judge the Jew as well as the Gentile (Rom. 2:1–3:8).

   a. God is absolutely impartial. Jews have no superiority when it comes to punishment for humanity's sin (Rom. 2:1–11).

   b. Possession of the Law is no protection; only doers of the Law are justified, and that Law is the Law written in their hearts (Rom. 2:12–24).

   c. Circumcision is no guarantee; in fact, it can convict you (Rom. 2:25–29).

   d. The inevitable question is, What is the advantage, then, of being a Jew? Jews are still the recipients of God's revelation, the inheritors of the covenant. It is *God's* faithfulness as righteous creator and judge of all, not *Israel's* faithfulness, that guarantees Israel's favored status (Rom. 3:1–8).

3. God's judgment falls on all without exception (Rom. 3:9–20).

   a. Scripture (i.e., TaNaK) says that everyone, Jew and Gentile, is equally "under sin" (Rom. 3:9–18). A *testamonia*—that is, a collection of scripture quotations—demonstrates Paul's point.

   b. Paul's objection to the Law is this: Whereas some have boasted that it confirms their special status before God and special favor from God, it really only brings consciousness of sin; it serves to show what sin is (Rom. 3:19–20).

If you are able to follow Paul's argument and you understand what he is saying in Romans 1:18–32, you are probably feeling more than a little depressed and pessimistic at this point about a human being's ability to do anything good or productive. Although he is somewhat subtle in his approach, Paul uses personification to describe sin as this monstrous ogre who has been given free rein to destroy humanity with its power. God has given all of humanity up to the power of sin, resulting in a cascading flood of evil activity. It's absolutely overwhelming! All of this, because humanity, at its beginning, chose not to honor God as God and creator of the universe? But this is a big deal! By refusing to acknowledge that they are creatures and that God is the only creator, humanity rejected all that God intended them to be.

This is why God "gave them up." Notice that Paul does not say that God punished humans. Rather, he says that God allowed them to go their own way. Later theologians, starting with Augustine in the fourth century C.E., will use the term **original sin** to describe this tendency toward sin, this flawed human condition. However, Paul did not have a fully developed doctrine of original sin. Instead, he simply wanted to establish why all of humanity, Jews and Gentiles, needed justification, that is, acquittal before God. Humanity knowingly broke the relationship with God by refusing to acknowledge God as God and itself as God's creation, and what we experience as the sinful human condition is the inevitable outcome of that choice.

---

### HOMOSEXUALITY AND THE NEW TESTAMENT

People sometimes mistakenly think that the Bible, and more specifically the New Testament, has a great deal to say about homosexuality and homosexual activity. In fact, the subject is seldom addressed, and when it is, homosexual activity is listed as just one among many activities (sexual and otherwise) that biblical authors considered unacceptable before God (e.g., Lev. 18:22; 20:13; 1 Cor. 6:9; 1 Tim. 1:10). Romans 1:18–32 is different insofar as it is the only New Testament text that treats this subject as part of a theological discourse. But even this text does not provide the kind of clear-cut answer that some people seek concerning the morality of homosexuality and homosexual behavior. Here is what the New Testament scholar Richard B. Hays has to say about this text:

> The fundamental human sin is the refusal to honor God and give God thanks (1:21); consequently, God's wrath takes the form of letting human idolatry run its own self-destructive course. Homosexuality, then is not a provocation of "the wrath of God" (Romans 1:18); rather, it is a consequence of God's decision to "give up" rebellious creatures to follow their own futile thinking and desires. . . .
>
> Paul singles out homosexual intercourse for special attention because he regards it as providing a particularly graphic image of the way in which human fallenness distorts God's created order. God the creator made man and woman for each other, to cleave together, to be fruitful and multiply. When human beings engage in homosexual activity, they enact an outward and visible sign of an inward and spiritual reality: the rejection of the creator's design. They embody the spiritual condition of those who have "exchanged the truth about God for a lie."

Homosexual acts are not, however, specifically reprehensible sins; they are no worse than any of the other manifestations of human unrighteousness listed in the passage (verses 29–31), no worse in principle than covetousness or gossip or disrespect for parents. . . .

One more thing must be said: Romans 1:18–32 performs a homiletical sting operation. The passage builds a crescendo of condemnation, declaring God's wrath upon human unrighteousness, whipping the reader into a frenzy of indignation against others. But then, in Romans 2:1, the sting strikes: "Therefore you have no excuse, whoever you are, when you judge others; for in passing judgment on another you condemn yourself, because you, the judge, are doing the very same things." (Richard B. Hays, Awaiting the Redemption of our Bodies: Drawing on Scripture and Tradition in the Church Debate on Homosexuality, *Sojourners* 20 [1991] 18.19).

Hopefully, this brief reflection demonstrates the care that must be used in taking New Testament texts and applying them to contemporary situations. A biblical text that might appear, on first examination, to be clear and unambiguous in its application to a particular issue will, more often than not, reveal a more nuanced meaning when examined in its literary and historical contexts. Paul could not have imagined the possibility that scientists would discover genetic factors that affect sexual orientation. Moreover, we should always be cautious of simple answers to complex moral questions. Particular faith traditions develop their own responses to moral issues over time. Certainly, the religious literature of each faith tradition enters into its response, but so do other theological, historical, cultural, scientific, and sociological factors. Because faith communities are embodied in a particular place and time, we should expect no less.

## JUSTIFICATION THROUGH FAITH

Having described the sad state of humanity apart from God and the desperate need for humanity's acquittal (i.e., justification), Paul then moves to his teaching on justification through faith (Rom. 3:21–4:25). From our study of his Letter to the Galatians, we already know that this teaching has little to do with later Christians' debates about faith versus works, about whether we "simply believe" or do good deeds. Paul's real concern is whether or not observance of Jewish law has any value in light of the gospel of Jesus Christ. Jews were obligated to keep Torah law, and still are, because it was commanded of them in their covenant relationship with God. But Paul wants to be clear: Obedience to Torah law is not sufficient to earn acquittal before God. It makes no difference whether a person is Jewish or Gentile. Only God can acquit, because humanity's sin—refusing to acknowledge God as God and creator of all—is a direct affront against God.

Again, as you read this next section of Paul's Letter to the Romans, you are invited to use the "read along" outline so that you can more easily follow Paul's argument. His teaching on justification by faith can be found in Romans 3:12–4:25.

---

### How Humanity Is Justified

1. God's righteousness (i.e., merciful acquittal of humanity) is revealed in the death of Jesus, which is our redemption, for all who believe. This is justification by faith (Rom. 3:21–26). Major points in the discussion:

   a. Jesus is our redemption (Rom. 3:24). The term **redemption** means "to buy back or to ransom," much as one might have redeemed a slave by paying the slave owner the price of the slave. The term grace means "free gift."

   b. Jesus is our sacrifice of atonement (Rom. 3:25a). The phrase "sacrifice of atonement" ought to remind the reader of Yom Kippur, the Jewish feast of atonement.

   c. God exercises forbearance in dealing with humanity's sin (Rom. 3:25b-26). When Paul writes about divine forbearance, he means God's patience in holding back his wrath.

2. This has consequences for the self-understanding of the Jews (Rom. 3:27–31). Major points in the discussion:

   a. There is no place for boasting in the Law or in observance of the works of the Law, even though Jews are obligated to do it as their part in keeping covenant with God (Rom. 3:27–28, 31).

   b. The new "law of faith" is the creator's call to all the people, Jews and Gentiles, to a proper response in their relationship with God. This is not an abandonment of Judaism, but a refounding of the covenant (Rom 3:29–30).

3. Abraham is presented as a type (Rom. 4:1–25).

   a. Abraham was justified not on the basis of his works but on the basis of his faith (Rom. 4:1–8; cf. Gen. 15:6).

   b. Abraham, whose name means "Father of Nations," was the father of all the uncircumcised who believe—as well as the circumcised who believe (Rom. 4:9–12).

   c. The promise depends not on the Law (i.e., something obtained as a right) but on faith, so that it may be a gift, and the promise may be guaranteed to all Abraham's descendants who follow his faith (Rom. 4:13–17).

   d. Abraham's trust in the seemingly impossible promise is a type of the Christian's experience of justification through faith in the death and resurrection of Jesus (Rom. 4:18–25).

---

As he did in his Letter to the Galatians, Paul appeals to Abraham as an example of justification by faith. Abraham is an ideal choice because, in narrative time, his story takes place before the story of Moses and the giving of the Law; thus, there can be no mistake: Obedience to the Law does not justify (i.e., acquit) humanity of its sin. Only God can justify. And who is justified? The one who believes—that is, trusts in or is open to God's free and undeserved gift. Thus, Paul uses Abraham as a type of the justified Christian (though, of course, these Jesus followers were not yet called "Christian"). The term *type* means "pattern or model," like a blueprint provides a model of something bigger and more perfect. In biblical interpretation, types usually involve a comparison between an Old Testament person or event and a New Testament person or event.

## THE LIFE OF THE JUSTIFIED

Finally, in the third major section of this letter (Rom. 5:1–8:39), Paul describes the life of the justified. He explains how God's gift has transformed their lives and how they are now freed from sin and death. He also provides his readers with a theology of baptism and expresses his hope in the destiny of humanity by God's grace. All of this, Paul says, comes to humanity through God's gracious gift of justification. Although we have a tendency to use the words *justification* and *salvation* interchangeably, notice that Paul distinguishes these terms. **Salvation** means "being made whole," and Paul uses the term to describe what comes to humanity when God's plan of salvation is finally accomplished. In contrast, justification by faith describes God's gracious act of restoring humanity's relationship with God, which was effected through the sacrificial death of Jesus and is available to all who believe (i.e., trust) in him. Again, an outline has been provided to help you better understand Paul's argument as you read this next section of his letter.

---

### *How Humanity's Destiny Is Changed Because of Justification*

1. The justified Christian experiences peace and hope on account of God's love, which is poured out in Jesus Christ (Rom. 5:1–11). The measure of God's love is shown in the fact that Christ died for us while we were still sinners.

2. God's gift of justification means freedom from death and sin (Rom. 5:12–21). Major points in the discussion:

   a. Adam is a type of Christ: Just as one man (Adam) brought sin, and consequently death, into the world, so one man (Jesus Christ) brings life (Rom. 5:12–14).

   b. The interplay of "one" and "many" (Rom. 5:15–19) demonstrates the extent to which sin and death affected humanity but also the extent to which Jesus' death brings justification for all.

   c. "Grace" translates as divine favor, which expresses the character of God (Rom. 5:20–21). Paul's emphasis is on the free gift of grace.

3. Transformation of self is possible through union with Christ (Rom. 6:1–23).

   a. Paul poses an imaginary objection: If righteousness comes from faith, not deeds, then Christians need not worry about evil deeds. Wrong! (Rom. 6:1–2).

   b. Baptism, a symbol of transformation, is identified with Christ's death and resurrection; the baptized go into death with Jesus in order to walk in a new way of life (Rom. 6:3–14).

> c. The notion of slavery implies service: One is either a slave of the Law/sin/death or a slave of righteousness, which comes through faith in Jesus Christ (Rom. 6:15–21). It is not really an issue of slavery versus freedom (what people today might understand as license to do what you want).
>
> d. Sanctification is dedication to God in Christ Jesus. The end (result) is eternal life (Rom. 6:22–23).
>
> 4. The discussion on freedom from the Law (Rom. 7:1–25) answers this question: What is the relationship of Christians to the Law?
>
>    a. Concerning baptism, Christians who have "died" are no longer bound by the Law (Rom. 7:1–6).
>
>    b. Concerning the relationship of the Law to sin, the Law makes one aware of sin (Rom. 7:7–8). The Law is a "moral informer."
>
>    c. The Law allows for the evil that already existed to become a conscious revolt against God (Rom. 7:9–12). The Law itself is holy, but sin (personified) took advantage of the Law in order to kill.
>
>    d. How could sin use something good in itself to destroy human beings? (Rom. 7:13–20) The problem is in human beings themselves! There is a split between what we desire and what we do.
>
>    e. Human nature consists of two elements at war with each other: the mind and the flesh (Rom. 7:21–25). Humanity's only salvation is in the love of God manifested in Jesus Christ.
>
> 5. The Christian life is lived in the Spirit and destined for glory (Rom. 8:1–39).

In describing the benefits of God's gift of justification for humanity, Paul has only one major point to make: Justification by faith means freedom from death and sin. This assertion necessarily leads to a discussion of the relationship between sin and the Law because Paul has already said that the function of the Law is to make sin known. However, you can see that he carefully avoids saying that the Law is sinful. Why? Because the Law is, and will remain, the visible expression of God's enduring covenant with Israel. Paul concludes this section of his Letter to the Romans with a beautiful proclamation of faith in the life-giving power of God's Holy Spirit and an intense prayer of longing for the fulfillment of God's plan of salvation and the glory that awaits those who love God.

## ROMAN CATHOLIC/LUTHERAN DIALOGUE ON JUSTIFICATION

Anyone who has studied the writings of Martin Luther or the history of the Reformation knows that Paul's Letters to the Galatians and the Romans are important texts for understanding the doctrine of justification, one of the central issues of debate during that time. Consequently, they are also important documents for modern Roman

Catholic/Lutheran ecumenical dialogue. You may want to refer to the *Joint Declaration on the Doctrine of Justification*, which was completed in 1998, for an example of the current debate on this question. An excerpt from the document follows:

### 3. THE COMMON UNDERSTANDING OF JUSTIFICATION

14. The Lutheran churches and the Roman Catholic Church have together listened to the good news proclaimed in Holy Scripture. This common listening, together with the theological conversations of recent years, has led to a shared understanding of justification. This encompasses a consensus in the basic truths; the differing explications in particular statements are compatible with it.

15. In faith we together hold the conviction that justification is the work of the triune God. The Father sent his Son into the world to save sinners. The foundation and presupposition of justification is the incarnation, death, and resurrection of Christ. Justification thus means that Christ himself is our righteousness, in which we share through the Holy Spirit in accord with the will of the Father. Together we confess: By grace alone, in faith in Christ's saving work and not because of any merit on our part, we are accepted by God and receive the Holy Spirit, who renews our hearts while equipping and calling us to good works.

16. All people are called by God to salvation in Christ. Through Christ alone are we justified, when we receive this salvation in faith. Faith is itself God's gift through the Holy Spirit who works through word and sacrament in the community of believers and who, at the same time, leads believers into that renewal of life which God will bring to completion in eternal life.

17. We also share the conviction that the message of justification directs us in a special way towards the heart of the New Testament witness to God's saving action in Christ: it tells us that as sinners our new life is solely due to the forgiving and renewing mercy that God imparts as a gift and we receive in faith, and never can merit in any way.

18. Therefore the doctrine of justification, which takes up this message and explicates it, is more than just one part of Christian doctrine. It stands in an essential relation to all truths of faith, which are to be seen as internally related to each other. It is an indispensable criterion which constantly serves to orient all the teaching and practice of our churches to Christ. When Lutherans emphasize the unique significance of this criterion, they do not deny the interrelation and significance of all truths of faith. When Catholics see themselves as bound by several criteria, they do not deny the special function of the message of justification. Lutherans and Catholics share the goal of confessing Christ in all things, who alone is to be trusted above all things as the one Mediator (1 Tim. 2:5f) through whom God in the Holy Spirit gives himself and pours out his renewing gifts. (*Joint Declaration on the Doctrine of Justification*, §3.14–18)

Although this agreement between the Roman Catholic Church and the Lutheran World Federation was designed to identify the common ground shared by these traditions, you can see, even in this short excerpt, that these two Christian traditions do not share exactly the same view on justification. Why? Certainly, there are many factors that contribute to these differences, but the most fundamental issue is how one understands Paul's theological anthropology.

As we have noted numerous times already, biblical critical methodologies seldom produce a single interpretation of a biblical text but rather result in a range of interpretations. The same is true for the Letter to the Romans, but this is not necessarily a limitation of the methodologies; instead, it is a recognition of the multilayered and sometimes ambiguous character of the biblical text. For example, concerning Paul's theological anthropology, Paul is not clear about whether he thinks that humanity, in and of itself, is capable of any good. In the first place, he says that humans were made capable of knowing God as God, but they chose not to acknowledge God as God, implying at least that they have the capacity to do good (Rom. 1:18–23). However, later he says that human beings, by themselves, are unable to win the inner war between what they want to do and what they ought to do, suggesting that it is not in their nature to be able to do good (Rom. 7:14–20).

Luther, reading Paul and drawing on the anthropology of Augustine, believed that people were so thoroughly corrupted because of original sin (the sin of Adam) that, by themselves, they were incapable of any good whatsoever. With this anthropology in mind, he taught justification *through faith alone*, emphasizing the radical nature of humanity's movement from death to new life. Luther understood that his movement was entirely of God's choosing, and one that makes humanity into a new creation. He was so strongly committed to this reading of Paul's teaching on justification that he went as far as to suggest that the Letter of James, which advocates salvation through faith *and works* (James 2:14), should be excluded from the New Testament.

Others have read Paul's Letter to the Romans and understood justification more as a "repair" of the natural powers of human beings, which are still available, albeit in limited capacity, after humanity's first sin. In other words, human beings are fundamentally good, and even though they are flawed on account of sin, they are still capable of doing what is right with the help of God's grace. This was the position of the Council of Trent during the time of the Reformation. It is also the current Roman Catholic position. According to this view, justification is a gradual process of moral and spiritual transformation. God is still the one who justifies, but human beings are able to cooperate in some way with divine grace to do good. Opponents of this view would say that it sounds like human beings are capable of saving themselves. However, its supporters would say that they are simply acknowledging the goodness of God's creation.

What about this problem of faith versus works? First, when Paul is writing about justification by works, he is not referring to doing good deeds. Second, Paul never says that faith *without works* is sufficient for salvation, nor does this accurately represent the position of the Lutheran World Federation. Rather, it is a matter of emphasis. Luther highlighted the benevolence of God toward creation by calling attention to humanity's inability to do any good on its own. On the other hand, Paul never says that *works alone* are sufficient for salvation. But neither is that the position of the Roman Catholic Church. Again, it is a matter of emphasis. The Roman Catholic view calls attention to the inherent goodness of creation by highlighting humanity's capacity to cooperate with God's grace. Thus, the differences between the two Christian traditions on the topic of justification derive from different interpretations of Paul's theological anthropology, which underlies his teaching on justification by faith.

Needless to say, the *Joint Declaration on the Doctrine of Justification* is not the final word on the doctrine of justification by faith in the ongoing ecumenical dialogue between the Roman Catholic Church and the Lutheran World Federation. However, it does provide a helpful model for dialogue between and among churches on a variety of doctrinal issues. They begin with an understanding of what they have in common, and only then, from a position of respect for each other, do they try to articulate their differences and the reasons for these differences. This model is also beginning to show promise in interfaith dialogues among Christians, Jews, and Muslims. If Paul could be here today, perhaps he would say of this activity that it is evidence of the power of the Spirit working for the rebirth of all of God's creation (Rom. 8:18–30).

## ISRAEL'S PLACE IN GOD'S PLAN OF SALVATION

In the fourth major segment of his Letter to the Romans (Rom. 9–11), Paul addresses an issue that has personal significance for him: the place of Judaism in God's plan for salvation. The subject is an emotional one because he himself is a Jew and his identity is firmly rooted in the ideals of Judaism. This subject is also important for contemporary Christians because they often do not recognize their roots in the Jewish faith, and history tells us again and again that lack of understanding of one's roots is the "feeding ground" for disregard, hatred, and fear in all its forms.

Paul's response to the question about Judaism's place in God's plan of salvation is written in the form of a **diatribe**. This is a rhetorical device that involves the creation of a hypothetical dialogue partner who poses objections or questions that the author might expect the audience to raise. The author states the question or objection as if someone in the audience is putting it forward and then proceeds to answer it. In this way, the hypothetical dialogue partner allows the author to fully develop his argument and convince even his opponents of his position.

Paul introduces this diatribe by expressing extreme grief over the unbelief of his own people. You can sense the extent of his anguish as he wishes that he could take their place (Rom. 9:1–5). Then, through a series of questions and answers, Paul reasons how it is that God could keep the covenant with Israel even though some of his Jewish brothers and sisters refuse to believe in Jesus as the fulfillment of that covenant. So that you can more easily follow Paul's argument, you might want to read this section of the letter with the following outline close at hand.

---

### *Israel's Place in God's Plan of Salvation*

1. *Question:* Did God's word fail? *Answer:* No. Rather, it is God's free choice that certain ones are children of the promise: Isaac over Ishmael, Jacob over Esau (Rom. 9:6–13).

2. *Question:* Then is God unjust? *Answer:* No. God is not unjust, since God has the right to show mercy to whomever God chooses (Rom. 9:14–18).

3. *Question:* Then does God have a right to find fault with Israel? *Answer:* How dare you! Paul indicates that we do not have a right even to raise this question. However, he also says that God has patience with the "vessels" God has created (Rom. 9:19–29). Remnant is covenant terminology, referring to the small group among the exiled Judeans who stayed faithful to God's covenant during and after the Babylonian Exile.

4. *Interlude:* Paul interrupts his diatribe to speak again about justification by faith (Rom. 9:30–10:17). In particular, he wants to highlight the irony of the situation for Jews and Gentiles. The Gentiles who did not pursue righteousness received it through faith; the Jews who pursued the Law of righteousness did not attain it because they thought that it could be done by works—that is, by observing Jewish law. Notice what Paul says about the source of faith: "[F]aith comes through what is heard and what is heard comes through the word of Christ" (Rom. 10:17).

5. *Question:* Then did the Jews not hear or understand? *Answer:* Yes, they did (Rom. 10:18–21). Notice how Paul uses scripture to make his point.

6. *Question:* Then has God abandoned his people? *Answer:* No. Paul says that the remnant from among the elect of Israel achieved righteousness—but by grace, not by works (Rom. 11:1–10).

7. *Question:* Has Israel stumbled, so as to fall (i.e., be lost forever)? *Answer:* No. As a result of its stumbling, salvation has come to the Gentiles. Eventually, the Jews will be made jealous and be saved (Rom. 11:11–16). The term first fruits refers to the Jews' practice of offering the first and best of the harvest in sacrifice to God, as a symbol of the whole harvest being offered to God.

Paul concludes this diatribe with a message to the Gentile believers, telling them not to become overconfident by thinking that they are somehow better or more privileged than their Jewish brothers and sisters. To make his point, he uses the image of wild olive branches being grafted onto an olive tree. Grafting is a process still used today to create new varieties of apple trees or roses, for example. It is done by making a groove or slit in a major branch of one plant variety and inserting a small twig from another variety before sealing up the cut.

Thus, Paul compares God's inclusive family to the olive tree. The root is God's covenant relationship from which Israel emerges. The natural branches are Jewish Christians like Paul, whom he otherwise calls the remnant (see above), and the wild olive shoots are the Gentiles who have been incorporated into the people of God by grace. And this is the context for Paul's warning: The root supports the branches! If the natural branches can be broken off, how much more easily can the branches that have been grafted on be broken off (Rom. 11:17–24). Paul concludes with some additional comments concerning Judaism's place in God's plan of salvation: God's call is irrevocable, he says, and Israel continues to be God's beloved. When the full number of Gentiles has been brought in, Judaism itself will be saved (Rom. 11:25–29).

## PAUL AND THE LAW IN A POST-HOLOCAUST WORLD

One of the most persistent Christian stereotypes of and misconceptions about Paul and his teaching on the Law is that Paul rejected his Jewishness and "converted" to Christianity after his experience of the risen Christ on the road to Damascus

(Acts 9:1–19). People also mistakenly say that Paul considered the Mosaic Law to be meaningless and irrelevant. Some go so far as to say that Paul rejected the Law because the Jews were so caught up with "picky details" that they missed the point about living a moral life. Hopefully, after reading some of Paul's own writings, you recognize that these stereotypes are clearly wrong. Paul was a devout Jew who continued to embrace his Jewishness even as he preached his gospel to the Gentiles.

People's misconceptions about Paul's teaching on the Law are sometimes called "rejection and replacement" theology. You could say that this is shorthand for a variety of views that, in the end, sound something like this: The Jews rejected Jesus Christ, and therefore God replaced them with Christians as God's chosen people; thus, the Jewish people no longer have a place in God's plan of salvation. About now you might be saying, "Isn't this just an academic dispute?" No! "Should I even care?" Yes! Here's why. Strands of interpretation that develop and persist over time, and even get embedded in notions of what it means to be Christian, can have profound and sometimes disastrous consequences in the end. Scholars of Holocaust studies say that such deeply rooted societal prejudices against Jewish people, whether acknowledged or not, made it possible for Hitler and his supporters to exterminate as many as six and a half million European Jews from 1933 to 1945.

Scholars who concern themselves with questions about the anti-Jewishness of the New Testament and its interpreters point to the Holocaust—and the atrocities that took place in concentration camps at Auschwitz, Birkenau, Belzec, and Chelmno, to name a few—as a watershed event. They argue that Christians can no longer, in good conscience, read and interpret the New Testament in the same way, naively accepting anti-Jewish biases as if they were of no consequence. Sidney G. Hall III, a Holocaust studies scholar and a participant in Jewish Christian dialogue, says it best:

Remembrance poster at Yad Vashem Holocaust Memorial in Jerusalem, Israel. Photo by Catherine Cory.

Auschwitz presents Christians with an ultimatum—to reject intolerant theology and to shed the cloak of anti-Judaism worn for two thousand years. After the Holocaust one must recognize that "no longer is it a case of the illegitimacy of Judaism. Unless [Christians] succeed in finding within the New Testament some area which is substantially free of anti-Judaism, the issue becomes the illegitimacy of Christianity" (Gager, *The Origins of Anti-Semitism*, 202). But is it possible for Christianity to cast off its rejection and replacement theology and uphold the foundations on which Christian tradition rests? Yes! Such a theology can be accomplished and it can be demonstrated through Paul. (*Christian Anti-Semitism and Paul's Theology*, 21)

After establishing the need for a new look at Paul's writings, Hall investigates a number of passages from the Letters to the Romans and the Galatians that traditionally have been interpreted as Paul's abrogation (i.e., public rejection) of the Law. He gives particular attention to Romans 10:4: "For Christ is the end of the Law, that there may be righteousness for everyone who believes." Concerning this statement, Hall, along with a number of other biblical scholars, argues that the Greek word *telos*, here translated as "end," is better translated as "goal" or "aim." The reason? The context for this statement in Romans is an argument for the inclusion of the Gentiles in God's plan of salvation (*Christian Anti-Semitism and Paul's Theology*, 112), not the exclusion of the Jews. Thus, Hall says of Paul's teaching on the Law:

In his Jewishness [Paul] knew that God had not nullified the law for Jews. Nor had God rejected the Jewish people. But something new had been fully realized that confirmed what the law had promised all along: the Gentiles are incorporated into the people of God, not by faith grounded in the law, but by the righteousness of God through Jesus Christ. Jews did not have to accept Christ as their Messiah. Gentiles did not have to accept Torah in order to be children of God. God had provided another way for Gentiles to share with Israel the promise to Abraham. In Paul's vision, the gospel embraces Jews as Jews and Gentiles as Gentiles. . . . Thus the core of Paul's gospel is not Christ-centered but God-centered. Christ is the channel through which God imparts the reality of righteousness to the Gentiles. . . .

But my study of Paul has also unearthed the reality that the tables have been turned. What Paul feared might happen has indeed occurred. Christians "claim to be wiser than [they] are" (Rom. 11:25). The branches who have been grafted onto the tree "have become proud" in the grafting (11:20) and have not continued in the kindness God has shown them (11:22). The tenebrous irony of the church's understanding of Paul is that this apostle of inclusiveness has been misrepresented as the primary textual authority of Christian exclusionism. Paul was aware of the possibility for this misunderstanding when he wrote to the Gentiles, "Note then the kindness and the severity of God: severity toward those who have fallen, but God's kindness to you, provided you continue in his kindness; otherwise you too will be cut off" (11:22). As a Christian it pains me to say, therefore, that the only correct way to read Romans, indeed Paul, in the church today is to see that those who "boast," those "unenlightened in their zeal for God," those who are "hardened"—are many Christians! Those who have ears to hear, listen to Paul's words to the church after Auschwitz: "You that boast in [Christ], do you dishonor God by your boasting? For, as it is written, 'The name of God is blasphemed among the [Jews] because of you'" (cf. 2:23–24).

For Paul, Christianity does not exist without Judaism. Had Hitler been successful, Christianity would have ceased to exist. Out of the embers Paul confronts one with the near destruction not only of the Jewish people but also of Christian faith. His particular claim for Christians is that God is an inclusive God. His God brings resurrection out of the dark entombment of anti-Jewish Christianity. It is a mystery that in the darkness of oven chambers God's light has shown what real faith is not, and thus what faith should be. With God's help, one can bear witness to Paul's gospel today—that faithful Christians are those who embrace Jews as Jews and Christians as Christians. Indeed, faithful Christians are those who embrace God's inclusive promise of authentic existence for all humanity and the cosmos. (*Christian Anti-Semitism and Paul's Theology*, 127–128, 129–130)

## CHURCH AS THE BODY OF CHRIST

Up to this point in our investigation of the New Testament, we have not seen very many direct references to church or many explanations of the nature of church. You may recall, for example, Matthew's account of the confession of Peter, in which Peter declares Jesus to be the messiah and Jesus responds by saying that he will establish his *ecclesia*, meaning "assembly" or "gathering," on rock (Matt. 16:17–20). Later Matthew's Jesus delivers a discourse that describes the church in terms of reconciliation (Matt. 18:1–35). We encountered another description of church in Acts of the Apostles, where Luke says that the early Christian communities shared all things in common (Acts 2:40–47). They did not allow anyone to be in need, Luke adds. They provided mutual support, and they shared prayer, especially Eucharist.

Paul's letters give us many more images to help us understand the nature of church, and perhaps the most important is **body of Christ**. In his Letter to the Romans, Paul uses the image of Christ's body to explain how the many become one in Christ and how people with various gifts come together for the common good (Rom. 12:3–8). Thus, for Paul, church is best described as an "organic" sharing in the life of Christ, not as individuals but as a community of faith whose members are connected to one another through their mutual commitment to Christ. Further, not paying attention to the community and its welfare is to deny Christ and ultimately to harm oneself because the individual believer does not have life apart from the body. You can see, then, that Paul's understanding of church has important implications for the way Christians ought to live today.

The remainder of Paul's Letter to the Romans, apart from its long closing section (Rom. 16:1–27), is devoted to advice about how to live a holy life. The Roman Christian community is to act with genuine love (Rom. 12:9) and a holy zeal (Rom. 12:11), attentive to the needs of everyone, whether within the community or without (Rom. 12:13). No one is to act arrogantly (Rom. 12:16) or out of vengeance (Rom. 12:19–20). They should not resist governing authorities because they act in God's name (Rom. 13:1–3), and they should pay their taxes (Rom. 13:6). *Note:* This teaching was conventional for first-century C.E. Roman cultures. Paul also provides a summation of the commandments of the Jewish covenant, saying, "Love does no wrong to a neighbor; therefore, love is the fulfilling of the law" (Rom. 13:10). Concerning those in the community who observe Jewish religious practices, Paul says the others must be respectful (Rom. 14:1–6). No one should pass judgment on another, and everyone should work toward building up the other so that the community can live in peace and harmony (Rom. 14:10–15:6).

Clearly, these are not the standards of the world, and Paul knew that, but he also believed that baptism transforms the community of faith in such a way that its members have died to their old ways and now walk in newness of life (Rom. 6:5–11). But they must not let sin regain its power (Rom. 6:12–13). Thus, the words of Paul: "Do not be conformed to this world, but be transformed by the renewing of your minds, so that you may discern what is the will of God—what is good and acceptable and perfect" (Rom. 12:2).

## KEY TERMS

Theological
   anthropology
Original sin

Redemption

Salvation

Diatribe

Body of Christ

## QUESTIONS FOR READING

Read Romans 1:1–3:20. Provide evidence from the text to answer the following questions.

1. According to Romans 1:1–7, what does Paul mean when he uses the word *gospel*? What does he mean when he uses the word *apostle*?

2. What clues does the thanksgiving section (Romans 1:8–17) give us about the principal themes of the letter?

3. What does Romans 1:8–15 tell us about why Paul wanted to visit the Christian community at Rome?

4. According to Paul, why is the Christian community not permitted to condemn nonbelievers for their sinful way of life (Rom. 2:1–16)?

5. According to Paul, is there any advantage in being a Jew (Rom. 3:1–8)? Explain.

6. What is the purpose of the Law, as Paul understands it (Rom. 3:19–20)?

Read Romans 3:21–8:39. Provide evidence from the text to answer the following questions.

7. What does Paul mean by the statement "Now, apart from law, the righteousness of God has been disclosed" (Rom. 3:21)? How does it relate to his earlier statement: "The one who is righteous will live by faith" (Rom. 1:17)?

8. Why does Paul use Abraham—as opposed to others among the heroes of Judaism like Moses or Isaiah—as an example of justification by faith (Rom. 4:1–25)?

9. What does Paul mean when he says that "the promise rests on grace" (Rom. 4:16)?

10. Explain Paul's interpretation of Adam as a type of Christ (Rom. 5:12–21). *Hint:* The word *type* means "pattern" or "example."

11. What is Paul's understanding of the meaning and significance of baptism (Rom. 6:1–4)?

12. What does Paul mean when he says that the members of the Roman community have "become slaves of righteousness" (Rom. 6:18)?

13. What does Paul mean when he says, "Now we are discharged from the Law" (Rom. 7:6)?

14. How does Paul reconcile the fact that the Law is holy with his admission that people come to know sin through the Law (Rom. 7:7–25)?

15. What does Paul mean by the "sufferings of this present time" (Rom. 8:18)? How does he make sense of them or give them meaning?

Read Romans 9–16. Provide evidence from the text to answer the following questions.

16. What is the problem that concerns Paul in Romans 9:1–5? Why is this difficulty so great in his mind?

17. Paul's attempt to answer the problem described in question 16 consists of a series of hypothetical objections followed by his own responses. Explain *in your own words* how Paul responds to each of these objections:
    a. Has God's word (i.e., the covenant) failed (Rom. 9:6–13)?
    b. Does this mean that God is unjust (Rom. 9:14–18)?
    c. Then does God have a right to blame Israel (Rom. 9:19–29)?
    d. Perhaps Israel has not heard God's word or understood it (Rom. 10:17–21)?
    e. Has God rejected the people of Israel (Rom. 11:1–10)?
    f. Does the stumbling of Israel mean the Jews are forever fallen (Rom. 11:11–16)?

18. What does Paul understand to be the role of the Jews in God's plan of salvation (Rom. 11:7–12, 25–36)?

19. What does Paul understand to be the proper attitude of Gentiles toward Judaism (Rom. 11:13–24)?

20. From the paraenesis of this letter, make a summary list of rules for how the Christian ought to live (Rom. 12:1–15:13).

21. What would you say are the characteristics of church, based on Paul's imagery of the body of Christ (Rom. 12:3–8; cf. 1 Cor. 12:12–31)?

22. Examine carefully Paul's greetings to individuals of the church at Rome (Rom. 16:1–16). What conclusions, if any, can you make about how the early church in this area was structured or how it operated?

## QUESTIONS FOR REFLECTION

1. Describe Paul's view of human nature (without the gospel). Does Paul think that people are capable of knowing God? How? Are people basically good? If so, what is the origin or source of evil? What about your own anthropology? Compare your view of human nature and the source of evil in the world with Paul's view. How are they similar? How are they different?

2. How would you define *freedom*? Are there different kinds of freedom? How does your definition relate to Paul's understanding of freedom? How does it relate to your understanding of the purpose of law?

3. What would you say in response to a "committed Christian" friend who believes either that Judaism is irrelevant or that persecution of Jews is morally justified because "they refused to believe in Jesus"? In what ways would your response be similar to (or different from) Paul's response?

## ACTIVITIES FOR LEARNING

1. Construct a unified ethics for today's Christian communities around Paul's understanding of baptism as participation in the death of Jesus so that the believer might enter into new life with him (Rom. 6:1–4). What constitutes sin in this model? Make a list of behaviors that are considered morally right in this model and explain why. Make a list of behaviors that are considered morally wrong in this model and explain why. What is the goal of this ethic, or to what end would the believer do what he or she does?

2. Select a Christian church tradition with which you are familiar, your own or the tradition of a friend or family member. Find out whether the Christian church you selected has a teaching about original sin. How does this teaching explain the limitations of the human condition and humanity's tendency toward evil or sin? How does the position of this tradition compare to Paul's view that humanity was created with the capability of knowing God through the created world but chose not to honor God as God and creator of the world. You might begin your investigation by seeing whether or not the church tradition has an official summary of its basic beliefs. In some churches, this is called a catechism. You might also consider going to www.wabashcenter.wabash.edu/Internet/front.htm, where you will find links to the official websites of a large number of American Christian churches.

3. Do some research on the Jewish Holocaust of 1933–1945, also called *Shoah*. What were some of the events that led up to the Holocaust? What were some of the attitudes and/or dispositions that made the Holocaust possible? Who were the perpetrators of the Holocaust? Were there any heroes? One place to begin your research is the Simon Wiesenthal Center's Museum of Tolerance Online Multimedia Learning Center, located at http://motlc.wiesenthal.com/pages/index.html.

## SOURCES AND RESOURCES

Achtemeier, Paul J. *Romans.* Interpretation Commentary Series. Atlanta, Ga.: John Knox, 1985.
Bartlett, David L. *Romans.* Louisville, Ky.: Westminster John Knox Press, 1995.
Byrne, Brendan. *Romans.* Collegeville, Minn.: Liturgical Press, 1996.
Donfried, Karl P., ed. *The Romans Debate.* Peabody, Mass.: Hendrickson, 1991.
Esler, Philip Francis. *Conflict and Identity in Romans: The Social Setting of Paul's Letter.* Minneapolis, Minn.: Fortress, 2003.
Fitzmyer, Joseph A. *Romans.* Anchor Bible Series, vol. 33. New York: Doubleday, 1993.
Fredriksen, Paula, and Adele Reinhartz, eds. *Jesus, Judaism and Christian Anti-Judaism: Reading the New Testament after the Holocaust.* Louisville, Ky.: Westminster John Knox Press, 2002.
Grieb, A. Katherine. *The Story of Romans: A Narrative Defense of God's Righteousness.* Louisville, Ky.: Westminster John Knox Press, 2002.
Hall, Sidney B., III. *Christian Anti-Semitism and Paul's Theology.* Minneapolis, Minn.: Fortress, 1993.

Hays, Richard B. "Awaiting the Redemption of Our Bodies: Drawing on Scripture and Tradition in the Church Debate on Homosexuality." *Sojourners* 20 (1991) 17–21.

Horsley, Richard A. *Paul and Politics: Ekklesia, Israel, Imperium, Interpretation.* Harrisburg, Pa.: Trinity Press International, 2000.

Johnson, Luke Timothy. *Reading Romans: A Literary and Theological Commentary.* New York: Crossroad, 1997.

Karris, Robert J. *Galatians and Romans.* Collegeville, Minn.: Liturgical Press, 2005.

Keck, Leander E. *Romans.* Nashville, Tenn.: Abingdon Press, 2005.

Levine, Amy-Jill, and Marianne Blickenstaff. *A Feminist Companion to Paul.* London: T & T Clark International, 2004.

Neyrey, Jerome H. *Paul, in Other Words: A Cultural Reading of His Letters.* Louisville, Ky.: Westminster John Knox Press, 1990.

Roetzel, Calvin J. *The Letters of Paul: Conversations in Context.* 4th ed. Louisville, Ky.: Westminster John Knox Press, 1998.

Sanders, E. P. *Paul and Palestinian Judaism.* Philadelphia: Fortress, 1978.

_____.*Paul, the Law and the Jewish People.* Philadelphia: Fortress, 1983.

Talbert, Charles H. *Romans.* Macon, Ga.: Smyth & Helwys, 2002.

Wedderburn, A. J. M. *The Reasons for Romans.* Edinburgh, Scotland: T & T Clark International, 1988.

Westerholm, Stephen. *Understanding Paul: The Early Christian Worldview of the Letter to the Romans.* Grand Rapids, Mich.: Baker Academic, 2004.

Witherington, Ben, and Darlene Hyatt. *Paul's Letter to the Romans: A Socio-Rhetorical Commentary.* Grand Rapids, Mich.: Eerdmans, 2004.

Wright, N. T. *Paul for Everyone: Romans.* London: SPCK; Louisville, Ky.: Westminster John Knox Press, 2004.

# CHAPTER 18

# THE LETTERS TO THE COLOSSIANS AND EPHESIANS

The Letter to the Colossians
- AUTHORSHIP: Anonymous, perhaps a disciple of Paul; written under the pseudonym of Paul
- DATE OF COMPOSITION: 80–100 C.E.
- INTENDED AUDIENCE: Identified as the church in Colossae, perhaps a Gentile community founded by Epaphras, but the author provides few clues about the nature of the letter's recipients
- MAJOR TOPICS: The Colossian Error; Christology, Ecclesiology, and Eschatology; Catalogues and Household Codes

The Letter to the Ephesians
- AUTHORSHIP: Anonymous, perhaps a Jewish Christian; written under the pseudonym of Paul
- DATE OF COMPOSITION: 90–100 C.E.
- INTENDED AUDIENCE: Gentile Christian communities in Asia Minor (modern Turkey); probably not intended for any particular church community
- MAJOR TOPICS: Themes of the Letter; Marked with the Seal of the Holy Spirit

| | |
|---|---|
| 49–50 C.E. | The Jerusalem Conference is held to decide about the inclusion of Gentile believers. |
| 64 C.E. | Peter and Paul are martyred in Rome. |
| 65–70 C.E. | The Gospel of Mark is written. |
| 70–90 C.E. | The First Letter of Peter is written. |
| 80–90 C.E. | The Gospels of Matthew and Luke are written; Acts of the Apostles is written. |
| 80–100 C.E. | **The Letter to the Colossians is written.** |
| 90–100 C.E. | **The Letter to the Ephesians is written**, sometime after the Letter to the Colossians. |
| 90–100 C.E. | The Gospel of John is written; the Second Letter to the Thessalonians is written. |
| 100 C.E. | The pastoral letters (1 Timothy, 2 Timothy, Titus) are written. |
| 100–125 C.E. | The Second Letter of Peter is written. |

**c. 140 C.E.**      The Gospel of Thomas is written.

**150–180 C.E.**   The Gospels of James and Peter are written.

The next leg of our voyage through the New Testament letters that are attributed to Paul brings us to the Letter to the Colossians and the Letter to the Ephesians. The two cities named in these letters, Colossae and Ephesus, were located in Asia Minor (modern Turkey), only a little more than one hundred miles apart. Like the Second Letter to the Thessalonians, these two letters are thought to be Deutero-Pauline, that is, attributed to Paul but not actually written by him. They also share some literary features, as we shall see, and even some of the same content. Actually, biblical scholars think that the author of the Letter to the Ephesians copied parts of the Letter to the Colossians into his letter. For this reason, we will begin our investigation with the Letter to the Colossians.

## THE LETTER TO THE COLOSSIANS

The Letter to the Colossians is beautifully written, especially in its imagery about Christ as the firstborn of creation (Col. 1:15) and as the one in whom "all the fullness of God was pleased to dwell" (Col. 1:19). It also contains numerous ethical teachings, including catalogues of virtues and vices and a household code. The household code, in particular, is something that we have not yet encountered in our study of New Testament letters. However, before we explore these aspects of the Letter to the Colossians, let's review what biblical scholars have concluded about its authorship, date of composition, and initial audience.

## AUTHORSHIP AND DATE OF COMPOSITION

Until the modern period, most biblical scholars simply assumed that the Letter to the Colossians was written by Paul, as suggested by the letter's opening section. Those who continue to hold this view today do so on the basis of certain similarities in vocabulary and theology between the Letter to the Colossians and the authentic Pauline letters. For example, the author of the Letter to the Colossians addresses the community as "saints" (Col. 1:2, 4; cf. Rom. 1:7) and thanks them for their faith and love (Col. 1:4; Rom. 1:8). He also describes the church as the body of Christ (Col. 1:18; cf. Rom. 12:3–8; 1 Cor. 12:12–31). Likewise, in writing about the community's new life in Christ, he includes a formula like the one in Galatians 3:28: "There is no longer Greek and Jew, circumcised and uncircumcised, barbarian, Scythian, slave and free, but Christ is all and in all!" (Col. 3:11).

However, at least a modest majority of biblical scholars now believe that the Letter to the Colossians was not actually written by Paul. Their arguments include the observation that the letter contains a considerable amount of vocabulary that occurs nowhere else in the authentic letters of Paul. Some of this vocabulary occurs nowhere else in the New Testament or only in the Letter to the Ephesians. At the same time, the Letter to the Colossians lacks some of the language that we typically find in Paul's letters—for example, words like *righteousness, law, grace, belief,* and *salvation*. Most of the typically Pauline phrases appear in the opening, thanksgiving, and final greetings—segments that easily could have been copied by another author according to the pattern of earlier authentic Pauline letters. Additionally, when read in its original Greek language, the Letter to the Colossians reveals a writing style that is quite different from that of Paul's authentic letters. Thus, many biblical scholars conclude that this letter was written by some anonymous Christian under the pseudonym of Paul.

Judging from the content of this letter, the anonymous author apparently knew Paul's life story fairly well and had read at least some of his authentic letters. For example, he describes Paul as "in chains," probably referring to his imprisonment at Ephesus (Col. 4:3, 18; see Chapter 15 on the prison letters). Likewise, he refers to a number of people who are also mentioned in Paul's Letter to Philemon, one of the authentic prison letters of Paul. For example, Timothy is identified as a co-author of the Letter to the Colossians (Col. 1:1; Phlm. 1), Onesimus is named as Tychicus's travel companion (Col. 4:9: Phlm. 10), and Epaphras is described as one of their own (Col. 1:7; 4:12; Phlm. 23). Others who are mentioned only briefly are Mark, Aristarchus, Demas, Luke, and Archippus (Col. 4:10, 14, 17; Phlm. 2, 23). Because so many of the people who are named in the Letter to Philemon are also named in this letter—eight of ten; only Philemon and Apphia are missing—some scholars argue that the author of this letter had the Letter to Philemon in his hands when he wrote to the Colossians. With the Letter to Philemon front of him, he simply copied the names of Paul's colleagues into the new document.

Biblical scholars who believe that the Letter to the Colossians is one of Paul's authentic letters assign it a date of composition very near the end of his life, approximately 61– 63 C.E. However, we will follow the majority view, in which the Letter to the Colossians is identified as a pseudonymous work, written sometime between 80 and 100 C.E. Two factors come into play in assigning this date. First, the letter has a well-developed and sophisticated theology that reflects a relatively late date of composition. Second, it appears that this letter was already in circulation before the Letter to the Ephesians was written, requiring a date of composition before the end of the first century C.E. See below for a discussion on the dating of the Letter to the Ephesians.

## AUDIENCE

Before we talk about the audience of the Letter to the Colossians, we need to be clear that, like the author, the audience might be pseudonymous. That is, the pseudonymous author might have chosen Colossae as the literary destination for this letter because he knew that Paul had visited this city and he knew that there was a Christian community there. Thus, it is possible that the letter was never actually sent to this community. What we are reconstructing here is a portrait of the community, as the pseudonymous author envisioned it, based on clues in the letter itself.

The author of the Letter to the Colossians is somewhat vague about the identity of its audience. He does not claim to be the founder of the Christian community but rather names Epaphras as the one who taught them the gospel (Col. 1:7). Therefore, we can reasonably conclude that Epaphras was their founder. The author describes him as "our beloved fellow servant" and a minister on the community's behalf (Col. 1:7–8). The community itself appears to have been Gentile, since the author warns them against taking up circumcision and Sabbaths (Col. 2:11, 16) and reminds them that, in baptism, they "died" to "elemental spirits," perhaps referring to pagan rituals (Col. 2:8, 20; cf. Gal. 4:3, 8–9). In addition to the Christian community at Colossae, which is named in the opening of the letter, the author names the church at Laodicea as an eventual recipient of this letter (Col. 4:16; cf. Col. 2:1). Unfortunately, the Letter to the Colossians does not give us any clues about this community or its founder.

The author of the Letter to the Colossians indicates that the Laodicean Christian community also possessed a letter attributed to Paul (Col. 4:16). Although several letters by the name "To the Laodiceans" have circulated over the centuries, biblical scholars do not think that any of them is the letter mentioned here. Instead, they argue that this letter, if it ever existed, is no longer extant (i.e., preserved today). However, the author's request that they exchange their letters with each other is interesting because it suggests that, already by the time the Letter to the Colossians was written, Christian communities were collecting Paul's letters and sharing them with other churches. These letters most likely did not yet have the status of scripture—that would take a few more decades—but they were already seen as worthy of respect and useful for teaching.

## THE CITIES OF COLOSSAE AND LAODICEA

Colossae had once been an important manufacturing city in Asia Minor. It was famous for its wool and textile industry, and the name of the city was synonymous with the dark red dye used in wools. By Paul's time, however, the city had declined in importance and was described as only a small town. Colossae's population consisted of native peoples, Phrygians, and Greek settlers, but sometime in the first century B.C.E., it was home to a large Jewish community as well. Some scholars estimate that it numbered as many as 10,000 members by Paul's time. However, clues in the letter itself suggest that the Christian community at Colossae was predominantly Gentile. The city suffered considerable damage in an earthquake in 60 or 61 C.E. and apparently operated at reduced capacity after that.

Located northwest of Colossae, only eleven miles away, Laodicea was a major commercial city in the first century C.E. It had been founded during the reign of the Greek king Antiochus II (261–246 B.C.E.) and, under Roman rule, it had grown into a manufacturing center for clothing and carpets made from a special type of black wool produced in the area. Laodicea boasted a medical school known for the healing of eye diseases, and it served as a major banking center. The city itself was very wealthy, as evidenced by the fact that it rebuilt quickly and without aid from outside sources after the earthquake that destroyed Colossae.

## OUTLINE OF THE LETTER

The Letter to the Colossians is carefully composed, containing all of the standard elements of the New Testament letter in the expected order and without interruption or duplication. It is interesting to note that Paul's authentic letters are not always so neatly constructed.

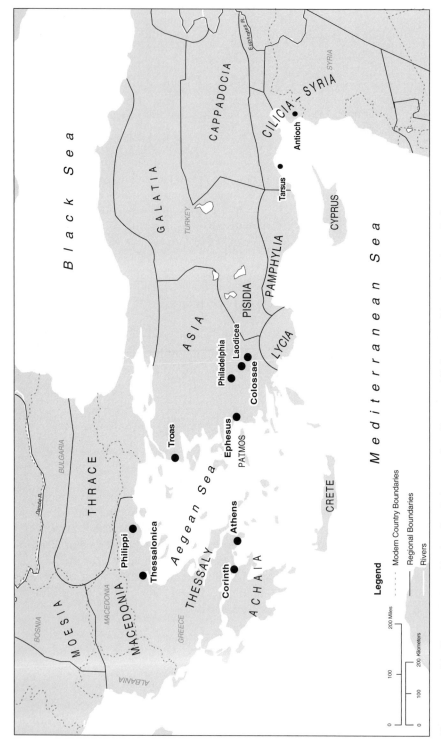

First-century Mediterranean world, showing Colossae, Laodicea, and Ephesus, with modern boundaries.

1. Colossians 1:1–2—Opening
2. Colossians 1:3–23—Thanksgiving
3. Colossians 1:24–3:4—Body
4. Colossians 3:5–4:6—Paraenesis
5. Colossians 4:7–18—Closing

When we investigate more deeply into the individual parts of this letter, we will find that the author incorporates a number of traditional materials that probably had already been circulating in some form among early Christian communities: a Christ hymn (Col. 1:15–20), a baptismal catechesis (Col. 2:6–15), some lists of vices and virtues (Col. 3:5–17), and a household code (Col. 3:18–4:1). The latter two were typical of popular (nonacademic) philosophical writings of the time.

## THE COLOSSIAN ERROR

Scholars have long been interested in figuring out what was going on in Colossae that prompted the letter writer to argue with such passion against those who would lead the Christian community astray (Col. 2:8–23). He warns the community about a false teaching, which he calls a philosophy, an empty deceit, and a human tradition (Col. 2:8). Whatever ritual practices were involved, they required observance of certain food regulations, asceticism (i.e., restricting food intake and other bodily pleasures), and festivals of the new moon and Sabbath, probably referring to participation in Jewish feasts (Col. 2:16, 23). The rituals about which the author is concerned apparently also involved the worship of angels (or worship with angels?) and elemental spirits (astrology?) (Col. 2:8, 18, 20). The author's repeated use of the term *mystery* (e.g., Col. 1:26–27; 4:3) suggests to some scholars that he is trying to correct their tendency toward the mystery cults (see Chapter 3). Likewise, his references to "knowledge" and the "fullness of God" (Col. 1:9; 2:9) prompt some scholars to think that the author of the Letter to the Colossians is concerned about a tendency toward Gnosticism (see Chapter 11).

Thus, the letter writer expresses concern about a community that appears to have made its own brand of Christianity by incorporating a mixture of elements from Judaism, paganism, magic, astrology, philosophy, and the mystery religions. A community like this is a good example of **syncretism**, which involves the incorporation of several different philosophies or religious practices under the umbrella of a single religion. However, because the author of the Letter to the Colossians is simply warning the community members about these errors and not actually saying that he has evidence of their involvement, we can reasonably conclude that the letter writer has experienced the consequences of Christian syncreticism, in whole or in part, elsewhere and wants to ensure that the same difficulties do not befall the recipients of this letter, if indeed he has a particular community in mind.

Syncretism is a phenomenon that affects every locale and every historical period because religions are always embedded in culture and culture affects how religion is practiced. Two obvious examples of Christian syncretism today are the Day of the

Dead (Día de los Muertos) celebrations in Mexico and the Santería religion of Haiti. However, there are many more, less exotic syncretistic practices that have become thoroughly embedded in American culture—for example, Easter eggs, Christmas trees, and Halloween on the eve of All Saints Day. Such melding of cultures and religious practices can be a profoundly enriching experience and an opportunity to witness the depth, breadth, and inclusiveness of God's revelation to all peoples. But syncretism can also threaten the core beliefs and practices of a particular religion. This is where a believing community's thoughtful reflection on the appropriation of culture is essential.

## CHRISTOLOGY, ECCLESIOLOGY, AND ESCHATOLOGY

The Letter to the Colossians addresses three major theological themes: Christology, ecclesiology, and eschatology. Each theme bears similarities to Paul's authentic letters but also goes beyond his teachings in significant ways. The first theme, Christology, refers to teachings about the person and mission of Jesus as the Christ that address these questions: Who is Jesus as the Anointed One of God? What is Christ's role in relation to God and the created world? The Christology of the Letter to the Colossians is most beautifully stated in a traditional hymn that the author incorporated into his letter immediately after the thanksgiving and before the body of the letter (Col. 1:15–20). Over the years, biblical scholars have devoted considerable time and energy to trying to reconstruct the original Christ hymn of the Letter to the Colossians. For our purposes, it is sufficient to say that the hymn contains two central Christological themes that are closely aligned to two parts of the hymn.

The first theme concerns Christ's relationship to creation and is treated in the first part of the hymn (Col. 1:15–17). Like personified Wisdom of the Old Testament, the Lord Jesus Christ is praised as "the image of the invisible God" (Col. 1:15), the firstborn of all creation (Col. 1:15), the one in whom all things were created and are held together (Col. 1:16–17) (see Chapter 4 on the personification of God's Wisdom).

The second Christological theme of this hymn concerns Christ's role in reconciling all things to God and is treated in the last part of the hymn (Col. 1:19–20). Christ is praised as the one who reconciled the believer through his death on the cross (Col. 1:20). He made peace (i.e., wholeness) in the entire created world through his crucifixion. The mention of blood in verse 20 is a reminder of ritual sacrifices in the Temple. Thus, the crucifixion is not understood simply as execution under Roman law; it has been reinterpreted to refer to a sacrificial offering to God.

Other special features of this letter's Christology include references to Christ-in-us as the mystery of God (Col. 1:27) and to the belief that Christians have already been raised with Christ (Col. 2:12), that Christ forgives sin (Col. 1:14), and that Christ is victorious over the principalities and powers of the world (Col. 2:15). None of these ideas is found in Paul's authentic letters. Likewise, the Letter to the Colossians is unique in the way that the author explains the meaning of suffering. He says that his suffering "fills up" what is lacking in Christ's afflictions (i.e., suffering) for the sake of the church. In this sense, the Christology of the Letter to the Colossians is closely related to the letter's ecclesiology.

*Ecclesiology* refers to teaching about the meaning of church and its mission in the world. The ecclesiology of this letter is different from that of the authentic Pauline letters in the fact that here "church" (in Greek, *ekklesia*) usually refers to the universal church—that is, the worldwide collections of churches—rather than to an individual, local Christian community (see, for example, Col. 1:18; 2:24). In addition, whereas Paul's authentic letters use the image of the body of Christ to describe the mutual and interdependent relationships of individual church members, this letter goes a step further, recognizing the universal church as the body of Christ and then identifying Christ as its cosmic head. Finally, while Paul focuses on the need of church members to build up the community and not be the cause of scandal, the author of the Letter to the Colossians urges church members to set their minds "on things that are above, not on things that are on earth" (Col. 3:2). In other words, the ecclesiology of the Letter to the Colossians produces a different kind of ethics than the ecclesiology of the authentic Pauline letters.

Both the Christology and the ecclesiology of the Letter to the Colossians are closely related to its eschatology. *Eschatology* refers to teachings about the end time and the destiny of humanity after death. Generally speaking, the New Testament contains two types of eschatology: future and realized. The eschatology of the Letter to the Colossians is what we call realized. Communities that hold this view believe that the end time is already under way. Thus, members of the community for which the Letter to the Colossians was written appear not to be occupied with waiting or preparing for the end time because they believe that it has already arrived, at least in a limited way. It is this kind of eschatology that accounts for statements like "you have died, and your life is hidden with Christ in God" (Col. 3:3).

## CATALOGUES AND HOUSEHOLD CODES

The Letter to the Colossians contains two types of moral teaching that were also used by some of the philosophers of that time, particularly the Stoics and the Cynics. These are **catalogues of virtues and vices** and household codes. For the most part, the catalogues were not the original creations of their authors. Rather, they were standard lists used for teaching good behavior or values (virtues) and for warning against bad behavior or tendencies toward evil (vices). When we see these lists in the New Testament letters, we should not assume that the letter writer has observed the community actually doing all of these things, good or bad. Instead, more likely than not, the author is saying, "If you wish to be moral people, these are the things that you must avoid (vices) and these are the things to which you must aspire (virtues)." Thus, catalogues of virtues and vices belong to the paraenesis of a letter. Colossians 3:5–6 is a good example of a catalogue of vices, while Colossians 3:12–15 is a good example of a catalogue of virtues. Among Paul's authentic letters, Galatians 5:19–23 is a good example of a catalogue of virtues, and Romans 1:28–32 is a good example of a catalogue of vices.

Likewise, household codes belong to the paraenesis of a letter and can be found in the writings of the philosophers. **Household codes** are moral instructions that focus on the relationship between superiors and subordinates. They emphasize the idea that the subordinate always owes respect and obedience to his or her superior.

Colossians 3:18–4:1 is a good example of a household code. Three pairs of relationships were typically included in household codes: wives who owe obedience to their husbands, children who owe obedience to their fathers, and slaves who owe obedience to their masters. Although such unequal relationships may sound quite offensive to modern ears, we should note that husbands, fathers, and masters were not given a "blank check" to abuse their power. Thus, the author of the Letter to the Colossians says that husbands must love their wives and treat them with kindness, fathers must not pick on their children for fear they cause them to be discouraged, and masters must treat their slaves justly because they themselves have a master in heaven (Col. 3:19, 21; 4:1). As we shall see, the Letter to the Ephesians and the pastoral letters also include household codes, but Paul's authentic letters have none.

## THE LETTER TO THE EPHESIANS

Among the letters associated with Paul, the Letter to the Ephesians has been grouped with his prison letters—including Philippians and Philemon, and now Colossians—because the author refers to himself as "a prisoner for Christ Jesus" (Eph. 3:1). However, most scholars today agree that it is a Deutero-Pauline letter. Like the Letter to the Colossians, the Letter to the Ephesians is famous for its beautiful and inspiring words about what it means to be church and for its description of Christ's role in reconciling everyone through his crucifixion. However, before we investigate these topics and themes, let's summarize what scholars have discovered about the authorship, date of composition and audience of the Letter to the Ephesians.

## AUTHORSHIP AND DATE OF COMPOSITION

Even before biblical scholars began to ask questions about the authorship of the Letter to the Colossians, they began to wonder whether Paul actually wrote the Letter to the Ephesians. The arguments against Pauline authorship are basically the same as the ones used for the Letter to the Colossians. This letter contains a considerable amount of vocabulary that occurs nowhere else in the authentic letters of Paul. Some of the vocabulary that distinguishes the Letter to the Ephesians from Paul's letters occurs nowhere else in the New Testament or only in the Letter to the Colossians. Likewise, the Letter to the Ephesians lacks some of the language that we typically find in Paul's letters—for example, words like *righteousness, law, grace, belief,* and *salvation.* Additionally, the Greek literary style of the Letter to the Ephesians is quite different from the style of Paul's authentic letters and much more like the style of the Letter to the Colossians.

To these arguments against Pauline authorship, biblical scholars have added a few more. For example, they have observed that the Letter to the Ephesians contains some understandings of eschatology and ecclesiology that are similar to those in the Letter to the Colossians (see above), but different from those in Paul's authentic letters. Even more convincing is the scholars' observation that the author of the Letter to the Ephesians appears to have copied certain phrases and short sections of text directly from the Letter to the Colossians. Here are a few examples.

| Colossians 4:7–8 | Ephesians 6:21–22 |
|---|---|
| *Tychicus will tell you everything* about me; *he is the beloved brother and a faithful minister* and a fellow servant in the Lord, the one whom I sent to you for this very purpose, so that you may know how we are and to encourage your hearts; | So that you also may know how I am and what I am doing, *Tychicus will tell you everything. He is the beloved brother and a faithful minister* in the Lord, the one whom I sent to you for this very purpose, so that you may know how we are, and to encourage your hearts. |
| Colossians 3:12–13 | Ephesians 4:1–2 |
| Put on then, as God's chosen ones, holy and beloved, compassion, kindness, *lowliness, meekness,* and *patience, forbearing one another* and, if one has a complaint against another, forgiving each other; as the Lord has forgiven you, so you also must forgive. | I therefore, a prisoner for the Lord, beg you to lead a life worthy of the calling to which you have been called, with all *lowliness* and *meekness,* with *patience, forbearing one another* in love. . . . |
| Colossians 2:19 | Ephesians 4:15–16 |
| . . . and not holding fast to the *head, from whom the whole body,* nourished and held together *by* its *ligaments* and sinews, grows with a *growth* that is from God. | But speaking the truth in love, we must grow up in every way into him who is the *head,* into Christ, *from whom the whole body,* joined and knit together *by* every *ligament* with which it is equipped, as each part is working properly, promotes the body's *growth* in building itself up in love. |

The words and phrases that you find in italics in the table above demonstrate how closely the author of the Letter to the Ephesians followed the Letter to the Colossians in his choice of Greek words and phrases. This degree of similarity is difficult to explain simply on the basis of shared oral remembrances.

Because of all these arguments against Pauline authorship, a significant majority of biblical scholars believe that the Letter to the Ephesians was written by an anonymous Christian under the pseudonym of Paul. It is possible that he came out of a Jewish Christian context because the opening blessing, "Blessed be God" (Eph. 1:3), is similar to the opening of Jewish prayers and because he distinguishes himself from his Gentile audience using the words *we* and *you* (Eph. 1:12–13; 2:10–11). However, the author may simply be reflecting his recognition that Paul was a Jewish Christian who preached the gospel to Gentile converts. If the Letter to the Colossians is dated between 80 and 100 C.E., then the Letter to the Ephesians may have been written sometime between 90 and 100 C.E.

## AUDIENCE

The Letter to the Ephesians gives few clues about the situation of the community to which the letter is addressed. In fact, early manuscripts do not even refer to the city itself (see the translator's note to Eph. 1:1). Thus, some scholars think that the letter was designed to be an encyclical letter—that is, a letter that is not intended for any one church but rather written to circulate among a group of churches (in this case, the churches of Asia Minor [modern Turkey]). The name of Ephesus may have gotten attached to the letter because the city was associated with the ministry of Paul (see Acts 19:1–41). The Christian community or communities for whom this letter was written apparently were operating within the same religious context as the community at Colossae. The repeated use of the term *mystery* suggests the mystery cults (Eph. 1:9; 3:3–5, 9; 6:19). The references to the "passions of our flesh," "knowledge," and the "fullness of God" may suggest some early form of Gnosticism (Eph. 2:3; 3:19). The letter writer describes his audience as Gentile (Eph. 2:11–13; 3:1).

## THE CITY OF EPHESUS

Because of its location on the western coast of Asia Minor and at the mouth of the River Cayster, Ephesus was an important commercial center for the eastern part of the Roman Empire in the first century C.E. The city was among the largest of the province, with a population estimated at 250,000. According to the Jewish historian Josephus, there was a substantial Jewish population in Ephesus. Acts of the Apostles suggests that Paul used Ephesus as his base of operations for two years during his missionary activity (Acts 19:1–41). In addition, early Christian traditions associate John, the author of the fourth gospel, with Ephesus. It is also said that Mary, the mother of Jesus, lived there for a time and died at Ephesus.

The city contained shrines in honor of a full range of Greek and Roman deities. Its most important religious site was the temple of Artemus, a Greek mother goddess and goddess of fertility, which was considered to be one of the Seven Wonders of the World. There was also a 25,000-seat theater in Ephesus. The library of Celsus was located there, along with temples for the imperial cult and shrines of the Egyptian deities. The city had also gained a reputation as a place to study magic. In other words, this was a fairly large, cosmopolitan city whose population was exposed to various cultures and religious practices and who valued learning and the arts.

## OUTLINE OF THE LETTER

A structural outline like the one you see on page 406 shows that the Letter to the Ephesians is carefully composed. However, it does not follow the typical letter format. It also lacks the personal character of other New Testament letters, which address particular problems within the churches. Thus, some biblical scholars have suggested that this document was a kind of "open" letter that could have been sent to any church.

Ancient theater at Ephesus, Turkey, which seated 25,000. The open-air stage is located at the lowest level in the center of this photo.

Archeological remains of statues, columns, and pedestals that line a walkway through the ancient city of Ephesus.

1. Ephesians 1:1–2—Opening

2. Ephesians 2:3–14—Blessing

3. Ephesians 1:15–23—Thanksgiving and prayer

4. Ephesians 2:1–3:13—Body

5. Ephesians 3:14–21—Prayer and doxology

6. Ephesians 4:1–6:20—Paraenesis

7. Ephesians 6:21–24—Closing

Like the Letter to the Colossians, this letter incorporates a number of traditional materials that likely circulated in other forms among the early Christian communities: the hymn, the baptismal catechesis and formula, the lists of vices and virtues, and the household code.

## THEMES OF THE LETTER

The Letter to the Ephesians appears to focus on and develop several of the same themes that we found in the Letter to the Colossians. For example, when you examine the Christology of this letter, you will see that it shares with the Letter to the Colossians the ideas that humanity was created through Christ (Eph. 2:10; Col. 1:16–17) and that Christ's death was a sacrificial offering to God (Eph. 5:2) for redemption and the forgiveness of sin (Eph. 4:32; Col. 3:1–3). Like the Letter to the Colossians, it also praises Christ's superiority over "all rule and authority and power and dominion" (Eph. 1:21–22; cf. Col. 1:16–18). At the same time, the Letter to the Ephesians moves outside of the Letter to the Colossians and Paul's authentic letters, calling Christ "our peace" and saying that his death creates "one new humanity in place of the two"—referring to the unity of Jews and Gentiles within the believing community (Eph. 2:14–16; cf. Col. 1:19–20).

Likewise, the ecclesiology of this letter is different from that of the authentic Pauline letters in the fact that here, as in the Letter to the Colossians, "church" refers to the universal church, the body of Christ, of which Christ is the head. At the same time, it uses some of Paul's other "church" imagery, albeit in a slightly different way. Thus, the author of the Letter to the Ephesians describes the church as God's temple and its members as God's household (Eph. 2:19–22; cf. 1 Cor. 3:16–17). There are also ways that this letter goes beyond the Letter to the Colossians, suggesting that the church is engaged with the activity of Christ on a cosmic scale. For example, the author explains that Christ sanctified the church and made her pure and without blemish (like a sacrificial offering or a heavenly bride) (Eph. 5:26–27). Further, he uses Christ's love for the church as the paradigm (i.e., the perfect example) of how husbands ought to love their wives (Eph. 5:25–30). The glory of God is said to reside in the church (Eph. 3:20), and it is described as the means by which the Wisdom of God is revealed in the heavenly world (Eph. 3:10).

## CHRIST AS HEAD OF THE CHURCH AND THE INTERDEPENDENCE OF MARRIAGE PARTNERS

Some Christians over the years have taken the metaphor "The husband is the head of the wife just as Christ is the head of the church" (Eph. 5:23) to mean that wives must be submissive to their husbands, who are the authority in all matters related to the home and family. However, there are other ways to interpret this text that both respect today's understandings of the importance of interdependency in marriage and honor the letter writer's metaphor of church as a marriage relationship. Here is an excerpt from Virginia Ramey Mollenkott's essay entitled "Emancipative Elements in Ephesians 5:21–33: Why Feminist Scholarship Has (Often) Left Them Unmentioned, and Why They Should Be Emphasized."

> Careful study of Eph. 5.21–33 would indicate that the word "head" is being used chiefly in the sense of "source". Just as Christ is the source of the church because there could be no church before there was a savior, so the husband who empties himself of patriarchal privilege is the source of the Christian marital structure and, in that sense, the source of the Christian wife. If Christ were actually the head of the church as its leader, ruler, and governor, as patriarchalists insist, then surely the church could not be as fragmented, fractious, and unjust as it has been ever since its structure was adapted to Greco-Roman social norms. To interpret "head" as "leader" rather than "source" is to blame the Christ for all the cruel faults of Christendom. Surely the burden of proof falls on those who insist on hierarchy where Jesus of Nazareth saw only a discipleship of equals! ("Emancipative Elements in Ephesians 5:21–33," 51–52)

Professor Mollenkott's essay raises some important questions about the right and wrong ways to interpret metaphors. It also reminds us that interpretation of biblical texts always has implications for other aspects of Christian life. For example, Ephesians 5:21–33 is often used as a basis for a Christian theology of marriage—the marriage relationship is a microcosm of Christ's relationship to the church—but it has also been used to sanction spousal abuse. Correct interpretation does matter!

The author of the Letter to the Ephesians is the only one among the New Testament writers to describe the unity of the church in seven aspects: one body, one Spirit, one hope (in their calling to be church), one Lord, one faith (referring to a set of doctrines), one baptism (referring to the sacrament of initiation into the church), and one God and Father of all (Eph. 4:3–6). The author also includes a list of ministers whose job it is to prepare people for the work of ministry: apostles, prophets, preachers, pastors, and teachers (Eph. 4:11–12; cf. 1 Cor. 12:28). These two statements have prompted some biblical scholars to say that the Letter to the Ephesians has a more highly developed ecclesiology, when compared to other books of the New Testament.

Finally, like the Letter to the Colossians, the eschatology of the Letter to the Ephesians might be described as "realized." The members of the community appear not to be preoccupied with waiting for the end time because they believe that it has already arrived, at least in a limited way. Thus, the author proclaims that Christ has already put "all things under his feet" (Eph. 1:22); that is, he has triumphed over all heavenly and earthly forces that oppose God. Likewise, the author of the letter sees the church community as already residing in some heavenly reality, seated alongside of Christ, with the angels (Eph. 2:6). Again, the most striking difference between this letter and Paul's authentic letters is the belief that the Christian has already been raised with Christ (Eph. 2:5–7).

## MARKED WITH THE SEAL OF THE HOLY SPIRIT

Both the Letter to the Colossians and the Letter to the Ephesians contain rich and beautiful imagery related to baptism. For example, the author, using a clothing image, urges people preparing for baptism, also called **catechumens**, to "put away" or "take off" their former way of life and "clothe" themselves with a new self that bears the likeness of God (Eph. 4:22–24; Col. 3:9–14). You may recall that Paul wrote about baptism in a similar way, urging people to "clothe" themselves with Christ (Gal. 3:27; Rom. 13:14). However, the Letter to the Ephesians is different from Paul's authentic letters in the way that it describes the baptized as being "marked with the seal of the promised Holy Spirit" (Eph. 1:13; 4:30). Although the receiving of the Holy Spirit is associated with baptism elsewhere in the New Testament, especially in Acts of the Apostles (e.g., Acts 10:47), the phrase "marked with the seal" may reflect some aspect of the baptism ritual, perhaps anointing with oil. Because of the pervasiveness of baptism imagery in this letter, some biblical scholars have suggested that the letter was used as part of the teaching preparation for the newly baptized or the soon-to-be-baptized. This kind of teaching is called **catechesis**.

## KEY TERMS

| | | |
|---|---|---|
| Syncretism | Household codes | Catechesis |
| Catalogues of virtues and vices | Catechumens | |

## QUESTIONS FOR READING

Read the Letter to the Colossians. Use evidence from the text to answer the following questions.

1. Find at least one passage (i.e., section or unit) in the Letter to the Colossians that suggests that Paul might not be its author. Be prepared to explain.

2. Find one passage in the Letter to the Colossians, apart from Colossians 1:15–20, that illustrates its Christology (teachings about the person and role of Jesus as the Christ). Be prepared to explain.

3. Find one passage in the Letter to the Colossians that illustrates its eschatology (teachings about the end). Be prepared to explain.

4. Find one passage in the Letter to the Colossians that illustrates its ecclesiology (teachings about the nature of church). Be prepared to explain.

Read the Letter to the Ephesians. Use evidence from the text to answer the following questions.

5. Find at least one passage (i.e., section or unit) in the Letter to the Ephesians that indicates that its initial audience comes out of the same religious context as the community at Colossae. Be prepared to explain.

6. Find at least two passages that reflect the author's use of traditional materials (creeds, lists of virtues or vices, baptismal formulas, hymns, or household codes). Can you make any conclusions about why the author might be interested in using these traditional materials?

7. Find one passage in the Letter to the Ephesians that illustrates its Christology (teachings about the person and role of Jesus as the Christ). Be prepared to explain.

8. Find at least one passage in the Letter to the Ephesians that illustrates its eschatology (teachings about the end). Be prepared to explain.

9. Find one passage in the Letter to the Ephesians that illustrates its ecclesiology (teachings about the nature of church). Be prepared to explain.

10. Find at least one passage in the Letter to the Ephesians that suggests that Paul might not be its author. Be prepared to explain.

## QUESTIONS FOR REFLECTION

1. If you were to create a written "portrait" of Jesus Christ based on your reading of the Letter to the Colossians, how would you describe him? Specifically, what does the Letter to the Colossians say about Christ's role or activity in relation to God? In relation to God's creation?

2. Given the positive and beautiful description of the purity and holiness of the church contained in the Letter to the Ephesians (Eph. 2:19–22; 5:25–30), how would you respond to someone who complains that today's churches are evil and not "of God" because the news regularly carries stories about clergy sex abuse, fraud, or other charges against church leaders?

## ACTIVITIES FOR LEARNING

1. Do a flow diagram of all or part of the Colossians Christ hymn (Col. 1:15–20; see Chapter 14 on how to construct a flow diagram). What does your diagram suggest about the meaning of the hymn or the significance of its message?

2. Do some research on Mexico's Day of the Dead (Día de los Muertos) celebrations or Haiti's Santería religion. What are some of its major beliefs or practices? What is its relationship with Christianity? How are Christian beliefs and practices enriched by this syncretism? What, if any, core beliefs and practices of Christianity might be threatened or compromised by this syncretism? Explain.

3. Do some research on the origins of Halloween, the Christmas tree, or Easter eggs. What, if anything, do these cultural practices add to Christians' understanding and/or appreciation of the feasts of All Saints Day, Christmas, or Easter, respectively? Is it possible that these cultural practices might be a detriment to Christian belief and practice? Explain.

4. Do a flow diagram of all or part of the Ephesians blessing, which some biblical scholars have described as a hymn (Eph. 1:3–14; see Chapter 14 on how to construct a flow diagram). What does your diagram suggest about the meaning of the blessing or the significance of its message?

## Sources and Resources

Barth, Markus, and Helmut Blanke. *Colossians: A New Translation with Introduction and Commentary.* Anchor Bible Series, vol. 34B. New York: Doubleday, 1994.

Donelson, Lewis R. *Colossians, Ephesians, First and Second Timothy, and Titus.* Louisville, Ky.: Westminster John Knox Press, 1996.

Harrington, Daniel J. *Paul's Prison Letters: Spiritual Commentaries on Paul's Letters to Philemon, the Philippians, and the Colossians.* Hyde Park, N.Y.: New City Press, 1997.

Hay, David M. *Colossians.* Nashville, Tenn.: Abingdon Press, 2000.

Krodel, Gerhard, ed. *The Deutero-Pauline Letters: Ephesians, Colossians, 2 Thessalonians, 1–2 Timothy, Titus.* Minneapolis, Minn.: Fortress, 1993.

Levine, Amy-Jill, and Marianne Blickenstaff, eds. *A Feminist Companion to the Deutero-Pauline Epistles.* London: T & T Clark International, 2003.

Martin, Ralph P. *Ephesians, Colossians, and Philemon.* Atlanta, Ga.: John Knox, 1991.

McDonald, Margaret Y. *Colossians and Ephesians.* Collegeville, Minn.: Liturgical Press, 2000.

Mollenkott, Virginia Ramey. "Emancipative Elements in Ephesians 5:21–33: Why Feminist Scholarship Has (Often) Left Them Unmentioned, and Why They Should Be Emphasized." In *A Feminist Companion to the Deutero-Pauline Epistles,* edited by Amy-Jill Levine and Marianne Blickenstaff. London: T & T Clark International, 2003.

Patzia, Arthur G. *Ephesians, Colossians, Philemon.* Peabody, Mass.: Hendrickson, 1990.

Smiles, Vincent M. *First Thessalonians, Philippians, Second Thessalonians, Colossians, Ephesians.* Collegeville, Minn.: Liturgical Press, 2005.

Stockhausen, Carol Kern. *Letters in the Pauline Tradition: Ephesians, Colossians, I Timothy, II Timothy, and Titus.* Wilmington, Del.: Glazier, 1989.

Thompson, Marianne Meye. *Colossians and Philemon.* Grand Rapids, Mich.: Eerdmans, 2005.

Wright, N. T. *Paul for Everyone: The Prison Letters: Ephesians, Philippians, Colossians and Philemon.* London: SPCK; Louisville, Ky.: Westminster John Knox Press, 2004.

# CHAPTER 19

# THE PASTORAL LETTERS

## OVERVIEW

- AUTHORSHIP: Pseudonymous
- DATES OF COMPOSITION: Probably 100 C.E., with the possibility that the Letter to Titus was written somewhat earlier
- INITIAL AUDIENCE: Named as Timothy and Titus, though these may be literary creations of the author; probably intended for pastors of churches in the eastern Mediterranean regions
- MAJOR TOPICS: Situation of the Churches; The Job of the Pastor; Ministry Roles in the Early Church

## TIMELINE

| | |
|---|---|
| **49–50 C.E.** | The Jerusalem conference is held to decide about the inclusion of Gentile believers. |
| **64 C.E.** | Peter and Paul are martyred in Rome. |
| **65–70 C.E.** | The Gospel of Mark is written. |
| **66–70 C.E.** | The Jewish War occurs, ending with the destruction of Jerusalem and the Temple. |
| **80–90 C.E.** | The Gospels of Matthew and Luke are written; Acts of the Apostles is written. |
| **80–100 C.E.** | The Letter to the Colossians is written. |
| **90–100 C.E.** | The Letter to the Ephesians is written, sometime after the Letter to the Colossians. |
| **90–100 C.E.** | The Gospel of John is written; the Second Letter to the Thessalonians is written. |
| **100 C.E.** | **The pastoral letters (1 Timothy, 2 Timothy, Titus) are written.** |
| **100–125 C.E.** | The Second Letter of Peter is written. |
| **c. 140 C.E.** | The Gospel of Thomas is written. |
| **c. 150–180 C.E.** | The Gospels of James and Peter are written. |

We have come to the end of the third leg of our voyage through the New Testament, the letters associated with Paul. Our last stop is the pastoral letters. Like the letters that follow these in the New Testament, the pastoral letters lack some of the elements that make us think of them as letters. They are generally thought to be pseudonymous works, reflecting a period of development in the early church that is at least a couple decades later than the time of the person to whom they are attributed. What makes the pastoral letters special, however, is that they give modern readers an opportunity to learn more about how early Christian communities functioned in the latter part of the first century C.E., when Christianity was beginning to develop its own identity, and what they valued in their shared life. It is a little bit like wandering off of the tourist path, accidentally peeking into someone's private garden, and then being invited in for a visit.

The New Testament contains three letters that are identified as pastoral—namely, 1 Timothy, 2 Timothy, and Titus. They are called **pastoral letters** because they are addressed to shepherds (i.e., pastors) of churches in Asia Minor and because they deal with community life, church organization, and religious practices. In fact, only two of the letters—1 Timothy and Titus—deal with church organization and community life. The third, 2 Timothy, represents the parting words of a famous teacher and preacher. All three letters are addressed to individual leaders of churches, even though their authors clearly intended them to be read by a wider audience. All three honor Paul as the authoritative voice for communities of faith. However, before we get too involved with the content of these letters, let's summarize what biblical scholars have concluded about their authorship, dates of composition, and initial audiences.

## Authorship

Although the opening greetings of the pastoral letters suggest otherwise, Paul probably did not write these letters. There are several reasons why scholars argue for this view. First, the pastoral letters contain vocabulary and concepts not previously found in Paul's letters—words like *piety, sound teaching, epiphany,* and *good conscience.* Second, the vocabulary and concepts that we typically find in Paul's letters—*body of Christ, covenant, the cross, freedom,* and *righteousness*—are absent from these letters. Third, 1 Timothy reflects a different understanding of the role of law than what is found in Paul's authentic writings (see 1 Tim. 1:8 and compare to Paul's view of the law in Galatians and Romans). Fourth, the details that the pastoral letters give us about Paul's travels and his ministry do not cohere with Acts of the Apostles or the letters that were actually written by Paul. Finally, two of these pastoral letters—1 Timothy and Titus—reflect a more fully developed church order (structure of leadership) than what can be found anywhere in Paul's time.

For these reasons, a considerable majority of biblical scholars agree that the pastoral letters are pseudonymous works, written in the name of Paul, but after his death. Again, although this might sound strange or even deceptive to our ears today, we need to remember that it was common practice among writers of ancient religious literature to ascribe their work to a famous person as a way of lending status to the work and honoring that person at the same time. Early Christian communities would not have seen this practice as a threat to the authority of the work. An added note: we will refer to the author of the pastoral letters in the singular simply for the sake of convenience. However, it is entirely possible, even probable, that these three letters were not written by the same anonymous author. Most notable are the differences between 2 Timothy and 1 Timothy and Titus.

# DATE OF COMPOSITION

When you read commentaries on the pastoral letters, you will see that the scholars' estimations of the dates of composition range from 60 to 160 C.E. Those who argue for the earliest dates believe that Paul actually wrote these letters. However, the arguments against Pauline authorship are fairly substantial. Those who argue for the latest dates think that it took that long for the early church to establish an organizational structure of ordained bishops and deacons. Against that view, we should note that 1 Timothy and Titus provide us with a list of qualifications for those who would be bishops and deacons, but they do not tell us that these persons were ordained for official positions of leadership or even what they actually did. Thus, the pastoral letters could easily represent a very early stage in the development of public ministry in the church, perhaps in the latter half of the first century C.E. Most biblical scholars take a middle ground, suggesting that these letters were written approximately 100 C.E. The pastoral letters are arranged not according to chronology but according to length. Thus, although the Letter to Titus was probably the first one written, the First Letter to Timothy comes first in the New Testament because of its length.

# THE RECIPIENTS OF THE LETTERS

Before we talk about the recipients of the pastoral letters, we need to be clear that their pseudonymous author might have chosen Timothy and Titus as the literary recipients of these letters because he knew that they were co-workers and companions of Paul during his missionary journeys. However, if these are pseudonymous works as we have described above, then we can safely say that the pastoral letters was never actually sent to Timothy and Titus, since they would have been deceased by the time the letters were written. In other words, the pastoral letters are literary fictions designed to honor Paul's memory and extend his message to a later generation of Christians, perhaps pastors and their churches in the eastern Mediterranean region. This is not to say that these works lack authority as sacred texts. Rather, we must allow for the possibility that writers of biblical texts were every bit as capable as their ancient counterparts (and as our contemporary writers) of using different kinds of literature, including literary fiction, to convey deep theological truths.

But who were these historical persons? Both Timothy and Titus were close companions of Paul during his missionary ministry. According to Acts 16, Timothy was of Jewish/Gentile parentage and converted to Christianity because of Paul. Later he was sent as Paul's representative to the churches at Thessalonica and Corinth, and he was with Paul in his imprisonment at Ephesus. He is named as the co-author of four of Paul's authentic letters: 2 Corinthians, Philippians, 1 Thessalonians, and Philemon. The introduction to 1 Timothy suggests that he was the pastor of the church at Ephesus at the time of its writing. Also according to Acts of the Apostles, we learn that Titus was a Gentile who converted to Christianity and who was one of Paul's companions at the Jerusalem Conference (cf. Acts 15). Paul sent him on a special mission to Corinth to deliver Paul's correctives (cf. 2 Cor. 8:16–24) and to begin the Jerusalem collection in that place. In the Letter to Titus, he is identified as the pastor of the churches in Crete.

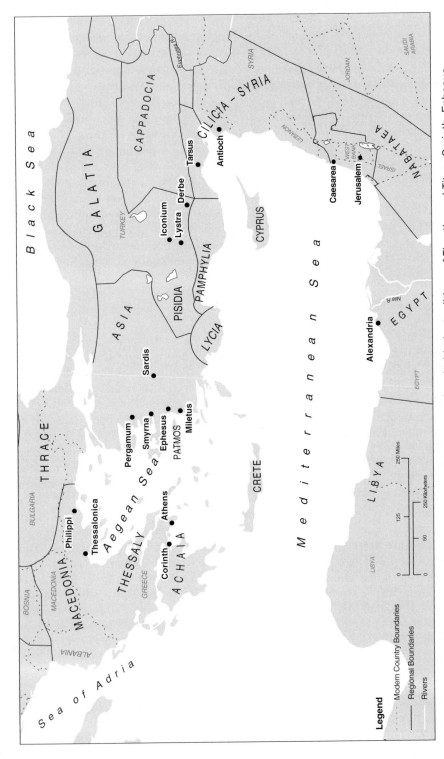

Eastern Mediterranean world, showing the cities and areas associated with the traditions of Timothy and Titus: Corinth, Ephesus, Thessalonica, Philippi, and Crete.

In sum, being of Gentile parentage, Timothy and Titus were themselves representatives of the churches that Paul established and served in his ministry. Because they were close companions of Paul in his lifetime, they were viewed as models of good and faithful church leadership. Perhaps you can imagine the first readers of these letters saying, "They learned to be good pastors by following Paul's example. We can learn to be good pastors and community members by following their example."

## OUTLINES OF THE LETTERS

The First Letter to Timothy and the Letter to Titus are similar in form and content. Both have some of the elements of a letter but not all. Because formal (i.e., structural) outlines are likely not to yield much insight into the meaning and significance of these letters, we will opt for thematic outlines instead. However, where appropriate, we will note the elements that have made people think of these documents as letters. An outline of 1 Timothy follows:

1. 1 Timothy 1:1–2—Opening
2. 1 Timothy 1:3–11—Thanksgiving (warning against false teachers)
3. 1 Timothy 1:12–2:15—Instructions on being a good pastor, on prayer, and on the proper conduct of women
4. 1 Timothy 3:1–16—Instructions on church order (qualifications for leadership)
5. 1 Timothy 4:1–5:2—Warning against false teaching and Timothy's role as teacher
6. 1 Timothy 5:3–6:2a—More instruction on church order
7. 1 Timothy 6:2b–21a—Warning against false teaching and Timothy's role as teacher
8. 1 Timothy 6:21b—Concluding blessing

The Letter to Titus is somewhat shorter than the First Letter to Timothy. It also bears greater resemblance to a standard letter because it has both a letter opening and a letter closing. An outline of the Letter to Titus follows:

1. Titus 1:1–4—Opening
2. Titus 1:5–9—Thanksgiving (Instruction on church order [qualifications of the bishop])
3. Titus 1:10–16—Warning against false teaching
4. Titus 2:1–3:11—Instruction on the proper behavior of the Christian community
5. Titus 3:12–15—Closing

As you can see from our outlines, both 1 Timothy and Titus address issues of church order and how one ought to live out his or her Christian faith in the community. Both also warn against false teaching and encourage the pastor to be the protector and preserver of right teaching. Structurally, both have standard letter openings, but only the Letter to Titus has a standard letter closing. Observe that neither letter has a thanksgiving section like the ones that we have come to expect in Paul's authentic letters.

Although the Second Letter to Timothy is similar to 1 Timothy and Titus in style, it follows more closely the form of Paul's authentic letters, and its content is somewhat different than that of the other two pastoral letters. It shares with 1 Timothy and Titus the concern about false teaching, but it does not address the question of leadership roles in the churches. More importantly, although it follows the form of a letter, some of its content sounds more like a farewell discourse—the parting words of a famous teacher to his forlorn disciples in the hours before he is about to die. An outline of 2 Timothy follows:

1. 2 Timothy 1:1–2—Opening
2. 2 Timothy 1:3–5—Thanksgiving
3. 2 Timothy 1:6–4:18—Body
   a. Encouragement for Timothy not to be ashamed of the gospel and of Paul, who is in prison (2 Tim. 1:6–18)
   b. Instructions about being willing to suffer for the gospel (2 Tim. 2:1–13)
   c. Warnings about false teachings and their teachers (2 Tim. 2:14–3:9)
   d. Encouragement for Timothy to be faithful to the ministry as Paul is about to die (2 Tim. 3:10–4:8)
   e. Personal notes about Paul's situation (2 Tim. 4:9–18)
4. 2 Timothy 4:19–22—Closing

In the sections that follow, we will focus on three major themes of the pastoral letters. The first is the situation of the churches for which these letters were intended—specifically the problems of false teachings and proper worship within the Christian community. The second is related: What is the job of the pastor who is responsible for the well-being of his community? The third topic concerns ministry roles in the early church. The pastoral letters provide us with an opportunity to glimpse the inner life of early Christian communities—how they were organized, what they valued in their shared life, and so on. We might ask ourselves whether the pastoral letters provide insights that might help contemporary Christian communities re-vision themselves for the world in which we live today.

## SITUATION OF THE CHURCHES

What do the pastoral letters tell us about the problems of the communities for which they were intended? For one thing, the pastors of these churches seem to be dealing with problems of false teaching (1 Tim. 1:3–7; 6:3–10; Tit. 1:10–16; 3:9). Apparently, the troublemakers called themselves "teachers of the law" (1 Tim. 1:7), but the letter writer calls them fomenters of "legal debates" (Tit. 3:9) who were interested in "Jewish myths" (Tit. 1:14) and genealogies (Tit. 3:9). Some of the writer's comments suggest that his opponents also lived a life of extreme asceticism, which involved celibacy and abstinence from food (1 Tim. 4:1–4, 7).

While some of these descriptions suggest that the false teachers of the pastoral letters were Jewish Christians who insisted that Gentiles become Jews before they could be members of the community or Gnostics like those behind the Gospel of Thomas, not all of these descriptors apply to any one group. It is also possible that the author of the pastoral letters had observed how Paul regularly commented about the presence of opponents in his authentic letters. Therefore, in his effort to imitate the form and content of Paul's letters, he created his own version of opponents, based on his knowledge of the churches in his own time. Another possibility is that he was trying to write an all-purpose polemic against heresies of any kind.

In addition to the issue of false teachings, the author of the pastoral letters apparently perceived that the churches had some problems related to proper conduct at worship. Thus, the First Letter to Timothy includes comments about how men ought to behave when praying and how women should "profess reverence for God" (1 Tim. 2:1–15). Notice that this writer, when compared to Paul, has a decidedly more negative view of women's place in the Christian community. Whereas Paul allowed women to pray and prophesy in public and even had female co-workers whom he called fellow apostles, the author of 1 Timothy says that "I permit no woman to teach" and that women "will be saved through childbearing" (1 Tim. 2:12, 15). The pastoral letters also contain advice for dealing with other kinds of problems and with peoples of all ages and social positions. The motive in each case is this:

An example of fifth-century church catacomb art that includes three persons standing with raised and outstretched arms, a position called the *Orans* (literally, "one who prays"). This fresco from San Gennaro Catacombs in Naples, Italy, features St. Varius with the deceased Comminia and infant Nicatiola. Several other examples can be found in the Catacombs of St. Calixtus in Rome *Picture Desk, Inc./Kobal Collection*.

"[A]ny opponent will be put to shame, having nothing evil to say of us" (Tit. 2:8). In other words, the community members' example of charity and proper conduct will convert their accusers or at least make them ashamed of their prejudicial behavior.

## THE JOB OF THE PASTOR

As we have already noted, the pastoral letters are addressed to pastors of churches, but what were these pastors charged to do? What was their role in the community? The writer of the pastoral letters had three things in mind. First, the pastor was responsible for restraining false teaching. Second, he was supposed to hold fast to the faith and the true doctrines of the church and be of good conscience/behavior (e.g., 1 Tim. 1:19; 4:16). Third, he was responsible for setting a good example for the rest of the community (Tit. 2:7–8; 1 Tim. 4:12–16). In other words, as the community's teacher, he was supposed to guard against heresy, and he was supposed to be a person of integrity when it came to his own faith and his behavior as a believer. Finally, he was supposed to live his faith in a public way so that, like Paul did with his communities, the pastor could say, "Imitate me."

Although not explicitly stated in the pastoral letters, we can assume that this notion of the pastor as an example for the community should never be seen as a source of pride or a reason for arrogance. The author of the pastoral letters took great pains to imitate the form and content of Paul's authentic letters, so we should assume that he also understood Paul's theology of ministry. Paul saw every hardship in his ministry as a way to more fully "know" (i.e., experience) Christ and share in his suffering until he could lose himself in Christ's ministry. Thus, he wrote to the Galatian churches: "I have been crucified with Christ; and it is no longer I who live, but it is Christ who lives in me" (Gal. 2:19b–20; cf. Phil. 3:7–11; Rom. 8:18–25). For Paul, Christ is the source of all boasting, so that he can say, "Imitate me," in complete humility. Among the pastoral letters, the Second Letter to Timothy addresses this issue of the right attitude or disposition of the pastor in the greatest detail, as you will see when you read the letter for yourself.

## MINISTRY ROLES IN THE EARLY CHURCH

The pastoral letters are unique among the books of the New Testament for their comments on leadership positions in the early church and their descriptions of the necessary qualifications of people who might be called on to take these jobs. If you recall reading Paul's letters, you know that he says very little about leadership roles within individual communities except for a brief mention of "bishops and deacons" in the opening greeting of his Letter to the Philippians (Phil. 1:1). However, most biblical scholars think these words, as they appear in the Letter to the Philippians, are better translated "overseers and helpers" because the Christian communities of the mid-50s did not yet have officially recognized leadership positions. This is not surprising because, in sociological terms, when a new group or movement first emerges, it tends to depend on the charism or vision of its founder for its direction. However, if a group is to endure beyond the passing of its founder, it needs a formal organizational structure. It also needs to work out job descriptions for its leaders and decide on the qualifications they need to have to perform their jobs well. The pastoral letters provide a window into the early church's transition from its earliest stages, when the community depended a great deal on the example and vision of its founder for its direction, to its later stages, when it began to develop a church structure that would ensure its survival for the long term.

Perhaps one of the most visible leadership positions in the early church was the **bishop**. The Greek term is *episkopos*, which means "overseer." Outside of Christianity, *episkopos* was used in a purely secular sense to refer to anyone who had a position of authority that involved responsibility for the welfare of others. For example, there was the overseer of slaves or the overseer of a trade association. When the term began to be used in early Christian churches, it referred to the head of a local church and was interchangeable with the term *pastor*. Thus, the bishop was the overseer of the church or the pastor (i.e., shepherd) of the flock. Early church writers like Clement of Rome tell us that bishops were selected by their communities and ordained by other bishops, giving them "official" status in the church. Although we do not know a great deal about the function of the bishop in the earliest decades of the church, it appears that he had two primary tasks: to act as the official teacher of the church and to preside at Eucharist, the Lord's Supper. Of course, as "overseer" of the church community, the bishop most likely had a variety of administrative functions as well.

Originally, it appears that there was a bishop for each local church community. However, as the early church grew in numbers, some churches were served by ordained persons who did not have the rank of bishop, and some bishoprics (i.e., the churches that the bishops oversaw) came to be viewed as more important than others. Sometimes these developments were due to the relative size and importance of the city in which the bishopric was located. Other times they had to do with the history of a church and its line of bishops. Especially important were those churches that could trace themselves and their bishops back to the earliest decades of the history of Christianity. Among these were the churches at Jerusalem, Alexandria (in Egypt), Antioch (in Syria), and Rome. These churches soon became the model of what it meant to be a Christian community, and their bishops were sought out for their wisdom in leadership of the larger church. Already in the second century C.E., Irenaeus of Lyons singled out the church at Rome for special recognition because that church could demonstrate **apostolic succession**, meaning that the teaching authority of its bishop could be traced back to the apostles, who had received their authority to teach from Jesus himself. However, it was not until the third century that Christianity (in the West at least) began to view the bishop of Rome as the bishop above all other bishops, later known as the pope.

Similar to the bishop, the **deacon** had an official capacity within the local church. The Greek word is *diakonos*, meaning "minister." Like the term *bishop*, the word *deacon* had a secular or generic meaning. Originally, it described anyone who served—for example, a table waiter. The First Letter to Timothy and the Letter to Titus tell us only the qualifications of the deacon and not his work, so we do not know what activities the first-century deacon performed within the church. However, by the end of the second century at least, the deacon came to be identified as the assistant to the bishop or a co-worker with the presbyter (see page 421). In these capacities, the deacon apparently performed a wide variety of tasks, depending on the needs of the community and responsibilities of the bishop. For example, the deacon assisted with the arrangements for Eucharist and other worship services, prepared people for baptism, provided assistance to the poor and sick in the church community, and even buried the dead. The deacon also helped with the administrative work of the church and acted as a messenger for the church. We know that deacons performed such services because they are mentioned in third- and fourth-century Christian writings.

Alongside of (or perhaps under) the deacon was the **deaconess**. Again, our principal sources of information about the role of deaconesses are writings of a later century—in this case, writings of third-century Christians. We know that deaconesses were accountable to the deacon. Because of cultural restrictions on interactions between men and women, they were usually given responsibility for the care of sick and elderly women in the Christian community. They also assisted with the baptism of women, since rules of modesty prohibited men from performing some of the rituals of baptism—full immersion in water and anointing with oil—on women. In some cases, it appears that they were responsible for teaching other women about the faith. They also helped arrange the seating of women at Eucharist.

Some biblical scholars question whether the New Testament says anything about the existence of deaconesses. For example, should the term *diakonos*, used to describe Phoebe in Romans 16:1, be translated generically as "minister"—that is, a table waitress—or more formally as "deacon," indicating an officially recognized position within the church. Likewise, should "the women too" in 1 Timothy 3:11 be understood to refer to deaconesses or to wives of deacons. Unfortunately, the pastoral letters do not provide enough evidence, one way or the other, to make any decisive conclusions about deaconesses in the New Testament church. However, in favor of the view that the New Testament church did have deaconesses is an argument of consistency. Why translate *diakonos* (a masculine noun) to mean "ordained deacon" when referring to a man but then translate it as "waitress or minister" when referring to a woman? If the New Testament writers intended to identify these women simply as table waiters, why not use the feminine form of this noun, as dictated by the rules of Greek grammar?

The First Letter to Timothy identifies another rather interesting group within the early church—namely, the widows. In ancient societies, the situation of the widow was quite desperate for the most part. Unless a widow was somehow independently wealthy, she had few choices for her livelihood except to return to her father's house or go to the home of one of her sons. Even if her family was willing to take her in, she was generally considered a burden. If her family was unwilling to take her or she had no living male family members, she was doomed to become a beggar or a prostitute. However, early Christianity inherited from its Jewish origins the command to "care for the widow and orphan," and as a result, Christian communities developed the practice of providing financial support to the widows of the church quite early in their history—at least by the end of the first century C.E., as is evident in 1 Timothy.

We know from several second- and third-century Christian writers that there existed an **order of widows**, which enrolled women who were "truly widowed"—that is, women who had no family to support them and who were at least sixty years of age. Given life expectancies of the time, perhaps averaging forty-five to fifty years, this age restriction meant that these widows were extremely old. Perhaps the reason for the minimum age limit was to ensure that these widows were not tempted later to remarry after they had been admitted to the order of widows. Although not ordained, each member of the order of widows was expected to take on the role of "prayer person" for the community. To abandon her holy position would be to go back on a commitment to God and to the community. In general, a member of the order had to be a moral person with a reputation for having raised her children well and lived a life of charity. In essence, she became the model and mentor for younger Christian women to teach them how to live their faith with their families and in their community.

Finally, the pastoral letters mention briefly the role of the **presbyter** or elder. The precise role of presbyters in the early church is not known. Perhaps their role was primarily ceremonial or symbolic, representing the apostles gathered around the bishop, who represented Christ, at Eucharist. Another possibility is that they were part of early Christianity's attempts to parallel the organization of the synagogue. The word *synagogue* means "assembly," as does the word *ecclesia*, which is also translated as "church." The synagogue had its elders, who served as leaders in various capacities, and scholars think that the presbyters might have played a similar role in the early church. Some presbyters were teachers, having gained authority for their ministry on account of their witness to the faith under the threat of martyrdom.

## LEADERSHIP ROLES IN THE EARLY CHURCH

Historians of the early church depend on a variety of sources to reconstruct the origins and development of leadership roles in the early church. The following excerpts are from the *Apostolic Constitutions*, a document that dates to approximately 380 C.E., though some of its content comes from an earlier document, the *Didascalia Apostolorum*, which is usually assigned a date of 250 C.E. The first is a prayer for the ordination of a deaconess. The second is instruction to nonordained church members, called the **laity**, concerning the authority of the bishop and those who assist him in the ministry of the church.

**BOOK VIII.XX.** Prayer for the Ordination of a Deaconess.

O Eternal God, the Father of our Lord Jesus Christ, the Creator of man and of woman, who didst replenish with the Spirit Miriam, and Deborah, and Anna, and Huldah; (6) who didst not disdain that Thy only begotten Son should be born of a woman; who also in the tabernacle of the testimony, and in the temple, didst ordain women to be keepers of Thy holy gates,—do Thou now also look down upon this Thy servant, who is to be ordained to the office of a deaconess, and grant her Thy Holy Spirit, and "cleanse her from all filthiness of flesh and spirit," (7) that she may worthily discharge the work which is committed to her to Thy glory, and the praise of Thy Christ, with whom glory and adoration be to Thee and the Holy Spirit for ever. Amen. (Roberts and Donaldson, *Ante-Nicene Fathers*, 7.492)

**BOOK II.XXVI.** According to what patterns and dignity every order of the clergy is appointed by God.

The bishop, he is the minister of the word, the keeper of knowledge, the mediator between God and you in the several parts of your divine worship. He is the teacher of piety; and, next after God, he is your father, who has begotten you again to the adoption of sons by water and the Spirit. He is your ruler and governor; he is your king and potentate; he is, next after God, your earthly god, who has a right to be honored by you. For concerning him, arid such as he, it is that God pronounces, "I have said, Ye are gods; and ye are all children of the Most High." (2) And, "Ye shall not speak evil of the gods." (3) For let the bishop preside over you as one honoured with the authority of God, which he is to exercise over the clergy, and by which he is to govern all the people.

But let the deacon minister to him, as Christ does to His Father; (4) and let him serve him unblameably in all things, as Christ does nothing of Himself, but does always those things that please His Father.

Let also the deaconess be honoured by you in the place of the Holy Ghost, and not do or say anything without the deacon; as neither does the Comforter say or do anything of Himself, but gives glory to Christ by waiting for His pleasure. And as we cannot believe on Christ without the teaching of the Spirit, so let not any woman address herself to the deacon or bishop without the deaconess.

Let the presbyters be esteemed by you to represent us the apostles, and let them be the teachers of divine knowledge; since our Lord, when He sent us, said, "Go ye, and make disciples of all nations, baptizing them in the name of the Father, and of the Son, and of the Holy Ghost: teaching them to observe all things whatsoever I have commanded you." (5) Let the widows and orphans be esteemed as representing the altar of burnt-offering; and let the virgins be honoured as representing the altar of incense, and the incense itself. (Roberts and Donaldson, *Ante-Nicene Fathers*, 7.401)

## KEY TERMS

| | | |
|---|---|---|
| Pastoral letters | Deacon | Presbyter |
| Bishop | Deaconess | Laity |
| Apostolic succession | Order of widows | |

## QUESTIONS FOR READING

Read the First Letter to Timothy and the Letter to Titus. Use evidence from the readings to support your responses to the following questions.

1. What does the author of 1 Timothy mean when he says that "the law is good" (1 Tim. 1:8–10)? To what kind of law does he refer? How does this compare with Paul's comments on the Law in Romans 7?

2. What does the author of 1 Timothy say about proper conduct at worship (1 Tim. 2:1–15) with regard to
   a. What kinds of prayer intentions are appropriate?
   b. How men should act?
   c. How women should act?

3. What kind of advice do 1 Timothy and Titus give to pastors concerning

    a. The treatment of older people and their role in the community (1 Tim. 5:1–2; Tit. 2:1–3)?

    b. How younger people in the community should behave (Tit. 2:4–6)?

    c. How slaves and masters should behave (1 Tim. 6:1–23; Tit. 2:9)?

    d. What wealthy people in the community should do (1 Tim. 6:17–18)?

    e. How the community should act toward political authorities (Tit. 3:1–2)?

4. What do 1 Timothy and Titus say about the requirements for admission to the church ministry role of

    a. Bishop (1 Tim. 3:1–7; Tit. 1:7–9)?

    b. Presbyter (1 Tim. 5:17–22; Tit. 1:5–6)?

    c. Deacon/deaconess (1 Tim. 3:8–13)?

    d. Widow (1 Tim. 5:3–16)?

Read the Second Letter to Timothy. Use evidence from the reading to support your responses to the following questions.

5. In 2 Timothy 1:3–7, the phrase "laying on hands" refers to commissioning for ministry (cf. 1 Tim. 4:14). The author of 2 Timothy suggests that certain gifts come with this "laying on hands." What are they? How will the commissioned person know that he has these gifts?

6. Several times the author of 2 Timothy describes Paul as suffering for a purpose. What does he think will come as a result of Paul's suffering?

7. The author of 2 Timothy describes Paul as using three images—the soldier, the athlete, and the farmer—to encourage a certain response from Timothy (2 Tim. 2:1–7). What point is he trying to make?

8. The author of 2 Timothy believes that the end time has already begun. What signs does he associate with its coming (2 Tim. 3:1–9)? How should Timothy respond in light of this news?

## QUESTIONS FOR REFLECTION

1. What insights might today's Christians glean from the pastoral letters that could help them deal with modern church problems? Identify a current church problem and provide an interpretation of some aspect of the teachings contained in the pastoral letters that might serve as a contemporary response to that problem.

2. Suppose that Christian churches today were organized in the same way as they were in the early church. What difference, if any, would this re-visioning of the church make for today's Christians? Explain.

## ACTIVITIES FOR LEARNING

1. Research the origin and development of ordained deaconesses or the order of widows in the early church. What were the admissions requirements for either of these groups? What role or function did they play in their larger church communities? Use the bibliography below to get started.

2. Investigate how your own church tradition or the church tradition of a friend or family member understands the role of the pastor and deacon. If possible, interview the pastor or a deacon within that church tradition, and ask for an explanation of how he or she views the responsibility of the pastor or deacon to the larger community. You might also try to locate official documents that describe that church tradition's views on the role of the pastor or deacon. One place to start your investigation is the Wabash Center website, *www.wabashcenter.wabash.edu/Internet/front.htm,* where you will find links to the official websites of a large number of American Christian churches.

## SOURCES AND RESOURCES

Bassler, Jouette M. *1 Timothy, 2 Timothy, Titus.* Nashville, Tenn.: Abingdon Press, 1996.

Cloke, Gillian. *This Female Man of God: Women and Spiritual Power in the Patristic Age, AD 350–450.* London: Routledge, 1995.

Collins, Raymond F. *1 and 2 Timothy and Titus.* Louisville, Ky.: Westminster John Knox Press, 2002.

Davies, Margaret. *The Pastoral Epistles: I and II Timothy and Titus.* London: Epworth Press, 1996.

Donelson, Lewis R. *Colossians, Ephesians, First and Second Timothy, and Titus.* Louisville, Ky.: Westminster John Knox Press, 1996.

Fee, Gordon D. *1 and 2 Timothy, Titus.* Peabody, Mass.: Hendrickson, 1988.

Hanson, A. T. *The Pastoral Epistles.* Grand Rapids, Mich.: Eerdmans, 1982.

Harding, Mark. *What Are They Saying about the Pastoral Epistles?* New York: Paulist Press, 2001.

Johnson, Luke Timothy. *Letters to Paul's Delegates: 1 Timothy, 2 Timothy, Titus.* Valley Forge, Pa.: Trinity Press International, 1996.

Karris, Robert J. *The Pastoral Epistles.* Wilmington, Del.: Glazier, 1979.

Kramer, Ross, and Mary Rose D'Angelo, eds. *Women and Christian Origins.* New York: Oxford University Press, 1999.

Krodel, Gerhard, ed. *The Deutero-Pauline Letters: Ephesians, Colossians, 2 Thessalonians, 1–2 Timothy, Titus.* Minneapolis, Minn.: Fortress, 1993.

Levine, Amy-Jill, and Marianne Blickenstaff, eds. *A Feminist Companion to the Deutero-Pauline Epistles.* London: T & T Clark International, 2003.

Neyrey, Jerome H. *First Timothy, Second Timothy, Titus, James, First Peter, Second Peter, Jude.* Collegeville, Minn.: Liturgical Press, 1983.

Oden, Thomas C. *First and Second Timothy and Titus.* Louisville, Ky.: John Knox Press, 1989.

Quinn, J. D. *1 and 2 Timothy and Titus.* Anchor Bible Series, vol. 35. Garden City, N.Y.: Doubleday, 1976.

Roberts, Alexander, and James Donaldson, eds. *Ante-Nicene Fathers,* vol. 7. Grand Rapids, Mich.: Eerdmans, 1982.

Roetzel, Calvin. *The Letters of Paul: Conversations in Context.* 4th ed. Louisville, Ky.: Westminster John Knox Press, 1998.

Stockhausen, Carol Kern. *Letters in the Pauline Tradition: Ephesians, Colossians, I Timothy, II Timothy, and Titus.* Wilmington, Del.: Glazier, 1989.

Thurston, Bonnie Bowman. *The Widows: A Women's Ministry in the Early Church.* Philadelphia: Fortress, 1989.

Witherington, Ben. *Women in the Earliest Churches.* Cambridge, England: Cambridge University Press, 1988.

Wright, N. T. *Paul for Everyone: The Pastoral Letters: 1 and 2 Timothy and Titus.* London: SPCK; Louisville, Ky.: Westminster John Knox Press, 2004.

Young, Frances. *The Theology of the Pastoral Epistles.* Cambridge: Cambridge University Press, 1994.

# OTHER LETTERS

Our journey through the New Testament brings us now to its last eight letters. On first view, these letters might look like the "leftovers" or, to use our travel metaphor, like little diversions or cultural curiosities along a major highway. And like those odd roadside stops that can range from Elvis memorabilia to motorcycle museums and jukebox collections or even the world's largest ball of string, these eight letters appear not to have any common themes, nor do they appear to be all that important except as entertaining distractions along the way. However, once we start exploring the details of these letters, we discover that these first impressions are far from reality. There are amazing treasures to be found in these little side trips!

Part IV of this book was dedicated to the letters associated with Paul. As we already noted, the New Testament includes thirteen letters to which Paul's name is attached, but most biblical scholars agree that only seven were actually written by Paul. The others were most likely written by later disciples of Paul who were both appealing to his authority and honoring his memory by writing under his name. Thus, we divided these thirteen letters into two groups—the authentic letters of Paul (also known as Pauline letters) and the letters attributed to Paul but not actually written by him (also known as Deutero-Pauline letters).

This part of our textbook will treat the eight remaining letters of the New Testament. Like the letters attributed to Paul, they appear to have been arranged according to length, longest to shortest:

Hebrews

James

1 Peter

2 Peter

1 John

2 John

3 John

Jude

The digit preceding the name of some of these books refers to the number of the letter, such as the First Letter of Peter and the Third Letter of John. The first of these letters, the anonymous Letter to the Hebrews, is different from the rest, partly because it is much longer but also because it had been (wrongly) associated with Paul for a time and because it is not really a letter.

The other seven letters in this collection are relatively short and have no connection whatsoever with Paul. Instead, they are named for apostles or disciples of Jesus. However, today most biblical scholars think that all of these letters are pseudonymous works. People sometimes are troubled by the suggestion that the persons identified with these books did not actually write them, perhaps because it raises questions about the authority or reliability of the book. However, we should remember that authenticity of authorship was of less concern to second- and third-century pastors and students of scripture than it is to people today. For them, the authority of these letters rested more in the fact that they were somehow tied to the traditions of these famous religious figures than in the fact that these figures actually wrote the letters.

Apart from Hebrews, the remaining seven letters in this group are identified as the catholic or general letters. Apparently, this designation was already in use by 300 C.E. and, for some of the letters, possibly earlier. The word *catholic* means "general or universal." Some have understood this designation to mean that the letters were intended for a general audience—that is, for churches in a region or even for any church in general—and not for a particular individual church. Others have understood it to mean that this group of letters was universally accepted among the churches. Today biblical scholars would question whether either of these explanations is appropriate, since it appears that some of these letters were written for individual groups and others were not universally accepted by the churches until relatively late in the process of canon formation. However, since they have been identified as such throughout the history of the tradition, you will see that the designation "catholic epistles" continues to be used today.

The next four chapters of this textbook address these other letters of the New Testament more or less in the order in which they appear in the canon, beginning with the Letter to the Hebrews in Chapter 20. The only exception is the Letter of Jude, which will be treated with the Letter of James because in the early Christian tradition the two men to whom they are attributed—James and Judas (Jude)—were brothers. When Part V is behind us, our voyage through the New Testament is almost complete. All that remains is the final book, Revelation.

# THE LETTER TO THE HEBREWS

## TIMELINE

| | |
|---|---|
| **64 C.E.** | Peter and Paul are martyred in Rome. |
| **65–70 C.E.** | The Gospel of Mark is written. |
| **66–70 C.E.** | The Jewish War occurs. |
| **70 C.E.** | Jerusalem and the Temple are destroyed. |
| **70–100 C.E.** | **The Letter to the Hebrews is written.** |
| **80–90 C.E.** | The Gospels of Matthew and Luke are written; Acts of the Apostles is written. |
| **80–100 C.E.** | The Letters to the Colossians is written. |
| **90–100 C.E.** | The Letter to the Ephesians is written, sometime after the Letter to the Colossians. |
| **90–100 C.E.** | The Gospel of John is written; the Second Letter to the Thessalonians is written. |
| **95–96 C.E.** | The Book of Revelation is written. |
| **100 C.E.** | The Letters of John and the pastoral letters (1 Timothy, 2 Timothy, Titus) are written. |

This fifth leg of our journey through the New Testament is about to take us in a new direction. Our tour of the letters associated with Paul took us to places that he visited and Christian communities that he established or at least knew in some personal way. However, we will soon discover, in our exploration of these remaining eight letters, that it will be difficult to associate them with places on the map or, in many cases, actual Christian communities. In other words, this next part of our travels will have a somewhat ethereal quality to it. We will not have an easy time of it as we try to situate these letters in space and time. Not to worry! We should still have an interesting adventure!

The Letter to the Hebrews is a rather unique and often misunderstood letter of the New Testament, if indeed it can even be called a letter. It has a closing greeting and blessing like the ones we would expect in a traditional letter, but it has no opening address (sender, recipient, greeting) or thanksgiving section. The author addresses his audience using "you" and "your" suggesting a written communication between two parties who know each other, but the content is quite impersonal, giving us few clues about the identity of the sender or recipients. He also uses the pronouns "we" and "us" as if including himself as a member of this community of recipients. Issues such as these can be frustrating to the biblical scholar who would like to know more about the background and literary genre of the Letter to the Hebrews. At the same time, this so-called letter is wonderfully exciting because of the skillful way that the author constructs his arguments and because of the profoundly inspiring statements he makes about Jesus as the Christ.

However, before we investigate these aspects of the Letter to the Hebrews, let us take some time to summarize what biblical scholars have been able to discover about the background of this letter.

## AUTHORSHIP AND DATE OF COMPOSITION

The so-called Letter to the Hebrews has no letter opening and therefore no named author. By the fourth and fifth centuries C.E., Christians thought that Paul had written this document. There were several reasons for this view. The lists of canonical books from this period identified it among fourteen books attributed to Paul, and a manuscript from the second century included it right after Romans in a collection of Paul's letters. The ending of Hebrews looks like the ending of many of Paul's authentic letters, and the mention of Timothy (Heb. 13:23) is consistent with Paul's practice of including references to Timothy in his letters (1 Thess. 3:2; Phlm. 1; 2 Cor. 1:1). Therefore, you can see how easy it would have been for people to assume that Paul wrote the Letter to the Hebrews.

Today almost all New Testament scholars agree that Hebrews was not written by Paul, since it differs considerably from his authentic letters in its elegant Greek literary style as well as its vocabulary and content. For example, Paul regularly uses the term *Christ Jesus* to refer to Jesus, whereas the author of Hebrews uses *Son, Christ,* or *Jesus,* but not *Christ Jesus.* Likewise, Paul's gospel is clearly focused on the crucified and resurrected Jesus, but Hebrews mentions his resurrection only once and in passing (Heb. 13:20). Instead, Hebrews is primarily concerned with showing that Christ is the new High Priest and most perfect Temple sacrifice, but Paul nowhere mentions these themes.

Biblical scholars have identified many more such examples to show that Paul did not write the Letter to the Hebrews. But then who did? The second-century writer Clement of Alexandria is supposed to have said that Luke, the gospel writer and author of Acts of the Apostles, wrote the Letter to the Hebrews (Eusebius, *Ecclesiastical History* 6.14.2–4). The third-century writer Tertullian ascribed it to Barnabas, Paul's co-missionary (*On Modesty* 20). The sixteenth-century Christian reformer Martin Luther attributed it to Apollos, who was a Jewish Christian missionary from Alexandria (Acts 18:24–28; cf. 1 Cor. 3:1–9, 21–23). Priscilla and Aquila (Acts 18:1–4, 26–27; cf. Rom. 16) have also been suggested on occasion.

Despite these very intriguing hypotheses, in the end we have to conclude that there is not enough evidence to determine exactly who wrote the Letter to the Hebrews. The late-second- and early-third-century writer Origen supposedly said, "God only knows who wrote it!" (Eusebius, *Ecclesiastical History* 6.25.11–14). At least we can say this much. Whatever the author's name, he (or she) probably was a Hellenistic Jewish Christian who had been trained within the Hellenistic educational system, since the author assumes a Platonic philosophical worldview—which consists of an eternal, stable heavenly realm and a transitory, illusory earthly realm—when constructing the arguments that are contained in the Letter to the Hebrews, and is very adept at using Jewish scriptures. For the sake of convenience, we will use masculine pronouns to refer to the author, since the likelihood is greater that he was a man. However, we should leave open the possibility that the author was female, as we have noted above.

Deciding on a date of composition for the Letter to the Hebrews is at least as difficult as determining its author. The author indicates that he was not among the first generation of Christians (Heb. 2:3), which would suggest a date at least as late as 60 C.E. He also makes numerous references to Jesus as the replacement of the Temple, its high priest, its sacrifices, and even Israel's covenant with God. This kind of theology is unlikely in the earliest decades of the Jesus movement, when the Jerusalem Temple was still operational and the Jesus followers still saw themselves simply as reformers within Judaism. However, we do begin to see it after the destruction of the Jerusalem Temple in 70 C.E. and especially in the last decade or so of the first century C.E. The Gospel of John is an obvious example.

But there is a problem with this theory. If you read the Letter to the Hebrews carefully, you will notice that the author writes about the Temple as if it is still standing and its sacrifices as if they are still being performed (see, for example, Heb. 8:7–13 and 10:1–2). Why would he do this if the Jerusalem Temple has already been destroyed at the time he is writing? Here's an even more difficult question. In light of his primary message about Jesus as the replacement of the Temple, its high priest, and its sacrifices, why does he not take advantage of the opportunity to reinforce his position by saying that the Jerusalem Temple had been destroyed to make room for Jesus? It would have been a brilliant argument!

Unfortunately, we have no good answers to these questions except to say that biblical scholars have observed the same phenomenon in the Babylonian Talmud, a Jewish writing composed during the third, fourth, and fifth centuries C.E., long after the Temple had been destroyed. In it, the rabbis describe in great detail a large number of regulations concerning the sacrifices offered in the Temple. Clearly, they knew that the Temple had been destroyed and that the sacrifices that the Law prescribed could not be fulfilled. Yet they continued to interpret the Law "as if" the Temple still existed, perhaps because they believed that God intended such sacrifice even though they were no longer able to provide it. By preserving the regulations associated with Temple sacrifices and acting "as if" these sacrifices were being carried out on earth, perhaps they believed that these acts of worship could continue to take place in the heavenly realm.

Because there is so little evidence to determine precisely when the Letter to the Hebrews was written, New Testament scholars give it a wide range of dates from 60 C.E., before the destruction of the Temple, to the mid-90s, shortly before Clement of Rome apparently referred to it in his writings, which are usually dated to the late 90s (1 Clement 17:1; 36:2–6). But most biblical scholars think Hebrews was written after the destruction of the Jerusalem Temple. Several assign it to the period of 70–100 C.E., while others narrow the range to approximately 80–90 C.E. Without additional information, we will follow the majority view and use 70–100 C.E. for the period in which this letter was written.

## AUDIENCE

Although the title "to the Hebrews" is likely a later addition—it was first found in late-second- and early-third-century manuscripts—the Jewish imagery and argumentation employed by the author confirm that its original audience was probably Jewish Christian. Some biblical scholars suggest that the location of this audience was Rome because the closing of the letter mentions greetings from some Italians in the author's company: "Those from Italy send you greetings" (Heb. 13:24). However, this reference could simply mean that these Italians were known to the author and to his audience, not that the audience was in Italy. Other biblical scholars have suggested Jerusalem because of the author's interest in the Temple. However, if a Jewish Christian community in Jerusalem was his intended audience, it would seem all the more necessary that he address the problem of the destruction of the Jerusalem Temple, and he does not. Beyond these two theories, there is little to be said about the identity of the group for which the Letter to the Hebrews was originally written.

Whether or not we can confidently identify the geographic location of the community for which the Letter to the Hebrews was written, biblical scholars are quite sure that it was addressed to a community that had undergone significant persecution in the past and was still traumatized by the effects of that persecution. Evidence in support of this theory can be found in Hebrews 10:32–34, where the author acknowledges that they had a "hard struggle with suffering." They were publicly abused and their property had been confiscated. Some were thrown into prison, and others suffered even as they supported those in prison. Apparently, their earlier conversion to the Jesus gospel came dramatically, in the power of the Holy Spirit, with miracles and ecstatic visionary experiences (Heb. 2:3–4; 6:4–5). Perhaps this first fervor made their suffering all the more traumatic. At any rate, the persecution was mostly over by the time this document was written except perhaps for some who were still in prison (Heb. 13:3) and for some kind of harassment by outsiders (Heb. 13:13).

Apparently these difficulties left the community for which the Letter to the Hebrews was written feeling vulnerable and "sluggish" in their faith (Heb. 6:12; cf. Heb. 5:11). Thus, one of the reasons for writing this document was to encourage the community and to warn against **apostasy** (i.e., renouncing the faith under threat of persecution). Giving up the faith was considered a very serious wrongdoing in the early church, when it was still a minority religious movement. The author of the Letter to the Hebrews describes the seriousness of the matter by saying that those who apostatize (i.e., renounce their faith) have committed an unforgivable sin and cannot ever be restored to repentance. Referring to their ecstatic experiences of the Holy Spirit when they first embraced the Jesus gospel, he adds that those who fall away, after having tasted the heavenly gift, "are crucifying again the Son of God and are holding him up to contempt" (Heb. 6:6). It is hard to imagine the author finding something harsher than this to say against the apostates. Their friends and families must have been heartbroken!

## OUTLINE OF THE LETTER

For some of the New Testament letters that we have studied thus far, we have provided a structural outline to show how well (or poorly) it conforms to the traditional pattern of the letter. For others, especially the longer ones, we have provided a content outline (identifying the various topics of the letter) because just identifying the five parts of a letter does not help us much in knowing how to interpret it. In the case of the Letter to the Hebrews, any attempt to create a structural outline shows us immediately that this document is not a letter, since it contains no opening address or thanksgiving. Likewise, when you look at the content of the letter, you see that it lacks the personal, relational character of other letters of the New Testament. Therefore, although the Letter to the Hebrews is traditionally called a letter, it is not.

What, then, is the genre of this document? Perhaps our content outline will give us some clues. Notice how the author builds his argument by alternating units of **exposition** (i.e., a theoretical discussion of a problem or theory) and **exhortation** (i.e., a statement urging someone to do something). The major themes of the book are identified in small capital letters to assist you in following the author's argument:

1. Hebrews 1:1–3—Introduction
2. Hebrews 1:4–2:18—Jesus as SON OF GOD, greater than the angels

   *Exhortation:* Stay faithful to the word you have heard as Christians (Heb. 2:1–4).
3. Hebrews 3:1–4:13—Jesus as the FAITHFUL HIGH PRIEST, worthy of more glory than Moses

   *Exhortation:* You must not forsake God and become hardened by sin (Heb. 3:7–15).

   *Exhortation:* You must persevere for the sake of the promised "rest" (Heb. 4:1–3).
4. Hebrews 4:14–5:14—Jesus as the MERCIFUL HIGH PRIEST, called and appointed like Aaron and Melchizedek

   *Exhortation:* You have become dull in your understanding and you need someone to teach you the basics of God's teachings again (Heb. 5:11–14).
5. Hebrews 6:1–20—God's promise, Abraham's hope, and the sure hope that comes through Jesus

   *Exhortation:* Let us move on toward perfection; a curse on the "fallen away" (Heb. 6:1–12).
6. Hebrews 7:1–28—Jesus as High Priest, GREATER THAN MELCHIZEDEK OR THE LEVITICAL PRIESTHOOD

7. Hebrews 8:1–10:39—Jesus, the HIGH PRIEST OF THE HEAVENLY SANCTUARY AND THE NEW COVENANT

   *Exhortation:* Let us approach God's house with full assurance of faith; warning to those who apostatize (Heb. 10:19–39).

8. Hebrews 11:1–40—The faith of the Ancients

9. Hebrews 12:1–13—Jesus as the SUPREME EXAMPLE OF FAITH

10. Hebrews 13:1–19—Final exhortations

11. Hebrews 13:20–25—Closing: final exhortation, blessing, greeting

## GENRE OF THE LETTER TO THE HEBREWS

Because this document has traditionally been identified as a letter, we will continue to use that term in its title. However, our content outline suggests that its genre is more like that of a theological treatise or a homily. A **theological treatise** is a carefully reasoned composition that expounds doctrine or teaching. As you can see, the Letter to the Hebrews has several lengthy sections of carefully reasoned argumentation about who Jesus is as the Christ and what his role is in God's plan of salvation. However, when you read the letter in its entirety, you will observe that the author's primary objective is to encourage people to hold fast to the Jesus gospel and to warn them against apostasy. For this reason, most scholars who study the Letter to the Hebrews suggest that it is better described as a homily or **sermon**. Acts of the Apostles describes the synagogue sermon as a "word of exhortation" (Acts 13:22). For all intents and purposes, this is also an accurate description of the Letter to the Hebrews. Our author has written a lengthy sermon and simply added an ending that makes it look like a letter.

## "FROM THE LESSER TO THE GREATER"

As we have already observed, the Letter to the Hebrews is constructed according to alternating patterns of exposition and exhortation. In our investigation into the audience of this document (see above), we were able to explore, albeit briefly, the "how" and "why" of the exhortations. But what about the expositions? What is the message that the author of the Letter to the Hebrews wants to convey, and how does he develop the argument? Our content outline (see above) shows that the author of Hebrews wants to assert that Jesus, as Son of God, is superior to and, in effect, has superseded or taken the place of the priesthood, the Temple, and the sacrifice of the Old Covenant. In this way, Jesus has effected a New Covenant with God's people. In the style of the rabbis, the various units of exposition are constructed according to an argument "from the lesser to the greater." We might describe this kind of argument like this: If something can be demonstrated to be true in a small matter, then we can say that it is even more true, when it concerns a greater matter that is analogous to the first.

For example, let's take a theological issue like revelation. Concerning the smaller matter, the author of Hebrews might say that God's revelation comes to humans through angels, the Law, and the Jewish priesthood. However, concerning the greater matter, *perfect* revelation comes through God's son, Jesus. If the first statement is accepted as true, then the second statement is more completely true. We could extend this argument to the goal or purpose of God's revelation, which is human salvation. If the partial revelation that came through the angels, the Law, and the Jewish priesthood resulted in salvation—that is, wholeness of covenant relationship with God—then the perfect revelation that came through Jesus will result in greater or fuller salvation for all God's people. Inserted at strategic points throughout the expositions, the author includes an exhortation of encouragement or a warning about not abandoning the Christian faith (apostasy). Thus, we see in the Letter to the Hebrews a good example of the direct relationship between theology and ethics. The author's particular kind of Christology—teaching about the nature and mission of Jesus as the Christ—demands a particular kind of response in action.

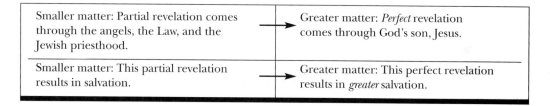

| Smaller matter: Partial revelation comes through the angels, the Law, and the Jewish priesthood. | Greater matter: *Perfect* revelation comes through God's son, Jesus. |
| --- | --- |
| Smaller matter: This partial revelation results in salvation. | Greater matter: This perfect revelation results in *greater* salvation. |

**Jesus as the Perfect High Priest**  In the "Questions for Reading" at the conclusion of this chapter, you will have an opportunity to explore for yourself some of the attributes that the author of the Letter to the Hebrews associates with Jesus, the perfect High Priest. You will also be able to see how he constructs these arguments "from the lesser to the greater." However, you will probably also experience how difficult it is for the beginning reader of the Letter to the Hebrews to fully appreciate the nuances of its arguments and the richness of its imagery. This is due, in part, to the author's heavy dependence on the TaNaK, the scriptures of Judaism, to support his arguments. Because most of us have a rather limited knowledge of the Old Testament, we are likely to miss important details in the development of the argument. One way to remedy this problem is to pay careful attention to the cross-references in your Bible and look up the author's quotations and allusions to the Old Testament as you go along, noting especially the original context of the quotation or allusion.

Another problem that makes it hard for beginning readers to make sense of the Letter to the Hebrews concerns the fact that most Christians today have little understanding of the meaning and significance of temple worship and cult sacrifices in the ancient world. Of course, the best remedy for this problem is to read the research of contemporary scholars who have studied these topics extensively. At a minimum, you may want to return to Chapter 5 of this textbook to get a brief overview of the significance of the Jerusalem Temple, its feasts, and its sacrifices as well as brief descriptions of the officials associated with the Temple.

**Greater than Moses**  Before we send you off on your own to read the Letter to the Hebrews, it might be helpful to work through a couple examples of the author's arguments concerning Jesus, the perfect High Priest of the Temple sacrifice. Let's start with the argument about Jesus as the *faithful* High Priest (Heb. 3:1–6). The author begins with the assertion that Jesus was faithful, just as Moses "was faithful in all God's house." Here he quotes Numbers 12:7. This quotation is part of a larger story in which we learn that Miriam, Moses' sister, and Aaron were complaining against Moses, challenging his authority as the spokesperson of God. The narrator of the story adds that Moses was the most humble (or devout) person on earth at that time.

Suddenly, Moses, Aaron, and Miriam hear God's voice telling them to come to the Tent of Meeting—the tent that held the symbols of the Exodus, the manna and the stone tablets of the commandments, while the Israelites wandered in the wilderness—where God will talk with them. When they arrive, God appears in a pillar of cloud and affirms Moses' superiority by saying that, unlike the prophets who know God's word only through visions, Moses gets to speak with God face to face and even is allowed to see God's form! Now Miriam herself was a prophet, and in punishment for her challenge to Moses' authority, God gave her a skin disease that lasted seven days. Notice, also, that God calls Moses "my servant" (Numbers 12:7).

Thus, in the context of the Book of Numbers, the quotation "was faithful in [or entrusted with] all God's house" (Numbers 12:7) describes how God affirmed Moses' superiority among the prophets and his responsibility for God's covenant people. Observe how the author of the Book of Hebrews builds on this quotation and the story behind it. He acknowledges the glory due to Moses because of his position of authority but also points out that Moses was given this authority *as a servant.* And, of course, a son has more authority in his father's household than any servant. Therefore, the author of Hebrews argues, Christ, *as God's Son,* has far greater authority than Moses and is deserving of more glory because he is the one truly and fully entrusted with God's household. Notice how the author of Hebrews deftly concludes his argument by saying, "and we are his house if we hold firm to the confidence and the pride that belong to hope" (Heb. 3:6). This is a call to the community for faithfulness and, in a subtle way, a warning against apostasy—unless they want to end up like Miriam!

**GREATER THAN MELCHIZEDEK** Let's take another example of an argument "from the lesser to the greater," this time showing how Jesus is the High Priest who is greater than Melchizedek (Heb. 7:1–28). In the context of the Book of Genesis, **Melchizedek** is a minor character in the Abraham stories (Gen. 14:17–20). In fact, if you are not paying attention, you might miss him entirely! He appears out of nowhere, after Abram (later to be known as Abraham) has successfully defeated his nephew Lot's enemies, collected the booty of war, and returned to his homeland, bringing Lot and his family with him (Gen. 14:13–16). The narrator of the story tells us that he is king of Salem and a priest of "God Most High"—that is, Abram's God—but we are not told how he became a priest of "God Most High." Since Genesis depicts Abram as the first and only person to encounter this God, at this point in the story we have to conclude that God somehow "hand-selected" Melchizedek for this job, perhaps even without his knowledge or understanding. Thus, in his capacity as priest, Melchizedek brings out bread and wine and offers a blessing over Abram. In turn, Abram offers him a tenth of the booty of war.

With this background in mind, let's observe how the author of the Letter to the Hebrews uses Melchizedek as a type (i.e., model or blueprint; see Chapter 4) of Jesus,

Victorious in battle, Abraham is depicted with angelic wings and dressed in military armor in this thirteenth-century fresco from Anagni Cathedral in Italy. He is blessed by Melchizedek as they participate in a sacrificial offering of bread and wine. The biblical story is Genesis 14:17–20. *Picture Desk, Inc./Kobal Collection.*

the perfect High Priest. First, he explains that Melchizedek's name means "king of righteousness" (Heb. 7:2). Of course, the audience of the Letter to the Hebrews would have understood what the author was doing and added, "But Jesus is *the* king of righteousness." Then the author reminds the reader that Melchizedek was the king of Salem—that is, "king of peace" (Heb. 7:2)—and the reader would have countered, "Yes, but Jesus is *the* king of peace." Next, he reminds the reader that the Book of Genesis does not tell us where Melchizedek came from or where he went after he completed his service as priest (Heb. 7:3). It's almost like he had no beginning and no end! And finally, he tells the reader that Abraham, the greatest figure of Israel's salvation story, acknowledged Melchizedek's superiority by accepting his blessing and giving him a tenth of his earnings, also called **tithing** or giving a **tithe** (Heb. 7:2, 4).

**GREATER THAN THE LEVITICAL PRIESTHOOD** Using the Melchizedek typology, the author of the Letter to the Hebrews develops a very elaborate double argument "from the lesser to the greater." Thus, he argues that Melchizedek's priesthood is greater than the **Levitical priesthood** (i.e., the priests who claim they are descendants of Levi, the brother of Joseph and son of Jacob; the priests of the Jerusalem Temple) and that Jesus' priesthood is greater than Melchizedek's priesthood (Heb. 7:4–28). Concerning the superiority of Melchizedek's priesthood over that of the Levites, he says that the Levitical priests collect tithes because the Law requires it, but Melchizedek is greater because he collected a tithe that was voluntarily given—from

Abraham, no less—and because he continues to live (at least we have no account of his death), whereas the Levitical priests will all die (Heb. 7:4–6). The author of Hebrews concludes this part of the argument by suggesting that even Levi and, as a consequence, all of the priests of Levi paid tithes to Melchizedek (Heb. 7:7–10). Of course, everyone knows that you pay tithes to a superior, not an inferior. Therefore, Melchizedek is superior to the Levitical priesthood.

Concerning the second argument, that Jesus' priesthood is greater than Melchizedek's, the author of Hebrews points to Psalm 110:4, suggesting that Jesus is the fulfillment of a prophecy concerning God's selection of a messiah who would be both priest and king:

> The Lord has sworn and will not change his mind,
> "You are a priest forever
> according to the order of Melchizedek." (Psa. 110:4)

Like Melchizedek, he argues, Jesus is not a descendant of the tribe of Levi, priests who receive their assignment to serve the Temple simply by virtue of their birth. Rather, God chose Jesus to be an everlasting priest on account of his resurrection. Thus, although Melchizedek might still be living, Jesus is greater because *he will never die* (Heb. 7:15–16). Finally, Jesus is greater than either Melchizedek or the Levitical priesthood because he became a priest not by the Law but *by God's oath* (Heb. 7:20–22, 28).

The **"Holy of Holies"** of the Jerusalem Temple, shown in a model located at the Holyland Hotel in Jerusalem. Photo by Catherine Cory. The author of the Letter to the Hebrews describes the earthly sanctuary (holy place) as "a sketch and shadow" of the heavenly sanctuary, where Jesus fulfills his more perfect ministry as priest and sacrifice (Heb. 8:5). The first tent or sanctuary to which the author refers was erected by Moses and transported through the wilderness during the Exodus (Heb. 8:5; cf. Exod. 25:40). Its more permanent counterpart in later centuries was the Jerusalem Temple.

In the course of his argument, the author also notes that Jesus came from the tribe of Judah from which the messiah was destined to descend (Heb. 7:13–14). He concludes the argument by stating that Jesus, as the perfect High Priest, does not need to offer sacrifices again and again because he offered himself once for all in the sacrifice of the crucifixion (Heb. 7:26–27). Thus, the perfect High Priest put an end to Temple sacrifice by himself becoming the perfect sacrifice.

These are only two of the many arguments "from the lesser to the greater" that can be found in the Letter to the Hebrews. Hopefully, by working together through these arguments, you now have some ideas about how to conduct your own analyses of other parts of the book. Perhaps, also, these examples will help you anticipate the richness of the imagery contained in the Letter to the Hebrews and the beauty of the author's arguments on behalf of Jesus, the High Priest, the perfect sacrifice, the one who presides over the heavenly sanctuary, and the guarantor of the New Covenant. There is nothing else to compare to it in the New Testament!

## THE LITANY OF THE ANCIENTS

While we could say much more about any one part of the Letter to the Hebrews, we cannot leave this book without commenting on its wonderful roll call of heroes of the Old Testament whom God approved because of their faith (Heb. 11:1–12:29). Immediately preceding this section, the author of this letter has been exhorting the community to approach with confidence the heavenly sanctuary (i.e., the holy place), which Jesus opened through his death (Heb. 10:19–22). He also has been urging community members to hold fast to their faith and not be like those who are lost (i.e., the apostates) (Heb. 10:23, 39). This is the context in which the author of the Letter to the Hebrews introduces his litany of the ancients. A **litany** is a series of prayers or blessings that begin or end with a common refrain. Observe the pattern:

*By faith*  Abel offered to God a more acceptable sacrifice than Cain's (Heb. 11:4).

*By faith*  Enoch was taken so that he did not experience death (Heb. 11:5).

*By faith*  Noah, warned by God about events as yet unseen, respected the warning and built an ark to save his household (Heb. 11:7).

*By faith*  Abraham obeyed when he was called to set out for a place that he was to receive as an inheritance; and he set out, not knowing where he was going (Heb. 11:8).

And so the author of the Letter to the Hebrews makes his way through the story of salvation from Abel, the son of Adam and Eve who was murdered by his brother, to the martyrs of the Maccabean period (second century B.C.E.), when King Antiochus IV tried to make the Jewish people abandon their religious practices and accept Greek culture by torturing and killing them. The Old Testament deuterocanonical or apocryphal books of the Maccabees tell the story of these brave men and women who gave up their lives rather than give up their faith.

The author's description of each of these faithful heroes provides the reader with a powerful reflection on the nature and object of faith. Faith, he says, is "assurance of things hoped for" and conviction about "things not seen" (Heb. 11:1). God approved each of these people because of their faith, even though they did not receive what was promised them in their lifetime. Abel offered sacrifice to God, even though it cost him his life (Heb. 11:4). In his faith, Enoch "pleased God" and was taken up to heaven without undergoing death (Heb. 11:5–6). Noah acted in faith by building the ark, even when he could not see what God was about to do (Heb. 11:7). Abraham, too, acted in faith when he answered God's call to go to the land that was promised to him, even though he did not know where he was going (Heb. 11:8–9). And so the author's reflection on faith moves forward through all the heroes of the faith, down to the example of the martyrs of the Maccabees. Each of these heroes waited in faith. Although they did not receive what was promised, they waited in anticipation of "something better" that God has planned for us (Heb. 11:39–40).

According to the author of the Letter to the Hebrews, this "something better" is fulfilled in the saving work of Jesus. He is the "pioneer and perfecter" of faith because he allowed himself to be shamed, even killed on a cross, for the sake of a promise that could only be seen from afar—his exaltation to the throne of God (Heb. 12:2–3). He is also the perfect model of endurance in the face of persecution. The author tells the members of this community that Jesus allowed himself to endure hostility so that they would not lose heart (Heb. 12:3). They should think of their sufferings as God's discipline—like a father disciplines his children—so that later they can enjoy "the peaceful fruit of righteousness" that comes to those who have been trained by their suffering (Heb. 12:7–11). Clearly, this message of education-through-suffering is not easy for people to hear, but the author of the Letter to the Hebrews apparently still saw reason for hope in the fact that, in their suffering, they were "surrounded by so great a cloud of witnesses" (Heb. 12:1), and even Jesus himself!

## KEY TERMS

| | | |
|---|---|---|
| Apostasy | Sermon | "Holy of Holies" |
| Exposition | Melchizedek | Litany |
| Exhortation | Tithing/tithe | |
| Theological treatise | Levitical priesthood | |

## QUESTIONS FOR READING

Read the Letter to the Hebrews. Use evidence from the biblical text to answer the following questions.

1. What functions (i.e., activities) and attributes (i.e., characteristics) does the author of the Letter to the Hebrews ascribe to Jesus as Son of God (Heb. 1:4–2:18)?

2. What functions (i.e., activities) and attributes (i.e., characteristics) does the author of the Letter to the Hebrews ascribe to Jesus as High Priest (Heb. 3:1–5:14)?

3. In the exhortations of Hebrews 5:11–14 and 6:1–12, what does the author encourage his readers to do, and how would he like them to behave? Why?

What does the author think about his readers' ability to accomplish these expectations?

4. In Hebrews 7:1–28, how does the author establish the superiority of Melchizedek's priesthood? In what ways is Christ superior even to Melchizedek?

5. According to Hebrews 8:1–13, how does the heavenly sanctuary differ from the earthly one? How is Jesus' heavenly ministry greater than that of the high priests of the earthly sanctuary? How does the New Covenant differ from the first covenant?

6. According to Hebrews 9:1–28, how does the ministry of the Levitical priests compare to the greater and more perfect ministry of Christ? In what sense, then, is he the mediator of a new covenant?

7. According to Hebrews 10:1–18, how is the sacrifice of Christ superior to the sacrifices under the Law?

8. In Hebrews 11:1–40, the author provides a summary of the salvation story from Abel through the prophets. What point (s) is he trying to make? How does this section fit into his larger argument?

9. Hebrews 13:1–19 is a paraenesis or moral exhortation similar to those we find in Paul's authentic letters. What values or virtues does the author hold up for his readers to achieve? What are some of the images he uses to illuminate these virtues?

10. Biblical scholars tell us that Hebrews 13:18–25 is a letter closing. How can you tell?

## QUESTIONS FOR REFLECTION

1. Carefully read some of the exhortation sections in the Letter to the Hebrews (see the outline above). What relevance, if any, do these exhortations have for Christians today? Give examples to explain.

2. How would you explain the Letter to the Hebrews' depiction of Jesus as the perfect High Priest in vocabulary and images that make sense to ordinary people today—perhaps to one of your friends who has little knowledge or understanding of these religious symbols?

## ACTIVITIES FOR LEARNING

1. Make a diagram (cartoon) or word picture of the Christology of the Letter to the Hebrews specifically in terms of its assertions about who Jesus is as Son of God and as High Priest. How does such a portrait translate into a believer's relationship with Jesus today? What attributes would you ascribe to him?

2. Make a diagram (cartoon) or word picture of the New Covenant's sanctuary and sacrifice as understood by the author of the Letter to the Hebrews. How does such a portrait translate into a believer's understanding of his/her salvation today?

3. Create a litany of modern "holy ones" who teach us the meaning of faith in our contemporary setting. Follow the pattern of Hebrews 11:1–40, and use the phrase "By faith. . . " to begin each entry. When you have completed your litany,

reflect on what you have written. What attributes or characteristics did you ascribe to faith? How do they compare with the characteristics of faith in the litany of the Ancients contained in the Letter to the Hebrews?

## SOURCES AND RESOURCES

Attridge, Harold W. *The Epistle to the Hebrews*. Philadelphia: Fortress, 1989.

Bourke, Myles. "The Epistle to the Hebrews." In *The New Jerome Biblical Commentary*, edited by R. E. Brown, J. A. Fitzmyer, and R. E. Murphy, 920–941. Englewood Cliffs, N.J.: Prentice Hall, 1990.

Donelson, Lewis R. *From Hebrews to Revelation: A Theological Introduction*. Louisville, Ky.: Westminster John Knox Press, 2001.

Eisenbaum, Pamela Michelle. *The Jewish Heroes of Christian History: Hebrews 11 in Literary Context*. Atlanta, Ga.: Scholars Press, 1997.

Gench, Frances Taylor. *Hebrews and James*. Louisville, Ky.: Westminster John Knox Press, 1996.

Hagner, Donald A. *Hebrews*. Peabody, Mass.: Hendrickson, 1990.

Harrington, Daniel J. *The Letter to the Hebrews*. Collegeville, Minn.: Liturgical Press, 2006.

Isaacs, Marie E. *Sacred Space: An Approach to the Theology of the Epistle to the Hebrews*. Sheffield, England: JSOT Press, 1992.

Isaak, Jon M. *Situating the Letter to the Hebrews in Early Christian History*. Lewiston, N.Y.: Mellen Press, 2002.

Koester, Craig R. *Hebrews: A New Translation with Introduction and Commentary*. Anchor Bible Series, vol. 36. New York: Doubleday, 2001.

Krodel, Gerhard, ed. *The General Letters: Hebrews, James, 1–2 Peter, Jude, 1–2–3 John*. Minneapolis, Minn.: Fortress, 1995.

Lindars, Barnabas. *The Theology of the Letter to the Hebrews*. Cambridge, England: Cambridge University Press, 1991.

Long, Thomas G. *Hebrews*. Louisville, Ky.: Westminster John Knox Press, 1997.

McDonnell, Rea. *The Catholic Epistles and Hebrews*. Wilmington, Del.: Glazier, 1986.

Pfitzner, Victor C. *Hebrews*. Nashville, Tenn.: Abingdon Press, 1997.

Schenck, Kenneth. *Understanding the Book of Hebrews: The Story behind the Sermon*. Louisville, Ky.: Westminster John Knox Press, 2003.

Wilson, Robert McLachlan. *Hebrews*. Grand Rapids, Mich.: Wm. B. Eerdmans, 1987.

# CHAPTER 21

# THE LETTERS OF JAMES AND JUDE

## OVERVIEW

The Letter of James
- AUTHORSHIP: Pseudonymous; written under the name of James, the brother of the Lord
- DATE OF COMPOSITION: Sometime around 80–100 C.E.
- INITIAL AUDIENCE: Unknown; some scholars suggest a community of Jewish Christians or a community of Gentile Christians who had knowledge of Judaism
- MAJOR TOPICS: True Religion and Acts of Favoritism; Faith and Works; Anointing of the Sick

The Letter of Jude
- AUTHORSHIP: Pseudonymous; written under the name of Jude, or Judas, the brother of James
- DATE OF COMPOSITION: Sometime between 90 and 100 C.E.
- INITIAL AUDIENCE: Unknown
- MAJOR TOPICS: Prophecies and Warnings

## TIMELINE

| | |
|---|---|
| **c. 61–62 C.E.** | James, the brother of Jesus, is stoned to death. |
| **65–70 C.E.** | The Gospel of Mark is written. |
| **66–70 C.E.** | The Jewish War occurs. |
| **70 C.E.** | Jerusalem and the Temple are destroyed. |
| **80–90 C.E.** | The Gospels of Matthew and Luke are written; Acts of the Apostles is written. |
| **80–100 C.E.** | **The Letter of James is written**; the Letter to the Colossians is written. |
| **90–100 C.E.** | **The Letter of Jude is written**; the Letter to the Ephesians is written, sometime after the Letter to the Colossians. |
| **95–96 C.E.** | The Book of Revelation is written. |
| **100 C.E.** | The Letters of John and the pastoral letters (1 Timothy, 2 Timothy, Titus) are written. |

Our journey through the New Testament takes us now to the Letters of James and Jude. It is fitting that we treat them together here because tradition has identified the first with James, the brother of Jesus, and the second with his brother, Judas or Jude. Paradoxically, these two letters take us back to where our journey began—Palestine. The early Christian traditions about James and Judas flourished mostly in Palestine and Jerusalem, where James was the head of the Jewish Christian church. The Letters of James and Jude belong to the category of letters called catholic, meaning "general" or "universal." These letters are also called apostolic letters, that is, letters attributed to one of the apostles. We will look at the Letter of James first and then the Letter of Jude.

## THE LETTER OF JAMES

Although the Letter of James is short and many scholars would not even call it a letter, it has received considerable attention over the years. In the period of the Reformation, Martin Luther called it "the epistle of straw" because of his negative assessment of its statements about faith and works. Today the same letter is lauded because of its strong and compelling exhortations about social justice. A distinctive feature of this letter is that it has very little to say about Christ and it does not contain very much language that could be considered "Christian," even though it has found a place in the Christian canon. What shall we make of this strange little letter? Again, before we investigate its content, we will summarize what scholars know about its author, date of composition, and audience.

## AUTHORSHIP AND DATE OF COMPOSITION

In the period of the early church, this letter was attributed to James, but which James? That is the question! There was James who was the brother of John and one of the sons of Zebedee (Mark 10:35–41), and James who was the son of Alphaeus (Mark 3:13–19), both of whom are counted among the apostles. But there was also James who was the brother of the Lord and who is named in the gospels and in Acts of the Apostles (Mark 3:31–32; 6:3; Matt. 13:55; Acts 15:1–21). The Gospel of James suggests that he was the stepbrother of Jesus, the son of Joseph from a previous marriage (G. James 9.2), but the New Testament describes him simply as the brother or kinfolk of Jesus. He had a position of authority in the early church, especially among Jewish Christians in Jerusalem, but he was not an apostle in the traditional sense of the word; that is, he was not one of the Twelve. And yet he was included in the list of people to whom Jesus appeared after the resurrection (1 Cor. 15:3–7). According to tradition, James was put to death sometime in the 60s C.E.

Most biblical scholars agree that the author of this letter was writing under the pseudonym of James, the brother of the Lord. Why do they think it was not actually written by James? The argument most frequently given concerns the vocabulary and literary style of the letter. The quality of Greek used by the author is quite elegant, suggesting someone who spoke Greek as his first language and who was educated in Hellenistic schools. Certainly, this would not have been the case for James, who came from Nazareth, a small village in Galilee. If he was literate—and quite likely he was not—his writing style would have carried the telltale signs of someone who was mentally translating from a Semitic language like Aramaic in order to write in Greek. Unfortunately, beyond his educational background, little more can be said about this anonymous author.

Closely related to the question of authorship is the issue of the letter's date of composition. Although it contains several sayings that sound a lot like gospel sayings, they have slightly different phrasing, suggesting that the author of the Letter of James did not know the actual written gospels but was familiar with oral traditions that eventually became part of the gospels. For this reason, biblical scholars think the letter was written at least before the beginning of the second century C.E. After that time, the written gospels would have been known fairly widely, and the author of the letter would have been inclined to copy from the written gospels rather than drawing on oral traditions, especially since we know that he copied his quotations of Jewish scriptures from the Septuagint. On the other end of the time frame, this author appears to know some version of Paul's teaching on faith and works, which likely would not have been widely circulated until after 60 C.E. Additionally, the letter describes teachers and presbyters as having official positions within the church, something that would have been unlikely before the latter part of the first century C.E. For all these reasons, biblical scholars give the Letter of James a date of composition between 70 and 110 C.E., but most often they date it in the last two decades of the first century C.E.

## AUDIENCE

Like many of the New Testament documents we have studied, the Letter of James provides few solid clues concerning the audience for which it was originally written. Because James was honored especially in Palestine and Jerusalem, this is the most frequently mentioned location for the letter. It contains imagery and vocabulary that are Jewish, and it is addressed to "the twelve tribes in the Dispersion" (James 1:1), suggesting a Jewish Christian audience. However, as we have already seen in Paul's letters, Gentile Christians who had been taught by Jewish Christian missionaries likely would have known and appreciated Jewish imagery as well. Acts of the Apostles and Paul's Letter to the Galatians both portray James as a church leader who wanted Gentiles to observe at least some parts of Jewish law if they wished to become Christians (Acts 15:12–21; Gal. 2:11–14). However, beyond these general observations, we probably cannot say much more about the original recipients of this letter.

## GENRE AND OUTLINE OF THE DOCUMENT

Anyone who does a careful reading of the Letter of James will notice that it does not follow the pattern of a letter except for its opening greeting. In fact, the document consists of collections of exhortations (commands for right behavior) on topics like avoiding temptation, not showing partiality, recognizing good teachers, and manifesting one's faith with good works. The following outline will help to identify the key topics and themes of the document:

1. James 1:1—Opening
2. James 1:2–18—The benefits of trials and temptation

Three sections of this letter—on favoritism, on faith and works, and on speech and wisdom (see above)—are written in the style of the diatribe. The diatribe is a literary technique that involves the creation of a hypothetical dialogue partner who poses objections or questions as if put forward by someone in the audience; the writer then proceeds to answer them. Thus, the hypothetical dialogue partner allows the author to fully develop his argument. Recall Paul's use of an extended diatribe in Romans 9–11, which he used in order to raise issues and advance his argument concerning Israel's place in God's plan of salvation (Chapter 17). We will treat two of these units in the following sections.

## TRUE RELIGION AND ACTS OF FAVORITISM

Already in the first section of the Letter of James, the author has been exhorting his audience, saying, "Be doers of the word, and not merely hearers who deceive themselves" (James 1:22). The "word" to which he refers is the gospel ("good news") of Jesus Christ. Using the metaphor of a mirror, he contrasts the doers of the word with those who merely hear. The latter—those who merely hear the word—look into the mirror and, seeing only themselves, turn away and quickly forget what they saw (James 1:23–24). However, doers of the word who look into the mirror, which is the "perfect law" (i.e., the gospel of Jesus Christ), and act on what they see will be blessed (James 1:25). Clearly, the author of James is not trying to establish a contrast between believers and unbelievers here. Rather, he is talking about those who fully embrace the gospel, which has the power to transform, and those who do not. Hence, his exhortation: "Welcome with meekness the implanted word that has the power to save your souls" (James 1:21). For James, meekness consists of a humble and listening heart, which is "slow to speak and slow to anger" (James 1:19).

It is in this context that the author of James introduces the word **religion** (James 1:26–27). The word is not commonly used in the New Testament, and unfortunately the letter writer does not define it for us. The phrase "pure and undefiled," which he uses to describe true religion, usually refers to cultic activity (worship practices) and regulations that ensure the suitability of this cultic activity as a means of communication with God. However, James describes "pure and undefiled" religion in terms of care for "the orphans and widows in their distress" (James 1:27), that is, the most vulnerable of society. This is the backdrop for James's diatribe on favoritism, which immediately follows.

Whether James has in mind a specific Christian community or is speaking generally about communities he has come to know somehow, he is critical of what he calls their "acts of favoritism" (James 2:1). He goes so far as to indicate that those who engage in this activity do not really believe in Jesus Christ. When and how are they playing favorites? James describes a scene in which a community is gathering for worship. Two strangers—one rich and the other poor—enter the worship space. The rich person is honored and given preferential treatment, while the poor person is treated as a slave or a castoff of society (James 2:2–4). James admonishes them with words that recall God's preference for the poor, as described in the Old Testament (e.g., Psa. 35:10; Isa. 61:1), and that resonate with the first beatitude of the Gospel of Luke, "Blessed are you who are poor" (Luke 6:20; cf. Matt 5:3):

> Listen, my beloved brothers and sisters. Has not God chosen the poor in this world to be rich in faith and to be heirs of the kingdom that he has promised to those who love him? But you have dishonored the poor. (James 2:5–6)

James's rhetoric is very harsh indeed. He goes on to tell his readers that they need to *really* fulfill the royal law (i.e., the gospel). They obey the commandments, or so they say. They do not murder or commit adultery, for example. But the author of this letter says that showing partiality is a violation of the great commandment: "You shall love your neighbor as yourself" (James 2:9; cf. Lev. 19:18). Further, he argues, to violate one point in the law is to violate the whole law. If his readers fail to love, they have broken the law every bit as much as if they were murderers or adulterers! (James 2:10–11). He also exhorts his readers to mercy. God will judge them according to the law of liberty (i.e., the gospel), he says, and if they judge others without mercy, so shall they be judged (James 2:12–13). Thus, for James, true religion consists of being a doer of the word in every way but especially in love and mercy toward those considered least in society.

---

### HONOR, SHAME, AND GOD'S CARE FOR THE POOR

A professor of the New Testament and a researcher in gender hermeneutics, Christina Conti analyzes some of the rhetorical techniques of the author of the Letter of James and employs socioeconomic hermeneutics to provide the following commentary on James 2:2–3:

> The author refers to the rich in an indirect way—as the "man with gold rings" and "the one who wears the resplendent dress"—to highlight the visual aspect of brilliance, which seems to be so blinding for the addressees. They prove to be unable to see beyond the external. The fact the descriptions of both the rich and the poor remain in the visual sphere is highly suggestive. Nothing is said about the inner self of either, for the simple reason that discrimination and partiality are precisely based on external aspects.
>
> The rich man is depicted as the stereotype of a patron, so the leaders seem to be looking for his favor. They invite the rich to sit "here," close to them. On the

contrary, they tell the poor person to "stand there," at a distance. What follows is remarkable, not only because of the place where the person is told to sit and what it implies, but also because of the wordplay involving the preposition *hypo* (under). The leaders tell the poor to sit literally "*under* my *under*-foot," that is under a footstool. There cannot be a lower position. The expression implies degradation—a loss of dignity as a human being. . . .

The bitter accusation that follows ("But you have dishonored the poor" [2:6]) emphasizes the pronoun "you," which instead of being implicit as is usual, appears explicitly at the beginning of the sentence. In that society, honor was the highest value. To deprive a man (especially a man) of his honor was to ostracize or marginalize him from society. The author wants to mark the contrast between God's attitude toward the poor and that of the addressees. While their option is for the rich, the option of God is for the poor. This point is in keeping with the tradition that saw the poor as objects of God's care and blessing." ("James," 542–543, Global Bible Commentary)

Reflecting on the socio-economic situation of her country of Uruguay, Dr. Conti describes how corruption and preferential treatment of the wealthy and powerful have harmed the economy, plummeted the middle class into the lower classes, widened the gap between rich and poor, and reduced a once viable democracy to rule by the rich for the rich. Her commentary serves as a prophetic voice, calling the church to be on the side of the poor just as God is on the side of the poor. How might the Letter of James, and our commentary on it, be a prophetic voice in our own cultural contexts?

## FAITH AND WORKS

The Letter of James is perhaps best known for its teaching on faith and works. The central question, of course, is whether James's teaching on faith and works represents a challenge to Paul's teaching on justification through faith or whether James intended only to clarify certain misunderstandings of Paul's teaching that had crept in over time. In working out a response to this question, two statements from the Letter of James might be helpful: "faith by itself, if it has no works, is dead" (James 2:17) and "show me your faith apart from your works, and I by my works will show you my faith" (James 2:18). First, recall that Paul argues for justification through faith and not by works. Simply stated, Paul's view is that human beings cannot set right their broken relationship with God by obeying the covenant obligations of Torah (i.e., justification by works of the Law) (Rom. 3:19–20) because only God can acquit humanity. Thus, people are justified by God *as a free gift* to all who believe (Rom. 3:21–26).

Is James contradicting Paul's teaching on justification through faith? On first reading, it would seem so. However, note that the Letter of James is not addressing the process or even the significance of justification but rather the *nature of faith*. The author's point is that "empty" faith—that is, faith that is not manifested in acts of justice and kindness—is not genuine faith (James 2:14–17). He wants to assert, instead, that faith is evidenced by one's good works (James 2:18). This is not substantially different from Paul's view on the quality of faith to which a believer is called. For example, Paul did not think that people could simply sit around thinking good thoughts about God. Instead, Paul says that "the only thing that counts is faith working through love" (Gal. 5:6)—that is, faith that manifests itself in love for God and love for the other. Believers are freed from the Law, but this does not mean that they have license for self-indulgence. Rather, they are to become slaves to one another through love (Gal. 5:13). Why? Paul says, "For the whole law is summed up in a single commandment, 'You shall love your neighbor as yourself'" (Gal. 5:14). As we saw above, this is the same reason that James gives for his admonition that his readers pay attention to the needs of the poor (James 2:9).

Likewise, the way that the author of the Letter of James uses the Abraham story to illustrate his teaching on faith and works appears, at first glance, to be in conflict with Paul's teaching on justification through faith, but in the end it is not. Recall that Paul appeals to the example of Abraham and even cites the Book of Genesis—"Abraham believed God and it was reckoned to him as righteousness" (Gal. 3:6; cf. Gen. 15:6)—to demonstrate *justification through faith*. However, the author of the Letter of James argues that Abraham was *justified by works* when he was asked to sacrifice his son Isaac (James 2:21; cf. Gen. 22:1–14). Crucial to understanding James' argument is the recognition that the story from which Paul draws the quotation "Abraham believed God and it was reckoned to him as righteousness" (Gen. 15:6) precedes the story of Abraham's sacrifice of Isaac (Gen. 22:1–14) in the Abraham narratives (Genesis 12–25). Again, James is not addressing the question of the nature of justification here. Rather, he is commenting on the quality of Abraham's faith. Already justified by God through faith, Abraham's trust in the promise is now tested—like fire purifies gold—when God asks him to sacrifice his only son, the son of the promise (Gen. 22:1). By obeying God as he did, Abraham's faith is brought to completion (James 2:22), and the scripture is fulfilled: "Abraham believed God and it was reckoned to him as righteousness" (James 2:23; Gen. 15:6). Thus, Abraham is an example of a person who is justified by faith *and* works in the sense that his story shows that his "faith was active along with his works" (James 2:22).

We have to acknowledge that James's choice of words to explain his teaching on faith and works is somewhat unfortunate. Because of Paul's concern about those who wanted to make Gentile converts observe Jewish law in order to become followers of Jesus, he probably would not have approved of James's use of the example of Abraham to say that the believer is justified by faith *and works*. Yet even in Paul's day, we can see clues in his letters that Jesus followers were taking his teaching on justification through faith, not by works, and wrongly concluding, "All things are lawful for me" (1 Cor. 6:12). Imagine a similar situation several decades later, when Christian believers were saying that God's justification has freed them from obligation to the Law. James' response would have sounded something like this: "Do you think that you have been freed from the Law? In fact, you are bound to the law of liberty and you will be judged by it!" (paraphrase of James 2:8–12). He goes on to say, "Judgment will be without mercy to anyone who has shown no mercy" (James 2:13) and "Faith by itself, if it has no works, is dead" (James 2:17). Thus, it is possible to conclude that, rather than contradicting Paul, James is trying to correct certain misconceptions that had arisen concerning Paul's teaching on justification through faith, not unlike what Paul was doing in his own day.

## Anointing of the Sick

At the conclusion of the Letter of James, the author gives advice about anointing the sick with oil (James 5:14). In the ancient world, oil was considered to have curative powers in and of itself, but, in this case, the elders (or presbyters) of the church use this medicine along with prayer. Today Christian churches that have a ritual of anointing the sick use this scripture as a basis for the practice. Take, for example, the Assemblies of God churches, which employ the practice of laying hands on the sick and anointing them with oil. In explaining the warrant for this practice, they refer directly to the New Testament and its references to oil being used for healing. In particular, see Mark 6:13, where the twelve apostles were sent out on a mission, and they "anointed with oil many who were sick and cured them." Likewise, concerning the anointing ritual itself, the Assemblies of God churches follow the directives outlined in scripture, in that order. Citing James 5:14–16, they say that the usual procedure is as follows: (1) a sick Christian calls for the elders of the church; (2) they pray over him, (3) and they anoint him with oil.

Concerning the theology of anointing, the Assemblies of God churches say that the anointing is merely a symbolic reminder of God's healing power. The actual healing takes place by the power of the Holy Spirit (see Acts 10:38). Why, then, do they use oil? Here is one explanation:

> In the Assemblies of God we believe neither the laying on of hands nor anointing with oil is indispensable for healing, for often in Scripture healing takes place without either. But at times the touch of a praying person and the application of oil are an encouragement to faith, and such a practice is enjoined by Scripture (James 5:14–16). (http://www.ag.org/top/beliefs/christian_doctrines/gendoct_12_sick.cfm)

Notice that the oil itself is not thought to have any medicinal powers. That is, the community members who use it do not consider it to be a healing drug. Rather, the oil provides the opportunity for the praying community to offer a "healing" touch, a gesture of consolation and encouragement to faith.

Certain branches of the Mennonite tradition also practice anointing of the sick. What follows is a description of the ritual and a brief explanation of the theology that informs their practice:

> The rite usually includes most or all of the following: singing of a stanza or two of a hymn; the reading of the relevant passage in James 5; an interpretation of the passage; a discussion of the meaning of prayer; opportunity for the sick person to give an expression of his faith, or to confess sin; the application of olive oil to the sick person's head; and prayer accompanied by the laying on of hands. The rite is intended to give expression to the sick Christian's faith (he himself is to call for the ceremony) and to stimulate his faith in the healing power of God. The oil is a mere symbol of this healing power. It is normally expected that the ill person has the assurance that God wishes to

raise him up, though this is not universally required; it may be merely the expression of a general faith coupled with a resignation to God's will. It is never a mandate to God demanding immediate or ultimate healing. Nor is it intended as a preparation for death. (http://www.mhsc.ca/index.asp?content=http://www.mhsc.ca/encyclopedia/contents/A557ME.html)

Notice that the ritual is intended to elicit faith (i.e., trust) in God's healing powers and provide an opportunity for confessing one's sins, but there is no expectation that God must heal the sick person. That outcome is left entirely to God's will.

A number of Christian churches—for example, the Lutheran Church Missouri Synod and the United Methodist Church— have an officially approved worship service for healing. However, the Catholic Church gives the ritual an even higher status by including **anointing of the sick** among its seven sacraments, the other six being baptism, Eucharist, confirmation, penance, marriage, and holy orders. The *Catechism of the Catholic Church* describes this sacrament as a communal celebration in which the community gathered together prays for the sick person while the priest anoints the hands and forehead of the sick person with holy oil and lays hands upon him or her. The sacrament is associated with the gifts of the Holy Spirit:

> The first grace of this sacrament is one of strengthening, peace, and courage to overcome the difficulties that go with the condition of serious illness or the frailty of old age. . . . This assistance from the Lord by the power of his Spirit is meant to lead the sick person to healing of the soul, but also of the body if such is God's will. (*Catechism of the Catholic Church* §1520)

As you reflect on this practice of anointing the sick, you might consider what purpose anointing serves, from a psychological or sociological perspective, for the sick and their loved ones. How do these purposes relate to various churches' theological perspectives on the ritual?

## THE LETTER OF JUDE

The Letter of Jude is very short and not often read by Christians today because its imagery is strange and difficult to understand and its application for the Christian life is not immediately apparent. Perhaps the early churches thought it was strange, too, because people like Clement of Alexandria, a second-century bishop, and Origen, a third-century theologian and Bible scholar, list the Letter of Jude among the "disputed books" of the New Testament, meaning that the churches' leaders were divided about whether or not it should be included in their sacred scriptures. By the fourth century C.E., however, its status must have been clarified because Athanasius included it in his canon in the Festal Letter of 367 C.E.

The author of the Letter of Jude is forthright about his reason for writing. He wants to appeal to his audience "to contend for the faith that was once for all entrusted to the saints" ( Jude 3). However, before we investigate the content of the Letter of Jude, let's summarize what biblical scholars know about its author, date of composition, and audience.

Decorated altar in the Armenian Orthodox Cathedral of St. James, located in the Armenian Quarter of the Old City in Jerusalem. This cathedral is built on the site of the tombs of St. James the Apostle and St. James the brother of the Lord. Armenian Christianity has a very long and rich tradition, tracing its roots back to the teaching and missionary activity of the apostles Thaddeus and Bartholomew in the latter half of the first century C.E. *Alistair Duncan (c) Dorling Kindersley.*

## AUTHORSHIP

The supposed author of this letter, Jude, identifies himself as the brother of James (Jude 1). This is probably the Judas of Mark 6:3, in which the narrator of the story tells us that the people of Jesus' hometown are offended by Jesus. They complain against him, saying, "Is this not the carpenter, the son of Mary and brother of James and Joses and *Judas* and Simon, and are not his sisters here with us?" (cf. Matt. 13:55). Some biblical scholars accept the view that Jude or Judas, the brother of James, actually wrote this letter. However, most have argued that the Letter of Jude was written under a pseudonym. One reason for this view, again, is the letter writer's elegant Greek style and the quality of his grammar. Certainly, a simple Palestinian peasant could not have written such a work! In response to this argument, others have suggested that Jude could have used a scribe who was educated in the Greek language.

Other arguments against Jude as the historical author of this letter include his use of the word *faith* to describe the doctrine (i.e., authoritative teachings) of the community (Jude 3, 20). Recall that earlier works of the New Testament use *faith* to describe an attitude or disposition of trust in God or Jesus, not a collection of teachings. Only in the latter part of the first century C.E. do we begin to see the word *faith* used in the way that the author of Jude uses it. Likewise, a reference to God, Jesus Christ, and the Holy Spirit in Jude 20–21 sounds almost **Trinitarian** (referring to the three-in-oneness of God). Christians today take Trinitarian language of God for granted, but in the earliest decades of Christianity, this kind of talk was problematic because it appeared to suggest the existence of three gods. Both of these details from the Letter of Jude suggest an anonymous author writing toward the end of the first century rather than the historical Jude writing in the mid–first century C.E. We should add, as a point of clarification, that it would take several more centuries for Christians to find the right vocabulary to describe the Trinitarian nature of God. See, for example, the Nicene-Constantinople Creed of 381 C.E. and the "Definition of Faith" from the Council of Chalcedon (451 C.E.).

The Letter of Jude contains at least one more piece of evidence that suggests it was written not by Jude (or Judas) but by a later anonymous author. This is the exhortation to go back and remember the predictions of the apostles of the Lord (Jude 17). The argument is as follows: If the author of the Letter of Jude was the historical Jude, the brother of James, he would have been living at the same time as the apostles, and any attempt to establish authority for his writings by referring people to the earlier exhortations of the apostles would have been nonsensical. Moreover, Jude would have been an authority in his own right, probably even the head of a Palestinian Christian church, as was James. Therefore, he would have had no reason to depend on the apostles to lend authority to his teachings. After all, as the brother of James, he was also the brother of Jesus. For all of these reasons, we will take the position that the Letter of Jude was written under a pseudonym and that the author is unknown.

## DATE OF COMPOSITION AND AUDIENCE

Because biblical scholars do not agree on the question of the authorship of the Letter of Jude, you can expect that they also do not agree on its date of composition. Those who think it was actually written by Jude, the brother of James, assign a date as early as 50 C.E. Those who treat the Letter of Jude as an anonymous work give it a date of composition ranging from 80 to 120 C.E. However, as already suggested by some of the arguments outlined in our "Authorship" section, most scholars assign it a date of approximately 90–100 C.E. Further support for this date of composition can be found in the Second Letter of Peter (see Chapter 22), which quotes extensively from Jude. Although we do not know exactly when 2 Peter was written, many biblical scholars give it a date as late as 125 C.E.

The Letter of Jude provides even fewer clues about its intended audience. The opening section of the document does not name a recipient but simply says, "To those who are called" (Jude 1). References to the author's opponents are equally vague—they are intruders, dreamers, and grumblers (Jude 4, 8, 16)—thereby eliminating another possible clue to the author's audience. Some biblical scholars have argued for a Palestinian Christian audience because the author's allusions to traditional Jewish stories appear to be based on the Hebrew scriptures rather than the Septuagint (the Greek translation of the Old Testament). Others have argued for geographic areas associated with Paul—most notably, Asia Minor (modern Turkey)—because of the author's attack on what sounds like libertarian behavior (motivated by the belief that people should have freedom to do whatever they want), which could be a misunderstanding of Paul's teaching on freedom from the Law (cf. Rom. 6:1–4 and 1 Cor. 6:12–20). However, since neither of these arguments is very strong, it would be better to say that we simply do not know its intended audience.

## GENRE AND OUTLINE OF THE DOCUMENT

Because Jude is so short, it may seem strange to consider outlining the document. However, in this case, the exercise can be helpful in determining the genre of the document. As we have seen many times before, there are several ways to outline any written work. This one attempts to highlight both the structure of the work and its major themes.

1. Jude 1–2—Opening
2. Jude 3–23—Body
    a. Occasion for writing: Keep the faith against intruders (Jude 3–4)
    b. Warnings against disobedience (Jude 5–7)
    c. More warnings and a description of the intruders (Jude 8–13)
    d. Prophecies about the coming of the intruders (Jude 14–19)
    e. Exhortation: Keep the faith (Jude 20–23)
3. Jude 24–25—Doxology

By outlining this document, we can see that the only part of the work that coincides with the letter genre is the opening. Is there a better way to describe the genre of this text? The author states clearly that his purpose in writing is to ask his audience "to contend for the faith that was once for all entrusted to the saints" (Jude 3). In simple terms, he is telling them to fight to protect the integrity of the teaching they had received against all attackers. Thus, the Letter of Jude is perhaps better described as an exhortation to orthodoxy (i.e., right teaching).

## PROPHECIES AND WARNINGS

The author of the Letter of Jude gives few clues concerning the identity of the intruders, if, in fact, he had an actual group in mind. The description of their wrongdoing is so generic and extreme—acting ungodly, behaving in licentious ways, perverting God's grace, defiling the flesh, rejecting authority, slandering the angels, and being grumblers and malcontents—that he may be painting a composite picture of anyone and everyone who might oppose the faith. The author wants to make clear, however, that the threat comes from within. That is, these folks have established for themselves a place within the Christian community and are now hidden among them (Jude 4). They even share in the community's "love feasts," but by participating they actually corrupt them (Jude 12). The love feast, also called the **agape meal**, is a term used in the early church for the Eucharist or the Lord's Supper. Perhaps this is why the author of Jude considers these intruders so dangerous—they are hidden among the faithful and even share in their Eucharist. Thus, instead of being a unifying force in the community, the Eucharist has become a tool for destruction.

Against these intruders and those who might be tempted to follow them, the author of Jude recalls several stories from the Hebrew scriptures and other nonbiblical Jewish literature in which God punishes the disobedient among God's people (Jude 5–13). He also reminds the community of the prophecies of Enoch and the apostles (Jude 14–19) as a way of saying that they should not be surprised about the presence of intruders in their midst because their arrival had been foretold as one of the events of the end time. In the Old Testament, Enoch is described as having walked with God; "then he was no more because God took him" (Gen. 5:21–24). For this reason, his name was later associated with the coming of the end time.

If you have not studied the literature of the Old Testament, you probably will not recognize most of the stories alluded to in Jude 5–11. However, with the aid of your Bible's footnotes or cross-references, you should be able to locate most of them: the Israelites who disobeyed God during their long Exodus journey (Jude 5; see Num. 14); the angels who came down to earth because they lusted after women (Jude 6; see Gen. 6); the people of Sodom and Gomorrah who refused hospitality to God's messengers (Jude 7; see Gen. 19); Cain, who killed his brother Abel (Jude 11; see Gen. 4); Balaam, who took part in an attempt to keep Israel from entering the Promised Land after the Exodus (Jude 11; see Josh. 24:9–11; Deut. 23:3–6; cf. Num. 21–22); and Korah, who rebelled and turned against Moses and Aaron (Jude 11; see Num. 16).

One of the references from the Letter of Jude that you will not find in the Bible is the story about the archangel Michael fighting Satan for Moses' dead body (Jude 9–10). Apparently, this story was preserved in a now-lost Jewish work called the Assumption of Moses. The detail about the fallen angels who are locked up under the earth until judgment day (Jude 6) can be found in a Jewish apocryphal work named 1 Enoch. These particular sections of the work—1 Enoch 10:4–6 and 12:1–13:10—date to the second century B.C.E., so the tradition had already been around for a long time before the Letter of Jude was written. Likewise, Jude's version of the prophecy of Enoch (Jude 14–15) has a parallel in 1 Enoch 1:9. It reads as follows:

> Behold, he will arrive with ten million of the holy ones in order to execute judgment upon all. He will destroy the wicked ones and censure all flesh on account of everything that they have done, that which the sinners and the wicked ones committed against him. (1 Enoch 1:9; Charlesworth, trans., *The Old Testament Pseudepigrapha*, 1.13–14)

You can see that both works—Jude and 1 Enoch—use highly apocalyptic vocabulary and imagery about judgment and the condemnation of the wicked in the end time.

Given all of Jude's strange and unfamiliar references, no wonder today's Christians are not attracted to this New Testament book. But this question still remains: Why did the early Christian churches see fit to include it in the New Testament canon? After you have had a chance to read the Letter of Jude, perhaps you might speculate on the answer to this question. What kind of Christian community, in what kind of social situation, might have found the message of this book inspiring or engaging? Are there situations that Christian communities face today for which this book might offer a message of admonition or hope?

## KEY TERMS

Religion                    Trinitarian                    Agape meal
Anointing of the sick


## QUESTIONS FOR READING

Read the Letter of James. Use evidence from the biblical text to answer the following questions.

1. Locate the elements of James that prompt people to think of it as a letter. What aspects of James indicate that it is not a letter?

2. What does the Letter of James have to say about the benefit of enduring or not giving in to temptation (James 1:2–16)? According to James, what is the source of this temptation?

3. What does James mean when he writes, "Be doers of the word, and not merely hearers . . . " (James 1:22)?

4. According to James, what kind of religion is worthless (James 1:26–27)? When is it pure?

5. James admonishes those who "show partiality," that is, favoritism (James 2:1–13). What kind of partiality is he referring to? What law are they violating?

6. What does James mean when he says that faith without works is dead (James 2:26)? How does this compare to Paul's teaching about justification by faith, not works?

7. James warns of two dangers that might affect teachers (James 3:1–12; 3:13–18). What are they? How will people know that a teacher has true wisdom?

8. In James 4:1–12, the author contrasts friendship with the world and friendship with God. What happens to the person who seeks friendship with the world? How does one attain friendship with God?

9. What does James say to those who thoughtlessly plan for their successful futures and those who accumulate riches (James 4:13–5:6)?

10. What is James's advice about the "coming of the Lord" (James 5:7–12)? What does he advise about how to care for the sick among them (James 5:13–15)?

Read the Letter of Jude. Use evidence from the biblical text to answer the following questions.

11. As you read the Letter of Jude, locate any words or phrases that the author uses to describe the community of faith to which he is writing. What do these words and phrases tell you about how he regards the community?

12. As you read the Letter of Jude, locate any words or phrases that the author uses to describe the intruders. What do these words and phrases tell you about how he regards the intruders?

13. What point does the author of Jude make when he contrasts the archangel Michael with the intruders in Jude 9–10?

14. What point does the author of Jude make when he calls the intruders "waterless clouds," "autumn trees," "wild waves of the sea," and "wandering stars" in Jude 12–13?

15. When Jude exhorts the community members to build themselves up on their most holy faith, what specifically does he want them to do (Jude 20–23)?

## QUESTIONS FOR REFLECTION

1. How would you describe the relationship between Paul's teaching on justification through faith alone and James's teaching on faith and works? Do you think James is trying to challenge or contradict Paul's teaching or is he simply correcting certain misperceptions of it? Give reasons to support your answer.

2. Speculate about why the early churches might have decided to include the Letter of Jude in the Christian New Testament. What kind of Christian community, in what kind of social situation, might have found this book meaningful? Are there situations in Christian communities today for which this book might be meaningful?

## ACTIVITIES FOR LEARNING

1. Biblical scholars have noticed that the Letter of James contains several sayings that appear to have their origins in the gospel traditions. Use your Bible's cross-references to locate at least three sayings that have parallels in the Gospel of Matthew. To what extent are these sayings from James similar to or different from their parallel sayings in the gospel?

2. Identify a church tradition that has a ritual or prayers of healing, including anointing with oil. It can be your own church tradition, the church tradition of a friend or family member, or one with which you have little experience. Find out what its ritual is like. Under what circumstances is the ritual performed? Who is eligible to participate? You might also try to locate official documents that describe that church tradition's views on prayers for healing and anointing with oil. A good place to start is the Wabash Center website, which has links to the official websites of a large number of American Christian churches. Go to www.wabashcenter.wabash.edu/Internet/front.htm. If possible, interview the pastor or someone who is active in ministry within the church tradition that you are investigating to learn what significance the community attaches to the ritual. Are there certain psychological or sociological concerns that the anointing addresses for the sick and their loved ones? How do these concerns relate to the church's theological understanding of the ritual?

3. Locate three or four contemporary definitions of religion. Encyclopedias of religion can be a good source, but you may even find some interesting definitions

on the internet. Analyze your definitions carefully. Isolate the basic elements of each definition. What statement does each definition make about the nature of religion and its sphere of operation? What needs does religion address? What are the benefits or outcomes of religion? Why do people participate in religion? In what ways do these definitions help to inform what the biblical author is saying about religion in James 1:26–27?

## Sources and Resources

Brosend, William F. *James and Jude*. New York: Cambridge University Press, 2004.

Charlesworth, James H., ed. *The Old Testament Pseudepigrapha*. Vol. I. New York: Doubleday, 1983.

Chilton, Bruce, and Jacob Neusner, eds. *The Brother of Jesus: James the Just and His Mission*. Louisville, Ky.: Westminster John Knox Press, 2001.

Conti, Christina. "James." In *Global Bible Commentary*, edited by Daniel Patte. Nashville, Tenn.: Abingdon Press, 2004.

Gench, Frances Taylor. *Hebrews and James*. Louisville, Ky.: Westminster John Knox Press, 1996.

Hartin, Patrick J. *A Spirituality of Perfection: Faith in Action in the Letter of James*. Collegeville, Minn.: Liturgical Press, 1999.

———. *James*. Collegeville, Minn.: Liturgical Press, 2003.

———. *James, First Peter, Jude, Second Peter*. Collegeville, Minn.: Liturgical Press, 2006.

Johnson, Luke Timothy. *The Letter of James: A New Translation with Introduction and Commentary*. Anchor Bible Series, vol. 37A. New York: Doubleday, 1995.

———. *Brother of Jesus, Friend of God: Studies in the Letter of James*. Grand Rapids, Mich.: Eerdmans, 2004.

Kraftchick, Steven J. *Jude, 2 Peter*. Nashville, Tenn.: Abingdon Press, 2002.

Martin, Ralph P. *James*. Waco, Tex.: Word Books, 1988.

Maynard-Reid, Pedrito U. *Poverty and Wealth in James*. Maryknoll, N.Y.: Orbis Books, 1986.

McDonnell, Rea. *The Catholic Epistles and Hebrews*. Wilmington, Del.: Glazier, 1986.

Patte, Daniel, ed. *Global Bible Commentary*. Nashville, Tenn.: Abingdon Press, 2004.

Perkins, Pheme. *First and Second Peter, James, and Jude*. Louisville, Ky.: Westminster John Knox Press, 1995.

Senior, Donald P., and Daniel J. Harrington. *1 Peter, Jude, and 2 Peter*. Collegeville, Minn.: Liturgical Press, 2003.

Sleeper, C. Freeman. *James*. Nashville, Tenn.: Abingdon Press, 1998.

Tamez, Elsa. *The Scandalous Message of James: Faith without Works Is Dead*. New York: Crossroad, 1990.

# CHAPTER 22

# THE FIRST AND SECOND LETTERS OF PETER

The First Letter of Peter
- AUTHORSHIP: Pseudonymous
- DATE OF COMPOSITION: 70–90 C.E.
- INITIAL AUDIENCE: Identified in the letter as churches in various regions of Asia Minor (modern Turkey); communities that were experiencing persecution of some sort
- MAJOR TOPICS: Baptism and Images of Church; How Christians Should Deal with the Problem of Suffering; Do We Have Martyrs Today?

The Second Letter of Peter
- AUTHORSHIP: Pseudonymous
- DATE OF COMPOSITION: 100–125 C.E.
- INITIAL AUDIENCE: Unknown; identified in the letter as the same communities for which 1 Peter was written
- MAJOR TOPICS: Peter's Last Will and Testament; Delay of the Parousia; Apostolic Tradition and the Authority of Sacred Scripture

## TIMELINE

| | |
|---|---|
| **64 C.E.** | Peter and Paul are martyred in Rome. |
| **65–70 C.E.** | The Gospel of Mark is written. |
| **66–70 C.E.** | The Jewish War occurs, and Jerusalem and the Temple are destroyed. |
| **70–90 C.E.** | **The First Letter of Peter is written.** |
| **70–100 C.E.** | The Letter to the Hebrews is written. |
| **80–90 C.E.** | The Gospels of Matthew and Luke are written; Acts of the Apostles is written. |
| **80–100 C.E.** | The Letter of James is written; the Letter to the Ephesians is written. |
| **90–100 C.E.** | The Gospel of John is written; the Second Letter to the Thessalonians is written; the Letter to the Ephesians is written, sometime after the Letter to the Colossians; the Letter of Jude is written. |
| **100 C.E.** | The Letters of John and the pastoral letters (1 Timothy, 2 Timothy, Titus) are written. |
| **100–125 C.E.** | **The Second Letter of Peter is written.** |

The next stop on our voyage through the New Testament will give us an opportunity to explore the First and Second Letters of Peter. These letters belong to a larger group of New Testament letters sometimes called the catholic (meaning "general" or "universal") epistles or the apostolic letters, that is, letters attributed to one of the apostles. The titles attached to 1 Peter and 2 Peter remind us that these letters celebrate the legacy of Peter, Jesus' most visible and vocal apostle—at least as the synoptic gospels and Acts of the Apostles tell his story.

While we could focus on any number of topics in our investigation of these two letters named after Peter, we will concentrate on two. Concerning the First Letter of Peter, we will investigate how the early church made sense of suffering for the faith: Why does God allow such suffering? Why is suffering necessary? What are the "benefits" of suffering? How should the suffering innocent person respond to his or her persecutors? In the Second Letter of Peter, we have an opportunity to read a literary work that is described as Peter's last will and testament. Except for Acts of the Apostles, these two letters are the only New Testament books that give sustained attention to Peter. We will investigate 1 Peter first, since most scholars believe it was written before 2 Peter.

## THE FIRST LETTER OF PETER

People travel for many reasons. Some travel for business, while others travel to relocate to another part of the country or another part of the world. Some travel to relax and find diversions from their otherwise busy and tension-filled lives. However, people who travel to learn the history of a place and who investigate its monuments and museums are bound to find testimony to painful or shameful moments in its past. In the United States, they might find a historical marker at the site of a massacre of Native Americans or a lynching of African slaves. They might also find stories about the persecution of immigrant peoples or the desecration of churches and synagogues or other religious sites within minority communities. These are, and ought to be, sources of shame for the perpetrators and the communities that stood by and allowed these atrocities to happen. However, reflecting on these events can be an opportunity to explore questions about the human condition, the nature of God and God's involvement in human history, and how and when justice will come to suffering innocent people. Our inquiry into the First Letter of Peter will provide just such an opportunity.

First, let's review what biblical scholars have concluded about the authorship and date of composition for the First Letter of Peter as well as its original intended audience.

## AUTHORSHIP AND DATE OF COMPOSITION

There are at least two theories about the authorship and date of composition of the First Letter of Peter. One theory ascribes the letter to Peter himself. Another holds that it is a pseudonymous work of a later date. Those who argue for a later date of composition and anonymous authorship do so because they think that Peter could not have known the addressees of this letter—churches in Pontus, Galatia,

Cappadocia, Asia, and Bithynia—since Acts of the Apostles gives no evidence that he traveled into this area of Asia Minor (modern Turkey). Other evidence suggests that some of the Christian churches to which 1 Peter is addressed had not yet been established in the time of Peter (d. 64 CE). The author's use of the term *Babylon* to describe Rome (1 Pet. 5:13; cf. Rev. 18:2) is another clue that Peter did not write this letter, since other references of this sort are not found until late in the first century C.E. Finally, scholars who hold the view that 1 Peter was written by someone other than Peter argue that a Galilean fisherman of the first century C.E. would have been incapable of writing the cultivated Greek with the numerous citations from the Greek Old Testament that are found in 1 Peter.

Another argument for assigning a later date of composition to 1 Peter is the observation that it contains testimony to publicly recognized leadership roles in the churches—specifically, presbyters or elders who receive compensation for their service to the churches (1 Pet. 5:1–2). Evidence from other parts of the New Testament and from other early Christian literature indicates that such leadership positions did not exist until the end of the first century C.E. Since this letter also bears certain similarities to Pauline letters, some scholars suggest that it was written by someone who was copying the style of Paul's letters. But this kind of "copying" would not have been possible until the latter half of the first century, after Paul's letters had circulated for a while. Finally, 1 Peter's allusions to widespread persecutions argue against Peter's time, since we know of no general empirewide persecutions then. There was such a persecution in the latter part of the reign of Emperor Domitian (81–96 C.E.), however.

Those who argue that Peter himself wrote this letter do so because Peter was associated with Rome and they think that Rome could have begun to exercise authority over the churches of Asia Minor (modern Turkey) within Peter's lifetime. They also argue that the church in Bithynia has very early origins (Pliny, *Epistulae* 10.96), although some of the other churches mentioned in the opening of the letter may not have existed in the time of Peter. In response to the objection that a fisherman like Peter would not have had the literary training to write this letter, scholars who support Petrine (adj., referring to Peter) authorship argue that secretaries were commonly given considerable license in the composition of letters (cf. 1 Pet. 5:12). Finally, they argue that 1 Peter is primitive in its theology and in its understanding of the organization of the church. Thus, these scholars would suggest a date of 62–64 C.E., during Emperor Nero's persecution of Christians at Rome, shortly before Peter was martyred.

While acknowledging that biblical scholars remain somewhat divided on questions of the authorship and date of composition for the First Letter of Peter, we will follow the majority view, which says that this is a pseudonymous work written sometime between 70 and 90 C.E..

## AUDIENCE

The churches to which this letter is addressed were in Pontus, Galatia, Cappadocia, Asia, and Bithynia (1 Pet. 1:1). Unfortunately, we do not know the exact locations of these church communities or even the number of churches involved because the places named here are not cities but regions or provinces. Working clockwise, the first province, Pontus, is located in northeast Turkey on the southern shore of the Black Sea. The next two, Galatia and Cappadocia, are located to the south of Pontus. The fourth, Asia, was in the area now known as western Turkey, and the fifth, Bithynia, was the province adjacent to Pontus on the southern shore of the Black Sea in north central Turkey.

The author of 1 Peter calls the members of these communities "exiles of the Dispersion" (1 Pet. 1:1). This phrase usually refers to Jews in the Diaspora (i.e., Jews living outside of Palestine). However, in this case, they are Gentiles (see 1 Pet. 1:14, 18; 2:9–10; 4:3–4) who have recently converted to belief in Jesus Christ (see 1 Pet. 1:14; 2:2; 4:12) but are in danger of giving up their faith under threat of persecution. In response to such persecutions, the letter writer uses the language of the

Regions of Pontus, Galatia, Cappadocia, Asia, and Bithynia within modern Turkey. The First Letter of Peter is addressed to churches in these areas.

Jewish covenant between God and Israel to describe the members of the church community: They are a chosen race, a royal priesthood, a holy nation, and a people set apart (1 Pet. 2:9). He also calls them "visiting strangers" and "resident aliens" (1 Pet. 1:1; 2:11)—terms that suggest communities in a marginalized or alienated situation in relation to the larger society. These descriptors are similar to the ones that contemporary Christian theologians sometimes use when they talk about the church as in the world but not of the world. Its members reside here for a time but their destiny is with God in eternity.

## OUTLINE OF THE LETTER

As we have observed with other New Testament books, the exercise of outlining can help us make some interesting observations about the book's form (structure) or its content. In this case, we discover that the First Letter of Peter has an opening and a closing, which make it look like a letter, but in other ways, it is not really a letter.

1. 1 Peter 1:1–2—Opening
2. 1 Peter 1:3–9—Blessing
3. 1 Peter 1:10–2:10—Concerning the special status of God's holy people
4. 1 Peter 2:11–3:12—Proper conduct when living among outsiders
5. 1 Peter 3:13–5:11—Proper conduct in the face of oppression
6. 1 Peter 5:12–14—Closing

Observe, for example, that this letter does not have a thanksgiving section. Instead, it has a blessing. In terms of content, too, 1 Peter sounds less like a letter and more like a sermon. These homiletic overtones, together with the letter's baptismal imagery (e.g., 1 Pet. 1:3; 2:23; 3:18–22), prompted some scholars of past decades to conclude that 1 Peter was, in whole or part, a homily intended for the celebration of baptism. This view is less popular today, with most scholars agreeing that it is a letter, albeit not conforming entirely to the form of a letter. Whether or not 1 Peter is a sermon or a letter, it invites its readers to appreciate their special relationship as God's holy people, exhorts them to live in a way proper to their calling, and encourages them to stand firm in the face of persecution.

## BAPTISM AND IMAGES OF CHURCH

As we have already noted above, the First Letter of Peter contains several important allusions to the readers' election or "chosenness" that comes through baptism. In the blessing, the author describes it as "a new birth into a living hope through the resurrection of Jesus Christ from the dead, and into an inheritance that is imperishable" (1 Pet. 1:3). A bit later he says that they are "born anew not of perishable but of imperishable seed" (1 Pet. 1:23). He also compares baptism to the story of Noah and the flood (Gen. 6:11–8:22). The water of the flood destroyed all of the evil in the world except for the eight who were saved in Noah's ark. The water of baptism saves people "as an appeal to God for a good conscience [disposition], through the resurrection of Jesus Christ" (1 Pet. 3:21). In other words, for this author, baptism is a promise of participation in the resurrection of Christ, which in some sense is already a reality. The baptized inherit imperishability!

The letter writer uses similar imagery of election to describe his idea of church. To be sure, the letter writer's ecclesial imagery is deeply rooted in God's covenant with Israel. Although the church members are considered "aliens and exiles" among their neighbors (1 Pet. 2:11–12), his readers should know that they are "a chosen race, a royal priesthood, a holy nation, God's own people" (1 Pet. 2:9). The author of 1 Peter also describes the believing community as living stones that are being built into a spiritual house (1 Pet. 2:4–5), which has Christ as its cornerstone for those who believe (1 Pet. 2:6–8). For a community of faith that is undergoing persecution, as the letter seems to suggest, these images must have engendered hope and confidence in their status as God's special people.

## How Christians Should Deal with the Problem of Suffering

The dominant theme of the First Letter of Peter concerns an enduring problem: how to make sense of suffering and religious persecution. Whoever wrote this letter and whatever communities first received it, they appear to have known firsthand the realities of suffering for the sake of their faith. This is what 1 Peter teaches about suffering:

- Christians should consider themselves living in this world as a "stranger in a foreign land" (1 Pet. 1:1).
- Suffering purifies people's faith and makes it more genuine (1 Pet. 1:7).
- Christ's suffering has already delivered believers from the useless and unimportant things of life (1 Pet. 1:17–18).
- Christians should act respectfully, loving one another from the heart and conducting themselves blamelessly (1 Pet. 2:12; 3:8; 4:7–11).
- It is God's will that Christians obey governors, emperors, and all persons in authority (1 Pet. 2:13–15).
- Christians should answer evil or insult with a blessing (1 Pet. 3:9).
- If Christians suffer persecution for justice's sake, they cannot really suffer harm (1 Pet. 3:14).
- If someone challenges a Christian's reason for hope, he or she must answer respectfully. By treating one's persecutors kindly, it will make these persecutors ashamed (1 Pet. 3:15–16).
- Christians are already saved through baptism (1 Pet. 3:21).

- Christians should never be ashamed for suffering because they are Christian; they will also share Christ's glory (1 Pet. 4:16).
- Through suffering, a believer shares in the sufferings of Christians all over the world (1 Pet. 5:9).

It should not come as a surprise that the model for this theology of suffering is Christ himself. These are the words of the letter writer:

> For this you have been called, because Christ also suffered for you, leaving you an example, so that you should follow in his steps.
>
> "He committed no sin, and no deceit was found in his mouth."
>
> When he was abused, he did not return abuse; when he suffered, he did not threaten; but he entrusted himself to the one who judges justly. He himself bore our sins in his body on the cross, so that, free from sins, we might live for righteousness; by his wounds you have been healed. For you were going astray like sheep, but now you have returned to the shepherd and guardian of your souls. (1 Pet. 2:21–24)

The descriptive imagery of this text will likely remind the careful reader of the fourth Servant Song of the prophet Isaiah (Isa. 52:13–53:12). Compare the prophet's words to the preceding statement from 1 Peter:

> But he was wounded for our transgressions, crushed for our iniquities; upon him was the punishment that made us whole, and by his bruises we are healed. All we like sheep have gone astray; we have all turned to our own way, and the Lord has laid on him the iniquity of us all. . . . Yet it was the will of the Lord to crush him with pain. . . . The righteous one, my servant, shall make many righteous. (Isa. 53:5–6, 10–11)

By appealing to the prophet Isaiah in this way, the letter writer not only provides a context for understanding the suffering of Christ but also links Christ's suffering to the believing community's own suffering, exhorting it to have the same intention as Christ (1 Pet. 4:1).

The letter writer's theology of suffering so thoroughly penetrates every aspect of his life that it even extends to his description of baptism. Notice how he plays on imagery from the story of Noah and the flood (cf. Gen. 6–8):

> For Christ also suffered for sins once for all, the righteous for the unrighteous, in order to bring you to God. . . . He went and made proclamation to the spirits in prison, who in former times did not obey when God waited patiently in the days of Noah, during the building of the ark, in which a few, that is, eight persons were saved through water. And baptism, which this prefigured, now saves you—not as a removal of dirt from the body, but as an appeal to God for a good conscience, through the resurrection of Jesus Christ. (1 Pet. 3:18–22)

The author's reference to Christ making proclamation to the "spirits in prison" is not easily understood, but it may mean that, between the time of his death and the time of his resurrection, Christ preached to the people who had died before his coming so that they, too, could be saved (see also 1 Pet. 4:6, G. Pet. 10:41). Using the flood imagery, the letter writer also makes the point that the water that once symbolized total suffering and destruction now brings salvation. Likewise, the community's own suffering will bring salvation.

## DO WE HAVE MARTYRS TODAY?

Sometimes we look back at the early church and marvel over those who became **martyrs**, having witnessed to their faith to the point of death. The Greek word *marturia* means "witness." For those of us who live in relative comfort and safety, with freedom to worship as we please, martyrdom seems far removed from our lives. However, modern incidents of religious persecution actually occur relatively frequently, especially in countries devastated by persistent and widespread poverty and political oppression. Thus, just as they did in the time of the early church, the stories of the martyrs can edify us and strengthen our resolve to live our faith in a more intentional way.

Before we look at a few examples of contemporary Christian martyrdom, we should add a note of caution. Today's media employ the term *martyr* in a much broader and less nuanced way than we are using it here. Perhaps we can even say that their usage is contrary to our intention, especially when the term *martyr* is applied to radical religious persons who are willing to go to great lengths, even to the point of committing suicide, to inflict harm on or punish those whom they consider to be a threat to their religious agenda. This kind of activity is not restricted to a particular faith tradition or religious movement. Moreover, it represents an extreme response from people who perceive that their religious principles are under assault on a cosmic level by forces that oppose the will of God. This is not the way the early church used the term *martyr*, nor is it our intention here. Rather, we are using it to describe people who live the core values of their faith despite the threat of persecution and even death. For the author of the First Letter of Peter, that meant acting in love toward everyone, walking in the footsteps of Christ in all that they said and did, living always in hope, and never retaliating against those who did them harm.

Here is a contemporary story of martyrdom that is illustrative of the themes of the First Letter of Peter. On December 2, 1980, four North American women were murdered in El Salvador for working with the church of the poor in that country. These are excerpts from letters to their families in the months before their deaths.

> My fear of death is being challenged constantly as children, lovely young girls, old people are being shot and some cut up with machetes and bodies thrown by the road and people prohibited from burying them. A loving Father must have a new life of unimaginable joy and peace prepared for these precious unknown, uncelebrated martyrs. . . . I want to stay on now. I believe now that this is right. At times I miss the comfort of having many friends made over the years in Nicaragua. Here I am starting from scratch but it must be his plan and he is teaching me and there is real peace in spite of the many frustrations and the terror around us and the work, etc. God is very present in his seeming absence.
>
> —Words of Sister Maura Clarke, November 20, 1980

Sister Maura Clark

What does December bring for us here in El Salvador? . . . First of all, it will bring us the Advent season—a time of waiting, a time of hoping, a time of yearning. . . . On the First Friday in December we have a Mass for Anointing the Sick. This means that we take our jeep and minibus and go up and down the hillsides picking up the sick and bringing them to the celebration. . . . All this goes on as normally as possible. And yet if we look at this little country of El Salvador as a whole, we find that it is all going on in a country that is writhing in pain—a country that daily faces the loss of so many of its people—and yet a country that is waiting, hoping and yearning for peace. The steadfast

Sister Dorothy Kazel

faith and courage our leaders have to continue preaching the Word of the Lord even though it may mean "laying down your life" in the very REAL sense is always a point of admiration and a vivid realization that JESUS is HERE with us. Yes, we have a sense of waiting, hoping, and yearning for a complete realization of the kingdom, and yet we know it will come because we can celebrate him here right now.

—Words of Sister Dorothy Kazel, November 1980

The Peace Corps left today and my heart sank low. The danger is extreme and they were right to leave. . . . Now I must assess my own position, because I am not up for sui-cide. Several times I have decided to leave. I almost could, except for the children, the poor bruised victims of adult lunacy. Who would care for them? Whose heart would be so staunch as to favor the reasonable thing in a sea of their tears and helplessness? Not mine, dear friend, not mine.

—Words of Jean Donovan, November 1980

I don't know if it is in spite of, or because of the horror, terror, evil, confusion, lawlessness—but I do know that it is right to be here. That may be the only surety as, with Carla, I start a work that is going to put us in contact with some of the hurting, homeless, hungry and to God knows who else! . . . "Each of you has received some spiritual gift; use it for the good of all; activate the different gifts that God has distributed among you" (1 Peter 4:10). To activate our gifts, to use them in this situation, to believe that we are gifted in and for El Salvador now, that the answers to the questions will come when they are needed, to walk in faith one day at a time with the Salvadorans along a road filled with obstacles, detours, and sometimes washouts—this seems to be what it means for us to be in El Salvador. And it is good for us to be here.

—Words of Sister Ita Ford, June 1980

Jean Donovan

Sister Ita Ford

Here is another piece of the El Salvador story. Less than nine months before the murders of these four church women, on March 24, 1980, Oscar Romero, the Catholic archbishop of San Salvador, was killed by gunfire as he celebrated the Eucharist (i.e., the Lord's Supper) in the convent chapel of the Carmelite sisters at Divine Providence Hospital. Thus, he died as a martyr for his people after only three years as archbishop. Did he know that his service to the church in El Salvador would demand that he give his life? These are the words he spoke in an interview only one month before his death.

My life has been threatened many times. I have to confess that, as a Christian, I don't believe in death without resurrection. If they kill me, I will rise again in the Salvadoran people. I'm not boasting, or saying this out of pride, but rather as humbly as I can. As a shepherd, I am obliged by divine law to give my life for those I love, for the entire Salvadoran people, including those Salvadorans who threaten to assassinate me. If they should go so far as to carry out their threats, I want you to know that I now offer my blood to God for justice and the resurrection of El Salvador. Martyrdom is a grace of God that I do not feel worthy of. But if God accepts the sacrifice of my life, my hope is that my blood will be like a seed of liberty and a sign that our hopes will soon become a reality. My death will be for the liberation of my people and a testimony of hope for the future. A bishop will die, but the church of God, which is the people, will never die. (Cited in Plácido Erdozaín. *Archbishop Romero. Martyr of Salvador*, pp. 75–76. Maryknoll, NY: Orbis Books, 1981).

As you reflect on the stories of these and other modern martyrs, consider how their lives might be a living example of the message of 1 Peter. What, if anything, do these witnesses say about the Christian calling today? What would you do if you were in their shoes?

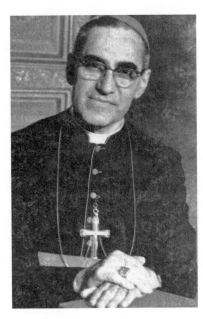

Bishop Oscar Romero

## THE SECOND LETTER OF PETER

The Second Letter of Peter is different, in many ways, from the First Letter of Peter. It is different in form (structure) and content. It is also different in style and quality of Greek grammar, leaving most scholars to conclude that 1 Peter and 2 Peter were not written by the same author. Little is known about the Second Letter of Peter in the earliest centuries of the church. It is first mentioned in an excerpt from the writings of Origen, a third-century theologian and Bible scholar, which is preserved in the writings of Eusebius, a fourth-century church historian (Origen, Commentary on John 5:3, in Eusebius, *Ecclesiastical History* 3.25.3). There Origen lists 2 Peter as among the "disputed books" of the New Testament. Although it is listed in Athanasius's canon in the Festal Letter of 367 C.E., apparently some churches of the fifth century C.E. still did not accept it as part of the New Testament. Today, of course, this letter is universally accepted among Christians as canonical.

Before we investigate the major themes of 2 Peter, let's summarize what scholars know about its author and historical context.

## AUTHORSHIP, DATE OF COMPOSITION, AND LOCATION

Most biblical scholars agree that the Second Letter of Peter is a pseudonymous work. However, its author apparently wanted to be true to the spirit of his hero, Peter, representing him as authentically as he can. In 2 Peter 1:1, for example, he is identified as Simon Peter—an early form of Peter's name—and in 2 Peter 1:18, the author says that he and his colleagues heard the heavenly voice say, "This is my Son, my Beloved," when they went with Jesus to the holy mountain, referring to the gospel story of Jesus' **transfiguration** (Mark 9:2–8 and parallels). Again, at the end of the letter, the author refers to "our beloved brother Paul" as if he were still alive at the time of this writing (2 Pet. 3:15). However, there is little evidence to suggest that the anonymous author of 2 Peter is the same person who wrote 1 Peter.

The Second Letter of Peter contains several pieces of evidence that point toward a date of composition in the late first century or early second century C.E. First, the author of 2 Peter knows that people had been collecting the letters of Paul, giving them the status of sacred scripture by the time this letter was written (see 2 Pet. 3:15–16). This practice certainly would not have happened in Peter's and Paul's lifetimes and perhaps would have been unlikely before the end of the first century or the early part of the second century C.E., as people were also beginning to recognize the gospels as sacred scripture. Second, the author of 2 Peter calls this his second letter to this community. If 1 Peter was written between 70 and 90 C.E., then 2 Peter must have been written later than that. Third, 2 Peter incorporates an "edited" version of a section of the Letter of Jude (compare 2 Pet. 2:1–22 and Jude 4–16), which most scholars think was written around 90 C.E. This would mean that 2 Peter had to have been written after 90 C.E. Finally, the author of 2 Peter knows the story of the transfiguration from the synoptic gospels, which was written to have occurred between 65 and 90 C.E. All of these clues suggest that 2 Peter was written no earlier than 100 C.E. and more likely somewhere around 125 C.E.

Even though most scholars agree that 2 Peter is pseudonymous, we can surmise that this anonymous author was writing from a place where Peter was honored after his death or where Paul's writings were known and traditions about Peter and Paul had come together. Biblical scholars suggest that Rome would be the best choice to satisfy these criteria. The author of 2 Peter says that the community (or communities) to whom he was writing are the same as those of 1 Peter—the eastern Mediterranean area then known as Asia Minor and today known as Turkey.

## OUTLINE OF THE DOCUMENT

As we saw with 1 Peter, the Second Letter of Peter is not really a letter. Although it has a letter opening, it is not directed to a particular community. Rather, the opening is a generic one that is intended for all Christians. Beyond the opening, this document has no formal (structural) elements of a letter. However, when we outline the document, we learn more about its genre.

1. 2 Peter 1:1–2—Opening
2. 2 Peter 1:3–21—Exhortation to live as God's holy ones
3. 2 Peter 2:1–22—Warning about false teachers
4. 2 Peter 3:1–16—Teaching about delay of the end time
5. 2 Peter 3:17–18—Closing exhortation

Notice that this so-called letter has no thanksgiving section. It also has no closing greeting or even a letter body. Instead, the document consists almost entirely of paraenesis (moral teaching).

## PETER'S LAST WILL AND TESTAMENT

If 2 Peter is not a letter, how shall we describe it? In the section called "exhortation to live as God's holy ones," the author has Peter say,

> I think it right, as long as I am in this body, to refresh your memory, since I know that my death will come soon, as indeed our Lord Jesus Christ has made clear to me. And I will make every effort so that after my departure you may be able at any time to recall these things. (2 Pet. 1:13–15)

Thus, the author of 2 Peter presents Peter as speaking to his beloved hearers shortly before his death. His goal is to remind them of all that he taught them so that after he dies, they will be able to remember his teachings. In other words, the author of 2 Peter is writing a last will and testament, the final words of a father or teacher to his loved ones.

We have already seen a testament in John's gospel—namely, the farewell discourses, when Jesus told his disciples about his impending death and promised them the Holy Spirit as their advocate (John 13:31–16:33). We saw another in 2 Timothy. While the content of each is different, the intention is the same: to console those who are left behind, to prepare them for the dangers they will face, and to exhort them to continue in the way they were taught. Therefore, when you read 2 Peter, keep in mind the literary setting of the testament. Consider how the author of 2 Peter would have wanted you to imagine Peter speaking these words, perhaps with a heavy heart. Imagine yourself sitting there with Peter's disciples and loved ones, who are hanging on his every word, trying to be brave but knowing that they are about to face difficult times. This is the literary context in which 2 Peter's warnings and exhortations should be understood and appreciated.

## DELAY OF THE PAROUSIA

Although not explicitly stated until late in this letter, the author's purpose in writing the Second Letter of Peter is to answer certain scoffers who challenge people's belief in the second coming of Jesus Christ, also known as the parousia. They try to argue that there is no promise of the parousia because "ever since our ancestors died, all things continue as they were from the beginning of creation" (2 Pet. 3:4). The "ancestors" probably are the apostles and eyewitnesses of the faith, though some scholars suppose that they are the patriarchs of the Old Testament. The author of 2 Peter counters the argument of these hecklers by saying that things have *not* stayed the same since the beginning of creation. After all, God used the waters of creation long ago to flood the world—a reference to the Genesis story of Noah and the flood (Gen. 6:5–8:19)—and God will use fire (another of the basic elements of the created world) to again destroy the world on the Day of Judgment (2 Pet. 3:5–7). The language is highly apocalyptic.

Further, the author of this letter appeals to the readers' recognition of his authority as an apostle—recall that he is writing under the pseudonym of Peter—and as one who had written to them earlier (2 Pet. 3:1) to remind them that they can trust in God's promise of the parousia because it was attested by the prophets and given by a "commandment of the Lord and Savior spoken through the apostles" (2 Pet. 3:2). He also reminds them that "with the Lord one day is like a thousand years, and a thousand years are like one day" (2 Pet. 3:8), meaning that the Lord's time is not like our time. Christ is not being slow in coming. Rather, he is being patient in order to give everyone an opportunity to repent before the Day of the Lord, when everything will be destroyed and a new heaven and earth will be established (2 Pet. 3:8–9, 13). In other words, they should consider "the patience of the Lord as salvation" (2 Pet. 3:15). In the meantime, they should live holy lives so that they will be pure and ready when the Day of God comes (2 Pet. 3:10–14). This is the author's answer to readers who are troubled by a delay of the parousia, which has now extended into another generation of believers.

For the author of 2 Peter, the problem of the delay of the parousia is not some sort of exercise in speculation about the future. Rather, it is closely allied with questions of theodicy. Is it possible to profess faith in a sovereign and just God in the face of so much evil? The author of 2 Peter says, "Yes!" Thus, he asserts that God has given the believers all that is needed for life and that, through God's promises, they will escape the corruption of the world (2 Pet. 1:3–4). By recalling God's past judgments on evil forces in the world—the wicked angels (Gen. 6:6–8), the world in the time of Noah (Gen. 8:18), and the people of the cities of Sodom and Gomorrah (Gen. 19:24)—he insists, "The Lord knows how to rescue the godly from trial and to keep the unrighteous under punishment until the day of judgment" (2 Pet. 2:9).

## APOSTOLIC TRADITION AND THE AUTHORITY OF SACRED SCRIPTURE

Scholars frequently cite the Second Letter of Peter when discussing theologies of biblical revelation because of its references to the power of apostolic witness, its comment about right interpretation of biblical prophecy, and its mention of the inspired character of sacred scripture. Perhaps the most well known of these references appears in the context of the author's statement of conviction concerning the return of Jesus Christ. Again writing under the pseudonym of Peter, he notes that the prophetic message (concerning the parousia) was more fully confirmed by the fact that they (i.e., Peter and the other disciples) were witnesses to the Transfiguration (2 Pet. 1:16–19; see Matt. 17:1–8; Mark 9:2–8; Luke 9:28–36), which he apparently interprets as a foreshadowing of the parousia. This statement, together with the author's pleading that the readers remember the "commandments of the Lord and Savior spoken through your apostles" (2 Peter 3:2), indicates that the apostolic tradition (teachings attributed to the apostles) had gained special status by the time that 2 Peter was written.

Concerning the inspired character of sacred scripture and the importance of right interpretation of biblical prophecy, biblical scholars quote the following from the Second Letter of Peter:

> First of all you must understand this, that no prophecy of scripture is a matter of one's own interpretation, because no prophecy ever came by human will, but men and women moved by the Holy Spirit spoke from God. (2 Pet. 1:20–21)

Although this statement is somewhat difficult to interpret, two things can be deduced from it about scripture and its interpretation. First, the author of 2 Peter asserts that biblical prophecy is trustworthy because the prophet is inspired by the Holy Spirit and speaks God's word. Second, he writes that individuals do not have the right to create their own interpretation of biblical prophecy. The literary context for this statement is an argument concerning the promises of the parousia. Immediately following the statement, the letter writer says, "But false prophets also arose among the people, just as there will be false teachers among you, who will secretly bring in destructive opinions" (2 Pet. 2:1). Later he says, "First of all you must understand this, that in the last days scoffers will come, scoffing and indulging their own lusts and saying, 'Where is the promise of his coming?'" (2 Pet. 3:3–4). Therefore, we can conclude that Peter's admonition about not creating one's own interpretation of biblical prophecy is aimed at his opposition, who held a different view about the coming of the parousia than his own, which he considered normative.

On the topic of the authority of scripture, one more quotation from 2 Peter is worthy of note. In an exhortation to live holy lives while awaiting the parousia, the letter writer reminds his readers that Paul's letters contained the same message. Acknowledging that some of Paul's writings are hard to understand, he adds a warning about those who would twist their meaning to their own destruction "as they do the other scriptures" (2 Pet. 3:16). Although the Greek word translated here as "scriptures" can simply mean "writings," some biblical scholars take this reference as an indication that early Christians were already recognizing Paul's letters as having the status of sacred scripture by the time that the Second Letter of Peter was written. If so, this quotation provides evidence of an early stage in the development of the New Testament canon.

## KEY TERMS

| | |
|---|---|
| Martyrs | Transfiguration |

## QUESTIONS FOR READING

Read 1 Peter. Use evidence from the text to support your answers.

1. The author of 1 Peter describes the members of the communities to which he is writing as "exiles," "aliens," and "sojourners in a foreign land." What does he mean? How do these terms relate to his description of Christians as "a chosen race" and a "holy nation" (1 Pet. 2:9)?

2. What is the "new birth" to which the letter writer refers in 1 Peter 1:3?

3. From your reading of 1 Peter, find at least two statements that express the author's understanding of the value of suffering and persecution, and explain them in your own words. What does he understand to be the role of the Old Testament prophets in making sense of suffering (1 Pet. 1:10–12)?

4. Explain what the author of 1 Peter means when he describes Christ and the Christian as "living stones" (1 Pet. 2:4–8).

5. What reason does the author of 1 Peter give for respecting government authorities (1 Pet. 2:13–17)?

6. Summarize 1 Peter's instructions to the Christian slave. What is the letter writer's justification for these instructions (1 Pet. 2:18–25)?

7. According to 1 Peter, how are Christians supposed to respond to injustices that are done against them (1 Pet. 3:13–17)?

8. What is the author's view about the immediacy of the end time (1 Pet. 4:7)? How does this issue relate to the problem of suffering?

9. What directives does the author give to the pastor of this community concerning how he should take care of the community (1 Pet. 5: 1–4)?

Read 2 Peter. Use evidence from the text to support your answers.

10. What does 2 Peter say about how people must "support" their faith (1 Pet. 1:3–11)? What do these activities have in common? According to the author of 2 Peter, what will happen to those who do not support their faith in this way?

11. Compare 2 Peter 1:16–18 to the synoptic versions of the story of the Transfiguration (Mark 9:2–8 and parallels). What elements of 2 Peter 1:16–18 are similar to the synoptic versions? What elements are different? What clues can you find to explain the message that 2 Peter intends to convey by using this story?

12. In 2 Peter 2:1–22, what attributes does the author assign to the false teachers? Speculate about why he portrays them in this way. What clues can you find in the text to determine the nature of the false teaching?

13. What does the author of 2 Peter want his audience to understand about the events of the end time (2 Pet. 3:1–15)? How does he want them to behave as they wait for the end time?

## QUESTIONS FOR REFLECTION

1. As you read the excerpts from the letters of the four North Americans killed in El Salvador (see above), you probably will recognize that they knew they were in great danger. What do you think motivated them to stay with the people? How do you think they maintained their courage?

2. If you were to find yourself in a situation similar to that of one of these modern martyrs, how would you respond? What would be your greatest obstacles? By what values or convictions would you be motivated to act?

## ACTIVITIES FOR LEARNING

1. Construct your own "theology" of suffering. What is your starting point; that is, what authoritative story (e.g., Jesus forgiving the people who crucified him in Luke 23:34) or what religious truth (e.g., God is just) provides the grounding for your theology of suffering? What is your understanding of the religious benefits of suffering for the Christian believer? How is the believer supposed to respond to his or her oppressors? Are there times or circumstances when the believer

ought to fight back against oppression? Why or why not? How does your theology of suffering compare to the theology of suffering in 1 Peter?

2. Locate other stories of contemporary martyrs like those of the four North American women and Bishop Oscar Romero, who were killed in El Salvador in 1980—For example, Dietrich Bonhoeffer, who was killed in 1945; Edith Stein, who was killed in 1942; the seven Trappist monks of Algeria, who were killed in 1996; and Etty Hillesum, who was killed in 1943. There are many other examples at http://www.catholicsites.com/beggarking/martyrs.htm. What were the circumstances surrounding their deaths? What in their life stories qualifies them to be called martyrs? What can you learn about their responses to the suffering imposed on them by their persecutors? What, if anything, in their stories inspires or motivates you to make different choices about how you live your life?

3. Imagine that you are the spiritual leader of a religious group today and you know you are about to die. Write a testament for your followers, one that will console those who are left behind and prepare them for the dangers they will face in the future. Also, decide on the message you want to pass on to future generations, and write a convincing exhortation that will inspire your followers to continue in the way they were taught.

## Sources and Resources

Achtemeier, Paul J. *1 Peter: A Commentary on First Peter*. Minneapolis, Minn.: Fortress, 1996.

Bauckham, Richard. *Jude, 2 Peter*. Dallas, Tex.: Word, 1990.

Bechtler, Steven Richard. *Following in His Steps: Suffering, Community, and Christology in 1 Peter*. Atlanta, Ga.: Scholars Press, 1998.

Boring, M. Eugene. *1 Peter*. Nashville, Tenn.: Abingdon Press, 1999.

Brett, Donna Whitson, and Edward T. Brett. *Murdered in Central America. The Stories of Eleven U. S. Missionaries*. Maryknoll, NY: Orbis Books, 1988.

Chester, Andrew, and Ralph Martin. *The Theology of the Letters of James, Peter, and Jude*. Cambridge, England: Cambridge University Press, 1994.

Craddock, Fred B. *First and Second Peter, and Jude*. Louisville, Ky.: Westminster John Knox Press, 1995.

Dalton, William J. "The First Epistle of Peter." In *The New Jerome Biblical Commentary*, edited by R. E. Brown, J. A. Fitzmyer, and R. E. Murphy, Englewood Cliffs, N.J.: Prentice Hall, 1990.

Elliott, John H. *A Home for the Homeless: A Sociological Exegesis of 1 Peter, Its Situation and Strategy*. Philadelphia: Fortress, 1981.

———. *1 Peter: A New Translation with Introduction and Commentary*. Anchor Bible Series, vol. 37B. New York: Doubleday, 2000.

Erdozaín, Plácido. *Archbishop Romero. Martyr of Salvador*. Maryknoll, NY: Orbis Books, 1981.

Hartin, Patrick J. *James, First Peter, Jude, Second Peter*. Collegeville, Minn.: Liturgical Press, 2006.

Hillyer, Norman. *1 and 2 Peter, Jude*. Peabody, Mass.: Hendrickson, 1992.

Kraftchick, Steven John. *Jude, 2 Peter*. Nashville, Tenn.: Abingdon Press, 2002.

Lapham, F. *Peter: The Myth, the Man and the Writings: A Study of Early Petrine Text and Tradition*. London: Sheffield Academic Press, 2003.

Michaels, J. Ramsey. *1 Peter*. Waco, Tex.: Word Books, 1988.

Neyrey, Jerome H. *2 Peter, Jude: A New Translation with Introduction and Commentary*. Anchor Bible Series, vol. 37C. New York: Doubleday, 1993.

Perkins, Pheme. *First and Second Peter, James, and Jude*. Louisville, Ky.: Westminster John Knox Press, 1995.

Senior, Donald, and Daniel J. Harrington. *1 Peter, Jude, and 2 Peter*, edited by Daniel J. Harrington. Collegeville, Minn.: Liturgical Press, 2003.

# THE THREE LETTERS OF JOHN

## OVERVIEW

- AUTHORSHIP: Anonymous; probably someone from the community for which the Gospel of John was written; identified as the presbyter in the second and third letters
- DATE OF COMPOSITION: Approximately 100 C.E.
- INITIAL AUDIENCE: The Christian community for which the Gospel of John was written
- MAJOR TOPICS: Was the Letter Writer Reading John?; Were the Secessionists Also Reading John?; God, Christ, and the Holy Spirit; Doctrine and Ethics

## TIMELINE

| | |
|---|---|
| 65–70 C.E. | The Gospel of Mark is written. |
| 66–70 C.E. | The Jewish War occurs. |
| 70 C.E. | Jerusalem and the Temple are destroyed. |
| 70–90 C.E. | The First Letter of Peter is written. |
| 80–90 C.E. | The Gospels of Matthew and Luke are written. |
| 90–100 C.E. | The Gospel of John is written. |
| 80–100 C.E. | The Letter of James is written; the Letter to the Colossians is written. |
| 90–100 C.E. | The Letter of Jude is written; the Letter to the Ephesians is written, sometime after the Letter to the Colossians. |
| 95–96 C.E. | The Book of Revelation is written. |
| 100 C.E. | **The Letters of John are written**; the pastoral letters are written. |
| 100–125 C.E. | The Second Letter of Peter is written |

The next stop on our journey through the New Testament will feel like a bit of déjà vu as we explore the Letters of John. These letters belong to a group of New Testament books called Johannine literature, meaning "literature that is associated with John or the Gospel of John." We will discover that the Johannine letters use much of the same symbolic vocabulary and imagery that we found in John's gospel. However, this distinctively Johannine language is employed in very different ways in the letters than in the gospel. What shall we make of these letters? And what is their relationship to the gospel by the same name? Before we tackle these questions, let's summarize what biblical scholars know about the authorship, date of composition, and audience for these letters.

## AUTHORSHIP

Early church tradition associated these documents, now known as the Letters of John, with the same John who wrote the Gospel of John. Most likely this connection was based on the recognition that the Gospel of John and the First Letter of John share similar style and vocabulary. However, the letters themselves give no clue to the identity of the author except that, in the opening of the Second and Third Letters of John, the author calls himself the presbyter (i.e., elder). Today most biblical scholars agree that the gospel writer John did not write these three letters. Rather, they think the letters are anonymous works, written by a disciple of John or some unnamed Christian who belonged to the community for which John's gospel was written. This would account for similarities in vocabulary between the Gospel of John and the First Letter of John and other details that link the First Letter of John to the Second and Third letters.

## DATE OF COMPOSITION AND AUDIENCE

We have already said that we know little about the authorship of the three Letters of John, but we know even less about their date of composition. How shall we proceed? Our investigation begins with the presupposition that the Gospel of John and 1 John were addressed to the same community at different stages in its development. Let's start with the date of John's gospel—approximately 90–100 C.E.—and then look for clues in 1 John that will help us establish a date relative to the gospel. Basically, there are two possibilities: Either 1 John was written before the Gospel of John, or the gospel was written before 1 John. Let's consider the arguments.

If you think back to Chapter 9 of this textbook, you will recall that the community for which the Gospel of John was written appears to have been relatively small, mostly Jewish Christian, and feeling beleaguered by opponents outside of the community. However, as you read the First Letter of John, you will see that community behind the letter has opponents who once belonged to the community and later left it over some kind of disagreement apparently concerning how the Gospel of John should be interpreted. Biblical scholars call these opponents **secessionists** because they were not forced out. Rather, they left on their own.

Scholars who say that the First Letter of John was written *after* the Gospel of John do so because they think it makes more sense to imagine a community that is, in its early stages, besieged by outsiders and, only later, when the community is established, is it divided over issues internal to the community. The opposite scenario, in which a newly formed Christian community suffers a split or schism over some issue of faith and later finds itself fighting outsiders, is much harder to imagine. Thus, those who think 1 John was written after the Gospel of John argue for a date of approximately 100 C.E., a decade after the gospel.

Scholars who argue that the First Letter of John was written *before* the Gospel of John do so because they view the theology of John's gospel to be more fully developed or more nuanced than that of the First Letter of John. For example, the Gospel of John describes Jesus as the Word of God. This concept is much more abstract and requires a great deal more sophistication to fully understand than does 1 John's phrase "word of life," which refers to a proclamation about the words and deeds of Jesus. Similarly, these scholars think that 1 John was written before the Gospel of John because the gospel's Christology is higher than that of 1 John. For example, the Gospel of John's Christology involves the preexistent Son of God becoming incarnate—taking on flesh—in the person of Jesus of Nazareth and later returning to the Father. Compare that view to the Christology of 1 John, which focuses on the saving power of Jesus' crucifixion. The first can be described as a high or three-stage Christology, while the second is a low or two-stage Christology (see Chapter 17). The operative approach here is to assume that two-stage or low Christologies might evolve into three-stage or high Christologies but not the other way around.

Given the weight of these two arguments, most biblical scholars think that 1 John was written after the Gospel of John. They respond to the argument in favor of an early date for 1 John by saying that 1 John does not represent a backward-thinking Christology. Rather, the author of 1 John was attempting to "correct" certain interpretations of John's Christology that he thought were going beyond the intended meaning of the gospel writer. The evidence used in support of these scholars' view comes, in part, from 2 John: "Everyone who does not abide in the teaching of Christ, but *goes beyond it* [emphasis mine], does not have God; whoever abides in the teaching has both the Father and the Son" (2 John 9).

For the purposes of our work, we will accept the view of the majority of biblical scholars who say that 1 John was written after the Gospel of John. But what about the other two letters? Again, most scholars agree that 1 John was probably written before 2 John because 2 John mentions only briefly, and without explanation, a false teaching that is addressed in greater detail in 1 John (1 John 4:1–6; cf. 2 John 7). Apparently, the audience of 2 John already knew the details about this heresy from its reading of 1 John and therefore needed no further explanation. However, 3 John has no connection with 1 John or 2 John except for the fact that the author of 3 John and the author of 2 John call themselves the presbyter or elder and both letters make a reference to hospitality. Thus, biblical scholars have concluded that these two letters were written by the same person, but 3 John could have been written earlier or later than either of the other two letters. In the absence of additional information about the sequencing of these letters, scholars assign a date of approximately 100 C.E. to all three.

## OUTLINES OF THE LETTERS

From our earlier investigations into the books of the New Testament, we have observed that outlines can sometimes enhance our understanding of a document and other times limit or narrow possible interpretations of the text. In this case, our first outline will show that, even though 1 John is identified as a letter, in fact it is not a letter—that is, it has none of the standard letter components: no opening, no thanksgiving, no body, and no concluding greetings. Here is one possible outline of 1 John:

1. 1 John 1:1–4—Prologue
2. 1 John 1:5–2:17—Walk in the light
3. 1 John 2:18–27—The antichrist and those who would deceive you

4. 1 John 2:28–3:24—You are God's children

5. 1 John 4:1–6—Test the spirits

6. 1 John 4:7–21—Love one another

7. 1 John 5:1–12—Those who are born of God

8. 1 John 5:13–21—Conclusion

Already in this outline, you can see language that is reminiscent of the Gospel of John. You might even notice that this book has some structural similarities to the gospel—most notably, a prologue. However, this outline also demonstrates how much of 1 John is devoted to exhortation to right behavior. Perhaps this is the reason people began calling it a letter even though it does not follow the letter form.

The Second and Third Letters of John are so short that they hardly need outlines to help us understand their content. However, the exercise of outlining can help to see more clearly the degree to which these two letters conform to the structure (form) of the letter. First, the Second Letter of John:

1. 2 John 1–3—Opening

2. 2 John 4–6—Thanksgiving

3. 2 John 7–11—Body

4. 2 John 12–13—Closing

In the thanksgiving, we find a number of themes that we expect to see in Johannine literature: "walking in the truth," "a new commandment," and "love one another." The author of 2 John also uses the phrase "from the beginning," which links this letter to the First Letter of John. Likewise, in the body of the letter, we find a greatly distilled version of the false teaching of the secessionists that was described in 1 John (see 2 John 7). Finally, the body of the letter includes a command not to welcome the deceivers, thus hinting at the notion of hospitality, which is a central theme in 3 John.

The Third Letter of John shares the same form as 2 John. However, unlike the Second Letter, which is addressed to a church—"the elect lady and her children"—this letter is addressed to an individual named Gaius. An outline follows:

1. 3 John 1—Opening

2. 3 John 2–4—Thanksgiving

3. 3 John 5–12—Body

4. 3 John 13–15—Closing

Based on the comments in this letter, it appears that **Diotrephes** was the leader of the church to which Gaius belonged, but Diotrephes was also someone who "likes to put himself first," meaning that he was full of pride and arrogance about his position of authority (3 John 9). At least, that was the writer's assessment. Apparently, Diotrephes refused to acknowledge the writer's authority and refused to give hospitality to his traveling preachers. **Gaius**, by contrast, was known for his generosity to missionaries. Hence, the reason for this letter.

# WAS THE LETTER WRITER READING JOHN?

If we assume that 1 John was written after the Gospel of John and then start comparing the vocabulary of 1 John to the vocabulary of the Gospel of John, it becomes apparent that the author of 1 John knew the Gospel of John. We can also imagine that he was interpreting (or reinterpreting) it as he wrote this First Letter. Here are a few examples:

> We declare to you what was *from the beginning*, what we have heard, what we have seen with our eyes, what we have looked at and touched with our hands, concerning the *word of life*. (1 John 1:1–2)

> *In the beginning* was the *Word* and the Word was with God and the Word was God. He was in the beginning with God. (John 1:1–2)

In this first example, notice how the author of 1 John designed his prologue with clear allusions to the prologue of John's gospel. The letter writer's audience would not have missed the connection either, but notice the difference of emphasis. By incorporating "sensing" verbs—hearing, seeing, touching—the letter writer is highlighting the tangibility of the "word of life," whereas John's gospel describes the Word's connection with the divine realm, making the Word appear transcendent and otherworldly. There are other interpretative changes as well. For the letter writer, the "word of life" is not the preexistent Son of God, as it is in the Gospel of John. Instead, the "word" is the proclamation (message) of eternal life, which is manifest in the words and deeds of Jesus (1 John 1:2). Thus, "from the beginning" means from the beginning of Jesus' ministry or from the beginning of John's community of faith, not the Son's preexistence with the Father.

The letter writer also has a somewhat different way of talking about discipleship than does the author of the Gospel of John. Recall that the gospel describes discipleship in terms of "abiding." The disciple is called to abide in Jesus as he abides in the Father and the Father abides in him. Unfortunately, John's language of "abiding" can sound very ethereal and heavenly, without much concern for the community—at least, some people might interpret it that way. Observe how the letter writer handles this topic:

> We declare to you what we have seen and heard so that you also may have fellowship [Greek; *koinonia*, meaning "partnership"] with us; and truly our fellowship is with the Father and with his Son Jesus Christ. (1 John 1:3)

Notice that the letter writer uses the word *koinonia* in place of "abiding." At the same time, he does not eliminate the word *abiding* from his vocabulary. He writes about God abiding in the believer (1 John 4:15) and about the message of God's love abiding in the believer (1 John 2:24). But when it comes to human activity, the test of true discipleship is partnership with the letter writer and those who stand with him.

The First Letter of John contains several other reinterpretations of Johannine vocabulary. For each of the following quotations from 1 John, see if you can locate the Johannine vocabulary and then compare the letter writer's use of that terminology to its usage in a similar quotation in the Gospel of John.

> God is light and in him there is no darkness at all. (1 John 1:5)

>> Again Jesus spoke to them, saying, "I am the light of the world. Whoever follows me will never walk in darkness but will have the light of life." (John 8:12)

> But if anyone does sin, we have an advocate with the Father, Jesus Christ, the righteous; and he is the atoning sacrifice for our sins. (1 John 2:1–2)

>> When the advocate comes, whom I will send to you from the Father, the Spirit of truth who comes from the Father he will testify on my behalf. (John 15:26)

> And this is [God's] commandment, that we should believe in the name of his son Jesus Christ and love one another just as he has commanded us. (1 John 3:23)

>> When [Judas] had gone out, Jesus said, . . . "I give you a new commandment, that you love one another. Just as I have loved you, you also should love one another." (John 13:31, 34)

We cannot reconstruct exactly what was going on in this community or what the letter writer was intending to convey when he took this Johannine vocabulary and reemployed as he did, but we can be fairly sure that he and his community had been reading the Gospel of John and using it as a source of religious authority for their shared life.

## WERE THE SECESSIONISTS ALSO READING JOHN?

When you read 1 John, you quickly recognize that the letter writer is writing to his beloved community, a group of people who are devoted to him and who think as he thinks. However, if you read very carefully, you can detect a second audience. The letter writer does not address this group directly. But if you imagine this scenario as a speech that is delivered orally instead of in a written document, you can almost see him standing among his close-knit community, consoling and encouraging them, but always having one eye on another group of people who have left this inner circle and now stand at a distance. You can imagine him periodically shifting his attention and raising his voice, saying, "Not like *those* guys!" These are the secessionists.

What does the letter writer tell us about the secessionists? Before we go any further, we have to be clear that this task of recreating a portrait of the secessionists from the writings of their chief opponent—when we have no literature from the secessionists themselves—is highly speculative and not very reliable. Yet, based on our reading of 1 John, there are at least a few things we can deduce about these people. The letter writer characterizes them as saying:

- We have fellowship with one another (1 John 1:6–7).
- We have no sin (1 John 1:8).
- We know Christ (1 John 2:4).
- We abide in Christ (1 John 2:6).
- We walk in the light (1 John 2:9).

If this reconstruction is accurate, you can easily see that the terminology used by the secessionists is typical of John's gospel. John's Jesus told the disciples that they must love one another as he has loved them and that the community would be known by its love for one another (John 13:34–35). Further, in John's gospel, sin is characterized by the refusal to believe in Jesus (John 8:24, 34–38), making it easy for members of the Johannine community to extrapolate from this teaching on sin and conclude that they, as believers, have no sin. Likewise, the Gospel of John describes the believer as knowing Christ (John 14:8–11), abiding in him (John 15:4), and walking in the light (John 8:12; 9:2–5). Thus, we can safely say that, like the letter writer and his community, the secessionists *also* were reading the Gospel of John and using it as a source of religious authority for their shared life.

What is the problem then? Why can't they just get along? The letter writer makes two charges against the secessionists: They hate the brothers and sisters (1 John 2:9), and they deny that Jesus is the Christ (1 John 2:22). These are pretty harsh accusations! In what sense do they hate the brothers and sisters? The letter writer says that they went out from their group; that is, they left these people behind (1 John 2:19). Worse yet, the ones who left were the rich of the community; they saw the needs of the community and they simply walked away (1 John 3:17). Well, at least that's how the letter writer saw it! And what about the second charge? The letter writer says that they deny Jesus is the Christ, but clearly the secessionists see themselves as Christians. Perhaps, then, the problem involves alternative understandings of the Christ, that is, different Christologies.

What are these differing Christologies? In 1 John 4:2, the letter writer describes what the community of 1 John believes about Jesus Christ. Apparently, it is also what the secessionists refuse to accept. Unfortunately, this Christological statement is ambiguous, even in Greek, and therefore cannot be translated easily. Thankfully, however, 2 John contains a statement that helps to clarify this Christological problem. The letter writer is warning against the deceivers who "do not confess that Jesus Christ has come in the flesh" (2 John 7). If these deceivers mentioned in 2 John are the same people as the secessionists of 1 John, and most biblical scholars agree that they are, then the best way to translate 1 John 4:2 is as follows: "Every spirit that confesses that *Jesus Christ has come in the flesh* is from God; and every spirit that does not confess Jesus is not from God." This reading is consistent with other parts of 1 John, like the prologue: "What we have heard, what we have seen with our eyes, what we have looked at and touched with our hands, concerning the word of life" (1 John 1:1).

The Second Letter of John helps to clarify that these secessionists were progressives in their Christology, not abiding in the "teaching of Christ" but going beyond it (2 John 9). Perhaps they negated the importance of Jesus' human career—in particular, his death for salvation. This would explain why the author of 1 John gives so much attention to the crucified Christ. For example, he writes that "the blood of Jesus his Son cleanses us from all sin" (1 John 1:7) and that Christ is "the atoning sacrifice for our sins" (1 John 2:2).

## GOD, CHRIST, AND THE HOLY SPIRIT

Although it would take several more centuries for the early Christian church to develop a coherent doctrine of the Trinitarian nature (three-in-oneness) of God, biblical scholars have observed that the author of the First Letter of John provides some interesting reference points for that discussion. We have already alluded to the author's presentation of God as Light (1 John 1:5), the one in whom the believer abides (1 John 5:14), and the one whose commandments the believing community must keep (1 John 3:21–24). He also describes God as love (I John 4:8), but this is not simply a romantic metaphor. The author goes on to write that God's love was revealed in the sending of his "only Son into the world so that we might live through him" (1 John 4:9). Moreover God's love does not consist in our love for God but rather in God's love for us insofar as he sent his son "to be the atoning sacrifice for our sins" (1 John 4:10). Finally, making a clear connection between theological reflection on the nature of God (doctrine) and how the community ought to live (ethics), he adds, "Since God loved us so much, we also ought to love one another" (1 John 4:11).

What is the role of the Holy Spirit in this fellowship that the believer shares "with the Father and with his Son Jesus Christ" (1 John 1:3)? The author of the First Letter of John asserts that the believers have been anointed by the Holy Spirit—perhaps a reference to baptism—and, in turn, have been given knowledge as a gift of the Spirit (1 John 2:20). Thus, the Spirit teaches them all things that are true (1 John 2:27) and allows them to know and "testify that the Father has sent his Son as the savior of the world" (1 John 4:14). Finally, the author of 1 John writes that it is the Spirit of truth who testifies that Jesus Christ came "by water and blood, not with the water only but with the water and the blood" (1 John 5:6). The statement is difficult to interpret. Biblical scholars have suggested, in the past, that the phrase "water and blood" refers to the sacraments of baptism and Eucharist. However, in the context of this letter, "blood" is elsewhere a reference to Jesus' atoning sacrifice on the cross (e.g., 1 John 1:7; 2:2; see also John 19:34–35). Therefore, if "blood" refers to the crucifixion of Jesus, then "water" must refer to his baptism in the Jordan River. In the Gospel of John, the evangelist describes the Spirit as descending on the Son from the moment of his baptism and continuing to abide with him, allowing John the Baptist to testify that he is the Son of God (John 1:31–34). Thus, there are three—the Spirit, the water, and the blood—that testify that Jesus Christ has come in the flesh (1 John 5:8).

Before we leave this topic, we should add a word about the *Johannine Comma*. In many of the manuscripts of the Vulgate (a Latin translation of the Bible) and in a few late Greek manuscripts that include the First Letter of John, the following text was inserted after 1 John 5:7 and at the beginning of 1 John 5:8: "There are three that testify in heaven, the Father, the Word, and the Holy Spirit, and these three are one. And there are three that testify on earth, . . . ." This addition, known as the

Johannine Comma, apparently first appeared in the fourth century C.E., perhaps in concert with the development of the doctrine of the Trinity. Again in the sixteenth century, it was picked up and incorporated into Greek texts that served as the basis for earlier English translations like the King James Version. Since modern text critics agree that the Johannine Comma is not part of the original text, you will only find it cited in the footnotes of more recent translations of 1 John, if at all. However, it is an important reminder that at least some scribes and theologians of the fourth century C.E. thought that 1 John provided a good reference point for commentary on the Trinitarian nature of God.

## DOCTRINE AND ETHICS

Concerning such theological questions as we have encountered in the Johannine letters, you might be tempted to ask, Who cares? Does Christology really matter all that much for how people live their lives? Does it have any relationship to how Christians behave? The letter writer says yes. In fact, he sees a direct connection between Christology and ethics. Recall 1 John's great commandment: "And this is [God's] commandment, that we should believe in the name of his Son Jesus Christ *and* [emphasis mine] love one another just as he has commanded us" (1 John 3:23). Later he says, "Everyone who believes that Jesus is the Christ has been born of God, and everyone who loves the parent loves the child. By this we know that we love the children of God, when we love God and obey his commandments" (1 John 5:1–2). Again, the letter writer is connecting right belief about Jesus to right behavior— love of the brothers and sisters.

The Jesuit biblical scholar Johannes Beutler has offered some reflections on the theological content of the Letters of John and its implications for today's society with its tendency to separate religion from ethics:

> In general, religion and ethics have become disassociated. Modern secular movements concentrate on the believer's personal spiritual growth, while charismatic groups primarily emphasize the sharing of spiritual experiences and group solidarity. Often, both groups disregard the social and political aspects of life. For Christian fundamentalists, the "world" is evil, and Christians must wait for the return of their Lord who will establish his kingdom at the end of time.
>
> The Letters of John, especially 1 John, seem to presuppose a similar situation. We may suppose that the communities where the letters originated were characterized by great inequality in wealth and social status. With tradition, we may think of the metropolis of Ephesus, one of the major centers of the Roman Empire in the East with its Jewish and Christian communities, as the setting of the redaction of these letters. The author's repeated invitations to love one's brother or sister become very concrete in 1 John 3; not sharing one's bread with one's hungry brother or sister is equivalent to murder.
>
> On the other hand, the author of 1 John is concerned with helping his addressees to develop a right understanding of faith. Commentaries have often distinguished between two aspects of possible doctrinal aberration among the addressees: a Christology that neglects the human nature of Christ, and a form of ethics that neglects the responsibility for one's brother or sister. The adversaries criticized by our author in

1 and 2 John may share a similar self-understanding and anthropology (see Beutler 2000, 20–24; Grayston 1984, 14–22). These adversaries seem to have come from the Johannine community but to have left it at a certain moment (1 John 2:18–19). There may be reason to assume that they were "ultra-Johannine" Christians who were deeply convinced that they possessed the Spirit beyond measure. As the "anointed ones" they no longer saw the need for redemption by the blood of Christ or for any salvific role of a "Christ" (the "Anointed One"). As spiritual persons they perhaps also felt they were no longer bound by any moral commandment, in particular the commandment to love one's brother or sister. ("1, 2, 3 John," 553–554, Global Bible Commentary)

The author of the Letters of John is not shy about expressing his displeasure with his adversaries over their apparent disassociation of right belief and right practice. Needless to say, his rhetoric indicates that he perceives the problem to be serious indeed. He goes so far as to call them "anti-Christs," "murderers," and "false prophets" (1 John 2:22; 3:11–15; 4:1). As you read 1 John, look for parallels in our contemporary cultures. What does 1 John have to say to those who want to separate their religious beliefs from their ethics? How does an individual or a community of faith achieve a consistent and coherent integration of doctrine and ethics?

## Key Terms

Secessionists                    Diotrephes                    Gaius

## Questions for Reading

Read 1 John. Use evidence from the text to answer the following questions.

1. Identify words or phrases in the prologue (1 John 1:1–4) that remind you of John's gospel. What point is the author of 1 John trying to make in his prologue? What word does he use to describe the relationship of the believer with the Father and the Son?

2. In 1 John 1:5–2:2, identify words or phrases that remind you of John's gospel. In this context, who is the light? What does it mean to walk in the light? What clues can you find to help us understand what kind of sin this writer has in mind? According to this letter, what role does Jesus have in relation to sin?

3. In the section on keeping the commandments (1 John 2:3–17), what point is the author trying to make? What does the author mean by the use of the words *commandment* and *world*? Do these terms have the same meaning that they had in John's gospel? If not, how are they different?

4. In 1 John 2:18–27, what is the meaning of the term *hour*? What clues, if any, does this section give us concerning the beliefs or activities of the antichrists? What makes them antichrists (i.e., opponents of Christ)?

5. In 1 John 2:29–3:24, the author describes what it means to say that we are "children of God." Explain. How is one able to distinguish children of God from children of the devil? What clues, if any, does this section give concerning the situation of the author's community?

6. According to 1 John 4:1–6, how does one test the spirits? Why is it necessary to test the spirits? What does the word *spirit* mean in this context? What is its relationship to the Holy Spirit? What is the "spirit of the antichrist"?

7. According to 1 John 4:7–21, why should Christians love one another? What does it mean to say that someone does not love? What is the author's understanding of what love is? Is it possible to say that you love God but hate your neighbor? Why or why not?

8. According to 1 John, how do people know that they abide in God? Who are those who have been "born of God" (1 John 5:1–5)?

9. What is the point of this statement: "There are three that testify: the Spirit and the water and the blood, and these three agree" (1 John 5:7)? What makes this saying difficult to interpret?

Read 2 John. Use evidence from the text to answer the following questions.

10. Having read 2 John, what clues, if any, can you find about the identity of the author? Why is he writing this letter?

11. What, if anything, does 2 John tell us about the audience for whom the author is writing?

12. From your reading of 2 John, what can you determine about the identity of the "deceivers"? What kind of people are they? What beliefs do they hold? What is the author's opinion of them?

Read 3 John. Use evidence from the text to answer the following questions.

13. Having read 3 John, what clues, if any, can you find about the identity of the author? Why is he writing this letter?

14. What, if anything, does 3 John tell us about the audience for whom the author is writing?

15. From your reading of 3 John, what can you determine about the identity of Diotrephes? What is the author's attitude toward him? Why?

## QUESTIONS FOR REFLECTION

1. In 1 John, the letter writer works from the assumption that there is a connection between Christology and ethics—that is, between what people understand about who Jesus is as the Christ and how they behave as Christian believers. What do you think about the letter writer's approach? Can you think of other examples that might demonstrate this connection between Christology and ethics?

2. In 3 John, the letter writer commends Gaius for his ministry of hospitality. In what ways might hospitality be a viable ministry of Christian believers today?

## Activities for Learning

1. Use a concordance to find all of the times that the author of 1 John uses the word *love*. Do the same thing with the Gospel of John. Study carefully the literary context for each of these occurrences. In what ways is the Gospel of John's use of the word *love* similar to or different from that of 1 John? Give examples to demonstrate.

2. Use a concordance to find all of the times that the author of 1 John uses the word *sin*. Do the same thing with the Gospel of John. Study carefully the literary context for each of these occurrences. To what does "sin" refer in the Gospel of John? To what does "sin" refer in 1 John? In what ways is the Gospel of John's use of the word *sin* similar to or different from that of 1 John? Give examples to demonstrate.

3. Biblical scholars have had difficulty knowing how to interpret 1 John 5:7–8, concerning the three things that testify on Jesus' behalf—the Spirit, the water, and the blood. From the commentaries in the bibliography below, select two different interpretations of 1 John 5:6–12. Explain the two interpretations in your own words. What evidence do biblical scholars give in support of their views? Which interpretation do you find more convincing? Why?

## Sources and Resources

Beutler, Johannes. "1, 2, 3 John." In *Global Bible Commentary*, edited by Daniel Patte. Nashville, Tenn.: Abingdon Press, 2004.

Brown, Raymond E. *The Gospel and Epistles of John: A Concise Commentary*. Collegeville, Minn.: Liturgical Press, 1988.

Culpepper, R. Alan. *1 John, 2 John, 3 John*. Atlanta, Ga.: John Knox, 1985.

Kruse, Colin G. *The Letters of John*. Grand Rapids, Mich.: Eerdmans, 2000.

Kysar, Robert. *I, II, III John*. Minneapolis Minn.: Augsburg, 1986.

Lewis, Scott M. *The Gospel according to John and the Johannine Letters*. Collegeville, Minn.: Liturgical Press, 2005.

Painter, John. *The Quest for the Messiah: The History, Literature, and Theology of the Johannine Community*. Nashville, Tenn.: Abingdon Press, 1993.

———. *1, 2, 3 John*. Collegeville, Minn.: Liturgical Press, 2002.

Patte, Daniel, ed. *Global Bible Commentary*. Nashville, Tenn.: Abingdon Press, 2004.

Rensburger, David K. *1 John, 2 John, 3 John*. Nashville, Tenn.: Abingdon Press, 1997.

———. *The Epistles of John*. Louisville, Ky.: Westminster John Knox Press, 2001.

Smith, D. Moody. *First, Second, and Third John*. Louisville, Ky.: Westminster John Knox Press, 1992.

Strecker, Georg. *The Johannine Letters: A Commentary on 1, 2, 3 John*, translated by Linda M. Maloney. Minneapolis, Minn.: Fortress, 1996.

Talbert, Charles H. *Reading John: A Literary and Theological Commentary on the Fourth Gospel and the Johannine Epistles*. New York: Crossroad, 1992.

Thompson, Marianne Meye. *1–3 John*. Downers Grove, Ill.: InterVarsity Press, 1992.

Von Wahlde, Urban C. *The Johannine Commandments: 1 John and the Struggle for the Johannine Tradition*. New York: Paulist, 1990.

# APOCALYPTIC LITERATURE

We are about to embark on the last leg of our journey through the New Testament, namely, the Book of Revelation. Some would say that we've left the best till last! Others wonder whether this book has anything of value to contribute to the New Testament. Of course, as we have noted several times with other books of the New Testament, the key to proper interpretation of Revelation is our ability to understand and appreciate its genre, that is, the type of literature we are reading. Only then do we know what expectations to have about its meaning. Therefore, before beginning our reading of the Book of Revelation, we need to ask about the apocalyptic genre.

We have already explored some apocalyptic themes very briefly when we studied the synoptic gospels (e.g., Mark 13 and parallels) and some of the letters attributed to Paul (e.g., 1–2 Thessalonians). In those documents, we saw expressions of concern about when the end time would come. We also read declarations of confidence in God's ability to rescue the righteous from the terrible events that would accompany the end. But what can we say about the apocalyptic genre? The English word *apocalypse* derives from a Greek word that means "revelation." In some Bible translations, the Book of Revelation is given the title Apocalypse, after its opening words. This title is appropriate because the book does contain revelations. John, the author of Revelation, presents them as a record of the visions (images) and auditions (voices) that came to him through divine beings, in most cases, an angel. These visions and auditions concern "heavenly things" and future events. However, John describes his work as a prophecy (Rev. 1:3).

Apocalypses were rather common from the third century B.C.E. through the second century C.E. Here are just a few, some from within Judaism, others from within Christianity: the Animal Apocalypse (1 Enoch 85–90); the Book of Watchers (1 Enoch 1–36); 4 Ezra; 2 Baruch; the Testament of Levi; the Testament of Abraham; the Apocalypse of Peter; the Shepherd of Hermas; and the Ascension of Isaiah 6–11. Typical of this genre, the seer (i.e., the recipient of the visions) receives revelations through mediation of some sort and then records them in writing. The revelations involve secrets of the cosmos (literally, "the world"). The secrets include the workings of the heavenly bodies, the fixing of the calendar, the names and activities of angelic beings, and the places of reward and punishment. In addition, they include secrets about the future: political and historical events, the destiny of God's people, and so on. Sometimes the seer is allowed to journey to heavenly locations, in which case the apocalypse describes the details of the heavenly journey. Most apocalypses also include a command to the seer to seal up the written account of the visions for some future time.

What rules of interpretation should we apply to apocalypses? Perhaps the best way to understand apocalypses is to investigate the precursors or forerunners of the genre. In recent decades, scholars have been debating whether apocalypses have their roots in the writings of the prophets or in wisdom literature. This question arose out of the fact that one can see features of both genres in a wide variety of Jewish and Christian apocalypses and, in particular, in the Book of Revelation. Let's review these two genres—prophecy and wisdom literature—and highlight some of their connections with the apocalyptic genre. Our goal is to better understand how we ought to read and interpret apocalyptic works like the Book of Revelation.

Let's start with prophetic literature and its parallels with the apocalyptic genre. Although the author of the Book of Revelation does not call himself a prophet, he describes his book as a prophecy (Rev. 1:3; 22:7, 10, 18, 19). Further, he seamlessly incorporates images and ideas from the writings of Old Testament prophets, most notably, Daniel and Ezekiel, in such a way that they seem to speak with one voice. Nowhere in the Book of Revelation does its author seem to suggest that the Jewish prophets of old had a different role or function than did the Christian prophets. Although people today sometimes assume that prophets of the Old Testament were, for the most part, predictors of the future, they were better known as God's spokespersons on behalf of the covenant. In that capacity, the prophets brought accusations against Israel and Judah when they failed to keep the covenant, and they warned of God's punishment against wrongdoers. They also delivered messages of consolation when the people of Israel and Judah thought God had abandoned them or when they were awaiting God's restoration of the covenant, after they had repented of their sin.

Prophetic literature sometimes can be difficult to interpret, because much of it is grounded in particular places and times. To fully appreciate the message of the prophets, you need to know the historical, political, and cultural contexts from which they wrote, and you need to know the major characters in the (unwritten) stories that stand behind the prophets' writings. If apocalyptic literature has its roots in prophecy, how then should we interpret it? First, like other biblical prophecy, we should read it as a call to conversion and a message of consolation for God's covenant people. Second, since biblical prophecy cannot be fully understood without reference to the situation in which it was written, likewise, apocalyptic literature must be read from the perspective of the historical, political, and cultural contexts of its author and his original, intended audience. Only then can we correctly reinterpret the text for today's believers. This process of reinterpretation requires careful and thoughtful reflection, but it is also in keeping with the prophets' role as the conscience of the people.

Other scholars argue that the apocalyptic genre has its roots in wisdom literature (see Chapter 4). Wisdom literature covers a wide variety of topics from proper etiquette in the king's court to the characteristics of a good wife and mother. However, from a theological or philosophical perspective, it devotes considerable attention to questions about universal truth, the meaning of life (and death), and what constitutes human good. It also addresses questions about the justice and the sovereignty of God: Why do righteous people suffer without warrant? Why do the wicked appear to go unpunished? What is the meaning of human suffering and where is God's justice? The term that describes this line of questioning is theodicy. All of us can relate to these questions, especially when the difficulties of life become too much to bear.

Biblical scholars have not yet conclusively answered the question about the origins of the apocalyptic genre. However, its parallels with biblical prophecy and wisdom literature give us a clearer sense of what to expect when we read apocalypses. To sum up, apocalypses do three things: (1) They console people in situations of persecution, (2) they present a particular interpretation of historical events that focuses on the justice and sovereignty of God and the triumph of good over evil, and (3) they persuade their hearers to keep covenant with God—that is, to live in a way that ensures that they will be among God's elect in the end time.

Finally, when you read an apocalypse, you should not expect to find a sustained story line that extends from the beginning to the end of the book. In terms of genre, it is not a narrative. Rather, it usually consists of a series of visions and auditions interspersed with dialogue. The Book of Revelation is a good example. You will observe that the document is not organized chronologically. Rather, its author describes several collections of visions: Some take place in the heavenly realm, and others are situated on earth; some pertain to the believing community as it anticipates persecution, and others relate to those who have endured the suffering and proved themselves faithful. Often the author will introduce a particular idea or image in an early vision and then return to it later in a series of expanded visions or auditions. Thus, when you read an apocalypse like the Book of Revelation, you must resist the temptation to impose a chronology on it. Any attempt to see the book as a linear map of the events of the end time will necessarily lead to misunderstanding of its message.

## SOURCES AND RESOURCES

Collins, Adela Yarbro, ed. "Early Christian Apocalypticism, Genre and Setting." *Semeia* 36 (1986): 1–174.

Collins, John J. *The Apocalyptic Imagination. An Introduction to Jewish Apocalyptic Literature.* Grand Rapids, Mich.: Eerdmans, 1998.

———., ed. "Apocalypse: The Morphology of a Genre." *Semeia* 14 (1979): 1–217.

Cory, Catherine A. *The Book of Revelation.* Collegeville, Minn.: Liturgical Press, 2006.

Martínez, Florentino, ed. *Wisdom and Apocalypticism in the Dead Sea Scrolls and in the Biblical Tradition.* Leuven, Belgium: Peeters, 2003.

Perdue, Leo G., Bernard Brandon Scott, and William Johnston Wiseman, eds. *In Search of Wisdom: Essays in Memory of John G. Gammie.* Louisville, Ky.: Westminster John Knox Press, 1993.

Wills, Lawrence M., and Benjamin G. Wright III, eds. *Conflicted Boundaries in Wisdom and Apocalypticism.* Atlanta, Ga.: Society of Biblical Literature, 2005.

# CHAPTER 24

# THE BOOK OF REVELATION

- AUTHORSHIP: John, an otherwise unknown Jewish Christian prophet, writing from Patmos
- DATE OF COMPOSITION: Approximately 95–96 C.E.
- INITIAL AUDIENCE: Most likely a group of Christian churches of Asia Minor (modern Turkey) that are addressed by name in the letters contained in Revelation 2–3
- MAJOR TOPICS: Symbolic Numbers and Colors in the Book of Revelation; The Vision of One Like a Son of Man; The Letters to the Seven Churches; The Vision of God's Throne and the Lamb; The Opening of the Seven Seals and the Blowing of Seven Trumpets; More Visions of God's Justice and Consolation; Visions of the Last Things; The New Jerusalem; The Conclusion of the Book of Revelation

## TIMELINE

| | |
|---|---|
| 27 B.C.E.–14 C.E. | Octavian (Augustus) is Roman emperor. |
| 14–37 C.E. | Tiberius is Roman emperor. |
| 37–41 C.E. | Gaius Caligula is Roman emperor. |
| 41–54 C.E. | Claudius is Roman emperor. |
| 54–68 C.E. | Nero is Roman emperor. |
| 65–70 C.E. | The Gospel of Mark is written. |
| 66–70 C.E. | The Jewish War occurs. |
| 68–69 C.E. | The Roman Empire is ruled by a quick succession of emperors, including Galba, Ortho, and Vitellius. |
| 69–79 C.E. | Vespasian is Roman emperor. |
| 70 C.E. | Jerusalem and the Temple are destroyed. |
| 79–81 C.E. | Titus is Roman emperor. |
| 80–90 C.E. | The Gospels of Matthew and Luke are written. |
| 81–96 C.E. | Domitian is Roman emperor. |
| 90–100 C.E. | The Gospel of John is written. |
| 95–96 C.E. | **The Book of Revelation is written**. |
| c. 180 C.E. | Irenaeus of Lyons writes *Against Heresies*. |
| c. 310 C.E. | Eusebius of Caesarea completes *Ecclesiastical History*. |

Here we are, finally, at the last stop on our voyage through the New Testament—the Book of Revelation. Some might say that we've left the best until last. Others might wonder why we should bother, because everything they've heard about this book confirms their view that it is confusing and without much merit for contemporary readers. Among those who have studied it, you find people who are fascinated by its many colorful and sometimes grotesque images. You will find others who view the book as an illustrated time line that will help them better prepare for the events of the end of the world. Still others see it as a kind of "war manual," that provides guidelines about how to prepare for the great battle of Armageddon.

We are going to take a somewhat different approach to the interpretation of the Book of Revelation. We are going to read it as a **theodicy**. Theodicy attempts to reconcile the existence of evil in the world with the belief that God is just and sovereign. People who explore this theological problem ask questions like this: If God is all-powerful, why does evil seem to prevail? If God is just, why do the innocent suffer harm and the wicked seem to enjoy success and happiness? In vivid, sometimes violent, but always dramatic imagery, the Book of Revelation answers these theodicy questions by asserting that God is sovereign over the whole world, including creatures that exist in the heavens, on the earth, and under the earth. It also expresses the conviction that God is just in every way and that God will vindicate the suffering holy ones (in God's own time) and utterly destroy the wicked. This is how the biblical author intended us to understand the Book of Revelation—from within the social and historical context in which it originated and as the type of literature it is, namely, apocalyptic.

However, before we delve too deeply into the imagery and message of the Book of Revelation, let's take a moment to survey what biblical scholars have come to know about its author, date of composition, and audience.

## AUTHORSHIP

Like some of the letters of the New Testament, and unlike the anonymously authored gospels, the person who wrote the Book of Revelation tells us his name. It is John (Rev. 1:1, 9). But this information does not answer our authorship question entirely, because John was a rather common name then as it is today. Two early church writers, Justin Martyr (c. 160 C.E.) and Irenaeus (c. 180 C.E.), identified this book with the apostle John whom they thought was the writer of the Gospel of John (see *Dialogue with Trypho* 81; *Against Heresies* 3.11.1–3; 4.20.11). However, most biblical scholars today think that the author of the Book of Revelation was neither an apostle of Jesus nor the author of the Gospel of John. One reason is that the Book of Revelation is written in a very different style and quality of Greek than the Gospel of John. Also, the Book of Revelation was most likely written at the end of the first century C.E., too late for the apostle John to be involved in its composition. At most, we can say that the author of the Book of Revelation was an early Jewish Christian prophet by the name of John, otherwise unknown in early Christian literature.

## DATE OF COMPOSITION AND AUDIENCE

Where was John when he wrote this book and to whom was he writing? He tells his readers that he received his visions while residing on Patmos, a small island in the Aegean Sea. Further, he tells his readers that he was there because he "proclaimed God's word and gave testimony to Jesus" (Rev. 1:9). Thus, we can probably assume that he had been exiled on Patmos and that his exile came as a result of his preaching activity—or at least he perceived it that way. Because he incorporates letters to seven churches of Asia Minor (modern Turkey) into his work (see Rev. 2–3), many biblical scholars assume that John had written the entire work with these churches in mind. Therefore, we can locate the original audience for this work in the eastern Mediterranean.

The Book of Revelation gives us an important clue about when it was written in its use of the term **Babylon** for Rome (Rev. 18:2; cf. 1 Pet. 5:13). This term recalls the sixth-century B.C.E. Babylonian Exile, during which time the Babylonians deported people from Judea and destroyed the Jerusalem Temple. The connection between Rome and Babylon might not be obvious to you at first. However, we find other examples of this practice in Jewish literature written toward the end of the first century C.E.—more specifically, after the Roman armies had destroyed Jerusalem and the Temple in 70 C.E. (see 2 Esdras. 3:1–2, 28–31 and 2 Apocalypse of Baruch 10:1–3; 11:1; 67:7), Because the Book of Revelation makes this same connection between Rome and Babylon, scholars generally agree that it had to have been written after 70 C.E.

The early church writer Irenaeus (*Against Heresies* 35.30.3) says that Revelation was written toward the end of Emperor Domitian's reign (81–96 C.E.). Apparently during that time, Domitian had begun to persecute Christians on a rather large scale. Some were charged with atheism and others with drifting into "Jewish ways," but it appears that Domitian's primary goal was to protect the status of Roman civil religion and his own position as emperor (Eusebius, *Ecclesiastical History* 3.18.4; Suetonius, *Lives of the Caesars*, Domitian, 8.10–15; Cassius Dio, *Roman History* 67.14.2). Thus, without evidence to the contrary, it is reasonable to assume that the Book of Revelation was written in approximately 95–96 C.E.

## OUTLINE OF THE BOOK

As we have noted many times before, there are almost as many outlines of a given biblical book as there are scholars studying it. Unfortunately, the authors of these biblical books did not provide us with their outlines, so modern readers use whatever clues they can find in the text to uncover the intent of these authors and then construct outlines accordingly. In turn, these outlines serve as a tour guide for studying the biblical books in an organized way. The outline provided here is designed to highlight the Book of Revelation's patterns built around the symbolic number seven.

1. Revelation 1:1–8—Introductory materials
2. Revelation 1:9–7:17—First cycle of visions
   a. Initial vision of One like a Son of Man (Rev. 1:9–20)
   b. The seven letters to the seven churches of Asia Minor (Rev. 2:1–3:22)

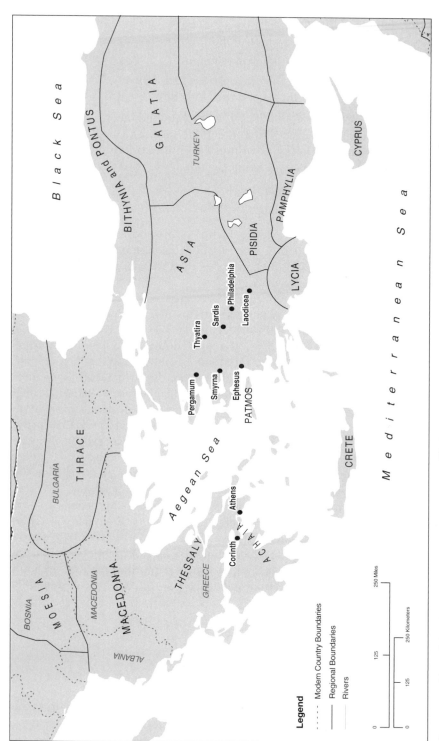

The seven cities of the Book of Revelation and the island of Patmos, including modern boundaries.

    c. The vision of God's throne and the Lamb (Rev. 4:1–5:14)

    d. The opening of the seven seals (Rev. 6:1–7:17)

  3. Revelation 8:1–11:19—The seven trumpets

  4. Revelation 12:1–16:21—Second cycle of visions

    a. Vision of the woman and the dragon (Rev. 12:1–17)

    b. Vision of the beasts of the sea and the land (Rev. 13:1–18)

    c. Vision of the Lamb and imminent judgment (Rev. 14:1–20)

    d. Visions of the seven bowls (Rev. 15:1–16:21)

  5. Revelation 17:1–18:24—Fall of Babylon (interlude)

  6. Revelation 19:1–20:15—Visions of the last things

  7. Revelation 21:1–22:5—Vision of the New Jerusalem

  8. Revelation 22:6–20—Concluding materials

The apocalyptic genre is already evident in the outline above, particularly in the lists of visions (see the introduction to Part VI of this textbook for more on the apocalyptic genre). Observe that the content of these visions pertains to the "last things," judgment, and reward for the righteous.

    Throughout Revelation, the author John is presented as the **seer**, that is, the recipient of the visions. The visions are given to him by an angel, who tells him to record them in a book (Rev. 1:19; cf. Rev. 22:10)—a characteristic feature of apocalyptic literature. As the book progresses, we learn that John is invited on a journey into the heavenly realm to witness the opening of the seven seals and worship before God's throne (Rev. 4:1), another characteristic feature of apocalyptic literature. Remember, however, that the purpose of apocalypses is not to predict the future. Rather, through the use of symbolic imagery, apocalypses are designed to console people in situations of persecution. They also provide an interpretation of historical events that focuses on the justice and sovereignty of God and the triumph of good over evil. Finally, apocalypses are designed for the edification of a community of believers. As such, apocalypses persuade their hearers to keep covenant with God—that is, to live in a way that assures that they will be among God's elect in the end time.

    In the remainder of this textbook chapter, we will focus on a few scenes from the Book of Revelation as a way of illustrating its central message: God is just, God is sovereign (i.e., all-powerful), and God will destroy the wicked and vindicate (i.e., prove right) the holy ones. However, before beginning this analysis, a brief introduction to the symbolism of Revelation's colors and numbers is in order. Without this information, you will likely miss some important aspects of the theological message of the Book of Revelation.

## SYMBOLIC NUMBERS AND COLORS IN THE BOOK OF REVELATION

Numbers and colors are used liberally throughout the Book of Revelation, and readers sometimes mistakenly take them literally rather than symbolically, as intended by its author.

Here are the most commonly cited numbers, together with their symbolic meanings:

| Three | A few, a limited number, or a limited time |
|---|---|
| Four | Fullness, especially as it relates to the breadth of the universe (e.g., four corners of the world) or universality |
| Seven | Perfection, fullness, and perfect orderedness; in Genesis, the number of the completeness of creation |
| Ten | Sometimes denotes a limited number; also recalls the ten kings of Daniel 7:24 who oppressed God's holy ones |
| Twelve | Fullness or completeness, especially the notion of bringing diversity into unity; can also symbolize the twelve tribes of Israel or the twelve apostles |
| Thousand | Myriads, a number too large to count |

These numbers—as well as multiples, combinations, or fractions of these numbers—occur throughout the Book of Revelation. For example, 3½ is ½ of 7, which is a perfect number, and it usually symbolizes a limited period of suffering after which the persecuted will be rescued. Likewise, the number 144,000, which is a multiple of two symbolic numbers (12 and 1,000), represents the enormously large number of victorious ones who are marked with the Lamb's seal. Beyond the general patterns described here, literary context will help us understand the significance of each number.

The colors of the Book of Revelation are also symbolic. Again, the context will help us understand their significance, but this list of symbolic colors will help us get started.

| White | Purity or ritual cleanness (see Chapter 5); victory or triumph over the forces of evil and death |
|---|---|
| Red | Bloodshed and violence |
| Scarlet | Royalty but also violence and bloodshed |
| Purple | Kingship and royalty |
| Black | Associated with the famine that follows war and civil unrest (see Rev. 6) |
| Pale Green | Associated with death (see Rev. 6) |

You will notice that Christ is usually wearing white garments, as are the martyrs who make up his heavenly army (e.g., Rev. 19:11–21). In contrast, the dragon who wreaks havoc on the earth is red (Rev. 12:1–6), and the whore Babylon wears scarlet and purple (Rev. 17:1–6). Thus, as a reader of the Book of Revelation, you should be able to recognize who is on each side in the great battle between good and evil just by paying attention to the colors that the author uses.

Now that we have a basic understanding of the symbolism of numbers and colors in the Book of Revelation, we are ready to investigate a few of its key scenes. By following the general pattern of our analyses here, hopefully you will be able to explore other sections of the Book of Revelation on your own.

## The Vision of One Like a Son of Man

In the first vision of the Book of Revelation, John tells his readers that he sees an unnamed heavenly being (Rev. 1:9–20). However, before he conveys this vision, he makes sure that his audience knows that they share something in common: "I John . . . who share with you the distress, the kingdom, and the endurance we have in Jesus" (Rev. 1:9). The word translated here as "distress" can also mean "persecution" or "tribulation," referring to the troubles that will accompany the end time. The word translated as "kingdom" can also mean "kingly reign" or "sovereignty," referring to their hope in God's power to triumph over evil in the end time. Finally, the word translated here as "endurance," refers to the way that Christians ought to respond to the troubles that they face. For John, this is participation in the Christian life.

This first vision consists of three parts: the account of the vision itself (Rev. 1:11–16), John's response to the vision (Rev. 1:17–18a), and an interpretation of the vision (Rev. 1:18b–20). The imagery of the vision is highly symbolic, much of it coming from the writings of Daniel and Ezekiel (see the footnotes or cross-references in your Bible). The **One like a Son of Man** (i.e., a heavenly being in human form) is an allusion to Daniel 7:13. The heavenly being's snow-white hair reminds us of Daniel's description of the "Ancient of Days," who is God (see Dan. 7:9). The remainder of John's description of the heavenly being—dressed in a long robe with a golden sash, with feet that gleamed like polished metal and eyes that blazed like fire (Rev. 1:13–15)—has parallels with Daniel's vision of a heavenly being in human form who comes to deliver a message about the conflict of nations (see Dan. 10:5–6).

Not only did John use imagery from the Book of Daniel for his description of One like a Son of Man, he likely also borrowed from the Book of Ezekiel. In his heavenly visions, Ezekiel describes God's torso—the language is metaphorical, because God does not really have human body parts—as gleaming like amber and God's feet as having the appearance of fire (see Ezek. 1:27; 8:2). Ancient peoples believed that a person's power to act resided in the hands and feet and that a person's will, intellect, and judgment resided in the eyes and heart. Thus, when John describes the heavenly being's feet as "burnished bronze" and his eyes as "a flame of fire" (Rev. 1:14–15), he is trying to show that One like a Son of Man manifests full power, intellect, and judgment (Rev. 1:14–15). John also describes the heavenly being as clothed with a long robe and girdle (i.e., a piece of fabric tied around the waist) (Rev. 1:13), which is reminiscent of the dress of the priests of the Jerusalem Temple (see Exod. 28:4; 39:29; Wis. 18:24). From the heavenly being's mouth comes a sharp two-edged sword, an apocalyptic symbol of end-time judgment (Rev. 1:16).

Later, when the heavenly being interprets the vision for John (Rev. 1:18–20), he reveals himself as the resurrected Christ, the one who was dead but now lives (Rev. 1:18). He also provides John with an explanation of the symbolic images contained in the vision. For example, he explains that the seven stars, which John saw, in the heavenly being's hand (Rev. 1:16), are the guardian spirits of the seven churches (Rev. 1:20)—ancient peoples believed that cities prospered because their guardian angels protected them. Likewise, he tells John that the seven golden lamps, which he saw standing all around the resurrected Christ (Rev. 1:12), are the seven churches (Rev. 1:20). The number seven is especially significant here. In Greco-Roman culture, the rainbow was thought to consist of seven colors. In the second century C.E., some of the Roman emperors included seven stars on their minted coins as a symbol of world domination. Seven is a symbol of perfection, completion, and fullness.

Thus, the message of this vision is ultimately one of hope and confidence in the One who possesses power over anyone and anything that might affect the churches. Just as the heavenly being in the vision walks among the lamps, the risen Christ continues to dwell among the church communities, and just as he holds the stars in his hand, the risen Christ continues to be responsible for their protection.

## THE LETTERS TO THE SEVEN CHURCHES

Immediately following this first vision, the author of the Book of Revelation incorporates seven letters to Christian churches of Asia Minor (modern Turkey): Ephesus, Smyrna, Pergamum, Thyatira, Sardis, Philadelphia, and Laodicea (Rev. 2:1–3:22). Based on archeological evidence, we know that these cities, and presumably their churches, actually existed in the first century C.E. The four cities of Smyrna, Ephesus, Sardis, and Pergamum were centers of the provincial assembly of the Roman Empire in Asia Minor. Ephesus was a very large city, an important commercial hub, and a center for the worship of Roman and Greek deities. Sardis and Smyrna had large Jewish communities. Pergamum was an important center for the arts and for learning. It also held a large shrine to Asclepius, the healing god. Thyatira was famous for the making and trading of a special kind of wool as well as for its shrines to Apollo and Helius, a sun god. Philadelphia was an agricultural center for its area. Laodicea had a large medical facility that specialized in treating eye diseases.

With some important exceptions, these letters to the churches follow a rather strict literary pattern, which can be outlined as follows:

- To the angel of the church in _____
- write: _____
- I know your works _____
- But I have this against you: _____
- To everyone who conquers I will give _____
- Let anyone who has an ear listen to what the Spirit is saying to the churches.

While John serves as the scribe (i.e., secretary) for the seven letters, the author of each letter is the one described after the phrase "write." In most cases, there is a connection between these descriptors and the first vision of the Book of Revelation. Can you figure out the identity of the author of these letters? Notice, also, the concluding statement, "Let anyone who has an ear. . . . " Sometimes this statement appears in the second-to-last position in the letter, but always it should remind us of the Old Testament prophet's message that the people must listen to God's call for repentance or suffer punishment.

When you read the seven letters (Rev. 2:1–3:22), you will see the greatest differences in form and content in the sections that begin "I know your works" and "But I have this against you." The first of these sections usually represents a message of consolation, while the second is a message of condemnation. This is where John describes what he thinks is wrong with these Christian communities in his day. See if you can figure out the nature of their wrongdoing. As you read these letters, you might also want to consider whether or not these problems have any counterpart in our modern cultures. Finally, you will notice that some of the letters have only one of these sections. That is, they have either the "I know your works" section or the "But I have this against you" section, but not both. What, if anything, does this variation in the form of the letter tell us about John's assessment of that particular Christian community?

## THE VISION OF GOD'S THRONE AND THE LAMB

The second vision of the Book of Revelation (Rev. 4:1–5:14) is a **theophany**, that is, a revelation or manifestation of God. It comes immediately after the seven letters to the churches and is linked to them by the promise that those who conquer (i.e., keep the faith) will be allowed to sit beside the risen Christ on his heavenly throne (Rev. 3:20–22). The typical features of a theophany include a vision of the throne of God or an angel messenger of God, heavenly voices, cosmic manifestations of the power of God (lightning, fire, thunder, etc.), the seer falling into a trance, and an interruption of the time sequence (e.g., time stands still). The setting for these visions is usually a mountain. The vision described in Revelation 4:1–5:14 belongs to a special category of theophanies called a **throne vision**.

Although the imagery included in this throne vision might seem strange to us—perhaps like something out of *The Wizard of Oz*—it is typical of Hellenistic royal court scenes. The "sea of glass" that John sees in front of the throne (Rev. 4:6) recalls the immense polished floors of a royal throne room of his day—though, of course, better and more dramatic—since this was God's throne room. The scroll in the hand of God is comparable to the depictions of the Roman emperor with a libellus, a petition or letter in the form of a scroll (Rev. 5:1). The twenty-four elders who place their crowns at the base of God's throne (Rev. 4:10) recall court rituals from the Hellenistic period in which vassal kings cast their crowns at the feet of the emperor as a sign of obedience and respect. John does not identity the twenty-four elders, though biblical scholars have suggested that they might represent the twelve tribes of Israel and the twelve apostles of Jesus. In support of this theory, you will notice that the twelve tribes and the twelve apostles appear together in the final vision of the New Jerusalem in Revelation 21–22. The twenty-four elders' acclamation, "You are worthy, our Lord and God" (Rev. 4:11), was also the standard address used to greet the Roman emperor when he entered the throne room. Here it is applied to God.

In this throne vision, John also sees "four living creatures" who are the attendants to God's throne (Rev. 4:6). In the Jewish hierarchy of angels, the four living creatures are called **watchers** or merkabah angels. Sometimes they are portrayed as angels of fire who support the throne of God, but here they are "full of eyes all around and inside" (Rev. 4:8), perhaps a symbol of their constant watchfulness over the throne of God. The song of the four living creatures, "The one who was, and who is, and who is to come" (Rev. 4:8; cf. Rev. 1:8), recalls the opening of the Book of Revelation and focuses attention on John's belief that God is eternal. Although John does not explain the significance of the faces of the four living creatures (Rev. 4:7), he probably borrowed the imagery from Ezekiel 1:5–14. In later Christian art and literature, the symbols of the four living creatures became associated with the four gospels: the lion (Mark), the ox (Luke), the man (Matthew), and the eagle (John).

This second vision of the Book of Revelation actually consists of two scenes. We have already examined the first scene—the worship of God in God's throne room (Rev. 4:1–11). The second scene concerns a scroll (Rev. 5:1) and the question that is announced by an angel, "Who is worthy to open the scroll and break its seals?" (Rev. 5:2). John does not tell us the contents of the scroll, but since it is located in the "right hand of the one seated on the throne" (Rev. 5:1)—that is, in God's hand of power—we can assume that it contains what God wills *and* what God has the authority to make happen in the world. When the identity of the one who will open the seals is finally revealed, we discover that it is "a Lamb standing as if it had been slaughtered" (Rev. 5:6). The lamb, of course, recalls Jerusalem Temple sacrifice, whether that of Passover or Yom Kippur (see Chapter 5). But this lamb is not an ordinary lamb. This lamb is standing *as if* it had been slaughtered, meaning that you might think it is dead, but it is not! It has somehow survived or transcended

The Lamb of God Surrounded by the Four Watchers and the Multitude in White. *Douce 189 folio 22v from the Douce Apocalypse, thirteenth century, England/Bodleian Library Oxford.*

death, and through its death, it has ransomed God's holy ones from among all the peoples of the world and transformed them into "a kingdom and priests serving our God" (Rev. 5:9–10).

Here, and in every other vision of the heavenly realm in the Book of Revelation, everyone—the angels, the twenty-four elders, the martyrs, and sometimes even John—is engaged in continuous worship of God. Everything is peaceful and joyful, and no one tires of singing God's praises. Thus, John asserts the sovereignty of God in the heavenly realm. However, in the earthly realm, the situation is quite different, as we shall see!

## THE OPENING OF THE SEVEN SEALS AND THE BLOWING OF SEVEN TRUMPETS

Following the throne vision, John recounts visions of the opening of the seven seals (Rev. 6:1–8:5) and the blowing of the seven trumpets (Rev. 8:6–9:21; 11:14–19), which signal the establishment of God's kingdom on earth. At the conclusion of these two cycles of visions, when the seventh angel blows its trumpet, John hears voices from around God's throne proclaiming, "The kingdom of the world has become the kingdom of our Lord and of his Messiah" (Rev. 11:15). He also hears the twenty-four elders praying, "We give you thanks, Lord God Almighty, who are and who were, for you have taken your great power and begun to reign" (Rev. 11:17). Their song of triumph ends with a declaration that God's time of judging the dead, punishing those who destroy the earth, and rewarding God's holy ones has come (Rev. 11:18).

However, between the announcement of the opening of the first seal (Rev. 6:1) and this heavenly song of triumph (Rev. 11:18), the earth and its inhabitants are bombarded by war, famine, and disease (Rev. 6:1–8); by earthquakes, eclipses of the sun and moon, and meteor showers (Rev. 6:12–17); and by every kind of plague imaginable, including monstrous locusts that have scorpion tails and look like horses armed for battle (Rev. 9:1–12; cf. Rev. 9:13–21). Though not completely destroyed, every aspect of the earth is affected, including the humans who have not been marked with the seal of God on their foreheads (Rev. 9:4).

Who are the ones who are marked with the seal of God, who are spared this terrible destruction? They are 144,000 of God's holy ones (Rev. 7:4). Composed of multiples of 12 and 1,000, it is a symbolic number that is both absolutely perfect and too great to count. Thus, John asserts the sovereignty and justice of God on earth.

## MORE VISIONS OF GOD'S JUSTICE AND CONSOLATION

Precisely how God's justice and sovereignty will be manifest on earth is the subject of the second half of the Book of Revelation (Rev. 12:1–22:5). The second cycle of visions (Rev. 12:1–16:21) begins with a vision of a pregnant woman, clothed with the sun and wearing a crown of stars, who is chased by a great red dragon (Rev. 12). Red is the symbol of violence and bloodshed. This vision is followed immediately by visions of two horrible beasts—one from the sea (representing the Roman Empire) and another from the land (representing the emperor)—who get their power from the dragon (Rev. 13). John shares a "secret" with his audience when he reminds the reader that this second beast bears the number of its name, 666 (Rev. 13:18). Even today there is much speculation about the meaning of this number and the identity of the person to whom John was referring. However, most biblical scholars think that John intended it as a reference to Emperor Nero (reigned 54–68 c.e.), who, like Domitian, had a reputation for persecuting Christians. In Hebrew numerology, the sum of the letters of his name is 666. If this topic is of interest to you, you may want to do some research into the number of the beast of the land in the Book of Revelation.

Immediately following these nightmare visions, John receives several more visions designed to give hope and consolation to the Christian communities. The first is a vision of the Lamb (i.e., the resurrected Christ) standing on Mount Zion (i.e., Jerusalem on high) with the 144,000 who have been rescued from the earth and who enjoy the Lamb's protection (Rev. 14:1–5). This vision, in turn, is followed by visions of seven angels pouring bowls of plagues onto the earth (Rev. 15:1–16:21). Filled with violence and destruction, these visions certainly sound terrible to our ears, but the communities for whom John was writing probably did not perceive them that way. As a persecuted people, they would have seen them as reminders of the Exodus, when God sent plagues upon the Israelites' enemies. For the Egyptians the plagues of the Exodus were devastating, but for the Israelites they were miracles of God's loving kindness. John wants his audience to view these visions in the same light: as testimony of God's beneficence on behalf of the persecuted holy ones.

Likewise, the interlude, which describes John's visions of the whore Babylon and the funeral dirges that are sung on her behalf (Rev. 17:1–18:24), is rich in symbolism and replete with warnings against those who made alliances with Rome. For now, it is enough to remember that, throughout all of these visions, John is articulating the central concerns of apocalyptic literature: that God is just and God is sovereign. Therefore, John must explain why God allows the suffering of the righteous. He must also assert that God will destroy the forces of evil—symbolized by the dragon and its two beasts—and all those who align themselves with them. This is the subject of the final cycle of seven visions in the Book of Revelation.

## VISIONS OF THE LAST THINGS

The Book of Revelation concludes with a final series of seven visions concerning the last things (Rev. 19:1–22:5). All of these visions are primarily concerned with the judgment that is about to come upon the wicked and the promised reward for the righteous in the end time. Since these visions are described in highly mythical language, we should interpret them as symbolic responses to John's concern about the justice and sovereignty of God and not as historical descriptions of the end of the world.

John begins this section of his recorded visions with another glimpse of the heavenly liturgy (i.e., worship service) that was already under way when he was first taken into God's throne room (Rev. 4:1–11) and that is still in progress with no signs of ending (Rev. 19:1–10). Only the content of the prayer has changed. Now the heavenly voices praise God for passing judgment against the great whore Babylon (i.e., Rome) and for avenging the blood of the martyrs (Rev. 19:1–3). They also praise God's sovereignty and announce the upcoming marriage of the bride and the Lamb. From the context, it is clear that the Lamb is the exalted Christ and the bride is a symbol for the faithful Christian community. Notice that her bridal dress is the "righteous deeds" of the holy ones (Rev. 19:6–8). Thus, once again, John asserts the sovereignty and the justice of God. God is all-powerful, reigning over all, and God rewards the righteous!

Such is the lens through which John presents the first six visions of the last things; each is an elaboration of his proclamation concerning the justice and sovereignty of God. These visions are summarized below in order to guide your reading. As you study each one, pay attention to its contribution to this theme. What does it say about the reward of the righteous? What does it say about the punishment of the wicked? What does it say about the manifestation of God's kingdom on earth and the defeat of evil? Notice that the fourth and fifth visions form an intercalation—one vision is inserted within another—with the understanding that they be read together. In this case, the outer vision should be interpreted in the light of the inner vision.

1. Revelation 19:11–16—The appearance of the parousia Christ, the judge of nations, riding a white horse and accompanied by a heavenly army.

2. Revelation 19:17–18—The eschatological banquet, a symbol of God's vengeance against the wicked.

3. Revelation 19:19–21—The punishment of the beast and the pseudoprophet and the death of their followers in the battle at Har (literally, "mountain of") Megiddo.

4. Revelation 20:1–3—Part I of the vision describing God's punishment of the forces of evil: Satan is seized and thrown in the abyss.

5. Revelation 20:4–6—Intercalated vision. The vision of the **millennium**, the thousand-year reign of Christ and his victorious martyrs

6. Revelation 20:7–10—Part II of the vision describing God's punishment of the forces of evil: Satan is thrown into the place of fire with the two beasts and their followers.

7. Revelation 20:11–15—A vision of God enthroned for judgment.

In dramatic fashion, these six visions express John's conviction that God is sovereign and God will reward the righteous and punish the wicked. The only question that remains is, What will the fullness of God's reign look like? The answer comes in the seventh vision, the vision of the New Jerusalem.

## THE NEW JERUSALEM

At the conclusion of the sixth vision in this series, John describes how death and Hades (i.e., the abode of the dead) are destroyed (Rev. 20:14). In the opening of this same vision, he notes that the earth and sky fled away (Rev 20:11), meaning that the slate has been wiped clean for the transformed **cosmos** (literally, "world," referring to the created universe), which is about to appear. This is the setting for John's final vision, the vision of the New Jerusalem (Rev. 21:1–22:5). In this vision, John sees a new heaven and a new earth and the holy city, a **New Jerusalem**, coming out of heaven from God (Rev. 21:1–2). Notice that this vision is not about the coming of an otherworldly reality but rather about the restoration of a transformed *this-worldly reality*. In other words, in John's seventh vision of the last things, "heaven" has come down to earth!

John uses three groups of images to describe the New Jerusalem: the bride, the Temple, and the new creation. First, the New Jerusalem is compared to a bride who has prepared herself for her husband (Rev. 21:2, 9; cf. Rev. 19:4–6). The prophets of the Old Testament used this traditional bridal image to describe the restoration of the historical Jerusalem, when God's people would return from the Babylonian Exile. See, for example, Isaiah 49:18: "Lift up your eyes all around and see; they all gather, they come to you. As I live, says the Lord, you shall put all of them on like an ornament, and like a bride you shall bind them on." See also Isaiah 52:1 and 61:10. This bride and bridegroom imagery is quite amazing. Simply stated, it means that the relationship between Christ, the Lamb, and the believing community is characterized by love, intimacy, fidelity, and fruitfulness. What an awesome mystery—the Christian community is called to be the beloved and adored wife of the Lamb.

Second, the New Jerusalem is compared to the Jerusalem Temple (Rev. 21:10–27). Historically, the Temple had become the symbol of God's covenant with Israel, the "place" where God came to dwell with his people, and the center of Judaism in the ancient world. However, in this final vision of the Book of Revelation, the entire city becomes God's Temple (Rev. 21:9–21). The cubic shape of the city recalls both the Holy of Holies in Solomon's Temple (1 Kgs. 6:20; 2 Chr. 3:8–9) and the plan of the Temple described by Ezekiel (Ezek. 41:21; 43:16; 45:1; 48:20). There are differences, too. For example, the high priest's breastplate was supposed to have twelve stones representing the twelve tribes, but here the twelve stones of the New Jerusalem bear the names of the twelve apostles of the Lamb (Rev. 21:14; cf. Exod. 28:21). Instead of Jews alone making pilgrimage to Jerusalem, all peoples will come streaming to the city (Rev. 21:24). There will be no need to close the gates of the city for protection, because no evil will threaten it (Rev. 21:25). There will also be no need for a temple in the city to mediate God's presence because God and the Lamb will dwell directly with the people (Rev. 21:22). Again, what a beautiful and hopeful image of peace, safety, and security for God's beloved people!

Finally, the New Jerusalem is compared to a new creation (Rev. 22:1–5). Again, the imagery is traditional. The river recalls the second creation story in Genesis, which provided the setting for God's creation of a human from the dust of the earth (cf. Gen. 2:9–10), as well as Ezekiel's vision of a river of water flowing from the Temple (Ezek. 47:1–12) and Zechariah's vision of water coming from Jerusalem when God's day of judgment comes (Zech. 14:8). John's observation that there is a tree of life on one side and another of the river (Rev. 22: 2) recalls the tree of life that God placed in the garden, also from the second creation story (cf. Gen. 2:9). It is the same tree from which Adam and Eve were banished after their sin (Gen. 3:22). In other words, John's vision of the New Jerusalem is paradise restored!

John further observes that these trees produce fruit twelve months of the year and that they have leaves that are good for healing of the nations (Rev. 22:2). The language is closely related to the words of the prophet Ezekiel: "Their leaves will not wither nor their fruit fail, but they will bear fresh fruit every month, because the

The Twelve Apostles Seated on the Foundations of the Walls of the New Jerusalem. From the twelfth-century commentary on the Apocalypse, Revelations XXI.14, by Haimo, Bishop of Auxerre, Germany. *Bodley 352 folio 4v/Bodleian Library Oxford.*

water for them flows from the sanctuary. Their fruit will be for food, and their leaves for healing" (Ezek. 47:12). The point of this part of the vision is this: God will provide all they need for nourishment and for well-being. John adds "of the nations," making the vision all-inclusive. John's observation that there is nothing accursed in the city (Rev. 22:3) and there is no darkness (Rev. 22:5) recalls an end-time prophecy about the lifting of the curse on Jerusalem so that it can finally live in safety (cf. Zech. 14:7–11). In sum, John's vision of the New Jerusalem concerns the establishment of a new creation—or better, a return to the first creation, before there was sin and evil in the world. It is a return to the Garden of Eden!

### THE VISION OF A NEW HEAVEN
### AND A NEW EARTH IN ASIA

Some of the visions of hope, particularly the vision of the New Jerusalem, raise difficult questions about the enormous gap that exists between the "hoped for" and reality. This is especially true in parts of the world where poverty is rampant and people lack the basic necessities of life like clean water, food, and a place to live. In "Revelation 21:1–22:5: An Asian Perspective," Choan-Seng Song offers a reflection on the vision of the New Jerusalem, beginning with the story of Yati. Yati is twenty-three years old; lives in Tangerang, Indonesia; and works in a factory making tennis shoes that are sold in the United States. She wants to become a secretary someday, but her dream will probably never become a reality because her long hours of work (50–60 hours per week) provides a salary of less than $80 in U.S. currency per month, leaving her with only enough to rent an unfurnished, single-room, lizard-infested shack, which she shares with two roommates. Asked about her dream of becoming a secretary, she answers, "I can't. This is all there is for me." Song continues:

> But the distance between Asia's exploited people and God's reign of justice and freedom, between the old heaven and the old earth and a new heaven and a new earth, is enormous. We cannot cover that distance with one giant leap. Nor can we reduce it by taking a shortcut. It takes all the tribulations, both personal and communal, for John the seer finally to envision that new heaven and earth. And he knows that the churches have to be tested and tried before they can be given glimpses of a new heaven and a new earth. It must be the same for Christians in Asia. There is a vision of a new heaven on earth, that part of the mother earth called Asia. But they cannot just wish that vision into becoming a reality. Nor can they hail it from nowhere. They have to become actively engaged in efforts to redress the causes of the crisis. They have to commit themselves "to try our best, with the belief in Christ as the life of the world" (*People of Asia, People of God, A Report of the Asia Mission Conference 1989* [Hong Kong: Christian Conference of Asia, 1990] 130)....
>
> What John is engaged in is the theology of **Immanuel**, a theology that God shares our human sufferings, that God is involved in the tribulations of the universe. That theology of Immanuel, translated into Asia, insists that for God to be God, God must be the God to be heard in Yati's story, to be perceived in the groaning of a natural world devastated by human greed. And for us human beings to be human beings, we must be able to resonate with that God in Yati's story and in the groaning of lands, forests, and rivers polluted by our industries and economic activities. This Immanuel—this God with creation and creation with God—is a new heaven and a new earth. ("Revelation 21:1–22:5: An Asian Perspective," 217–218)

## THE CONCLUSION OF THE BOOK OF REVELATION

And how does the Book of Revelation end? It ends with a promise from Jesus Christ: "I am coming soon!" (Rev. 22:20), to which the author, on behalf of the readers, answers, "Amen," meaning "so be it." We would have to say that there is no better message of hope for the persecuted. However, the time is *coming*; it is not yet here. Therefore the author adds a prayer of petition, "Come, Lord Jesus" (Rev. 22:20). In Aramaic, the prayer is *marana tha*. Christians still use this petition in their Advent prayers, during the four weeks before Christmas. Thus, the Book of Revelation ends with intense expectation for the coming of the parousia Christ, when God's reign is fully established on earth and everyone can live in peace and security, without suffering or tears. Marana tha!

## KEY TERMS

| | | |
|---|---|---|
| Theodicy | Seer | Theophany |
| Babylon | One like a Son of Man | Throne vision |

| | | |
|---|---|---|
| Watchers | Cosmos | Immanuel |
| Millennium | New Jerusalem | |

## Questions for Reading

Read the Book of Revelation. Use evidence from the text to demonstrate your answers.

1. From the prologue (Rev. 1:1–3) and the introduction to the first vision (Rev. 1:9–11), what do we learn about the author of the Book of Revelation? What kind of literature does he think he is writing?

2. In the letter opening that follows the prologue, John uses a pattern of three descriptors to explain his Christology (Rev. 1:4–6). What are the three things he says about who Jesus Christ is? What are the three things he says about what Jesus Christ does? Who is the "One who is and who was and who is to come" (Rev. 1:4, 8)?

3. From the first vision of the Book of Revelation, make a list of descriptors for One like a Son of Man (Rev. 1:9–20). How do we learn that One like a Son of Man is the exalted Christ? Can you speculate about the effect that this vision might have had on the initial readers/hearers of the Book of Revelation?

4. For each of the letters to the churches, explain in a sentence or two the nature of the accusations that John is bringing against that church. If he has no complaint against a particular church, why not?
   a. Ephesus (Rev. 2:1–7)
   b. Smyrna (Rev. 2:8–11)
   c. Pergamum (Rev. 2:12–17)
   d. Thyatira (Rev. 2:18–29)
   e. Sardis (Rev. 3:1–6)
   f. Philadelphia (Rev. 3:7–13)
   g. Laodicea (Rev. 3:14–22)

5. At the conclusion of each of the seven letters to the churches (Rev. 2:1–3:22), John adds a promise to those who keep the faith. How would you characterize these promises? Provide two examples to demonstrate.

6. In the second vision of the Book of Revelation (Rev. 4:1–5:14), John is permitted to see the heavenly throne room. Who is seated on the throne? How do you know? Who is the "Lamb standing as if it had been slain" (Rev. 5:6)? How do you know? What is the significance of John's description of the Lamb? *Hint:* Horns were a symbol of power, and eyes were a symbol of knowing or insight.

7. Make a list of the events that accompany the opening of each of the seven seals (Rev. 6:1–8:5). Based on the assumption that John is writing about the historical and political situation of his time, what can you conclude about the significance of these seven signs?

8. Make a list of the events that accompany the blowing of each of the seven trumpets (Rev. 8:6–9:21; 11:14–19). Based on your reading of the biblical text, what can you conclude about the significance of these seven trumpets?

9. The vision of the woman and the dragon (Rev. 12:1–17) is actually an intercalation of two visions. Locate the two visions. What is the relationship of the inner

vision to the outer vision? What, if anything, can we say about the identity of the woman? Who is the dragon? Can you speculate about the purpose or primary message of this intercalated vision?

10. Most biblical scholars think that the visions of the beast of the sea and the beast of the land (Rev. 13:1–18) describe the Roman Empire and Rome's emperor, respectively. What aspects of the text appear to support this view? According to the biblical text, what is the relationship between the beast of the sea and the beast of the land? What is the relationship between the dragon and the beasts of the sea and land?

11. Make a list of the events that accompany the pouring out of each of the seven bowls (Rev. 15:1–16:21). Based on your reading of the biblical text, what can you conclude about the significance of these seven bowls?

12. Most biblical scholars think that the vision of the whore Babylon (Rev. 17:1–18) describes Rome and its leadership. What, then, is the meaning of the clothes she is wearing and the beast she is riding? What is the symbolism of the cup she holds? Can you speculate about the purpose or primary message of this vision?

13. Revelation 18:1–24 is a dirge (funeral song) that is sung by three groups: the kings of the earth, the merchants, and the shipmasters. Whose funeral is it? What are these three groups grieving?

14. In the visions of the last things, who is the rider of the white horse who is called "Faithful and True"? What is his role in the end time (Rev. 19:11–16)?

15. In the visions of the last things, what is the symbolic meaning of the thousand-year period of the binding of Satan (Rev. 20:1–10)? To what event is the author referring when he speaks of the time in which Satan will be released from prison?

16. According to the vision of the New Jerusalem at the end of the Book of Revelation, what attributes will this New Jerusalem have (Rev. 21:1–22:5)? What makes the New Jerusalem of the Book of Revelation distinctive from the old Jerusalem?

## QUESTIONS FOR REFLECTION

1. If the Old Testament prophets were spokespersons for God, calling people to return to the covenant, in what ways would you say that the Book of Revelation is prophetic literature?

2. In what ways might John's vision of the New Jerusalem (Rev. 21:1–22:5) be a source of hope for oppressed peoples today?

3. Some people find the Book of Revelation to be disturbing and dangerous. Others see it as extremely attractive and appealing. How would you account for these differing views?

## ACTIVITIES FOR LEARNING

1. After studying the form and content of the seven letters to the seven churches (Rev. 2:1–3:22), write your own contemporary "letter to the churches." Use the same form as the letters in the Book of Revelation, but change the content to

reflect the situation of a present-day faith community. It can be an actual Christian community or a fictional "true-to-life" community. How do you think your audience might respond to your prophetic letter?

2. Over the years, people have developed a wide range of interpretations of the number of the beast, 666 (Rev. 13:18). Locate as many of these interpretations as you can. You are likely to find the strangest ones by doing an internet search, but you also will want to consult some academic commentaries on the Book of Revelation to learn what biblical scholars think about the symbol 666. In a few sentences, describe the rationale for each interpretation that you were able to find. Which, if any, of these interpretations is consistent with a contextualist reading of scripture—that is, an interpretation that takes into account the historical, political, and cultural setting out of which John was writing and the literary genre he was using? Explain.

3. Using John's vision of the New Jerusalem (Rev. 21:1–22:5) as a model, write your own vision of the New Jerusalem with imagery and symbolism that might be relevant for contemporary Christians. Alternatively, find a recent artist's rendition of the vision of the New Jerusalem. What does your contemporary version of this vision say about humanity's hope for a new and restored relationship with God?

## SOURCES AND RESOURCES

Bauckham, Richard. *The Theology of the Book of Revelation*. New York: Cambridge University Press, 1993.

Blount, Brian K. *Can I Get a Witness? Reading Revelation through African American Culture*. Louisville, Ky.: Westminster John Knox Press, 2005.

Collins, Adela Yarbro. *The Apocalypse*. Wilmington, Del.: Glazier, 1979.

———. *Crisis and Catharsis: The Power of the Apocalypse*. Philadelphia: Westminster, 1984.

Cory, Catherine A. *The Book of Revelation*. Collegeville, Minn.: Liturgical Press, 2006.

Faley, Roland J. *Apocalypse Then and Now: A Companion to the Book of Revelation*. New York: Paulist, 1999.

Fiorenza, Elizabeth Schussler. *The Book of Revelation: Justice and Judgment*. Philadelphia: Fortress, 1985.

González, Catherine Gunsalus, and Justo L. González. *Revelation*. Louisville, Ky.: Westminster John Knox Press, 1997.

Harrington, Wilfrid J., O.P. *Revelation*. Collegeville, Minn.: Liturgical Press, 1993.

Jeske, Richard L. *Revelation for Today: Images of Hope*. Minneapolis, Minn.: Fortress, 1983.

Koester, Craig R. *Revelation and the End of All Things*. Grand Rapids, Mich.: Eerdmans, 2001.

Mounce, Robert. *The Book of Revelation*. Grand Rapids, Mich.: Eerdmans, 1998.

Perkins, Pheme. *The Book of Revelation*. Collegeville, Minn.: Liturgical Press, 1983.

Pilch, John. *What Are They Saying about the Book of Revelation?* New York: Paulist, 1978.

Rhoads, David. *From Every People and Nation: The Book of Revelation in Intercultural Perspective*. Minneapolis, Minn.: Fortress, 2005.

Russell, D. S. *Prophecy and the Apocalyptic Dream: Protest and Promise*. Peabody, Mass.: Hendrickson, 1994.

Schüssler Fiorenza, Elizabeth. *Revelation: Vision of a Just World*. Minneapolis, Minn.: Fortress, 1991.

Smith, Robert H. *Apocalypse: A Commentary on Revelation in Words and Images*. Collegeville, Minn.: Liturgical Press, 2000.

Song, Choan-Seng. "Revelation 21:1–22:5: An Asian Perspective." In *Return to Babel: Global Perspectives on the Bible*, edited by John R. Levison and Priscilla Pope-Levison. Louisville, Ky.: Westminster John Knox Press, 1999.

Talbert, Charles H. *The Apocalypse: A Reading of the Revelation of John*. Louisville, Ky.: Westminster John Knox Press, 1994.

Thompson, Leonard L. *Revelation*. Nashville, Tenn.: Abingdon Press, 1998.

Witherington, Ben. *Revelation*. Cambridge, England: Cambridge University Press, 2003.

# GLOSSARY OF TERMS

**Abiding:** Also translated as "remaining," "dwelling" or "staying." In John's gospel, this word describes a relationship so intense that one party of the relationship appears to dwell in the other. It is used of Jesus' relationship with the Father and the disciples' relationship with Jesus.

**Abraham:** Known as Abram until God changed his name to Abraham, "Father of Nations." He was the first of the patriarchs of Judaism. His story is told in the Book of Genesis. Later Paul uses him as an example of justification through faith.

**Agape meal:** A term used in the early church for the Eucharist or the Lord's Supper. *Agape* means "love."

**Age of Enlightenment:** See *Enlightenment, Age of.*

**Agent of God:** A messenger or representative of God who "stands" in the place of God in a particular situation and who speaks God's words. The biblical prophets were agents of God. Scholars of John's gospel use this notion to explain Jesus' special relationship to the God the Father: Jesus does and says only what the Father tells him to do, namely, judge and give life (John 5:19–24).

**Allegorical sense (of scripture):** One of the "Four Senses" in medieval interpretation of scripture, it was concerned with finding a metaphor (comparison) that could help explain how the biblical text pointed to the Christ event (his incarnation, death, and resurrection) or his presence in the sacraments.

**Allegory:** A method of biblical interpretation in which the persons, places, and events of a biblical story are given a symbolic or spiritual meaning beyond their literal meaning, usually one having to do with humanity's journey to salvation.

**Anagogical sense (of scripture):** One of the "Four Senses" in medieval interpretation of scripture, it was concerned with learning what the biblical text taught about humanity's final goal, heaven, or how it related to one's reflection on these final things.

**Anna:** According to the Gospel of James, the mother of Mary, who would later become the mother of Jesus.

**Annunciation:** The Christian feast, celebrated on March 25, which recalls Luke's story of the angel who comes to Mary to announce the conception of Jesus through the Holy Spirit (Luke 1:26–38).

**Anointing of the sick:** A ritual practiced within some Christian churches in which a sick person approaches the community for prayers of healing. The community (or its representative) lays hands on the person (a gesture of prayer) and anoints him or her with oil.

**Anthropology:** The study of or teachings about the nature of humanity, including the development of human culture.

**Anthropology, theological:** Religious teachings about the nature of human beings vis-à-vis God, as well as their origin and destiny.

**Apocalypse:** A genre or type of literature that includes revelations about heavenly realities, the end of the world, and God's ultimate triumph over the forces of evil.

**Apocalyptic:** Pertaining to a religious worldview that expects the imminent end of the world. It includes the belief that the end time will be accompanied by a final conflict between God and the powers of evil and that God will establish a new world order.

**Apocrypha:** A Greek word meaning "hidden" or "concealed." Protestant traditions use it to refer to seven books and parts of two other books that are not part of the Hebrew canon. These include the Old Testament books of Tobit, Judith, Wisdom of Solomon, Ecclesiasticus (Sirach), 1 and 2 Maccabees, and Baruch and parts of the books of Daniel and Esther.

**Apollos:** A Jewish Christian from Alexandria in Egypt who, after his conversion, used his skills as a rhetorician to preach the gospel about Jesus. He is mentioned in Acts 18 and several times in 1 Corinthians.

**Apostasy:** The act of abandoning or rejecting one's faith, usually under threat of persecution. Apostasy was considered to be one of the three unforgivable sins in the early church, along with murder and adultery.

**Apostle:** From a Greek word meaning "one who is sent." In the New Testament, it usually refers to the twelve who were chosen and sent out by Jesus to proclaim the good news of God. However, Paul called himself an apostle, even though he did not know Jesus during his human existence, because he was sent by the risen Jesus.

**Apostolic:** Adjective; describes things that are associated with the apostles.

**Apostolic succession:** Referring to the teaching authority of the bishops of the early Church, which could be traced back to the apostles, who had received their authority to teach from Jesus himself.

**Ascension:** Jesus' ascent into heaven after his resurrection. According to Luke and Acts of the Apostles, this happened forty days after Easter, a symbolic number signifying change or transition.

**Asceticism:** Depriving the body of pleasures by fasting or engaging in other spiritual practices in order to focus one's attention on spiritual matters.

**Augustus Caesar:** Also known as Gaius Octavian, he was emperor of Rome from 27 B.C.E. through 14 C.E. During his reign, Jesus of Nazareth was born.

**Babylon:** Originally, a reference to the city associated with the Babylonian Exile, during which time the Babylonians deported people from Judea and destroyed the Jerusalem

Temple. In New Testament literature, an allusion to Rome and the empire it represented.

**Babylonian Exile:** The deportation that took place after the Babylonian conquest of Judah in 586 B.C.E. The people were allowed to return from exile in approximately 530 B.C.E.

**B.C.E.:** An abbreviation for "before the Common Era"—that is, before the common period in which Judaism and Christianity existed together. It replaces the abbreviation B.C., especially among biblical scholars, because it more properly represents Judaism's ongoing place in history.

**Beatitudes:** Brief statements of blessing that begin "Blessed are you . . ." or "Happy are they . . . ." The most famous beatitudes are found in Matthew's Sermon on the Mount (Matt. 5–7) and Luke's Sermon on the Plain (Luke 7).

**Beloved disciple:** Literally, "the one whom he loved;" in John's gospel, the disciple whom Jesus loved. He is considered to be the author of John's gospel insofar as the traditions behind the gospel are associated with his memory.

**Bible:** From the Greek term *ta biblia*, meaning "the books." It is most often used to describe the collection of sacred writings of Judaism or Christianity.

**Biblical critical methods:** A general term used to describe the various analytical approaches biblical scholars use to study the Bible.

**Bishop:** Translated from the Greek term *episkopos*, which means "overseer," anyone who had a position of authority that involved responsibility for the welfare of others. Among early Christians, the head of a local church.

**Blasphemy:** Words or actions that are perceived to show disrespect for God or holy things.

**Body of Christ:** An image that Paul uses to describe church and to explain how the many become one in Christ and how people with various gifts come together for the common good (1 Cor. 12:12–31; Rom. 12:3–8).

**Book of Glory:** John 13:1–20:31; the second of two major units of the Gospel of John, which tells the story of the passion, death, and resurrection of Jesus and is punctuated by an extended farewell discourse.

**Book of Signs:** John 1:19–12:50; the first of two major units of the Gospel of John, which recounts Jesus' miracles (known as "signs") and includes several large sections of dialogue and discourse.

**Caesar Augustus:** See *Augustus Caesar.*

**Canon:** A term that means "rule" or "standard," like a measuring stick. It is used to refer to the collection of authoritative writings of a particular group of people. Although we do not know the exact date of the final assembly of all the canonical books of the Christian Bible, the first list that corresponds to today's canon was not recorded until the fourth century C.E.

**Canonical criticism:** An area of study and a set of methods that focus on the final stage of Bible formation, the canon. Its goal is to interpret particular biblical texts in light of the canon as a whole and its overarching theological themes.

**Catalogues of virtues and vices:** Standard lists used for teaching good behavior or values (virtues) and for warning against bad behavior or tendencies toward evil (vices). They are found in several books of the New Testament but also in the writings of the philosophers of that time, particularly the Stoics and the Cynics.

**Catechesis:** Religious instruction for the newly baptized or the soon-to-be-baptized.

**Catechumens:** People who are preparing for baptism in the Christian faith.

**Catholic:** A term meaning "general" or "universal." Traditionally, seven letters of the New Testament—James, 1 Peter, 2 Peter, 1 John, 2 John, 3 John, and Jude—are known as catholic letters.

**C.E.:** An abbreviation for "Common Era"—that is, the common period in which Judaism and Christianity existed together. It replaces the abbreviation A.D., especially among biblical scholars, because it more properly represents Judaism's ongoing place in history.

**Centurion:** An officer in the Roman army during the first century C.E. He was in charge of a century, that is, a division of one hundred men.

**Chiasm:** A rhetorical technique employed in ancient Greek literature; also called inverted parallelisms. They are constructed in such a way that the first unit of text corresponds to the last unit of the same text, the second unit corresponds to the second to the last unit of the text, and so on. If the chiasm has an even number of units, the outermost elements are highlighted. If the chiasm has an odd number of units, then the focal point is the central element.

**Chief priests:** Members of the leading priestly families in Jerusalem.

**Chloe:** Mentioned only in 1 Corinthians, apparently her slaves or household members had passed through Corinth sometime before Paul wrote this letter and alerted him to problems in the church at Corinth (1 Cor. 1:11).

**Christ:** From a Greek word meaning "anointed." The title was used to describe an anointed royal figure. Its Hebrew equivalent is *messiah.*

**Christ of Faith:** Referring to the resurrected Jesus as he was revealed through the faith experiences of people who had come to believe in him.

**Christology:** From the Greek words *Christos,* which means "anointed," and *logos,* which means "teaching" or "word." Christology refers to the study of the person and nature or function of Jesus as the messiah or Christ.

**Commentary:** A study resource that contains the results of biblical scholars' analyses of the content of particular books of the Bible. It is arranged as a series of comments on small units or individual verses of the biblical book under investigation.

**Concordance:** A study resource that lists every word of the Bible, arranged alphabetically, together with citations (chapter and verse) indicating where that word occurs.

**Confession:** (1) An admission of wrongdoing; (2) a declaration of faith.

**Contextualist:** Adjective; describes an approach to the interpretation of the Bible that takes into account the historical, cultural, and literary contexts out of which particular biblical books were written.

**Cosmos:** A Greek word meaning "world." In many cases, it carries the sense of an ordered universe that exists as an integrated whole.

**Cosmology:** The study of or teachings about the nature of the universe, usually from a philosophical perspective.

**Covenant:** A contract or agreement between a person in authority and his/her subjects. Judaism understands itself to have its identity in the covenant(s) God made with Israel, most notably the covenant with Moses at Sinai. Christianity understands Jesus to be God's establishment of a new covenant, making its members the new Israel.

**Creed:** A brief statement of belief. The more fully developed creeds are summaries of the faith communities' doctrines (official teachings).

**Crispus:** Mentioned in Acts of the Apostles and 1 Corinthians, he was a ruler of the synagogue in Corinth before he was baptized by Paul (Acts 18:8; 1 Cor. 1:14).

**Cult:** The system of worship or rituals that characterize a particular religious group.

**Cultural hermeneutics:** A hermeneutical (i.e., interpretational) perspective that takes the reader a step further into the meaning of a biblical text by drawing on traditional myths, stories, and imagery of cultures that are less like the postindustrial Western world and more like the traditional cultures of the Bible (e.g., African and Asian cultures).

**David:** Son of Jesse and second king of Israel after Saul, he reigned from approximately 1005 to 965 B.C.E. Some consider him the greatest king in Israel's history.

**Deacon:** Translation of a Greek word meaning, "minister" referring to anyone who serves. In second- and third-century Christian circles, the assistant to the bishop or a co-worker with the presbyter.

**Deaconess:** Female deacons of the early church who were responsible for assisting at the baptisms of women and for caring for the sick and elderly women of the community.

**Dead Sea Scrolls:** Scrolls that were discovered between 1947 and 1960 most of which were found in eleven caves around Qumran near the Dead Sea. Some are documents of the Essene community; others are copies of Jewish biblical books and commentaries on Jewish biblical texts.

**Deconstruction:** Drawing on the insights of the French philosopher Jacques Derrida, this method of interpretation critiques commonly held assumptions about the way the world is organized and gives priority of importance to things that people otherwise consider secondary: femaleness over maleness, metaphorical meanings over literal meanings, fiction over historicity, and irrationality over rationality. It works from the presupposition that language is fluid and has within itself the tendency for its meaning to implode or collapse in on itself.

**Deuterocanonical:** Meaning "second canon," this term is usually used by the Roman Catholic Church and some Eastern Christians to refer to literature that was given biblical status at a second or later stage of development. These books—Tobit, Judith, Wisdom of Solomon, Ecclesiasticus (Sirach), 1 and 2 Maccabees, and Baruch and parts of the books of Daniel and Esther—were part of the Septuagint Bible and the early Christian versions of the Old Testament but were not included in the TaNaK.

**Deutero-Pauline:** Adjective; refers to letters attributed to Paul but not actually written by him. In most cases, these letters are thought to be written by a disciple of Paul as a way of honoring his memory.

**Diaspora:** Meaning "to scatter," this term was used to refer to Jews living outside of Palestine after the Babylonian Exile (586 B.C.E.).

**Diatribe:** A rhetorical device that involves the creation of a hypothetical dialogue partner who poses objections or questions that the author might expect the audience to raise. By answering the objections or questions, the author is able to more fully develop his argument.

**Didymus Judas Thomas:** The person to whom the Coptic Gospel of Thomas is attributed. In extracanonical literature, he is described as the twin brother of Jesus, most likely intended to be understood in a spiritual sense. The Greek word *Didymus* and the Aramaic word *Thomas* both mean "twin."

**Diotrephes:** A church leader mentioned only in 3 John. The elder who wrote the letter charges him with putting himself before others and refusing to offer hospitality to the elder's emissaries (3 John 9–10).

**Disciple:** From a Greek word meaning "learner." In the New Testament, it refers to a follower of Jesus or another religious figure who acts as teacher.

**Docetism:** A tendency, often associated with Gnostic Christianity, in which people think of Jesus as only "seeming" to suffer. The effect of this tendency was to focus on Jesus as pure spirit and as divinity, to the exclusion of his humanity.

**Domitian:** The emperor of Rome from 81 to 96 C.E. Biblical scholars think that the Book of Revelation was written during a period of persecution toward the end of his reign.

**Double meanings:** A literary technique employed in the Gospel of John in which Jesus is described as saying something that is deliberately ambiguous, usually having both a plain meaning and a symbolic meaning. The other characters in the story usually comprehend only the plain meaning of Jesus' words, but the intended audience understands their symbolic meaning.

**Double tradition:** In source critical analyses, segments of text that are almost identical in wording in two of the three synoptic gospels.

**Doxology:** A brief prayer of praise that usually begins "Glory to God . . . ."

**Dualism:** Pairs of ideas that are considered to be polar opposites of one another. E.g., light and darkness, good and evil, body and spirit.

**Ecclesia:** A Greek word meaning "assembly." In the New Testament, it has been translated as "church."

**Election:** God's choice of Israel as God's own people, which is ritualized in the covenant. In the New Testament, it also pertains to Jesus, who is God's elect one, and to the Jesus followers.

**Emmanuel:** See *Immanuel.*

**Emperor cult:** A social or civic religion of the Greco-Roman world in which emperors who excelled in their activities as rulers were given divine honors and official recognition that the deities worked through them.

**Enlightenment, Age of:** A worldview or intellectual movement associated with eighteenth-century Europe that emphasized reason in philosophy and empirical evidence in science and history. It gave rise to modern scientific methods and challenged certain religious claims about God and the salvation story.

**Epilogue:** A speech or a dramatic scene added to the conclusion of a story to explain what happened after the original story ended.

**Epiphany:** An appearance or manifestation of a divine being, perhaps an angel or God.

**Eschatology:** From the Greek words *eschaton,* which means "end," and *logos,* which means "teaching." Eschatology describes a teaching about the end time.

**Essenes:** A Jewish movement that existed from the second century B.C.E. until the Jewish War (70 C.E.). Some lived as monks and were associated with Qumran near the Dead Sea in Israel, but others married and lived in cities and villages throughout Palestine. Both groups were concerned about ritual purity and strict observance of community rules.

**Evangelist:** Related to the Greek word *euangelion,* which means "good message," this term describes a preacher of the gospel or, in the case of the New Testament, a writer of one of the four canonical gospels.

**Exegesis:** The analysis and interpretation of a biblical passage for the purpose of understanding the meaning of the text and the intent of the author of the text.

**Exhortation:** A statement urging someone to do something.

**Exodus:** Meaning "departure" or "going forth," it refers to the story of Moses leading God's people out of slavery in Egypt; the second book of the Bible.

**Exorcism:** A process, usually involving prayer or religious ritual, by which an evil or unclean spirit is driven out of a person or place.

**Explanatory note:** A literary technique in which the narrator of a story appears to "step aside" to talk directly to the audience in order to explain certain details of the story. The rhetorical effect is to make the reader a privileged participant in the story.

**Exposition:** A theoretical discussion of a problem or theory.

**Extant:** Adjective; still in existence.

**Extracanonical:** With reference to the Bible, religious writings that they are not part of the canon of Christianity and not authoritative for Christian faith; also called noncanonical.

**Faith:** A set of religious teachings to which a believer must give mental assent; trust in someone or something; disposition or attitude of openness and receptivity toward another.

**Farewell discourse:** A literary form in which a holy man or great teacher is portrayed as delivering the sum of his teaching or his last will and testament to his disciples immediately before his death.

**Felix, Antonius:** Governor of Palestine from 52 to 60 C.E. According to Acts of the Apostles, Felix presided over Paul's trial in Caesarea but chose not to decide his case, leaving him in prison till the end of his term (Acts 23:23–24:27).

**Feminist criticism:** A hermeneutical (i.e., interpretational) perspective from which biblical scholars study biblical texts. In this case, special attention is given to questions of gender and how assumptions about gender affect meaning.

**Festus, Porcius:** Governor of Palestine from 60 to 62 C.E. According to Acts of the Apostles, Festus tried to rectify Paul's situation of imprisonment, left unresolved by his predecessor, Felix. However, when Paul appealed to the emperor, Festus sent him under guard to Rome (Acts 25:1–26:32).

**First fruits:** Referring to the feast of Weeks; the first and best of the harvest is given to God in recognition that the whole harvest belonged to God.

**Form criticism:** An area of study and a set of methods used to uncover the oral traditions that an author might have used in the composition of a document. When biblical scholars first developed this methodology, they hoped to uncover the *Sitz im Leben* ("setting in life") of these oral traditions and, in this way, reconstruct the story of the earliest Christian communities. Eventually, they abandoned this objective as unattainable, but form criticism is still an important first step for redaction criticism.

**Form, literary:** Smaller units within a genre of literature or art that share similarities in structure, content, or technique. For example, the parable is a literary form within the gospel genre.

**Frame stories:** Two similar stories (same plot, similar characters, etc.) that provide a "frame" around a collection of stories and teachings that highlight a certain theme.

**Fulfillment citations:** Statements that begin with the phrase "All this took place to fulfill what had been spoken through the prophet" or "As it was written." In the case of the New Testament, the majority of these statements come from the Old Testament.

**Fundamentalist:** Adjective; describes a way of interpreting scripture that is designed to preserve certain fundamentals (basic doctrines) of the faith. This approach is often associated with a literalist interpretation of scripture.

**Gaius:** (1) Mentioned in 1 Corinthians as a person whom Paul baptized (1 Cor. 1:14), perhaps the same person who is described in the Letter to the Romans as Paul's host and a host of the whole church (Rom. 16:23); (2) Mentioned in Acts of the Apostles as one of Paul's occasional traveling companions (Acts 19:29); (3) Recipient of the Third Letter of John (3 John 1).

**Galilee:** The northern part of Palestine, which was ruled by Herod Antipas in 4 B.C.E. to 39 C.E. According to the gospels he was responsible for the death of John the Baptist.

**Genre:** A type or category of artistic expression. This term is used in a wide range of studies of literature and fine arts to describe categories of work that share the same structure, content, or artistic technique. For example, the novel is a genre.

**Gentile:** Any non-Jewish person.

**Glory/glorification:** A major theme of John's gospel: Jesus reveals the Father's glory by performing miracles, he glorifies the Father by doing what the Father sent him to do, and he is glorified in his death and exaltation.

**Glossalalia:** Speaking in tongues; the act of speaking in a language that is unfamiliar or incomprehensible. In the New Testament, Paul writes about *glossalalia* as one of the gifts of the Holy Spirit.

**Gnosis:** Greek word meaning "knowledge." Gnostics of the early Christian centuries claimed to know the truth about the human self, their status as the saved, and the way of their salvation, that is, how they could return to the divine realm, which was their place of origin.

**Gnostic myth:** A symbolic narrative that explained how God sent a savior, one of the divine powers, down to earth to help the enlightened soul return to the heavenly realm. The Gnostic myth took many forms, but its common elements are the heavenly origin, fall, incarnation, awakening, and return of the human spirit (sometimes called the mind) to God.

**Gnosticism:** A movement in early Christianity and Judaism whose members believed salvation was gained through special knowledge (*gnosis*) that was made available only to a certain elite. Its worldview was based on a philosophical system that favored the world of ideas over the world of matter.

**God-fearer:** Literally, "one who fears or reveres God." In Acts of the Apostles, it is used of Gentile proselytes to Judaism. They were among the first Gentiles to become Jesus followers.

**Gospel:** From the Anglo-Saxon *god-spell*, which means "good tidings"; a translation of the Greek word *euangelion*, which means "good message" (of Jesus Christ); the first four books of the New Testament (Matthew, Mark, Luke, and John).

**Grace:** From a Greek word meaning, "a gift" or "something that brings happiness or good fortune." For Christians, God's love freely given to humanity; God's favor or benevolence.

**Greco-Roman period:** Roughly speaking, the first century B.C.E. through the first century C.E., when the Mediterranean world was under the power of the Romans but still greatly influenced by Greek culture.

**Griesbach hypothesis:** A theory that attempts to explain the literary relationship among the synoptic gospels (Matthew, Mark, and Luke)

by arguing that Luke had Matthew's gospel available to him when he wrote his gospel and that Mark used both Matthew's and Luke's gospels in the composition of his gospel.

**Hellenization:** The influence of Greek thought, language, and culture on indigenous peoples. This process began with Alexander the Great (322 B.C.E.) and continued through the reigns of his Hellenistic successors and into the time of the Roman Empire.

**Heresy/heretical:** A theological teaching that is not consistent with the endorsed or approved teaching of the religious tradition to which the person belongs.

**Hermeneutics:** From a Greek word meaning "interpretation." Here it refers to the field of theological study that deals with the interpretation of scripture. It includes the study of both the principles of biblical interpretation and the process through which such interpretation is carried out in order to make the biblical text relevant for modern readers.

**Herod Antipas:** Son of Herod the Great; king of Galilee and the area to the east of the River Jordan from 4 B.C.E. to 39 C.E. The synoptic gospels describe him as the one who beheaded John the Baptist.

**Herod the Great:** King of Palestine from 37 to 4 B.C.E. Matthew's gospel describes him as seeking to kill Jesus at the time of his birth (Matt. 2:16–18).

**High Priest:** The head of the Jerusalem Temple and, during the Greco-Roman period, the most powerful person of the ruling class in Judea.

**Historical Jesus:** A term used in theology and biblical scholarship to refer to the man named Jesus of Nazareth who lived in Palestine in the first century C.E. It describes only what can be known about Jesus as a historical person, not what can be understood about him as an object of faith.

**Hour, the:** Generally, a specific time; the end time or day of judgment. In John's gospel, the moment of Jesus' death and exaltation, understood as a single event.

**Holy of Holies:** The innermost room of the Jerusalem Temple, where the Ark of the

Covenant was preserved and where God was believed to reside. Only the High Priest was permitted to enter this place and then only on the feast of Yom Kippur (Day of Atonement).

**Household codes:** Moral instructions that focus on the relationship between superiors and subordinates with particular emphasis on the respect and obedience that the subordinate owes to his or her superior.

**"I am" sayings:** Statements or sayings that begin with the phrase "I am." Among New Testament books, these are most commonly found in the Gospel of John, where they are attributed to Jesus.

**Immanuel:** Meaning "God-with-us," this term was applied to Jesus by early Christian writers.

**Incarnation:** The Christian teaching about the preexistent Son of God who took on flesh to live among humans.

**Inerrancy:** Literally, "without error." Christian churches' understanding of inerrancy is directly dependent on their understanding of inspiration. For some, inerrancy means that the Bible contains no errors or inconsistencies of any sort. For others, the Bible's inerrancy consists in its being a trustworthy guide to salvation, but it does not mean that the Bible is devoid of errors in areas of science, history, literary correctness, and so on.

**Infancy narratives:** Stories about the birth and early childhood of important persons. In the case of the canonical gospels, that person is Jesus.

**Inspiration:** When it pertains to the Bible, it describes the belief that God is its author. Some church traditions understand inspiration as God's direct dictation, which is transcribed in written form by human secretaries. Others understand inspiration to mean that the Bible is God's word communicated through human authors who are real authors, using their own language and historical and cultural expressions to convey what God wanted to reveal to humanity.

**Inspiration, verbal:** The belief that the Bible represents the words of God dictated to the human author, who acted as a scribe or secretary, writing down exactly what God told him to write.

**Intercalation:** A literary technique in which a story is inserted within another story. Typically, the "inner" story explains the "outer" one or focuses its interpretation in a special way.

**Interpolation:** In the case of the New Testament, a segment of text added by some later editor or copyist.

**Irony:** A literary device designed to catch the readers' attention and make them feel like insiders to the story. *Verbal irony* occurs when a character of the story says something that he or she intends to be sarcastic, derogatory, or unflattering but the reader recognizes that it is a profoundly truthful statement. *Situational irony* can be seen in an event that has a negative or demeaning meaning to the unaware but that readers recognize as revealing an entirely different meaning.

**Jewish Christians:** Biblical scholars' term for Jews of the earliest Christian centuries who became Jesus followers. Some call them Christian Jews, because they retained their Jewish identity and religious practices even as they became Christians.

**Joachim:** According to the Gospel of James, the father of Mary, who would later become the mother of Jesus.

**Johannine community:** The initial audience of John's gospel and the early Christian community, which looked to the Beloved Disciple as its spiritual leader.

**Judaizers:** A term that biblical scholars gave to Jewish Christians of the early church who argued that Gentiles must keep all of Jewish Law, if they wished to become Jesus followers.

**Judea:** In New Testament times, the southern part of Palestine. According to the gospels, Jesus traveled to this region and eventually was crucified in its capital, Jerusalem.

**Justification:** Literally, "setting right." This term is important in the writings of Paul that explain how human beings are brought into right relationship with God; also translated as "righteousness."

**Justification by works:** Phrase used by Paul in his Letters to the Galatians and the Romans to describe the view held by some that observance of Jewish Law could actually acquit a person of all failures against the covenant.

**Justification by faith:** Phrase used by Paul in his Letters to the Galatians and the Romans to argue against his opponents who accepted justification by works: no one is acquitted before God, except by God's free gift, which is Jesus Christ, for those who believe.

**Kerygma:** From a Greek word meaning "proclamation," this term refers to the preaching of the message about Jesus as the Christ to people who are just being introduced to the faith.

**Kingdom of heaven/God:** This phrase does not refer to a place, like an earthly kingdom, but rather to a state of being, in which God's rule is made manifest among the created world and evil is conquered.

**Koinonia:** Literally, "fellowship" or "partnership." In the New Testament, Paul uses this term to represent his notion of church.

**Laity:** Members of a religious community who are not ordained clergy.

**Law of Moses:** Referring to Torah, properly understood as "instruction." This phrase describes the obligations placed on God's people as part of the covenant associated with Moses.

**Legend:** As a literary genre, a story that may have some basis in history but that was not intended to convey history or, at least, it cannot be verified by independent oral traditions or written records. Its purpose is to inspire and edify.

**Levites:** Originally, descendants of the tribe of Levi; in the New Testament period, they were attendants in the Jerusalem Temple.

**Levitical priesthood:** The priests who claimed to be descendants of Levi, the brother of Joseph and son of Jacob; the priests of the Jerusalem Temple.

**Liberation hermeneutics:** A hermeneutical (i.e., interpretational) perspective from which biblical scholars study biblical texts. In this case, special attention is given to the relationships of power and economic inequity described in the text. The starting point for liberation hermeneutics is the belief that God is on the side of the poor and oppressed.

**"Lifted up" sayings:** In John's gospel, statements made by Jesus that include the verbs "to lift up" or "to be lifted up" ( John 3:14–15; John 8:28; John 12:31–33). An example of double meaning, it signifies Jesus' lifting up in crucifixion and his lifting up in exaltation.

**Litany:** A series of short prayers or blessings that begin or end with a common refrain.

**Literal sense (of scripture):** One of the "Four Senses" in medieval interpretation of scripture, it is not so much "what the words say" as it is the events as narrated or what the author intended to say.

**Literalist:** Adjective; describes an approach to the interpretation of the Bible that works from the assumption that scripture is fully and in every detail what God intended and thus can have no errors or contradictions. Sometimes called *verbal inspiration.*

**Literary form:** See *Form, literary.*

**Logos:** A Greek word meaning "a word," "a teaching," or "reason." It was used by Greek philosophers to refer to the rational principle that creates and governs the universe, giving it vitality and order. The term is used in the Gospel of John to refer to the preexistent Christ.

**Logion (pl. logia):** literally, a word or a saying; in Christian literature, usually referring to sayings of Jesus. The plural form is *logia.* The Coptic Gospel of Thomas is a collection of *logia* attributed to Jesus.

**LXX:** The Roman numeral 70; the abbreviation for the Septuagint, the Greek translation of the Old Testament. It received this designation because, according to legend, the Egyptian king Philadelphus (285–246 B.C.E.) requested a Greek translation of the Law (Torah) for his library at Alexandria. In response, the Jerusalem High Priest Eleazar sent 72 Jewish elders (six from each of the twelve tribes) who completed the job in 72 days, to the satisfaction of all involved.

**Magi:** Scholars of the esoteric sciences (e.g., magic, astrology, dream interpretation) from the East, described by Matthew as coming to Bethlehem to seek out the newborn Jesus.

**Magnificat:** Mary's hymn of praise to God, which was also her response to the greeting of Elizabeth before the birth of Jesus (Luke 1:46–55).

**Martyr:** From a Greek word meaning "witness." Martyrs chose death rather than renounce their faith under threat of persecution. They were honored among the first "saints" of the early Christian church.

**Martyrdom:** From the Greek word meaning "witness," this term refers to the notion of witnessing to the faith even to the point of being willing to give up one's life.

**Melchizedek:** A minor character in the Abraham stories (Gen. 14:17–20), in early Christian interpretation, he is a type for Christ, the perfect High Priest (Heb. 7:1–28). His name means "king of righteousness" and his title is king of Salem, which means "peace."

**Messiah:** A Hebrew word meaning "anointed one." In the Old Testament, it was used to designate anyone who was anointed: kings, priests, and even prophets. Because of the prophecy made to David about a future heir to his throne (2 Sam. 7), messianic expectation became a significant aspect of ancient Judaism.

**Messianic secret:** A term used to describe scenes in Mark's gospel where someone identifies Jesus as the messiah or Son of God, or otherwise calls attention to his activities on behalf of God's reign, and Jesus tells them not to tell anyone.

**Midrash:** A Jewish technique of commenting on scripture in which the interpreter takes each individual word or phrase of the biblical text and gives it a new contemporary meaning.

**Millennium:** A period of 1,000 years.

**Misunderstanding:** A literary technique employed in the Gospel of John in which the characters who interact with Jesus are portrayed as comprehending only the plain meaning of his words and therefore misunderstanding his true intent.

**Moneychangers:** People whose job it is to exchange one kind of currency for another for a fee.

**Moses:** According to the Book of Exodus, the person who was called by God to lead God's people out of slavery in Egypt. He was known as the greatest of God's prophets and the one who knew God face to face (Deut. 34:10).

**Mystery:** Meaning "secret" or "hidden." Paul uses it to describe the mystery of God's plan of salvation, which is so vast and rich that humans cannot comprehend it. When used in the plural form (mysteries), it usually refers to the mystery religions and the secret rituals that were used for initiation.

**Mystery cults:** In the Greco-Roman world, religions of the common people that included initiation rituals, myths about death and rebirth, and the belief or expectation that a person could conquer the powers of chaos and fate through knowledge of and identification with the god or goddess. Examples include the Eleusian mysteries and the cults of Mithras and Dionysus.

**Myth:** Religious stories that employ symbols and metaphoric language in order to articulate religious truths that otherwise cannot be easily understood through logical reasoning. They tell the truth about fundamental human experiences and answer questions that transcend reason, but they were never intended to be read as historical fact.

**Narrative criticism:** An area of study and a set of methods used to explain how a story makes meaning. The narrative critic inquires about the narrator, characters, plot, and setting of the story as well as the rhetoric used to tell the story.

**Nero:** Emperor of Rome from 54 to 69 C.E. Biblical scholars think that he is the one to whom the author of the Book of Revelation was referring when he wrote of the beast of the land (Rev. 13:18).

**New Jerusalem:** Referring to the final vision of the Book of Revelation, it represents the restoration of paradise on earth, after evil and death have been destroyed (Rev. 21:1–22:5; see also garden of Eden in Genesis 1–2).

**New Testament:** The second of two major segments of the Bible. It is a Christian convention, suggesting that God's covenant (testament) with Israel has been fulfilled or expanded by God's new covenant, which is embodied in the incarnation, death, and resurrection of Jesus Christ.

**Old Testament:** The first of two major segments of the Bible. It is a Christian convention and would not be considered an appropriate descriptor of the biblical text from the perspective of Judaism because it suggests that God's covenant with Israel is no longer valid or effective.

**One like a Son of Man:** A heavenly being in human form (see Dan. 7:13). In the Book of Revelation, One like a Son of Man is Christ.

**Order of widows:** In early Christianity, an enrollment of women who were widowed, had no family to support them, and were at least sixty years of age. They prayed on behalf of the community and served as mentors to the younger women. In return, the community provided them with financial support.

**Original sin:** A Christian doctrine, first articulated by Augustine of Hippo (354–430 C.E.), concerning humanity's tendency toward sin. Although the doctrine itself is nowhere mentioned in the Bible, two scripture texts are often cited as the basis for this doctrine: Genesis's story of the serpent in the garden (Gen. 3:1–24) and Paul's argument concerning humanity's responsibility for the spread of evil in the world, which derives from it (Rom. 1:18–32).

**Orthodox/orthodoxy:** Usually described as "right thinking" or "right belief," this term refers to traditional rules or officially approved teachings of a particular group.

**Palestine:** The name that the Greeks and later the Romans gave to the land of Israel, previously known as Canaan.

**Parable:** A fictional story used for comparison. Its imagery is drawn from nature or common life, and it has a surprise or "twist" that makes the reader/hearer ponder its deeper, metaphorical meaning.

**Paraclete:** A Greek word meaning "advocate" or "intercessor," usually in a trial setting. John's gospel uses this term to refer to the Holy Spirit, whom Jesus sent to be his continued presence in the world.

**Paraenesis:** Moral exhortation or teaching.

**Parousia:** A Greek word meaning "coming." It refers to the second coming of Christ, an event that was expected to correspond with the end-time judgment of the world and punishment of the wicked.

**Passion/passion narrative:** A term used to refer to the suffering and death of Jesus. The gospel story of Jesus' arrest, trial, and crucifixion is called a passion narrative.

**Passover:** An annual Jewish observance of the Exodus event in which the Hebrew people gathered to sacrifice the lamb, placing blood on their lintels and doorposts so that the Angel of Death would "pass over" their homes but kill the firstborn of the Egyptians. It is a feast of remembrance, celebrated in anticipation of full liberation for Israel.

**Pastoral/pastoral letters:** Adjective; describes things related to pastors or shepherds. In the New Testament, this term describes the First and Second Letters to Timothy and the Letter to Titus.

**Patron-client system:** A way of organizing society in which the patron, someone more powerful and of higher status, provides protection and provisions in return for services from the client.

**Pauline:** Adjective; refers to authentic writings of Paul.

**Pentecost:** Meaning "fiftieth," for the seven weeks plus a day between the Feast of Unleavened Bread and this pilgrimage feast; also called the feast of Weeks; the Christian feast that commemorates the descent of the Holy Spirit on the apostles as told in Acts 2:1–47.

**People of the land:** Originally, male Jews who were not part of the ruling class; also used in Jewish scriptures as a derogatory reference to uneducated people of the lower classes who did not or could not keep Jewish law.

**Pharisees:** A religious group of first-century C.E. Judaism that was noted for its skill in interpreting the Law. According to Josephus, Pharisees were well respected among the people because of their pious way of life and their religious purity.

**Pontius Pilate:** Procurator of Palestine from 26 to 36 C.E. The gospels describe him as presiding at the trial of Jesus and sentencing him to death by crucifixion.

**Postresurrection narratives:** Collections of stories about people who witnessed Jesus' empty tomb or saw the risen Christ. They are narrated as proof of the resurrection.

**Preexistence:** Existence at an earlier time and in a different state. The Gospel of John describes the preexistence of the Word, who is the Son of God, as having been with God from the beginning (John 1:1–5).

**Preferential option for the poor:** In liberation theology and liberation readings of scripture, the conviction that God is on the side of the poor and oppressed and that anyone who wishes to be in a relationship with God needs to be on the side of the poor, too.

**Presbyter:** An elder. The presbyters' role in early Christian communities is unclear; some were teachers, others may have served a symbolic role as representatives of the apostles surrounding the bishop, a representative of Christ, at Eucharist.

**Priests:** In New Testament literature, this term usually refers to guardians of the Jerusalem Temple who were responsible for various duties associated with its operation, including offering sacrifices. Their positions were passed on through their fathers.

**Priscilla (or Prisca) and Aquila:** Jewish Christians from Pontus in Asia Minor who were tentmakers by trade, but who also shared in Paul's ministry of evangelization. They are mentioned in Acts 18, 1 Corinthians 16, and Romans 16.

**Prologue:** An introduction to a longer literary work that serves as a preface, explaining the events that led to the production of the document or summarizing its main points.

**Prophets:** People who served as spokespersons for God. In the Bible they are also known as seers, visionaries, or men of God. In the phrase "Law and Prophets," the term refers to a collection of books in the Hebrew Scriptures (also the Old Testament) that tell the stories of the prophets and the prophecies associated with them.

**Proselyte:** A person who is newly converted to a faith tradition or a worldview.

**Pseudonymity:** A literary practice, common in ancient religious literature, in which anonymous authors would write under the name of a famous religious figure of the past. Several of the New Testament documents were written under pseudonyms.

**Q:** An abbreviation for the German word *Quelle*, meaning "source." Together with the Gospel of Mark, Q is posited as a hypothetical source (or sources) for the synoptic gospels of Matthew and Luke.

**Reader-response criticism:** An area of study and a set of methods used to analyze the reader's experience of reading a document and the way that the reader makes meaning of the text in the process of reading.

**Real presence:** Referring to the Christian celebration of Eucharist and the belief held by many, though not all, that Christ is really and fully present in the consecrated bread and wine and/or in the ritual of blessing and sharing the bread and wine as a remembrance of Jesus' last supper with his disciples.

**Realized eschatology:** Teachings about the end, in which its adherents believe that the end-time reign of God has already come, at least in a partial way, and that its realities are already present in the world. The Gospel of John contains realized eschatology.

**Redaction:** Editing.

**Redaction criticism:** An area of study and a set of methods used to uncover the various layers of redaction (i.e., editing) in a written document. The redaction critic starts with the results of source criticism and form criticism and then analyzes the document in order to understand how and why the author gathered and ordered various oral traditions and written materials as he did.

**Redemption:** A transaction that results in someone or something being released from bondage or indebtedness of some sort. For Christians, having been bought back from the bondage of sin through the death and resurrection of Jesus.

**Religion:** In a general sense, a term used to describe one's obligation to perform or participate in certain sacred rituals for the welfare of the community. Thus, it involves ceremonies that express reverence for God or the gods and expectations for good moral behavior. This term is used only rarely in the Bible.

**Remnant:** The small piece that is left over after part has been removed; a small group among exiled Judeans who stayed faithful to God's covenant during and after the Babylonian Exile. Paul uses it with reference to Jewish Christians, who are the remnant of God's true covenant (Rom. 11:5).

**Reversal theology:** A term that biblical scholars give to the "reversal of fortune" theme found in the Gospel of Luke: God raises up the poor and brings down the mighty.

**Righteousness:** In Paul's writings, right relationship with God (i.e., a properly ordered relationship) or "acquittal," as in a court of law. See also *justification*. In other books of the New Testament, obedience to God's will; doing all that the law demands.

**Rites:** Ceremonial rituals or formal religious practices.

**Sabbath:** The seventh day of the week, which Jews dedicate to rest and abstaining from work. It is patterned after the first creation story in Genesis, which describes God as resting on the seventh day (Gen. 2:2–3).

**Sacrifice:** From a Latin word that means "to make holy," it is an offering that humans make to God to give God thanks, to petition for favors or protection, and to ask forgiveness for wrongdoing.

**Sadducees:** A religious group of first-century-C.E. Judaism. Composed primarily of priests, it controlled the Sanhedrin in Jerusalem. We know little about the Saducees' teachings except that they rejected the notion of afterlife and immortality of the soul. They accepted only the Torah as God's law and therefore were considered to be narrow or strict interpreters of Jewish law.

**Sage:** Someone who is wiser or more knowledgeable than one would ordinarily expect; a religious person whose wisdom comes from God.

**Salvation:** The act of being healed or made whole. Paul uses the term to describe what comes to humanity when God's plan of salvation is finally accomplished. In the New Testament, it is associated with the establishment of God's kingdom.

**Samaria:** The central part of Palestine, whose capital was originally also called Samaria, but was renamed Sebaste in 30 B.C.E., in honor of the Roman emperor Augustus whose Greek name was Sebastos.

**Samaritans:** Although their origins are unknown, biblical scholars think they represented a conservative branch of Judaism, taking only the Pentateuch as their scriptures and strictly observing Sabbath regulations. They worshiped at Mt. Gerazim in Samaria, not in the Jerusalem Temple.

**Sanhedrin:** The supreme judicial council of the Jews in Jerusalem. Jesus was tried before this group, condemned for blasphemy, and subsequently put to death by the Romans.

**Scribes:** Professional copyists who were responsible for reading and writing all documents, whether commercial, personal, or religious. They were also the secretaries and clerks of the royal courts.

**Secessionists:** People who left or removed themselves from a group in a dispute over an issue that divided the community.

**Second Temple Judaism:** A period in Jewish history from the rebuilding of the Jerusalem Temple at the end of the Babylonian Exile in the latter part of the sixth century B.C.E. to its destruction by the Romans in 70 C.E.

**Seer:** A recipient of visions; a visionary. The term is associated with early prophets of the Jewish scriptures.

**Septuagint:** The Greek translation of the Old Testament. See *LXX*.

**Sermon:** A written or spoken speech on a religious topic; a word of exhortation.

**Signs source:** Part of a theory concerning the sources that the author of the Gospel of John used in the construction of his gospel; a collection of miracle stories that is no longer extant.

**Social science criticisms:** A variety of approaches to the study of scripture—for example, drawn from the social sciences, archeology, and anthropology—all of which relate to the social-historical background of the biblical text, its author, or its original audience.

**Solitary one:** In the Coptic Gospel of Thomas, the true disciple of Jesus, that is the one who has detached himself from the things of the world to become pure mind.

**Solomon:** Son of David and king of Israel who reigned approximately 961–928 B.C.E.

**Son of God:** Describes a person with a special relationship to God. Old Testament kings, angelic beings, and righteous people were called sons of God. In the New Testament, the title is ascribed to Jesus, who is God's son.

**Son of Man:** (1) A human being; (2) the heavenly warrior/judge who battles the evil one at the end of time and subsequently is given power, honor, and glory; (3) in the gospels, the one who must suffer, die, and be raised up.

**Sophia:** A Greek word meaning "wisdom." An attribute of God, personified as the feminine co-creator and throne partner of God in Proverbs and Wisdom of Solomon.

**Soteriological (Adjective):** From the Greek word *soter*, which means "savior," it describes teachings about the death of Jesus as the means of salvation for humanity.

**Source criticism:** An area of study and a set of methods used to uncover the written materials that an author might have used in the composition of a document. Related to the study of the gospels, this methodology is used to explain the literary relationship among the synoptic gospels (Matthew, Mark, and Luke).

**Stephanas:** Mentioned in 1 Corinthians, he and his household were baptized by Paul (1 Cor. 1:16). Paul speaks appreciatively of his service to the churches and urges the community at Corinth to honor his authority with obedience (1 Cor. 16:15–16).

**Structuralism:** An area of study and a set of methods that use the assumptions and techniques of semiotics to analyze the symbol systems of language and how the meanings and relationships of symbols make communication possible.

**Suzerainty treaty:** an ancient covenant or agreement between a king and his subjects. He would promise to give them protection from their enemies or other favors. In return, they had to abide by certain rules set by the king.

**Symbolic discourse:** An extended speech that contains highly metaphorical language or themes that cannot be fully appreciated except by people who share the author's worldview.

**Synagogue:** In Judaism, the location where people gathered; a gathering consisting of a minimum of ten adult males. They assembled for worship, the study of scripture, and the administration of the affairs of the local Jewish community. Synagogues originated as early as the Babylonian Exile after the Temple was destroyed. There were no sacrifices offered in the synagogue.

**Syncretism:** A cultural accommodation whereby several different philosophies or religious practices are incorporated under the umbrella of a single religion.

**Synoptic:** From the Greek word *synoptikos*, which means "seeing the whole together." The Gospels of Matthew, Mark, and Luke are called synoptic gospels because they tell the same general story of Jesus in the same kind of way and with more or less the same chronology.

**Synoptic problem:** A term that describes scholarly attempts to understand the literary relationship among the synoptic gospels (Matthew, Mark, and Luke), where evidence suggests that one or more of these authors was copying from a common source.

**Tabernacles:** A Jewish pilgrimage feast that celebrates the fall harvest of fruits and olives; also known as Booths or Sukkoth, because the Jewish pilgrims lived in tents during the seven-day feast to remind them of their journey in the desert during the Exodus.

**TaNaK:** The sacred scriptures of Judaism. The name is an acronym based on the scriptures' three parts: Law (the Hebrew word is Torah), Prophets (the Hebrew word is Nevi'im), and Writings (the Hebrew word is Ketuvim).

**Tax collectors:** Pertaining to the New Testament, people who were responsible for collecting taxes on behalf of the Roman Empire. They were despised by indigenous peoples at least in part because they made their living by collecting more taxes than they were contracted to deliver and pocketing the surplus.

**Temple:** In the literature of the New Testament, the term usually refers to the Jewish Temple in Jerusalem. Jews believed that it was God's dwelling place, also called the "house" of God, and the place where God "came down" to be with Israel.

**Testament:** Meaning "covenant" or "agreement," this term can refer both to the legal agreement that a person makes to ensure that his property is properly disposed after death and to the parting words of the deceased. However, in the Bible, testament refers to God's covenant relationship with humanity.

**Text criticism:** An area of study and a set of methods used to reconstruct, insofar as possible, the original wording of an ancient document based on the evidence of later manuscript copies.

**Theodicy:** An attempt to explain how God can be a just God when evil exists in the world and people experience unwarranted suffering.

**Theological treatise:** A carefully reasoned composition that expounds a religious doctrine or teaching.

**Theophany:** A revelation or manifestation of God.

**Theophilus:** Meaning "lover of God." In the Gospel of Luke and Acts of the Apostles, Luke names him as the one to whom these documents were addressed (Luke 1:3; Acts 1:1).

**Throne vision:** A special category of theophany in which the visionary is allowed to see the throne of God.

**Tiberius:** Claudius Caesar Augustus, stepson of Octavian (Augustus) and Roman emperor from 14 to 37 C.E.

**Timothy:** Paul's colleague whom he described as his "beloved and faithful child in the Lord" (1 Cor. 4:17). Biblical scholars believe that he was an important collaborator in Paul's ministry, because he is mentioned as a coauthor in four of Paul's letters: 1 Thessalonians, 2 Corinthians, Philippians, and Philemon.

**Tithing/tithe:** Dedicating a tenth of one's earnings to God as an offering.

**Torah:** Translated literally, "the Law," referring to the Law of Moses; the first five books of the Old Testament, also called the Pentateuch.

**Tradition:** A custom or belief that has been handed down from generation to generation; in a religious sense, a body of Christian doctrine (teachings) that is revealed over time as the word of God.

**Transfiguration:** The scene recorded in the synoptic gospels in which Jesus' appearance is changed so that he looks like a being of light. This event is generally interpreted as a preview of the resurrection.

**Travel narrative:** Luke 9:51–19:27; a large unit of text that does not have a parallel in the other synoptic gospels, so named because its narrative setting is Jesus' journey to Jerusalem.

**Trinitarian:** Referring to Christian belief in the three-in-oneness of God (Father, Son, and Holy Spirit).

**Triple tradition:** In source critical analyses, segments of text that are almost identical in wording across all three synoptic gospels.

**Tropological sense (of scripture):** One of the "Four Senses" in medieval interpretation of scripture, it could also be called the moral sense except that it was not primarily concerned with searching out a list of ethical regulations within scripture but rather with responding to its call to conversion.

**Two-source hypothesis:** A theory that attempts to explain the literary relationship among the synoptic gospels (Matthew, Mark, and Luke) by suggesting that Mark's gospel and another, no longer extant source called Q were used by Matthew and Luke in the creation of their gospels.

**Type/typology:** A form of biblical interpretation in which an Old Testament character or event is viewed as a pattern or blueprint for a New Testament character or event. It is used primarily as a way of saying that the Old Testament history anticipated the coming of Jesus as the Christ.

**Variant:** A difference in wording that a text critic finds when comparing two or more ancient manuscripts.

**Verbal inspiration:** See *Inspiration, verbal.*

**Visitation:** The Christian feast, celebrated on May 31, which recalls Luke's story of the Mary's visit to her cousin Elizabeth after she learned that Elizabeth was pregnant with a son who would later be known as John the Baptist (Luke 1:39–56).

**Watchers:** In the Book of Revelation, the four living creatures who support the throne of God and are "full of eyes all around and inside" (Rev. 4:8), perhaps a symbol of their constant watchfulness over the throne of God.

**Weeks:** A Jewish pilgrimage feast that celebrates the spring harvest of grain. Its name is derived from the fact that it was celebrated seven weeks after the Feast of Unleavened Bread (Passover).

**"We passages":** Segments of Acts of the Apostles, in which the author changes from third-person narration ("he" and "they") to first-person narration ("we" and "us"), suggesting that the author was present with Paul during these travels (see Acts 16:10–17; 20:5–15; 21:1–18; and 27:1–28:16).

**Wisdom literature:** Among the writings of Hebrew Scriptures (or the Old Testament), these books—Proverbs, Psalms, Song of Songs, Ecclesiastes, Sirach (Ecclesiasticus), Job, and the (deuterocanonical) Wisdom of Solomon—address practical questions about proper behavior as well as bigger questions about the meaning of human existence and the problem of suffering.

**Yom Kippur:** The Jewish Day of Atonement, a day of fasting on which God's people ask forgiveness for their past wrongs.

**Zealots:** People who have "zeal" for God and for the establishment of God's kingdom; a Jewish political resistance movement that rallied against Rome in the years preceding the Jewish War (70 C.E.).

# TEXT CREDITS

**Chapters 4, 7, 8, 9, 14, 16, 22, 23:** Excerpts in these chapters are reprinted from NRSV.

"Revised Standard Version of the Bible, copyright 1952 [2nd edition, 1971] by the Division of Christian Education of the National Council of the Churches of Christ in the United States of America. Used by permission. All rights reserved."

"The Catholic Edition of the Revised Standard Version of the Bible, copyright © 1965, 1966 by the Division of Christian Education of the National Council of the Churches of Christ in the United States of America. Used by permission. All rights reserved."

"Common Bible: Revised Standard Version of the Bible, copyright ©1973 by the Division of Christian Education of the National Council of the Churches of Christ in the United States of America. Used by permission. All rights reserved."

"Revised Standard Version of the Bible, Apocrypha, copyright © 1957; The Third and Fourth Books of the Maccabees and Psalm 151, copyright © 1977 by the Division of Christian Education of the National Council of the Churches of Christ in the United States of America. Used by permission. All rights reserved."

"New Revised Standard Version Bible, copyright © 1989, Division of Christian Education of the National Council of the Churches of Christ in the United States of America. Used by permission. All rights reserved."

"New Revised Standard Version Bible: Catholic Edition, copyright © 1989, 1993, Division of Christian Education of the National Council of the Churches of Christ in the United States of America. Used by permission. All rights reserved."

"Common Bible: New Revised Standard Version Bible, copyright © 1989, Division of Christian Education of the National Council of the Churches of Christ in the United States of America. Used by permission. All rights reserved."

"New Revised Standard Version Bible: Anglicized Edition, copyright © 1989, 1995, Division of Christian Education of the National Council of the Churches of Christ in the United States of America. Used by permission. All rights reserved."

**Chapter 17:** p. 388 From CHRISTIAN ANTI-SEMITISM AND PAUL'S THEOLOGY by Sidney B. Hall. Copyright © 1993 by Fortress Press. Reprinted by permission of Augsburg Fortress.

**Chapter 21:** pp. 445–446 From GLOBAL BIBLE COMMENTARY ed. by Daniel Patte. Copyright © 2004 by Abingdon Press. Used by permission of the publisher.

**Chapter 22:** pp. 464–466 Courtesy of Mr. Scott Wright, EPICA, on behalf of the Religious Task Force on Central America and Mexico.

**Chapter 23:** pp. 483–484 From GLOBAL BIBLE COMMENTARY ed. by Daniel Patte. Copyright © 2004 by Abingdon Press. Used by permission of the publisher.

**Chapter 24:** p. 505 Excerpt from "New Jerusalem" by Coan-seng Song in RETURN TO BABEL: Global Perspectives on the Bible ed. by Priscilla Pope-Levison and John R. Levison. Copyright © 1991. Published by Westminster John Knox Press and reprinted by permission of Presbyterian Publishing Corp.

# INDEX

Aaron, 86, 434, 453
Abel, 437–38, 453
Abiding, 211, 479–80
Abraham (Abram), 29, 82–84,
    255, 325–27, 380, 434–37
    and Sarah, 82–84, 255
    justified by faith and works,
        446–48
Acrocorinth, 351
*Acts of Paul and Thecla*, 295
Acts of the Apostles, 6, 66,
    272–84. *See also* Gospel
    of Luke
    authorship, 273–74
    baptism, 281, 335
    date and audience, 274
    financial contribution
        to Jewish Christian
        Community, 283
    on Gentiles, 155, 279
    God's covenant with
        Israel, 89
    Holy Spirit, 279–81
    liberation theology, 280–81
    life of early church, 281–83
    literary features, 275–76
    Luke and, 273
    Paul and, 6–7, 67, 78, 179,
        276–79, 283
    Peter and, 276–79
    Philip and, 103, 216
    scientific history and,
        235–40
    "we" passages, 273, 276–79
    women in, 68, 335
Adam, 339, 360, 381, 384
Adam and Eve, 28, 159, 503
Adultery, 164
Aegean Sea, 492
*Against Heresies* (Irenaeus), 9,
    28, 130, 262, 491–92
Agape Meal, 452–53
Age of Enlightenment, 27,
    32–34, 46, 50

Agent of God, 210–11
Akhmim, Egypt, 260
Albinus, 237
Alexander of Alexandria, 29
Alexander the Great, 62, 66,
    115, 303, 334
Alexandria (Egypt), 419
Alexandria school, 27–29
*Allegorical Interpretation*, 28
Allegorical sense of
    scripture, 31
Allegory, 27, 326–27
Almsgiving, 164
Anagogical sense of
    scripture, 31
Ananias, 277
*Anchor Bible Dictionary*, 56
"Ancient of Days," 496
Andrew, apostle, 216
Angel of Death, 86
Angels, 83, 159, 399, 453,
    498–500
Animal Apocalypse
    (Enoch), 487
Anna, 254–55
"Anointed one," 116–17,
    400–401, 484
Anointing of the sick,
    448–49
Annunciation, 184–85
Anthropology, theological,
    376–79, 384
Anti-Christ, 313–14
Anti-Judaism, 263–65, 386–89
Antioch, in Pisidia, 318
Antioch, (Syria), 180, 281, 419
Antiochene School, 28–29
Antiochus II, 397
*Antiquities* (Josephus), 237, 253
Aphrodite, 351
Apocalptic literature, 19,
    171–72, 487–89,
    490–505
Apocalypticism, 116

Apocalypse, defined, 140–41,
    487. *See also* Book of
    Revelation
Apocryphon of James, 244
Apocryphon of John, 244
Apollo, 257, 497
Apollos, 82, 283, 348–49,
    353, 429
Apostasy, 430–31, 434
*Apostolic Constitutions*, 421
Apostles. *See also* Acts of the
    Apostles; individual
    apostles
    defined, 170, 375
    disciples and, 170
    letters of, 6–7
    ministry of, 129
    Paul's apostleship, 320, 375
Apostolic Fathers, 7
Apostolic succession, 282, 419
Apostolic witness, 471–72
Apphia, 341–43, 396
Aquila, 273, 283, 348–49,
    355–57, 429
Aquinas, Thomas, 31–32
Aramaic language, 55, 66,
    442, 505
*Archbishop Romero, Martyr of
    Salvador* (Erdozain), 467
Archelaus, Ethnarch, 103
Archippus, 341–43, 396
Ark of the Covenant, 86, 92
Aristarchus, 396
Ascension, 192
Asceticism, 246
Asclepius, 497
Asia (Western Turkey), 458–61
Asia Minor, 254, 260, 280, 318,
    373, 397, 404, 412, 459,
    492, 497–98
Assemblies of God Church, 448
Assyria and Assyrians, 62,
    92–93, 104
Astrologers, 159, 161